Labor, Employment, and the Law

A Dictionary

CONTEMPORARY LEGAL ISSUES

Labor, Employment, and the Law

A Dictionary

Christopher Thomas Anglim

ABC-CLIO
Santa Barbara, California
Denver, Colorado
Oxford, England

Library of Congress Cataloging-in-Publication Data

Anglim, Christopher.
Labor, employment, and the law : a dictionary / Christopher Thomas Anglim.
p.cm. — (Contemporary legal issues)
Includes bibliographical references and index.
1. Labor laws and legislation—United States—Dictionaries.
I. Title.II. Series.
KF3317.A541997344.7301'03—dc2197-20803

ISBN 0-87436-825-1

(alk. paper)

03 02 01 00 99 98 97 10 9 8 7 6 5 4 3 2 1 (cloth)

ABC-CLIO, Inc.
130 Cremona Drive, P.O. Box 1911
Santa Barbara, California 93116-1911

This book is printed on acid-free paper ♾.
Manufactured in the United States of America

This book is dedicated to my parents, Richard and Mary Ann Anglim,
and my siblings, Kathleen and John.

Contents

Preface

The law governing employment and labor matters has its own distinct vocabulary, developed over an extended period of time by courts, legislatures, and regulators. Many of these concepts were inherited from Anglo-American common law, while others emerged from case law and labor statutes such as the Wagner Act and the Taft-Hartley Act. Both employment and labor law can be complex, therefore *Labor, Employment, and the Law: A Dictionary* seeks to provide concise and accurate definitions of the concepts used in these fields for those seeking such information in a single reference volume. These definitions are based on the important cases, statutes, regulations, and commentaries in labor and employment law.

This dictionary reflects the changes and new developments in contemporary U.S. workplace relations. The nation's economic structure is indeed undergoing a dramatic transformation from manufacturing to service industries. The United States also finds itself in an increasingly competitive and complex economic environment. Employment is also affected by changes in the nature of the work force and workplace technology. All of these major socioeconomic changes create challenges that our legal system attempts to deal with by applying the law to a given situation. This dictionary endeavors to incorporate the contemporary trends in the law of employment relations. This book, however, is not designed to substitute for legal advice in any particular case, which would require a thorough knowledge of specific facts. The law also often varies from state to state. If you have a specific legal concern, you should consult an attorney.

An Overview

Law reflects the culture in which it exists. Understanding law extends beyond merely learning legal rules to understanding the context in which they operate. Generally—and certainly in comparison to the laws of other industrialized nations—the employment relationship is not extensively regulated in the United States, even in contemporary times. During the twentieth century, however, public policy in the United States has shifted to favor a system that combines reliance on market forces with regulation. The development of American labor and employment law can be explained by four fundamental themes. First, social movements affect the development of law. These include the labor movement, which advocated the National Labor Relations Act of 1935 (also known as the NLRA and the Wagner Act), and the civil rights movement, which advocated the passage of the Civil Rights Act of 1964. Laws prohibiting discrimination on the basis of race, religion, sex, or disability, for example, can be analyzed as an expression of social value judgments on the permissible grounds for evaluating potential employees. Second, society attempts, through the law, to control concentrations and abuses of power, whether in the hands of government or private business. Antitrust laws, for example, are intended to prevent undue concentrations of power in private business. Regulation is also thought necessary to correct the imbalance of bargaining power between employers and employees by protecting the right of workers to form unions and engage in collective bargaining and by writing into every employment contract such standards as minimum wages, maximum hours, limits on the use of child labor, and guarantees of safe and healthy workplaces. Congress, for example, regulates labor conditions through the Fair Labor Standards Act of 1938 and the Occupational Safety and Health Act of 1970. Third, the law may serve as a means for adjusting claims of conflicting rights. The Wagner Act balanced labor's right to organize with the right of businesses to keep their facilities operating. Fourth, some laws are intended to correct deficiencies in the operation of labor markets. Labor markets are not perfectly competitive and some form of regulation may actually improve the efficiency of labor markets. Unemployment insurance and adjustment assistance laws force employers to absorb some of the costs of their termination decisions, which would otherwise be imposed on society.

This work is entitled *Labor, Employment, and the Law: A Dictionary* because it covers terms from both labor law and employment law, two distinct but related bodies of law. Both labor and employment law regulate issues involving work and the conditions of work. Though both labor law and employment law contend with work-related issues, there are crucial differences between the two. Employment law applies to all workers, while labor law regulations apply to workers who have chosen or are seeking to be represented by unions. Labor law emphasizes the employer-employee-union relationship, focusing on union representation and collective bargaining. Labor law covers group action, the relationship between organized capital and organized labor, or the relationship between the individual and the labor organization. Traditional labor law includes the rules of collective organization and collective bargaining in the private sector. Labor law consists largely of the amended National Labor Relations Act, but it has become increasingly complicated as several federal and state statutes have been enacted to regulate many aspects of the employer-employee relationship.

SOURCES OF LABOR AND EMPLOYMENT LAW

The modern public law of employment relations is derived from four main legal sources: constitutional law, statutory law, case law, and regulatory law. The U.S. Congress' constitutional authority to regulate labor relations is based on the broad grant of power to oversee commerce that is found in article 1, section 8, clause 3 of the U.S. Constitution: "The Congress shall have the power to . . . regulate commerce with foreign nations, and the several states." Under this provision, the U.S. Supreme Court has upheld congressional authority to control labor relations through measures such as the Wagner Act, and to regulate wages and hours through such statutes as the Fair Labor Standards Act of 1938.

Congress has the authority to prohibit discrimination in employment through important statutes such as Title VII of the Civil Rights Act of 1964. That statute, enacted under the Commerce Clause, has been upheld by the U.S. Supreme Court. The Thirteenth, Fourteenth, and Fifteenth Amendments to the U.S. Constitution have also been utilized as authority for the statutes prohibiting discrimination. The civil rights acts of the nineteenth century (now often referred to as Section 1981, Section 1983, and Section 1985), enacted to give effect to those amendments, have been used since the 1960s to combat private acts of discrimination based on race.

There is no single comprehensive statute covering labor law and employment law in the United States. Instead, there is a series of statutes on both the federal and state levels, each dealing with a specific issue or area concerning employment. This dictionary includes federal or state statutes governing employment relations. These statutes govern matters in five broad categories: labor-management relations (covering issues such as collective bargaining); equal opportunity (prohibiting discrimination due to race, color, national origin, sex, religion, disability, or age); wages and hours (mandating minimum wages and maximum hours); health and safety (enforcing safety in the workplace); and benefits (regulating welfare or pension funds). In addition to federal and state statutes, many cities have local ordinances that regulate issues such as cigarette smoking in the workplace. Many statutes also authorize administrative agencies to implement the laws.

Case law is a body of reported judicial cases containing the interpretation of statutes by the courts. This dictionary includes representative cases in employment and labor law. The great majority of reported case law in these areas is composed of decisions of the National Labor Relations Board (NLRB) and their review by the courts of appeal and the U.S. Supreme Court.

Regulatory law is made by various state or federal agencies to carry out the intent of a statute. The agencies issue regulations to guide the activities of those regulated by the agency, to manage the actions of their own employees, and to ensure uniform application of the law. For example, the Wagner Act created the NLRB, which administers that act, and Title VII established the Equal Employment Opportunity Commission, the agency responsible for the act's administration. The NLRB and the National Mediation Board, especially, have broad discretion in the interpretation and application of labor-related statutes. This dictionary will focus on the regulatory law that effects labor and employment law.

In addition to administrative regulations, the president has issued a series of executive orders regulating government procurement contracts, imposing nondiscrimination and affirmative action on contractors and subcontractors who engage in business with the federal government. Both Executive Order 11246 (24 September 1965) and Executive Order 11375 (13 October 1967) prohibits discrimination based on color, religion, sex, and national origin and imposes affirmative action requirements in federal government contracts.

Along with these three formal types of law, there is an informal law—an almost customary form of law called "industrial jurisprudence." It consists of the actions arising out of the daily collective bargaining relationship of the parties and the administration of the contract. Also called the common law of industrial relations, industrial jurisprudence may be based on an arbitration award or accepted by the parties themselves as a basis for working out their relationship.

SCOPE OF LABOR LAW AND EMPLOYMENT LAW

The principles of modern labor law have been developed by the U.S. Congress, the National Labor Relations Board, and the courts under three major pieces of legislation: the Wagner Act or National Labor Relations Act of 1935, the Taft-Hartley Act or the Labor-Management Relations Act of 1947, and the Landrum-Griffin Act or Labor-Management Reporting and Disclosure Act of 1959. Together, these statutes form the present National Labor Relations Act (NLRA), upon which American labor law is based. The NLRA protects the rights of workers to form independent trade unions and engage in collective bargaining. This statute is also intended to eliminate unfair economic conduct by either labor or management, leaving the conditions of employment subject to whatever private agreement may emerge from the use of lawful economic pressure. The NLRA does not specify working conditions that employers must provide. Nor does it contain any assurance that employees could retain their job rights if "just cause" for termination exists. As originally enacted, it preserves as much freedom of thought and action as possible while curbing the sort of employer excesses that had led to general strikes and significant labor disruptions early in the century. The Taft-Hartley Act (1947) was enacted by Congress to curb perceived union excesses. Today's labor law jurisprudence, largely based on federal statutory law, governs such aspects of the labor-management relationship as collective bargaining, collective bargaining agreements, labor disputes, concerted activities, labor organizations, wages and hours, and unfair labor practices.

American labor law differs from the labor law of other nations because of five features. First, it is decentralized, largely because unions seek elections based on the smallest organizing unit. Unions acquire bargaining authority on a plant-by-plant basis, often among a subgroup of workers in a plant. Second, the system is based on an adversarial model and on the political idea that an essential premise of the NLRA is that worker organizations would help American democracy by providing a "countervailing power" to otherwise overwhelming business domination. Third, American employers are more hostile to unions than their counterparts in other major industrial nations. Fourth, unions are predominantly multiemployer organizations who represent employees of several competing firms, which makes it difficult for any firm to share proprietary or nonpublic financial information with, or to secure variable labor terms from, the multiemployer union. And fifth, unions are institutionally insecure. They are threatened because of the growing nonunion employment sector. Challenges to unions are posed by such legal devices as decertification elections, the employer's ability to test majority support by withdrawing recognition, and duty-of-fair-representation lawsuits brought by employees complaining of the union's representation in grievances or collective bargaining. Democracy requirements for the conduct of internal union elections and the maintenance of union discipline also undermine their security.

Employment law is the only law governing employment issues in the 83 percent of American workplaces that are not unionized. Nonunionized workers are governed by a complex system of employment laws. It is essentially an extension of tort and contract law, modified by statute, especially in the health and safety areas. State court decisions have held that the unorganized worker's relationship with the employer is contractual. In most cases, the "contract" is invisible: the terms and conditions are fixed unilaterally by the employer, subject to the minimums prescribed by statute.

Employment law emerged from the classical common law of the master-servant relationship. Under that law, the "inferior status" of employees is considered a fundamental assumption in the relationship. Modern employment law, which governs the employer-employee relationship, is based on status, contract, and legislation. An individual's rights are determined in part by their status. In some cases, the worker's rights are affected if the person is an adult as opposed to a minor, an apprentice as opposed to a journeyman, or an alien as opposed to a citizen.

The employment relationship is also governed by contract, in that it is created by an express or implied contract of employment, which states the rights, powers, duties, and liabilities of the parties between themselves and others, including termination and discharge and wages and other compensation.

Modern American employment law has dramatically changed from traditional arrangements, in which nonunionized workers had few rights in the workplace. This change was the result of recent statutes and case law on both the state and federal levels. Employment law, therefore, includes those statutes and other legal rules, not covered by labor law, that govern the employment relationship, such as wage and hour laws, laws barring discrimination in employment on the basis of race or sex, health and safety laws, workers' compensation laws, pension laws, unemployment compensation laws, and social security regulations. These relatively recent federal and state statutes have tended to make the rights of employers and employees more equal in workplace issues.

One example of where employment law has changed is in the area of employment-at-will. Employment-at-will means that an employee not covered by a union contract or a written individual employment contract may be terminated by his or her employer at any time for any or no reason. Partly in response to civil rights laws and laws regulating the conditions of employment such as the Occupational Safety and Health Act, the previously entrenched employment-at-will rule has been successfully changed in court. By the end of the 1980s, virtually every state had adopted one or more exception to the at-will rule. An increasing number of states recognize a tort action for terminations that violate "public policy." Thus, an employer can be sued, for example, if it discharges an employee because the employee must be absent from work for jury duty, refuses to commit perjury, or declines to act in violation of professional standards. The various exceptions to the "at-will doctrine" place employers at a significant risk of liability for discharges not based on some valid reason.

Employment law largely governs the so-called McJobs, the low-wage, no-benefit jobs that have become increasingly common in the American economy. Currently, one-third of all American workers—and almost 20 percent of full-time, year-round workers—receive poverty-level wages. Employment law also covers the increasing numbers of contingent and other nonstandard workers. A major problem involving these workers is how to balance employers' needs for flexibility with workers' needs for adequate income protections and job security. They also raise important questions about how best to apply the public laws that these arrangements attempt to evade, including labor protection and labor relations statutes.

The law of wrongful discharge is a crucial element of employment law and includes recently developed limitations on the employer's established right to fire employees at will. The legal theories and policy reasons for wrongful discharge protections are based on either contract law—the employer promises not to discharge the employee except for good cause—or tort law—retaliatory discharge doctrines prohibit employers from terminating employees who refuse to commit various types of illegal acts. Many states allow an employee who has difficulty obtaining new employment to sue his or her former employer for defamation because of the dissemination of information about an erroneous discharge that affects the employee's reputation.

LITIGATION OF EMPLOYMENT ISSUES

Litigation in the employment context concerns private lawsuits by the employee against the employer, the employer against the employee, and third persons against the employer. Currently, the most litigated area in employment relations law is wrongful discharge, which involves employees who sue their employer for unfairly terminating them. One of the grounds for wrongful discharge is if the employee was terminated in violation of a contract in which an employer has agreed employees would be terminated only for just cause. An employee who is wrongfully discharged in breach of contract is entitled to damages if a monetary loss has resulted from the discharge.

In many states, discharging employees for certain reasons—because of jury duty, for example, or in retaliation for assisting law enforcement or refusing to drop a criminal investigation—is illegal because it violates public policy. In that case, the employee has a right of action. However, discharge in retaliation for activities such as competition with the employer or refusal to take a drug or alcohol test does not violate public policy. Generally, the discharge of an employee is illegal if it violates public policy, and the employee may recover back pay, even if the court does not order reinstatement.

One of the most common forms of litigation by an employer against its ex-employees involves employees who divulge trade secrets and confidential information. An employee is under an obligation during and after the termination of his or her employment not to divulge any of the employer's trade secrets. However, trade secrets and confidential information, in order to be protected, must be the particular secrets of the employer as distinguished from the general secrets of the trade. Confidential information or customer information, in some cases, may constitute a trade secret.

The doctrine of respondeat superior usually is the basis of an employer's liability for injuries to third persons caused by acts or omissions of its employees. Under the doctrine of respondeat superior, courts have held employers liable to third persons for injuries caused by their employees, but only those committed within the employees' scope of employment. The liability of an employer for its employee's wrongful acts has been based on the grounds that, where one of two innocent persons must suffer for the wrong of a third, the loss must fall to him who has enabled the third person to do the wrong. Ordinarily, in order to render a person liable for injuries under the doctrine of respondeat superior, the relation of employer and employee must be shown to have existed at the time of the injury, and in respect of the very transaction out of which the injury arose. An employer may also become liable to a third person for failure to exercise ordinary care in furnishing a reasonably safe tool or appliance. An employer is also liable for torts committed by its employee in obedience of express orders or committed in the employer's presence or with the employer's assent or acquiescence.

Under the common law "fellow servant" exception to the respondeat superior doctrine, developed in the early nineteenth century, masters were not liable for harm caused by fellow servants, even though acting within the scope of employment, if the fellow servants were negligent. By the late nineteenth century, state legislatures recognized the unfair hardships this rule caused workers. State workers' compensation laws were enacted to limit the application of the fellow servant rule and provide compensation without fault.

Courts have also recognized negligence in selecting or retaining employees as a tort cause of action. An employer may be liable for injuries to a third person resulting from the incompetence or unfitness of an employee if the employer negligently selected an incompetent or unfit employee. An employer also may be liable for negligently placing an employee with known dangerous propensities in a position where he or she could injure a third party. Retaining an employee who is, or should be, known to be incompetent, habitually negligent, or otherwise unfit, constitutes negligence on the part of the employer. It will render the employer liable for injuries to third parties caused by the improper actions of the employee.

THE DEVELOPMENT OF LABOR LAW AND EMPLOYMENT LAW

American employment and labor law originated in the English common law's general legal principles governing the relationship between master and servant. Servants lived on the property of their masters and often worked for a single master for their entire lives. The law regarded the relationship between servants and their masters as analogous to those between children and parents. Masters were held to be responsible for the wrongful acts of their servants and also obliged to provide their servants with competent fellow servants and reasonable protection from harm.

English legal doctrines, first imported by colonial America, continued to be followed by the United States after it won its independence. As urbanization and industrialization expanded in the nineteenth century, workers became less dependent on their employers for food, shelter, clothing, and other necessities. A new set of relationships emerged that was more closely related to commercial contracts.

The duration of the employment contract is a key legal issue. In the mid-nineteenth century, the concept of employment-at-will developed, meaning that employment relationships could be terminated "at will" by either party. The employee was free to quit at any time for any reason, and the employer was free to discharge the employee at any time for any reason. During the 1960s, the courts in many jurisdictions recognized the hardships that the rule often caused and began creating several exceptions to it. The employment-at-will doctrine also has been limited by statute (including civil rights legislation) and public policy considerations. The three major exceptions to the at-will doctrine are breach of an express or implied promise, including representation made in employee handbooks; wrongful discharge in violation of public policy; and breach of the implied covenant of good faith and fair dealing. Almost every state accepts at least one of these exceptions.

THE LAW GOVERNING WORKING CONDITIONS

Contemporary American labor laws provide far fewer protections against injury, illness, and unemployment than those of almost any other leading Western industrial nation. American laws also exclude more workers from their coverage. Both phenomena may be due to the fact that American unions did not form or ally themselves with a party of socialist orientation and had less "class consciousness," which caused the American labor movement to be organized mainly around the job for economic purposes rather than around the working class for political purposes.

Early federal labor statutes were largely concerned with "conditions of labor" issues such as wages and the hours of work. At the state level, workers' compensation laws enacted in the early twentieth century often were the first attempts to regulate working conditions in a comprehensive manner. The first major body of federal legislation on working conditions was enacted during the New Deal. The Social Security Act (1935) established a program of contributory social insurance whereby employees, employers, and the self-employed make contributions, which are placed in a special trust fund. The Fair Labor Standards Act (1938) established standards for a minimum wage, overtime pay, and child labor, and turned the regulation of these matters over to the U.S. Department of Labor. The Wages and Hours Administration of the Department of Labor enforces the statute throughout the country, subject to certain limitations. It may also bring a class action lawsuit for large groups of employees who claim that they have been wrongfully denied proper compensation.

Beginning in 1970, Congress and state legislatures began enacting new statutes regulating employment conditions. The Occupational Safety and Health Administration was created that year with the passage of the Occupational Safety and Health Act (OSHA). OSHA imposes, for example, a "general duty" on employers to maintain safe conditions at the workplace. For example, employers must furnish employees a workplace free from certain recognized hazards. The act authorizes the U.S. Department of Labor to prescribe and enforce safety and health standards in businesses that affect interstate commerce and to send inspectors into the field to enforce them. Since Americans currently work more hours than people in other industrialized countries except Japan, work conditions are a major factor in the economic well-being of citizens. But despite OSHA and a number of similar legislative attempts at reform—the Employment Retirement Income Security Act (1974), the Federal Mine Safety and Health Act (1977), the Worker Adjustment and Retraining Notification Act (1988), the Employee Polygraph Protection Act (1988), and the Family and Medical Leave Act (1993)—the occupational health and safety record of U.S. companies failed to improve significantly. The result is increased costs for private business, workers, and the economy.

The Family and Medical Leave Act (FMLA), the newest "minimum labor standard," is based on the same principles as child labor laws, Social Security, health and safety laws, and the Federal Labor Standards Act. It provides that employers with 50 or more workers must allow employees to take unpaid, job-protected leaves of absence for up to 12 weeks upon the birth or adoption of a child, to care for a family member with a serious health condition, or because of a serious health condition that renders the employee unable to perform the functions of his or her position. The FMLA also entitles the employee to reinstatement at the end of the leave. It does not require employers to pay salary or wages during the period of the leave, but it does require that they maintain health benefits. Perhaps the most profound impact of the FMLA will be on employers' absenteeism control policies. FMLA provides that employees with "serious health conditions" may take their 12 weeks of unpaid leave on an intermittent basis or arrange a reduced work schedule. Intended, in part, to "balance the demands of the workplace with the needs of families, to promote the stability and economic security of families, and to promote national interest in preserving family integrity," the FMLA has the potential to significantly improve the lives of working Americans and employers.

State and federal governments have enacted several statutes designed to assure the provision of minimal working conditions to all workers. These include the Equal Pay Act, the Age Discrimination in Employment Act, OSHA, the Employment Retirement Income Security Act, and Title VII of the Civil Rights Act of 1964. Every state has statutes conferring still additional minimum terms, such as advance notice prior to plant closing or mass layoff of greater than the 60 days advance notice required by the Worker Adjustment and Retraining Notification Act of 1988.

Health and safety laws such as OSHA are an enduring part of the American law governing working conditions. These statutes are likely to be strengthened over time, with more emphasis on workplace health factors. For example, restrictions may be imposed on employers whose employees work with Video Display Terminals (VDTs). The claim is that VDTs are hazardous to the employees' health, either because of radiation, eyestrain, or the stress of spending long periods of time in front of a VDT.

Workplace privacy is an area of emerging concern. Employees have become increasingly sensitive about employer intrusiveness on their privacy and have brought several lawsuits seeking redress. The most frequently asserted privacy claims, however, have been for the common law tort of invasion of privacy. There are four separate types of these cases: (1) public disclosure of private facts, (2) intrusion upon seclusion, (3) false light, and (4) appropriation of name or likeness. Each of these claims has been asserted in the employment context.

Advocates of privacy regulation argue that workers should have the right to preserve areas of privacy even on the job. Such protections are common in the government sector, and some have suggested that similar rules be extended to the private workplace. Congress has passed laws restricting the use of polygraphs (lie detectors) and the interception of telephone calls as tools for investigating employee misconduct. In recent years, bills have been introduced in every session of Congress to regulate electronic surveillance of employees while at work. It is also likely that there will be further legislation in the area of employee dignity and privacy in the workplace, covering such areas as searches of employee lockers and vehicles, access by an employee to his or her personnel records, and the use of polygraph tests.

Drug testing of employees is an increasingly common practice. Government employees are protected by the Fourth Amendment of the U.S. Constitution and some states have statutes that restrict random testing and require "reasonable suspicion" of illegal drug use unless the employee works in certain safety or security-sensitive positions. Employees in the private sector do not have such protections unless they are covered by a collective bargaining agreement or work in a state that has enacted a statute regulating drug testing.

THE LAW GOVERNING LABOR-MANAGEMENT RELATIONS

Labor law, the law governing unionized employment situations, is primarily based on the Railway Labor Act (RLA) (1926), the Wagner Act (1935), the Taft-Hartley Act (1947), and their subsequent amendments. The principal labor law is the Wagner Act, which applies to all employers in private industries affecting commerce, with the exception of the railroad and airline industries, which are regulated by the RLA. Because Congress intended that labor law be national in scope, both the Wagner Act and the RLA broadly take precedence over all state regulations of labor relations in the industries they cover. The states have enacted "mini Wagner Acts" for industries not regulated by federal law, and public sector labor relations laws for the employees of state and local governments. The federal government has a separate labor relations statute for its employees.

Unions have struggled throughout much of American history to organize American workers, often meeting with frustration and hostility. During the late nineteenth and early twentieth centuries, relations between management and labor were particularly poor. Workers attempted to improve working conditions through collective action, but most companies tried to thwart the workers' organizing efforts. This ongoing conflict led to an era of social unrest and violence, and in some cases, open warfare erupted between the companies and employees. No industrial country has a worse history of such unrest than the United States.

American courts first began hearing cases on the issue of collective bargaining by employees in the early nineteenth century but did so using common law doctrines embodied in state laws as guiding principles. The common law conspiracy doctrine was used by nineteenth-century courts to prevent unionization. As "combinations" intent on raising wages and reducing hours, unions were considered illegal conspiracies in restraint of trade. As a result, unions were outlawed as criminal conspiracies, and all worker attempts at self-protection were deemed illegal ends through the common law "unlawful means-unlawful ends" test. Gradually, by the mid-nineteenth century courts began to abandon the criminal conspiracy doctrine and, instead, used injunctions to prevent or break strikes, pickets, and boycotts. Injunctions were frequently sought by employers because they often not only ended the actual strike but also significantly reduced the willingness of other workers to strike.

Freedom of contract was also used to firmly establish the employment-at-will doctrine. Prior to the Civil War, the states generally had not expressly adopted the principle that employers could terminate employees at will. By the 1880s, however, the doctrine was firmly established, a development that promoted maximum freedom for employers in making business decisions, and hence greater stability and order for employers.

The courts also frequently used the Sherman Antitrust Act to prohibit union tactics involving organizing and economic pressure. That statute, which was enacted to control monopoly practice by business, was applied instead to union activities. Judges frequently issued injunctions under the act on the grounds that unions or strikes were illegal combinations in restraint of trade. Many employers also actively opposed unionization and compelled job applicants to sign a "yellow dog contract," which was a pledge not to join a union.

Labor unions actively supported legislation regulating workplace safety, child labor, conditions for women laborers, maximum hours for the workday, and minimum wages. Many state legislatures responded to these concerns with protective legislation. The courts, however, consistently invoked the freedom of contract doctrine, under the substantive due process theory, to strike down many of these statutes. Labor unions responded by lobbying Congress to obtain federal labor legislation. One of the first statutes to be upheld was the Railway Labor Act of 1926, which prohibited railroads from interfering with the right of their employees to organize and bargain collectively. Truly significant legal changes occurred in the next decade.

During the 1930s, a combination of many factors—the Great Depression, judicial and legislative recognition of the imbalance in bargaining power in employment relations, the rejection of laissez faire economics and the acceptance of Keynesian economics, the necessity for government intervention, and, perhaps most significant, changes in the personnel of the U.S. Supreme Court—brought about remarkable changes in the acceptance of labor legislation. One crucial new statute was the Norris-LaGuardia Act (1932), which effectively allowed for continued growth of the labor movement by prohibiting courts from issuing injunctions in labor disputes. The main provision of the act rejected the injunction as a remedy in labor disputes. It declared that federal courts were not the proper governmental body to formulate substantive labor policy, and it repudiated the federal common law of labor relations. The act also outlawed provisions of "yellow dog contracts" and declared that the right to organize and bargain collectively was public policy.

Several federal statutes were enacted during the New Deal era, most important of which was the Wagner Act. Also known as the National Labor Relations Act of 1935, it gave employees the right to organize and bargain collectively. It also provided the means of enforcing the rights that had previously been recognized in Section 7(a) of the National Industrial Recovery Act. With the passage of the Wagner Act, Congress ended its laissez faire attitude toward labor relations and began regulating collective bargaining. The act was amended by the Taft-Hartley Act of 1947 and the Landrum-Griffin Act of 1959.

Intended to promote labor peace, to limit employer interference with union activity, and, primarily, to require employers to bargain with unions designated by a majority of the appropriate employees, the Wagner Act altered the form and effectiveness of strikes by making them negotiable, predictable, and less likely. It both empowered and restricted worker activity by recognizing the strike as a tool to facilitate bargaining and, at the same time, providing employers with the right to continue production despite a strike. The Wagner Act had no provisions restricting union power. Both it and the National Industrial Recovery Act contributed to the doubling of union membership between 1933 and 1937.

To administer and interpret its unfair labor practice and representation provisions, the Wagner Act created the National Labor Relations Board (NLRB). The NLRB, whose members are appointed by the president and confirmed by the Senate, was intended by both the Wagner Act and the Taft-Hartley amendments to reflect political influences. It has been expected to make political decisions in accordance with the political outlook of its members, who were expected to support the policies of the president who appointed them. They serve five-year staggered terms. Routine cases are decided by panels of three board members, but cases of particular importance are decided by the whole board.

A Republican victory in the 1946 congressional elections represented a significant shift in American labor policy as embodied in the Taft-Hartley Act of 1947. Its passage was considered a victory of business interests over organized labor. That act expanded the employer's rights to both influence the outcome of representation elections and to appeal rulings involving unfair labor practices and the duty to bargain. Taft-Hartley also added provisions to the Wagner Act to protect employers as well as employees: prohibiting certain union conduct, giving employees the right to refrain from union activities, reviving the use of the injunction to prevent unfair labor practices, and reorganizing the NLRB. The act also limited the union security provisions of the Wagner Act by outlawing the closed shop and the automatic check-off, and substituted these for a form of union shop. Taft-Hartley restrained union growth and constrained certain strategies that unions found successful in the 1930s, such as the sit-down strike. Taft-Hartley also created the Federal Mediation and Conciliation Service, which was charged with helping to settle labor-management disputes through conciliation and mediation.

During the 1950s, the Eisenhower NLRB tended to stress individual rights as opposed to collective bargaining. This tendency is also represented by the passage of the Labor-Management Reporting Act (the Landrum-Griffin Act) in 1959. This statute attempted to increase regulation of internal union affairs and, more specifically, impose a greater measure of internal union democracy. The act was designed to protect the rights of employees by regulating internal union conduct through a bill of rights for union members and by requiring certain union financial disclosures, regulating the use of trusteeships over local unions, and mandating remedies for financial abuses by union officers. The bill of rights provision provides that union members have enforceable rights of free speech at union meetings and to run for union office free of unreasonable restrictions in fairly conducted elections. The statute also expanded Taft-Hartley provisions on picketing and boycotts. Management interests successfully lobbied to amend the act, broadening the coverage of the secondary boycott provisions of the Wagner Act and restricting the right of unions to picket in order to obtain representation rights.

John F. Kennedy's election in 1960 insured liberal appointments to the NLRB, especially that of Frank W. McCulloch, a Chicago lawyer and social activist with an expansive view of workers' collective rights, as chairman. Indeed, the McCulloch board was well ahead of the labor movement itself in promoting an early form of codetermination through such rulings as the 1967 *Fibreboard* case that appeared to invite unions to participate in business decisions that had previously been considered strictly managerial.

During the 1960s, organized labor thrived in a buoyant economy, rising worker militancy, undoubted union political clout, and a friendly government in Washington. In each of the national elections from 1958 through 1964, organized labor's candidates did exceedingly well and labor's reputation as a political and lobbying force was at its peak. At the same time, the labor movement experienced both collective bargaining successes and organizational failures. President Kennedy's Executive Order 10988 (1962) helped facilitate expansion in public employee unionism. Also during the 1960s, many unions were forced to defend themselves against charges of union corruption, featherbedding, and excessive power. By the late 1960s, many Republican congressmen and business interests sharply criticized the NLRB for its alleged improper use of its powers in resolving labor-management disputes and favoritism toward unions at the expense of management. In 1968, Senator Sam Ervin launched a hostile investigation of the NLRB, but no action resulted from this investigation.

The spirit that had infused the unions in a previous era inspired the civil rights, antipoverty, and antiwar movements, resulting in a broad range of social legislation, including the Civil Rights Act of 1964. But Walter Reuther, president of the United Auto Workers (UAW), saw the AFL-CIO as stagnating and led a reform effort, which became known as the American Labor Alliance (ALA). His actions led to the UAW's disaffiliation from the AFL-CIO in 1968. During this same period, the International Brotherhood of Teamsters became the largest of the nation's international unions.

Changing political fortunes significantly affected labor policy during the 1970s, with the NLRB increasingly reluctant to follow a liberal agenda during the Nixon, Ford, and Carter years. Business interests accelerated their concerted attack on the NLRB, which had begun in 1968 in opposition to the McCulloch board's controversial pro-union decisions. The corporate-sponsored Labor Law Reform Group, in particular, began an extensive and heavily funded attack on federal labor policy and the labor movement in a manner similar to business antiunion efforts in the 1930s.

During the early 1970s, most labor unions opposed wage and price controls. The unions, in their organizational effort, focused greater attention on public employees, who had become increasingly militant and more willing to organize. The union movement also worked to reform the labor statutes in order to provide more effective remedies against employers willing to resist union organizing and bargaining efforts by violating the existing statutes.

Ronald Reagan's victory in 1980, though unrelated to any prominent labor-management issues, provided a vehicle for ideological attacks on the basic premises of the original Wagner Act and for the marginalization of collective bargaining and trade unionism. The Supreme Court also consistently favored individual over collective rights and private property and efficiency over claims of workplace equity.

In the 1980s, deregulation in transportation produced nonunion competition for the organized sector. That competition, in turn, may have contributed to increased litigation in the organized sector. Union membership continued to decline during the Reagan and Bush administrations, with only 16.1 percent of the workforce unionized in 1990. Because of the decline in the numbers of organized employees, courts and legislatures placed increasing importance on the rights of individual employees outside the union environment. The labor movement complained that American law was failing both to protect labor organizing and to defend existing unions from a new open shop movement.

The mass layoffs of the 1970s and 1980s, particularly in the nation's older industrial areas, led Congress and the state legislatures to enact a series of statutes dealing with these issues, including the Workers Adjustment and Retraining Notification Act (1988). This act emulates legislation and case law already in existence in western Europe and Japan that provides employees with notice, consultation, and other rights in connection with layoffs triggered by economic considerations.

Supporters of organized labor have been encouraged by new prospects for reform in the U.S. system of workplace representation. President Clinton's election in November 1992 and the subsequent creation of the Commission on the Future of Worker-Management Relations in 1993, chaired by John Dunlop, are seen as particularly significant developments by union supporters.

Presently, there is piecemeal protection already provided by federal and state anti-discrimination laws, workplace safety statutes, and workers' compensation statutes, all of which significantly restrain arbitrary firings. There are also efforts to provide comprehensive statutory coverage of employee discharge. Federal legislation protecting against wrongful discharge is still in the early stages of evolution in the United States. As a result of the proportionate increase in nonunion employees, wrongful discharge litigation has become more important in employment law.

EQUAL OPPORTUNITY OR ANTIDISCRIMINATION LAW

As social concern for the well-being for all citizens has grown, Congress and the courts have attacked the persistent problem of employment discrimination with a body of statutes and cases that comprise the jurisprudence now variously known as equal opportunity, antidiscrimination, or employment discrimination law. Legislation has been adopted to combat unfair labor conditions and discrimination, such as the Civil Rights Act of 1964, the Equal Employment Opportunity Act of 1972, and the Age Discrimination in Employment Act of 1967. The Civil Rights Act of 1866 and the Civil Rights Act of 1871 have also been interpreted by the courts to prohibit employment discrimination.

For many years, African Americans struggled to overcome unfair treatment. In 1896, the U.S. Supreme Court in *Plessy v. Ferguson* essentially ratified the practice of racial segregation in public accommodations. Following this decision, states were free to segregate the labor market and labor opportunities based on *Plessy's* "separate but equal" doctrine until it was overturned by the Supreme Court in *Brown v. Board of Education* in 1954. Although *Brown* applied only to public schools, the Court extended its rejection of the "separate but equal" doctrine to many other public facilities. Job segregation on the basis of race and gender was open and legal until 1965, when the Civil Rights Act of 1964 became effective.

Congress significantly changed the law of employment in the 1960s and 1970s. The centerpiece of employment discrimination legislation is Title VII of the Civil Rights Act (1964), as amended by the Equal Employment Opportunity Act (1972), and the Civil Rights Act of 1991. Both of these amendments provided additional protections against discrimination. Title VII prohibits discrimination in both private and public sector employment based on race, color, religion, sex, and national origin. It covers employers with 15 or more employees, employment agencies, and unions with 15 or more members. Title VII and related legislation played a significant role in desegregating America's workplaces. Equally important were the landmark U.S. Supreme Court cases that have applied the provisions of the Civil Rights Act. In its 1971 *Griggs v. Duke Power Co.* decision, the Court declared that any testing program conducted by an employer in the hiring process must be relevant to the job being filled. *Griggs* has been extended by later cases, such as *Harless v. Duck*, which was decided by the U.S. Sixth Circuit Court of Appeals in 1980.

Antidiscrimination law prohibits two forms of discrimination. The first is intentional discrimination. Because direct evidence of discriminatory motive is often lacking, employees/job applicants are also permitted to mount a case through circumstantial evidence by attacking the reasons for the challenged decision as articulated by the employer or through statistical proof of a "pattern or practice" of discrimination.

Equal employment opportunity became an increasingly significant employment issue for several groups during the 1960s and 1970s. Through antidiscrimination legislation, Congress also required that men and women be paid equally for performing the same jobs, outlawed discrimination against pregnant women and the disabled, and ended discrimination on the basis of age. Equal employment opportunity law is oriented to group rights, or at least to group cases, that may be enforced through class action lawsuits.

How to remedy past discrimination fairly has remained a persistent issue in American society. Affirmative action, which is a remedial concept, offers one solution. It demands that the employer take positive action in areas such as recruitment, hiring, transfer, and upgrading in order to improve work opportunities for groups that have been deprived of opportunities because of discrimination.

In the area of sex discrimination, comparable worth and sexual harassment on the job are areas of current legal concern. Sex discrimination refers to inequities in hiring, work assignments, salaries, promotions, and other conditions of work based on gender, including exclusion from social and peer networks where business is conducted, information is shared, or decisions are made. The concept of equal pay for equal work has helped remedy this problem somewhat. However, the fact that men and women have historically been segregated in different occupations makes comparison of "equal work" difficult. In recent decades, women have fought sex discrimination by seeking access to traditionally "male" jobs under affirmative action plans. The Supreme Court has made several landmark decisions in the sex discrimination area, including ruling that women are not to be required to make larger contributions to pension plans in order to obtain the same monthly pension benefits as men. These decisions include the *City of Los Angeles Department of Water and Power v. Manhart* in 1978 and *Arizona Governing Committee v. Norris* in 1983. Sexual harassment is a specific type of sex discrimination that includes unwelcome sexual advances, requests for sexual favors, and other verbal or physical conduct of a sexual nature that adversely affects the work environment.

Various courts have interpreted Title VII as offering no protection to lesbians and gays against sexual orientation discrimination. These include the Fifth Circuit case of *Smith v. Liberty Mutual Insurance Co.* and the Ninth Circuit case of *DeSantis v. Pacific Telephone and Telegraph,* both in 1979. Some states and localities have passed statutes prohibiting sexual orientation discrimination.

One of the newest controversial issues involving sexual discrimination concerns fetal exclusion policies. Some employers have claimed that scientific research supports excluding fertile women from jobs requiring exposure to toxic substances, and that these policies are the least costly defense against damage suits. The U.S. Supreme Court decided in *Auto Workers v. Johnson Controls* in 1991 that one company's fetal exclusion policy constituted illegal sexual discrimination because it excluded only certain fertile women, not all workers at risk, and gave priority to fetal rights over workers' rights. The only exception the court recognized were those rare circumstances in which reproductive potential prevents the actual performance of job duties.

Many older adults have difficulty obtaining and retaining a job due to age discrimination. Since its passage in 1967, the Age Discrimination in Employment Act (ADEA) has been broadened beyond protection for the older worker in the workplace to protection of pension benefits, the elimination of the maximum age cap, and reduction of expenditures for social security. But unlike some other discrimination laws, there are no true class-action lawsuit procedures under the ADEA.

In recent years, new forms of discrimination have been identified and remedied, including protection under Title I of the Americans with Disabilities Act (ADA), which prohibits employment discrimination against disabled workers. The ADA states that all private and public employers with 15 or more employees are prohibited from disability-based discrimination. The statute prohibits both intentional and disparate impact discrimination. All employment standards having an adverse impact on individuals with disabilities must be job-related and consistent with business necessity. The ADA also imposes affirmative obligations on employers by requiring them to provide "reasonable accommodations" for qualified individuals with a disability. The reasonable accommodation duty may in particular circumstances include making existing facilities used by employees readily accessible to and usable by individuals with disabilities. The ADA, along with other federal and state laws prohibiting employment discrimination of the disabled, has been extended to include people with AIDS (acquired immune deficiency syndrome). Many states have also passed legislation that specifically prohibits AIDS-based employment discrimination and some even prohibit HIV (human immunodeficiency virus) testing for employment reasons.

There are several controversial issues related to employment law that still await resolution. One of the most heated of these concerns the rights of undocumented workers. Under the Immigration Reform and Control Act of 1986, it is illegal to knowingly hire an undocumented worker despite the economic usefulness of these workers in this country. Another controversial issue is discrimination on the basis of sexual orientation. Neither the federal government nor most states currently prohibit this type of discrimination. Also, both legislatures and the courts are considering the rights of smoking and nonsmoking workers in the light of established employment discrimination law.

While the inequalities of earnings based on gender and race have been reduced in the United States, considerable differences remain. The gap in earnings between men and women has declined in recent years, though women continue to earn less. The gap by race has fallen among women, but the earnings of African American men relative to that of white men were no better in 1993 than they were in 1970.

In the 1990s, the two most important pieces of legislation affecting employment provided new forms of protection against discrimination. The Americans with Disabilities Act (1990) provides extensive protection against employment discrimination for both the physically and mentally disabled. The second, the Civil Rights Act of 1991 (the Danforth-Kennedy Act) was prompted by a series of Supreme Court decisions that interpreted civil rights legislation narrowly, which Congress found objectionable. This act, however, went beyond reversing the decisions and allowed for applicants and employees to obtain punitive and compensatory damages already available in racial discrimination and wrongful discharge actions in sex, religious, and disability discrimination cases.

Current Trends and Issues in Labor and Employment Law

The United States now has the lowest effective rate of unionization in the developed world. It also lacks those other institutions—worker-based political parties, mandated "works councils" or other forms of worker representation inside the firm, and general wage regulation—that elsewhere supplement or substitute for union power. The United States also has the lowest level of general social protections and highest level of wage inequality, after-tax poverty, and working-class electoral abstention in the developed world.

While the NLRA has changed little since the Taft-Hartley Act, the social, political, and economic forces forming the context in which labor law operates, and indeed, give meaning to or alter the meaning of the law, have significantly changed. For example, the move from an industrial society to an information or service society has tremendous legal implications.

There are fewer factories employing 5,000 or more blue-collar employees in one location working at repetitive jobs. There are also blurring distinctions between blue- and white-collar workers, and between professional and nonprofessional workers. Workers are becoming better educated and more technologically oriented, U.S. firms are continuing to face stiff international competition, and technology is increasingly complicated. But as the country moves from an industrial to an information or service society, it is becoming increasingly less unionized. This trend may be due to three factors: (1) employers continue to aggressively resist unionization, (2) employers often try to introduce "substitutes" for unionization such as employee participation plans, and (3) traditional unions and their organizers often have had difficulties adjusting to the realities of the changed economy in the present legal context. The ability of unions to "take wages out of competition" has been made increasingly difficult because of competition in global product markets; the deregulation of previously unionized industries such as airlines, trucking, and telecommunications; and technological change altering needs for skilled labor and reducing the advantages of local producers.

Technology, especially, is radically changing the American workplace. Current labor law hinders unions in this environment because the distinction between so-called mandatory and permissive subjects of bargaining, especially, often prevents unions from addressing critical issues of workplace technology. Technology, therefore, is altering the balance of power in the workplace, weakening the power of unions in ways that the framers of the Wagner Act could not have foreseen while underscoring the urgent need for labor law reform.

THE FUTURE OF LABOR AND EMPLOYMENT LAW

The future of labor law is closely linked with the future of unions themselves. Despite the common notion that unions are obsolete, labor organizations continue to play a vital role in society. The basic ideas of the Wagner Act—that workers should enjoy the right to association inside and outside the workplace and that collective worker organizations can contribute to the vitality of the American economy—remain relevant and sound goals today. The Wagner Act's fundamental promises were that workers shall have the right to self-organization; to form, join, or assist labor organizations; to bargain collectively through representatives of their own choosing; and to engage in other concerted activities for the purpose of collective bargaining or other mutual aid or protection. Worker organization and collective bargaining continues to provide workers with the means to participate in the framing and administering of the law that has the greatest impact on their daily lives, the law that governs at the workplace. Labor law and a strong labor movement will continue to be of crucial importance in America's development as an advanced economic democracy.

A declining proportion of workers is covered by collective bargaining agreements. The decline of union density, therefore, creates a gap in worker representation that cannot be filled by human resource management and government regulation. Government regulations, however, have become more extensive, and reliance on administrative and judicial remedies to resolve disagreements has increased. The growth of federal workplace regulations leaves less room for local parties to determine the workplace rules that best meet their needs in their particular situation. Through unions, working people formulate policies that are expressed in the form of shop rules and embodied in agreements with employers. Without union representation, employees have no independent organization through which to discuss workplace issues with management. Human resource managers, whose job is to oversee decisions and actions that affect the relationship between the organization and employees, represent the employer's interests. One of the most challenging issues in the years ahead is likely to be whether the American employment relations system can evolve into a system that is less adversarial and more cooperative.

ABSENTEEISM The failure of a worker to report for work when scheduled. It may be an unexcused absence when the worker does not call in to say he or she will be absent, or, it may be an excused absence when a worker calls in and provides a reason acceptable to management, such as illness.

Some employers have developed "no fault" absenteeism control plans under which employees are allowed a given number of unexcused and excused absences, late arrivals, and early departures in a given time period but are disciplined for any additional absences or for arriving late or leaving early, regardless of the reason and even though they may be "excused." The theory of these plans is that the company need not determine whether the absence was acceptable. If workers exceed the limits set out in the no fault plan, they would undergo progressive discipline—verbal warning, written warning, short suspension, longer suspension, and eventually discharge. Workers move from step to step along the progressive discipline process for each unexcused absence, but they are able to regress along the chain by maintaining good attendance records for given periods of time.

Employers seek to control absenteeism because of the costs it causes in paid leave and worker's compensation benefits, replacement workers, diminished product quality, and higher prices for goods and services

See also **Progressive Discipline.**

ACQUIRED IMMUNE DEFICIENCY SYNDROME (AIDS) A lethal sexually transmitted disease that attacks the body's immune system, rendering the victim vulnerable to infections. It is, at present, incurable. AIDS raises several employment-related legal issues, which reflect society's evolving perception of the disease.

In the early 1980s, when AIDS and how it was transmitted were poorly understood, employers were concerned over the costs of maintaining insurance and the possible spread of the disease to other employees. So they fired employees who tested positive for HIV, the AIDS virus. AIDS victims have successfully argued that they are persons with disabilities and therefore protected by the Rehabilitation Act of 1973. Under this act, the Ninth Circuit Court of Appeals ordered a school district to return an HIV-positive teacher to classroom duties.

Under current law, employers cannot legally test either potential or current employees for HIV/AIDS. In fact, no examination may be conducted or inquiry made into whether an applicant has a disability before an offer of employment is made. Medical examinations may be conducted if all entering employees in the same job category are treated the same way without regard to disability. The Americans with Disabilities Act does not prohibit HIV testing at this stage, but will generally prevent an employer from using a positive test result to discriminate.

Unlawful discrimination includes actions such as segregating a person with HIV from other employees, using qualification standards that tend to screen out persons with disabilities, failing to provide reasonable accommodation, and denying an employee with HIV disease equal access to health care benefits offered by the employer. In general, an employer may test an employee or applicant for AIDS only if being AIDS-free is a bona fide occupational qualification (BFOQ). An employer must present substantial evidence to prove a BFOQ. He or she must prove that any criterion for employment that tends to screen out persons with the HIV disease is related to the performance of the essential functions of the job in question and is consistent with business necessity. If an employer receives test results, he or she is prohibited from disclosing the results of the test to any other person.

AIDS and health care workers involve two distinct issues: (1) health care workers are more likely than persons in other professions to come into contact with infectious diseases affecting their own health and (2) they are also discriminated against on the grounds that an infected health care worker poses a threat to himself and others. Some of the vigorously debated issues in this area include the precautions that should be taken to reduce the risk of HIV transmission to patients and what information health care workers must disclose to patients.

There are some findings, however, that indicate that the risk of becoming infected with HIV based on transmission from an infected health care worker is infinitesimal. As of 1995, only one health care worker has ever been documented as the source of HIV transmission to a patient.

See also **Americans with Disabilities Act of 1990; Bona Fide Occupational Qualification; Rehabilitation Act of 1973.**

ADMINISTRATIVE LAW JUDGE (ALJ) The representative of a federal agency who is responsible for conducting hearings and making recommendations to the National Labor Relations Board (NLRB) or other government agency. Administrative law judges were, until August 19, 1972, known as trial examiners.

If an unfair labor practice has been charged, a field examiner from the NLRB conducts a preliminary investigation of the charge, and the ALJ hears the case. He or she acts independently from the NLRB, which reviews the decision on appeal, and the general counsel, who investigates and prosecutes cases. The recommended order will either present the appropriate remedy or dismiss the complaint.

The ALJ is, in effect, a judge in a court of first impression, although the hearing procedures in NLRB complaint ("C") cases are less formal than those in a court of law. Among other powers, the ALJ administers oaths and affirmations; grants applications for subpoenas; rules on offers of proof and receives relevant evidence; takes or causes depositions to be taken; regulates the course of the hearing; disposes of procedural requests and similar matters; renders and files decisions; calls, examines, and cross-examines witnesses; and takes any other action necessary under the board's rules and regulations. The ALJ's opinion may be appealed by either party to the NLRB.

See also **Charge; National Labor Relations Board; Unfair Labor Practice.**

AFFIRMATIVE ACTION Equal employment practices that go beyond simply avoiding discrimination and attempt to undo or compensate for past discrimination. They are not only used to eliminate existing and continuing discrimination against protected classes, but also to remedy lingering effects of past discrimination, and to create means to prevent future discrimination. Affirmative action occurs whenever an employer hires or promotes an employee in a manner that legally favors a Title VII protected class. It is a remedial concept involving positive action taken by an employer in areas such as recruitment, hiring, transfer, upgrading, rates of pay, and selection for training to improve work opportunities.

In employment, there are two basic types of affirmative action: coercive and voluntary. Coercive plans may be imposed as a condition of government contracts or grants under Executive Order 11246 (1965), or to benefit the disabled under the Rehabilitation Act (1973). They may also be court-imposed remedies under Title VII of the Civil Rights Act (1964). Affirmative action may, for example, be implemented voluntarily by private industry or as a result of a court order, legislative provision, or a settlement with the Equal Employment Opportunity Commission. It includes conciliation agreements settling employment discrimination charges brought under Title VII of the Civil Rights Act of 1964.

Affirmative action involves "results-oriented actions" a contractor, by virtue of its contracts, must take to ensure equal employment opportunity. Where appropriate, it includes goals to increase the employment of members of protected classes. It may also provide relief such as back pay and retroactive seniority. Written affirmative action plans are required of certain federal contractors under Executive Order 11246 (1965). Federal contractors are also required under the Rehabilitation Act (1973), as amended, to take affirmative action to employ and promote disabled persons. Qualified disabled veterans must be given similar attention by the terms of the Vietnam Era Veterans Readjustment Assistance Act (1974), as amended. State and local governmental entities may be subject to special affirmative action requirements if they receive federal funds under the Revenue Sharing Act of 1972 and the Intergovernmental Personnel Act.

Until 1969, affirmative action plans were implemented to ensure equal individual opportunity and group representation. But at that point, the Nixon administration introduced goals or quotas in hiring. These quotas became, and remain, controversial political issues, and affirmative action plans have often encountered serious opposition. Employers and unions have, in the past, argued that affirmative action programs caused discrimination against those who are already employed. Both the Reagan and Bush administrations opposed affirmative action programs, especially quotas, and Senator Orrin Hatch (R-Utah) once sponsored a constitutional amendment prohibiting federally and state-mandated racial quotas.

Over time, the nature and purpose of affirmative action have been interpreted by the courts and applied inconsistently. Some believe that, within reason, a preference should be given to members of those protected classes that "have in the past been discriminated against." Others believe that only those individuals who have actually been discriminated against should be awarded a remedy through affirmative action preference. The resulting confusion led to what became known as "the quota mentality." Though the regulations creating judicially acceptable affirmative action plans specifically reject this approach, several "reverse discrimination" cases have been brought alleging that decision makers have indeed established a quota system.

The U.S. Supreme Court declined to accept the Reagan administration arguments that programs that provide preference to minority groups at the expense of white employees are never permissible unless the individuals who benefit have personally suffered discrimination. Although the court was sharply divided in each case, the decisions permit affirmative action plans that attempt to compensate for past discrimination through preferential hiring and promotion of members of minority groups. [*Local 28 of Sheet Metal Workers' International Association v. Equal Employment Opportunity Commission* (1986)] Programs that provide preferential treatment to minority employees during layoffs, however, seem less likely to be approved by the courts. [*Wygant v. Jackson Board of Education* (1986)]

The effectiveness of affirmative action has been limited by the inherent vulnerability of the legal bases of these plans, as well as the strength of the opposition to affirmative action. [*Detroit Police Officers v. Young* (1981), *Underwood v. D.C. Armory Board* (1987), and *Hayes v. North Star State Law Enforcement Officers Association & City of Charlotte* (1993)] But despite limitations, organized opposition, and mishandling by many firms, it has had some success in providing members of protected classes with an equal opportunity for employment. Women and minorities have made impressive gains in entering the labor force. Both current demographic conditions and future projections indicate that it will be difficult for employers to staff their workplaces if they discriminate against minorities.

The Supreme Court has significantly limited the use of affirmative action programs that favor protected classes. [*Adarand Constructors v. Federico Pena* (1995)] The Court ruled that federal affirmative action programs must be examined under a "strict scrutiny" standard. Under this standard, a program favoring racial minorities over other races would fail to be constitutional only if it was found to serve "compelling government interest" and was "reasonably tailored" to serve that interest.

Affirmative action is likely to remain a contentious legal issue in the employment area. Two examples of this are *Texas v. Hopwood* (1996) and the litigation involving California's Proposition 209. The *Hopwood* case was brought by four white Texas residents who sought admission to the University of Texas Law School. The admission process was designed to obtain a minimum 10 percent Hispanic representation and 5 percent African American. No other minority group received any preference. Applications were color-coded according to race, separate faculty committees were used to evaluate applications on the basis of race, separate waiting lists were maintained for different racial groups, and different test score admission thresholds were applied to the preferred minorities. The four plaintiffs were rejected, although no applicant from the preferred minority groups with the same test scores was rejected. When the plaintiffs challenged the admission process, the law school defended its actions by advancing two compelling interests—remedying past discrimination and providing a racially diverse student body. The Fifth Circuit rejected both justifications. It held the school had not demonstrated that race-based admissions programs were, in fact, designed to remedy the present effects of its own past discrimination. And in regard to diversity, it broadly rejected that justification, stating "the use of ethnic diversity simply to achieve heterogeneity . . . is unconstitutional." The U.S. Supreme Court subsequently refused to hear the case. The *Hopwood* case has raised substantial confusion and concern in the academic and legal community and its impact, if any, on affirmative action plans in employment matters remains unclear.

In 1996, California voters passed Proposition 209, a ban against the use of racial, ethnic, and gender preferences by public agencies, including in public employment, public education, and public contracting. While it was initially enjoined from taking effect, Proposition 209 was late upheld as constitutional by the Ninth Circuit Court of Appeals. It is highly likely that the case will be reviewd by the U.S. Supreme Court.

See also **Civil Rights Act of 1964; Equal Employment Opportunity Commission; Protected Class; Rehabilitation Act of 1973; Vietnam Era Veterans Readjustment Assistance Act.**

AFRICAN AMERICANS: EMPLOYMENT ISSUES

A person with origins in any of the Negroid racial groups of Africa who is not also of Hispanic origin is considered an African American. Under Title VII, African Americans are a protected class.

A heritage of slavery has long relegated African Americans to second-class citizenship, limiting them largely to the most unskilled, unattractive, and poorly paid occupations. African Americans have long been severely underrepresented among the ranks of professionals, managers, sales workers, and skilled laborers. In contrast, African Americans are heavily concentrated in unskilled positions such as factory work and unskilled labor. Their current economically disadvantaged position is directly related to racial discrimination in employment and other critical areas.

The basic citizenship rights of African Americans were legally established during the Reconstruction era. Throughout much of the twentieth century, African Americans were able to improve their conditions despite severe adversity and largely without legal support. Nonetheless, African Americans were restricted to unskilled, low status, low-paying jobs. Until World War II, they were rarely hired in factories except as janitors or as laborers. After *Brown v. Board of Education* (1954), their situation improved, and since 1960, African American employment has increased, especially in white-collar, artisan, and manufacturing occupations.

Until the passage of Title VII of the Civil Rights Act of 1964, African Americans had no effective legal means to challenge employment discrimination. Title VII established the Equal Employment Opportunity Commission, an executive agency empowered to investigate and resolve complaints of discrimination. African Americans have also pursued claims of racial discrimination under the Civil Rights Act of 1866 (also known as "Section 1981"), which says "all persons . . . shall have the same right to make and enforce contracts . . . as is enjoyed by white persons." This statute, which has been interpreted to protect the rights of African Americans to contract for employment, provides an alternative remedy to Title VII in employment discrimination cases. It is enforced by a private civil action and no administrative agency participation is required.

But even if all legal employment bias were ended, this would still not assist many of the African Americans in the nation's underclass who lack the skills or education necessary for the available jobs. In 1997, some 11 percent of the U.S. civilian labor force was African American, yet some 9.8 percent of African Americans were unemployed, compared to 4.2 percent for whites. The unemployment rate for African-American teenagers was 34.3 percent, compared to 17.0 percent for all teenagers. Labor force participation is higher for African American women (63.7 percent) that white women (59.6 percent), and in 1997, the median income for African American families was 76.5 percent of that for white families.

This inequality is partially due to the fact that African Americans are concentrated disproportionately in the inner cities of 12 major urban centers and scattered throughout the rural South, areas where jobs are frequently scarce. Obtaining the available entry-level jobs is made more difficult by the necessity of competing with large numbers of new immigrants, especially illegal immigrants, who also settle disproportionately in inner city areas.

Recent reports from the U.S. Census Bureau indicate that the quality of life for African Americans is improving. For the first time since the census bureau began keeping track in 1959, the poverty rate fell below 30 percent of all African Americans in 1995. African Americans are the only racial group whose inflation-adjusted median income exceeds what it was in 1989, the year before the last recession. In 1989, households headed by African American married couples earned 79 percent as much as their white counterparts. By 1995, the gap was 87 percent. Also, the proportion of African American adults ages 25 to 29 who have completed high school has reached that of the same age group among whites.

Large gaps remain between African Americans and whites in educational attainment, income, and poverty rates. African Americans continue to face disproportionate problems of discrimination, unemployment, and welfare dependency. There is also a possibility that the gains could be reversed if the economy enters into a recession.

See also **Civil Rights Act of 1866; Civil Rights Act of 1964; Equal Employment Opportunity Commission; Protected Class.**

AGE DISCRIMINATION Any negative actions in hiring, training, promoting, disciplining, compensating (including health benefits), or terminating based on the person being 40 years of age or older. Discrimination in the workplace on the basis of age is prohibited by the 1967 Age Discrimination in Employment Act (ADEA).

Most age discrimination cases are based on the disparate treatment theory, which was articulated by the U.S. Supreme Court in *Griggs v. Duke Power* (1971). A plaintiff seeking relief under the ADEA must allege disparate treatment "as the theory for employment discrimination, in which the employee is charging that the employer treated the employee less favorably than others because of the employee's age." Although the Court has held that the ADEA authorizes disparate treatment claims, it has not ruled whether disparate impact is available to ADEA plaintiffs.

To prove age discrimination with this theory, and employee must establish the employer's intent, by either direct or indirect evidence. Direct evidence is actual, documented employer actions and policies, such as a mandatory retirement age, or the refusal to hire employees past a certain age. Indirect evidence is usually inferred from statistical data that consistently shows less favorable treatment of older employees, such as inequitable hiring, advancement, and salary increases. It can also be inferred from comments that imply that age was a factor in employer treatment of older employees.

See also **Age Discrimination in Employment Act of 1967; Disparate Treatment; *Griggs v. Duke Power Co.***

Age Discrimination Act of 1975 Federal statute prohibiting discrimination based on age and protecting persons from being excluded from participation in, being denied the benefits of, or being subject to discrimination because of age in programs or activities receiving federal financial assistance. State and local activities are covered by the statute of the jurisdiction involved. Federal funding may be terminated for entities that do not comply with the provisions of the act. The Department of Health and Human Services has issued regulations to enforce the law. Unlike the Age Discrimination in Employment Act of 1967, which protects persons who are age 40 or older, this statute does not specify age requirements.

See also **Age Discrimination in Employment Act of 1967.**

Age Discrimination in Employment Act (ADEA) of 1967 Federal statute prohibiting employers, unions, employment agencies, and apprenticeship and training programs from discriminating against employees and job applicants on the basis of age. It specifically protects persons who are 40 or older. ADEA also prohibits employers from discriminating on the basis of age between two persons who are both within the protected age group. The statute has been enforced by Equal Employment Opportunity Commission (EEOC) since July 1, 1979.

The prohibitions against age discrimination found in ADEA, as with the prohibitions found in Title VII, forbid discrimination in hiring, discharges, promotions, and all other terms and conditions of employment. Age-based discrimination is permitted, however, if age is a bona fide occupational qualification reasonably necessary for the normal operation of that particular business. Other exceptions are made for bona fide retirement, pension or retirement plans that are not intended to evade the ADEA. The same approach used in Title VII litigation to establish discrimination generally will be followed in ADEA litigation. Generally, a plaintiff builds a prima facie case (sufficient to establish a fact unless it is disputed) of age discrimination by demonstrating that (1) the plaintiff was in a protected age group, (2) the plaintiff was qualified, (3) the plaintiff was nevertheless adversely affected, and (4) the defendant sought someone else with similar qualifications to perform the work. Persons who believe that they have been discriminated against on the basis of age may, under the ADEA, either file civil suits or use the EEOC's complaint procedure. As the proportion of elderly people in the American population has grown, complaints of age discrimination have increased.

Employers with 20 or more workers employed for at least 20 weeks a year are subject to the act, as are labor unions with 25 members, employment agencies, and apprenticeship and training programs that provide referral services to employers in interstate commerce. States and political subdivisions and federal employees, except military personnel, are also covered by the statute.

Under the ADEA, mandatory retirement of employees based on age is illegal unless age is a bona fide occupational qualification. This mandatory retirement ban does not apply to executives who receive annual retirement benefits of at least $44,000 at age 65; tenured college and university personnel 70 years of age; and state and local government fire fighters and law enforcement employees subject to applicable state and local retirement laws. The mandatory retirement ban for college and university faculty, fire fighters, and law enforcement employees was repealed on December 31, 1993, when studies on the impact of eliminating mandatory retirement were completed.

Title VII doesn't prohibit discrimination against persons under age 40 because young people have not had a history of being unfairly discriminated against in contrast to women, the elderly, racial, and ethnic minorities. Some state laws, however, prohibit discrimination against age groups not covered by Title VII.

See also **Age Discrimination; Bona Fide Occupational Qualification; Civil Rights Act of 1964; Equal Employment Opportunity Commission.**

AGE OF MAJORITY The age at which a person is legally an adult. It is also the age at which, according to law, persons are bound by their words and acts. For most legal purposes, the terms child, infant, minor, or juvenile are used interchangeably to denote those who have not yet attained the age of majority, also called "full age" or "legal age."

Each state determines its own age of majority. In most states, the age of majority is 18. Until 1971, the age of majority in almost every state was 21. Since the enactment that year of the Twenty-Sixth Amendment, which gave 18-year-olds the right to vote in federal elections, all but a few states have lowered the age of majority from 21 to 18. The opposite of majority, minority, usually designates someone under 18.

The effect of the age of majority, even within a single state, varies with respect to the activity involved. The state has the power to set ages of qualification for a wide range of activities, including making contracts and working for wages.

Laws that make decisions for very young children are justified out of necessity, since these persons cannot make decisions for themselves. In the employment context, every state has child labor laws, which are intended to protect the health, safety, and educational interests of minors. They restrict the types of jobs that children may hold, the age at which they may hold them, and the hours of employment, along with other conditions. Because every state has its own set of child labor laws, the state employment office or department of labor is the best source of information on the law in a particular state for a particular set of circumstances.

Under certain circumstances, minors can be emancipated, that is released from some or all of the legal restrictions of childhood and receive the rights and duties of adulthood. Emancipation may be granted by a court or under other conditions such as an agreement without court approval.

See also **Child Labor Laws.**

AGENCY SHOP A specific provision of a collective bargaining agreement (a union security measure) that requires every company employee—union and nonunion alike—to pay the union an amount equal to the union's customary initiation fees and monthly dues. It does not require any employee to become a formal member of the union, to be a member before becoming hired, to take any oath, or to follow any internal rules and regulations of the union. The payment to the union is to defray the expenses of the union (as bargaining agent) in negotiations and contract administration.

The U.S. Supreme Court upheld Section 8(a)(3) of the National Labor Relations Act (NLRA) (as amended by the Labor-Management Relations

Act of 1947, also known as the Taft-Hartley Act), which permits agency shop arrangements that condition employment upon payment of charges for union representation instead of membership fees. [*NLRB v. General Motors* (1963)] However, the Court also ruled that the states may prohibit the agency shop under the authority of Section 14(b) of the NLRA in *Retail Clerks, Local 1625 v. Schermerhorn* (1963).

The first agency shop provisions were allowed under the National War Labor Board during World War II. The agency shop became better known following the arbitration award involving Ford Motor Company and the United Automobile Workers Union. The National Labor Relations Board held that the agency shop is a "valid union security agreement" under the NLRA in *Public Service Co. of Colorado* on April 14, 1950.

See also **National Labor Relations Act; National Labor Relations Board; Union Security Clause; United Automobile Workers.**

AGRICULTURAL WORKERS Individuals whose occupation is work in farming operations, primarily in such activities as cultivation and tillage of the soil and dairying. These operations also include any practices, which are performed either by a farmer or on a farm, incidentally to or in conjunction with such farming operations. [*Farmer's Reservoir & Irrigation Co. v. McComb* (1949)]

Federal law has long recognized agricultural exemptions in statutes on wages, hours, labor relations, child labor, Social Security, unemployment compensation, and workers' compensation. Section 2(3) of the National Labor Relations Act (NLRA), for example, which excludes from its coverage "any individual employed as an agricultural laborer" may have been a concession to agricultural interests in Congress who would have opposed not only the NLRA but also the Social Security Act and the Fair Labor Standards Act (FLSA) had the three statutes not included an agricultural exclusion. It may also be attributable to some concern that employment relations on most farms are too local to fall within federal regulation, or that the perishability of crops is such that strikes would give agricultural employees too strong a bargaining weapon and unionization would make farm operations unduly costly, or that (somewhat inconsistently) farm workers do not need unionization since their relationship with the employer is a friendly and intimate one (akin to the excluded domestic servant or close relative of the employer).

The FLSA requires that certain agricultural employers pay an agricultural minimum wage, set since January 1978 at the same rate as the general minimum wage. An agricultural employer who uses 500 man-days of agricultural labor during any calendar quarter of a particular year must pay the agricultural minimum wage to certain agricultural employees in the following calendar year. Agricultural employers who are required to pay the agricultural minimum wage must pay it to all agricultural employees except: (1) members of his or her immediate family, unless the farm is incorporated; (2) local hand-harvest piece-rate workers who come to the farm from their permanent residences each day, but only if such workers were employed less than 13 weeks in agriculture in the preceding year; (3) children age 16 and under whose parents are migrant workers, and who are employed as hand-harvest piece-rate workers on the same farm as their parents, provided that they receive the same piece-rate as other workers; and (4) employees engaged in the range production of livestock.

See also **Fair Labor Standards Act; National Labor Relations Act; Social Security Act.**

***ALEXANDER V. GARDNER-DENVER* (1974)** The U.S. Supreme Court opinion that was interpreted as a major change in the Court's position in the three Supreme Court decisions in 1960 known as the Steelworkers Trilogy. However, a closer examination of the case seems to indicate that it was not a wide departure from the earlier federal law of arbitration.

The *Alexander v. Gardner-Denver* case involved the discharge of an employee for alleged poor performance. The employee contested his discharge through the negotiated grievance procedure, where he claimed he had been discharged because of his race. At the same time, he filed a complaint with the local Equal Employment Opportunity Commission (EEOC) charging racial discrimination. The employee lost at arbitration and the EEOC discovered no reasonable grounds for finding that he had been discriminated against. Following these two decisions, the employee carried his complaint to the federal courts.

The U.S. Supreme Court ruled that the arbitration award had not exhausted the grievant's legal remedies, a conclusion based on the fact that an individual can pursue multiple avenues of remedy in civil rights cases. Rights arising out of the Civil Rights Act of 1964 rather than the collective bargaining agreement do not require judicial deferral to arbitration. This is true even though the remedy is originally sought under the grievance arbitration procedures of a collective bargaining agreement.

Several points made by the Court in *Gardner-Denver* were not new, and the direction the decision pointed was anticipated in several earlier decisions. Some of the significant issues—multiple remedies and limited deferral in civil rights cases, distinctions between the rights of an individual and those of the union organization, and distinctions between contractual rights and statutory rights—required further examination.

The U.S. Supreme Court in *Gardner-Denver* held that civil rights guaranteed by the Civil Rights Act of 1964 are not a part of the collective bargaining agreement and that while a union may waive certain statutory rights related to the progress of collective bargaining, there can be no waiver of employee rights under Title VII of the Civil Rights Act. Individual employees have a statutory right to trial under Title VII that is not prevented by submission of a claim to final arbitration under the nondiscrimination clause of the collective agreement. Congress intended for individuals to pursue their rights independently under Title VII and all other applicable state and federal statutes. The Court recognized an essential difference between the law of the shop (a contract right interpreted through arbitration) and the law of the land (a statutory right interpreted by the federal courts).

The *Gardner-Denver* decision suggested guidelines for judicial deferral to arbitration awards. The arbitration decision itself can be submitted as evidence and accorded such weight as the Court deems appropriate. Relevant factors in considering deferral include the existence of provisions in the agreement that conform to the intent of Title VII; the degree of procedural fairness in the arbitration hearing; the adequacy of the record with respect to discrimination; and the special competence of particular arbitrators. If the arbitration gives full consideration to an employer's Title VII rights, it may be given great weight in the courts, which have been granted ultimate authority for resolution of such disputes by Congress.

See also **Civil Rights Act of 1964; Grievance; Grievance Arbitration; Steelworkers Trilogy.**

ALIENS: EMPLOYMENT ISSUES Aliens are foreign-born individuals in the labor force who are not American citizens. They may be (1) resident aliens, or legal immigrants, admitted for permanent settlement under statutory quotas and preferences, (2) temporary workers, such as doctors, scientists, entertainers, and other particularly qualified persons, admitted for specific periods, and (3) illegal aliens, the largest group of immigrants in today's economy. Aliens who work in the United States for American employers are considered employees under the National Labor Relations Act, even if they are in the country illegally. Illegal aliens are also entitled to minimum wages and overtime under the Fair Labor Standards Act (FLSA).

The U.S. Supreme Court has recognized the exclusion of aliens as a fundamental act of national sovereignty, and Congress has restricted immigration to the United States since 1882. Despite these restrictions and several recent congressional attempts to limit illegal immigration, the United States still attracts a large number of undocumented aliens.

The Civil Rights Act of 1866 protects aliens from invidious discrimination. Thus, in the absence of a bona fide business reason for refusing employment—the requirement that aliens possess work permits or permission to remain in the United States, for example—a refusal to hire based on citizenship alone may violate this statute. However, noncitizen aliens are not part of a protected class under Title VII of the Civil Rights Act of 1964. The Supreme Court ruled in *Espinoza v. Farah Manufacturing Co.* (1973) that the act does not prohibit discrimination based on citizenship or alienage. Employment practices that discriminate among aliens based on race, color, religion, sex, or national origin, and hiring Anglo-Saxon aliens over aliens of Mexican ancestry, is prohibited by Title VII.

The Immigration Reform and Control Act (IRCA) (1986), which amended the Immigration and Nationality Act, substantially changed the federal law on employing aliens. IRCA prohibited, for the first time, the hiring or continued employment of "unauthorized aliens" and required that employers verify and document the identity and employment eligibility of every employee. The employer is required to verify the eligibility of every new hire and record the verification on an I-9 form, regardless of an employer's certainty that the new hire is eligible to work in the United States. The hiring or continued employment of an "unauthorized alien," or failure to abide by IRCA's verification and recordkeeping rules, may subject an employer to civil or criminal penalties. IRCA also prohibits employment discrimination based on an individual's national origin or citizenship status. This provision was included because of concerns over employment discrimination against Hispanic citizens.

In federal employment, the Supreme Court in *Hampton v. Wong* (1976) ruled that although the president and Congress can restrict employment of aliens in the national interest, prohibiting employment of resident aliens must be based on an adequate showing of legitimate reasons. Executive Order 11935 (September 3, 1986), which requires citizenship status for federal employment, has been upheld by the courts on the basis that the president is authorized to issue executive orders to prohibit aliens from civil service employment.

Undocumented aliens generally do not take jobs from legal workers but instead work under exploitative conditions unacceptable to most legal workers. Faced with economic realities, employers will choose among three options: ignore sanctions, absorb the costs of improving working conditions to attract U.S. citizens, or move operations abroad. Many American employers largely ignore sanction laws such as the minimum wage, the FLSA, and the Occupational Safety and Health Act, because of the economic advantages gained in employing illegal aliens.

See also **Civil Rights Act of 1866; Civil Rights Act of 1964; Fair Labor Standards Act; Hispanics: Employment Issues; Immigration Reform and Control Act of 1986; Minimum Wage; National Labor Relations Act; Occupational Safety and Health Act; Overtime.**

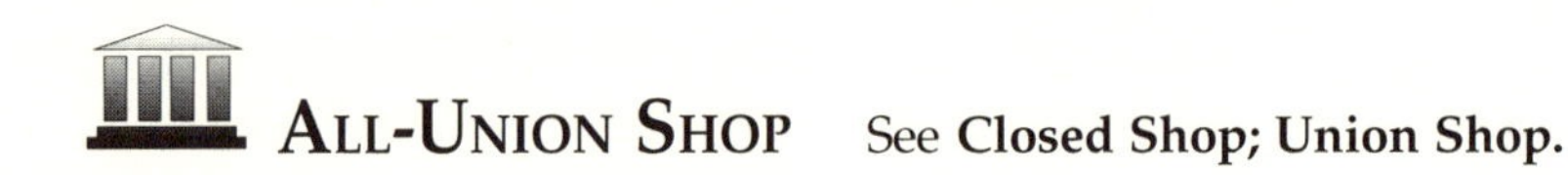

ALL-UNION SHOP

See **Closed Shop; Union Shop.**

ALLY DOCTRINE

The ally doctrine is an exception to the provisions of the National Labor Relations Act (NLRA) prohibiting the secondary boycott when two employers are "allies," so that a union may picket both of them, even if the dispute is only with one of them. Under the ally doctrine, an employer who performs struck work for or assists a struck employer in some way is considered his ally. "Struck work" is that work which otherwise would have been done by the striking employees of the primary employer. The ally is considered a primary employer for the purpose of the secondary boycott provisions of the NLRA because such an employer has ceased to be neutral. The ally doctrine was first pronounced in *Douds v. Metropolitan Federation of Architects* (1948).

A secondary boycott is the use of economic pressure (such as picketing) against an employer with whom the union has no dispute on its own terms of employment in order to induce that employer to cease doing business with another employer (the primary employer) with whom the union has an ongoing labor dispute. Secondary boycotts are principally regulated through Sections 8(b)(4)(B) and 8(e) of the NLRA. Congress, in passing these provisions as part of the Labor-Management Relations Act (LMRA) of 1947 (the Taft-Hartley Act), made the secondary boycott an unfair labor practice so that neutral employers would not become enmeshed in labor disputes between a union and the primary employer in which they were not involved and could not resolve.

The ally doctrine provides an exception to the NLRA's secondary boycott prohibition if the following facts are present:

1. The second (secondary) employer's employees are doing the struck work
2. There is an arrangement between the primary and secondary employer by which this work is done
3. The primary and secondary employer both receive an economic benefit from the arrangement—the secondary employer is doing work it would have done but for the strike, and the primary employer is able to avoid the full effect of the strike

An example of when the ally doctrine applies is when a struck employer subcontracts work to another employer and such work would normally be performed by the striking employees, the subcontractor is considered an ally of the struck employer and may be picketed just as the primary employer. When an employer is treated as an ally of the primary employer, instead of as a neutral, it is subject to all of the pressures through the inducement of its employees to strike to which the primary employer is properly subjected, just as if its employees were replacements who went to work in the primary plant. The ally is considered a primary employer for the purpose of the secondary boycott provisions of the statute, because such an employer has ceased to be neutral.

The mere fact that two companies have the same owners does not necessarily make the two companies a single employer or allies. Some crucial factors to analyze in order to determine whether the ally doctrine would apply in this context are: whether the companies have a common labor relations policy and whether there was a significant integration of operations and management.

The leading case applying the ally doctrine is *NLRB v. Business Machine and Office Appliance Mechanics Conference Board Local 459 (Royal Typewriter*

Co.) (1955), which was heard by the second circuit of the U.S. Court of Appeals.

See also **Labor-Management Relations Act of 1947; National Labor Relations Act; Secondary Boycott; Unfair Labor Practice.**

ALTERNATIVE DISPUTE RESOLUTION (ADR)

Procedures for settling disputes by some method other than a lawsuit. ADR techniques—such as mediation, fact-finding, and arbitration—are commonly used in the labor relations field.

ADR involves the use of a third party neutral or a panel of neutrals to help resolve disputes that might otherwise be resolved though litigation or not be resolved at all. One advantage of ADR is that it applies "substantive expertise," that is, the neutral party is well versed in the subject of the dispute, in addition to "process expertise," or knowledge about the process of conflict resolution. ADR is intended to relieve court congestion and avoid undue cost and delay, facilitating access to justice. More than 600 large corporations such as Federal Express and Coors Brewing Company use ADR, largely because they have found employment litigation so expensive. (The court costs for a jury trial in employment disputes can range from $50,000 to $100,000.)

In mediation, the parties meet with a mediator who helps them evaluate the issues and settle their dispute. Mediators have no authority to impose their decisions. They are, however, neutral parties, frequently professionals in their fields, and provide opinions and guidance in the search for a settlement. Mediation is usually more informal and less time consuming than litigation.

In arbitration, as opposed to mediation, parties make a prior agreement that the arbitrator's decisions will be binding (a mediator does not make a final decision, but rather attempts to lead the parties to reach an agreement). Arbitration has been used in several types of commercial disputes and in complex cases that a layperson jury would find difficult to resolve. Arbitration proceedings often resemble trials. The process of presenting evidence and advocating one's position is relatively formal, although the rules of evidence and procedure are more informal than those used in court.

See also **Mediation.**

AMERICAN FEDERATION OF LABOR-CONGRESS OF INDUSTRIAL ORGANIZATIONS (AFL-CIO) A national federation of craft and industrial labor unions representing employees in the United States and Canada. This federation of craft and industrial unions, and unions with a mixed structure, was created in 1955 by the merger of the American Federation of Labor and the Congress of Industrial Organizations.

Formed in 1886, the American Federation of Labor (AFL), initially led by Samuel Gompers, emphasized a trade unionism that avoided political ideology and focused on what could be won through bargaining with management. The AFL sought immediate improvements in wages and employment conditions within the existing economic system. It had no political ideology and strove to avoid becoming formally affiliated with a political party as the European unions had done. In the early twentieth century, for example, the chief goals of the AFL's minimalist political approach were abolishing the injunction and removing the courts from policing strikes.

By the late 1890s, the AFL was the nation's leading labor organization. In the prosperous years following the depression of 1893–1896, membership in AFL unions doubled. AFL leaders strove to transform their craft unions into more centralized, bureaucratic organizations—not only capable of wielding greater power through national combination and mutual support but also more restrained in their strike policies. Not "final emancipation" from the "wages system" but the business unionism of collective bargaining became the AFL's goal.

American trade unionism, as represented by the AFL, has been described as "bread and butter unionism" because of the wage consciousness of the trade unions. The traditionally economic focus of American unions, as opposed to the class-based political programs of the European unions, is due in part to a sense of upward mobility and a lack of class consciousness among American workers. The AFL resorted to political action chiefly to prevent hostile judicial interventions in labor disputes. Labor's efforts in national politics led to landmark labor legislation passed during the Wilson administration (1913–1921), especially the Clayton Act and the Seamen's Act, both intended to reverse hostile judge-made law. Through this legislation and comparable state legislation, the AFL hoped to reduce rather than extend the scope of government regulation of industrial relations.

By the end of the nineteenth century, the power and prestige of the AFL were utilized to help the skilled craftsmen organize by occupation. The AFL was primarily a federation consisting of independent national unions organized by craft or trade (i.e., carpenters or plumbers) rather than by industry (i.e., all workers in the steel industry). This narrow form of organization gave the AFL strength to survive antiunion pressure from employers in a period when industrial unionism had yet to develop. But the masses of workers, who had often been regarded by the crafts unions as unorganizable, were not affiliated with any type of labor union until the 1930s. Relentless pressure was exerted within the AFL to organize workers in the steel, packing house, and rubber industries, and during the 1930s, labor leaders such as John L. Lewis and Philip Murray began organizing workers in mass production by industry rather than on a crafts basis.

Expanding employment was concentrated in mass production industries, such as the rubber and auto industries. There, skilled workers were in the minority. The workers in the rubber and automobile industries organized and applied for membership in the AFL but wanted to form industrial rather than craft unions in their industries. Six unions within the AFL formed in November 1935 to organize unorganized workers in mass production industries and encourage their affiliation with the American Federation of Labor, including the United Steelworkers and the United Autoworkers. The existing craft international unions demanded that the charters of the applicants exclude jurisdiction over workers in occupations claimed by the crafts. This concession was unacceptable to the new internationals and to certain older AFL industrial internationals such as the United Mine Workers, the Amalgamated Clothing Workers, and the International Ladies' Garment Workers. The issue could not be resolved within the framework of the old AFL.

The industrial unions, led by John L. Lewis, then formed a Committee of Industrial Organizations (CIO). The effort to organize by industry was resisted by the most powerful AFL leaders, who clung desperately to their principles of crafts organization. After the proposal for industrial unionism was defeated at the AFL convention in 1935, eight unions founded the CIO within the AFL. The executive council of the AFL charged that the Committee for Industrial Organization promoted "dual unionism" (independent rival organizations). Efforts at reconciliation failed, and in 1937 the AFL expelled the CIO. The CIO then changed its name to the Congress of Industrial Organizations (CIO) and became a separate federation of unions in 1938. The CIO then sought to unionize the workers in America's basic industries.

By 1941, the CIO had successfully organized many large corporations in the automobile, rubber, textile, and glass industries, often after long, bitter struggles for recognition by those respective industries. After the CIO won major breakthroughs in the steel and auto industries, it had as nearly as large a membership as the AFL. The distinction between the two federations started to disappear when the AFL began to charter industrial unions and the CIO began to charter craft unions, and the two found themselves competing for the same workers in all trades and industries. By 1945, most of the workers in the nation's mass production industries had been unionized.

One of the most important postwar developments was the merger of the two federations in 1955, after jurisdictional disputes were resolved by a "no-raiding agreement" between the two federations in 1949. The merger united approximately 130 international unions representing some 15 million members. It did not include the United Mine Workers of America, some railroad unions, and various smaller organizations expelled from the CIO for Communist domination. The 1955 convention of the AFL-CIO established the administrative structure and governing policies of the organization. As a compromise, the new name merely combined the names of the two organizations to become the American Federation of Labor-Congress of Industrial Organizations.

But the political climate also changed dramatically in the 1950s. Organized labor and the progressives were defeated in their battles against the Labor-Management Relations Act of 1947 (also known as the Taft-Hartley Act) and for an Economic Bill of Rights. Union corruption uncovered by Senate investigations led Congress to enact further legislation to restrict labor and led the AFL-CIO to expel certain internationals, including the International Brotherhood of Teamsters, with its more than 1.5 million members, for corrupt practices. Congress passed the Labor-Management Reporting and Disclosure Act of 1959 (also known as the Landrum-Griffin Act) in an attempt to protect union funds and the fairness of elections through monitoring and reporting procedures. During the 1960s, the United Auto Workers under Walter Reuther broke away from the AFL-CIO to join with the Teamsters under the Alliance for Labor Action. Reuther hoped to reinvigorate a labor movement, which he believed was ignoring social goals. The effort stagnated, however, after Reuther's death in 1970.

The principal organizational levels in the contemporary union movement are the AFL-CIO Federation, national unions, and local unions. The primary functions of the federation are lobbying on behalf of the union movement, educating the public on labor's viewpoints, and resolving disputes among affiliated unions. The primary roles of a national union are organizing additional local unions within its jurisdiction and negotiating collective bargaining agreements.

The primary governing body of the AFL-CIO is the biennial convention, where national unions are represented in proportion to their membership. The executive council, which usually meets three times a year, consists of a president, secretary-treasurer, and 27 vice-presidents, each of whom is a president of national union. An executive committee consisting of six vice presidents selected by the council meets regularly with the president and secretary-treasurer to discuss policy matters. In addition, a general board consisting of the executive council and a principal officer of each affiliated union meets at least once a year to decide policy questions referred to it. The federation is supported by a per capita tax on affiliated unions and organizing committees. The federation engages in organizing efforts, educational campaigns on behalf of the labor movement, the settlement of jurisdictional disputes among its affiliates, and the political support of legislation deemed beneficial.

Lane Kirkland was elected president of the AFL-CIO on November 19, 1979, following the retirement of its first president, George Meany. During his tenure as president, Kirkland focused on foreign policy, which often resulted in organized labor supporting the Reagan and Bush administrations on defense matters while criticizing their domestic policies. Kirkland and the AFL-CIO almost single-handedly kept Poland's Solidarity movement alive in the 1980s, smuggling money and equipment into that country when even the U.S. government was reluctant to become involved.

By the 1980s, unions had become less influential in American political and economic life than they were 20 or 30 years before. Changing patterns of employment by industry and occupation have tended to reduce union membership. Employment in the highly unionized segments of the economy has grown slowly in recent years; at the same time, it has grown rapidly in industries and occupations with historically low levels of unionization. Technological change and foreign competition have threatened many blue-collar jobs, and employers have become increasingly successful in efforts to prevent unionization. These patterns are expected to remain constant in the future.

Union membership as a percentage of the American labor force has been declining since 1954. In 1987, the AFL-CIO represented 14 million of the nation's 17 million union members. Today, the AFL-CIO is composed of 88 national unions and more than 60,000 local unions. It has a membership of approximately 13 million. Approximately 14.5 percent of America's civilian employees are members of the AFL-CIO international and national affiliates. The unionized workforce is becoming increasingly diversified. Women by 1995 constitute 39.2 percent of the union membership. African Americans account for 15 percent, and Hispanics 8 percent.

By the 1990s, organized labor found both its membership and its political influence in sharp decline. Since at least 1984, Kirkland and other labor leaders have attributed American labor's decline to adverse National Labor Relations Board decisions and hostile court interpretations of the National Labor Relations Act. Kirkland at one point stated that he preferred "no law" to the labor law of the Reagan-Bush era. Labor's leadership seems to believe that the affirmative protections of labor law are empty promises, while prohibitions against secondary boycotts excessively restrict what unions can do to assist each other in confronting employers who have violated the law.

AFL-CIO leaders often blamed their losses on Republican presidential administrations. Confronted with a dwindling membership and, beginning in 1995, a Republican-controlled Congress actively promoting a probusiness agenda, the leaders of 11 major unions concluded that Kirkland had to retire. Ironically, some of the unions Kirkland brought back into the AFL-CIO—including the United Auto Workers, the International Brotherhood of Teamsters, and the United Mineworkers of America—opposed his reelection in 1995.

Criticized for not changing with the times, Lane Kirkland retired as AFL-CIO president in August 1995. His longtime deputy, Thomas Donahue, was elected as the federation's president by the AFL-CIO Executive Council. In the first contested election for president of the AFL-CIO in the federation's history, Donahue was defeated at the group's October 1995 convention by John Sweeney, then president of the Service Employees International Union. Sweeney has focused the federation's resources on political activism during the 1996 elections and on large-scale union organizing efforts, such as its drive to organize the hotel, hospital, and construction workers of Las Vegas.

See also **Clayton Antitrust Act; Collective Bargaining; Industrial Relations; Labor Dispute; Labor Organization; National Labor Relations Act; National Labor Relations Board; United Auto Workers.**

AMERICANS WITH DISABILITIES ACT (ADA) OF 1990 A federal statute enacted that prohibits discrimination against persons with disabilities in public accommodations and in terms and conditions of employment. The act addresses the physical barriers and social attitudes that prevent the 43 million physically and mentally disabled Americans from having access to public places and from equal employment. It is a major piece of social legislation that significantly affects all aspects of American society.

A person is considered disabled, and covered by the ADA, if (1) he or she has a "physical or mental impairment [including orthopedic, visual, speech, and hearing impairments] that substantially limits one or more major life activities"; (2) he or she has a history or record of such impairment; or (3) he or she has a physical or mental impairment that is considered a disability (this provision protects a person with a disability that limits a major life activity only as a result of the "attitude" of others toward the impairment).

The ADA is divided into five titles, and many of the employment issues arising from the ADA are covered in Title I. Title I covers all employers with 25 or more employees on July 26, 1992, and as of July 26, 1994, it applied to employers with less than 25 but more than 15 employees. However, some organizations are exempt from ADA requirements: corporations fully owned by the U.S. government, Indian tribes, and tax exempt private membership clubs that are not labor organizations.

The ADA prohibits employment discrimination against "qualified individual[s] with disabilities" in all aspects of employment, including testing, job applications, hiring, assignments, evaluation, disciplinary actions, training, promotions, medical examinations, layoff/recall, terminations, compensation, leave, and benefits. Since the ADA protects only "qualified individuals with a disability," an employer is not required to hire or retain an individual with a disability who is unable to perform the "essential functions" of the position. An essential function is a job task that is fundamental, as opposed to a task that is only marginally related to the position. This is determined by examining the duty in the context of the total work environment.

After the essential functions of the job are determined, the ADA requires that employers must make "reasonable accommodations" to help the disabled employee perform the essential functions of the job, such as modifying equipment or permitting the use of a guide dog at work. An employer is not obligated to lower standards or modify programs to hire an employee with a disability if no accommodation would allow the person to meet legitimate job standards, or if the only sufficient accommodation imposes an undue hardship on the employer. "Undue hardship" means that the remedial action involves "significant difficulty or expense." The factors used in determining whether there is undue hardship include the nature and cost of the accommodation, the overall financial resources of the business, and the type and operation of the business. Claims of undue hardship are determined on a case-by-case basis, because the ADA does not provide an all-encompassing definition of reasonableness or hardship.

The employment provisions of the ADA are enforced by the Equal Employment Opportunity Commission (EEOC) in a manner similar to its enforcement of the Civil Rights Act of 1964. The commission has the authority to investigate alleged violations of the ADA, and persons who believe that their rights under the ADA have been violated must file charges with the commission within 180 days of the action. These persons also have the right to file a private lawsuit against the offending party.

The full ramifications of the ADA will not be apparent for some time. Interpreting the statute's requirement for reasonable accommodation will likely create many legal issues. Recently, a U.S. district court in New York provided some insight into these provisions. Even though the case, *D'Amico v. New York State Board of Law Examiner* (1993), was not decided under the employment title of the ADA, it indicates that employers considering refusing an accommodation should consider obtaining the support of a medical expert. It is clearly the disabled employee's responsibility to request an accommodation when needed, and the employee's request triggers the employer's duty to reasonably accommodate the employee's disability as it affects the performance of the assigned job duties. The employer may choose the easiest or least expensive accommodation, but the employer is required by the EEOC guidelines to give primary consideration to the disabled employee's preference. The employer will be required to make a good faith effort to come up with a workable means of accommodation satisfactory to the disabled employee.

Some courts have been willing to extend the ADA's "is regarded as having such an impairment" language to include transsexuals as those who are regarded as handicapped by others. This includes a case in the U.S. district court in the District of Columbia in which an employment offer was rescinded after it was learned that the prospective employee was a preoperative transsexual. [*Jane Doe v. United States Postal Service* (1985)] The Washington Supreme Court, however, ruled that a transsexual employee, without evidence of discrimination, is not handicapped under the Washington Statute Against Discrimination. An employee's duty to accommodate the transsexual is limited to the steps reasonably necessary to enable job performance by the employee.

The ADA is not the final solution to disability-based discrimination. It is, however, a substantial step toward addressing the problems of less-than-equal opportunity for many disabled persons and represents a major commitment by the federal government to creating equal opportunity for all its citizens.

See also **Civil Rights Act of 1964; Equal Employment Opportunity Commission.**

ANTITRUST LAWS Federal and state statutes intended to limit interference with free trade and competition. Antitrust laws are intended to promote competition and to encourage the production of quality goods and services at the lowest prices. They explicitly prohibit unlawful restraints of trade, price fixing, and monopoly. In the early twentieth century, they were frequently applied to labor organizations as agencies acting in restraint of trade.

The Sherman Antitrust Act (1890), the first and most significant American antitrust statute, made agreements in restraint of trade and monopolization illegal. It also made violators liable for civil remedies, criminal penalties, actions by the U.S. district attorneys, and to treble damage actions in private lawsuits. It was initially applied more often to unions than to employers and was regularly used by federal courts as the authority for enjoining union-led boycotts. In 1908 the Supreme Court sustained the applicability of the act to unions and union activities in *Loewe v. Lawlor* (the 1908 "Danbury Hatters' case").

Some years later, the Supreme Court in a case involving a labor dispute, articulated the true rationale of the Sherman Antitrust Act: "It was enacted in the era of 'trusts and of combinations' of business and capital organized and directed to control of the marketing of goods and services, the monopolistic tendency of which had become a matter of public concern." [*Apex Hosiery Co. v. Leader* (1940)] The legislative history of the Sherman Act, however, was unclear as to whether the statute was intended to cover unions or intended to leave the issue for the courts to decide.

The Clayton Act contained two sections (Section 6 and Section 20) that appeared to exempt all unions, all collective bargaining, and all peaceful concerted activities from antitrust laws. The U.S. Supreme Court, however, persisted in applying antitrust laws against labor unions in cases such as *Duplex Printing Press Co. v. Deering* (1921), which involved a secondary boycott. To make clearer what had appeared to be its intention in Sections 6 and 20 of the Clayton Act, Congress enacted the Norris-La Guardia Act, which forbids the issuance of injunctions in cases involving peaceful labor disputes.

Present-day federal antitrust laws do not prohibit labor organizations from exercising the rights guaranteed by the National Labor Relations Act; however, labor unions are not entirely immune from liability for federal antitrust violations. Whether labor union activities violate the Sherman Act depends on whether the union acts alone or in combination with business groups. A union commits an antitrust violation when it has contracted, combined, or conspired with a nonlabor group, usually competitors of a business, to unlawfully restrain the marketing of goods or services. [*United States v. Hutcheson* (1941)] Since the Supreme Court held that the Clayton Act and the Norris-LaGuardia Act are constitutional in *Hutcheson*, the Sherman Act has played a rather limited role in the regulation of unions.

See also **Clayton Antitrust Act; *Loewe v. Lawlor* (1908); National Labor Relations Act; Norris-LaGuardia Act; Sherman Antitrust Act of 1980.**

APPRENTICESHIP An arrangement whereby an employee enters into an agreement with an employer and a union, and sometimes vocational schools, to learn a skilled trade by work experience and technical instruction. An apprentice is a person who agrees to work for a specified time in order to learn a trade, craft, or profession in which the employer, traditionally called the master, agrees to instruct him or her. Apprentices are full-time employees who receive training in all aspects of a trade. An individual who successfully completes the apprenticeship program, which takes from one to six years, attains journey-worker status. To protect job opportunities for journey workers, unions usually restrict the number of apprentices to a certain percentage of practicing journey workers.

Apprenticeship programs are administered by employers, unions, or jointly by employers and unions. An apprenticeship must be formed from an agreement, sometimes referred to as an indenture, that meets the requirements of a valid contact. If the contract cannot be performed within a year, it must be in writing, in order to satisfy the statute of frauds, an old English law adopted in the United States which requires that certain agreements to be in writing. Both the apprentice and the employer must sign the agreement, along with the parents or guardian of a minor apprentice. The contract must include the provisions required by law and drafted for the benefit of the minor, such as those relating to his or her education or training. A breach of the apprenticeship contract may justify the award of damages. Unless authorized by statute, there can be no assignment, or transfer, of the contract of apprenticeship to another, binding the apprentice to a new service.

The formal apprenticeship system began in the United States in 1937 with the passage of the National Apprenticeship Act. Administered by the U.S. Department of Labor, the act sets federal and state standards on job duties and training, equal employment opportunity, and safety for apprenticeships.

Title VII of the Civil Rights Act of 1964 specifically prohibits discrimination on the basis of race, color, religion, sex, or national origin by an employer, union, or joint labor-management committee in the control of apprenticeships. Some of the practices found to be discriminatory are not job-related—discriminatory recruitment efforts and discriminatory applications of admissions requirements.

See also **Civil Rights Act of 1964.**

APPROPRIATE BARGAINING UNIT The persons employed in a certain group of jobs at the time of a representation election, who have been deemed by the National Labor Relations Board (NLRB) as entitled to vote, whether they wish to settle the terms and conditions of employment on an individual basis or whether they wish to have one or another employee representative.

A union can be certified as the bargaining representative of a group of employees only if those employees constitute an appropriate bargaining unit. In determining whether a proposed bargaining unit is appropriate, the NLRB will determine whether the employees share a community of interests, based on factors such as: (1) similarity in the scale and manner of determining earnings; (2) similarity in employment benefits, hours of work, and other terms and conditions of employment; (3) similarity in the kind of work performed; (4) similarity in the qualifications, skills, and training of the employees; (5) frequency of the contact or interchange among the employees; (6) geographic proximity; (7) continuity or integration of the production processes; (8) common supervision and determination of labor relations policy; (9) relationship to collective bargaining; (10) desires of the affected employees; and (11) extent of union organization within the firm. For example, all production and maintenance employees would form one appropriate bargaining unit, while all office clerical employees would form a distinct and separate appropriate bargaining unit.

An employer's duty to bargain collectively extends only to a union that represents the employees in an appropriate bargaining unit. The right of a union to represent is the authority to bargain for a group of employees in this unit. To obtain a representation election, the union must agree to represent all the employees in the appropriate bargaining unit, the group held by the NLRB and state and local boards to constitute the unit appropriate for bargaining purposes. When no official designation of certification is made, it is the unit accepted by the employer for bargaining purposes.

However, an employer, must also bargain even where a union seeks recognition for an inappropriate unit if (1) the requested unit is smaller than the unit the employer believes to be appropriate, and the union has a majority in both the requested and the appropriate units; (2) the requested unit is ambiguous; (3) or the employer fails to base its refusal of recognition on the inappropriateness of the requested unit; (4) an employer cannot refuse to bargain based on an erroneous belief that a bargaining unit is inappropriate, even if that belief is a good-faith belief; and (5) an employer is not justified in refusing to bargain when a unit description, although unclear, leaves no doubt as to the claim of representation of the majority of employees.

See also **Certification; National Labor Relations Board.**

ARIZONA GOVERNING COMMITTEE FOR TAX DEFERRED COMPENSATION PLANS V. NORRIS (1983)

The defendants in this case administered a deferred compensation plan for employees in Arizona. The plaintiffs brought a class action lawsuit on behalf of all current and future female employees, those who are enrolled in the plan or will enroll in the future. The employer offered employees the option of receiving retirement benefits from one of several companies selected by the employer. All of these companies paid women lower monthly retirement benefits than men who had made the same contributions because women lived longer according to actuarial statistics.

The plaintiffs brought this lawsuit under Title VII of the Civil Rights of 1964, which plainly forbids the use of gender-distinct conditions of employment. The Supreme Court held that this practice had little or nothing to do with useful or genuine business considerations but instead demeaned individuals because they were women. Thus the Court held that the defendants violated Title VII. It not only ruled that all retirement benefits must be calculated without regard to the sex of the beneficiary; it also held that an employer cannot even offer its employers a sexually disparate term or condition of employment, even though (1) the employer offers nondiscriminatory alternative terms and conditions; (2) the employer does not offer the sex-based term as a device to demean, humiliate, or harm women; and (3) the stereotype is scientifically accurate. Benefits derived from contributions made prior to this decision may be calculated as provided by the existing terms of the Arizona plan.

The court in *Norris* found that the defendants engaged in "per se discrimination." Per se discrimination occurs when an employer's policy, term, condition, or practice is blatantly discriminatory. A unique aspect of the *Norris* case is that the discriminatory treatment involves "per se" but "unintentional" discrimination, demonstrating that on rare occasions, the court can find discrimination "per se" that does not involve a discriminatory intent.

See also **Civil Rights Act of 1964; Class Action; Retirement.**

ASIAN AMERICANS: EMPLOYMENT ISSUES Asian Americans are people whose ethnic origins lie in the continent of Asia, including the Indian subcontinent. However, those originating from the Middle East are not included within the scope of "Asian" or "Asian American."

Classification based on race is considered a "suspect classification" (statutory classifications which, because they give distinct treatment to a group that has historically been the victim of discrimination are subject to "strict scrutiny"), because of the long history of both public and private racial discrimination in the United States. In addition to African Americans, any other racial group may, if made the object of a classification intended to disfavor that group, invoke strict scrutiny. *Yick Wo v. Hopkins* (1886) was a case involving a suspect administrative discrimination against Asian Americans.

Chinese immigrant laborers in the 1870s, like immigrant laborers from other countries, have been blamed for economic and social problems and subjected to discrimination. In *Yick Wo,* the Supreme Court found a violation of equal protection in the discriminatory administration of a laundry licensing regulation. In that case, a San Francisco ordinance barred the operation of hand laundries in wooden buildings, except with the consent of the Board of Supervisors. The board granted permits to all but one of the non-Chinese applicants, but to none of the nearly 200 Chinese applicants. The U.S. Supreme Court said that Congress's plenary power to exclude aliens was a proposition it did not think open to controversy. [*Chinese Exclusion Case* (1889)] A major early limitation of federal power, involving Asian immigrants, is that no alien can be expelled from the United States unless he or she has been accorded a fair hearing. [*Japanese Immigrant Case* (1903)] The federal government has been immune to challenges for alleged discrimination in granting benefits to immigrants—this included excluding aliens from federal service employment. [*Hampton v. Mow Sun Wong* (1976)]

The infamous Japanese Exclusion case, involved 100,000 Japanese Americans, many of whom were U.S. citizens, who were incarcerated without due process under Executive Order 9066, signed by President Roosevelt in 1942. This was the last case in which a racial or ethnic classification survived strict scrutiny. [*Korematsu v. United States* (1944)] Almost universally, *Korematsu* became regarded by constitutional scholars as one of the worst betrayals of Americans' constitutional rights.

Title VII of the Civil Rights Act of 1964 prohibits race discrimination, including members of groups who trace their ancestry to Asia. In recent years, Asia along with Latin America has contributed the largest inflow of migration. Economic factors such as poverty and the hope of finding employment often supply the motive for migration to the United States. Between 1980 and 1990, the Asian population grew from 1.5% to 2.9% of the total U.S. population.

See also **African Americans: Employment Issues; Civil Rights Act of 1964.**

AUTHORIZATION CARD A statement signed by an employee authorizing a union to act as his or her agent in collective bargaining. Support for a union is usually indicated by these signed, dated cards. Authorization cards signed by 30 percent of the employees in a bargaining unit is required before the National Labor Relations Board (NLRB) will direct that an election be held. However, a union may be recognized as the bargaining agent without an election, on the basis of authorization cards signed by a majority of the employees in an appropriate bargaining unit. The U.S. Supreme Court in *NLRB v. Gissell Packing Co.* (1969) ruled that while an NLRB-conducted secret ballot election is the preferable statutory route to bargaining status, other routes (such as authorization cards and strike support) are acceptable under appropriate circumstances. The NLRB, therefore, is not precluded from considering card strength in issuing a bargaining order.

Authorization cards may also be used to establish bargaining rights even though a union loses an election. For example, in cases of sufficient employer unfair labor practices, if the union can show prior majority strength (usually through authorization cards), and if the possibility of undoing the effects of past practices and of insuring a fair election is slight, the NLRB may issue a bargaining order if it finds that this course would best reflect employee sentiments.

The card may take the form of a union membership card, a membership application, a dues check-off authorization, or a card designating the union as the worker's bargaining representative. The NLRB recognizes dual-purpose cards that designate the union as the bargaining representative and also express the employees' desire for a representational election. However, an employee who signs an authorization card is not obligated to vote for the union in a representation election.

See also **Appropriate Bargaining Unit; Collective Bargaining; National Labor Relations Board.**

***Auto Workers v. Johnson Controls* (1991)** In this case, the U.S. Supreme Court held that an employer's fetal protection policy violated the Pregnancy Discrimination Act of 1978 and Title VII of the Civil Rights Act by excluding women from jobs that may be hazardous to unborn children. This case may have been the most important sex discrimination case since the enactment of Title VII, because the Court applied an "equal treatment" analysis and rejected arguments asserting that the reproductive safety of working women and their fetuses established an employer justification for sex-specific fetal protection employment policies.

The court in *Johnson Controls* established a new legal principle for the law of sex discrimination: sex-specific fetal protection policies are expressly discriminatory and thus unlawful unless they are justified under a narrow interpretation of Title VII's Bona Fide Occupational Qualification (BFOQ) defense. The Court found the bias in the company's policy "obvious" because "fertile men, but not fertile women, are given a choice as whether they wish to risk their reproductive health for a particular job." The Court concluded that no BFOQ exception could be based on excluding fertile women for safety reasons in this case, as the unconceived fetuses of female employees "are neither customers nor third persons whose safety is essential to the business of battery manufacturing. . . . Decisions about the welfare of future children must be left to the parents who conceive, bear, support, and raise them rather than to employers who hired those parents." The court held that the "essence of business" (that which is at the core of the business's existence) and not the cost and safety concerns of the company, is the test applicable to a BFOQ defense. In other words, employers may not limit employment in particular jobs to persons of a particular sex, religion, or national origin unless the employer can show that the desired sex, religion, or national origin is necessary for performing the job. On the issue of tort liability, the court held that compliance with lead standards established by the Occupational Safety and Health Administration, full disclosure of possible risks, and the employer not acting negligently ensure employer liability will be "remote at best."

The underlying problem that Johnson Controls' policy sought to address is a serious one. Approximately 15 to 20 million workers in the United States are exposed to toxic workplace hazards that cause reproductive injury. In this decision, the Court offered little or no protection to women from the reproductive hazards of the workplace. Critics have argued that while this decision has remedied the sex discrimination problem, it failed to address the serious problem of reproductive harm caused by toxic exposure. Even though employers may not be able to totally eliminate toxic workplace hazards, they should take actions to reduce workplace hazards and minimize risks to workers of both sexes.

See also **Bona Fide Occupational Qualification; Civil Rights Act of 1964; Occupational Safety and Health Administration; Pregnancy Discrimination Act of 1978; Sex Discrimination in Employment.**

AWARD

As a verb, *award* means to concede, to give by judicial determination, or to rule in favor after an evaluation of the facts. Thus, a jury awards damages; the court awards an injunction; and one awards a contract to a bidder. As a noun, *award* refers to the decision or determination rendered by arbitrators or commissioners, or other private or extrajudicial decision makers, in a controversy submitted to them. It also refers to the document embodying such decision.

Any award should be reasonable, timely, consistent, and definite. The courts may review an arbitration award in a proceeding to confirm it or to enforce it, or in a proceeding to correct, modify, or vacate it. The court's jurisdiction to review a labor arbitration depends on the terms of the statute under which the review is sought. A court has jurisdiction to enforce final and binding awards rendered pursuant to the arbitration awards under the National Labor Relations Act provisions authorizing lawsuits for the violation of such agreements.

An arbitration award in a labor controversy may be confirmed or enforced in a judicial proceeding only if it is final and definite and is substantially in compliance with the terms of the agreement for arbitration. An arbitration award in a labor case can be impeached in judicial review or enforcement proceedings only upon a clear showing that the award was not within the spirit and provisions of the submission agreement, or upon a showing of fraud, corruption, or similar irregularity, or denial of a hearing.

See also **Grievance Arbitration; Injunctions Against Unions; Labor Management Relations Act of 1947; National Labor Relations Act.**

Back Pay Generally an award of an employee's lost wages, and in some cases fringe benefits, back pay is an award that the employee would have earned but for his or her discharge in violation of a legal right, either one based on statute or acquired by contract. These awards can take two forms: (1) a legally enforceable decree ordering an employer to pay an employee retroactively a designated increase in salary that occurred during a particular period of employment or (2) a decision rendered by a judicial or administrative body that an employee has a legal right to collect an accrued salary which has not been paid out to him or her.

Back pay may be awarded from litigation involving employment discrimination or labor-management issues. Federal civil rights legislation allows for back pay awards to compensate the victim for economic losses suffered as a result of discrimination. Back pay can be awarded to an employee in any of the following cases:

- Improper layoff or discharge under the collective bargaining agreement. Back pay is generally made pursuant to an order by the National Labor Relations Board or an arbitration award.
- Piece-rate adjustments following a grievance under the employment contract. Back pay is generally made pursuant to an arbitration award.
- Violation of the legal minimum wage under federal, state, or local law. Back pay is available from a lawsuit under the minimum wage statute and is enforced by the courts.
- Violation of federal laws prohibiting unfair labor practices.
- Employment discrimination. Back pay is enforced by the courts under Title VII, Section 1981, Section 1983, the Age Discrimination in Employment Act, the Federal Revenue Sharing Act, the Rehabilitation Act, and the Equal Pay Act.

See also **Age Discrimination in Employment Act; Award; Equal Pay Act of 1963; Grievance Arbitration; Minimum Wage; Rehabilitation Act of 1973; Unfair Labor Practice.**

Bakke Case See ***Regents of the University of California v. Bakke* (1978).**

Bankruptcy Amendments and Federal Judgeship Act of 1984 Federal statute enacted to remedy defects in the Bankruptcy Reform Act of 1978, sections of which had been declared unconstitutional by the U.S. Supreme Court. Among other things, the statute made it more difficult for a company in Chapter 11 bankruptcy proceedings to reject its labor contracts. While the amendments were pending in Congress, the Court ruled that a bankruptcy court could permit a Chapter 11 debtor to reject a labor contract if the contract seriously burdened the company and, on balance, the best interests of the company, its creditors, and its employers favored annulment of the contract. [*NLRB v. Bildisco & Bildisco* (1984)] Congress responded by establishing procedures that a company must follow before it can reject a collective bargaining agreement under Section 1113 of the 1984 Amendments. After filing for bankruptcy but before applying to break the contract, the company must meet with labor representatives to discuss changes in the contract that would be needed to enable the company to continue operating. The company must also supply the employees' representatives with the information they need to evaluate the proposed changes and bargain in good faith for the requested concessions. The amendments also require court approval before a debtor can reject a collective bargaining agreement. The statute allows rejection only if the union has refused the debtor's proposed contract modifications "without good cause" and if the balance of equities clearly favors rejection of the union contract.

The Courts have ruled in cases such as *In re: American Provision* (1984) that while Section 1113 protects the interests of companies, the rights of employers must also be protected before a bargaining agreement may be rejected.

See also **Collective Bargaining Agreement.**

Bargaining Unit See **Appropriate Bargaining Unit.**

BELKNAP, INC. V. HALE (1983) The U.S. Supreme Court held that strike replacements who were promised permanent employment but were discharged to enable the return of striking employees had the right to seek relief in state court for breach of contract and misrepresentation. The Court also said that there was no basis for finding that the contract cause of action conflicted with either the strikers or the employer, or that it would frustrate any policy of the federal labor laws.

In this case, Belknap Inc. is a corporation engaged in the sale of hardware products and certain building material. The bargaining unit consists of Belknap's warehouse and maintenance employees. The employee's bargaining representative is the International Brotherhood of Teamsters. The union and Belknap had a contract that expired. In the preliminary negotiations for a new contract, the parties reached an impasse and subsequently the union members went on strike. Shortly after the strike began, Belknap hired replacements for the strikers, agreeing that these replacement employees would be permanently employed. Yet, the company and union reached a settlement and Belknap laid off the replacements. Because of the layoff, Hale, one of the strike replacements, brought a class action lawsuit on behalf of himself and the other replacements against Belknap for misrepresentation and breach of contract by firing them as a result of the settlement with the union.

The case is also significant in how it attempts to articulate the appropriate boundaries of state labor regulation under the National Labor Relations Act. The Court determined that the state law, under these particular facts, took precedence over federal law. It noted that the state had an interest in protecting its citizens from misrepresentations and that the rights of the replacements in this case were of only "peripheral concern" to federal law. While *Belknap* did not in any way limit the jurisdiction of the National Labor Relations Board, it did increase the availability of remedies in state court by allowing ordinary tort or breach of contact suits in these types of labor disputes.

See also **National Labor Relations Act; Strike Replacements.**

BENEFITS Virtually any form of compensation that is (1) in a form other than wages and (2) paid for in whole or in part by the employer, even if provided by a third party (such as an insurance company).

Different benefits serve different social and economic needs. Generally, benefits fall into three categories: statutory, compensatory, and supplementary. Statutory benefits—those required by law— include social security, workers' compensation, and federal and state unemployment insurance. Compensatory benefits are wages paid for time not worked, such as vacations, holidays, sick leave, and coffee breaks. Supplementary benefits most commonly include health insurance, pension plans, and life insurance.

Benefits originally resulted from either collective bargaining or were adopted by employers unilaterally out of altruism or as a means of discouraging union organizing. They have become widely adopted and are one of the most important areas in collective bargaining.

Since World War II, employee benefits have become increasingly important aspects of employee compensation. Health care became a more commonly offered benefit. Previously, some lost-income benefits were available during an illness or accident, and perhaps an informal arrangement existed for employees to receive medical care at a company clinic or other local facility. But formal medical insurance was uncommon. To meet the increased need, employers began providing formal health care plans to employees and their families, through either commercial insurers or Blue Cross-Blue Shield organizations.

From 1960 to 1974, employers established and expanded upon typical benefit plans, such as paid leave, retirement income, health care, and survivor and disability insurance. Catastrophic medical coverage of employees rose dramatically. Also during this period, more generous early retirement pension benefits and expanded survivor income payments were added to benefit packages.

The Employee Retirement Security Act (ERISA) (1974) was the first of a series of tax and benefit laws that dramatically changed benefit plans. These statutes focus on improving and guaranteeing the provisions of existing benefits rather than mandating new ones. Pension provisions concerning eligibility requirements, vesting, discrimination rules, and survivor benefits were strengthened and institutionalized.

Historically, a more common statutory approach to employee benefits has been not to require employers to provide a benefit but to impose certain obligations once an employer chooses to offer one. For example, except in Hawaii, no law currently requires employers to offer health care coverage to their workers. Once an employer provides this benefit, however, ERISA requires the provision of continuation coverage rights. If an employer provides health coverage through the purchase of insurance, every state requires some minimum level of coverage through its insurance law, although the specific coverage requirements differ greatly from state to state.

From 1975 to the present, two major trends characterized the benefits environment: substantial changes in the demographics of the labor force and massive government regulation of benefits. During this period women joined the labor force in large numbers, and it became less common for women to leave the labor force for a significant period following childbirth. In recognition of the changing demographics, employers have provided several new benefits and offered employees more opportunities to choose benefits to suit their family needs. The newly emerging benefits include parental leave (time off for parents to care for newborn or adopted children), child care (employer-provided facilities or financial assistance), and flexible schedules. Benefit choices among a variety of medical plans or among plans in multiple benefit areas also attracted considerable attention as the "typical" family of the 1950s and 1960s became less common and the needs of the new nontraditional families could no longer be satisfied by a traditional set of benefits.

One of the benefit regulations enacted during this period is that employers must offer workers over age 65 the same health insurance coverage they offer to younger workers and their spouses. In addition, if participation in the plan is mandatory, the employer may not compel older workers to pay any more than younger workers to belong. If participation is voluntary, premiums charged to older workers cannot be greater than actuarial tables show costs for older workers to be in relation to costs for younger workers.

Title VII of the Civil Rights Act of 1964, as amended by the Pregnancy Discrimination Act of 1978, requires employers that offer health coverage to include coverage for pregnancy and childbirth. The Pregnancy Discrimination Act requires that "women affected by pregnancy and related conditions must be treated the same as other applicants and employees on the basis of their ability or inability to work." In the area of health insurance benefits, this means that employers who provide health insurance must provide the same coverage to women who can't work because of childbirth or their "disabilities" related to pregnancy as they provide to all employees for other disabilities.

The Consolidated Omnibus Budget Reconciliation Act (COBRA) (1986) requires employers or insurance companies to offer employees the opportunity to continue health insurance (and that of the spouse and dependents) if the employee is terminated for any reason except gross misconduct. Although the statute applies only to employers with 20 or more employees, many states have their own laws covering smaller employers. COBRA has specific requirements regarding when the employee must be notified of the right to continued coverage, when the employee must notify the employer of his or her intention to exercise those rights, the maximum premium the employee may be charged, the minimum period of extended coverage (which is 18 months), and the reasons coverage can be terminated prematurely.

Until recently, however, Congress has resisted universal government-mandated benefits, and employers provide most benefits either unilaterally or as a result of collective bargaining with unions representing their workers. But the Family and Medical Leave Act (1993) requires covered employers to grant leaves of absence for the birth or adoption of a child, or for serious health conditions of the employee or close family members. This represents a significant departure from past practice.

See also **Child and Other Dependent Care; Civil Rights Act of 1964; Consolidated Omnibus Budget Reconciliation Act of 1985; Employee Retirement Income Security Act of 1974; Family and Medical Leave Act of 1993; Holiday; Leave of Absence; Pregnancy Discrimination Act of 1978; Retirement; Unemployment Compensation; Vacations.**

BEREAVEMENT LEAVE

See **Leave of Absence.**

BLACK LUNG BENEFITS LEGISLATION

Black lung disease is not a medical term and has no precise medical meaning. It is, instead, a description of autopsy findings on coal workers, whose lungs often take on the color of the dust they breathe while performing their jobs. The black lung controversy has both a medical and a political dimension. Regarding the medical dimension, conservatives argue that black lung refers to coal workers' pneumoconiosis (CWP), a relatively rare disorder diagnosed only by pulmonary x-ray. Company doctors have traditionally believed that pulmonary ailments among coal miners were normal and that the symptoms signified a benign condition. Liberals argue that black lung refers to more than CWP; they define black lung disease as any respiratory or pulmonary disorder related to work in the mines. They rely on the fact that many miners whose x-rays for CWP are negative experience disabling shortness of breath, coughing, and black sputum.

Until 1969, virtually all coal miners with job-related disease had only one possible recourse, their state's workers compensation program. In 1969, following months of agitation by miners for special black lung legislation, a nationwide wildcat strike, and a new black lung law in West Virginia, Congress passed the Coal Mine Health and Safety Act, the first and only federal workers' compensation law in American history. Black lung compensation in 1969 was only a cautious beginning. The law was strengthened in 1972 and 1977 and produced a well-funded program.

The Black Lung Benefits Reform Act of 1977 liberalized the eligibility requirements in the black lung benefits program established by Title IV of the Federal Coal Mine and Safety Act of 1969 (now the Federal Mine Safety and Health Act of 1977) and the Black Lung Benefits Act of 1972. It facilitated access to benefits, including monthly payments and medical treatment for coal miners totally disabled by pneumoconiosis or black lung disease. Benefits were also provided to dependents and survivors of coal miners with the diseases. Other major changes in the law included reconsideration of claims previously rejected under more restrictive criteria, a redefinition of total disability, and alteration of the standards of evidence proving disability.

The act was amended by the Black Lung Benefits Amendments of 1981, which tightened the eligibility requirements for claims filed after December 29, 1981.

See also **Workers' Compensation.**

BLACK LUNG BENEFITS REVENUE ACT OF 1981

See **Black Lung Benefits Legislation.**

BLUE-COLLAR WORKER

A term often used to describe a manual worker, specifically, production and maintenance workers employed in a plant as distinguished from white-collar workers employed in an office. Blue-collar workers are usually paid by the hour or on an incentive basis. Blue-collar jobs require less education and skills, have less skill variety, task identity, task significance, and less autonomy than professional jobs. Under the 1980 standard occupational system, the blue-collar designation was eliminated and replaced with the new categories of "precision production, craft, and repair" and "operators, fabricators, and laborers."

Blue-collar workers are employed in three categories of occupations: (1) skilled craft workers, including jobs requiring special manual skills and comprehensive knowledge of the process involved, which they acquire through on-the-job training and experience through apprenticeship or formal training programs; (2) wholly unskilled work, or work that involves semiskilled production operations; and (3) service-maintenance workers, who perform duties resulting in the comfort, convenience, hygiene, or safety of the general public or the upkeep and care of buildings or grounds of public property. Over the past 40 years, blue-collar employment has declined as white-collar employment has increased. Between 1950 and 1960, white-collar employment increased by nearly 28 percent compared to less than 6 percent for manual workers. In 1978, white-collar workers comprised 49.8 percent of the total number of persons employed, compared to 32.6 percent for blue-collar workers.

Blue-collar workers have always made up the largest proportion of the membership in American unions. Although the unions' wage gains of the 1950s and 1960s brought them into the middle class, American blue-collar workers have been losing ground since the 1970s due to inflation, reductions in benefits, and shrinkage of manufacturing industries.

See also **Apprenticeship; White-Collar Worker.**

BONA FIDE OCCUPATIONAL QUALIFICATION (BFOQ)

An employer's defense to a charge of unlawful discrimination that allows for intentional classification of applicants or employees in the narrow circumstances where such classification is "reasonably necessary to the normal operation of that particular business or enterprise." The Civil Rights Act of 1964 limits this exclusion on the basis of gender, national origin, and religion. Race is specifically excluded from this defense. Title VII of the Civil Rights Act of 1964 and the Age Discrimination in Employment Act both provide for bona fide occupational qualifications. However, an employer must establish that a particular gender, religion, national origin, or age is required for performing the job by proving a relationship between the classification and job performance, the necessity of the classification for successful performance, and that the job performance affected is the essence of the employer's business operation.

The Equal Employment Opportunity Commission and the courts have narrowly construed the BFOQ application. Gender or race may be a proper job qualification in the case of actors or actresses, and gender for work in restrooms or fitting rooms. The U.S. Supreme Court, in *Dothard v. Rawlinson* (1977), decided that under certain conditions, the use of women as prison guards would pose security problems in an all-male penitentiary. In most other situations, BFOQ's are not granted.

The BFOQ exception under federal employment discrimination law is a specific statutory rule that permits an employer to exclude particular protected group members but nevertheless seek to justify the exclusion based on the character or circumstances of the job. Employers may impose other job requirements that do not expressly preclude the employment of particular protected group members. Lacking a specific BFOQ exception, however, those requirements are subject to challenge, either for being unequally applied against particular protected group members or on the basis of their unlawful adverse impact against protected group members, even if equally applied to all applicants or employees.

Personal privacy concerns have been the most common grounds of employers to assert a sex-based BFOQ. Sex has been found to be a BFOQ for the jobs of nurse's aide in a female nursing home, nurse in the labor and delivery section of an obstetrical hospital, janitor in a men's bathhouse, washroom attendant, and security guard where the duties involved searching male employees. Establishing this type of BFOQ involves providing evidence concerning the stressful and embarrassing confrontations that could arise absent the necessary sex-based distinction and can only be demonstrated when the employer shows those job responsibilities cannot be reassigned so as to minimize or eliminate the clash between the personal privacy concerns at issue and Title VII's antidiscrimination mandates.

See also **Age Discrimination in Employment Act; Civil Rights Act of 1964; Equal Employment Opportunity Commission.**

BONUS Monetary or nonmonetary compensation paid in addition to wages, usually as a reward for extra effort, loyal service, or as a gift. Valid reasons for a distribution of a bonus include work performance, need, or demonstrated loyalty. A regular weekly cash payment in addition to an employee's base pay cannot be a bonus. Though certain types of bonuses and similar payments are excluded from the regular rate of pay, the mere fact that part of an employee's regular compensation is labeled as "bonus" does not preclude that part from being added to the employee's other earnings in determining his regular rate. Gifts and bonuses may not be credited toward overtime compensation owed under the Fair Labor Standards Act.

There are several special types of bonuses. An attendance bonus (also called attendance money) is extra compensation in the form of a bonus to employees who establish an exceptional record of attendance. However, fines for absences and bonuses for attendance are not widespread. Production and incentive bonuses are promised to employees to induce them to work more steadily, rapidly, or efficiently, or to remain with the employer.

A bonus can be either discretionary or nondiscretionary. If the bonus is discretionary, it is a gift and the employee has no enforceable right to such a bonus. If it is nondiscretionary, it a form of compensation earned by the employee, subject to the conditions of the bonus.

An employer may not grant bonuses to encourage or discourage union membership or activity. Thus, an employer unlawfully discriminates where it unilaterally reduces Christmas bonuses the day after a union wins a representation election, or where it gives a Christmas bonus only to office and supervisory employees after the unionization of its production and maintenance workers.

See also **Compensation; Fair Labor Standards Act; Wage.**

BOULWARISM Consistently bargaining on a "take it or leave it" basis, this bargaining practice is now considered bad-faith bargaining. [*General Electric v. NLRB* (1969)] This collective bargaining approach was followed by the General Electric Company and named after its vice president for employee and public relations, Lemuel Boulware, who conceived the strategy. It essentially follows this procedure:

The company begins by soliciting input from its low-level supervisors on the desires of the employees and the type and levels of benefits that employees expect. The company researches the costs and other management values of these benefits. A company proposal is formulated consisting of an entire package of bargaining terms. This proposal is then released to the public in a major publicity campaign designed to convince the public in general and employees in particular of the wisdom and fairness of the proposal. During collective bargaining, the company places its entire package on the table immediately and adopts a "firm, fair" position—that the company is not prepared to move from its proposal unless the union can show some error in the underlying data supporting the package.

This process is criticized because it involves the presentation of a non-negotiable demand designed to satisfy the needs of the other negotiating party in order to shortcut the negotiation process. Today, Boulwarism is considered an unfair labor practice by the National Labor Relations Board. Boulwarism is also now considered ineffective as a negotiation tool because the company comes into the bargaining process with a closed mind on the issues involved and because the company is seen as bypassing the union to deal directly with the employees.

See also **Collective Bargaining; National Labor Relations Board; Unfair Labor Practice.**

BOYCOTT

Refusal to deal with or purchase the products or services of a business as a means of exerting pressure in a labor dispute. A boycott is a concerted action by employees and a union or customers or other employers to refuse to transact business with an employer. It is generally part of an economic or strike strategy against an employer because of unfair labor practices or action that the union believes is harmful to its welfare. Participating in or inducing a boycott by employees is legal "primary concerted activity" when the intended object of a boycott is the party with whom the employees have a dispute—for example, a group of discharged employees sending letters requesting a boycott of their former employer to support their reinstatement.

The legality of a boycott often depends on whether it is a primary or secondary boycott. Only where the refusal to patronize is directed against the employer directly involved in the dispute is it a primary boycott. Where the economic pressure is exerted through parties not directly involved in the dispute, or where failure to patronize or handle the products or supply the services affects third parties, a boycott is generally held to be secondary. The National Labor Relations Act (NLRA) significantly limits a labor organization's right to boycott employers other than the one with which the organization has a labor dispute.

Section 8(b)(4) of the NLRA, which prohibits secondary boycotts, forbids unions from threatening or coercing a secondary employer (such as by threatening to picket that employer) or asking the secondary's employees not to work on products manufactured by the "unfair" employer with which the union has a dispute. The union does not violate this section if the appeal to the secondary employer is a request that it use management discretion to cease doing business with the primary, and is not a request to engage in a work stoppage. A peaceful request accompanied by a threat to engage in lawful conduct against the secondary employer is not prohibited. [*NLRB v. Servette* (1964)] In that case, a peaceful request to a secondary employer was accompanied by a threat to engage in handbilling, a protected activity. Since the threat was that the union would engage in lawful conduct, the "threat" was not a prohibited activity.

The courts have not interpreted Section 8(b)(4)(B) of the NLRA as broadly prohibiting peaceful consumer picketing. Consumer picketing at a secondary site is forbidden if it is intended to persuade consumers to cease all purchases from the secondary employer in order to force the secondary to cease doing business with the primary employer and thus to influence the primary to settle the union dispute on the union's terms. Peaceful consumer picketing is permitted at a secondary, when it merely asks the public to withhold its patronage of the primary's products that come from the secondary employer.

Federal antitrust statutes forbid certain boycotts as restraints of trade. Consumer boycotts, or union appeals to the consumer public not to purchase certain products, and secondary boycotts, or union pressure exerted against an individual to force him to cease doing business with another employer (the latter being the ultimate target or primary employer) do not violate antitrust laws.

The term "boycott" originated from the agrarian land agitation in Ireland around 1880–1881. Irate tenants developed this procedure against Captain Boycott, an agent for an Irish landlord who was harsh in his treatment of his tenants. Persons given the Boycott treatment were cut off from all social dealings with their neighbors; no one was permitted to work for them, supply them with goods or services, or to aid them in any other way. This method was effective and widely used at that time.

See also **Antitrust Laws; Concerted Activity; National Labor Relations Act; Unfair Labor Practice.**

BRADWELL V. ILLINOIS (1872) Myra C. Bradwell (1831–1894) was a legal editor and an early leader in the struggle for women's rights, especially in the legal profession. Moving from Memphis to Chicago, she began to study law with her husband in order to become his assistant but later decided to establish her own practice. She passed the Illinois state bar in 1869, but her application to the bar was rejected because she was a married woman and therefore not bound by attorney-client contracts. The court based its ruling that Bradwell could not practice law because of the "disability imposed by [her] married condition" at least in part on common law, still somewhat viable in the nineteenth century—the law of coverture. Under the principle of coverture, the husband and wife are one person under the law and therefore the very legal existence of the woman is suspended during the marriage. Bradwell argued that the principle of coverture was no longer viable, or at the very least, that it had been so greatly whittled away by the courts that it no longer served as a bar to a woman's entry into the legal profession. The court ruled, however, that "the sex of the applicant, independently of coverture, is, as our law now stands, a sufficient reason for not granting this license."

Bradwell appealed to the U.S. Supreme Court. The nation's highest court, however, upheld the Illinois decision, saying that it could not interfere with each state's right to regulate the granting of licenses within its borders. The court, in basing its decision on the "Slaughterhouse Cases" (in which it refused to apply the Fourteenth Amendment to protect the African American plaintiffs), held that "There are privileges and immunities belonging to citizens of the United States . . . and it is these and these alone which a state is forbidden to abridge. But the right to admission to practice in the courts of a state is not one of them." In concurring with the majority, Justice Joseph Bradley said that "the paramount mission and destiny of women are to fulfill the noble and benign office of wife and mother. This is the law of the creator." Many later commentators believed that the prospect of women practicing law was perceived as a threat to male lawyers and those few men whose wives or female relatives might wish to enter the profession.

In 1872, Illinois passed a statute guaranteeing all persons, regardless of sex, the right to select the profession they wished and the state bar subsequently accepted Bradwell's application.

Technically, then, the U.S. Supreme Court's Bradwell decision in 1872 was somewhat moot as to Myra Bradwell. But what Bradwell had sought by her appeal was not merely a ruling that would have permitted her to practice law but rather a Supreme Court decision saying that nowhere in the nation could any woman be barred from practicing the profession of her choice based on her sex. Thus, although Bradwell lost her Supreme Court case, the new Illinois statute passed in response to her case removed the statutory prohibition against women becoming lawyers.

Only recently have women become lawyers in substantial numbers. In 1963, 3.6 percent of the total law school enrollment was women, 9.5 percent in 1971, and one-third by 1980.

See also **African Americans: Employment Issues; Common Law: Employment Doctrines.**

BUILDING TRADES The skilled trades in the building industry, which include carpenters, painters, electricians, plumbers, hod carriers, bricklayers, and stone masons. These crafts are generally highly organized, with a well-developed apprenticeship system, though many commentators now criticize construction trades as anachronisms, occupations that reflect a now-outdated craft mode of production.

Appropriate bargaining units in the construction industry are determined according to function and community of interest. Employees within a proposed skilled grouping need not exercise pure craft skills, progress in their trade on the basis of apprenticeship programs, or maintain strict jurisdictional integrity within the grouping in order to justify the proposed unit. Nor does some sharing of functions with other skilled groups make the proposed craft unit inappropriate. The fact that some employees perform duties not strictly within their job descriptions will not alter a clearly identifiable homogeneous group of employees.

Separate bargaining units for each of various job sites overseen by a construction general contractor are appropriate where the contractor conducts each project as an independent, autonomous operation. Employees on a project may be organized as highly integrated crews that perform various jobs rather than along craft or departmental lines. Truck drivers who perform occasional tasks of construction but whose primary task remains the transportation of materials will not be included in appropriate unit of construction workers.

Construction trade locals will enroll all workers in a single craft within a specific geographic area: a city, metropolitan area, a state, or several states. As in other industries with geographically narrow markets, the local unions take the initiative in negotiating contracts. In the construction industry, though, jobs are temporary, work is seasonal, and without effective seniority protection. Job distribution is often controlled by business agents who cultivate friendly relations with contractors and make side deals so that the agent's own supporters get the most lucrative jobs. Dissenters and troublemakers who file grievances on the job or in the union may find it difficult to obtain any work.

Construction unions, the backbone of the old American Federation of Labor (AFL), were probably the labor movement's strongest industrial entities through much of its history and played an important role in shaping the American system of labor law. The dominance of the construction and other nonmanufacturing unions in the 1930s led the philosophy and policies of organized labor (identified as those of the AFL) in a conservative direction. But construction unions grew during the thirties and the proportion of construction workers who were unionized continued to increase in the post–World War II era. After 1947, however, unionization in construction sharply declined. At the beginning of 1985, construction unions had dropped far below the 1930 rate of 64.5 percent of employment unionized to 22.3 percent.

Since 1945, one of the most important legal issues for the building trades has concerned common situs picketing. The National Labor Relations Board has found common situs picketing to be a primary (and not an illegal secondary boycott) and lawful since it complied with the following four-part criteria known as the *Moore Dry Dock* standards: (a) the picketing is strictly limited to times when the situs of dispute is located on the secondary employer's premises; (b) at the time of the picketing the primary employer is engaged in its normal business at the situs; (c) the picketing is limited to places reasonably close to the location of the situs; and (d) the picketing discloses clearly that the dispute is with the primary employer. [*Sailors Union of the Pacific (Moore Dry Dock Co.)* (1950)] These rules have been applied by the courts and acknowledged by the U.S. Supreme Court. [*Local 761, International Union of Electrical Workers v. NLRB (General Electric Co.)* (1961)]

Common situs picketing has proved to be a special problem in the construction industry, where the property on which employees are at work is generally owned by another and where many different employers (a general contractor and subcontractors) have their employees working in close proximity. The extent of allowable picketing at a construction site was limited by the U.S. Supreme Court in *NLRB v. Denver Building and Construction Trades Council* (1951).

For years, organized labor—particularly the construction unions—supported federal legislation to permit common situs picketing by a single construction union addressed to all other crafts at the job site. In 1975, Congress did pass such legislation, but it was vetoed by President Gerald Ford.

Because of the close working interrelation among the several unions at one construction site, a picket line at the primary employer's would necessarily affect the secondary employees, possibly persuading all employees to refuse to work. This tactic would place great pressure on the primary employer to accede to union demands and would stand a good chance of success—particularly because employee response in the construction industry is likely to be automatic.

There seems to be confusion in the law regarding common situs picketing. The Supreme Court held in *Denver Building Trades* (1951)that picketing is illegal where one of its objects is to interfere with the secondary employer and its employees and their relationship with the primary employer. This decision, however, is difficult to reconcile with the ally doctrine and the Court's subsequent ruling that common situs picketing at an industrial site where the employer maintains separate gates for outside contractors does not violate the statute. The AFL-CIO Building Trades Department has pressed for legislation that would reverse *Denver Building Trades* and perhaps permit common situs picketing. The concern of the building trades unions has increased in recent years as nonunion construction work has spread, but every effort on their part to lobby for common situs picketing has been unsuccessful. Business interests that oppose the reversal of *Denver Building Trades* believe that unions would have considerable power to organize entire building sites by involving employers (other subcontractors) who have no interest in the dispute.

See also **Ally Doctrine; Apprenticeship; Appropriate Bargaining Unit; Community of Interest; Craft Union; Picketing.**

BUMPING

See **Layoffs.**

BUSINESS CYCLE

The cycle of fluctuations, including booms and recessions, in business activity. Theories on the causes of business cycles consider various possible factors, but none has conclusively delineated the underlying causes of these fluctuations. Historically, the number of members in American labor unions has corresponded with changes in the business cycle.

The American economy has grown somewhat erratically, particularly in the second half of the twentieth century. Since the end of World War II, eight cycles have been identified. On average, the overall economy has expanded for 50 months and contracted for 11 months. The length of postwar expansions averages twice those of prewar periods, and postwar contractions are half as long. There are three possible explanations for this postwar economic stabilization: smaller shocks to the postwar economy, a decrease in the proportion of output composition from highly cyclical sectors, and shifts in how the information was compiled. An analysis of recession-recovery cycles from the 1950s to the present shows that the recovery periods of the 1990s differ from earlier recoveries in the relative weakness of consumer spending. This difference may be attributed to the fewer people venturing to establish high-spending households, more people returning to or remaining in parental homes, and a lower consumer confidence index.

Business downturns typically reduce union membership, while upturns usually bring with them a rise in membership. During the cycles of the 1980s, though, union membership fell with the downturn but, significantly, failed to revive during the upturn. Between 1980 and 1982, a period dominated by recession, unions lost nearly 1.4 million members; between 1982 and 1984, a period of strong economic recovery, unions lost yet another 1.25 million members. These numbers seem to reinforce the view that American trade unions are in a state of permanent membership decline, as measured by the percentage of labor markets organized.

BUSINESS NECESSITY A standard used to justify an employment practice that is nondiscriminatory on its face but has a discriminatory impact. A business necessity is a justification for an otherwise prohibited employment practice that is essential for the safety and efficiency of the business and for which no reasonable alternative with a lesser impact exists.

In *Griggs v. Duke Power Co.* (1971), the U.S. Supreme Court held that a policy that had a discriminatory impact might be justified on grounds of business necessity. The test for business necessity requires proof that an employment practice is related to job performance. Other courts have added interpretations of business necessity as justified on the basis that (1) the challenged practice is essential for the safe and efficient operation of the business and (2) no acceptable alternative with lesser impact is available. The concept of business necessity cannot be justified on the basis of inconvenience, annoyance, or expense to the employer.

Whether evidence of business necessity is sufficient to justify certain employment practices depends on the facts of the case in question. For example, a district court found that the "legitimate employment goals of safety and efficiency" were "significantly served by—even if they do not require" the employer's rule barring narcotic users (including persons on methadone). The U.S. Supreme Court agreed, finding that the rule was sufficiently job-related to be a bona fide occupational qualification under Title VII of the Civil Rights Act of 1964. There have been many qualifying decisions since *Griggs*. Other decisions insist that the employment qualification "must not only foster safety and efficiency, but must be essential to that goal," and "there must be available no acceptable, alternative policies or practices which would better accomplish the business purpose advanced, or accomplish it equally well with a lesser differential impact." An employer cannot make a "business necessity" defense simply by showing that taking actions to end discrimination forbidden by Title VII will impose higher costs on him or her.

See also **Bona Fide Occupational Qualification; Civil Rights Act of 1964; Safety.**

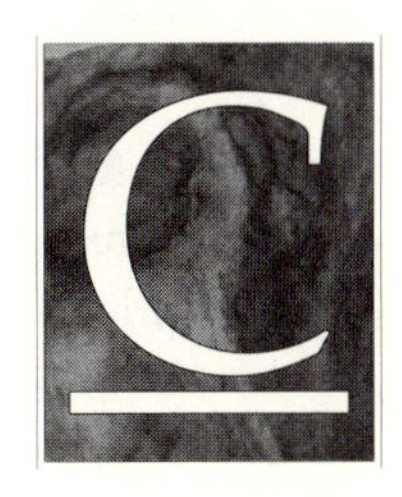

Cafeteria Plans Also called flexible benefits plans, cafeteria plans allow employees to choose between two or more types of benefits. These programs allow employees to design the benefits portion of their compensation package according to their needs. Like cafeterias, cafeteria plans offer a range of choices, providing employees with the opportunity to satisfy their own compensation preferences within a given dollar allowance.

In cafeteria plans, employees are typically provided individual cash funds that they can distribute among various benefits or retain as cash, although there is a core list of fixed benefits that cannot be exchanged for cash. The most common choices are: health and dental coverage, long-term disability benefit coverage, additional retirement income, qualified legal services plans, and the option of receiving cash instead of benefits. Comprehensive legal plans typically cover most legal services needed by an average person, such as assistance in document preparation, sale or purchase of a home, and consumer disputes.

An estimated 2.75 million employees in the United States are currently covered by cafeteria plans. The advantage of cafeteria plans is that they allow employees to choose a complement of benefits that contributes to their job satisfaction and avoid spending a substantial amount of money on fringe benefits they have little use for. The disadvantage is that they present bookkeeping problems for the employer and result in the inclusion of a high proportion of high-risk employees in various insurance plans.

The statutory and tax requirements of cafeteria plans are stated in Section 125 of the Internal Revenue Code. The Internal Revenue Service held that elective cafeteria plan contributions are not compensation included in the employer's qualified retirement plan contributions' deduction limits because of their similarity to 401(k) contributions. Group legal benefits included in a cafeteria plan are subject to taxation according to Sections 120 and 125 of the Internal Revenue Code.

See also **Benefits; Compensation.**

CAREER LADDER Jobs that progress from an entry level to an increasingly responsible position within an organization. Career ladder systems are implemented by organizations to alleviate the problems of low morale and to establish career advancement programs. The construction of a career ladder includes identification of promotion paths and the establishment of criteria for job progress and promotion. The career ladder system redefines job descriptions, reclassifies positions through consolidation, integrates cost-control measures, enhances employee morale, improves employee retention, and establishes equity in all administrative tasks within the organization. Career ladders are useful in establishing an organization's policy in equal opportunity matters, specifying organizational responsibilities, clarifying individual responsibilities, and establishing the basis for administration of the promotion program.

However, the once clearly defined career ladder is becoming more blurred in the contemporary American workplace. To advance in their careers, employees traditionally had to obtain a job in management. Now, in a strategy that has the potential to reshape the landscape of careers and compensation, more large corporations are designing ways to promote and reward people without making them bosses. The trend is generating new opportunities and higher salaries for many occupations by creating "dual" career ladders (that is, a choice between management, professional, and technical career ladders). It is also creating a new set of corporate ladders that ascend into hierarchies of relatively untested titles and positions rather than into management ranks. It is advantageous, because it provides additional opportunities for growth for veteran employees.

CASUAL WORKER A person who is irregularly, intermittently, periodically, or seasonally employed. Casual employees are workers employed on an as-needed basis. These workers are employed only for a short period of time, are not attached to a regular company, do not accumulate seniority, and do not vote in National Labor Relations Board (NLRB) elections.

The NLRB, in its bargaining unit determinations, distinguishes casual employees, who lack a sufficient community of interest with regular employees to be included in the bargaining unit, from regular part-time employees, who are included in the unit. Thus, the NLRB has excluded from bargaining units as casual employees seasonal employees employed during the holidays who perform the same kind of work as permanent employees but are paid at a lower rate and do not receive employee benefits granted to permanent employees. Workers' compensation laws in many states do not apply to casual employees, who are regarded as temporary employees with no reasonable expectation of substantial future employment. Casual work has often been identified as unskilled work, with irregular and low earnings.

Casual workers are covered by the Worker Adjustment and Retraining Notification Act (WARN). The U.S. Department of Labor has ruled that casual workers must be given notice of a plant closing or mass layoff on the same terms as other employees, even though their work may be temporary. However, the department does not count casual workers in determining whether a mass layoff or plant closing has occurred, because both of these events are determined by a stated percentage of regular full- and part-time employees losing their jobs. No advance notice is required when the closing involves a temporary facility or the closing or mass layoff results from the completion of a particular project, so long as the affected employees were hired with the understanding that their employment was limited to the duration of the facility or particular project.

WARN covers companies that employ 100 full-time or 100 or more full- and part-time employees who work a total of at least 4,000 hours per week.

See also **Layoff; National Labor Relations Board; Seniority; Worker Adjustment and Retraining Notification Act of 1988; Workers' Compensation.**

CEASE AND DESIST ORDER A ruling or order issued by the National Labor Relations Board (NLRB) under Section 10(c) of the National Labor Relations Act or by a state agency requiring an employer or union to end an unfair labor practice and to undo the effects of the violation as much as possible. A cease and desist order specifies the action the employer or union is to stop. It may also include the affirmative action to be taken to remedy the situation. Such orders assume the force of law only when formally enforced by a federal court of appeals. Where there is evidence that the union has a tendency toward unlawful conduct, the cease and desist order may not only prevent concerted illegal activity directed at the employer in the case in question but also against any other employer in the union's jurisdiction. [*NLRB v. Local 138, Operating Engineers* (1967)]

The NLRB may issue a cease and desist order enjoining an employer from intimidating its employees by threatening the use of physical violence, threatening adverse economic consequences resulting from support of a union, or using law enforcement to intimidate employees or interfere with union activities.

The NLRB may issue a cease and desist order if an employer implements an espionage system in order to interfere with protected employee rights, even if the surveillance system could have been used for a proper purpose, such as preventing employee theft of company property, if the employees are unaware that surveillance is occurring. The NLRB may also issue a cease and desist order if an employer interrogates its employees about their union membership or that of other employees, thereby interfering with, restraining, or coercing employees in the exercise of their organizational rights. An employer may also be ordered to stop interrogating employment applicants if such interrogation has a coercive impact on the exercise of employees' rights.

The NLRB also has the authority to protect employees from union violence, coercion, and threats. It may order a union to cease and desist from engaging in secondary activity, unlawful recognitional picketing, or seeking to enforce an unlawful hot cargo agreement. [*Bricklayers Local 18* (1971)]

See also **Cease and Desist Order; Hot Cargo Agreement; Jurisdiction; National Labor Relations Board; Unfair Labor Practice.**

CERTIFICATION Official designation by a labor board of a labor organization entitled to bargain as the exclusive representative of employees in a certain unit. A union may be certified by the National Labor Relations Board (NLRB) or an appropriate state agency as the bargaining representative of only those groups of employees that constitute an appropriate bargaining unit. Normally, the NLRB will certify a union as a bargaining representative after a valid secret-ballot representation election. When a union receives a majority of the valid votes cast, the NLRB issues a certification of representation. The NLRB can conduct such an election, under Section 9(c)(1) of the National Labor Relations Act (NLRA), only when a petition has been filed requesting one. A petition for certification of representation can be filed by an employee or a group of employees or any individual or labor organization acting on their behalf, or it can be filed by an employer. When a union fails to receive a majority of the valid votes cast, the board issues a certification of results.

Certification is ordinarily issued after all remaining representation issues have been resolved. Thus the NLRB must issue certification of the election results including, where appropriate, a certification of a bargaining representative when (1) no election objections were filed, the number of challenged ballots is insufficient to affect the election results, and no runoff election is required; or (2) the regional director of the NLRB has directed the opening and counting of challenged ballots and the issuance of a revised count of ballots, and no objections to that revised tally are filed within seven days after it is given to the parties.

During the one-year period following a union's certification, the NLRB will not direct an election in any bargaining unit or any subdivision. Section 9(c)(3) of the NLRA. A certification year begins on the date of the parties' first bargaining session, unless there is a significant delay in the commencement of bargaining due to the union's inexcusable procrastination or due to the other party's showing of bad faith. An employer may not refuse to bargain with the union during its certification year on the basis that a majority of the employees have repudiated union representation. The rule is the same whether the union lost majority support as a result of the employer's unfair labor practice, or through no fault of the employer. [Section 8(a)(5) of the NLRA and *Brooks v. NLRB* (1954)]

The NLRA provides favored treatment (such as protection against the concerted activity of other unions) to unions that have been certified rather than merely informally recognized under Section 8(b)(4) of the NLRA.

See also **Appropriate Bargaining Unit; Concerted Activity; National Labor Relations Act; National Labor Relations Board; Unfair Labor Practice.**

CERTIFICATION PROCEEDING An administrative hearing before the National Labor Relations Board (NLRB), pursuant to the National Labor Relations Act, to help determine questions of union representation for a certain group of employees. When the petition for certifying a union is filed, the NLRB must investigate and conduct a hearing if necessary. The purpose of both the investigation and the hearing is to determine issues such as the following:

1. Whether the NLRB has jurisdiction to conduct an election
2. Whether there is a sufficient showing of employee interest to justify an election

3. Whether a question of representation exists
4. Whether the election is sought by an appropriate unit of employees
5. Whether the representative named in the petition is qualified
6. Whether there are any barriers to an election in the form of existing contracts or prior elections

Under the current practice of the NLRB, approved by the U.S. Supreme Court in *Linden Lumber v. NLRB* (1974), an employer may refuse a union's request for recognition even in the face of substantial evidence of majority employee support for the union, such as authorization card signatures or a strike by a majority of the employees. Authorization cards are somewhat suspect and "fear may . . . prevent some [employees] from crossing a picket line; or sympathy for strikers, not a desire to be represented by a particular union, may influence others." The Court approved the board's abandonment of a good faith test for employer refusals to bargain in this context. The Court also rejected the contention that the failure of the employer to file a representation petition demonstrates the lack of a good faith doubt of the union's majority status.

See also **Appropriate Bargaining Unit; Authorization Card; Collective Bargaining; National Labor Relations Act; National Labor Relations Board.**

CHARGE A written claim filed by any person (usually an employee, an employer, or a labor union) alleging that an unfair labor practice was committed in violation of the National Labor Relations Act (NLRA). The charge is filed with the regional director of the National Labor Relations Board (NLRB). The charge must, by statute, relate to conduct occurring within the prior six months. It is investigated by a field representative of the regional office, who interviews witnesses and prepares a report, and a decision is then made by the regional director whether a complaint is to be issued against the charged party. A charge may be withdrawn, but the regional director must first give consent, and only after determining that the public interest will be served. The NLRB will issue a formal complaint if it determines that an unfair labor practice occurred. [Section 10 of the NLRA] A determination by the regional director not to issue a complaint may be appealed to the general counsel, whose decision whether or not to issue an unfair labor practice complaint is in all cases unreviewable, either by the board members or by a court.

See also **Hot Cargo Agreement; Jurisdiction; National Labor Relations Act; National Labor Relations Board; Unfair Labor Practice.**

CHILD AND OTHER DEPENDENT CARE

Daycare services provided for the care of children so parents can work. The need for nursery, daycare, and before- and after-school care for children was created by the increased number of working mothers, one of the fastest growing segments of the labor force.

The labor force participation rate of women with children has increased dramatically over past four decades. In 1950, the participation rate for women with children under six was 12 percent; in 1978 the figure was 42 percent. In 1988, two-thirds of the 30 million wives in the labor force were mothers; half of all women with children aged one and younger worked or looked for work, and six of every ten children had mothers who worked or looked for work.

Government support for child-care services has included federal programs for daycare for low-income families, food subsidies for child-care centers, and tax credits for child-care expenses. Child-care services have seldom been included in employee benefit packages. But as pressure to expand employee benefits increases, the larger number of mothers available for work and tax relief for employer-paid daycare benefits will motivate companies to provide for these services.

Under the Family and Medical Leave Act (FMLA), fathers and mothers are equally entitled to family leave following the birth or adoption of a child. Moreover, if both parents are eligible employees of employers covered by FMLA, they may take their leaves simultaneously or sequentially, depending upon their preference. This means that new parents in households where both parents work are eligible for a total of 24 weeks of child-care leave, as long as the parents work for different employers. Spouses who work for the same employer are eligible for a total of 12 weeks together.

Unions often negotiate for assistance with child care. Since many women are delaying having children, a growing number of families care for young children and aged parents at the same time. The union-negotiated financial assistance plans that address this situation include dependent care assistance plans, which allow employees to set aside pretax salary for child or elder care, and a child- and elder-care fund. The employer contributes money to this fund, and the employees later choose how to spend it. Options include child-care centers and dependent-care subsidies.

See also **Benefits; Family and Medical Leave Act of 1993; Women: Employment Issues.**

CHILD LABOR LAWS

CHILD LABOR LAWS The practice of employing minor children in gainful occupations. The term also refers to the employment of children who are too young to work for hire, employed at jobs unsafe or unsuitable for children or harmful to their welfare. The age of 16 is generally accepted as the transition from childhood to youth for purposes of regulation.

"Oppressive child labor" is defined by Section 3(l) of the Fair Labor Standards Act of 1938 (FLSA) to include all labor of children under the age of 16, or under the age of 18 in any occupation determined by the U.S. Department of Labor to be particularly hazardous to a child's health or well-being.

During the early years of industrialization in the United States, child labor was not only considered necessary to maintain production but also socially valuable, since it kept children from mischief and idleness and prevented orphaned children or the children of poor families from becoming public charges. Children as young as six or seven were employed in factories (often hired along with their parents) and mines. In fact, all of the employees in the first cotton-spinning mill in the United States, established in Pawtucket, Rhode Island, around 1790, were children between the ages of 7 and 12. Because all workers put in long hours, it was not thought excessive to work children 12, 13, or more hours per day for six days a week.

The first state laws regulating child labor were advocated by reformers out of a concern for the education of factory children. These laws usually required factory owners to provide a basic education for the children they employed, set a maximum working day for children, and establish a minimum age, usually between 10 and 13, for factory employment. Massachusetts enacted the first child labor law in 1836, setting the minimum age of 15 for employment of children in factories.

The early laws, however, were minimal by current standards and were not strictly or consistently enforced. During the nineteenth century, most teenagers would have worked, though not necessarily in a factory or similar workplace. Almost half of the workforce was engaged in agriculture, and indeed, much "child labor" occurred on family farms with the parents serving as the "employers."

The first federal statute in this area was the Child Labor Act (also known as the Owen-Keatings Bill), which forbade the interstate shipment of products made by child labor. This law was declared unconstitutional by the U.S. Supreme Court. In 1933, child labor was regulated by the National Industrial Recovery Act, an act that was also declared invalid. In 1938 Congress passed the FLSA, which established a 16-year minimum age in all but hazardous occupations. It also allowed children ages 14 and 15 to work in numerous types of jobs while attending school. The Supreme Court in *United States v. Darby Lumber Company* (1941) upheld the statute as constitutional.

The issue of child labor laws cannot be viewed apart from a broad range of economic, social, and political considerations. Existing public policies on youth employment and schooling have developed slowly over an extended period of time and thus reflect both historical and contemporary concerns. Because child labor standards and school-leaving laws have been laws for so long, little critical attention has been paid to their existence or effects.

Child labor laws raise several complicated questions: When is a person "mature"? To what degree should persons, as they approach maturity be allowed to make decisions for themselves? Can the transition from school to work be eased through work/study programs?

On the state level, child labor has been a subject of great legislative interest in recent years. All states have statutes that regulate the employment of children, and if both federal and state statutes apply, the law setting the higher standard must be followed. The recent trend has been toward making these statutes more restrictive by limiting permissible hours of work and expanding applicability of certain provisions to include additional minors and strengthening of penalty provisions. For example, in 1992 North Carolina adopted night work restrictions for 16- and 17- year-olds during the school year.

Child labor has also recently become an issue of international legal significance. Many American garment manufacturers have recently adopted codes of conduct that prohibit child labor in the overseas production of the goods they import. These codes are intended to avoid the exploitation of child workers. A U.S. Department of Labor report, however, seems to suggest that greater efforts must be made to enforce and monitor compliance with these codes in order to ensure their credibility.

See also **Fair Labor Standards Act.**

CIVIL RIGHTS ACT OF 1866 Also known as Section 1981, this statute guarantees to all persons, regardless of race, the right to make and enforce contracts, to sue, to give evidence, and to enjoy full and equal benefits of the law. [*McDonald v. Santa Fe Trail Transportation* (1976)] Congress originally passed this statute in 1866, following the abolition of slavery in the Thirteenth Amendment. The purpose of the Reconstruction Era civil rights acts, such as Section 1981, was to grant civil rights to the newly freed slaves. Section 1981 affects all employee-employer relationships, because all such relationships are based on contract.

For several years, the Section 1981 guarantee that all persons have the right to make and enforce contracts has been interpreted by federal courts to prohibit race discrimination in all aspects of the employment relationship. In *Patterson v. McLean Credit Union* (1989), the U.S. Supreme Court narrowly limited the section's coverage, ruling that the statute did not apply to harassment or to discrimination in terms or conditions of employment, or termination. Rather, the court said that Section 1981 applied only to race discrimination in the enforcement of contracts. The Civil Rights Act of 1991 reversed the *Patterson* decision by adding language to Section 1981 expressly providing that the statute applies to all aspects of contractual relationships including "the making, performance, modification, and termination of contracts and the enjoyment of all benefits, privileges, terms, and conditions of the contractual relationship."

An employee who wishes to pursue a claim of intentional discrimination based on race or ethnicity is covered by both Section 1981 and Title VII of the Civil Rights Act of 1964.

See also **Civil Rights Act of 1964; Civil Rights Act of 1991.**

CIVIL RIGHTS ACT OF 1871 Also known as Section 1983 or the Ku Klux Klan Act, this statute was enacted to enforce the provisions of the Fourteenth Amendment, which states that "No state shall make or enforce any law which shall abridge the privileges or immunities of citizens of the United States; nor shall any State deprive any person of life, liberty, or property, without due process of law; nor deny to any person within its jurisdiction the equal protection of the laws."

The statute itself does not create new rights. It does, however, provide a remedy for the violation of established rights. Section 1983 prohibits invidious discrimination by governmental employers on the basis of race, national origin, religion, or gender, but it does not cover private employers. Many significant employment discrimination cases brought under Section 1983 have included claims against police departments, fire departments, and public schools.

Section 1983 was intended to provide a civil action to protect persons against misuse of power possessed by virtue of state law and made possible because the defendant was acting under the authority of the state. This law applies only where the defendants act under "color of state law." Officers and employees of the states and their political subdivisions will generally be acting under "color of state law" when they deprive people of civil rights in the fulfillment of the tasks and obligations assigned to them or made possible by the power conferred on them by the government. A person deprives another of a constitutional right, within the meaning of Section 1983, if he commits an affirmative act, participates in another's affirmative act, or omits to perform an act he is legally required to perform. The statute also provides that individuals may be sued and held personally liable for the harm caused by such deprivation.

Where Section 1983 does apply, it prohibits discrimination based on race, color, sex, religion, or national origin. Persons of all races may bring a lawsuit under Section 1983. If the defendants are a state or local government or any enterprise operating under "color of law," a plaintiff who is the victim of racial discrimination in employment may obtain relief under Section 1983. Class action lawsuits can be used in proper cases to remove patterns and practices of racial discrimination in public employment.

In Section 1983 lawsuits alleging disparate treatment employment discrimination, the courts have applied the following analysis from the Title VII case *McDonnell Douglas v. Green* (1973). It states that the plaintiff establishes a prima facie case (that is, sufficient to establish a fact unless it is disputed) of this type of discrimination by proving that (1) he or she is a member of a protected class, (2) he or she applied and was qualified for the job (or promotion, or job retention, or other beneficial action) at issue, and (3) the job (or other benefit) was given instead to a member of a different class. Once this proof has been made, the burden of proof shifts to the employer, who must state a legitimate nondiscriminating reason for not selecting the plaintiff. If the employer does not do so, the plaintiff prevails.

The right of applicants to employment in state and local government, as well as in enterprises operating under "color of law," to be free from racially discriminatory tests and examinations can be protected in a Section 1983 action.

See also **Class Action; Disparate Treatment Discrimination.**

CIVIL RIGHTS ACT OF 1964 The federal statute, as amended, that prohibits discrimination on the basis of race, color, religion, sex, handicap status, national origin, and Vietnam War veteran status. The Civil Rights Act of 1964 was enacted by Congress under the authority of the Commerce Clause of the U.S. Constitution, as well as the Thirteenth, Fourteenth, and Fifteenth Amendments to the Constitution. The statute was later upheld by the U.S. Supreme Court. Of the 11 titles of this statute, Title VII is the provision that prohibits all employment discrimination based on race, color, religion, sex, or national origin. In so doing, Title VII became this century's most important federal statute on employment discrimination. It recognized the importance of work in American society by prohibiting discrimination in all aspects of the employment relationship. It makes it unlawful for employers, labor unions, and employment agencies in industries affecting interstate commerce to discriminate in employment or union membership against any individual because of race, religion, sex, or national origin.

Originally, Title VII applied to employers of 100 or more employees. Currently, employers with 15 or more employees are covered. The statute as amended by the Equal Employment Opportunity Act of 1972 prohibits discrimination in employment by most employers, labor unions, and employment agencies. The 1972 amendments extended the coverage of this act to all state and local governments. The statute became effective July 2, 1965, one year after its enactment.

Title VII established the five-member Equal Employment Opportunity Commission (EEOC), which administers the act. Title VII emphasizes conciliation as the method of settling discrimination complaints and makes provisions for a system of federal-state cooperation in promoting equal opportunity by reliance on state laws (or local enactments in some cases) whose terms are compatible with the federal statute. If negotiation or conciliation fails to redress complaints, victims of discrimination may bring a lawsuit in U.S. district court. The EEOC is authorized to seek injunctive and other relief in federal court. The attorney general retains such authority in cases against a government, government agency, or a political subdivision.

The Civil Rights Act of 1964 was also the first statute to explicitly protect racial minorities employed by private employers. The Supreme Court in *Griggs v. Duke Power Company* (1971) clearly enunciated the intent of Congress in enacting Title VII: "to achieve equality of employment opportunities and remove barriers that have operated in the past to favor an identifiable group of white employees over other employees." Race and color, therefore, are not factors that an employer may consider in deciding whether to hire or promote someone, or in any other terms or conditions of employment. The Supreme Court in *Griggs* interpreted the Civil Rights Act of 1964 as not only applying to the deliberate wrongdoer, but to the attitudes and practices which even well-intentioned individuals may exhibit.

At first Title VII was thought to prohibit only intentional discrimination or disparate treatment. Despite the intent of the statute, many previously segregated jobs continued to be segregated, even though they were made available to all qualified workers. One problem involved the definition of the term "qualified workers." Some employers required a high school diploma or its equivalent in order to qualify for a job, even though the diploma was not necessary to perform the work competently. As a result, these employers continued racial segregation in practice if not in theory. This situation reflected the impact of long-term racial discrimination in education and throughout American society. For these reasons, the courts began to recognize claims of discrimination based on the disparate impact of seemingly neutral employment criteria [*Griggs*] and thereby vastly expanded the scope of protection given racial minorities.

Title VII also prohibits religious discrimination in employment practices as well as procedures that deny equal employment opportunity on the basis of religion. Employers must make reasonable accommodations for religious observance or practices of employees or job applicants, unless it is demonstrated that the accommodation would impose a hardship on the employer. Cases have been pursued under Title VII involving the accommodation of Sabbatarians, atheists, and religious objectors to membership in unions. The challenge in religious discrimination in employment cases is balancing the various claims of individual rights, employer needs, government interests, and religious freedom.

Title VII was amended by major legislation such as the Equal Employment Opportunity Act of 1972, which extended coverage to state and local governments; the Pregnancy Discrimination Act of 1978; the Civil Rights Restoration Act of 1987; and the Civil Rights Act of 1991.

Certain categories of employers are excluded from coverage of the act, at least in part. These include: religious organizations, with respect to employment of persons connected with religious activities, and educational institutions with a religious affiliation, on the basis of religion with regard to all their employees. Title VII also expressly exempts both Native-American tribes and certain tax-exempt private clubs from its coverage.

See also **Discrimination in Employment; Disparate Impact Discrimination; Disparate Treatment Discrimination; Equal Employment Opportunity Act of 1972;** ***Griggs v. Duke Power Co.;*** **Pregnancy Discrimination Act of 1978; Religious Discrimination; Sex Discrimination in Employment.**

CIVIL RIGHTS ACT OF 1991 Significantly strengthens the rights of plaintiffs in employment discrimination lawsuits by reversing parts of seven U.S. Supreme Court decisions that were unfavorable to victims of employment discrimination and by expanding the remedies under Title VII of the Civil Rights Act of 1964 to include compensatory and punitive damages in intentional discrimination cases. Damages are awarded not merely to compensate victims but also deter illegal conduct and wrongdoing. The statute also limits compensatory and punitive damages to between $50,000 and $300,000, depending on the size of the employer's workforce.

The Civil Rights Act of 1991 reverses in part decisions from the following cases:

- *Wards Cove Packing Co. v. Atonio* (1989), which required the employer to "demonstrate that the challenged practice is job-related . . . and consistent with business necessity"
- *Patterson v. McLean Credit Union* (1989), which held that Section 1981 of the Civil Rights Act of 1866 covers all forms of racial employment bias including bias after hiring
- *Martin v. Wilks* (1989), which prohibits challenges to consent decrees
- *Price Waterhouse v. Hopkins* (1989), which held that any intentional discrimination is unlawful, even if the same action would have resulted without discriminatory motive
- *Lorance v. AT&T* (1989), which allowed employees to challenge a seniority system
- *EEOC v. Aramco* (1991), which extended Title VII coverage to American citizens employed by American companies overseas
- *West Virginia University Hospitals v. Casey* (1991), which allowed the recovery of expert witness fees

In addition to amending Title VII and the Civil Rights Act of 1866, the new statute amended the Attorney Fees Awards Act of 1976, the

Americans with Disabilities Act of 1990, and the Age Discrimination in Employment Act of 1967. It also includes provisions that allow for payment of interest in delayed awards and extension of the filing time for suits against the federal government, establishment of a "glass ceiling" commission, and coverage of Senate and presidential staffs by federal civil rights law.

See also **Age Discrimination in Employment Act of 1967; Americans with Disabilities Act of 1990; Civil Rights Act of 1866; Consent Decree.**

CIVIL RIGHTS RESTORATION ACT OF 1988

This statute was enacted in order to overturn the U.S. Supreme Court decision in *Grove City College v. Bell* (1984), which limited enforcement of antidiscrimination laws against educational institutions. Specifically, the Court had ruled that compliance with Title IX of the Education Amendments of 1972 prohibiting sex discrimination was limited to the particular program or activity receiving federal funds and was not an institution-wide requirement.

The statute broadly extends the protections against race, sex, and age discrimination. It invalidates the Court's narrow interpretation and extends compliance coverage to include the institution, governmental entity, or private employer under Title IX, the Rehabilitation Act of 1973 , the Age Discrimination Act of 1975, and Title VI of the Civil Rights Act of 1964. The Rehabilitation Act was also amended to include as individuals with handicaps protected under the law those persons with contagious disease or infection who do not pose a direct threat to the health or safety of other individuals and who are able to perform the duties of the jobs. The statute further provides that programs and entities that receive direct or indirect federal assistance are subject to civil rights laws on an institution-wide rather than on a program-specific basis.

See also **Age Discrimination Act of 1975; Civil Rights Act of 1964; Rehabilitation Act of 1973.**

CIVIL SERVICE

A central personnel bureau within a governmental unit established to assure equal opportunity for all job applicants on all levels of government.

A civil service has a function similar to a corporate personnel unit in that it advises, formulates policy, and regulates employment procedures. Used synonymously with merit system, it also refers to a government employment system that regulates the selection of government employees by examination or the assessment of fitness, ability and experience, advancement, and retention. The federal government, most states, and some cities have their own civil service commissions, which create job descriptions and screen the applicants. This system is merit-based, opposed to a system, such as a patronage system, that employs based on a candidate's connections.

Often, though, the designation "civil service" merely distinguishes civilian from military government employment. Civil service positions can be filled either through patronage or under a merit system.

Congress passed the Pendleton Act in 1883 to eliminate patronage in federal employment and institute efficient and objective federal personnel policies. A product of the nineteenth century progressive movement, the Pendleton Act sought to replace the spoils system, under which the president could dispense federal jobs as rewards for political patronage, with a "merit system" that would base selection and promotion on competence. The Pendleton Act also established the U.S. Civil Service Commission to implement merit selection, management, and adjudication of complaints by applicants and employees. Although the Pendleton Act was amended repeatedly over the years, Congress made its most dramatic revisions when it passed the Civil Service Reform Act in 1978.

Several administrative positions in the federal civil service require examinations, but not all. The Federal Job Information Center, which has offices nationwide, maintains records of what positions are available, the necessary qualifications, and application forms. Not all federal jobs, however, are offered through the Information Center. Individuals who are already employed in an agency usually receive the first notice on openings and have an advantage in hiring.

In addition to the federal civil service laws, virtually every state has some version of a merit system applicable to all or most of its civil service, and most states have some form of competitive testing. Many states provide their public employees statutory protections exceeding those applicable to federal employees. For example, these statutes prohibit discrimination on the basis of an expunged juvenile record, marital status, parenthood, sexual orientation, or weight.

Federal civil service employees may be removed for just cause according to the Lloyd-LaFollette Act in 1912. Gradually, the "just-cause" standard has been extended to virtually all federal and state, and most local government employees.

See also **Civil Service Reform Act of 1978.**

CIVIL SERVICE REFORM ACT (CSRA) OF 1978

The first federal statute to comprehensively reform the federal civil service system since the passage of the Pendleton Act in 1883. The Civil Service Reform Act of 1978, which consisted of nine titles, became effective on January 1, 1979. Title II divided the Civil Service Commission into two bodies: the Office of Personnel Management (OPM) and the Merit Systems Protection Board (MSPB), with an office of the Special Counsel authorized to assist whistleblowers. The OPM was given responsibility for the administration and enforcement of the civil service, including maintaining the system of competitive examinations and position announcements. The MPSB was assigned the quasi-judicial role of protecting employees against unjust actions.

The CSRA also transferred many of the functions regarding Title VII of the Civil Rights Act of 1964, the Rehabilitation Act of 1973, and the Age Discrimination in Employment Act to the Equal Employment Opportunity Commission (EEOC). Prior to this time, the EEOC only had enforcement authority in matters involving private sector employment. The CSRA, therefore, added a new avenue for pursuing discrimination complaints.

The statute made several other major changes to the federal civil service: merit system principles and sanctions for prohibited personnel practices were codified; whistleblowing protections were added; a senior executive service for senior-level personnel was created to cover top level federal employees; compensation for middle-level managers was tied to performance rather than seniority; and the substance and procedures of employee discipline were revised. The CSRA reaffirmed the federal government's commitment to "merit principles" of fair and open competition, equal opportunity based solely on ability, equal pay for equal work, and freedom from prohibited personnel policies.

The CSRA prohibits discrimination on the basis of race, color, religion, national origin, age, handicap, marital status, or political affiliation;

influencing political activity through coercion or reprisal; interfering with or obstructing any competitor's application; using unauthorized influence to increase or decrease an applicant's prospects; engaging in nepotism; retaliating for whistleblowing or exercising the right to appeal; discriminating on the basis of conduct unrelated to job performance; or violating any regulation on merit system principles.

The merit principles and prohibited personnel practices have incorporated by reference into the civil service system the protections of Title VII, the Equal Pay Act, the Americans with Disabilities Act, and the Age Discrimination in Employment Act. In the 1972 amendments to Title VII, Congress extended the protections of Title VII to the federal government.

The statute was passed in reaction to public perceptions that the civil service was encumbered with employees who should have been removed for incompetence or misconduct but remained in their jobs because the existing disciplinary system was too cumbersome to be effective.

See also **Age Discrimination in Employment Act; Civil Rights Act of 1964; Equal Employment Opportunity Commission; Rehabilitation Act of 1973; Whistleblower.**

CIVILIAN LABOR FORCE

All employed or unemployed persons in the civilian noninstitutional population, 16 years of age and older, who have a job and those who do not work but are willing, able, and available, and "actively seeking" work. The civilian labor force does not, however, include people who want to work but, because of the state of economy, have abandoned the job search, believing that their efforts would be fruitless. These people are called "discouraged workers." (The higher the unemployment rate at any given time, the higher the number of discouraged workers, and vice versa.) Women in general as well as younger and older men are most likely to be affected by this phenomenon. The definition of the civilian labor force, however, does include all persons who want to work full time but can only find part-time jobs. In other words, the definition of the civilian labor force is a matter of opinion, resulting in controversies over who should be included and who should not.

The civilian labor force, both male and female, has been declining for several years. In 1991, the labor force fell almost six million short of the level it would have reached had the 1970–1990 growth trend been maintained. The relatively moderate rise in the unemployment rate in the early

1990s partly reflects the slowing growth of the labor force. If the labor force had continued to grow at its trend rate, with job creation proceeding at its normal rate, the unemployment rate would have surpassed 10 percent.

Despite the smaller number of working Americans, the economy of the United States continues to have difficulty providing a sufficient number of jobs for those who need them. Moreover, matching job seekers with available jobs can be difficult, since the composition of the labor force has been changing rapidly. Increasingly, a greater proportion of newcomers to the labor force are expected to be women, minorities, and immigrants. Members of these groups have frequently had difficulty obtaining the necessary job training and a fair chance to compete for the available jobs.

See also **Unemployment.**

CLASSIFICATION A term common to civil service systems that describes groups of jobs involving the same kind of work, arranged according to such factors as skill required, pay range, and the level of difficulty and responsibility of the positions (i.e., clerk typist I, clerk typist II). Classification can be defined as the logical and reasonable grouping of duties and responsibilities so that similar positions would have similar treatment titles and salaries.

See also **Civil Service.**

CLASS ACTION A civil lawsuit brought by or defended against a large group of persons who are interested in the matter being contested. In a class action suit, also known as a representative action, one or more persons may sue or be sued as representatives of the class without needing to include every member of the class. The plaintiffs must present questions of law and fact that are common to the class, and the representative parties must show that they clearly and adequately represent the class.

The class action procedure is available in federal court under Rule 23 of the Federal Rules of Civil Procedure and in most state courts under a similar rule. Rule 23(a) states that a class action is available only if "the class is so numerous that joinder of all members is impracticable." For example, where the other requirements stated in Rule 23 were met, the fact that almost two hundred female employees had been affected by a company's alleged discriminatory maternity leave policy was sufficient to justify class treatment of the plaintiff's case. Class actions are frequently brought under Title VII of the Civil Rights Act of 1964. While private persons may file a lawsuit, either individually or as a class action, a charge must first have been filed with the Equal Employment Opportunity Commission (EEOC) or appropriate state agency in order for that agency to settle the matter. After a specified period, the EEOC may issue a "right to sue letter."

The representative of the class must follow the procedural and certification requirements of bringing a class action lawsuit. Other members of the class do not generally have to follow the requirements for filing a lawsuit except for the 90-day rule in the event of class decertification.

Courts have tended to allow class actions in Title VII lawsuits without much proof that many individuals were similarly situated. They have found that Title VII claims are class actions by their very nature, since they challenge the defendants' actions toward a specific class or group mentioned in the statute. Courts have refused to recognize a class, however, in Title VII where there were so few employees involved that they could easily be joined as plaintiff parties.

Rule 23(b)(3) has an "opt-out" clause in class actions, under which members of a plaintiff class remain members unless they expressly exclude themselves. A unique exception to this rule is found in Rule 16(b) of the Fair Labor Standards Act (FLSA), which states that no employee may be a party to an FLSA lawsuit unless he or she has consented in writing and filed that consent with the courts.

See also **Civil Rights Act of 1964; Equal Employment Opportunity Commission; Fair Labor Standards Act.**

CLAYTON ANTITRUST ACT (1914) A federal statute, enacted in 1914, intended to prohibit applying the antitrust provisions of the Sherman Antitrust Act to labor unions and to limit the jurisdiction of the courts to issue injunctions in labor disputes. Section 6 of the Clayton Act stated that the "labor of a human being is not a commodity or article of commerce. Nothing contained in these laws shall be construed to forbid the existence and operation of labor organizations instituted for the purposes of mutual help." The act further stated that labor unions were neither illegal combinations or conspiracies.

The Clayton Act outlawed the use of injunctions in labor disputes "unless necessary to prevent irreparable injury to property or to a property right . . . for which injury there is no adequate remedy at law."

Section 20 of the act provided that "no restraining order or injunction shall be granted by any court of the United States in any case between employers and employees." Samuel Gompers, president of the American Federation of Labor praised the statute as labor's "Magna Carta," but judicial interpretation during the 1920s changed that opinion. The U.S. Supreme Court, in *Duplex Printing Press Co. v. Deering* (1921), narrowly interpreted the Clayton Act provision protecting labor activity, leaving unions nearly as susceptible to federal antitrust law as they had been before the act. This restrictive judicial treatment of the Clayton Act led Congress to more definitively prohibit injunctions against peaceful labor activities through the Norris-La Guardia Act (1932) and the National Labor Relations Act (1935).

See also **Antitrust Laws; *Duplex Printing Press Co. v. Deering;* Injunctions against Unions; National Labor Relations Act; Norris-LaGuardia Act; Sherman Antitrust Act of 1980.**

CLOSED SHOP

A union security arrangement where the employer is required to hire only employees who are union members and discharge any employee who drops union membership. In a closed shop, union membership is required prior to employment by the company and is a condition of continued employment. When additional workers are needed, the employer must request that the union send applicants for consideration. The closed shop was made illegal by the Labor-Management Relations Act of 1947 (the Taft-Hartley Act) amendments to the National Labor Relations Act (NLRA), now known as Section 8(b)(2) of the NLRA. The closed shop was made illegal because it discriminates in the hire or tenure of employment to encourage union membership, and is not protected by Section 8(a)(3) of the NLRA, which prohibits employer unfair labor practices.

Another union security arrangement is the union shop, which differs from the closed shop. In a union shop, employees are not required to belong to a labor union before they are hired, but they are required to join within a specified period of time (by law, not less than 30 days). Of the union security devices, the closed shop gives the union the greatest power. It permits the union to determine the eligibility of job applicants (as well as which workers keep the jobs they already hold) by controlling admission to union membership and by expelling workers who fail to comply with internal rules and regulations.

See also **Union Security Clause; Labor-Management Relations Act of 1947; National Labor Relations Act.**

CODE OF ETHICAL PRACTICES A code of union ethics, drafted by the ethical practices committee of the American Federation of Labor-Congress of Industrial Organizations (AFL-CIO) in 1957 and later adopted by the AFL-CIO convention, that sets standards of trade union behavior. Suspected violations of these standards by affiliated unions may be investigated and recommendations for remedial action made to the executive council of the Federation. The code covers issues such as the financial responsibility of union officers, racketeering, and union democratic processes.

See also **American Federation of Labor-Congress of Industrial Organizations.**

COERCION Economic or other pressure, including antiunion speeches or literature, exerted by employers against employees to prevent their joining a union or engaging in concerted activities protected by law. The employment relationship, characterized by complete economic dependence of the employee upon the good will of the employer, makes such antiunion statements inherently intrusive on employee free choice. However, communications are not coercive and are not an unfair labor practice unless they contain a threat of reprisal or a promise of benefit. Thus, an employer's speech or leaflet can itself be considered "interference, restraint or coercion" if it explicitly threatens the loss of employment, loss of pay, loss of promotion, or violence if the listener votes for the union or if the union wins the election. If the language is ambiguous, it can still be held to constitute an unfair labor practice.

Coercion also includes intimidation by the union or fellow employees to compel affiliation with a union. A union's threats during an election campaign are outlawed along with the employer's, including threats that a union loss or a vote against the union will result in physical harm to a person or his or her property or family. Promises by the union, on the other hand, are considered different from employer promises, and courts are more willing to find employer promises coercive or restrictive of employee free choice.

Section 8(a)(1) of the National Labor Relations Act (NLRA) states that it is an unfair labor practice for an employer to "interfere with, restrain, or coerce a reasonable employee in the exercise of the rights guaranteed in Section 7" to organize and bargain collectively and to engage in peaceful concerted activities. The NLRA states four classes of employer actions that were thought to be particularly objectionable. All were considered specific types of the broader Section 8(1) violation: employer domination of a union; employer discrimination in hiring, firing, or working conditions to encourage or discourage union membership; employer discrimination for filing charges or giving testimony before the National Labor Relations Board; and employer refusal to bargain with a majority union. Section 8(1) can also be violated by conduct more specifically prohibited in the sections that follow it, such as threats of employer reprisal for voting for a union, employer surveillance of employees in their union activities, and employer questioning of employees on their union activities.

See also **Company Union; Concerted Activity; National Labor Relations Act; National Labor Relations Board; Unfair Labor Practice.**

COLLECTIVE ACTION Lawsuits brought by an employee or a group of employees authorized by Section 16(b) of the Fair Labor Standards Act (FLSA) as a unique form of representative action to recover minimum wages, overtime pay, and damages. A collective action can be commenced by the filing of a lawsuit by any one of the individual claimants on behalf of all the plaintiffs specifically named as parties if written consents to be plaintiffs in this action are filed in a timely manner. [*Burrell v. LaFollette Coach Lines* (1981)] The statute forbids nonemployees from being a party in such lawsuits, with the exception of the U.S. Department of Labor, which specifically is empowered to bring suit on behalf of an employee or group of employees under 16(c) of the FLSA. These lawsuits are also known as FLSA representation lawsuits.

See also **Fair Labor Standards Act.**

COLLECTIVE BARGAINING A method of determining terms and conditions of employment between union representatives of employees and representatives of the employer. While "bargaining" means to negotiate terms, collective bargaining refers to the process whereby the union and the employer negotiate on the wages, hours, benefits, working conditions, and other terms of employment to be included in an agreement that controls the relations of the parties for a specified period of time.

Often the union is first to announce its demands, after which management studies them and makes a counter offer. Then the two sides usually negotiate until they work out an agreement, each side generally having to modify or abandon some of its initial demands. Once an agreement has been reached, the terms are recorded in a written contract that sets forth the agreed-upon wages, hours, and other employment conditions, including what type of union security arrangement will be in force.

Sections 8(a)(5) and 8(b)(3) of the National Labor Relations Act (NLRA) require bargaining in good faith by every employer and union party in a representation relationship. Though the meaning of good faith bargaining is somewhat ambiguous, the NLRA basically defines good faith bargaining as the obligation to meet and discuss terms with an open mind but without being required to come to an agreement. The duty to bargain in good faith is defined in Section 8(d) of the NLRA as the mutual obligation of the employer and the union (1) to meet at reasonable times and to confer in good faith on wages, hours, and other terms and conditions of employment; and (2) execute a written contract incorporating any agreement reached, if requested by the other party.

During the collective bargaining process, all of the parties must, upon request, make available all relevant and necessary information to support their bargaining positions. Each party, in other words, must substantiate its claims. [*NLRB v. Truitt Manufacturing Co.* (1956)]

The parties are permitted to bargain on specific "bargaining subjects," which are included in the collective bargaining agreement. There are two classifications of bargainable subjects: (1) *mandatory (or compulsory) subjects*, which include wages, hours, and any other terms and conditions of employment, and (2) *permissive subjects*, which may be included in the collective bargaining agreement but on which the parties are not forced to bargain. The scope of the bargaining unit, legal liability clauses, and matters internal to the union are all permissive bargaining subjects. The distinction between mandatory and permissive subjects was approved by the U.S. Supreme Court in *NLRB v. Borg-Warner, Wooster Div.* (1958). The distinction is important. The parties must bargain in good faith on mandatory bargaining subjects and can maintain their posture until an impasse is reached. The parties may negotiate on permissive bargaining subjects, but they may not insist that their position be agreed to by the other party in order to reach agreement on a contract.

A nonbargainable subject is one in which no bargaining is permitted. This may occur because the subject *must* be included in the contract on request or because it *may not* be included in the contract.

Certain kinds of behavior during collective bargaining is prohibited by Section 8 of the NLRA as unfair labor practices. They include the refusal to even meet with the other parties for purposes of collective bargaining, a refusal to execute a written contract embodying terms the parties agree to, changes in wages and other working conditions under negotiation, and a refusal to turn over information required by the other party to assist in legitimate bargaining.

The union's power to act as an exclusive representative of all unit employees gives it a duty to fairly and in good faith represent the interests of all within the unit. The union has a duty of fair representation in both the collective bargaining and contract administration functions of its representatives, meaning that it has the duty to "serve the interests of all members without hostility or discrimination towards any, to exercise its discretion with complete good faith and honesty and avoid arbitrary conduct." [*Vaca v. Sipes* (1967); *Steele v. Louisville & N.R.R.* (1944)] Newer case law, nonetheless, has found the union's duty of fair representation to be relatively greater in contract administration than in contract negotiation. [*Price v. Teamsters* (1972)]

The number of subjects covered by collective bargaining is considerably greater in the United States, where the system encourages unions to strive for more at the bargaining table, than in Europe and Japan. The American system of decentralized bargaining and the wage-conscious behavior of unions also encourages American employers to resist union organizational activities. As a result, there are many more organizational and recognition disputes in the United States than in other industrialized countries. The extent to which federal statutes authorizing lawsuits for violating collective bargaining agreements preempts state-based actions has generated several important cases.

Collective bargaining is an effective vehicle for advancing the workplace interests of unionized workers—a claim proven by the fact that the largest union-nonunion compensation differential in the industrialized world exists in the United States. But for more than 50 years, collective bargaining in the United States has centered around the right of employees to withhold their labor when all other means have failed. Under the NLRA the strike is the primary way of resolving disputes where a union and employer are unable to agree on contract terms. However, workers today who exercise their right to strike are often fired and permanently replaced. Critics of collective bargaining believe that the process fails to protect workers and that employee protections should be provided through labor market–wide government mandates. They argue that bargaining outcomes have increased employer incentives to transfer their operations to non-union locations.

See also **Collective Bargaining Agreement; Fair Labor Standards Act; National Labor Relations Act.**

COLLECTIVE BARGAINING AGREEMENT A formal contract entered into by an employer or groups of employers with their employees represented by a union, as opposed to an agreement arrived at by individual bargaining. It is an enforceable contract or mutual understanding between a union and company or their representatives establishing the terms and conditions of employment, usually for a specified period of time. There is no "standard" collective bargaining agreement. The scope and coverage of each contract is tailored to the needs and desires of the employees, union, and company involved.

Most agreements include provisions on the parties involved (including the bargaining unit and union security), conditions of employment (such as seniority, grievance procedures, wages, hours, vacations, and holidays), and the procedure to be used in settling disputes that may arise during the term of the contract. Often a no-strike clause is included. Collective bargaining agreements typically provide for arbitration, because the contract cannot cover all aspects of the employer-employee relationship. As a result, an extensive body of law has arisen on arbitration under collective bargaining agreements.

The collective bargaining agreement is a special type of contract because it must conform to both basic contract law and national labor policy as reflected in federal labor statutes passed by Congress and interpreted by court decisions. The Supreme Court in the Steelworkers Trilogy cases in 1960 stressed the importance of collective bargaining agreements as a matter of public policy when it held that "a collective bargaining agreement is an effort to erect a system of industrial self-government."

The collective bargaining agreement is not an employment contract. Employees are hired separately and individually. Once in the bargaining unit, however, they are regulated by the collective bargaining agreement.

See also **Benefits; Duty of Fair Representation; Hours; Impasse; National Labor Relations Act; Union Security Clause; Wage.**

COLLUSION A conspiracy engaged in by an employer and the certified representative of his or her employees to defraud the employees represented while providing the semblance of a genuine bargaining relationship.

A union violates its duty of fair representation if its actions are "arbitrary, discriminating, or in bad faith." [*Vaca v. Sipes* (1967)] This duty applies to both the negotiation and administration of collective bargaining agreements. [*Ford Motor Co. v. Huffman* (1953)] Both a union and the employer are liable for the union's breach of its duty of fair representation if they act in collusion with each other. [*Jones v. T.W.A.* (1974); *United Independent Flight Officers v. United Airlines, Inc.* (1985); *Bautista v. Pan American* (1987)]

See also **Collective Bargaining Agreement; Duty of Fair Representation.**

COMMISSION ON CIVIL RIGHTS An independent, nonpartisan, fact-finding agency of the executive branch established under the Civil Rights Act of 1957, the Commission on Civil Rights makes findings of fact but has no enforcement authority. It investigates discriminatory actions based on color, race, religion, sex, age, disability, and national origin, and it has the authority to hold hearings and to issue subpoenas for documents and witnesses. Since it lacks enforcement powers that would enable it to apply specific remedies in individual cases, the commission refers the many complaints it receives to the appropriate government agency for action.

The commission also evaluates federal statutes and federal equal opportunity programs and serves as a national clearinghouse for civil rights information. Many of its findings and recommendations, which it submits to the president and Congress, have been enacted, either by statute, executive order, or regulation. The new structure was the direct result of President Reagan's unprecedented attempt to fire his critics on the commission and replace them with members of his own choosing. The new arrangement emerged as a compromise between a Democratic-controlled Congress and the Reagan Administration. In 1983, the commission was transformed from a six- to an eight-member body, with four members appointed by the president and four by Congress. The commission maintains state advisory committees and consults with representatives of federal, state, and local organizations.

COMMISSION ON THE FUTURE OF WORKER/MANAGEMENT RELATIONS Also called the Dunlop Commission after its chair, former Labor Secretary John Dunlop, the commission investigated contemporary labor-management relations and American law and recommended changes to improve productivity through increased labor-management cooperation and employee participation in the workplace.

The commission examined three basic issues: (1) What, if any, new methods or institutions should be encouraged or required to enhance workplace productivity through labor-management cooperation and participation? (2) What, if any, changes should be made within the current legal framework and practices of collective bargaining to enhance cooperative behavior, improve productivity, and reduce conflict and delay? (3) What, if anything, should be done to encourage labor and management to resolve workplace problems themselves rather than resorting to state and federal courts or government regulatory bodies?

The Dunlop Commission called for any significant reforms in the framework of American employment relations. Proclaiming a participatory, high-performance economy as its goal, the commission declared in its preliminary report that "employee participation, rights freely to exercise or refrain from [union] representation, and dispute resolution is a seamless whole for the future of worker-management relations."

Labor unions are central to the economy envisioned by the Dunlop Commission. A strong and open work environment "where a union is present" maximizes the productive value of participatory employment practices, such as self-managed teams and quality circles. But the commission found that outdated labor laws allow corporations to suppress the workers who dare to exercise their rights to unionize and to promote an adversarial rather than cooperative labor-management relationship.

The Dunlap Commission said that the evidence presented to it demonstrated that current labor law was not encouraging collective bargaining or protecting workers' rights to choose whether or not to be represented by a union. In light of this finding, the panel recommended four changes in collective bargaining procedures to enhance cooperation and reduce conflict and delay: (1) expedite representation elections after the National Labor Relations Board (NLRB) determines that an election should be held; (2) give the NLRB statutory authority to obtain prompt injunctions to remedy discriminatory actions against employees that occur during an organizing campaign or negotiations for a first contract; (3) assist employers and newly certified unions in achieving first contracts through an upgraded dispute resolution system that provides for mediation and empowers a tripartite advisory board to use a variety of options to settle unresolved disputes ranging from self-help to binding arbitration; and (4) encourage railroad and airline management representatives—whose bargaining is covered under the Railway Labor Act and not the National Labor Relations Act—to seek their own solutions for improving the performance of collective bargaining in their industries.

See also **Collective Bargaining; Labor-Management Cooperation; Labor-Management Relations; Quality Circles.**

COMMITTEE FOR INDUSTRIAL ORGANIZATION (CIO)

See **American Federation of Labor-Congress of Industrial Organizations.**

COMMITTEE ON POLITICAL EDUCATION (COPE)

A division of the American Federation of Labor-Congress of Industrial Organizations (AFL-CIO), COPE exists primarily to provide support for candidates for political office who have received the endorsement of labor unions. Its activities are supported by voluntary contributions.

COPE was formed with the merger of the AFL and the CIO in 1955, which led to the combination of the AFL's Labor League for Political Action and the CIO's Political Action Committee. COPE's major purpose is to encourage union members and their families to actively participate in the political life of their community in order to protect their rights as union members and citizens. COPE organizations also participate actively in the nomination, support, and election of candidates, endorsing those who favor organized labor's legislative objectives.

Frequently the involvement of unions in politics emerges as a political issue. Unionists argue that they have no choice in the matter because the American legal-political system has often been hostile to unions, so therefore, at least some political activity is essential in order to preserve meaningful collective bargaining.

In 1996, the AFL-CIO ran an energetic campaign to support President Clinton's reelection and to help the Democrats recapture control of Congress, which that party lost in 1994, partially because 40 percent of union members ignored their leadership and voted for Republican Congressional candidates. The AFL-CIO, stressing issues such a Medicare and Medicaid, conducted an extensive campaign of television ads and grass-roots organizing. The unions had not launched such an all-out nationwide political effort since 1968, when they supported Hubert Humphrey's presidential campaign.

See also **American Federation of Labor-Congress of Industrial Organizations.**

COMMON LAW: EMPLOYMENT DOCTRINES

Common law is the system of law based on legal precedents and principles established by judicial case law rather than statutes or administrative regulations. However, much of English common law has now been enacted as or replaced by statutory law.

The common law defined a "master" as one who employs another person to perform services and who controls or has a right of control over the other's conduct in performing such services. By definition, the master had the power to control, choose, and direct the servant as to the object to be accomplished as well as the power to control the details of the work. These common law definitions are still important in determining who is an employer and employee.

During the early history of the American unions, the courts were the primary sources of public policy. In the absence of labor legislation, the judiciary created labor policy by applying common law rules. Thus the courts controlled the labor movement from its origins in the late eighteenth century through the early twentieth century. The landmark "Philadelphia Cordwainers" case (1806) was significant in that it was the first to apply the English common law doctrine of criminal conspiracy to union activities in the United States. Though the use of the conspiracy doctrine did not completely prevent workers from striking to improve working conditions, it did limit trade union activities.

Nowhere else among industrial nations was the judiciary as influential in labor relations as in nineteenth-century and early twentieth-century America, and no other issue occupied the attentions of trade unionists as consistently for several decades as judge-made law. When labor struggled for legitimacy in a court-dominated era, labor's leaders transformed older republican "rights" arguments into the common law's liberal mold, relinquishing a vision of law actively reconstructing the industrial world.

Law reshaped labor's language and outlook in conservative directions, but organized labor also eventually reshaped the law. The unions built on the antislavery legacy and created an alternative constitutional vision. They exploited the ambiguities of common law doctrines and used the radical aspects of constitutional tradition to create an alternative version of labor's rights. Industrial disorder and workers' powerful and articulate defiance of judge-made law gradually persuaded state and national lawmakers and political elites that the old legal order was untenable and that labor's constitutional claims demanded recognition. The workers' mass defiance of the official legal order persuaded New Deal lawmakers to adapt much of labor's alternative "law" and "Constitution" as their own.

See also **Conspiracy Doctrine.**

COMMON SITUS PICKETING Common situs picketing is a form of picketing in which employees of a struck company who work at a common site with employees of at least one neutral employer may picket only at the entrance to the work site. The employees of the neutral employers must enter the work site through other gates. Picketing is restricted to the entrance of the struck employer so as not to encourage a secondary boycott by employees of the neutral employers. Common situs picketing is found most often in the construction industry.

The most difficult cases under the National Labor Relations Act's (NLRA's) secondary boycott provisions are those in which a union has picketed a common site because employees of both the struck employer and neutral employers are working there. The basic rules on picketing in common situs situations were laid down in the *International Rice Milling* (1951), *Denver Building Trades* (1951), and *Moore Dry Dock* (1950) cases. The Supreme Court in *International Rice* found that the action of the pickets in refusing to allow delivery persons of a neutral employer to enter the mill—the primary site of the labor dispute—was not in violation of the NLRA's secondary boycott provisions. In the *Denver Building Trades* case, the Supreme Court rejected the contention that the general contractor and its subcontractors on a construction project were "allies" for the purpose of the secondary boycott prohibition. In applying the boycott provisions, the Court said, the contractor and the subcontractors must be treated as separate employers. So the picketing of a construction project in support of a strike against a subcontractor was considered a violation of the secondary boycott ban if it had the effect of inducing the employers of the general contractor or other subcontractors to stop work.

The National Labor Relations Board (NLRB) gradually developed a series of standards for determining the legality of common situs picketing. The tests used in the 1950 *Moore Dry Dock* case are:

1. Picketing must be limited to times when the primary (struck) employer's employees actually are present at the common site.
2. Picketing must be limited to places "reasonably close" to the operations of the primary employer's workers.
3. The pickets must show clearly that their dispute is with the primary employer alone.
4. The primary employer's workers must be engaged in the employer's normal business at the common site.

In 1953, the NLRB added another condition to the permissibility of common situs picketing. It held that a union engaging in such picketing must show that the struck employer has no permanent place of business in the area that can be picketed. Created in the *Washington Coca Cola Bottling Works* case in 1953, this rule later was rejected as too "mechanical" by the U.S. Court of Appeals in New Orleans and the District of Columbia in *Otis Massey* (1950) and in T*ruck Drivers and Helpers Local 728 v. NLRB* (*Campbell Coal)* (1957). In 1967, the NLRB abandoned the rule, stating in *International Brotherhood of Electrical Workers, Local 861 (Plauche Electric Co.)* that the availability of an establishment of the struck employer in the area, along with the place of picketing, would merely be one factor to consider in determining the legality of the picketing.

A year later, the NLRB ruled that the *Moore Dry Dock* standards themselves may not be applied on an indiscriminate per se basis but may be regarded merely as aids in determining the underlying question of statutory violations. On this basis the NLRB held in a case involving New Power Wire and Electric Corporation that a union did not violate the NLRA by picketing the premises of neutral employers who were working even though the employees of the struck employer were absent from some of the picketed premises for substantial periods of time.

See also **National Labor Relations Act; National Labor Relations Board; Picketing; Secondary Boycott.**

COMMONWEALTH V. HUNT (1842) One of the landmark cases in labor history, this case limited the use of the conspiracy doctrine in labor disputes and supported the right of labor organizations to perform their legitimate functions. It established the principle that the legality of a combination of workers depends on the purposes they seek and the means they use to attain these goals—what became known as the "means-ends doctrine." In ruling that unions engaged in strikes were not guilty of conspiracy in restraint of trade and that it was legal for a union to strike for higher wages, American labor won its first significant judicial victory.

This case enunciated the theory of "the law of labor combinations," in which a conspiracy is a combination of two or more persons to accomplish, by concerted actions, some purpose not in itself unlawful by unlawful means. The law of labor combinations has the same meaning as the conspiracy doctrine and probably comes from the English combination laws passed in the fourteenth century.

The significance of *Hunt* is that it marked the beginning of the end of the criminal conspiracy doctrine in labor disputes. It was the foundation for the application of a new legal principle: the doctrine of illegal means and ends. However, judges had considerable discretion when examining union means and objectives, and criminal conspiracy charges could still be used to deter trade union activities. Subsequent to this decision, trade unionists were occasionally charged as participants in criminal conspiracies.

Despite the *Hunt* decision, labor's victory remained incomplete. When a court believed that a union was seeking an unlawful objective or was using unlawful means to achieve a lawful objective, judicial action was undertaken to terminate the union activity. In fact, there were more labor conspiracy cases in the second half of the nineteenth century than in the first half.

See also **Concerted Action; Conspiracy Doctrine; Labor Dispute.**

Commonwealth v. Pullis (1806) The English common law doctrine of criminal conspiracy was first applied to union activities in *Commonwealth v. Pullis* (also known as the Philadelphia Cordwainers' case) in 1806. After some master shoemakers unilaterally reduced the price they paid journeymen for boots, a group of journeymen shoemakers (known as cordwainers) demanded the old price be reestablished. This involved a price increase of 25 cents to 75 cents, depending upon the type of boot involved. When the masters refused, some journeymen shoemakers decided to strike. During the strike, eight journeymen were arrested and indicted for actions constituting a "combination and conspiracy to raise their wages." The court found the striking journeymen guilty and the union was fined. In this case, the judge applied the English common law doctrine of criminal conspiracy. He ruled that "a combination of working men to raise their wages may be considered in a twofold point of view; one is to benefit themselves. . . . The other is to injure those who do not join the [combination] . . . the rule of law condemns both."

The court in the Philadelphia Cordwainers' case held that a combination of workers striking to raise wages or obtain other more favorable terms of employment was an illegal conspiracy that could be suppressed by the state. Following the case, strikers were subjected to prosecution for criminal conspiracy in other eastern states and became less effective. Though the doctrine did not completely prevent workers from striking to improve working conditions, it greatly inhibited trade union activities.

See also **Strike.**

COMMUNITY OF INTEREST A criterion utilized by the National Labor Relations Board (NLRB) to determine whether a group of employees constitutes an appropriate bargaining unit—a group of workers that may appropriately decide whether to be represented by a single union, under Section 9(b) of the National Labor Relations Act.

In determining whether the bargaining unit is appropriate, the NLRB must find that the employees in the unit share a community of interest. For example, the board looks for similarities in such factors as duties, wages, hours, benefits, skills, training, working conditions, and common supervision. The NLRB is also concerned that the unit neither includes employees with a substantial conflict of economic interest nor omits employees who share a unit of economic interest with employees in the election or bargaining group. This determination is made on a case-by-case basis. [*Black & Decker Manufacturing Co.* (1964)]

The NLRB also seeks to determine whether those who will be included in the bargaining unit—employees in a particular unit or department of a factory, or the plants workers as a whole—have a community of interest that is distinct from the interests of those who will be outside the bargaining unit. This doctrine reflects the classic craft-industry division in American labor history. For example, all of the electricians, and no one else, may be seen as having a community of interests sufficient to justify their recognition as an appropriate bargaining unit, even if they are only a few dozen among thousands of other employees in the same factory. The electricians' decision to join a particular union, however, may frustrate their fellow employees, who may want to include the electricians in their union. Thus one possible issue in an NLRB determination is whether employees with special craft skills should be separated from other employees for purposes of voting and bargaining.

Though other employees are guaranteed the right to unionize, current American labor law states that neither managerial nor supervisory employees may organize to pursue collective bargaining without their employer's consent. The NLRB has consistently excluded managerial employees from rank-and-file units in order to avoid creating units with substantial conflicts of economic interests. In *Julien P. Friez & Sons* (1943), for example, the NLRB excluded expediters from a unit of rank and file employees on the basis that they were closely related to management.

See also **Appropriate Bargaining Unit; Collective Bargaining; National Labor Relations Board.**

COMPANY UNION

An organization of employees, usually of a single company, that is dominated or strongly influenced by management. Ordinarily, the purpose of these organizations was to keep outside unions from organizing the employees and to ensure a dependable and willing labor supply.

Before the National Labor Relations Act (NLRA) was passed in 1935, recognition of a company union was a favored means of avoiding a true adversarial relationship. In the late 1920s and early 1930s, employers confronting the challenge of unionization frequently took the initiative in organizing employee committees or associations to represent the employees in resolving grievances over wages and working conditions. The employer often dominated such groups of "employee representatives" by instigating their creation, shaping their rules and organization, influencing policy by placing company representatives in official positions, inducing or requiring employees to join the organization, controlling its finances, and giving it special privileges (such as time for solicitation and meetings). Congress believed that such employer domination and support interfered with the freedom of employees in selecting their collective bargaining representatives and substituted for the voice of the employees at the bargaining table the voice of the employer, engaged in a dialogue with itself.

In 1935, Congress enacted what is now Section 8(a)(2) of the NLRA, guaranteeing employees the right to organize and bargain collectively. The act makes it an unfair labor practice and unlawful for an employer to support a company-established or preferred union financially or with other assistance. To exercise such involvement constitutes a prohibited employer interference with the right of employees to form "unions of their own choosing." [*Hertzka v. Knowles* (1974) and *NLRB v. Clappers Manufacturing, Inc.* (1974)] Since the 1930s, company unions have largely ceased to exist.

After the demise of the company union, there has been very little litigation under Section 8(a)(2). The major issues became, instead of "employer domination," (1) the fine line between the company's illegal "support" and its legal—and desirable—"cooperation" with the union; and (2) the limitations upon employer in dealing with one union when a second union is engaged in organizing.

Section 8(a)(2) has recently reemerged as a major issue as worker participation plans such as quality of work life (QWL) programs and quality circles have become more popular. The National Labor Relations Board (NLRB) recently decided two cases that applied the section to worker participation issues. Both *Electromation, Inc. v. Teamsters Local 1049* (1992), which arose in a nonunionized workplace, and *E.I. DuPont deNemours & Co. v. Local 900 of the International Chemical Workers Assn.* (1993), which arose in a unionized workplace, are regarded as landmark cases.

The *Electromation* case reaffirms the protections of labor organizations and employees. Without impairing legitimate worker participation efforts, worker participation programs were considered legitimate to the extent that they are concerned with improving quality, productivity, or such matters as customer relations, rather than working conditions. The NLRB, in *Electromation,* defines a group as a labor organization if (1) the employees participate, (2) the organization exists, at least in part, for the purpose of "dealing" with employers, and (3) those dealings concern "conditions of work" or other statutory subjects. Further, if the organization is intended to represent employees, then it meets the statutory definition of "employee representation committee plan" under Section 2(5) of the NLRA.

In *DuPont,* the NLRB found that management had used the employee committees that the company had established in its cooperative program to undermine the union's representational capacity, rather than truly to cooperate. The NLRB recognized both (1) the importance of cooperative efforts such as QWL programs, and (2) that productivity and efficiency issues are legitimate subjects for employee committees. The committees in this case, however, became involved in activities properly within the union's authority and the company bypassed the recognized labor union in violation of its duty under Section 8(a)(5) to bargain with the recognized labor union. Further, because management closely controlled how the employee committees functioned, the company therefore dominated these labor organizations in violation of Section 8(a)(2).

See also **National Labor Relations Act; Quality Circles; Quality of Work Life; Unfair Labor Practice.**

COMPANYWIDE BARGAINING Collective bargaining agreements that cover all of a company's employees. Companywide bargaining takes place between a company with many plants and a single union representing employees of a particular craft or all employees of an industrial unit. Terms and conditions of employment are generally uniform, except for provisions to handle purely local conditions.

Two or more nominally separate business entities are regarded as a single employer when they are so structurally interrelated that they constitute one integrated enterprise. The major factors determining single-employer status are the interrelation of operations, common management, centralized control of labor relations, and common ownership. Two or more corporations owned or controlled by the same shareholder or shareholders can be treated as a single, integrated employer where the common owner controls the labor relations and personnel policies of the corporations.

Whenever a parent corporation and its wholly owned subsidiaries are engaged in what is fundamentally the same industry or business enterprise, the National Labor Relations Board is likely to find that the parent and subsidiaries are a single employer. In making its finding, the board will look for (1) common officers and directors; (2) unified and integrated labor relations policies; (3) common supervisory, technical, or professional personnel; and (4) the sharing of employees and equipment.

See also **National Labor Relations Board.**

COMPARABLE RATE The idea that men and women should receive equal pay when they perform work that involves comparable skills and responsibility or is of comparable worth to the employer. Comparable rates are used in wage negotiations where it is necessary to compare identical or similar occupations or occupations with similar job characteristics. These may be within the same plant or in other plants in the community or in the industry. The comparison of such rates may provide a basis for settlement when individual job classifications are being considered in wage negotiations.

Proponents of comparable worth, also known as "pay equity," argue that it is the only means of remedying the history of sex discrimination that has depressed wages in particular jobs traditionally held by women. Opponents argue that comparable worth legislation would upset the market forces of supply and demand, which they claim are more important in setting wages than patterns of discrimination.

See also **Comparable Worth; Sex Discrimination in Employment.**

COMPARABLE WORTH The doctrine that men and women who perform work of the same inherent value should receive comparable compensation. The concept generally means that compensation should be based on the worth of a job to the employer as measured by such factors as skill, effort, responsibility, and working conditions under a bias-free system of job evaluation.

Comparable worth theory is based on the principle of "equal pay for work of comparable worth" as distinct from "equal pay for equal work." The well-documented disparity between men's and women's earnings has generated intense debate over the concept of comparable worth, that is, equal pay for work judged to be of equal value. Government, business, labor unions, and the courts have all considered whether workers in dissimilar jobs of comparable worth—measured by such criteria as working conditions, degree of difficulty, and knowledge and responsibility required—should receive equal wages and how wage adjustments can be implemented. Proponents of comparable worth argue that the relative pay of women is affected significantly by prejudice or tradition and that it should be increased by administrative or judicial action. One method of increasing the relative pay for jobs filled predominantly by women is to adjust wages on the basis of job evaluations. According to this approach, holders of jobs judged to be of comparable worth should receive equal pay, whether or not the current market wages are identical. Opponents of comparable worth believe that pay tends to reflect productivity and working conditions, and that the current pay differential simply reflects the operation of market forces. According to this view, to receive increased pay, women must choose different lines of work and stay in the paid labor force longer without interruption.

To some extent, the comparable worth debate began with the Equal Pay Act (EPA) of 1963. The EPA applies to gender-based discrimination only where men and women perform substantially the same work. It had both ideological and practical limits, which gave rise to calls for comparable worth in the 1990s. Though opponents have used market-based arguments, proponents have argued that market outcomes have been tempered by customary notions of justice or fairness.

Title VII of the Civil Rights Act of 1964, enacted one year after the EPA, prohibits gender discrimination in all aspects of employment, including compensation, without requiring that the work in question be equal work (an equal work requirement.) Title VII's broad language spurred Congress to pass the Bennett Amendment in order to maintain the restrictions of the EPA. The Bennett Amendment to Title VII permits differentiation on the basis of sex in determining compensation if the differentiation is authorized by the EPA.

Judicial interpretation of the amendment's ambiguous language became a crucial issue in the comparable worth debate. In *County of Washington v. Gunther* (1981), many expected the U.S. Supreme Court to resolve the question of whether there is a cause of action under Title VII of the Civil Rights Act of 1964 for women paid less than men for jobs that are not equal but are of comparable worth. Although the Supreme Court did not rule on the issue of comparable worth, it held that "claims of discriminatory undercompensation are not barred by Section 703(h) of Title VII merely because the female jail guards who brought the lawsuit "do not perform work equal to that of male jail guards." The Court held that the female employees were working substantially equal jobs and therefore had a viable wage discrimination claim under Title VII. In other words, the Court held that the plaintiffs can prevail by proving that their wages were depressed because of intentional sex discrimination, even though their jobs were not equal to jobs held by higher-paid men. Most federal district courts and many federal appellate courts have been unwilling to extend Title VII to cover comparable worth claims, including *Gerlach v. Michigan Bell Telephone Company* (1980) and *AFSCME v. State of Washington* (1985). The Equal Employment Opportunity Commission, in ruling on a 1985 case, comparing a municipal housing authority's 85-percent female administrative staff and its higher-paid, 88-percent male maintenance staff. It found no violation of Title VII and rejected the pure comparable worth doctrine.

Both Minnesota and California have comparable worth statutes for state employees. Minnesota, for example, requires "equitable compensation relationships between female dominated [70 percent], male dominated [80 percent], and balanced classes of employees" using a standard of comparability of the value of the work in relationship to other positions in the executive branch. Comparability means the value of work measured by the composite of the skill, effort, responsibility, and working conditions normally required.

See also **Civil Rights Act of 1964; Equal Employment Opportunity Commission; Equal Pay Act of 1963.**

COMPENSABLE INJURY A work injury for which the injured worker or his or her beneficiaries can collect compensation benefits under workers' compensation laws or under an employer's private insurance plan. Generally, an injury caused by work (work-related) is a compensable injury. The typical state workers' compensation statute defines a compensable injury as a disease arising out of and in the course of employment and excludes ordinary diseases to which the general public is exposed outside of the employment.

The three factors that determine whether an injury is covered by workers' compensation are the scope of the risk, the injury's relation to employment, and factual cause. Most workers' compensation acts require a "personal injury or death by accident arising out of and in the course of employment." Courts use five basic risk doctrines to determine the scope of risk: proximate cause, peculiar risk, increased risk, actual risk, and positional risk. They also require a sufficiently close relationship (in time, place, and circumstances) between one's employment and the injury. The employee need not be acting within the course and scope of employment when an employment-related injury occurs. Even if the employee's work produced an injury that occurs or manifests itself while the employee is not at work and off the employer's premises, the injury is covered. However, accidents that occur while the employee is traveling to or from work are generally not covered, because these accidents occur outside the course of employment.

The language "personal injury by accident" posed special problems in cases involving diseases, mental illnesses, and injuries to artificial limbs. Initially, occupational diseases were excluded from workers' compensation coverage because they were believed to be an area for private health insurance. Injuries to artificial limbs were not considered "personal injuries," and disabilities from disease that developed over extended periods of time were excluded from coverage because no personal injury "by accident" had occurred. Recently, however, the need for occupational disease coverage has been recognized by judicial interpretation of the statute and by special provisions in the compensation acts. The courts have recognized that mental illness, too, may be caused, at least in part, by one's employment.

Though the coverage formula addresses "personal injury," workers' compensation legislation also provides compensation for work-related deaths. Most of the issues that apply to personal injury cases also apply to deaths.

See also **Workers' Compensation.**

COMPENSATION The total earnings an individual receives from the employment relationship. Compensation includes direct payments (base pay plus any merit pay, incentives, cost of living allowances, and stock options) and indirect payments (benefit plans such as vacations, holidays, health and life insurance, and pensions). Compensation may also refer to recompense for loss or damage, as in workers compensation cases or in cases involving unfair dismissal.

In certain kinds of employment, minimum wages have been established by law. An employee's right to compensation may also, in some circumstances, emerge from custom or practice in the particular field of employment. The employee's compensation also depends upon a contract, express or implied. The type, amount, and schedule of compensation is ordinarily one of the terms of the employment contract, set by agreement between the parties. The employment contract must be a voluntary act for both the employer and the employee, resulting in a common understanding. Thus a contract binding a person to pay for personal services, for example, cannot be implied or inferred unless the party furnishing the services had reason to expect compensation.

The relationship between employer and employee regarding unpaid wages is that of debtor and creditor. Where the business of an individual employer is later incorporated, the individual employer is liable for wages up to the time of the incorporation, and the corporation is liable for wages earned after that time.

See also **Benefits; Holiday; Minimum Wage; Workers' Compensation.**

COMPENSATORY TIME OFF Special time off allowed to employees in lieu of overtime pay, or in compensation for extra time worked by the employee for which no overtime can be paid. Also known as "comp time."

The practice of allowing public employees to take time off in payment for overtime hours, at a rate of one and one-half hours compensatory time off for every hour of overtime worked, as opposed to paying them promptly in cash for overtime hours, has been permitted under Section 7(o) of the Fair Labor Standards Act (FLSA) only when the comp time is granted to the employees during the same pay period as the overtime.

Private employers generally are not allowed to grant compensatory time off instead of paying overtime. State and local government employers, however, may grant comp time within certain limits. Comp time must be given at the rate of one and one half times the overtime hours worked. After 160 hours of overtime (240 hours of comp time), however, the employee must be paid any additional overtime in cash. For emergency and safety personnel the limit is 320 hours of overtime (480 hours of comp time).

An employer may not attempt to persuade an employee to waive overtime pay or accept comp time instead of money. Unless the employee is exempt from overtime, the employee must be paid time and one-half for overtime hours, pursuant to Section 7(e) of the FLSA. The employee cannot agree to waive payment of overtime, and any agreement to do so is invalid. The employee is allowed to sue the employer for back overtime payments, even if the employee signed an agreement to waive them.

See also **Fair Labor Standards Act; Overtime.**

COMPETENCE Proven ability, knowledge, or skill in handling of a specific job. In order to function effectively, each employee is required to master a basic set of skills pertaining to his or her particular job and to be able to accomplish these skills within a certain, specified degree of competence. The standard of comparison is the degree of skill, efficiency, and knowledge possessed by those of ordinary skill, competency, and standing in the particular trade or business in question. In entering employment, the employee implicitly agrees that he possesses and will exercise this degree of skill.

An employee owes his or her employer the duty of exercising a reasonable degree of care, skill, and judgment in the performance of the duties of his or her employment. This duty does not depend upon any express obligation assumed by an employee but is implied from the contract of employment. Though the employee is not held responsible for mere errors of judgment, it is a widely recognized rule that an employee is liable directly to his employer for whatever injury or damage occurs because of the employee's failure to exercise reasonable care and diligence or because of his misconduct. Even the employer's habitual negligence is no excuse for similar negligence by the employee.

The employer, however, is not an insurer for unforeseeable events. He or she is not liable for damage, in other words, resulting from actions or events that cannot be anticipated by common experience. He or she is bound merely to the exercise of reasonable care, skill, and judgment.

COMPLAINT A formal statement by a regional director of the National Labor Relations Board (NLRB), after the investigation of a charge, that it has a prima facie case (such as will prevail unless contradicted and overcome by other evidence) involving an unfair labor practice in violation of the National Labor Relations Act (NLRA). The complaint states the basis for the NLRB's jurisdiction and the alleged unfair labor practices committed by the employer or the union.

Section 10(b) of the NLRA states in part: "Whenever it is charged that any person has engaged in or is engaging in any such unfair labor practice, the Board, or any agent or agency designated by the Board for such purposes, shall have power to issue and cause to be served upon such person a complaint stating the charge in that respect."

After the regional director issues an unfair labor practice complaint, and the respondent is allowed to file an answer, the case is tried in a court-like proceeding before an administrative law judge. Typically, the unfair labor practice case is heard in the locality where the alleged illegal conduct occurred. While the "prosecuting" party is technically the General Counsel, the case against the respondent is conducted by attorneys from the appropriate regional office.

Only about 10 percent of all unfair labor practice charges filed result in formal complaints. Approximately 80 percent of the complaints are against employers and 20 percent against unions.

See also **Administrative Law Judge; Charge; National Labor Relations Act; National Labor Relations Board; Unfair Labor Practice.**

COMPREHENSIVE EMPLOYMENT AND TRAINING ACT (CETA) OF 1973

See **Jobs Training Programs, Federal.**

COMPULSORY ARBITRATION

See **Grievance Arbitration.**

CONCERTED ACTIVITY

Action by one or more employees for the legitimate furtherance of their common interests, usually for the purpose of improving their wages, hours, and working conditions. These activities are largely protected by Section 7 of the National Labor Relations Act (NLRA) as well as state labor relations acts. However, concerted activity will be protected only if it satisfies four requirements: (1) there must be a work-related complaint or grievance; (2) the concerted activity must further some group interest; (3) a specific remedy or result must be sought through such activity; and (4) the activity should not be unlawful or otherwise improper. [*Shelly & Anderson Furniture Manufacturing Co. v. NLRB* (1974)] Unprotected concerted activities include work slow-downs, sit-down strikes, wildcat strikes, damage to business or to plant and equipment, trespass, violence, refusal to accept work assignments, physical sabotage, and a refusal to obey rules.

An individual employee's actions may be concerted, even without the explicit involvement of other employees, if the surrounding circumstances indicate that the employee is acting on behalf of other employees and not solely for personal benefit.

Section 7 of the NLRA generally protects employees engaged in union solicitation, organization, or bargaining (most of the reported cases involving employer discipline for exercising Section 7 rights involve employees who are engaged in union solicitation, organization, or bargaining and thus are protected by the statute). This statutory protection also exists where there is no union on the scene, and employee conduct will be protected only if the activities were for mutual aid or protection. Thus, a spontaneous walkout because a group of employees believe it's too cold to continue work is a protected concerted activity, even though there is no union and employees are nonunionized. [*NLRB v. Washington Aluminum Co.* (1962)] Protected concerted activities include both the employees who jointly seek support for a union, and those who jointly criticize it. [*Cooper Tire & Rubber Co. v. NLRB* (1971)]

The Railway Labor Act, like the NLRA, grants employees the right to organize and bargain collectively through representatives of their own choosing without interference by the carrier.

See also **National Labor Relations Act; Railway Labor Act.**

CONCESSION BARGAINING Sometimes called employee or union givebacks, concession bargaining usually describes those instances when unions agree to modify terms in the existing contract in exchange for job security or other employment protection. During the 1980s, for example, many unions agreed to modify their demands on such issues as work rules and seniority provisions in exchange for greater job security.

See also **Job Security; Seniority.**

CONFIDENTIAL EMPLOYEE An employee who, although he or she may have no supervisory responsibilities, has access to information on the organization's labor relations policy and is therefore ineligible for inclusion in a bargaining unit or coverage by a bargaining agreement. The secretary to the director of labor relations, for example, would be considered a confidential employee. Labor relation statutes often specifically exclude confidential employees from the bargaining unit.

The National Labor Relations Board first defined "confidential employee" in the *B.F. Goodrich Company* case in 1956. The U.S. Supreme Court, in *NLRB v. Hendricks County* (1981), ruled that there was a reasonable basis in law for excluding confidential employees from bargaining units. They are excluded from coverage under many public sector bargaining statutes.

CONFLICT OF INTEREST A situation in which an employee is engaged in outside but closely related business activities that cause economic harm to the employer. If the employee refuses to abandon these activities, the legitimate business interests of the employer require that he be able to terminate the services of the employee.

Implicit in the employment contract is the understanding that the employee will be faithful to the employer's interest during this employment. When an employee deliberately acquires an interest adverse to the employer, he is disloyal and discharge is justified. Where an employee engages in a business that makes him a competitor and rival of his employer, no matter how much or how little time and attention he may devote to it, he is deemed to have an interest that conflicts with his duty to the employer. For this cause he may be dismissed. However, if the employee, during the time of the employment contract, has plans to engage in a competing business after the contract expires, this does not legally justify a discharge (absent a lawful noncompetition agreement).

Whether an employee may be justifiably discharged for engaging in a business that does not compete with that of his employer depends on the circumstances. A discharge may be justified where the contract of employment calls for the "exclusive services" of the employee. Without such a provision, the discharge will be justifiable if it appeared that his activities tended to injure the business of his employer or that he is unable to give his time and attention to the discharge of his duties.

Employers such as local governments are able to deny employment to individuals in the protected classes when they create a conflict of interest sufficient to create a reasonable belief in their inability to provide loyal service to the employer.

See also **Protected Class.**

CONGRESS OF INDUSTRIAL ORGANIZATIONS See **American Federation of Labor-Congress of Industrial Organizations.**

CONSENT DECREE An agreement by the defendant to cease activities asserted as illegal by the government. Upon approval of this agreement by the court, the government's action against the defendant is dropped. It is also a court judgment entered when the parties stipulate that they agree that the decree is a just determination of their rights based upon the real facts of the case, if such facts had been proved. It binds only the consenting parties and is not binding on the court.

In the labor context, the procedure is used by the National Labor Relations Board to end litigation in a disputed case by having the company *or* union enter into a settlement with each other. The litigants consent to the entry of the decree, and once a federal circuit court has reviewed and entered the decree, no further appeal is open to the parties.

When determining whether to issue a judgment based on a stipulation, a trial court is not confined to the agreed-upon facts in the stipulation but may consider additional facts necessary for a full understanding of the issues and for a clarification of the terms used in the stipulation. A court may choose not to enter a consent judgment and, without rendering a judgment, dismiss an action that appears to be a collusive suit, particularly where there is an important issue to be decided that should be resolved only by a true adversary hearing.

A court, in its discretion, may also relieve parties from a stipulation where adherence would inflict a manifest injustice upon one of the parties or where the stipulation had been entered into under a mistake of law. Generally, however, a court does not disregard or set aside a stipulation.

When the parties voluntarily settle a class-based employment discrimination claim, the settlement is reviewed and adopted by the trial court as a consent decree. Typically, the settlement includes an express statement that the defendant has not violated the law but agrees voluntarily to take measures for the benefit of the class. In the equal employment opportunity—affirmative action context, consent decrees are broad pledges from employers, usually obtained by the Equal Employment Opportunity Commission (EEOC) to implement affirmative employment plans. Two of the more prominent cases involved the voluntary plan of nine major steel companies and the United Steelworkers in 1974 to remedy race and sex discrimination and the consent decree involving the American Telephone and Telegraph Company, the EEOC, and the Department of Labor, signed on January 18, 1973. If the affirmative action plan is not properly constructed, the employees affected can intervene to protest. Individuals cannot challenge the decree, however, if they were fully informed of their interest in litigation and notified of the opportunity to intervene and participate at the time of the litigation but chose not to do so.

See also **Equal Employment Opportunity Commission; United Steelworkers of America.**

CONSOLIDATED OMNIBUS BUDGET RECONCILIATION ACT (COBRA) OF 1985

Requires most employers to offer to employees who leave the company, voluntarily or not, or whose work hours are significantly reduced, the option of remaining members of the company's group health plans. (Employees who are terminated for gross misconduct, however, are not covered by COBRA.) In addition, the employer must offer continued coverage to the employee's spouse and dependent children if they are covered under the company's health plan.

COBRA applies to group health plans maintained by all employers except charities, federal government agencies, state and local government agencies that do not receive funds under the Public Health Service Act, and employers that "normally employed fewer than 20 employees on a typical business day during the preceding calendar year." State and local governments that receive funds under the Public Health Service Act are also covered by COBRA. In some states, local laws are similar to COBRA; in others, they entitle employees to more extensive coverage than does COBRA.

Under COBRA, an employer-provided health plan is defined as any plan through which the employer provides medical care to employees, former employees, and/or these employees' spouses and dependent children. The medical care may be provided directly or through insurance, reimbursement or other means. Plans that are typically covered by COBRA include group hospitalization, surgical, major medical, and dental insurance plans.

The length of the required continuation coverage depends on the nature of the "qualifying event," an event that would have resulted in the loss of coverage under the plan but for the right to choose continuation of the coverage. The employee's termination or reduction in hours is one such qualifying event. Under most circumstances, the employee who leaves the company may extend coverage for up to 18 months, at his or her own expense. (The employer must provide the employee 45 days after he or she elects to continue coverage before requiring the first payment. The employee is normally required to make subsequent payments within 30 days of the payment due date for each period.) The employer is also required to extend the coverage for up to 36 months if the qualifying event is the death of the employee, divorce or separation, loss of dependent-child status, or eligibility for Medicare.

COBRA continuation coverage ends automatically on the last day of the beneficiary's maximum coverage period (i.e., after 18, 29, or 36 months, depending on the event that began continuation coverage). The employer may also terminate the beneficiary's coverage if the beneficiary fails to pay the required premiums on time.

In most cases, continuation coverage also ends when the beneficiary becomes covered by another group plan. Under recent amendments to

COBRA, however, there are exceptions to this rule. Employers may not terminate a beneficiary's coverage before the end of the continuation period even if the employee joins another group plan, if the new plan excludes or limits the beneficiary from coverage because he or she has a preexisting medical condition.

Coverage under the employer's health plan normally ends for the employee if he or she becomes eligible for Medicare. The former employee's eligibility for Medicare, however, sometimes begins a 36-month continuation period for the spouse and dependent children.

CONSPIRACY DOCTRINE The doctrine developed by English common law that some actions, perfectly lawful when performed by an individual (such as a worker's demand for an increase in pay), may become unlawful when performed by a group (such as several workers acting in concert to demand an increase in pay).

The conspiracy doctrine emerged after the Bubonic Plague of 1349 killed a third of England's workforce. Because of the labor shortage, the Statute of Laborers was passed in 1350 which required all except "gentlemen born" and students to work at wages fixed by local officials, with criminal penalties for violations. As it was unlawful for an individual to seek higher wages, an English court in *Rex v. Journeymen Tailors* ruled that any combination of persons seeking wage increases constituted a criminal conspiracy. Under the common law of the time, any conspiracy was unlawful.

In England, the crime of criminal conspiracy emerged in several statutes. The Combination Acts of 1799 and 1800, for example, extended the coverage of a 1720 act to all working men. It made any agreement to seek increased wages or to withhold services a crime, subject to imprisonment for three months. It was not until 1875 that the Conspiracy and Protection Act abolished the criminal conspiracy doctrine in England.

English and American courts widely applied the doctrine to prevent the combination of workers to enhance their wages, hours, and conditions of employment, while employers used it as a legal weapon to curb union growth. In a landmark decision, the Massachusetts Supreme Court in *Commonwealth v. Hunt* (1842) held that labor combinations were not in themselves illegal. The court dismissed a criminal conspiracy indictment, stating that the aim of inducing all in the same occupation to join the same "society" was lawful and that the indictment stated no "dangerous or pernicious aim." The case enunciated a test that assessed tactics, motive, and intent. *Hunt* also ruled that the closed shop, which requires a worker to join the union prior to employment, was a lawful objective.

The *Hunt* decision broke the tradition of relying on the criminal conspiracy doctrine to thwart union growth. Although the court did not abolish the doctrine, it refused to rule that the objectives of workers were improper. This ruling made using the conspiracy doctrine against labor unions more difficult, and the criminal-conspiracy doctrine began to fall into disuse. But the demise of the criminal conspiracy doctrine did not end labor conflict. In England, the battle continued in Parliament. In the United States, it was fought in the courts on two fronts: lawsuits for civil court injunctions and review of remedial legislation by Congress and state legislatures.

Other legal doctrines were soon developed to replace the criminal conspiracy doctrine as a tool to curtail union growth, such as the prima facie tort doctrine (making a person civilly liable for the infliction of intentional harm, resulting in damage, without excuse or justification, by an act or series of acts which would have otherwise been lawful). It held that the intentional infliction of economic harm upon another party is a tort, unless justified by a legitimate purpose. This doctrine was applied against union picketing and strikes. After *Hunt,* prosecutions against unions were based on the illegality of methods used or ends sought rather than on the issue of conspiracy.

See also **Closed Shop; Common Law: Employment Doctrines; *Commonwealth v. Hunt* (1842); Injunctions against Unions.**

CONSTRUCTIVE DISCHARGE

As opposed to an express discharge, a constructive discharge occurs if working conditions are such that a reasonable person in the worker's circumstances would feel compelled to resign. A constructive discharge occurs when an employee involuntarily resigns in order to escape intolerable and illegal employment requirements—action by an employer to terminate an employee, not by actual discharge, but by making conditions so unbearable that the employee is forced to "quit." Ordinarily, an employee who quits a job does not have a claim for breach of contract or retaliatory discharge. If, however, the conditions that caused the employee to quit constitute a constructive discharge, courts will treat the employee as if he or she had been fired.

To constitute a constructive discharge, the employee's resignation must be related to the employer's actions or inactions, rather than for personal reasons. The employee does not need to prove that the employer intended to force the resignation, but the constructive discharge must be the reasonable and foreseeable result of the employer's conduct. Relatively minor abuse of an employee is insufficient to establish a constructive discharge. Rather, the adverse working conditions must generally be ongoing, repetitive, and severe.

In unionized settings, the constructive discharge doctrine has existed for 50 years. In these cases, an employer who knows or suspects that an employee is engaged in protected activity (such as union organizing) imposes or acquiesces in the imposition of discriminatory work conditions on the employee. When the employee reacts by quitting, he or she has been constructively discharged in violation of Section 8(a)(3) of the National Labor Relations Act.

Under the doctrine of constructive discharge, a plaintiff alleges that the defendant's unlawful conduct made plaintiffs "working conditions . . . so difficult or unpleasant that a reasonable person in the employee's shoes would have felt compelled to resign." [*Held v. Gulf Oil Company* (1982)] In one common scenario, an employer shows an indifference to and toleration of sexually harassing conduct toward an employee by other employees. [*Easter v. Jeep Corporation* (1984)] The U.S. Supreme Court has ruled that in order to prove constructive discharge, the plaintiff must prove a more severe case of harassment than the minimum necessary to prove "hostile working environment," which would support a case of sexual harassment. [*Landgraf v. USI Film Productions* (1993)]

Being demoted or passed over for an expected promotion is by itself rarely thought so humiliating as to constitute a constructive discharge, even though the employee continues to work with persons who are aware of the adverse action. [*Jurgens v. EEOC* (1990)]

Generally, courts have held that reinstatement and back pay are the preferred remedies to front pay (monetary relief for any future loss of earnings resulting from past discrimination ordered if reinstatement is impractical) for two reasons: (1) they enforce national policy against discrimination in employment, and (2) avoid windfalls for victims of discrimination. Some state courts are taking a dim view of the large verdicts won under the constructive discharge theory. A California appellate court said that "this area of the law is quickly running out of control" and warned that "if the legislature fails to act in this area, we can see that, in due course, business enterprises will flee the state." [*Hunio v. Tishman Construction Corporation* (1994)]

See also **National Labor Relations Act; Protected Activity.**

CONSUMER CREDIT PROTECTION ACT OF 1968 A federal statute requiring disclosure of all terms and conditions of finance charges in consumer credit transactions. Because credit use has become common for consumers, and their need for protection in that area is significant, the most important consumer protection in recent years is consumer credit protection. This statute reflects congressional concern over the unscrupulous and unfair use of wage garnishments by creditors. It was enacted to protect consumers by informing them and to protect employees from "predatory extensions of credit."

The Truth in Lending Act consists of the first five chapters of the Consumer Credit Protection Act. These chapters set forth general provisions and deal with credit transactions, credit advertising, credit billing, and consumer leases. Under Title III of the act, the earnings of an employee that may be garnisheed are limited in either a federal or state court. That limit may vary depending on the circumstances.

The statute applies to all employers. It limits the amount of an employee's wages that can be attached by court order and withheld by his or her employer for payment of a judgment. For court orders other than for support of a spouse or dependent, the limit is 25 percent of weekly disposable earnings or the amount that is 40 times the federal minimum wage, whichever is less. For support orders, up to 60 percent of the employee's disposable earnings can be attached (only 50 percent if the individual is already supporting another spouse or dependent child). Some states allow less of an employee's wages to be attached than does federal law. In that case, only the lesser amount can be withheld from the employee's wages. Amounts payable for federal and state taxes, however, are not subject to these limits.

In addition, the act prohibits discrimination against or discharge of an employee whose wages are subject to any one indebtedness. "One indebtedness" refers to a single debt, regardless of the number of loans made or creditors seeking satisfaction. This provision has been interpreted to prohibit discharge until the employer is in fact required to withhold funds for a *second* indebtedness; mere receipt of a garnishment order is not enough if no withholding is actually required. [*Brennan v. Kroger Co.* (1975)] Some states prohibit an employer from disciplining or discharging an employee, even if his or her wages have been attached for numerous debts.

CONTINGENT COMPENSATION Also called variable pay, or nontraditional reward systems. Contingent compensation schemes tie rewards to performance—individual, unit, or corporate—to motivate employees toward performance improvement. These programs seek to improve quality, reduce compensation costs, and enhance employee commitment, involvement, and teamwork. Contingent compensation includes gainsharing plans (where all employees are involved in resolving problems in costs, quality, and productivity, and share these gains with organizational members usually in the form of a cash bonus); knowledge-based pay or skill-based pay (where workers are paid based on the types of jobs they can perform, that is their knowledge and mastery of different jobs in the organization); performance-based pay (any compensation system tying pay or pay increases to some measure of individual performance and organizational effectiveness); bonuses (a payment in excess of an employee's regular pay); profit-sharing (a system or procedure whereby an employee pays compensation or benefits to employees in addition to their regular wages, based on the profits of the company); and noncash incentives (methods other than wages for stimulating worker effort and output).

"Variable pay" is compensation, whether wages or salaries, in which payment fluctuates according to some standard. The standard may be a preset formula, as in the case of gainsharing; it may be the achievement of specific goals, as in the cases of group or individual incentives; it may be the whole performance of an individual over a certain period, as in the case of the merit bonus; or it may be the level of earnings of the entire organization, as in the case of profit sharing.

These compensation arrangements have become increasingly popular. In recent years, more gainsharing, pay-for-knowledge, small-group incentives, lump-sum bonus, and two-tier plans have been adopted, and that trend is likely to continue.

See also **Bonus.**

CONTINGENT WORK Any job in which an individual does not have an explicit or implicit contract for long-term employment or one in which the minimum hours worked can vary in a nonsystematic manner. Contingent work, also called alternative or flexible staffing, generally refers to a range of employment practices that includes part-time, temporary, and home-based employment, self-employment, and contracting out. It is characterized by a low degree of job security, because there is no commitment between the employer and employee for long-term employment and no guarantee of recall, and because the work varies and the hours are unpredictable.

Conditional and transitory employment relationships are initiated by a need for labor, usually because a company has an increased demand for a particular service, product, or technology at a particular place and at a specific time. Part-time, temporary, self-employed, contract, at home, and leased workers are considered "contingent" because they supplement the core employees. Their relationship with an employer is much weaker than that of traditional full-time permanent employees. The employer can easily adjust their work schedules to accommodate short-term changes in product or service demand and employ them at reduced levels of compensation and benefits. As a result, these workers have no significant stake in or attachment to a company.

In 1995, the U.S. Department of Labor estimated that between 2.2 to 4.9 percent of the workforce was in contingent arrangements. Contingent workers were found more than twice as likely as noncontingent workers to be under the age of 25, and they were slightly more likely to be women and African American.

See also **Job Security.**

CONTRACT See **Employment Contract.**

CONTRACT BAR RULES A general rule established by the National Labor Relations Board (NLRB) that it will not disturb a valid existing collective bargaining agreement during its term. The bar precludes the NLRB from honoring a request for a representation election by a rival union or a petition for a decertification election. Under the NLRB's contract bar rules, a current and valid contract between an employer and a union ordinarily will bar an election sought by a rival union. Elections will be prohibited until a valid existing collective bargaining agreement, effective for a period of not longer than three years, nears its expiration date. The NLRB will not deal with representation questions unless a petition is filed at least 60 days before but not more than 90 days before the expiration of a current contract.

The three-year contract bar rule was established in *General Cable Corporation* (1962), which replaced the previous two-year maximum established in *Pacific Coast Association of Pulp & Paper Manufacturers* (1958). Exceptions to the rule are made under some circumstances, including the following: the contract is not in writing or is not signed, the contract contains an illegal union security clause, the bargaining unit is not appropriate, the contract discriminates between employees on racial grounds, or the employer's operations have changed substantially since the contract was executed.

One of the major objectives of the National Labor Relations Act (NLRA), as amended, is to promote stable employer-union relationships. The contract bar doctrine serves the NLRA's objective of encouraging and protecting industrial stability. Therefore, where continuity of representation, or industrial stability, is not the key issue, as in affiliation elections, contract bar rules do not apply.

The contract bar doctrine is not required by the NLRA, however, or by any regulations of the board. It is simply NLRB policy, applied or waived at the board's discretion. The doctrine has, however, been followed in a long line of decisions by the NLRB. These decisions have developed a complex set of rules on when a contract will operate as an election bar and when a rival union's election petition will be recognized and processed. Although the contract bar principle is not statutory, it has received judicial approval.

The burden of showing that a contract is a bar to an election is placed on the party making that claim. The NLRB will determine the legality of a contract based on the contract itself and will not admit extrinsic evidence on the issue. Therefore, unless a clause is clearly illegal, the contract will remain a bar to representation petitions. A contract that contains a clause in violation of the NLRA, however, will not bar a representation election. Once the NLRB has made a ruling on the effect of an existing contract, failure to appeal the ruling may waive the issue.

See also **Collective Bargaining Agreement; National Labor Relations Act; National Labor Relations Board.**

Contract Wage Payment A method of wage compensation where the worker agrees to perform a fixed job for a specified amount of money.

The minimum wage provision of the Fair Labor Standards Act is read into and becomes part of every employment contract that is subject to the terms of the statute. Under those provisions, an employee who is covered by the act is a creditor of his employer for any unpaid portion of the minimum wage, regardless of any agreement between the parties respecting compensation. Thus, parties are free to enter into agreements on hours of work and compensation, but the agreement cannot be used to pay less than the minimum wage, depriving employees of their statutory rights. Such an agreement is invalid, even though the employee has supposedly accepted and acquiesced in the lower payment, and even though the employee is designated as an independent contractor.

See also **Compensation; Fair Labor Standards Act; Independent Contractor; Minimum Wage.**

Contract Work Hours and Safety Standards Act (1962) A federal statute adopted in 1962, to replace the Eight-Hour Laws applicable to laborers and mechanics on public works and federally financed construction projects. The Eight-Hour Laws required that such workers be paid time and one-half for work in excess of eight hours a day. The Contract Work Hours and Safety Standards Act required that they be paid time and one-half for work both in excess of eight hours a day and 40 hours a week. There is a penalty of $100 per day for each worker employed in violation of these requirements.

A 1969 amendment to the statute provides that no laborer or mechanic shall be employed in working conditions that are "unsanitary, hazardous, or dangerous to his health or safety," as determined by the U.S. Department of Labor. The blacklist penalty may be imposed for repeated willful or grossly negligent violations. These standards have since been largely supplanted by the Occupational Safety and Health Act of 1970.

See also **Occupational Safety and Health Act of 1970.**

Cooling-Off Period A required period of delay following legal notice of a pending labor dispute during which employees are forbidden to strike or walkout. This time is intended to allow the parties to consider the issues involved and, in some cases, to vote on the company's "last offer." The period also allows the parties time to exert all good faith efforts to reach a settlement through peaceful negotiations and avoid economic force.

Both federal or state statutes have provisions that postpone strike or lockout action and allow mediation agencies an opportunity to settle the dispute. The statutory objective—to resolve disputes through peaceful bargaining—is reinforced by the request that the party seeking to terminate or modify the contract provide notice to the Federal Mediation and Conciliation Service and any state mediation agency within 30 days after the initial notice is given to the other party.

If the president believes a strike or lockout threatens the nation's health and safety, he or she is authorized by the national emergency provisions of the Labor-Management Relations Act of 1947 (the Taft-Hartley Act) to direct the attorney general of the United States to seek an injunction from the federal courts for an 80-day cooling-off period (or 30-days for Railway Labor Act cases). The intent of Congress in drafting a cooling-off provision has been interpreted to mean that regardless of the merits of the parties' positions, a national emergency strike or lockout had to be delayed in order to maximize the possibility of a peaceful settlement. [*United Steelworkers v. United States* (1959)] Wages and work conditions are usually frozen under conditions set by the previous contract during this time, and every effort is made to settle the dispute. If at the end of the 80-day period there has been no settlement, the strike or lockout may legally be resumed.

See also **Federal Mediation and Conciliation Service; Labor Dispute; Lockout; Mediation; Railway Labor Act; Strike.**

COST OF LIVING ADJUSTMENT (COLA) A provision in a collective bargaining agreement that relates wage increases to the cost of living during the period of the agreement. Most COLA clauses provide for a portion of Consumer Price Index increases to be reflected in the increase. COLA might result in a 0.4 percent increase in wages. COLA clauses are designed to prevent dramatic declines in real wages. They are sometimes referred to as "escalator clauses."

See also **Collective Bargaining Agreement.**

COUNSELING A service provided by employers to help workers find reasonable solutions to personal and work-related problems. This type of assistance recognizes the value of workers to the organization and the social responsibility of the employer to help employees contend with problems that affect job performance. Trained counselors and other professionals may be employed by the company to render such assistance.

Employee counseling services may include help in resolving financial, legal, physical, mental, family, marital, and drug and alcohol problems; work-related issues include compensation and benefits, interpersonal matters, retirement, and working conditions.

Counseling services may also include career counseling to promote career development of employees. Performance-centered counseling is done by assessing the individual's contribution to the organization's goals and subsequently helping the individual to be even more effective. In the process, the organization benefits and the individual is assisted in his or her development as well.

***COUNTY OF WASHINGTON V. GUNTHER* (1981)** The first case in which the U.S. Supreme Court ruled that women bringing claims of sex-based wage discrimination are not required under Title VII of the Civil Rights Act of 1964 to satisfy the "equal work" standards of the Equal Pay Act.

In *Gunther,* female prison guards contended they were paid substantially lower wages than their male counterparts. The district court, however, concluded that the jobs of the male and female prison guards were not "substantially equal," since the male guards performed more duties, i.e., they supervised ten times the number of prisoners as female guards. Alternatively, the female guards alleged their lower salaries resulted from the defendant's intentional sex discrimination, as evidenced by the employer's failure to pay them adequately according to both job evaluations and labor-market surveys. The employer argued that a lawsuit for sex-based wage discrimination, could not be maintained under Title VII unless the evidence shows that the equal pay for equal work standard of the Equal Pay Act was violated.

The Supreme Court disagreed. The court held that the plaintiffs stated a Title VII claim, even though women did not perform work equal to that of male jail guards. Though it expressly stated that the plaintiff's claim was not based on the controversial concept of comparable worth, the Court held that jobs need not be substantially equal in order to maintain a Title VII claim for pay discrimination. The case was remanded (sent back) to the district court for a determination on the merits of the Title VII claim, but the parties settled before the trial was held. The *Gunther* court, however, did not address the issue of whether or how much comparable worth would constitute a recognized cause of action.

Since *Gunther,* every federal circuit court considering the issue has refused to impose liability based on comparable worth. [*American Nurses Association v. State of Illinois* (1986); *AFSCME v. State of Washington* (1985); *Spaulding v. University of Washington* (1984); *Kouba v. Allstate Insurance Co.* (1982); *Bonner v. City of Pritchard* (1981); and *Christensen v. State of Ohio* (1977)] These cases hold that the theory of comparable worth by itself does not provide a basis for a Title VII suit. Employers who, nonetheless, conduct comparable worth studies may be unnecessarily exposing themselves to wage discrimination lawsuits. This is especially true where the employer that conducts the study fails to act on the results.

See also **Civil Rights Act of 1964; Comparable Worth; Equal Pay Act of 1963; Sex Discrimination in Employment.**

CRAFT A trade that requires skill, manual ability, understanding of the principles of the trade, and a fixed training period or apprenticeship. The craftsman practices a handicraft that requires relatively skilled work, as opposed to the laborer, whose work demands strength or exertion rather than skill. Typesetting, carpentry, and plumbing are examples of crafts.

Early unionization efforts began among the skilled craftsmen, such as the tailors, printers, and boot- and shoemakers. They had the education that unskilled workers lacked and they were committed to their trade because of the time they had invested in apprenticeships. By the early 1800s labor organizations composed of skilled workers emerged in American cities.

See also **Apprenticeship; Craft Union; Labor Organization.**

CRAFT UNION A labor organization that limits its membership to workers in a particular craft or trade (such as molders and carpenters) or a group of closely related skilled tasks. Craft unions may be purely local or national in scope. Crafts such as carpenters, shoemakers, and printers formed associations in Philadelphia, New York, and Boston in the late 1700s. These early local associations typically sought to secure higher wages, enforcement of apprenticeship standards, and employment of union members. Cooperation among unions within a city began when the craft unions in Philadelphia joined together to form a city central organization in 1827.

Organized crafts workers in the late nineteenth century had substantial control over production and enjoyed significant functional autonomy on the job. The early American labor organizations reflected the interests and values of the crafts workers, who founded them.

By the mid nineteenth century, product markets in the United States had become less localized and more national, due to the development of railroads. The emergence of national markets became the primary factor in the development of national labor unions. Other factors included (1) in creased geographic mobility of labor, resulting in competition for jobs between migratory journeymen and local trade union members; (2) the formation of employer associations, which confronted unions behind a united front; and (3) the division of established trades and reduction in the need for skilled laborers created by the factory system.

During the mid and late nineteenth century, several national unions were formed. Some of these still exist, such as the plasterers, cigarmakers, bricklayers, and masons. There were also three major attempts to form national labor federations (associations of national and local labor unions). Two of these organizations, the National Labor Federation and the Knights of Labor (which sought to organize both skilled and unskilled workers) eventually failed. A third, the American Federation of Labor (AFL), which was formed in 1886, succeeded. The AFL represented skilled craftsmen organized on an occupational basis. Within the federation, the principle of trade autonomy was stressed, and power was centralized within the national unions.

Collective bargaining was not the original preference or objective of emerging unions in the United States. Instead, the goal was "crafts unilateralism," a concept with roots in the European guilds. Under crafts unilateralism, each craft determined both the pay rates and the rules under which its members would work. Then, by organizing the entire supply of qualified labor into closed-shop unions, they ensured that the employers would bargain with them. If the unions were successful in "taking wages out of competition," their primary objective, no employer could obtain equal quality labor for less money and, therefore, would have no strong reason to resist paying union wages. Early strikes were called most often when an employer attempted to depart from the prevailing pay scales and work rules.

Craft unions welcomed collective bargaining only when they found that, both because of the mobility of labor in the United States and the size and ruthlessness of impersonal corporate employers, they were unable to enforce the closed shop and prevent competition in the labor market. Although collective bargaining was adopted as the substitute objective of the crafts unions that were unable to impose their unilateral will, the ultimate development of collective bargaining occurred after 1935 among the industrial unions exemplified by the unions of the Congress of Industrial Organizations. The strengths of the crafts organization gave rise to its major drawback: an abiding particularism that made each trade look to itself and attempt to separate itself from unskilled workers.

In the early twentieth century, craft unions played a major part in workers lives, performing social welfare and labor-supply functions crucial to the welfare of working people. These included union-controlled and union-financed unemployment insurance, retirement programs, burial funds, apprenticeship programs, and hiring halls. After the Great Depression of the 1930s, which destroyed many union social welfare programs, many of these union functions were absorbed by government and corporations.

The jurisdiction and membership of many of the former AFL craft unions expanded. As American industry increasingly relied on technology in production, the crafts unions had to make similar changes in order to maintain their strength and bargaining position in the industry. Many crafts unions enlarged their jurisdiction to include new members. Thus the International Association of Machinists, a craft union, has brought production workers in the aircraft industry into the union.

The National Labor Relations Board (NLRB) has broad authority in determining units appropriate for collective bargaining under Section 9(b) of the NLRB, whether it be an employer unit, craft unit, plant unit, or subdivision unit. The issue then becomes one of providing a separate unit for identifiable craft workers. In determining whether a proposed unit is appropriate, the general inquiry is whether the employees share a community of interests. Two of the factors relied on by the NLRB to make this determination are similarity of work performed and similarity of employees' qualifications, skills, and training. In determining whether craft bargaining, as opposed to industrial bargaining, should be used to represent a certain group of employees, the NLRB will look to functions that include

(1) whether the proposed unit consists of a "distinct group of skilled craftsmen" or comprises a "functionally distinct department" working at a trade for which there is a tradition of separate representation, and (2) the history and pattern of collective bargaining. [*Mallinckrodt Chemical Works* (1966)]

See also **American Federation of Labor-Congress of Industrial Organizations; Apprenticeship; Collective Bargaining; Craft.**

CRIMINAL CONSPIRACY DOCTRINE See **Conspiracy Doctrine.**

CUTBACK See **Layoff.**

CYCLICAL UNEMPLOYMENT See **Unemployment.**

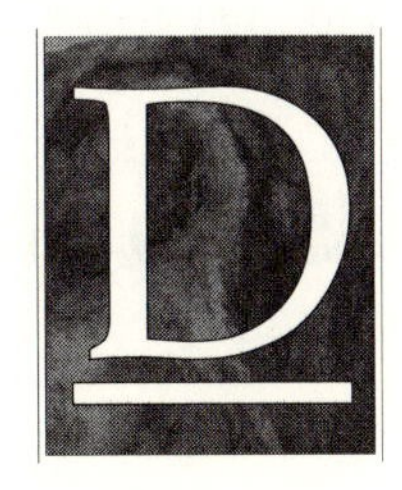

DAMAGES The amount claimed or judicially allowed as compensation for injuries sustained or property damaged through the wrongful acts or negligence of another. Damage suits are civil claims for alleged injury resulting from actions in violation of law. Early in the twentieth century, the U.S. Supreme Court interpreted Section 7 of the Sherman Antitrust Act to allow a company to sue the union for treble damages if its business was injured by actions in violation of the law. In *Loewe v. Lawlor* (1908), the U.S. Supreme Court held that individual union members were liable for damage suffered by an employer resulting from a violation of the Sherman Act.

Under the National Labor Relations Act (NLRA), unions and employers may file damage suits for contract violations. Section 303 of the NLRA states that "whoever shall be injured in his business or property" because of an unfair labor practice may sue in federal court "without respect to the amount in controversy" or in state court and "shall recover the damages by him sustained and the cost of the suit." By including this language, Congress essentially stated that the conduct outlawed in Section 8(b)(4) of the NLRA is subject to redress not only by the National Labor Relations Board (NLRB) but also as a federal tort in the federal and state court. The dual remedial scheme was designed to deter prohibited union conduct such as the secondary boycott and strikes over recognition and work assignment. Damages, however, are awarded against union assets, not those of the employee or union members under Section 301(b) of the NLRA.

A plaintiff may assert a claim by either filing a charge with the NLRB or commencing a lawsuit. A party pursuing an unfair labor case in court is not obliged to "make an election," which means that it may pursue both remedies at the same time or in sequence.

Damage suits against unions have also been filed by unions as well as nonunion employees who believe that they have been deprived of certain rights protected by the union constitution, or state or federal laws.

See also **Compensation; *Loewe v. Lawlor* (1908); National Labor Relations Act; National Labor Relations Board; Secondary Boycott; Sherman Antitrust Act of 1880.**

DANBURY HATTERS' CASE

See *Loewe v. Lawlor* (1908).

DARLINGTON CASE

In *Textile Workers v. Darlington Mfg.* (1965), a landmark case known as the "Darlington Case," the U.S. Supreme Court considered the issue of whether an employer violated Sections 8(a)(3) or 8(a)(1) of the National Labor Relations Act (NLRA) by going out of business and thus must compensate its employees for any losses suffered as a result of the violation. In that case, Roger Milliken and members of his family owned controlling shares of Deering Milliken, a textile distributor, which in turn controlled 17 textile manufacturers operating 27 mills. Milliken also controlled indirectly one of those manufacturers, the Darlington Manufacturing Company, which operated one mill. After threats that unionization at Darlington would result in its closing, and after a union victory in an election, the Darlington board of directors voted to close down, sell the physical assets, and go out of business. The National Labor Relations Board (NLRB) concluded that the entire Deering Milliken operation was a single business enterprise and that the shutdown violated the NLRA, even conceding that the employer had some economic reasons independent of unionization for going out of business and that unionization was considered by the company in economic terms. The court of appeals reversed, holding that even antiunion motivation would not render illegal a complete or partial (that is, one of several plants) shutting down. The case went to the U.S. Supreme Court.

The Supreme Court held that complete shutdown by an employer who does not have a purpose of discouraging unionization elsewhere violates neither Sections 8(a)(3) nor 8(a)(1) of the NLRA. In so holding, the Court laid down important tests for violations of those sections.

According to the opinion, Section 8(a)(1) is violated only when interference with employees' Section 7 rights outweighs the business justification for the employer's action. A violation of Section 8(a)(1) presupposes an action by the employer which is unlawful even absent a discriminatory motive. Furthermore, "some employer decisions are so peculiarly matters of management prerogative that they would never constitute violations of Section 8(a)(1), whether or not they involve sound business judgment, unless they also violated Section 8(a)(3). A decision to terminate completely a business was one of these prerogatives, the Court ruled.

The next issue was whether the shutdown violated Section 8(a)(3). According to the Court, even if it is clear that the employer has closed the plant because of a desire to avoid the union, the closing violates Section 8(a)(3) only if the closing is intended to yield a future benefit to the employer. In articulating this standard, the court said that an unfair labor practice under Section 8(a)(3) is established if the persons exercising control over the plant which is being closed for antiunion reasons: (a) have an interest in another business, whether or not it is engaged in the same line of commercial activity as the closed plant, buy which the employer may benefit from the discouragement of unionization in that business; (b) close the plant with the purpose of achieving that result; (c) occupy a relationship to the other business which might lead employees to believe that plant would be closed if they engage in union activities, then an unfair labor practice under Section 8(a)(3)has been established.

This future benefit can be found in the cases of run-away shops—moving a plant from one location to another, or closing a plant in order to increase business at another location—or in cases where the employees could cause the plant to reopen by renouncing the union. Where no future benefit is involved, there is no violation of Section 8(a)(3). The Court's reliance on the "future benefit" theory was unprecedented.

The court remanded the case back to the NLRB both for a determination of the purpose and of the effect of the closing on other aspects of the employer's business based on "future benefits" criteria and for consideration of the issues of whether this particular plant was a part of a larger single enterprise controlled by the owners of the plant and of whether the closing was intended to chill unionization in those other plants. The NLRB was instructed that it must look to an actual showing of a motivation to chill unionization elsewhere; a finding that such a closing would necessarily have such an impact would not suffice.

It is not apparent why the Supreme Court established these standards for Sections 8(a)(1) and (3) of the NLRA, other than a reluctance to find that a plant shutdown violates the statute. The *Darlington* shutdown has been distinguished from run-away shops and partial closings. If an employer moves its business in order to discourage union membership or to avoid collective bargaining, it violates Section 8(a)(3); but if it moves for legitimate economic reasons, such as lower wage rates in the new geographic area, it does not violate the NLRA. This distinction, while reasonable in theory, often makes unfair labor practice liability dependent on the company's expressed rationale for moving its operations.

When the NLRB received the case back on remand, it concluded that the closing of the Darlington mill was a partial shutdown and that it was at least partially intended to deter unionism in the other mills controlled by the Milliken family. A divided Fourth Circuit Court of Appeals enforced the NLRB's order. While the *Darlington* case has had its greatest use in cases involving partial shutdowns, it appears not to have been applied to cases involving subcontracting or plant relocations. Some commentators believe that *Darlington* requires that the employer, to violate Section 8(a)(3) of the NLRA, must act with the expressed purpose of "chilling unionism" among its remaining employees in cases involving subcontracting and its new employees in cases involving relocation.

See also **Concerted Activity; National Labor Relations Act; National Labor Relations Board.**

DAVIS-BACON ACT OF 1931 Also known as the "Prevailing Rate of Wage Act," this federal statute imposes special minimum prevailing wage obligations on employers engaged in federally financed construction. The Davis-Bacon Act, passed in 1931 and amended in 1935, 1940, and 1964, requires the payment of the wage rates and fringe benefits prevailing in the locality where construction, alteration, or repair of public buildings or public works is being done under federal or federally financed contract.

Prevailing rates and fringe benefits are determined by the U.S. Department of Labor and apply to all contracts and subcontracts of more than $2,000 in the United States. Violations of the statute may result in the withholding of payments to the contractor, cancellation of the contract by the government agency, and denial of awards of government contracts. The Wage Appeals Board, established in February 1964, reviews appeals of decisions on prevailing wage determinations and enforcement cases.

The Davis-Bacon Act is intended to protect local contractors and workers from outside contractors employing cheaper itinerant workers. In addition, since contracts are usually awarded to the lowest qualified bidder, it was intended to discourage employers from paying lower wages.

The statute has been severely criticized for two reasons: (1) Since union wage rates and benefits are often specified as those prevailing in a geographic area, nonunion contractors paying lower rates lose their cost advantage in bidding on contracts. Consequently, the cost of federal construction in some cases is higher than otherwise would be the case. (2) Studies indicate that the Davis-Bacon Act does result in higher costs for federal construction.

DEATH BENEFIT

A payment, usually a lump sum, to an employee's beneficiaries in the event of his or her death. The payment may be provided by a pension plan or another type of employer-sponsored welfare plan, or by a union to its members. In insurance, the more common term for death benefit is life insurance.

Death benefits are provided by workers compensation legislation to certain classes of beneficiaries. These benefits include burial expenses and compensation for the beneficiaries, calculated according to the statutory formula of the particular jurisdiction. The right to a death benefit is a right created by statute, and it is not dependent upon any rights of the deceased worker. Therefore, a worker's release, compromise, settlement, or unfavorable compensation decision would not prevent the claims of beneficiaries. A beneficiary's claim is legally separate and distinct from the worker's claim for compensation during his or her lifetime, and the employee generally has no right to control or dispose of the claims of the beneficiaries.

Death compensation benefits, like disability benefits, are generally computed on the basis of statutorily fixed percentages of a worker's average wage. Most compensation statutes impose maximum limits on death benefits. The formulas and methods employed in computing death benefits for all dependents vary considerably, so generalizations on exact compensation are inappropriate.

See also **Workers' Compensation.**

DEAUTHORIZATION

Also known as a union shop deauthorization election, this procedure, under Section 9(e) of the National Labor Relations Act (NLRA), is similar to a decertification election. It permits employees, on a petition of more than 30 percent in the bargaining unit, to vote on the question of withdrawing from the union the authority to require union membership as a condition of continued employment.

The procedure was probably a counterpart of the original provision in the Labor-Management Relations Act of 1947 (the Taft-Hartley Act) that required elections to "authorize" the union to bargain for a union shop. Because it was found burdensome and useless, the union shop authorization election was repealed in 1951, which meant that unions were automatically authorized to bargain for and to incorporate the union shop into the labor contract. However, Section 9(3)(1) of the NLRA, which establishes the process after the fact to withdraw that authorization, was not removed. That section requires the National Labor Relations Board to "take a secret ballot of the employees in such unit and certify the results thereof to such labor organization and to the employer."

See also **Appropriate Bargaining Unit; Decertification; National Labor Relations Act; National Labor Relations Board.**

DECERTIFICATION Procedure for removing a union as the certified bargaining representative of employees in an appropriate bargaining unit. A petition alleging that the union no longer represents the majority of the employees must be filed with the National Labor Relations Board (NLRB). The NLRB will order a decertification election only if 30 percent of the employees in a unit support the petition. The contract bar and other NLRB election rules apply to the decertification elections in the same manner that they apply to representation elections. The union need not have been certified initially; it may have secured representational rights through voluntary employer recognition. The unit in which the election is held must be the same as the established bargaining unit; a smaller election may not be held to certify a segment of the unit.

In extreme cases, the NLRB has, upon motion of the employer, revoked the certification of an incumbent certified union. This has been done when a union, in the course of negotiations, repeatedly inflicted or threatened severe physical harm to company negotiators, supervisors, employees, and property. The NLRB may also revoke a union's certification if after a hearing it can be shown that the union has discriminated on the basis of race, religion, national origin, or sex in representing employees in contract negotiations or grievance processing, thereby violating its duty of fair representation.

When the election is lost by the certified agent, or the NLRB determines that the certified agent is no longer a "representative," the union loses its status and is "decertified."

See also **Appropriate Bargaining Unit; Contract Bar Rules; Duty of Fair Representation; National Labor Relations Board.**

DEFINED BENEFIT PLANS AND DEFINED CONTRIBUTION PLANS Defined benefit plans promise a specific benefit that can be determined in advance and is payable to the plan participants when they retire. The amount of the monthly benefit may be determined by a formula based on years of participation or on average of earnings when they retire. No individual accounts are maintained, as is done in the defined contribution plans. Typical defined benefit plans provide a specified amount at retirement based on years of service with the employer and the years of highest salary, with an exponential increase in benefits in the later years of employment. (Employers are obligated to provide benefits based on these calculations.) As a result, an employee with 15 years experience at company A who at age 50 moved to company B and worked another 15 years would, quite likely, receive less in combined pension benefits than if he had remained at company A for the full 30 years. Defined benefits plans are subject to funding requirements established by the Employee Retirement Income Security Act (ERISA).

Defined contribution plans generally specify an employer contribution but not a formula for determining benefits as in a defined benefit plan. Instead, individual accounts are set up for participants, and benefits are based on amounts credited to these accounts plus investment earnings.

Since the passage of ERISA, both defined benefit pension assets and defined benefits payments have increased enormously. Defined benefit coverage, however, remained relatively stable because of the following factors: (1) ERISA requires employers to insure their defined benefit plans with the U.S. Pension Benefit Guaranty Corporation, thus increasing costs for operating pension plans; and (2) other ERISA requirements, such as vesting and other minimum benefits standards, may also have increased the cost of administering defined benefit plans. Declining employment in industries that historically have favored defined benefit plans, such as manufacturing firms that participate in collective bargaining, may also have slowed the growth of these plans. The increase in the numbers of smaller, service-oriented firms, which are usually not collective bargaining participants, has also played an important role in the growth of defined contribution plans.

See also **Employee Retirement Income Security Act of 1974.**

DEMOTION The process of moving an employee to a position lower in the wage scale or in rank. A demotion may be involuntary, in the form of a penalty for inefficient or careless work, or voluntary and without prejudice to the employee, when it results from a curtailment of production. In the latter case, demotion is similar to downsizing.

Demotions are one of the management actions considered a "normal part of the employment relationship," according to *Cole v. Fair Oaks Fire Protection District* (1987). To be actionable, they normally have to involve "outrageous conduct" by the employer, unless they are discriminatory demotions based on factors such as age, race, or national origin. Discriminatory discharges are prohibited by Title VII of the Civil Rights Act of 1964. A case of outrageous conduct could be proved in a retaliatory demotion and infliction of emotional distress, according to *Mourad v. Automobile Club Insurance Association* (1991).

See also **Downsizing.**

DEPARTMENT OF LABOR See **U.S. Department of Labor.**

DISABILITY

The inability to engage in any substantial gainful activity by reason of any medically determinable physical or mental impairment which can be expected to result in death or which has lasted or can be expected to last for a continuous period of not less than one year. Disability can be categorized as short-term or long-term, temporary or permanent, and partial or total.

Workers' compensation statutes generally provide four general classifications of disability: (1) permanent total, (2) temporary total, (3) temporary partial, and (4) permanent partial. These classifications in conjunction with the employee's average wages and the statutory formula provide the basis for disability benefit computation.

Disability is also defined under other laws. The Americans with Disabilities Act of 1990 defines a "qualified individual with a disability" as an "individual with a disability who, with or without reasonable accommodation, can perform the essential functions of the employment position that such individual holds or desires."

Persons are generally classified as having a work disability if they have a health problem or disability that prevents them from working or limits the kind or amount of work they can do, or if they have a service-connected disability or retired or left a job for health reasons. The following types of impairments would ordinarily be considered as preventing substantial gainful activity: loss of use of two limbs; diabetes; multiple sclerosis; inoperable and progressive cancer; damage to the brain resulting in loss of judgment, intellect, or memory; psychosis or severe psychoneurosis; permanent and total loss of speech.

See also **Americans with Disabilities Act of 1990; Workers' Compensation.**

DISCHARGE

See **Termination.**

DISCOURAGED WORKER

An unemployed individual who does not look for employment because he or she believes that jobs are not available or that no jobs are available for which he or she could qualify.

DISCRIMINATION IN EMPLOYMENT

The employer may discriminate among employees on the basis of factors such as proven ability, past performance, or job skills. The employer may not, however, discriminate on the basis of criteria prohibited by employment discrimination law.

Antidiscrimination statutes prohibit unfavorable treatment of two broad groups of persons: (1) those who share a particular status or condition characteristic, including those over 40, or female, or union members; and (2) those who have engaged in certain conduct, such as military service or going out on strike. These categories are not mutually exclusive.

The primary federal statute prohibiting employment discrimination is Title VII of the Civil Rights Act of 1964. It prohibits discrimination by employers—state governments and their political subdivisions and agencies, and the federal government, employment agencies, labor organizations, joint labor-management committees, and other training programs—on the basis of race or color, religion, sex, pregnancy, and national origin. Title VII also prohibits forcibly resisting the Equal Employment Opportunity

Commission (EEOC) or its representatives in the performance of their official duties as well as coercive practices by unions designed to cause an employer to engage in unlawful discrimination. It does not, however, apply to discrimination in nonemployment matters. And since the statute's antidiscrimination provisions are limited to employment actions based on race, color, religion, sex, and national origin, it does not extend to discrimination based solely on factors such as citizenship or alienage, nepotism, alcoholism, effeminacy in men, or post-employment "blacklisting."

In prohibiting discrimination based on national origin, Title VII generally protects employees of African, Asian, European, or Latin American *origin,* but it does not prohibit discrimination based on *citizenship status.*

Every state regulates employment, not only through statutes prohibiting discriminatory practices (known as fair employment practice laws), but also through statutes that govern conduct in a variety of circumstances. In some instances, the EEOC must defer to its state counterpart in the initial attempt to resolve discrimination complaints. Both state and federal laws have time limitations for filing charges of discrimination and the recovery of wages owed.

Title VII is only one of several federal statutes that prohibit employment discrimination. Race discrimination, for example, is prohibited by Section 1981 (the Civil Rights Act of 1866) in the making, performance, modification, and termination of contracts and in the enjoyment of all benefits, privileges, terms, and conditions of the contractual relationship. These statutes may afford broader remedies than Title VII. There may be other concerns as well, especially considerations on filing a court action, that make it necessary or advantageous to forego a Title VII action in favor of suing under another statute.

See also **Civil Rights Act of 1964; Equal Employment Opportunity Commission.**

DISPARATE IMPACT DISCRIMINATION

Also known as "adverse impact " discrimination, disparate impact discrimination is a substantially different rate of selection in hiring, promotion, or other employment decisions that works to the disadvantage of members of a race, sex, or ethnic group. Proof of discriminatory impact alone can justify a finding of liability, without proof of intent, under the Civil Rights Act of 1964. A plaintiff establishes a prima facie case (one which is sufficient on its face to establish a fact unless it is contradicted by other evidence) of disparate impact discrimination by proving that the defendant has adopted an employment standard that selects employees in a pattern significantly different from that of a protected class in the relevant labor force. That is, the plaintiff must show that the standard has a discriminatory effect. See Civil Rights Act of 1991 and *Griggs v. Duke Power Co.* (1971).

Disparate impact discrimination is a more complicated type of discrimination than disparate treatment discrimination, because it involves employment practices that are facially neutral (not expressly discriminatory for or against certain groups) in their treatment of different groups but that in fact fall more harshly upon one group than another and cannot be justified by business necessity. The U.S. Supreme Court first accepted the concept of disparate impact discrimination in its landmark *Griggs* case. In *Griggs,* the Court considered an employer's requirement that persons seeking certain jobs have a high school diploma and pass a battery of tests. The plaintiffs were able to prove that in the labor market in question, the lack of a high school diploma was significantly associated with being African American, so that this facially neutral requirement in fact operated to prevent African Americans from obtaining a certain category of jobs.

Employee selection procedures that may have an adverse impact on a protected class include such measures as scored tests; height, weight, and physical requrements; nonscored objective criteria such as specific education, license, performance, or experience; and such subjective criteria as "leadership," "aggressiveness," interest, or personality.

The Equal Employment Opportunity Commission (EEOC) sometimes uses as a gross measure of adverse impact whether the selection rate for any race, sex, or ethnic group is less than four-fifths (or 80 percent) of the selection rate for the group with the highest selection rate. The EEOC regards this rule as a guideline, as opposed to a legal definition, without the force of law. Nonetheless, the four-fifths rule, along with the *Griggs* case, has been used to invalidate several objective screening devices because they had disparate impacts on protected classes. Some courts have not followed the four-fifths rule to assess the sufficiency of the disparity for the prima facie case. [*Clady v. County of Los Angeles* (1985)] The four-fifths rule has been criticized by some courts as capable of producing anomalous results, and the U.S. Supreme Court has refused to identify any single measure for assessing the sufficiency of the two groups being compared. [*Watson v. Fort Worth Bank & Trust Co.* (1988)]

See also **Civil Rights Act of 1964; Civil Rights Act of 1991; Disparate Treatment Discrimination; Equal Employment Opportunity Commission;** ***Griggs v. Duke Power Co.;*** **Protected Class.**

DISPARATE TREATMENT DISCRIMINATION The most easily understood type of discrimination, disparate treatment discrimination involves expressly treating some people less favorably than others because of their race, color, religion, sex, national origin, disability, or veteran status. Disparate treatment includes, for example, the situation where the job applicants of a particular race are required to pass tests that the applicants of another race or sex are not required to take.

Disparate treatment theory is based on motive. The employee must establish that the employer acted intentionally to treat the employee's class or the individual employee differently. In contrast, motive is irrelevant in disparate impact discrimination, where hiring practices disproportionately disadvantage a group defined by race, color, religion, sex, or national origin. The plaintiff has the burden of establishing a prima facie case (one which is sufficient on its face to establish a fact, unless it is contradicted by other evidence) of disparate treatment by producing either direct or circumstantial evidence of the employer's motivation. Direct or "smoking gun" evidence may include the supervisor's comments about the plaintiff's race or sex. To establish a circumstantial case, the plaintiff must prove that (1) he or she is within a protected class (e.g., is of a particular race); (2) he or she applied for a job for which the employer sought applicants; (3) he or she was qualified for the job; (4) he or she was denied the job; and (5) the employer continued to accept applicants for the job. [*McDonnell Douglas Corp. v. Green* (1973); *McDonald v. Santa Fe Trail Transportation Co.* (1976)]

In *Watson v. Fort Worth* (1988), the U.S. Supreme Court held that even subjective or discretionary employment practices may be invalidated in some cases under a disparate impact theory. In *Watson*, the plaintiff argued that her continuing exclusion from upper management, though not enough to prove disparate "treatment" could still prove that the bank's wholly discretionary system of internal promotions had a disparate "impact" on minorities. The Court held that subjective promotion criteria can establish a type of discrimination that straddles the line between disparate treatment and impact. *Watson* seems to suggest, then, at least in the Title VII context, that a combined showing of even statistically insignificant imbalances in a workforce, subjective employment evaluation processes, and evidence of the presence of "subconscious stereotypes" may be sufficient to get a disparate impact discrimination claim to a jury.

A prima facie case of disparate discrimination in an employee discipline or discharge context may be established under Title VII by the plaintiff's proof that employees who are not members of the same protected group were treated more leniently by the employer under comparable circumstances—that is, they were not fired or were given lesser punishment for similar misconduct. [*McDonald v. Santa Fe Trail Transportation Co.* (1976)]

In the case of a discharge, an employee presents a prima facie disparate treatment case by showing (1) membership in a group protected by Title VII; (2) satisfactory performance in that position; (3) termination of employment or discipline on a job despite satisfactory performance; and (4) that the employer attempted to replace the employee with someone better qualified or, in a discipline situation, that other employees were disciplined less severely. [*McDonald v. Santa Fe Trail Transportation Co.* (1976)]

The four-part burden of proof applicable to disparate treatment Title VII cases has been applied in discriminatory discharge cases under the Age Discrimination in Employment Act. [*Loeb v. Textron, Inc.* (1979); *Pena v. Brattleboro Retreat* (1983)]

A prima facie case of discriminatory discharge under the Rehabilitation Act of 1973 is established by showing that the plaintiff is an "otherwise qualified handicapped individual" and by demonstrating that the plaintiff was terminated because of her handicap. [*Reynolds v. Brock* (1987)]

See also **Age Discrimination in Employment Act; Equal Employment Opportunity Commission; Protected Class; Rehabilitation Act of 1973.**

DIVERSITY Although white males have historically dominated the American business mainstream, the demographics of the American workplace has dramatically changed in recent years. The proportion of both women and ethnic minorities in the labor force has greatly increased, and an increase in heterogeneity—or diversity—has occurred. In the past, these different groups were usually defined in terms of race, gender, and ethnicity. Today, the term "minority" would include any person who is different from the "norm," such as homosexuals and the physically and mentally disabled. Organizations committed to diversity base their missions on the principle that members of these groups should not be discriminated against as a matter of public policy and common decency.

Traditionally, diversity was conceptualized as a "melting pot." Managers assumed that different people would somehow assimilate and become more homogeneous. Today, most managers recognize that employees do not leave their deep-seated preferences and values at home when they come to work. In fact, differing cultures, value systems, and ages may create communication barriers. The challenges posed by diversity, then, are to accommodate the different lifestyles, values, work styles, and family needs of these groups without compromising the goals and operations of the organization.

Unfortunately, efforts to manage diversity have not always lived up to expectations. Although diversity programs are increasing in number, so are the problems of resistance and backlash. Now that businesses have intensified efforts to hire and promote more females and minorities, white males often feel frustrated, resentful, and afraid, largely due to the poor implementation of the well-intended efforts to manage diversity.

The Civil Rights Act of 1991 changed the parameters of lawful diversity management. Although Section 107(a) of the act does not appear to forbid completely the use of race-, sex-, or national origin-conscious measures to increase the participation of women and minorities in the workforce, employers must now exercise extreme caution whenever they take these factors into consideration. Neither benevolent intentions nor sound business judgment alone will relieve an employer from liability for reverse discrimination when race, sex, or national origin are motivating factors, however slight, for an employment decision in violation of the statute.

One option for achieving diversity is to develop a formal affirmative action plan that meets the requirements of antidiscrimination statutes, Equal Employment Opportunity Commission regulations, and case law. The process begins a self-analysis to determine the extent to which women and minorities are underrepresented in the employer's workforce compared to the proportion of qualified women and minorities in the workforce at large. If the self-analysis reveals a significant underrepresentation, the employer should attempt to discover why the disparity exists and take reasonable steps, including the establishment of race-, sex-, and national origin-conscious goals and timetables, to increase the number and percentage of women and minority employees.

Considering the Civil Rights Act of 1991 and the traditional willingness of the courts to uphold certain race- or sex-conscious measures that comply with the spirit, if not the letter, of Title VII of the Civil Rights Act of 1964, it appears that employers are not completely prevented from making efforts to achieve a truly diverse workforce. The law and the changed composition of the U.S. Supreme Court do, however, significantly increase the risks of liability associated with both formal and informal diversity programs and further restrict the tactics an employer may use to change the demographic composition of its workforce. In designing programs to increase racial, sexual, and ethnic diversity in the workforce, employers must be careful that they do not commit reverse discrimination.

Opponents of diversity programs argue that if employers believe a nondiverse workforce is more productive than a heterogeneous one, they should be allowed to reject job applicants on grounds that are currently prohibited, such as race or gender, as a matter of business judgment.

See also **Affirmative Action; Civil Rights Act of 1964; Civil Rights Act of 1991; Equal Employment Opportunity Commission; Women: Employment Issues.**

DOMESTIC EMPLOYMENT IN A PRIVATE HOME

Domestic services performed as an employee of a householder-employer. Domestic service is only that work that services the needs of a household. [*Durrow v. W.C.A.B. Heckard's Catering* (1993)] The Zoe Baird/Nannygate incident, in which it was discovered that President Bill Clinton's nominee for Attorney General had failed to pay the legally required social security taxes for her nanny who was an illegal alien, is an example that hiring part-time or full-time household help sometimes involves complicated tax, immigration, and labor issues. Employers of domestic service employees face substantial legal risks in failing to pay social security or federal unemployment taxes, state employment taxes, or in ignoring the immigration laws. The possible consequences include not only a lawsuit by the former employee, but also being compelled by the Internal Revenue Service or various state agencies to file late payroll tax returns and to pay all taxes, penalties, and interest.

See also **Domestic Service Employee.**

DOMESTIC PARTNERSHIPS

Generally, an exclusive relationship between two persons of the same sex or between opposite-sex partners who live together and are financially interdependent. Beginning in the mid-1980s, a few private employers, city and state governments, and unions began to give unmarried couples of the same or opposite sex the opportunity to participate in employer-sponsored benefits on the same basis as married couples. Often, under such an arrangement, the employee must sign an affidavit attesting that the partner is aged 18 or older and shares living quarters with the employee in an exclusive, committed relationship in which the partners are responsible for each other's common welfare.

Corporate America has been slow to offer domestic partner benefits. Companies that have declined to provide them have generally cited one of five reasons: fear of rising benefit costs, few employee requests for domestic partner benefits, lack of senior management support, anxiety over moving into an unknown area, and concern over the possibility of lawsuits. As of mid-1995, more than 350 employers offered full medical/dental plans to domestic partners. Some organizations do not offer coverage for opposite-sex domestic partners because heterosexuals have the option to marry legally, whereas homosexuals do not.

Some jurisdictions allow same-sex partners to "register" their relationships with the local authorities just as married couples register their marriages. In 1993, the Boston City Council passed the Family Registration Act, which permits homosexual couples to register as domestic partners. As enacted, the act does not provide health benefits for gay and lesbian companions of Boston city employees.

One of the most difficult questions under statewide employment antidiscrimination laws is whether a prohibition of sexual orientation discrimination forbids an employer from tying job benefits to marriage, a practice that necessarily discriminates against gay and lesbian employees. The courts have uniformly agreed that a ban of sexual orientation discrimination does not require an employer to provide benefits to a homosexual employee's lifetime partner as the employer does for a heterosexual employee's spouse.

The leading case on the issue of employee benefits for gay and lesbian life partners is a 1985 California Court of Appeal decision, *Hinman v. Department of Personnel Administration* (1985). *Hinman* argued that the California Department of Personnel Administration's policy granting dental benefits to the spouses of married employees but not to the partners of homosexual employees violated the California Constitution's equal protection clause. The court, finding that a distinction based on marriage creates no classification according to sexual orientation, rejected the argument on the threshold question. *Hinman's* reasoning did not specifically rely on any specific provision of the California Constitution or any statute. Thus it has been easy for courts in other states to adopt *Hinman*, as well as to apply its reasoning to other forms of employee benefits tied to marriage, such as health insurance. The *Hinman* line of cases is problematic because none of the courts has considered a disparate impact theory of sexual orientation discrimination. Every court has discussed the tying of employee benefits to domestic partners in terms of whether it treats homosexuals differently from heterosexuals.

These courts have concluded that unmarried homosexuals are treated identically to unmarried heterosexuals in a classification by marital status. A disparate impact argument would probably destroy the *Hinman* line of precedent. Because not all antidiscrimination statutes allow disparate impact claims, courts would be forced to distinguish between different state laws. *Hinman* itself was an equal protection claim under the California Constitution, which does not allow disparate impact claims. Thus, *Hinman* would have no persuasive value for a disparate impact claim brought under the gay rights laws of Rhode Island, Vermont, Minnesota, New Jersey, Wisconsin, Massachusetts, Connecticut, or the District of Columbia, because disparate impact claims are cognizable under all of these statutes. *Hinman*'s precedential value to California law is unclear because, although the state's Fair Employment of Housing Act does permit disparate impact claims, no court has decided whether Section 102.1 of the Labor Code also does.

Gay rights advocates believe a disparate impact theory should lead a court to hold that tying employee benefits to marriage constitutes discrimination on the basis of sexual orientation. The proposed basic test for a disparate impact claim is, first, whether a facially neutral employment policy has a discriminatory effect on a protected class and, second, whether there is no business necessity that justifies that policy. State marriage laws guarantee that the first prong of the test is fulfilled. An employer's policy of providing health insurance, dental insurance, or any other benefit to the legal spouses of employees necessarily discriminates against gays and lesbians because they cannot be legally married.

The real issue in establishing a disparate impact claim lies in the second prong of the test. A disparate impact claim would fail if there were sufficient business reason for an employer to tie benefits to marriage as opposed to domestic partnership. When the *Hinman* court considered the argument that an employer could choose to ignore the marriage standard completely and allow all of its employees to register domestic partners for benefits purposes, it responded that this course of action would be impracticable for employers:

> The responsible agencies would have to establish standards which would reach the very foundations of the privacy rights of both homosexual partners in order to properly determine whether the relationship meets some arbitrary standard equating with marriage, and still exclude other unmarried non-spouses, such as roommates, acquaintances or companions. Yet, an employer could bypass this problem simply by defining a 'domestic partner' (for example, as someone with whom an employee has lived for more than a year), asking its employees whether they meet this standard, and then applying the same standard to both heterosexual and homosexual employees. Thus, there would be no problem of an 'arbitrary standard' equating with marriage because under this argument, the employer would not be creating marriage 'equivalent' for gays and lesbians.

Thus, the employer would ignore marriage completely and create a uniform standard for all employees.

Increasingly, private companies are offering health benefits to domestic partners. One of the issues, then, becomes whether these benefits are taxable. Including an employee's domestic partner in a health benefit plan is considered a taxable fringe benefit, unless the domestic partner was recognized as a spouse under state law or qualified as a dependent under Section 152(a), according to IRS Letter Ruling 96-3011. In that case, an international law firm contributed to a health plan for its full-time employees and their spouses and children. The firm amended the plan to extend coverage to domestic partners of employees who attested to their relationship. Section 106 of the Internal Revenue Code excludes from gross income employer-provided coverage under an accident or health plan. The exclusion is limited to contributions for the employee, the employee's spouse, and the employee's dependents, under IRS Regulations 1.106-1. The IRS concluded that favorable tax treatment applied only if the domestic partner was recognized as the employee's spouse or could qualify as a dependent. Marital status is determined under local law according to the IRS. Therefore, if the domestic partner and the employee were not legally married, the domestic partner cannot be the employee's spouse for tax purposes.

DOMESTIC SERVICE EMPLOYEE

The Fair Labor Standards Act was amended to cover such employees, defined as employees who perform home-related noncommercial labor in private family homes and whose work, but for the availability of outside paid help and the economic means of the homeowner to compensate the same, would be done by tradition and necessity, in every household, by members of that family unit. [*Marshall v. Cordero* (1981)]

DOUBLE BREASTING A practice, usually confined to the construction industry, wherein a single employer operates two subsidiaries, one unionized and the other nonunion. Unionized firms believe that under this arrangement they can better compete with open shop firms.

Unions frequently allege that employers use double-breasted operations to avoid dealing with unions, and therefore violate Section 8(a)(5) of the National Labor Relations Act (NLRA) by refusing to bargain with the duly authorized union, in claims to the National Labor Relations Board (NLRB). Unions also allege double-breasting violates Section 301 of the NLRA and provisions of the Employee Retirement Income Security Act and antitrust statutes.

The U.S. Supreme Court, in *Peter Kiewit & Sons Co.* (1979), ruled that the two subsidiaries in that case were a single employer for the purposes of the NLRA but left the issue of the appropriateness of bargaining unit to the NLRB as the expert body. In applying the test of the employees' community of interest, the NLRB found that the employees of each subsidiary had distinct interests and therefore formed separate bargaining units. This finding meant that the nonunion company could lawfully ignore the collective bargaining agreement. Unions have responded to *Kiewit* by attempting to limit the growth of double-breasting through several legal tactics. For example, unions have sought to have the parent and the subsidiaries declared "alter egos." If successful, the "corporate veil" can then be pierced and the nonunion segment bound by the obligations of the unionized company.

See also **Antitrust Laws; Collective Bargaining Agreement; Community of Interest; National Labor Relations Act; National Labor Relations Board; Employee Retirement Income Security Act of 1974; Open Shop.**

DOWNSIZING Reducing the size of the employer's labor force by laying off employees. Demotions, downgrades, and transfers are the most frequent actions companies have taken to reduce layoffs. Hiring freezes have become the more popular method of downsizing in recent years for many companies. Salary reductions, early retirement incentives, and voluntary separation plans have also been used.

Increasingly, companies have sought ways to assist the employees affected by downsizing. Most employers offer outplacement assistance and some offer extended health care benefits. The options that have grown less popular among downsizing employers include extended severance pay and job retraining.

See also **Layoff.**

DRESS CODE Employers often regulate the appearance of their employees by regulating their dress. They may require uniforms and establish rules regarding eyeglasses, head coverings, earrings, and certain types of religious clothing. As with grooming rules, dress codes have been challenged as discrimination based on gender, race, and religion under Title VII of the Civil Rights Act of 1964, and also under state law. Dress codes should bear some relationship to the job, but even when they do relate to the job, they may be discriminatory if they affect members of a protected group more than they do other employees.

There is little direct regulation of dress codes. An employer may require an employee to wear a uniform or similar attire, but policies that have the purpose or effect of unreasonably discriminating against employees on the basis of gender, religion, or other proscribed factors will violate Title VII.

Dress codes challenged under Title VII as discriminatory on the basis of gender have involved requiring uniforms for women only, requiring uniforms that subject the wearer to sexual harassment, and requiring women to wear contact lenses. The imposition of a dress code by an employer may constitute illegal sex discrimination, although the courts are divided on the issue. Case law holds that, absent business necessity, the imposition of a dress code violated Title VII where only women were forbidden to wear slacks on the job, were forbidden to wear glasses, were required to wear sexually provocative uniforms, were required to wear smocks, or were required to treat their uniforms, which were provided by the employer, as income. Where differing treatment is unjustified by business necessity, and nondiscriminatory alternatives for achieving the same purpose are available to the employer, discriminatory dress regulations will violate Title VII.

However, if particular dress regulations are reasonably related to business needs and justified by accepted social norms, they are lawful even if they are different for men and women. Thus, it was not an unlawful employment practice to require male—but not female—store employees to wear ties. Similarly, an employer's prohibition on pantsuits for female employees in its executive office but not in its general office was not sex discrimination. An employer may impose different standards of appearance on female and male employees if the standards are reasonable and enforced for both sexes.

The Equal Employment Opportunity Commission has held that an employer's dress code can constitute religious discrimination if unjustified by business necessity. Thus it was unlawful to terminate a Black Muslim for wearing high-necked dresses substantially covering her legs and arms while permitting other employees to wear unusual or attention-getting clothing. In contrast, Title VII's exemption for religious entities who employ individuals to perform the entity's activities permitted a church-operated retirement home to prohibit its receptionist from wearing a head covering required by her Muslim religion. The nursing home sought to provide a Christian environment for its residents and required that its employees' actions, attitudes, and appearance conform with the environment. The exception applies even when the job in question is not sectarian or ecclesiastical in nature.

See also **Civil Rights Act of 1964; Equal Employment Opportunity Commission; Protected Class; Religious Discrimination; Sexual Harassment; Sex Discrimination in Employment; Women: Employment Issues.**

DRUG ABUSE AND EMPLOYMENT

During the 1970s, as a means of monitoring drug use at treatment centers, automated and increasingly sophisticated tests were developed to measure drugs in urine. These techniques were applied later in other settings, such as the military, which began drug testing in 1981. By the mid 1980s, drug testing was widely adopted in both public- and private-sector employment.

"Drug-free workplace" statutes require employers to prohibit drug abuse in the workplace and to take certain steps to discourage drug use. They impose very limited duties on employers and do not require drug or alcohol testing except in the case of certain regulated employers. Consequently, the drug-free workplace laws, standing alone, do not determine whether an employer should or may engage in drug or alcohol testing.

The federal Drug-Free Workplace Act of 1988 was designed to help employers combat drugs in the workplace and requires certain employers to develop and distribute to their employees policies that, among other things, prohibit "the unlawful manufacture, distribution, dispensation, possession, or use of a controlled substance" in the workplace. The policy must also inform employees of the actions the company will take against employees who violate the drug-free policy.

The act applies to two kinds of employers: those that seek and enter into contracts with the federal government to provide goods or services worth $25,000 or more, and those that obtain federal financial assistance grants of any amount. Under the act, most government contractors must (1) have a policy prohibiting drug use and require employees to abide by it; (2) establish a drug-free awareness program for employees; (3) sanction or require participation in a drug rehabilitation program for any employee convicted under a criminal drug statute; and (4) make a good-faith effort to maintain a drug-free workplace. Significantly, the statute does not require drug testing.

The main requirement of the Drug-Free Workplace Act—that employers develop and distribute a policy prohibiting illegal drugs in the workplace—has been widely followed by businesses in the private sector, including by many companies not required to do so. And many employers already have employee assistance programs or drug-abuse treatment programs to which they refer employees with drug-abuse problems.

The most important factor affecting the legality of drug testing for private sector employees is whether the testing is government mandated. If so, then this "state action" or "governmental action" will permit employees to assert constitutional arguments similar to those raised by public sector employees. The degree to which the job involves public safety is often controlling. For example, the testing of applicants and employees in nuclear power plants has been upheld by the courts. However, the employer is free to prohibit drug or alcohol use or possession at work, hold current drug and alcohol users to the same performance standards as nonusers, and require the employee's behavior conform to the Drug-Free Workplace Act.

Two federal statutes offer limited protection to drug and alcohol abusers as "handicapped individuals": the Rehabilitation Act of 1973, which applies to federal contractors and recipients of federal funds, and the Americans with Disabilities Act of 1990 (ADA), which covers all employers of fifteen or more workers. The ADA is neutral on the issue of drug testing; it does not require, prohibit, or encourage employers to implement drug-testing programs. Indeed, the act's rather limited requirements are mild in comparison with the strict monitoring programs that the federal Department of Transportation first imposed in 1989 on employees in the transportation industry. In addition, the ADA allows pre-employment drug tests, since the statute provides that drug tests shall not be considered medical examinations, which may be conducted only after the applicant has accepted employment.

Employer drug testing has been challenged on several constitutional grounds, including the right of privacy. As the case of *Webster v. Motorola* (1994) indicates, at least some employees do have a right to privacy in this area. Increasingly, random drug testing is being recognized by the court as appropriate for employees in safety-sensitive positions only.

See also **Americans with Disabilities Act of 1990; Rehabilitation Act of 1973.**

Dunlop Commission

See **Commission on the Future of Worker/Management Relations.**

Duplex Printing Press Co. v. Deering (1921)

A U.S. Supreme Court case involving a secondary boycott by the International Association of Machinists representing employees of newspaper publishers in New York in support of efforts by machinists in Battle Creek, Michigan, to unionize a printing press manufacturer, the only one of four major national printing press manufacturers that had remained unorganized. Owners of two of the unionized plants told the union that unless the fourth was organized, they would terminate their contracts.

The Michigan factory followed an open shop policy, purportedly refusing to discriminate against either union or nonunion employees. The union, whose goals were a closed shop (where only union members could be employed), an eight-hour day, and the union scale of wages, called a strike at the factory. When only a few of the workers joined in the union's efforts, the union attempted to boycott the company's products, threatened customers with sympathetic strikes, and encouraged employees of the customers to strike against their employers. The Duplex Company brought an antitrust action against the union for unlawful restraint of trade.

The Supreme Court narrowly interpreted the Clayton Act provisions protecting labor activity from antitrust liability. The Court held that Section 6 merely provided that the Sherman Act conferred no antitrust immunity where unions "depart from . . . normal and legitimate objects." The court then interpreted Section 20 as applying to "a case between employers and employees," and this protected only workers in a proximate relation to the dispute—the employees of the primary employer. Thus it appeared that only primary union activity would be protected, and even that protection might be lost if the court deemed the union's object "illegitimate." The Court specifically ruled that secondary boycotts violated the Sherman Antitrust Act and were therefore not a "legitimate union activity" protected under the Clayton Act. The Court held that the Clayton Act did not shelter the secondary boycott because there was no direct-employment relationship between the defendant union and the company that was the ultimate object of the boycott.

Duplex significantly impaired organized labor's efforts through its narrow interpretation of the Clayton Act. Thus, a probusiness judiciary continued to impose its social and economic biases as the law on labor relations. Congress responded to *Duplex* by enacting the Norris-LaGuardia Act in 1932. This statute limited the federal court's injunctive power in labor disputes and established a policy of governmental neutrality in labor disputes as a means of aiding the growth of organized labor.

See also **Antitrust Laws; Clayton Antitrust Act; Closed Shop; Norris-LaGuardia Act; Open Shop; Secondary Boycott; Sherman Antitrust Act of 1980; Strike.**

Duty of Fair Representation

A union with the status of exclusive bargaining representative under the National Labor Relations Act (NLRA) has the responsibility to represent fairly all employees in the bargaining unit. This duty governs both the union's collective bargaining with the employer and its enforcement of the resulting collective bargaining agreement. The duty of fair representation requires the union to serve the interests of all union and nonunion bargaining-unit members without hostility or discrimination, to exercise this responsibility in good faith, and to avoid arbitrary conduct—whether or not members of the bargaining unit are members of the union or voted for the union and whether or not they are members of some racial or ethnic minority group.

The duty of unions to represent employees without discrimination was first enunciated in a Railway Labor Act case, *Steele v. Louisville Railroad* (1944), where the Supreme Court struck down a bargaining agreement that discriminated against African American members of the bargaining unit.

In *Steele,* the Court found that the principle of exclusive representation included an implied obligation to represent employees in bargaining fairly and without hostile discrimination.

This duty is no less exacting than the duty the U.S. Constitution imposes upon a legislature to provide equal protection to those for whom it legislates. A union may exercise a wide range of discretion in bargaining, but it must exercise that discretion "fairly, impartially, and in good faith." The courts have found that the same duty exists in the provisions of the NLRA. [*Syres v. Oil Workers, Local 23* (1955)]

In the grievance-processing context, the U.S. Supreme Court has ruled that duty of fair representation does not require that every grievance be carried to arbitration [*Vaca v. Sipes* (1967)], lest arbitration become so expensive that it will lose its usefulness. The union has considerable discretion, but it may not arbitrarily ignore a grievance or handle it in a perfunctory fashion. The union must act honestly and in good faith. A court may not second-guess the union regarding whether a grievance warrants arbitration. In *Vaca,* since there was no evidence that any union officer was personally hostile to the employee who presented the grievance or that the union acted in bad faith, no breach of the duty occurred when the union refused to arbitrate the employee's grievance.

The union may commit an unfair labor practice if it refuses to process an employee's grievance, but that does not limit court jurisdiction because there is no federal preemption in those situations.

The Supreme Court in *Vaca* also established the principle that liability for damages resulting from a breach of duty and an employer should be apportioned according to the damage caused by the fault of each. In other words, courts cannot charge a union with damages that result from an employer's breach of contract. Damages, thus, must be apportioned between the employer and the union according to the fault of each.

An employee may sue in federal court or state court to enforce an individual right under the collective bargaining agreement. Several judicial remedies are available when an employee sues his or her employer and perhaps the union as well, in a breach of bargaining agreement and breach of fair representation suit. If the union is found to have breached its duty, the court may order an employer to arbitrate, the remedy called for in the bargaining agreement, but the court may also decide itself whether the bargaining agreement has been breached and can award damages. According to *Vaca,* availability of the latter alternative is required by sound policy because in some cases a portion of damages will be attributable to the union's default and the normal arbitration award will not include those damages. Also, issues concerning the merits of the breach of contract claim may have been completely litigated in the lawsuit, and it would be inefficient for the court to not render a decision on those issues.

The Court held in *Hines v. Anchor Motor Freight, Inc.* (1976) that even an arbitration award in favor of an employer will not bar an employee lawsuit against it for breach of a collective bargaining agreement if that award is tainted by the union's breach of duty to represent the grieving employee fairly. In *Hines,* the plaintiff employees alleged that evidence favorable to them had not been presented in the arbitration hearing because the union had handled their case in bad faith. There was no allegation that the employer contributed to the union's breach of duty.

In *Bowen v. United States Postal Service* (1983), without adequate explanation the union failed to take a grievance to arbitration, thus violating its duty to represent fairly an employee who had been discharged. The trial court apportioned damages between the union and the employer. The employer was charged with lost wages from the time of the discharge to the time an arbitrator would have ordered the employee reinstated. The union was charged with the lost pay for the period after the employee would have been reinstated by the hypothetical arbitration. Calling the union's decision not to invoke contractual arbitration a "waiver," the majority on the Supreme Court agreed with the trial court's apportionment of damages. The majority emphasized the need to protect the employer's reliance interest.

Many lower courts have required employees seeking to bring fair representation actions against the union, or who would rely on a union breach of fair representation to justify proceeding individually against the employer, or to exhaust their internal union remedies. In *Clayton v. United Auto Workers* (1981), the Court held that lower courts have some discretion in deciding whether to require employees to exhaust internal union remedies. The factors considered are whether union officials are so hostile to the employee that he or she could not hope to obtain a fair hearing on the claim; whether the internal union procedures are adequate to offer the employee full relief; and whether exhaustion of internal procedures would unreasonably delay the employee's opportunity to secure a judicial hearing on the merits of the claim.

A union's obligation to fairly represent employees is subject to reasonable limitation, but it is enforceable in a lawsuit under Section 301 of the NLRA. A union breaches its duty of fair representation only when its conduct toward a bargaining unit member is arbitrary, discriminatory, or in bad faith. [*Vaca v. Sipes* (1967); *Humphrey v. Moore* (1964)]

See also **Collective Bargaining; Collective Bargaining Agreement; Exhaustion of Remedies; National Labor Relations Act; Railway Labor Act; *Steele v. Louisville & Nashville R.R. Co.* (1944).**

EARLY RETIREMENT See **Retirement.**

EASTEX INC. V. NLRB (1977)

A case involving Eastex employees who sought to distribute a union newsletter in nonworking areas of their employer's property during nonworking hours. The newsletter urged employees to support the union and discussed a proposal to incorporate the state right-to-work statute into the Texas state constitution and a presidential veto of an increase in the federal minimum wage. The newsletter urged the workers to act to protect their interests. Eastex refused to allow distribution of the newsletter because the sections on the right-to-work provisions and the minimum wage veto had nothing to do with its relations with its employees. The union filed an unfair labor practice charge with the National Labor Relations Board (NLRB) alleging that Eastex's refusal interfered with the employees' exercise of their rights under Section 7 of the National Labor Relations Act. The administrative law judge ruled in favor of the employees, holding that Eastex restrained the employees right under Section 7 to engage in "concerted activities for the purpose of . . . mutual aid or protection." The NLRB adopted the administrative law judge's order and the U.S. Fifth Circuit Court of Appeals enforced its order. Eastex appealed to the U.S. Supreme Court, which affirmed the lower court's opinion.

The Court addressed two issues: (1) whether distribution of the newsletter is the kind of concerted activity protected by Section 7, and (2) whether the fact that the activity occurs on the employer's property creates a "countervailing interest" that outweighs Section 7 rights. The Court agreed with the NLRB that distribution of the portion of the newsletter on the right-to-work provision was protected because union security is "central to the union concept of strength through solidarity." The board also properly acted within its discretion when it held that distribution of the section on the presidential veto was also protected. In agreeing with the NLRB that the employees were allowed to distribute the newsletter on the employer's premises, the Court relied on *Republic Aviation Corporation v. NLRB* (1945), which held that an employer may not prohibit its employees from distributing union organizational literature on company premises. The organizational activity in *Eastex* case was protected because it was conducted by employees already rightfully on the employer's property.

See also **Concerted Activity; National Labor Relations Act; National Labor Relations Board; Right-To-Work Laws; Unfair Labor Practice.**

Economic Strike A work stoppage resulting from a dispute over wages, hours, requests that the employer recognize a union, or other terms of employment. It is a strike used exclusively as an economic weapon to assert pressure on the employer.

Economic strikers retain this status even though their protest may be partially devoted to an unfair labor practice issue. The main focus of the workers' expressed concerns, however, must be on economic issues. Noneconomic strikers are those employees who strike to protest employer conduct found by the National Labor Relations Board to be an unfair labor practice. An economic strike, under certain circumstances, may become an unfair labor practice.

During an economic strike, an employer may replace striking employees with new workers in order to operate during the strike. An employer is not required to reinstate economic strikers whose positions have been filled by permanent replacements. The employer's right to replace economic strikers, however, does not extend to withholding from them the right to return to their unoccupied jobs simply because they went out on strike.

Economic strikers who unconditionally apply for reinstatement when their positions are filled by permanent replacements remain employees and are entitled to full reinstatement when the replacements leave unless they have, in the meantime, acquired regular and substantially equivalent employment, or unless the employer has a legitimate and substantial business reason for not reinstating them.

Economic strikers are eligible to vote in a representation election conducted during the strike unless the election is held more than twelve months after the beginning of the strike.

See also **National Labor Relations Board; Permanently Replaced Employees; Reinstatement Rights of Economic Strikers; Strike.**

EFFECTS BARGAINING Labor-management negotiations over effects of employer decisions. Effects bargaining is allowed by an interpretation of a labor relations statute by an administrative agency or a court that effectively states, that although a certain issue may not be a mandatory subject of bargaining, the employer is obliged to bargain over the effect of the unilateral decision on that issue. Thus, even though an employer may unilaterally reduce the number of workers employed, the order of layoffs (which workers go first) can be a mandatory subject of bargaining.

EMPLOYEE Generally, any person who works for a wage or salary and performs services for an employer.

In labor-management relations, the term has been variously defined to establish rights and duties under the various provisions of federal law. For example, the term is differently interpreted and applied in the Fair Labor Standards Act and the Social Security Act. The status of the employee is central to National Labor Relations Act (NLRA) protections. The NLRA defines "employee" to include not only persons currently on an employer's payroll but also persons whose work has ceased because of an ongoing lawful strike or an unfair labor practice and who have not obtained other regular and substantially equivalent employment. [*NLRB v. Fansteel Metallurgical Corp.* (1939)] The U.S. Supreme Court expressly defines "employee" as any employee unless excluded. [*NLRB v. Town & Country Electric, Inc.* (1995) and *Ameristaff Personnel Contractors, Inc.* (1995)]

The Labor-Management Relations Act of 1947 (the Taft-Hartley Act) amends Section 2(3) of the NLRA so that the definition of employee excludes certain categories of workers, such as supervisors. Prior to this act, supervisors were considered employees, and the employer could not discriminate against them for engaging in union activity. Since 1947, employers are free to demand that supervisors refrain from union activities and from taking out union membership. The employer may discharge a supervisor for either offense without violating Section 8(a). Nonetheless, supervisors may join unions, and employers may choose to recognize these unions. Supervisors, however, are excluded from National Labor Relations Board (NLRB) jurisdiction and the regulation of their strike weapons and bargaining rights are left to the state.

The U.S. Supreme Court, in *NLRB v. Bell Aerospace* (1974), concluded that Congress intended to exclude *all* persons properly defined as "managerial employees" from NLRA protection, regardless of whether their policy-formulating activities affect the company's labor policies. The criteria for determining which employees are "managerial employees" center not on job titles, but on the employee's actual "job responsibilities," authority, and relationship to management:

> Those who formulate and effectuate management policies by expressing and making operative the decisions of their employer, and those who have discretion in the performance of their jobs independent of their employer's established policy. . . . [M]anagerial status is not conferred upon rank-and-file workers, or upon those who perform routinely, but rather it is reserved for those in executive positions, those who are closely aligned with management, as the representatives of management.

Besides supervisors, other workers exempted from the NLRA definition of employees include agricultural workers, domestic service workers, individuals employed by spouse or parents, independent contractors, and persons employed by employers subject to the Railway Labor Act

The Supreme Court recognizes employees are a special class with certain rights because (1) an employee generally depends upon one employer for a job and occupies a relatively weak bargaining position in the American economy, (2) employment provides for such crucial needs as material survival, social welfare benefits (including healthcare, disability insurance, and pensions), political power, and social status, and (3) unlike other market exchanges, employment involves an exchange of human value.

See also **Fair Labor Standards Act; Independent Contractor; National Labor Relations Act; Railway Labor Act; Social Security Act; Strike; Supervisor; Unfair Labor Practice.**

EMPLOYEE ASSISTANCE PROGRAMS Employer-provided services to assist workers in handling personal problems such as alcohol or drug abuse. These programs may include health care, education, prevention, counseling, and assistance in the control of specific conditions (e.g., alcoholism, hypertension, smoking, and fitness). They are offered because employers recognize that an employee's personal problems may adversely affect job performance and attendance.

Often an employee assistance program serves as a problem assessment and referral service rather than a treatment program. Several unions have actively sought to implement these programs in collective bargaining agreements.

The confidentiality of employee records becomes particularly important at the workplace when the employer has an employee assistance plan or otherwise compiles data on individual employee drug abuse and its consequences. Presently, there is no comprehensive federal legislation on employee privacy, and the statutory law in this area varies in its coverage.

It is unclear whether the Consolidated Omnibus Budget Reconciliation Act of 1985 extension of benefits provision applies to employee assistance plans, where counseling and referrals are provided to employees either by an employee or by a counseling service engaged by the employer.

See also **Consolidated Omnibus Budget Reconciliation Act of 1985.**

EMPLOYEE HANDBOOK A document produced by an employer articulating the rights and duties of the employees and the procedures that must be followed at the workplace.

Employee handbooks are often provided to new employees in orientation programs. They generally contain a brief statement about the organization and, in order to fulfill legal obligations, articulate the company's policies on issues as vacations, hours of work, complaint resolution, discipline procedures, company rules, benefits, and bonuses.

Employee handbooks, manuals, and policy statements may modify the existing employment relationship or become a part of a new employment relationship. This, however, does not apply in unionized workplaces. Courts have found that policies in employee handbooks create legally enforceable employer obligations. In litigation involving certain nonunionized workplaces, former employees frequently assert that the employer breached promises made in an employee handbook. Under certain circumstances, courts have held that employer handbooks may form an implied contract limiting the employer's right to terminate his employees because the language constitutes some form of job security.

Some courts have ruled that a handbook or manual becomes part of the employment contract if the language is definite and is communicated to the employee, or if an employment handbook contains detailed procedures for discipline and discharge. Many courts also recognize that if the employee handbook expressly states that the employer will terminate only for good cause, then the courts will recognize that the employment-at-will rule has been modified. In the landmark case *Toussaint v. Blue Cross & Blue Shield of Michigan* (1980), the Michigan Supreme Court ruled in favor of an employee when the company failed to follow the disciplinary procedure in its employee handbook prior to terminating the individual.

The New Jersey Supreme Court ruled in *Woolley v. Hoffmann-La Roche, Inc.* (1985) that the company's policy manual statements on job security created a binding contractual obligation. It also ruled that when an employer does not want its manual provisions to be binding, it should state prominently "that there is no promise of any kind by the employer contained in the manual, regardless of what the manual says or provides, and that the employer promises nothing and remains free to change working conditions without anyone's agreement." This language is known as a disclaimer, which an employer may include to prevent the handbook from becoming a part of a binding contract or a continued guarantee of employment. If a disclaimer is prominently displayed within the handbook or manual, courts will generally uphold the disclaimer. Some courts, however, have ruled that at-will employment could be refuted by evidence in an employee handbook that the parties expressly or implicitly intended the employment to be for a specific term and that termination could be for good cause only.

If a policy is about to change or disclaimers will be added to a manual to change a policy—such as changing the grounds of discharge from "at will" to "just cause"—employees must be adequately informed of these changes. In *Biggers v. Wittek Inc.* (1993), employees were not informed that the company severance policy distributed in 1987 had been altered in 1989. When the company closed a factory in 1991, the employees wanted their severance pay to be based on the more generous 1987 policy. The court ruled in favor of the employees.

There are certain provisions that handbooks may not include without violating a statute or regulation. The National Labor Relations Board, for example, has ruled that a company's policy requiring that its employees agree in writing to abide by its nonunion policies violated the National Labor Relations Act. The board further ordered the company to rescind the "employee's acceptance form" and remove all signed forms from employees' personnel files. The board, however, did not require the "Company's Position on Labor Unions" be removed from the handbook. [*La Quinta Motor Inns, Inc.* (1989)]

See also **Job Security; National Labor Relations Act; National Labor Relations Board; Personnel Files.**

EMPLOYEE HONESTY Refers to employees' duty to refrain from lying, cheating, and stealing. Employee honesty is a crucial issue for employers, because employee theft and dishonesty costs U.S. companies at least $15–25 billion annually. The incidence of employees who steal ranges from less than 30 percent to more than 70 percent, depending upon the industry or company involved and the survey methods used. Employers must balance the need to reduce employee theft with the need to minimize the risk of legal liability in such areas as screening job applicants, implementing programs to reduce theft, conducting in-house investigations, preventing or defending wrongful discharge claims, handling references for discharged workers, and recovering losses. The Employee Polygraph Protection Act forbids the use of polygraphs except for those operating security services (such as armored car firms) or involved in businesses related to national defense and security in which polygraph testing by agents of the federal government is conducted. The statute does not govern the use of honesty tests.

Many employers have developed methods in their personnel selection programs to increase the probability of selecting honest job applicants. Employers that screen employees for attitudes toward theft believe the result is a more honest workforce, fewer terminations for employee theft, and lower inventory shrinkage losses. These programs now include selection interviews, reference checks, credit checks, criminal background checks, and written honesty tests. Not only are the professionally developed honesty tests the most scientifically valid of these selection procedures, they are also inexpensive, typically inoffensive, and nondiscriminatory in the context of equal employment opportunity laws and regulations.

Recently, the potential impact of psychological tests on the right to employee privacy has been increasingly explored. [*Soroka v. Dayton-Hudson* (1991)] Pre-employment honesty tests, when confined to appropriate workplace contexts, generally do not seem to cause an unwarranted invasion of privacy. Most job applicants who take an honesty test during the selection process do not find it offensive, nor do they have negative opinions about the testing process.

Recent court decisions on employee privacy have tended to hold that an informed and carefully delineated employee screening policy can significantly lessen the company's vulnerability to privacy-related litigation. Few states, by statute, prohibit or restrict the use of paper and pencil honesty or psychological profile tests.

Besides employee privacy, another critical issue with honesty testing is avoiding illegal discrimination. The Civil Rights Act of 1964, in Section 703h, prohibits employers from conducting or acting upon the results of any professionally developed ability tests to discriminate on the basis of race, color, religion, sex, or national origin. However, there is no case law on personality tests, including honesty tests, where a federal or state court or administrative agency found illegal discrimination. This fact seems to reinforce the argument that honesty tests appear to have no adverse impact on any protected class. Psychological testing has also been challenged as violating state and federal disability statutes, with varying results. The case often turns on the issue of whether the employee or applicant is disabled as a result of the psychological condition at issue.

See also **Civil Rights Act of 1964; Protected Class; Wrongful Discharge.**

EMPLOYEE OWNERSHIP Employees' financial holdings in the company. In the United States, employee-owned companies in the form of producers' cooperatives, in which the employees commonly own and manage the business, developed as early as 1791. They increased dramatically in the nineteenth century. Firms organized along traditional lines also have made small amounts of company stock available to selected employees through fringe benefit stock options and bonus plans since the 1920s. The employee stock ownership plan is one form of employee ownership. In recent years, some factories have been purchased by employees from the employer to avoid factory closings.

See also **Employee Stock Ownership Plans.**

EMPLOYEE PARTICIPATION PROGRAMS (EPPs) With the direct support of employees, many employers have implemented or considered implementing employee participation programs. EPPs take a number of forms and have been variously referred to as quality circles, employee involvement committees, and employee teams. Despite their differing titles, EPPs typically are workplace committees composed of management representatives and workers and charged with addressing certain workplace issues. Management's goal in establishing EPPs is enhancing employee productivity and loyalty by increasing employee involvement in workplace decisions. EPPs are increasingly popular because employees gain a sense of involvement and empowerment in the workplace, and employers benefit from useful front-line input and improved quality, efficiency, and morale.

Employee participation committees are increasingly being considered by nonunion companies, based on the worker council concept used in Europe. These committees are elected by employees and terminated only when workers choose to do so. Although they may not bargain over wages, hours, or benefits, they have legal rights to information and the ability to consult with management on its labor policies. Nevertheless, in two well-known 1992 rulings, *Electromation, Inc.* and *E. I. duPont de Nemours & Co.*, the National Labor Relations Board (NLRB) held that in some circumstances an EPP may constitute an unfair labor practice because it may be an unlawful employer-dominated labor union (i.e., a company union).

The employer is forbidden by Section 8(a)(2) to dominate or support any employee group falling within the National Labor Relations Act's (NLRA) definition of a labor organization:

> Any organization of any kind, or any agency or employee representation committee or plan, in which employees participate and which exists for the purpose, in whole or in part, of dealing with employers concerning grievances, labor disputes, wages, rates of pay, hours of employment, or conditions of work.

In its only opinion on the issue, *NLRB v. Cabot Carbon Co.* (1959), the U.S. Supreme Court held that if an employee group "deals with the employer" on any of the enumerated topics, the employee group has no ultimate control over the disposition of the issue and therefore will be per se a "labor organization," except when such an organization is an independent entity. The NLRB has applied a fairly strict test to employee participation plans and has been unwilling to narrowly interpret the *Cabot Carbon* case. However, the NLRB has upheld many employee participation plans and has indicated that it does not object to these programs. In *Sparks Nugget, Inc.* (1977), the NLRB determined that an employee committee established by management to resolve grievances was not a labor organization because it was adjudicative in nature—it resolved grievances rather than simply propose solutions for management's review. All decisions of the committee were final. Thus, the committee was a management tool performing a function for management rather than interacting with it.

Employee participation programs play a large role in American industry today. The focus of most current employee participation plans, including team quality circles and total quality programs, is ostensibly on quality, efficiency, and customer satisfaction. Even though these matters might not appear to be issues for collective bargaining, employee participation programs inevitably become involved in issues that must be dealt with in collective bargaining. [*Electromation v. Teamsters Local 1049* (1982)] Programs that deal such issues risk violating Sections 8(a)(2) and 2(5) of the NLRA. Section 8(a)(2) prohibits employer efforts to create employee representation plans that deal with employers on "conditions of employment," because the employer veritably controls such groups and thereby undermines the rights of workers and unions.

See also **Company Union; Labor Organization; National Labor Relations Act; National Labor Relations Board; Quality Circles.**

EMPLOYEE POLYGRAPH PROTECTION ACT (EPPA) OF 1988 A federal statute that prohibits employers from requiring employees to take lie detector tests and prohibits discharge of employees who refused to take lie detector tests. The EPPA prohibits most employers from requiring or even requesting that a job applicant or employee submit to a polygraph or lie detector test as a condition of employment. Prior to the passage of the EPPA, the pre-employment polygraph examination was frequently used for employment selection in many industries. Between 70 and 80 percent of polygraph tests at the time were pre-employment tests.

The EPPA applies to most employers except those with employees directly responsible for security matters (such as armored car personnel and maintainers of security alarm systems) and those in the prescription drug business with employees who directly handle drugs. It specifically does not apply to public employers or to private employers with subcontracts with the U.S. Department of Defense, the U.S. Department of Energy, and government agencies responsible for the national security. Public employers, however, are subject to many constitutional, statutory, or regulatory restrictions on the use of polygraphs.

Nor does the statute apply in cases where an employee is reasonably suspected of workplace theft or of intentionally causing a monetary loss to his or her employer, or if the employee had access to the property in question. In that case, strict testing requirements must be followed. Advance notice must be provided to the employee of his or her legal rights, including questions that may not be asked and the right to discontinue the test at any time. The act permits an employer to use the test as a basis for adverse employment action only if there is additional evidence against the employee. Employees who are unlawfully fired or denied a promotion on the basis of a lie detector test are entitled to reinstatement to their jobs or the promotion they were denied with back pay and full benefits. The employer is also subject to a fine of up to $10,000 for illegally requiring the employee to take a lie detector test. The EPPA is administered and enforced by the U.S. Department of Labor. In addition, the EPPA allows for private actions by the affected applicants or employees.

The statute recognizes certain crucial differences between polygraph exams and paper and pencil honesty tests. First, a polygraph involves being attached to a blood pressure cuff, chest bands to measure respiration, electrodes to measure electrodermal responses, and sometimes other leads—procedures that many examinees find intimidating. A paper and pencil honesty test, in contrast, simply involves writing answers to job-related questions in a test booklet. Because they are so commonly used in education, people have often become desensitized to paper and pencil tests and typically do not find them offensive.

Secondly, the underlying theory of the polygraph rests upon two assumptions: that past behavior predicts future behavior and that the truthfulness of responses to questions on past behavior may be assessed by physiological changes in respiration, blood pressures, and electrogalvanic or electrodermal responses. While the first assumption is plausible and widely used in other personnel assessment procedures (e.g., structured interviews, biographical data forms), the second assumption is highly controversial. Assessment of the meaning of "deceptive" responses, usually combined with the examiner's observations of the behavior of the examinee during the exam, is subjective and can lead to substantial inter-examiner variability.

EMPLOYEE PRIVACY A concept derived from the broader concept of the right to privacy, which is founded on federal constitutional principles, federal statutes, state constitutions, state statutes, and common law. Existing privacy law pertaining to the workplace (including the constitutional, statutory, and common principles on the topic) typically focuses on the procedures of personal data collection—its management, dissemination, review and correction, and employee access to that information. It does not address issues regarding the content of psychological tests. The extent to which the right to privacy extends to employee privacy rights is a relatively new area of law.

The right to privacy has been extensively argued in relation to physiologically based drug-screening tests (such as urinalysis and blood tests) and has frequently been supported at the district and appellate court levels. The right to privacy in relation to drug-screening tests was considered by the U.S. Supreme Court in *Skinner v. Railway Labor Executives' Association* (1989) and *National Treasury Union v. Von Raab* (1989). In both cases, the Court found that although the Fourth Amendment was applicable to the drug and alcohol testing mandated by the relevant agencies, random urinalysis without an individualized suspicion requirement qualifies as an exception to Fourth Amendment requirements.

In 1974, Congress passed two major privacy statutes. One is the Family Education Rights and Privacy Act of 1974, which provides for parental access to children's school records and requires written parental consent before those records are released to third parties. This act has no bearing on employment testing. The second statute is the Privacy Act of 1974, which was designed to protect the privacy and confidentiality of federal employees' records, particularly against Freedom of Information Act claims. The focus of the Privacy Act is current federal employees rather than job applicants. It sets four general privacy and confidentiality requirements: (1) employee records may not be disclosed to third parties without the employees' consent; (2) employees have the right of access to their own records upon request; (3) records may be corrected or amended upon request; and (4) if a request to amend the records is denied, employees should have access to a review hearing. Although there are many exceptions and qualifications to these requirements, they form the basic law on federal employee privacy rights.

In addition to constitutional and statutory protections of employment privacy rights, common law privacy rights account for a major share of litigation in the area of employment privacy. Common law privacy rights generally encompass four distinct causes of action: (1) public disclosure of private facts, (2) placing an individual in a false light before the public eye, (3) commercial appropriation of an individual's name and likeness, and (4) unreasonable intrusion upon an individual's seclusion. [*Restatement (Second) of Torts,* Sections 652B–652E]

See also **Common Law: Employment Rules.**

EMPLOYEE REPRESENTATION PLANS Programs designed to provide employees a sense of participation in the management of the company. Employee representation plans entail the formation of committees, elected by the employees, that will meet with members of the management to consider problems of mutual concern, primarily the application or enforcement of company policy, grievances, and working conditions. The plans are not designed to develop procedures for collective bargaining, but rather to provide an opportunity for the exchange of ideas or experience before a final decision by management.

During the 1920s, many employee representation plans were implemented in order to prevent unionization at the employers' businesses. The Employers Association during that period argued that management through the employee representation plans fostered the belief among workers that ultimately the interests of management and labor were identical. Many plant managers strongly believed that these plans (also called company unions or works councils) made their managerial authority democratic and legitimate. The typical company unions centered around periodic meetings between employee and managerial representatives of a single enterprise or plant. The subjects of consultation included individual grievances, production problems, and less frequently, wages and benefits.

The framers of the National Labor Relations Act of 1934 (NLRA) believed that company unions merely rubber-stamped management's decisions, and in most cases the employer drafted the organization's constitution and bylaws, oversaw election of employee representatives, and participated in or officiated at meetings of the organization. Company unions were also a part of management's overall coercive campaigns against independent unions. Therefore, the NLRA expressly prohibited company unions.

In the 1990s, many of these old issues were revived in the context of the collaborative "workplace of the future" debates. The many new proposals for workplace collaboration raised concerns among labor supporters about possible employer domination of the union. The debate focuses, at least partially, on what legal framework would best safeguard workers from domination, engender continuing labor-management trust, and develop worker decision-making authority and bargaining power. Specifically, some have proposed permitting employers to establish employee representation plans that would not violate Section 8(a)(2) of the NLRA if the plan meets specified requirements, including, for example, an agreement to submit to binding arbitration disputes over rights under individual employment contracts and under agreements between the employer and the employees' representatives.

See also **Benefits; Collective Bargaining; Company Unions; Employment Contract; Grievance; Grievance Arbitration; Management; National Labor Relations Act.**

EMPLOYEE RETIREMENT INCOME SECURITY ACT (ERISA) OF 1974 The first comprehensive pension reform statute enacted by Congress, ERISA transformed the federal law governing most fringe benefits and profoundly impacted how retirement and benefit plans were created. ERISA does not require employers to establish pension plans; rather, it sets minimum standards for employee participation, portable pension plans, vesting rights, funding, reporting, and disclosures that all plans must meet. Although ERISA's emphasis is on retirement savings and pension plans, it also regulates, through the federal tax code and the federal labor code, other employee fringe benefits such as health care, disability, accident and death benefits.

Mismanagement of pension funds led Congress to enact ERISA in order to remedy abuses in private pension systems, to ensure the soundness of employee plan investments, to guarantee benefits under employee benefit plans, and in short, to ensure that all employees covered by pension plans receive the benefits as promised.

ERISA contains four titles. Title I, which deals with the protection of employee rights, consists of six parts: Reporting and Disclosure, Participation and Vesting, Funding, Fiduciary Responsibility, Administration and Enforcement, and Continuation of Health Coverage. Title II amended the Internal Revenue Code and deals with the tax consequences of coverage. It divides responsibility for administration and enforcement among the U.S. Department of Labor, the Internal Revenue Service, and the Pension Benefit Guarantee Corporation and establishes a system of insurance for pension plan termination.

Under ERISA, employees covered by private pension and welfare plans are assured of receiving benefits in accordance with their credited years of service. In addition to the establishment of minimum vesting requirements, the law also establishes registration and reporting requirements, rules for the administration of the plans with penalties for violations, fiduciary responsibilities, funding requirements, improvements in provisions covering the self-employed, and provisions for individual retirement accounts. ERISA supersedes the Welfare and Pension Plans Disclosure Act of 1959.

Despite its broad coverage, ERISA does not cover all retirement plans; government retirement plans, Railroad Retirement Act plans, church plans, and unfunded excess benefits plans are not covered.

See also **Benefits; Pension; Retirement; Welfare and Pension Plans Disclosure Act of 1958.**

EMPLOYEE STOCK OWNERSHIP PLANS (ESOPs)

Plans designed to give employees a stake in the company by providing an opportunity for them to purchase stock or receive stock bonuses. Through the ESOP, management hopes to instill a sense of ownership and create ties that will result in increased productivity, low turnover, and possibly opposition to unionization.

Employee stock ownership and profit-sharing plans have been two major strategies in employers' efforts to persuade employees to identify their interests with those of the company. But in most instances, employee stock purchases are not sufficient to give employees any significant voice in company policy, and ESOP stock is often a special class of nonvoting common stock.

ESOPs are governed by the IRS Code and the Employee Retirement Income Security Act of 1974. A plan is generally considered an ESOP if it is qualified under the tax code and if it is designed to invest primarily in qualifying employer securities. Qualifying employer securities generally means common stock, issued by an employer or commonly traded entity, that is readily tradable. An ESOP is a legal entity that receives either company shares donated in the names of the employees or cash that is used to purchase shares from the company. Corporations are allowed a tax deduction for part or all of their donations to ESOPs. ESOPs may borrow funds from a financial institutions and use the money to acquire additional shares in the company.

ESOPs originated from company profit-sharing efforts in the early 1900s, when many employers offered profit sharing as a means of discouraging unionization. These employers believed that sharing profits would unite workers and management in pursuit of the same goal: improving company performance. But unions were suspicious of profit sharing. Samuel Gompers, first president of the American Federation of Labor, believed that employers with profit-sharing programs "pared down wages of their employees" so that even with profit sharing, their employees' compensation was below that of others in the same industry.

During the stock market boom in the 1920s, some employers shifted their emphasis from profit sharing to ESOPs. Employers believed that by giving workers ownership in the firm, they would encourage greater productivity. However, the stock market crash and the beginning of the Great Depression made many of these early ESOPs worthless.

ESOPs have enjoyed a resurgence since the 1970s, but this time with the support of organized labor. During the late 1980s, many companies implemented ESOPs to thwart hostile takeovers. During the late 1980s, unions in the steel, airline, trucking, railroad, and construction industries became actively involved in ESOP plans in order to save jobs. All of these ventures were designed to produce both income and employment security.

See also **Compensation; Employee Retirement Income Security Act of 1974.**

EMPLOYEE THEFT See **Employee Honesty.**

EMPLOYEES, DISMISSAL OF

The firing or termination of an employee. This is a permanent separation of an employee from the payroll by an employer.

Usually when a decision is made to discharge an employee, a letter is written that states the specific reason or reasons for the dismissal and the types and dates of prior warnings, performance evaluations, and notices of suspension. Some attorneys argue that the employer should not state the reasons for discharge. While this advice is legally correct, it appears unfair and thus may encourage lawsuits. The letter of dismissal is frequently discussed during an exit interview.

In some cases, the personnel office may allow the employee to choose between quitting and being fired. If the option to quit is offered and accepted, the employee is often required to sign a legal release of all claims against the employer in exchange for the opportunity to resign. Even so, although both parties decide to call the decision to quit "voluntary" even though it is initiated by the employer, it is legally considered a discharge.

Traditionally, employee-employer relations were "at-will," which meant that either party could terminate the employment relationship for any reason and at any time without providing advance notice to the other party. In recent years, however, an increasing number of employees have initiated wrongful discharge lawsuits against their employers. Although no federal statute governs this area, many states have created employee protection legislation. Discriminatory discharge, which includes discharge for union activity, or because of race, color, religion, sex, or national origin, is prohibited under the Civil Rights Act of 1964.

Under contract theory, opportunities to recover damages, particularly for rank-and-file employees, are limited. If the employee bases the claim solely on the contract, the employee can only recover damages based on employee compensation; the employee cannot recover damages for the emotional distress suffered as a result of the job loss. Moreover, contract-based damage awards may be insufficient even to pay the plaintiff's legal expenses. Most states permit the recovery of damages for emotional distress in common law retaliatory discharge cases. Some states recognize discharge in violation of public policy as an intentional tort, for which emotional distress damages are usually available. For example, *Cagle v. Burns & Roe* (1986).

Nevertheless, the discharged employees frequently seek relief under a breach of contract theory, which is a cause of action now recognized by 34 states. Such claims are usually based on an employee handbook, personnel policy, or some other document that creates the terms of a binding contract. In one of the earliest cases to recognize this theory, the Michigan Supreme Court held that a employee manual stating that it was company policy to discharge only for just cause created a contractual term binding the employer. In other cases, courts have found contractual protection for employees because of promises made at the time of hire. [*Toussaint v. Blue Cross & Blue Shield* (1980)] Merely a history of good performance reviews and promotions, combined with promises of continued employment, has sometimes led courts to grant contract protection for employees. [*Kestenbaum v. Pennzoil Co.* (1988), *Cleary v. American Airlines, Inc.* (1980)]

See also **Employee Handbook; Exit Interview; Personnel Policy; Termination; Wrongful Discharge.**

EMPLOYER Generally, a person, association, or corporation that employs workers. In a small company, the employer is frequently the owner and manager. In a large organization, the functions of the employer are divided among the foreman, manager, president, and stockholders.

In the labor-management field, the term *employer* is generally confined to the meaning in a particular statute, and legislators provide different definitions to meet their objectives. The Labor-Management Relations Act of 1947 (the Taft-Hartley Act) modified Section 2 of the National Labor Relations Act (NLRA) to include within the definition of employer "any person acting as an agent of an employer." These provisions permit the term employer to refer to both actions that are implicitly authorized and, more important, actions that are within the "apparent authority" of the actor. Thus an employer may be held responsible for the actions of one of his supervisors—even if the action was unauthorized—as long as the supervisor was acting within the scope of his or her duty. An employer may escape liability for isolated or sporadic instances of antiunion conduct by his supervisors, though, as long as the employer has not approved the conduct.

The NLRA does not apply to the following groups of employers: the federal government or any wholly owned government corporation or any federal reserve bank, any state or political division of a state, employers subject to the Railway Labor Act, and labor organizations, except when they act as employers.

See also **Labor Organization; Labor-Management Relations Act of 1947; National Labor Relations Act; Supervisor; Railway Labor Act.**

EMPLOYER-EMPLOYEE RELATIONSHIP The relationship that exists in, or arises out of, the employment of employees by an employer. The term has been used synonymously with labor-management relations, industrial relations, and labor relations. However, the term "industrial relations" is customarily used to describe a formal, organized relationship resulting from collective bargaining, while the term employer-employee relations is applied to all employment relationships, whether with organized or unorganized employees. Also, the employer-employee relationship occasionally is defined as the contractual agreement of the employer with the individual employee, as distinguished from the relationship with the union through the collective bargaining agreement.

Until the New Deal era, the employer traditionally managed the workplace with relatively little government regulation. The law pertaining to the employer-employee relationship has evolved over the past century to reflect changing legal, social, and economic conditions. Most of these reforms have led in the direction of equalizing rights between employers and employees. The employment relationship became increasingly subject to statutory regulation, including the areas of minimum wages, maximum hours, workplace safety, and discrimination.

See also **Collective Bargaining; Collective Bargaining Agreement; Employee; Employer; Labor-Management Relations.**

EMPLOYMENT CONTRACT The relationship between employee and employer derives from the relationship between servant and master in English common law. And like the master-servant relationship, the relationship between employer and employee is contractual. Whether an employment contract exists depends on whether the three elements of a contract are present: offer, acceptance, and consideration. The usual "offer" is found in the employer's express or implied promise to pay for services. "Acceptance" may be either the act of working or a promise to perform services. "Consideration" is provided by wages and by the benefit flowing from the services.

The employee-employer relationship may be created by express contract, but need not be; it may also be created by conduct showing that the parties recognize that one is the employer or master and the other is employee or servant. Generally, a master is a person who controls or has the right to control the details of the work of another person engaged in providing services for the master. Whether a particular person is the master of another becomes important when the other person commits a tort. A master may be liable to third parties for a servant's torts under the doctrine of respondeat superior. This liability is not based upon fault or agency, but rather on the public policy that a business enterprise should not be able to disclaim responsibility for actions that may fairly be said to be characteristic of its own activities. Courts have sometimes admitted as evidence of the master-servant relationship the fact that one performs services for another. Also, when a person is found in possession of property of another, using it in the service of the owner, he or she is presumed to be the servant of the owner.

Modern contract law offers employees some protection against wrongful discharge. Historically, employees were deemed to have no rights under an implied contract of employment because there was no "mutuality of obligation." This doctrine, however, has generally been repudiated. In determining the terms of an oral or an implied contract, courts look to the intent and expectations of the parties. Another contractual remedy available to wrongfully discharged employees is the implied covenant of good faith and fair dealing. Although only a few states currently recognize this claim, it is attractive from the employee's perspective because the employee may receive compensatory and punitive damages.

Both unions and employers may now pursue allegations of breach of contract in state and federal courts under Section 301 of the National Labor Relations Act . [*Textile Workers Union v. Lincoln Mills of Alabama* (1957)] Before the section was added as an amendment to the Labor-Management Relations Act of 1947 (also known as the Taft-Hartley Act), employers found it difficult to sue in state courts because the collective bargaining agreement was commonly regarded as a gentleman's agreement rather than a court-enforceable contract, and because the court often insisted that unions, as voluntary unincorporated associations, must be sued in the name of each individual member—a daunting task. Section 301, which made collective bargaining agreements enforceable in the federal courts, was prompted by congressional concern that unions were acting irresponsibly and often in violation of their collectively negotiated contract provisions. Ironically, as in the Lincoln Mills case, it was unions who have used this provision successfully by insisting that unwilling employers proceed to arbitration when there is a Section 301 dispute over the meaning of the collective bargaining agreement. Indeed, most of the actions on the enforcement of agreements have been brought by unions, mainly because they are actions to employ arbitration or to enforce an arbitrator's award. [*United Steelworkers of America v. American Manufacturing* (1960); *United Steelworkers of America v. Warrior & Gulf Navigation Co.* (1960); and *United Steelworkers of America v. Enterprise Wheel & Car Corp.* (1960)]

In addition to contractual rights, the notion of property rights in employment has emerged. Before the Industrial Revolution, most workers aspired to be self-employed, and time spent as an apprentice or employee of another was a step towards independence. Even in the nineteenth century, a worker who lost a job might have been able to survive by working a plot of land. But in today's urban environment the loss of a job can be catastrophic. The contemporary law on employer-employee relationship, while based on the common law, reflects modern realities. No possession recognized by today's courts as property is more important to the average citizen than his or her job.

Property rights in public sector jobs are established by a state law creating a term of office or establishing specific laws for which a public employee may be discharged, or through an express or implied contract providing protection from arbitrary dismissal. For example, a tenured faculty member at a public school, college, or university has a constitutionally protected property right because tenure is a promise of continued employment. If, however, an employee is provisional, probationary, or untenured, he or she does not have a property right in the employment.

See also **Apprentice; Employee; Employer; Employer-Employee Relationship; Grievance Arbitration; Property Rights; Wrongful Discharge.**

EMPLOYMENT TERMINATION MODEL ACT (1991)

Beginning in the second half of the nineteenth century, and continuing for nearly a century, the American rule was that absent a fixed-term employment contract, employers "may dismiss their employees at will for good cause, for no cause, or even for a morally wrong cause." [*Payne v. Western & A.R.R.* (1884)] Over the past two decades, however, 40 of the 50 states have approved modifications in the employment-at-will doctrine. By the 1980s, most states had recognized at least one of three theories supporting a cause of action for wrongful discharge: tort, breach of an expressed or implied contract, and more rarely, breach of the implied covenant of good faith and fair dealing. The tort claim usually involves a discharge in violation of an established public policy, e.g., the employer fires an employee for refusing to commit perjury or engage in a price-fixing conspiracy for the employer. Contract breaches occur when an employer dismisses an employee despite an oral assurance of job security at the time of hiring or a policy statement in an employee manual that discipline will only be imposed for good cause.

The Employment Termination Model Act, drafted by the Uniform Law Commission, is a compromise. Employees are granted an expanded substantive right (that is, an actual as opposed to a procedural right) to "just cause" protections against discharge. This right cannot be waived except by an individually executed agreement guaranteeing the employee a minimum schedule of graduated severance payments, depending on length of service. At the same time, the range of available remedies is sharply limited to reinstatement, with or without back pay, and severance pay when reinstatement is not feasible. Compensatory and punitive damages are eliminated. Because of this latter provision, attorneys' fees are allowed a prevailing plaintiff. If they were not, practically no rank-and-file worker could obtain legal representation except on a pro bono basis. The new statutory right of action also abolishes several subsidiary tort claims. Finally, the preferred method of enforcement is arbitration managed by appropriate state administrative agencies, instead of litigation, the former method being a speedier, less formal, more expert, and less expensive procedure.

The model act is intended, in part, to protect employers from the uncertainties of wrongful discharge case law. Current wrongful discharge litigation is so unpredictable that several states are seriously considering the model act. At least 14 states have drafted or considered legislation in this area, and many more are likely to follow suit. Those who support the act believe that it will not only improve the law but also minimize the differences that now exist in the different state laws. Many observers believe that consistency in the state laws, particularly on the substantive rights of employees, will help both employees and employers, since their mutual rights or obligations would be more uniform and predictable.

The act also establishes just-cause discharge guidelines. Employees may be terminated for "good cause," including technological changes and reductions in business. For the first time, however, employers may be required to prove that these justifications are based on legitimate business conditions.

See also **Back Pay; Employee; Employee Handbook; Employer; Employment-at-Will; Employment Contract; Reinstatement; Tort; Wrongful Discharge.**

EMPLOYMENT TESTING Any performance measure used as a basis for any employment decision. Employment testing includes all formal scored, quantified, or standardized techniques of assessing job suitability, including specific qualifying or disqualifying personnel history or background requirements, specific educational or work history requirements, scored interviews, biographical information forms, interviewer's rating scales, and scored application forms. Employment testing also refers to any written employment tests used to hire, transfer, promote, train, refer, or retain employees are governed by the statutes, case law, and administrative regulations prohibiting discrimination.

The U.S. Supreme Court sanctions standardized testing procedures, stating that "far from disparaging job qualifications as such, Congress has made such qualifications the controlling factor, so that race, religion, nationality, and sex become irrelevant. What Congress has commanded is that any such tests used must measure the person for the job and not the person in the abstract." [*Griggs v. Duke Power Co.* (1971)]

Standardized testing can help implement nondiscriminatory personnel policies. Discriminatory testing, however, is prohibited by federal civil rights law. General ability or intelligence tests that have a disproportionate impact upon groups protected by Title VII of the Civil Rights Act of 1964, in hiring, transfer, assignment, or promotion, violate Title VII unless they have a demonstrable relationship to successful performance of the job for which they are used. Tests assessing the physical skills of job applicants have been upheld when no disproportionate impact upon a protected group is shown and when the tests are proved to be job related. Where sex discrimination is alleged in tests for physical skills, courts will examine closely the defense of business necessity. In some cases, the courts have required employers to seek alternative means of selection.

See also **Civil Rights Act of 1964; Discrimination in Employment; *Griggs v. Duke Power Co.*; Sex Discrimination in Employment.**

EMPLOYMENT-AT-WILL

The common law at-will employment doctrine states that in the absence of an express contract to the contrary, an employee may be terminated for no cause or for any cause without the employer being legally liable. Even if the cause for termination were morally corrupt, there would be no liability. The doctrine also allows the employee to quit for any reason, in the absence of contract terms to the contrary, without being legally liable to the employer. Most often, the doctrine operates against the interest of the employee, because it grants the employer absolute discretion (except as otherwise limited by law) over terms and conditions of employment.

The employment-at-will doctrine became part of nineteenth-century American case law as the United States became increasingly industrialized. It was based on both the socioeconomic climate of the era and the legal emphasis on freedom of contract. Under traditional American common law, when an employment relationship was not based on a contract that expressly defined a term of employment, employment was presumed to be at the will of each party and terminable by either party without notice and for any or no cause. There were some early exceptions to this rule. If, for instance, the employment extended beyond the first year, the relationship was presumed to be renewed for an additional year. This exception to the doctrine helped avoid the injustices that could result in an agrarian society if the employer or the employee were allowed to capriciously terminate the relationship. Since the New Deal era, the courts have increasingly regulated an employer's right to discharge an employee at will. On the federal level, the National Labor Relations Act of 1935, also known as the Wagner Act, limited the scope of the discharge right by forbidding employers to discharge employees engaged in union activities. However, employees without a union were not protected.

Although the common law employment-at-will doctrine remains the basis of employment in many states, it has been limited by both statutory and judicial exceptions. Most state legislatures, Congress, and most state courts have imposed varying limits on the employer's right to discharge at will. On the federal level, statutory limitations to the at-will doctrine include Title VII (included in the Civil Rights Act of 1991), the Americans with Disabilities Act, the Age Discrimination in Employment Act, and the Fair Labor Standards Act. Many states have similar statutory protections for union membership, military service, political activity, and "whistleblowing."

In addition to statutory limitations, limitations have been imposed by the courts, either on tort grounds or on contract grounds. The recognized judicial limitations on employment-at-will include employment contract theories, public policy theories, the implied covenant of good faith and fair dealing, and various tort theories. Many employees allege a tort claim when challenging an at-will discharge because of the limitations placed on contract damages. Possible tort claims include intentional infliction of emotional distress, fraudulent misrepresentations, interference with contractual relations, and wrongful discharge—the most common tort claim. A wrongful discharge claim states that the discharge violated federal or state antidiscrimination statutes, public policy, or an implied covenant of good faith and fair dealing. An employee may allege that an employer fraudulently misrepresented various terms and conditions of employment in addition to misrepresenting job security. While employees often include the tort of intentional emotional distress in lawsuits against employers, these claims are often rejected because the employer's alleged act is not sufficiently "outrageous."

The most common judicial exception to the employment-at-will doctrine is the public policy exception. "Public policy" refers to the legal principle that holds that no citizen can lawfully do that which tends to injure the public or be against the public good. Generally, courts will recognize a public policy exception to the at-will doctrine in a case where an employee's discharge resulted from refusing to commit an unlawful act, exercising a statutory right or privilege, or performing a statutory obligation.

Under traditional contract theory, employees covered by written contracts of employment are protected by the terms of those agreements. An employer who discharges an employee in violation of the contractual terms therefore incurs potential liability. If the contract does not specify a definite term of employment in writing, however, the employee may be discharged at the will of the employer. Most states also recognize the implied contract theory as an exception to the employment-at-will doctrine. This theory is based on a court finding of an implied contract, often on the basis of an employer's policy statements, handouts, employee manuals, or conduct.

The trend in employment law leads away from the employment-at-will doctrine toward greater protection for employees through the increased use of contract, tort, and public policy claims in wrongful discharge suits. However, the present collection of statutes and case law on the subject allows a great disparity in the protections to the workforce and creates confusion. As long as the at-will doctrine exists and the number of workers covered by collective bargaining agreements declines, discharge-related litigation is likely to increase because the courts are increasingly more active in protecting employees from arbitrary or retaliatory dismissal. Also, many state courts are increasingly unwilling to strictly interpret the doctrine and frequently use the exceptions to counter the doctrine's inflexibility. Because litigation is neither efficient nor cost-effective, many states are considering adopting the Model Employment Termination Act to replace the at-will doctrine. Supporters believe that this act, drafted in 1991 by the National Conference of Commissioners on Uniform State Laws, will guarantee fair discharge rights for employees and ensure uniformity in the state law on the discharge of employees. As a general rule, the current law remains that a private employer, unless limited by statute, contract, or the collective bargaining agreement, is free to hire, manage, and fire any employee at will.

See also **Age Discrimination in Employment Act; Americans with Disabilities Act of 1990; Common Law; Employee; Employer; Employment Contract; Fair Labor Standards Act; Freedom of Contract; Job Security; National Labor Relations Act; Tort; Whistleblower.**

EQUAL EMPLOYMENT OPPORTUNITY ACT OF 1972

A federal statute enacted in 1972 amending Title VII of the Civil Rights Act of 1964. The amendment extended the coverage of Title VII to include, among others, state and local governments, educational institutions, employers with 15 and more employees, and labor unions with 15 and more members.

The act makes governments, governmental agencies, and political subdivisions subject to Title VII when they act as either an employer or an employment agency. However, the act stated that Title VII does not apply to the federal government or to religious organizations "with respect to the employment of individuals of a particular religion to perform work connected with the carrying on by such corporation, association, educational institution, or society of its activities."

The amendments empower the Equal Employment Opportunity Commission (EEOC) to seek conciliation agreements or, when it is unable to obtain an agreement, to seek injunctive and other relief in federal district court against an employer, union, employment agency, or joint labor-management committee. In cases involving state or local governments, the attorney general is authorized to bring a lawsuit. The act also requires the EEOC to notify an aggrieved party if a complaint is dismissed, if no complaint is issued, or if the commission does not enter into a conciliation agreement. The EEOC and the Justice Department retain concurrent jurisdiction for two years to settle unlawful employment practice cases. The commission has exclusive jurisdiction after the two-year period.

The act is frequently invoked to secure equal rights for female employees performing the same job as male employees, as well as to eliminate ability tests that discriminate against women and members of minority groups.

See also **Civil Rights Act of 1964; Equal Employment Opportunity Commission.**

EQUAL EMPLOYMENT OPPORTUNITY COMMISSION (EEOC) The major federal agency responsible for enforcing statutes that prohibit employment discrimination. It also promotes voluntary affirmative action programs by employers, unions, and community groups.

Title VII of the Civil Rights Act of 1964 established the EEOC, which is composed of five members appointed by the president. The commission is responsible for the administration and enforcement of Title VII, the Americans with Disabilities Act, the Equal Pay Act, and the Age Discrimination in Employment Act. It has jurisdiction over (1) employers with 15 or more employees for at least 20 calendar weeks in the year in an industry affecting commerce, (2) employment agencies that regularly secure employees for employers covered by the act, (3) state and local employment agencies receiving federal assistance, and (4) labor unions in an industry with 15 or more members or which operate a hiring hall.

Title VII makes the EEOC responsible for preventing the unlawful employment practices set forth in that statute. Under this broad mandate, Congress has given the EEOC the following specific powers and duties: (1) to receive or initiate written charges of alleged discrimination against employers, labor organizations, joint labor-management apprenticeship programs, and employment agencies; (2) to investigate charges received; (3) to order access to evidence; (4) to bring legal action for appropriate temporary or preliminary relief, pending final disposition of a charge; and (5) to determine if there is reasonable cause to believe that a charge is true. The purpose of the EEOC investigation is to give the agency an opportunity to mediate the dispute and to decide whether it should bring a judicial action on behalf of the complainant and other affected persons. The EEOC, in enforcing Title VII, cannot adjudicate claims or impose administrative sanctions. The EEOC attempts to enforce the law through conciliation agreements, but may file its own lawsuit. Most lawsuits, however, are ultimately filed by the charging parties.

After a complaint has been made and a hearing has been held, the agency may investigate and decide questions involving the alleged violation of federal statutes. In 1972, the Civil Rights Act was amended so that the EEOC may bring enforcement actions directly through the federal courts. The procedures for processing employment discrimination complaints under Title VII are the same for the Americans with Disabilities Act, including the procedures for processing retaliation violations.

The EEOC does not have jurisdiction over religious organizations, with respect to employment of persons connected with religious activities, or educational institutions with religious affiliation, on the basis of the religion of these employees.

See also **Affirmative Action; Age Discrimination in Employment Act; Americans with Disabilities Act of 1990; Civil Rights Act of 1964.**

***Equal Employment Opportunity Commission v. Wyoming* (1983)** Public employees were not included in the Age Discrimination in Employment Act (ADEA) when it was originally enacted, but the 1974 amendments expanded the act's coverage to governmental employees. Congress approached these amendments to the ADEA just as it had Title VII of the Civil Rights Act of 1964 two years earlier. State and local governments but not the federal government became covered by the act when the definition of employer was amended to include them. The U.S. Supreme Court upheld the constitutionality of the ADEA's application to states in *EEOC v. Wyoming* (1983). In this case, the state-employer challenged the federal regulation of its employment practices as an interference with the state's sovereignty as articulated in the Tenth Amendment. The court disagreed on the ground that the regulation was not a direct interference with the state's ability to operate its traditional governmental functions and thus Congress was operating within its constitutional authority.

See also **Age Discrimination Act of 1975; Civil Rights Act of 1964.**

Equal Pay Act (EPA) of 1963 A federal statute intended to eliminate differences in pay based solely on sex. The statute prohibits employers from paying wages at a rate less than the rate at which it pays wages to employees of the opposite sex in an establishment for equal work on jobs the performance of which requires equal skill, effort, and responsibility, and which are performed under similar working conditions, except where such payment is made pursuant to (1) a seniority system; (2) a merit system; (3) a system that measures earnings by quantity or quality of production; or (4) a differential based on any other factor other than sex, provided that an employer who is paying a wage rate differential in violation of this subsection shall not, in order to comply with the provisions of this subsection, reduce the wage rate of any employee.

The EPA was the first contemporary employment discrimination statute and was enacted as an amendment to the Fair Labor Standards Act (FLSA). The EPA covers the same groups of individual employees, private employers, and government employers as does the FLSA. The EPA was amended in 1972 to cover executive, administrative, and professional employees, all of whom remain exempt from the FLSA's minimum wages and overtime requirements. The EPA applies to all employers with two or more employees.

Currently, the statute is interpreted to mean that an employer may not discriminate against an individual in compensation because of race, religion, sex, or national origin. To prevail in a lawsuit, the plaintiff must establish that (1) the work occurred at the same establishment; (2) there was unequal pay; (3) the disparity in pay was on the basis of sex; and (4) the men and women involved performed equal work. It is not necessary to prove intent to discriminate. [*Sinclair v. Auto Club of Oklahoma* (1984)] The Third Circuit declared that "equal" means "substantially equal," not "identical," and all the circuits to consider this issue have adopted this standard. [*Schultz v. Wheaton Glass Co.* (1981)] The substantially equal test requires that jobs share a common core of tasks, that is, a significant portion of the two jobs must be identical. No more precise test or percentage requirement has emerged. To help determine when jobs share this core, Congress, in drafting the EPA, specifically chose the concepts of skill, effort, responsibility, and wage structures among a wide range of very different jobs. The courts have construed the EPA's equal work requirement as applying only to jobs within a group of jobs with similar duties and responsibilities.

The EPA was initially administered by the U.S. Department of Labor but has been enforced by the Equal Employment Commission (EEOC) since 1979. An employee may file a claim with the EEOC, which must bring a lawsuit within two years of the violation (three years if the violation was willful). Or an employees may bring a private lawsuit. But once the employee files a complaint with the EEOC, he or she may not bring a private lawsuit unless the EEOC does not pursue the case. Employees who win may be reinstated or promoted and receive double back and attorneys' fees and court costs. The court can order the employer to halt the practice and impose a fine of up to $10,000. For subsequent and willful offenses, the fine may be greater and a prison sentence imposed.

See also **Equal Employment Commission; Fair Labor Standards Act; Seniority.**

EQUAL PAY FOR EQUAL WORK The principle that job rates should not be dependent upon factors unrelated to quantity or quality of work, such as race, sex, and other similar factors.

Employers are prohibited from paying discriminatory wages or salaries by several federal and state job discrimination laws. Private and public employers are prohibited from committing "compensation" discrimination based on race, color, religion, sex, and national origin under Title VII of the Civil Rights Act of 1964; based on age under the Age Discrimination in Employment Act; and based on disability under the Americans with Disabilities Act. Though most claims involving sex discrimination in pay are brought under both the Equal Pay Act and Title VII, there are substantive, procedural, and remedial differences in the statutes that should be considered in determining whether to sue under one or both of these acts and in formulating a successful defense under each statute.

See also **Age Discrimination in Employment Act of 1967; Americans with Disabilities Act of 1990; Civil Rights Act of 1964; Equal Pay Act of 1963.**

EQUAL PROTECTION Though similar to substantive due process, the two concepts are not completely identical. Equal protection scrutiny is used in judicial analysis even when no liberty or property interest can be established. If state action discriminates based on suspect classes (such as race or national origin), or discriminates based on fundamental rights (which is essentially the same concept as liberty interests under substantive due process analysis), the government must have a compelling state interest to justify the discrimination. [*Loving v. Virginia* (1967)] Classifications based on gender are subject to an "intermediate standard of review." The Supreme Court in *Craig v. Boren* (1981) defined this standard as follows: "Classifications by gender must serve important government objectives and must be substantially related to achievement of those objectives." [*U.S. Railroad Retirement Board v. Fritz* (1980)] When no suspect classification or exercise of fundamental rights is involved, the state is required to show only a "rational relation" to a legitimate purpose in order to justify disparate treatment.

Homosexual orientation is considered a suspect classification and the courts are increasingly finding no rational basis for considering sexual orientation in employment, including the hiring of public school teachers. [*Jantz v. Muci* (1991)] The courts have applied this protection to federal employees. In one case, an employee of a White House contractor fired for homosexuality was entitled to recover on the basis of equal protection unless the government can show a rational basis for the termination. [*Swift v. United States* (1986)] One of the most controversial equal protection employment issues involves homosexuals in the military. Some courts have held that army regulations prohibiting reenlistment of homosexual soldiers violate equal protection, especially in jurisdictions where discrimination against homosexuals is recognized as creating a suspect class. [*Watkins v. U.S. Army* (1989)] Other courts, however, have ruled that the army may justify its policy of discharging gay service members under the equal protection rational basis standard. [*Pruitt v. Cheny* (1991)]

See also **Discrimination in Employment; Disparate Treatment Discrimination; Sexual Orientation; Substantive Due Process Rights.**

ERISA

See **Employee Retirement Income Security Act of 1974.**

Escalator Clause

See **Cost of Living Adjustment.**

Escape Clause

See **Maintenance of Membership.**

Espinoza v. Farah Manufacturing (1973)

In this case, the U.S. Supreme Court held that Title VII of the Civil Rights of the 1964 does not forbid discrimination against job applicants on the basis of citizenship, as opposed to national origin. Therefore, citizenship requirements will generally be sustained under the act. The court distinguishes between citizenship and national origin for Title VII analysis. However, an employment action based on citizenship may be national origin discrimination if the employer's *intent* is to discriminate based on national origin or if there is an adverse effect on a group of individuals of a certain national origin.

On the basis of a long-standing antialien hiring policy, Farah Manufacturing Company rejected the employment application of a lawfully admitted resident alien who remained a Mexican citizen. The Supreme Court rejected Espinoza's national origin discrimination allegation, holding that Espinoza was denied employment on the basis of citizenship, not national origin. Citing the legally approved policy of excluding noncitizens from federal jobs, the Court reasoned that this policy could be reconciled with Title VII's prohibition against national origin discrimination only if citizenship and national origin were conceptually different. Based on this analysis, the Court concluded that Congress did not intend to prohibit discrimination based on citizenship under Title VII. Even though the Court distinguished between the concepts of citizenship and national origin, it did so cautiously, emphasizing that "there may be many situations where discrimination on the basis of citizenship would have the effect of discriminating on the basis of national origin."

In *Espinoza*, the Fifth Circuit held that a private employer's failure to hire an applicant because she is not a U.S. citizen did not fall within the prohibition of Title VII against employment discrimination on the basis of national origin. The Supreme Court agreed on this point but observed that a citizenship requirement might violate Title VII if it was "but one part of a wider scheme of unlawful national origin discrimination" or had "the purpose or effect of discriminating on the basis of national origin." The *Espinoza* decision was relied on in *Guerra v. Manchester Terminal Corporation* (1974), a case involving denial of job preferences and fringe benefits to Mexican nationals who maintained their families in Mexico.

Espinoza was decided before the Immigration Reform and Control Act (IRCA) was enacted in 1986. IRCA made it an unfair immigration-related employment practice for an employer or other entity to discriminate against any individual other than an unauthorized alien in hiring, recruitment, or referral for employment, or to discriminatory discharge an individual because of the individual's citizenship. However, IRCA does prohibit citizenship discrimination if citizenship is required by statute, regulation, executive order, or a government contract, or if the attorney general has determined that citizenship is essential for an employer to work with any agency of any level of government. Furthermore, any employer may hire, recruit, or refer a U.S. citizen or national over an alien if the applicants are equally qualified. The U.S. Supreme Court held that aliens were included in a special class of "employees" because of the breadth of the term "individual." Although not specifically stated by the Court, the reliance on the terms "individual" and "employee" in the Court's decision implies that there are certain rights that belong to a person with the status of an employee, separate from rights and protections associated with citizenship. A special, protected status for employees is also suggested by the fact that most labor laws, including Title VII, cover employees but exclude other workers, such as independent contractors or volunteers.

See also **Civil Rights Act of 1964; Immigration Reform and Control Act.**

EXCLUSIVITY Also known as exclusive representation, exclusivity is the right acquired by an employee organization to be the sole representative of all employees in the bargaining unit. Most collective bargaining statutes in the United States provide for exclusivity. A labor organization becomes certified as exclusive representative by an agency such as the National Labor Relations Board or the Federal Labor Relations Authority if it has been selected as the bargaining agent by a majority of the employees constituting an appropriate unit in a secret ballot election.

See also **Collective Bargaining: Duty of Fair Representation; National Labor Relations Board.**

EXECUTIVE ORDER 10988 Executive Order 10988, issued by President John F. Kennedy on January 17, 1962, dealt with employee-management cooperation in the federal service. It provided the mechanisms for determining bargaining representation and forms of recognition for employees. It also established the means in the U.S. Department of Labor and the U.S. Civil Service Commission to give technical assistance to federal agencies in carrying out the provisions of this order. It was superseded by Executive Order 11491 in 1969.

EXECUTIVE ORDER 11491 An order issued in 1969 by President Richard M. Nixon. It revised Executive Order 10988, issued by President John F. Kennedy in 1962, which established the first government labor relations program by extending limited collective bargaining rights to federal employees.

See also **Collective Bargaining.**

EXEMPT EMPLOYEE An employee who is not subject to the provisions of the Fair Labor Standards Act (FLSA). For the most part, employees whose compensation is based on an annual sum, rather than on an hourly rate, are considered exempt employees. The minimum wage and overtime pay provisions of the FLSA do not apply to any employee who is an executive, administrator, professional, or outside salesman.

Whether an employer is exempt under the FLSA's so-called white-collar exemption is determined by the employee's actual work activities, not by an employer's characterization of those activities through a job title, job description, or other formality, or by the nature of the employer's business.

A "primary duty" rule applies to the exemption for executives, administrators, and professionals. Regarding executives, this rule means that an employee will not qualify for the exemption unless his or her duties are managerial. Likewise, an administrator's primary duties must be "administrative" and a professional's primary duties must be "professional." The level of discretion an employee is allowed and the amount of time the employee devotes to these duties are both crucial factors in determining an employee's primary duty.

See also **Fair Labor Standards Act.**

EXHAUSTION OF REMEDIES Federal labor policy requires, under the exhaustion of contractual remedies policy, that individual employees wishing to assert contract grievances attempt to use the contract grievance procedure negotiated by employer and union to redress grievances. [*Alexander v. Gardner-Denver* (1974); *Republic Steel Corp. v. Maddox* (1965)] Regardless of any other circumstances, an employee may not assert that an employer has repudiated a grievance procedure until he has attempted to use that procedure. Section 101(a)(4) of the National Labor Relations Act (NLRA) states that a union member may be required to exhaust all union remedies. However, an employee may attempt to argue that he is not covered by the procedure.

The duty to exhaust contractual remedies before bringing a lawsuit under Section 301 of the NLRA also applies to unions. [*National Post Office Mail Handlers v. U.S. Postal Service* (1979)] Exhaustion of contractual remedies is not required where the employer's conduct amounts to repudiation of the contract. [*Vaca v. Sipes* (1967)] However, an employer's decision to lay off an employee and subsequent refusal to reinstate him or her as required under the collective bargaining agreement did not constitute repudiation of the grievance procedure.

The employer's obligation to exhaust contractual remedies depends on whether the employer has the right to invoke the grievance procedure, which is oriented toward resolution of employee grievances. In addition, an employer is not required to exhaust contractual grievance procedures before bringing suit against a union if the union repudiates its obligations under that agreement. [*California Trucking Association v. Brotherhood of Teamsters & Auto, Truck Drivers* (1981)]

See also **Collective Bargaining Agreement; Grievance; National Labor Relations Act.**

EXIT INTERVIEW

A crucial component of the employee termination process, the exit interview should be conducted by the personnel manager or assistant personnel manager, and it should inform the employee of the type of personal reference he or she can expect. The latter is crucial. Lawsuits claiming libel, slander, invasion of privacy, and "intentional infliction of emotional distress" have occurred because former employees have been surprised by what the former employer said in a reference.

Many firms ask their employees to sign a consent form authorizing the company to grant a designated type of reference. The consent forms often contain an outline of what will be included in a personal reference. For example, it might indicate that the company will report that the employee did satisfactory work but was discharged for excessive absenteeism.

Most firms will discuss with the employee any vested pension plan rights, continued fringe benefits, or other financial considerations. Many companies paying to extend health insurance benefits beyond what is required by law, even in cases of discharge for cause. This relatively simple act may be more effective than any other in causing employees to believe he or she is being treated fairly. The premiums paid for the extended insurance are insignificant compared with the potential expense of a lawsuit. Many employers also voluntarily grant a modest severance pay, especially to longer-term employees, even if the discharge is for cause. Often firms ask the employee to express any concerns or complaints, which allows him or her the opportunity of complaining without filing a legal complaint or lawsuit, and the exit interviewer may learn about problems that were not previously known by the personnel department.

See also **Benefits; Employees, Dismissal of; Pension; Termination.**

Factory Laws When industrial production began in Europe and the United States, employers adopted in the newly established factories hours common to agriculture and handicraft production. Men, women, and children labored at their machines 12, 14, and even 16 hours a day. Soon, the injurious effects of such work periods became evident, particularly with regard to women and children. It may have been appropriate for people to work extended hours in the healthy environment of farms or even in leisurely handicraft shops, but it was quite inappropriate for them to be confined indoors on unhealthful, wearing, high-speed machine production. So by the late nineteenth century, Germany had a government-administered insurance system for sickness and industrial accidents (the first version of workers' compensation statutes) as well as old age pensions, child labor laws, and condition of labor laws. The United States lagged behind most of the rest of the industrialized world in adopting similar legislation.

American political Progressives of the nineteenth and early twentieth century, influenced by German thought and practice, sought to improve workplace conditions. In 1842, Massachusetts limited the factory hours of children under 12 years of age to 10 hours a day and in 1867 limited the weekly hours of children under 15 to 60 hours. In New York, factory work by women was limited to 60 hours, and night work was abolished in 1905. In both England (1909) and Massachusetts (1912), minimum wage statutes and labor agencies were established. By 1923, 16 other states had adopted similar measures. Progressive state administrations passed workers' compensation laws to force employers to assist those who were injured at their work. Employers became increasingly aware of industrial safety issues; nonetheless, safety statutes were necessary to ensure uniform compliance.

Additional state statutes were enacted to safeguard women workers in industry, to prohibit child labor, to assist mothers with dependent children who lacked other means of support, and to provide pensions for the aged. State laws prohibited company stores and payment in scrip, and adopted measures to facilitate and secure the payment of wages such as lien, stockholder liability, pay-period, and hours laws. Various states also enacted corporate insolvency statutes that conferred a preference on workers' wages. But even American experiments with social security statutes were still insignificant compared to the advances in other industrial countries.

The factory laws were a set of labor statutes that attempted to relieve poverty by ending the era when employers could offer whatever wages they pleased. Maximum-hours laws were first enacted to protect children and women, and women were also the first beneficiaries of minimum wage laws. Trades particularly dangerous to health became increasingly regulated by maximum-hours law. A New York statute limiting bakers to ten hours a day was challenged on the constitutional issue of freedom of contract. [*Lochner v. New York* (1905)] Employers argued that if an employee wished to make a contract to work more than the statutory ten hours, his freedom as well as the employer's was violated by the state statute. In 1905, the U.S. Supreme Court upheld this view and declared the New York statute invalid. In 1908, however, the Court upheld the Oregon law limiting women to ten hours per day. [*Muller v. Oregon* (1908)] Many states subsequently passed hours statutes and a few adopted wage laws for women and prohibited child labor.

Enforcement of the factory laws was not rigorous, and the federal courts quickly constructed new constitutional barriers against them. Furthermore, progressive state laws placed any state that adopted them in an unfavorable competitive position. When New York, for example, outlawed child labor or sweatshops, many employers moved to New Jersey. Some states, particularly in the South, eagerly invited "runaway" companies to escape the social legislation and higher labor costs of the progressive states. For this reason, many Progressives who were successful in their own states turned to the federal government for assistance.

The American Federation of Labor (AFL) frequently criticized many Progressive-era (1900–1914) labor statutes and social and industrial "reform legislation." Samuel Gompers, president of the federation, condemned this legislation as ensnaring labor in webs of "superlegalism" like those spun by injunction judges. This approach exemplifies the Gompers-led AFL abandonment of the republican rights approach of the Gilded Age labor movement in favor of a liberal, laissez-faire approach of protest and reform.

See also **Child Labor Laws; Freedom of Contract; Hours;** ***Lochner v. New York*** **(1905); Minimum Wage; Pensions; Workers' Compensation.**

FAIR EMPLOYMENT PRACTICE LAWS Federal, state, and municipal statutes and ordinances designed to prohibit employers from discriminating in the hiring of employees because of race, color, religion, sex, or national origin. Typically, they allow an employee who has been discriminated against by his or her employer to file a complaint with a certain administrative agency. After investigating the complaint, the agency may, if the facts warrant, conduct a hearing. If the evidence shows that the employer has engaged in a practice prohibited by the statute, the agency issues a cease and desist order, an enforceable order that is subject to judicial review.

There is a notable lack of case law on fair employment practices legislation. The administrative agencies charged with enforcing these statutes frequently attribute this situation to employer cooperation and employee willingness to accept administrative rulings without demanding court review. Their validity, it seems, has been assumed by contemporary courts.

The U.S. Supreme Court has long held that the right to work for a living in the common occupations of the community constitutes the very essence of the personal freedom and opportunity protected by the Fourteenth Amendment. [*Traux v. Raich* (1915)] The Supreme Court later held that fair employment practices laws are constitutional in *Railway Mail Association v. Corsi* (1945). In this case, the New York statute prohibiting labor organizations from discriminating by reason of race, or color, or creed in the admission of members was held not to violate either the due process or equal protection clauses of the Fourteenth Amendment. The Court said that a judicial holding that fair employment practices laws violated the Fourteenth Amendment would distort the policy behind that amendment, which was adopted to prevent state legislation designed to perpetuate discrimination on the basis of race or color. Furthermore, the Court said there was no constitutional basis for finding that a state could not protect workers from discrimination solely on the basis of race, color, or creed by an organization operating under the protection of the state. Justice Felix Frankfurter, in his concurring opinion, wrote that "a state may choose to put its authority behind one of the cherished aims of American feeling by forbidding indulgence in racial or religious prejudice to another's hurt. To use the Fourteenth Amendment as a sword against such State power would stultify that Amendment."

The Civil Rights Act of 1964, through Section 1104 of Title XI, provides that nothing contained in any title of the act shall be construed as indicating an intent of Congress to occupy the field and preempt state laws on the same subject; nor shall any provision of the act be interpreted as invalidating any state statute unless that state law is inconsistent with the purposes or any provision of the act.

The states perceived a need to prohibit certain types of discriminatory conduct by employers. All but four states now have some form of fair employment practices statute or civil rights statute that forbid certain types of employment discrimination. Many cities also have some type of fair employment practice law. Many states extend greater protection against discrimination to their citizens than is available under federal law. Because of the specific limitations placed on federal agencies by the U.S. Supreme Court in the case of *Espinoza v. Farah Manufacturing Co.* (1973), states cannot rely on these agencies in defending their citizens against forms of discrimination not specified by Congress. Consequently, many states use their legislative powers to offer their citizens greater protection that is often more comprehensive or broader than federal law and to require that an employer meet the more rigorous state requirements. Some states, however, have fewer protections. Alabama and Mississippi have no comprehensive fair employment practice statutes for private employers and no fair employment agencies.

See also **Cease and Desist Order; Civil Rights Act of 1964; Due Process; Equal Protection; *Espinoza v. Farah Manufacturing Co.***

FAIR LABOR STANDARDS ACT (FLSA) (1938)

A major labor relations statute intended to eliminate "labor conditions detrimental to the maintenance of the minimum standards of living necessary for health, efficiency, and well-being of workers." The FLSA establishes wage, hour, and employment standards that affect most workers in the United States. These standards include those that set minimum wages, overtime compensation, and the age at which children may work. This federal statute, also known as the Wages and Hours Law, was enacted by Congress in 1938 and covers all workers in businesses engaged in interstate commerce or producing goods for interstate commerce. The statute was intended to provide substantive guarantees for these employees by providing minimum standards below which workers should not fall.

The FLSA set up a Wage and Hour Division in the Department of Labor. The new division appointed a committee to determine proper rates of pay for various industries. The statute also established a maximum of 44 working hours a week for the first year, 42 hours for the next, and 40 thereafter. Similarly, minimum wages of 25 cents per hour for the first year, 30 for the second, and 40 for the ensuring six years were mandated. Employees were entitled to time and a half pay if they worked overtime.

The statute has been amended several times to increase the minimum wage. As of 1996, the minimum wage is $ 4.75 and will increase to $5.15 in 1997. State legislatures have enacted their own wage and hour statutes. Sometimes their minimum wage exceeds federal requirements, and some of these state statutes cover employees who are not under the jurisdiction of the FLSA.

See also **Minimum Wage.**

Fair Representation See **Duty of Fair Representation.**

Fair Share The amount of a nonmember's compensation that he or she is compelled to contribute to a union to support its collective bargaining activities. The fair share arrangement, frequently justified on the basis that the union is required to represent all employees fairly, is specified in the collective bargaining agreement.

See also **Agency Shop; Collective Bargaining; Collective Bargaining Agreement; Maintenance of Membership.**

***Fall River Dyeing and Finishing Corp. v. NLRB* (1987)** A textile dyeing and finishing plant began having financial difficulties, which led it to lay off all of its production employees. It disposed of most of its assets and hired a professional liquidator to sell the rest. Before this was completed, a former employee and a former customer formed a partnership and purchased the remaining assets and inventory. The company then advertised for employees and supervisors. Its initial hiring goal was 50 to 60 workers. The company hired 21 employees,

18 of whom had been with the original firm. The union that had represented the workers with the original firm demanded recognition. Eventually, the new company had 55 employees, 36 of whom had been with the original firm. The new company refused to bargain with the union, claiming that it was not a "successor employer." Under the concept of successorship, if a new employer is a legal successor, it has an obligation to bargain with the union representing the former employer's employees. A successor employer, however, has no obligation to set the initial terms and conditions of employment. Once an employer's successorship status has been determined, it must bargain with the incumbent union on the same basis as the predecessor employer.

The Supreme Court held that the question of successorship is determined by several factors—namely whether the business of both employers is essentially the same, whether the employees of the new enterprise are performing the same jobs in the same working conditions under the same supervisors, and whether the new entity has the same body of customers. The court enunciated the following test: "[the] . . . emphasis on the employee's perspective furthers the Act's policy of industrial peace. If the employees find themselves in essentially the same jobs after the employer's transition and their legitimate expectation in continued representation by their union are thwarted, their dissatisfaction may lead to labor unrest." Accordingly, the court also noted: "to a substantial extent the applicability of [successorship] . . . rests in the hands of the successor. If the new employer makes a conscious decision to maintain generally the same business and to hire a majority of its employees from the predecessor, then the bargaining obligation of Section 8(a)(5) [the duty imposed by Section 8(a)(5) of the National Labor Relations Act for employers to bargain in good faith] is activated."

A mere decline in jobs and job classifications with a smaller management hierarchy will not undermine a finding of successorship. However, the Court has held that although a successor employer has a duty to recognize the union of the predecessor, the National Labor Relations Board (NLRB) cannot impose the labor contract upon the successor employer, because to do so would contradict the case law instructing the NLRB to avoid imposing contract terms upon labor and management.

In the earlier case of *NLRB v. Burns Security* (1972), the U.S. Supreme Court stated that in some situations: "it may not be clear until the successor employer has hired his full complement of employees that he has a duty to bargain with a union, since it will not be evident until then that the bargaining representatives represent a majority of the employees in the unit." In *Fall River,* however, the court held that a full complement is not essential. Instead, it found that the NLRB's "substantial complement" rule—which fixes the moment when the determination of majority is made—is reasonable in the successorship context.

See also **National Labor Relations Board; Successor Employer.**

FAMILY AND MEDICAL LEAVE ACT (FMLA) OF 1993

Hailed as a significant advance in employee rights, the FMLA is a federal statute intended to allow employees to balance their work and family life by taking reasonable unpaid leave for specified family reasons. It provides that employers with 50 or more employees are required to allow their employees up to 12 weeks of unpaid, job-protected leave per year to take care of a sick child or parent, or because of an employee's own serious health problems. Family/medical leave is unpaid, although the employee may be eligible for sick leave or long-term disability payments and workers compensation benefits under those benefits or insurance plans. The act took effect on August 5, 1993.

The statute specifically applies to employers with at least 50 employees, including government agencies. Employees are considered eligible for leave after at least one year of employment and after having worked at least 1,250 hours. Leaves for up to 12 work weeks may be taken during any 12-month period. The leave may be continuous or, when a serious illness affects the employee, either intermittently or in the form of a reduced schedule. In other cases, flexibility in scheduling leaves must be approved by the employer.

Any eligible employee may take family/medical leave for any of the following reasons: the birth of a son or daughter and to care for the new baby; the placement of a child with the employee for adoption or foster care; to care for a spouse, son, daughter, or parent with a serious health condition; or because of the employee's own serious health condition which prevents the employee from doing his or her job.

A "serious health condition" means any illness, injury, impairment, or physical or mental condition that involves (1) any period of incapacity or treatment in connection with inpatient care (overnight stay) in a hospital, hospice, or residential medical facility; (2) any incapacity requiring absence from work, school, or other regular daily activities of more than three calendar days that also involves continuing treatment by a health care provider; or (3) continuing treatment by a health care provider of a chronic or long-term condition that is incurable or will likely result in incapacity of more than three days if not treated.

The passage of the FMLA resulted from a long and often bitter congressional debate. Earlier family leave legislation had been passed in both 1990 and 1991, but on each occasion Congress was unable to override President George Bush's veto. During the 1992 presidential campaign, however, Governor Bill Clinton strongly supported family leave legislation, and the FMLA was the first significant piece of legislation signed by the new president. FMLA supporters believe that it provides a minimum standard for unpaid leave and that the realities of family life in the 1990s make it a necessary law. Opponents argue that decisions on such benefits are best left to employers and employees, and that the federal mandates established by the FMLA will do more harm than good. Though adhering to the requirements of the FMLA compelled many employers to substantially revise their family leave policies or to develop policies where none existed, employers generally reported no overwhelming positive or negative effects of FMLA compliance. Some employers have complained of added bureaucracy, lower production, and employee attitudes of entitlement resulting from the FMLA.

The U.S. Department of Labor is responsible for investigating alleged violations of the FMLA and for enforcing its provisions. The FMLA includes several provisions designed to ensure employer compliance. Employers cannot interfere with employees' right to exercise their provisions of the FMLA. Nor are they allowed to "discharge or otherwise discriminate" against employees who request or take unpaid leave. If employers violate these prohibitions, they are subject to lawsuits brought by individual employees and by the Department of Labor. Lawsuits must be brought within two years of the alleged violation, unless the violation is deemed willful, in which case, plaintiffs have three years to bring action against an employer.

Protection at the state level is now prevalent as well—some 27 states have enacted comprehensive family leave legislation. The FMLA does not affect any state legislation that provides greater leave benefits, including state laws currently in effect and those that may be passed in the future. The FMLA, however, will supersede state laws that provide lesser benefits than the FMLA.

See also **Workers' Compensation.**

FARM WORKERS

See **Agricultural Workers.**

FARWELL V. BOSTON AND WORCESTER RAILROAD (1842)

In this case, the Massachusetts Supreme Court articulated the principle that employees assume the ordinary risks involved in their employment. The court said that an employee "who engages in the employment of another for the performance of specified duties and services, for compensation, takes upon himself the natural and ordinary risks and perils incident to the performance of such services, and in legal presumption, the compensation is adjusted accordingly."

In other words, by accepting employment, the worker assumed the risk of negligence by fellow servants (or workers). This doctrine, which came to be called the Fellow Servant Rule, was an extension of the common law assumption of risk doctrine. Thus, the nineteenth-century common law rules left the burdens of injuries on the working people who suffered them, regardless of whether they had the ability to avoid the accident, to change the degree of danger, or even to object to the dangerous condition. For several years, the general employer duty to provide a safe workplace became increasingly limited by judicial exceptions and by the legal fiction that the working person was deemed to have assumed the risk in his or her bargaining for the job. It was against this background that modern workers compensation laws were enacted.

See also **Common Law: Employment Doctrines; Fellow Servant Rule; Workers' Compensation.**

FAVORITISM

Action by the employer or supervisor that is based on consideration other than fairness or equity to all employees. Favoritism occurs, for example, when a worker is promoted merely because he or she brings gifts to the supervisor rather than on the basis of objective standards, such as ability, production, qualification for the job, and length of outstanding performance. Favoritism also refers to an unfair labor practice by an employer who declares a preference among rival unions seeking to organize its employees. This action violates Section 8(a)(2) of the National Labor Relations Act because it constitutes interference with the employees right to choose freely which, if any, of the unions they wish to represent them.

Good business practice dictates that an organization's procedures and policies must be administered consistently. Though every disciplinary procedure must provide reasonable flexibility, this discretion must not be influenced by favoritism or discrimination. Disregard for the way similar situations were handled in the past, or the precedent being set for the future, creates inconsistency. Even when it is simply due to oversight, inconsistency tends to resemble discrimination or favoritism.

Compensation systems should be fair and understandable; that is, they must not allow for favoritism and must be free of race, sex, age, and any other form of discrimination.

See also **Discrimination in Employment; National Labor Relations Act.**

FEATHERBEDDING A term applied to those contractual requirements or work rules that employers believe require the employment of more workers than needed for the job and are therefore attempts to enhance safety and ensure quality work. The fear of workers that they might work themselves out of a job is another motivation for featherbedding.

Section 8(b)(6) of the National Labor Relations Act (NLRA) makes it an unfair labor practice for a union to "cause or attempt to cause an employer to pay or deliver or agree to pay or deliver any money or other thing of value, in the nature of an extraction, for services which are not performed or are not to be performed." The NLRA rule against featherbedding is limited to instances where a labor organization or its agents exact pay from an employer for services not performed or not to be performed. Thus, if the work is actually done by the employees, the provision is not violated. This is so whether or not the employer wants or needs the work, whether or not the persons receiving the payments performed the work, and regardless of the value and usefulness of the work to the employer's business.

The prohibition against featherbedding does not attempt to remedy situations where the work is designed solely to legalize continued payments that, prior to the Taft-Hartley Act, unions had exacted from employers without performing any work. The National Labor Relations Board (NLRB) has emphasized that the proscription against featherbedding is a limited one and as a result, its terms are to be strictly construed. [*American Newspaper Publishers Association v. NLRB* (1953)]

See also **National Labor Relations Act; National Labor Relations Board; Unfair Labor Practice.**

FEDERAL ANTI-INJUNCTION ACT

See **Norris-LaGuardia Act.**

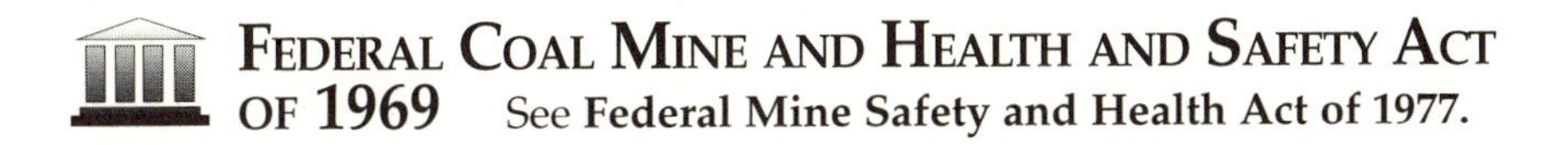

FEDERAL COAL MINE AND HEALTH AND SAFETY ACT OF 1969

See **Federal Mine Safety and Health Act of 1977.**

FEDERAL EMPLOYEES COMPENSATION ACT (1916)

One of two workers' compensation statutes covering federal employees that applies to the civilian federal employees. Enacted in 1916, the statute provides workers' compensation coverage for disability or death due to personal injury sustained while in the performance of duty or to employment-related disease.

The statute established the Federal Employees' Compensation Program, whose mission is to return federal workers to gainful employment through efficient and equitable claims management. The task of the Office of Workers' Compensation Program is to achieve this mission through effective intervention. The impetus to intervene is based chiefly on two assumptions: first, that quick and meaningful intervention, including medical diagnosis, is a critical step in limiting the period or severity of a disability and the time lost from work; and second, that workers with repeated occurrences of disability for extended periods of time can, with constructive, sensible, and sensitive rehabilitation, return to partial or full work roles.

The program in recent years has sought to improve the character and quality of its claims adjudication. It has become increasingly efficient, with little case backlog, and consistently adjudicates cases in a timely manner compared with other state and federal benefit programs. It now emphasizes effective return-to-work process and innovative claims management.

See also **Workers' Compensation.**

Federal Labor Relations Authority (FLRA)

An independent agency, created by Reorganization Plan No. 2 of 1978, that oversees the federal service labor-management relations program. The FLRA administers the statute that protects the right of federal employees to organize, bargain collectively, and participate in decisions affecting them through labor organizations of their own choosing. The FLRA also ensures compliance with the statutory rights and obligations of federal employees and the labor organizations that represent them in their dealings with federal agencies.

The FLRA provides leadership in establishing policies and guidance on federal service labor-management relations program. It determines the appropriateness of bargaining units, supervises or conducts representation elections, resolves the scope of negotiation issues, adjudicates unfair labor practice cases, prescribes criteria for compelling need, resolves exceptions to arbitration disputes, resolves issues on the granting of consultation rights to labor organizations on internal agency policies and government-wide rules and regulations, and establishes policy and guidance for Title VII of the Civil Service Reform Act, which it administers. The three members of the FLRA are appointed by the president and confirmed by the Senate.

The FLRA was established to meet two congressional objectives: to assure impartial adjudication of federal labor-management disputes, and to eliminate the fragmentation of authority in the federal labor relations program. Two major components of the FLRA are the Office of the General Counsel and the Federal Service Impasses Panel. The Impasses Panel is responsible for providing assistance in resolving negotiation impasses between agencies and unions. After investigating an impasse, the panel may either recommend procedures to the parties to resolve the impasse or assist them in resolving it through a variety of methods and procedures, including fact-finding and recommendations. If the parties cannot settle the dispute after assistance by the panel, it may hold hearings and take whatever action is necessary to resolve the impasse.

See also **Civil Service Reform Act of 1978; Grievance Arbitration; Labor-Management Relations; Unfair Labor Practice.**

Federal Labor Union

A local union chartered directly by the American Federation of Labor-Congress of Industrial Organizations (AFL-CIO), usually involving employees over which no affiliated national or international union claims jurisdiction. Historically, a federal labor union has often been a transitional form leading to the organization of a national union. At one time, there were many federal labor unions in the rubber, auto, chemical, and cement industries.

See also **American Federation of Labor-Congress of Industrial Organizations; Jurisdiction.**

FEDERAL MEDIATION AND CONCILIATION SERVICE (FMCS)

An independent agency created under Title II of the Labor-Management Relations Act of 1947 (the Taft-Hartley Act). Title II formalized some of the practices of the U.S. Conciliation Service and gave explicit statutory sanction to the FMCS. The FMCS assumed the function and duties of the U.S. Conciliation Service, which had operated within the U.S. Department of Labor since 1913. The director of the FMCS is appointed by the president and confirmed by the Senate.

Congress has made it federal policy that the settlement of issues between employers and employees through collective bargaining may be advanced by making available the means for conciliation, mediation, and voluntary arbitration through the FMCS. This agency represents the public interest in promoting the development of sound and stable labor-management relationships, preventing or minimizing work stoppages by assisting labor and management to settle their disputes through mediation; advocating collective bargaining, mediation and voluntary arbitration as the preferred processes for settling labor disputes; developing the art, science, and practice of dispute resolution and fostering constructive joint relationships of labor and management leaders to increase their mutual understanding and solution of common problems.

The FMCS helps prevent disruptions in the flow of interstate commerce caused by labor-management disputes by providing mediators to facilitate agreements in collective bargaining disputes in both the private and public sector. The service can intervene on its own motion or at the request of either side. Mediators have no law enforcement authority and rely wholly on persuasive techniques. The service also helps labor and management with the names of qualified third party factfinders or arbitrators who may be used in grievance arbitration. The work of the service is intended to strengthen the national labor-management relations policy favoring collective bargaining and responsible labor-management relations.

Section 8 of the National Labor Relations Act requires that parties to a labor contract file a dispute notice with the service and the appropriate state or local mediation agency, if agreement is not reached 30 days in advance of a contract termination or reopening date. The FMCS is required to avoid mediating disputes that would have only a minor impact on interstate commerce if state or other conciliation services are available to the parties.

The FMCS has the power to: (1) compel parties to arbitrate, to agree to arbitration, or agree to a particular arbitrator; (2) enforce an agreement to arbitrate; (3) influence, alter, or set aside decisions of arbitrators listed on the roster of labor arbitrators; and (4) compel, deny, or modify payment of compensation to an arbitrator. Furthermore, if either party claims that a dispute is not subject to arbitration, the FMCS will not decide the merits of such claim. Thus, neither the submission of a panel nor the appointment of an arbitrator should be construed as anything more than compliance with a request.

See also **Collective Bargaining; Grievance Arbitration; Mediation; National Labor Relations Act.**

FEDERAL MINE SAFETY AND HEALTH ACT OF 1977

The statute that imposed new and more stringent safety and health standards on employers in the mining industry. These standards are similar to those developed by the Occupational Safety and Health Administration under the U.S. Department of Labor.

In drafting the 1977 act, Congress recognized the important role of miners. It declared, in the findings and purpose section of the law, that it could not tolerate the "existence of unsafe and unhealthful conditions and practices in the Nation's coal or other mining industry." The statute further states that "the operators of such mines with the assistance of the miners have the primary responsibility to prevent the existence of such conditions and practices in such mines."

Regulations under the statute may limit a mine operator's ability to implement certain types of technology. Most equipment used in underground coal mines must be approved and certified by the Mine Safety and Health Administration (MSHA). Any change in an approved feature or certified component of a piece of equipment, which could include equipment retrofits, must be approved by the MSHA. Thus, coordination with the MSHA undoubtedly will be required where a coal industry employer wishes to modify certain equipment as a means of fulfilling its reasonable accommodation obligations.

Regulations promulgated under the act require coal operators to reassign miners who have developed pneumoconiosis (black lung disease). Once a miner develops black lung disease, he is classified as a "Part 90" miner with the right to be transferred to a less dusty environment, which may or may not entail transfer to a different job. Unlike disabled employees under the Americans with Disabilities Act, Part 90 miners essentially have an absolute right to transfer to an existing position (assuming the employer cannot maintain lower respirable dust concentrations in the employee's existing work area) with the same pay.

See also **Americans with Disabilities Act of 1990; Occupational Safety and Health Administration.**

FEDERAL-STATE JURISDICTION The division of jurisdiction over labor-management relations between federal and state governments. States are permitted to regulate labor-management issues not controlled by federal law and where state regulations would not interfere with federal labor policy. Federal-state jurisdiction on labor matters is governed by both statute and case law. Section 10(a) of the Labor-Management Relations Act of 1947 (the Taft-Hartley Act) authorized the National Labor Relations Board (NLRB) to relinquish jurisdiction over labor disputes to state tribunals, but it established conditions that no state was able to meet. Then in the 1957 *Guss v. Utah Board* case, the U.S. Supreme Court ruled that a state tribunal could act in a case within the NLRB's Taft-Hartley jurisdiction only where the NLRB had granted jurisdiction to the state under Section 10(a). A refusal by the NLRB to assert jurisdiction over a case, the Court said, did provide the state tribunal with jurisdiction.

The effect of this decision was to create a legal "no-man's land" in which no court or agency was authorized to hear the case; the NLRB would not assert jurisdiction, and the state courts were prevented from taking jurisdiction. Congress sought to correct the situation in the 1959 Landrum-Griffin amendment to the Taft-Hartley Act. Amendments to Section 14 provided that (1) the NLRB, by rule of decision or published rules, may decline to assert jurisdiction over any labor dispute involving any class or category of employers where the effect on interstate commerce is not substantial enough to warrant the exercise of jurisdiction; (2) however, the board may not decline to assert jurisdiction over any dispute over which it would have asserted jurisdiction under the standards prevailing on August 1, 1959; and (3) cases rejected by the NLRB under its jurisdictional standards may be handled by agencies or courts of the states and territories.

If a party to a dispute comes within the NLRB's standards for asserting jurisdiction, a state may not take jurisdiction over activities that potentially are subject to regulation under the Taft-Hartley Act except where violence or coercive conduct is involved. [*San Diego Building Trades Council v. Garmon* (1959)].

See also **Jurisdiction; Labor-Management Relations Act of 1947; National Labor Relations Act; National Labor Relations Board.**

FELLOW SERVANT RULE The doctrine in common law that held the employer could not be held liable for accidents suffered by an employee. It was assumed that the employer had explained the nature of the work, warned the workers of the hazards involved in the work, established rules designed to permit safe places of work, and hired workers with due care as to their ability.

Under the fellow servant rule, a master will not be held liable for injuries to a servant resulting from the negligence of a coservant. The fellow servant rule is a departure from the general doctrine that a master is responsible for injuries to a third party resulting from negligence or misconduct of the servant while the servant is performing tasks within the scope of employment. The rationale for this rule is that the servant assumes the risk of negligence of a fellow servant incidental to employment. Thus the risk was seen as an implied term of the employment contract.

Once the English and American courts had developed the fellow servant rule in the second quarter of the nineteenth century barring lawsuits by employees against their employers for the negligence of their coworkers, employees began to claim that they were or had worked as independent contractors in order to escape the rule, while defendant-employers insisted that plaintiffs, who would otherwise have qualified as independent contractors were indeed their employees and hence subject to the rule.

State constitutional and statutory provisions, such as workers compensation acts, have abolished the common law fellow servant rule in most jurisdictions.

See also **Common Law: Employment Doctrines; Employee; Employer; Employment Contract; Independent Contractor; Workers' Compensation.**

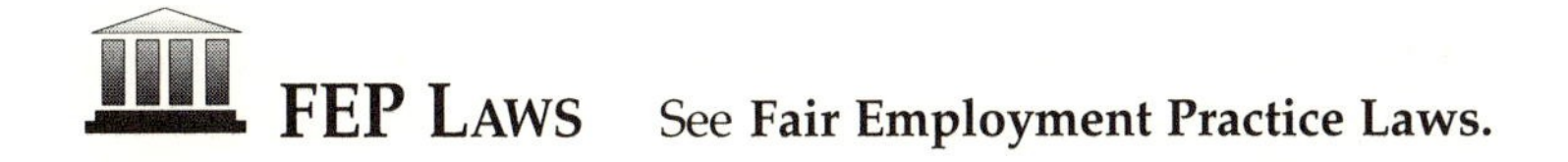

FEP LAWS See **Fair Employment Practice Laws.**

FIELD EXAMINER An employee of the National Labor Relations Board whose primary duties are to conduct certification elections and to conduct preliminary investigations of unfair labor practice charges.

See also **Certification; National Labor Relations Board; Unfair Labor Practice.**

FINAL OFFER ARBITRATION See **Grievance Arbitration.**

***FITZPATRICK V. BLITZER* (1976)** The U.S. Supreme Court in 1976 upheld the constitutionality of extending Title VII of the Civil Rights Act of 1964 to state and local governments and the authorization of lawsuits against agencies. The Court held that the extension was a proper exercise of congressional power under the Fourteenth Amendment, and that the amendment does not prohibit the award of back pay and attorneys fees against state employees. These employers were excluded from coverage when the Civil Rights Act of 1964 was originally passed, but Congress extended Title VII to state and local governments in the Equal Employment Opportunity Act of 1974.

See also **Award; Back Pay; Civil Rights Act of 1964; Equal Employment Opportunity Act of 1972.**

FLEXTIME A work scheduling method that allows employees to vary their arrival and departure time around a required number of work hours to meet their personal needs. Such plans may require all employees to be on the job during certain operating hours. This system is intended as both a way to stagger hours and a form of job enrichment. It allows workers to attend to family needs without using sick time, and it can reduce daycare expenses, increase time spent with family, and increase employee productivity and loyalty.

Most flextime schedules are based on a flexible workday rather than a work week or month. Often they consist of a core of hours when all employees must be present. Beyond those core hours, the employee may choose when to come and go, as long as the total hours worked remains the same. Some may take a two-hour lunch, while others may come in early and leave early.

Flexible time-off options include vacation buying and selling, which allows employees to purchase more time, sell unneeded time, or both. Corporations find that this approach addresses different employee needs but does not require the modification of existing vacation schedules and policies. Other corporations use either a system of unallocated time off or a "block time off" program, which allocates a total number of days off for any purpose.

FLSA See **Fair Labor Standards Act.**

FMCS See **Federal Mediation and Conciliation Service.**

Free Riders An employee within the bargaining unit who is eligible for union membership but does not join the union. Union members maintain that free riders receive all the benefits of the union contract obtained through the efforts of the dues-paying members in the collective bargaining process, yet do not pay the dues or fees that make these benefits possible. Therefore, free riders are said to have a financial advantage over dues-paying members. Opponents of compulsory unionism argue, however, that no worker should be forced to join a union as a condition of employment. The U.S. Supreme Court has held that one of the purposes of Section 8(a)(3) of the National Labor Relations Act was to eliminate the free rider by requiring a payment for the union's services as a bargaining agent.

See also **Benefits; Collective Bargaining; National Labor Relations Act.**

FREEDOM OF CONTRACT A constitutional doctrine developed by the U.S. Supreme Court in the nineteenth and early twentieth century, holding that certain types of labor-protective statutes violated the rights of employees to contract and therefore denied them rights protected under the Fourteenth Amendment. Since the freedom of contract was held as a property right, restrictions of that right contradicted the Fourteenth Amendment, which provides that "no state shall deprive any person of life, liberty, or property without due process of law." [*Allgeyer v. Louisiana* (1897); *Lochner v. New York* (1905)]

Laissez-faire economists traditionally have advocated a social and economic policy of the free market, freedom of contract, and the common law as a means of achieving social good, and even as desirable ends in and of themselves. Under American common law, noncontractual employment relationships could be terminated at the will of either party, employer or employee. At the turn of the century, the common law allowed employers to terminate an employment contract for any reason. At-will employment was appealing because of the privileged status of the freedom to contract. Courts reasoned that the parties were free to contract to any term they wished, so that in the absence of any exercise of that right, the employee was not legally bound to the employer; therefore, the employer should not be held to obligations without an express contract. In addition, courts feared the prolongation of servitude absent an independent contract would harm commerce in the industrial age and lead to lifelong servitude.

The U.S. Supreme Court gave the freedom of contract and the employment-at-will doctrines constitutional legitimacy in the case of *Adair v. United States* (1908). In *Adair*, a railroad company that had fired an employee for union membership challenged a federal statute, the Erdman Act, which criminalized dismissing an employees for being a union member and forbade the "yellow dog contract." The Supreme Court invalidated the law, ruling that it violated the Fifth Amendment guarantee of the freedom of contract. The at-will rule's association with antiunion cases such as this one is why many modern commentators and courts criticize it.

Unionists have long argued that freedom of contract doctrines harm the interests of employees, who lack the collectivity to give them strength in negotiations with management. Contracts were often offered to workers on a take it or leave it basis and the workers often have no real involvement in the process determining their working conditions.

No modern court continues to follow the freedom of contract/substantive due process doctrines developed by the courts in the late nineteenth and early twentieth century. The U.S. Supreme Court's strict adherence to the employment-at-will rule and the freedom of contract doctrine ended when the Court upheld the constitutionality of the National Labor Relations Act in *NLRB v. Jones & Laughlin Steel Corporation* (1937).

See also **Common Law: Employment Doctrines; Employment-at-Will; National Labor Relations Act;** ***NLRB v. Jones & Laughlin Steel Corp.;*** **Property Rights; Yellow Dog Contract.**

FRICTIONAL UNEMPLOYMENT See **Unemployment.**

FRINGE BENEFITS See **Benefits.**

FRONTIERO V. RICHARDSON (1973)

The "mere rationality" standard (that the law would be stricken only if the classification is "purely arbitrary") for gender-based classifications was explicitly applied by the U.S. Supreme Court in *Frontiero.* The statute at issue allowed a serviceman to claim his wife as a dependent, whether or not she was in fact dependent on him for any part of her support. A servicewoman, however, could not claim her husband as a dependent unless he in fact depended upon her for more than half of his support. The Court held that the statute violated the equal protection principle of the Fifth Amendment.

The Court held that classifications based on sex, like classifications based upon race, alienage, or national origin, are inherently suspect and must therefore be subjected to strict judicial scrutiny. It based its holding on three factors: (1) sex is an "immutable characteristic" whose use to determine rights seemed to violate the basic notion that "legal burdens should bear some relationship to individual responsibility"; (2) sex frequently bears no relation to ability to perform or contribute to society; and (3) Congress itself, by proposing the Equal Rights Amendment and passing other sexual-equality legislation, had concluded that gender-based classifications are inherently invidious.

Reviewed under this standard, the classification was invalidated. The only defense of it that the government could offer was that it promoted administrative convenience, since it would be less expensive and easier simply to presume that wives of servicemen are financially dependent on their husbands than to have an individualized hearing in each case. The Court flatly rejected administrative convenience as a justification for classification by gender. It then articulated an "intermediate" level of scrutiny for gender-based classifications.

FRONT-LOADED Providing a greater wage increase in the early period of a multiyear collective bargaining agreement than in the later period: for example, a 6 percent wage increase in the first year of a three-year agreement and a 5 percent increase in each of the two years following.

See also **Collective Bargaining Agreement.**

FULL CREW RULE A regulation stating the minimum number of employees required for a given operation. Originally designed as a safety precaution for both workers and the public, critics charge that full crew rules are now used by some unions to protect employees in jobs that are no longer essential. For example, railroad unions have been generally successful in having full crew rules enacted into state law, but railroad management believes, that the full crew rule requiring a firefighter to ride in the cab of a diesel engine is featherbedding.

See also **Featherbedding.**

FULL EMPLOYMENT Ideally, an employment level at which any person willing and able to work is able to find employment. There is considerable disagreement on the meaning of full employment, however, because of the frictional unemployment and seasonal unemployment that always exist. These factors make an unemployment rate of between 2 and 4 percent of the labor force about as close to full employment as can be expected in a free economy. The lowest unemployment rate experienced in the United States was 1.2 percent in 1944.

See also **Unemployment.**

***FULLILOVE V. KLUTZNICK* (1980)** The U.S. Supreme Court in *Fullilove* upheld a congressionally enacted 10 percent set-aside program for minority business enterprise. Significantly, however, six of the justices agreed that in affirmative action cases there must be a finding by a competent body of past constitutional or statutory violations.

The 1978 *Bakke* case had left the constitutionality of affirmative action in doubt, since four justices reached their decision on purely statutory grounds and the remaining five disagreed on the applicable rules. In *Fullilove,* all nine justices confronted the issue of the constitutionality of race-conscious affirmative action. By a vote of 6 to 3, the Court decisively established that government may use appropriately tailored, racially conscious measures to remedy the effects of past discrimination. Though the *Fullilove* decision involved a federal statute, the decision seems in principle equally applicable to affirmative action plans instituted by state entities.

The affirmative action plan at issue in *Fullilove* was one by which 10 percent of the federal funds granted for local public works projects were earmarked for the purchase of goods or services from minority-owned contractors (minority business enterprises). The statute defined as "minorities" African Americans, Spanish-speaking persons, Orientals, Native Americans, Eskimos, and Aleuts. The set-aside applied to slightly more than four billion dollars worth of federal grants, giving these businesses the right to four hundred million dollars worth of business. Grantees, however, were provided special "waiver" provisions, under which they could be relieved of the set-aside if they showed that their best efforts could not achieve the 10 percent minority participation.

The Supreme Court did not reach a majority opinion. The Court's judgment was announced in a plurality opinion by Chief Justice Warren Burger, joined by Justices Byron White and Lewis Powell. Burger found that Congress had the right to take measures to remedy the effects of past discrimination and that these measures need not be "colorblind." The set-aside was sufficiently "closely tailored" to the valid congressional objective of redressing past discrimination that it did not violate the equal protection clause (as applied to the federal government through the Fifth Amendment due process clause). The Chief Justice explicitly refrained from adopting either the "strict scrutiny" or the "middle-level scrutiny" standard, each of which had its proponents in *Bakke*. Instead, he merely stated that any preference based on racial or ethnic criteria must receive a "most searching examination." He added that the plan here would have survived even if the strict scrutiny standard applied.

The broad significance of *Fullilove* is that it confirms, by a larger majority, *Bakke's* endorsement of racial classifications as a means of combating past discrimination. Some of the particular issues on which *Fullilove* established new law are:

1. Use of racial classifications. Seven members of the Court believed that racial classifications may be used to combat the effects of past discrimination.
2. "Innocent" third parties. *Fullilove* held that at least some relative disadvantages of nonminorities will be tolerated by the Court as an unavoidable consequence of the need to remedy past discrimination.
3. Use of quotas. *Fullilove* explicitly endorses the use of quotas where necessary to abolish discrimination. On this point, *Fullilove* stands in sharp contrast to *Bakke*, where only four members of the Court were willing to approve the University of Davis quota scheme.
4. Tracing of discrimination. The majority in *Fullilove* permitted remedial action even where there was no finding that the party implementing the affirmative action (i.e., Congress) had been guilty of past discrimination. In fact, the Court did not impose a requirement that the past "societal" discrimination be traced to any particular entity. This probably means that a majority of the Court would allow any public entity to embark upon a suitable affirmative action without ever having itself discriminated.

See also **Affirmative Action; *Regents of the University of California v. Bakke* (1978); Discrimination in Employment; Due Process Rights.**

FUNERAL LEAVE

See **Leave of Absence.**

FURLOUGH A leave of absence from work or other duties. Usually it is initiated by an employee to meet some special problem. It is temporary, since the employee plans to return as soon as the furlough period is over.

The Civil Service Reform Act defines furlough as "the placing of an employee in a temporary status without duties and pay because of lack of work or funds or other nondisciplinary reasons."

See also **Civil Service Reform Act of 1978; Leave of Absence.**

GARDNER-DENVER See ***Alexander v. Gardner-Denver* (1974).**

GENERAL ELECTRIC V. GILBERT (1976) The U.S. Supreme Court held, in *Gilbert,* that an employer's generally comprehensive disability plan which excluded disabilities due to pregnancy from coverage did not violate Title VII of the Civil Rights Act of 1964's prohibition against sex discrimination in employment because the disability plan did not exclude anyone on the basis of gender. The court noted that while pregnancy is confined to women, it is "significantly different" from the typical covered disease or disability. In fact, "it is not a 'disease' at all, and is often a voluntarily undertaken and desired condition." The Court found that the exclusion was not a pretext for discriminating against women and that there is no proof that the "package" of risks covered by the plan was in fact worth more to men than to women. The Court, by so ruling, rejected the Equal Employment Opportunity Commission (EEOC) guidelines on sex discrimination, which held that pregnancy-related disabilities should be considered as any other disability covered by insurance or sick leave plans. The Court stated that EEOC guidelines may be considered in determining legislative intent, "but it does not mean that courts properly may accord less weight to such guidelines than to administrative regulations which Congress has declared shall have the force of law."

Congress reacted to *Gilbert* and to *Nashville Gas Co. v. Satty* (1977) by amending Title VII in 1978. This section reversed the Supreme Court decision and specifically outlawed discrimination based on pregnancy.

See also **Civil Rights Act of 1964; Equal Employment Opportunity Commission; Sex Discrimination in Employment.**

GLASS CEILING Those artificial barriers based on attitudinal or organization bias that prevent qualified individuals from advancing upward into management-level positions. In this instance, "qualified individuals" refers to women and minorities.

A glass ceiling is said to exist when women and minorities are not proportionately represented in the management ranks. While the number of women in management and administrative jobs increased from 24 percent to 37 percent in 1987, only 2 percent of top-level management jobs and 5 percent of corporate board memberships are held by women, due to the glass ceiling. The U.S. Department of Labor's glass ceiling initiative found that some 7 percent of women and 3 percent of minority groups were executives in Fortune 100 companies.

Some scholars believe that the well-known stereotypes of men as more competitive, more driven to acquire status and resources, and more inclined to take risks than women, and stereotypes of women as more nurturing, more risk adverse, less greedy, and less single-minded than men are true as generalizations and therefore largely responsible for differential workplace results.

Progress in removing the glass ceiling has been slow. The Glass Ceiling Commission in 1995 reported that 97 percent of the senior management at the Fortune 1000 industrial corporations were white males, and only 5 percent of the top managers at the Fortune 2000 industrial and service companies were women, virtually all of them white.

GLOBE ELECTIONS Special election to determine whether a particular group of employees desires to become part of a larger bargaining unit. The smaller unit to be "globed" must constitute an appropriate bargaining unit by itself. The name originates from the case of *Globe Machine and Stamping Co.* (NLRB, 1937). In that case, the National Labor Relations Board (NLRB) provided for special balloting to determine the representation wishes of employees. The situation involved a bargaining unit determination by the NLRB where a smaller craft unit and a larger industry unit were equally reasonable results. By permitting the employees in the smaller unit to indicate their preference, the NLRB was able to decide whether to leave the craft group in the smaller bargaining unit or to combine it with the larger group. In recent years, the NLRB has never found the factors evenly balanced and thus has not conducted Globe elections. Special protection for the crafts was provided by the Labor-Management Relations Act (LMRA) of 1947 (the Taft-Hartley Act).

See also **Appropriate Bargaining Unit; National Labor Relations Board.**

GOOD FAITH BARGAINING

Section 8(d) of the National Labor Relations Act (NLRA) defines good faith bargaining as negotiations in which two parties meet and confer at reasonable times, their minds open to persuasion, with a view to reaching agreement on new contract terms. Good faith bargaining does not imply that either party is required to make concessions or reach agreement on any proposal. Failure to bargain in good faith is an unfair labor practice, under Section 8(a)(5) of the NLRA. The U.S. Supreme Court has said that the essential element of good faith bargaining is "the serious intent to adjust differences and to reach an acceptable common ground." [*NLRB v. Insurance Agents International Union* (1960)]

See also **National Labor Relations Act; Unfair Labor Practice.**

GRIEVANCE

An allegation or complaint by an employee, union, or employer about any aspect of the employment relationship (e.g., that a collective bargaining contract or a traditional work practice has been violated). The grievance may be warranted or fancied, arbitrable or nonarbitrable under the employment contract. Issues regarding the interpretation and application of the collective bargaining agreement are subject to the grievance procedure, as provided in the contract.

An individual employee has the right to present a grievance to the employer and to have the grievance handled without the intervention of his bargaining representative. The outcome of the grievance, however, must not be inconsistent with the terms of the collective bargaining agreement in effect and the bargaining representative must be given an opportunity to be present at grievance meetings. [National Labor Relations Act, Section 9(a)] Workers and unions and managers all have an interest in the best possible operation of grievance systems. To the extent a grievance system works well—with due process and both the perception and the reality of "justice on the job"—it creates better labor-management relations.

See also **Collective Bargaining Agreement; Employment Contract; Grievance Arbitration; Grievance Procedure; National Labor Relations Act.**

GRIEVANCE ARBITRATION A procedure in which parties to a labor-management dispute submit the dispute to the judgment of a specified number of unbiased third parties called arbitrators. The details of grievance arbitration vary considerably among collective bargaining agreements, as does the power given to an arbitrator to decide grievances. Some bargaining agreements withdraw specified matters from the arbitrator's authority or place other kinds of limits on decisions that the arbitrator can make.

Arbitration saves the resources of all the parties involved, allowing them to avoid the formalities, delay, expense, and inconvenience of ordinary litigation. As a result, almost 95 percent of all labor contracts provide for some form of labor arbitration.

Most collective bargaining agreements include a clause stating that if the employer and the union cannot agree in a labor grievance or dispute, they will submit the matter to arbitration. As the last step of the grievance procedure, the arbitrator's task is to determine whether the contract or longstanding work practice, which frequently has the force of a contract provision, has been misinterpreted or misapplied. If an arbitrator is appointed to hear just one case, the arbitration is called temporary or ad hoc. A majority of collective bargaining agreements provide for ad hoc arbitration, where the parties will mutually agree on a particular arbitrator to decide the grievances that have occurred during the term of the agreement. A permanent arbitrator, on the other hand, is designated by the agreement to decide grievances during the term of the agreement—an arrangement is known as permanent arbitration.

The decision of the arbitrators is called an award, and the parties agree in advance that it is binding on both parties. Opinions and awards are usually in writing and contain a statement of the grievance, a summary of the evidence, and arguments on both sides, an explanation of the reasons why the arbitrator has reached a decision, and a statement of relief granted. If the losing party refuses to comply with an arbitration award, the winning party must either seek judicial enforcement in a breach of contract action, or resort to economic action to compel compliance with the award, with or without a bargaining agreement sanction.

Compulsory arbitration—where arbitration procedures are required by law—was not used in the United States until the National War Labor Board was established during World War II to prevent wartime strikes and lockouts. After the war, some states required compulsory arbitration or seizure in public utility labor disputes. But in those industries that affected interstate commerce, the Supreme Court determined that the federal government had jurisdiction, and federal labor policy made labor arbitration agreements enforceable through the courts.

See also **Award; Collective Bargaining Agreement.**

Grievance Procedure

Grievance Procedure The steps established, usually in the collective bargaining agreement, to resolve problems (which are known as grievances) that arise either in the application and interpretation of the contract or out of that agreement. The U.S. Supreme Court, in the *United Steel Workers v. Warrior & Gulf Navigation Co.* (1960) case, observed that "the processing of disputes through the grievance machinery is actually a vehicle by which the meaning and content is given to the collective bargaining agreement."

Grievances are often handled through elaborate systems with specific time limits at each step. The intent of the process is to settle a complaint, usually an allegation that the contract has been misinterpreted or misapplied, as quickly as possible without interrupting the employer's operations. The first step usually occurs at the shop level, where most grievances are settled. If an agreement is not reached at this level, the grievance may be appealed in successive steps. The number and type of these steps vary among contracts. The most important aspect of any grievance procedure is the final step, arbitration. Grievance procedures with arbitration are now routinely included in almost all private sector labor-management agreements and in most public sector agreements. But rather than being the goal of the grievance process, arbitration signifies its failure.

See also **Collective Bargaining Agreement; Grievance; Grievance Arbitration.**

Griggs v. Duke Power Co. (1971)

***Griggs v. Duke Power Co.* (1971)** A landmark Supreme Court decision which held that employment tests or criteria operating to exclude minority groups in hiring are prohibited under Title

VII of the Civil Rights Act of 1964 unless the requirements are shown to be related to job performance. In *Griggs,* prior to the passage of the Civil Rights Act, African Americans were employed only in the Duke Power Company's labor department, which consisted of the lowest paid jobs. In other departments, however, the company retained its policy of requiring a high school education. It permitted its employees to transfer from the labor department if they made satisfactory scores—the national median for high school graduates—on two professionally prepared aptitude tests. New employees were required to pass both tests and have a high school education. African Americans in the labor department brought a lawsuit charging the employer with racial discrimination under Title VII of the Civil Rights Act of 1964. The U.S. Supreme Court held that these requirements were not intended to measure ability to learn to perform a particular job. Further, the requirements operated to disqualify African American applicants at a substantially higher rate than white applicants. Formerly the jobs in question had been filled only by white employees as part of a long-standing practice of giving preference to whites.

In *Griggs,* the Supreme Court departed from a narrow interpretation of this provision—limited to intentional discrimination—and held that Title VII prevents employment criteria that disproportionately impact a protected class, regardless of intent. Objective screening criteria, such as the diploma and intelligence requirements at issue in *Griggs,* appear neutral with respect to race. But the screening criteria are invalidated if a plaintiff demonstrates that, in the aggregate, they disproportionately burden a protected class and if the employer then fails to show that they are "related to job performance" and justified by "business necessity."

Title VII and the *Griggs* decision began what developed into 30 years of frustration for many organizations. Before the *Griggs* decisions, for example, pre-employment testing was widely used in the selection process; after Griggs, its use declined sharply. In addition, everything from the employment application form to interview questions have been used in litigation as prima facie evidence of discrimination. Though some commentators believe that management generally did not implement affirmative action well in the wake of the *Griggs* decision, many legal experts have convincingly argued that the Supreme Court's seemingly confused series of opinions is responsible for much of this mismanagement.

See also **African Americans: Employment Issues; Civil Rights Act of 1964; Employment Testing; Protected Class.**

GROUP INSURANCE A program designed to provide low-cost protection to large groups of employees through a plan, generally negotiated with an insurance company, to cover life, accident, sickness, hospitalization, and medical benefits. The plan may be jointly financed by the employer and the employees (contributory). Group insurance plans may be inaugurated where there is no union or negotiated within the collective bargaining process in unionized environments.

Health insurance in the United States began nearly 200 years ago with hospital care for seamen paid for by compulsory wage deductions. Group health insurance developed during the early twentieth century in response to growing industrialization, the increasing size of companies' workforces, and the employers' and labor unions' realization that workers needed economic protection against the unforeseeable losses that result from premature death and disability. But it was not until 1929, with the development of Blue Cross, that health insurance began to resemble its current form. In the 1970s and 1980s, enrollment greatly increased in "managed care plans"—Health Maintenance Organizations and Preferred Provider Organizations. These plans were a direct response to the sharp increase in healthcare costs. Health care is now comprehensive, providing hospital, surgical, and medical benefits, and also may include coverage for dental care, eye care, mental health, and home health care.

Approximately 35.7 million people under the age of 65 were not covered by health insurance in 1990, according to the Bureau of Labor Statistics—an increase of two million persons since 1988. That increase, along with rising costs for health care services, has intensified interest in reforming the health care system. Throughout the 1990s, Congress considered legislation designed to improve access to and reduce the cost of health care and to modify the tax treatment of health care benefits. Many of these proposals are various reforms of the current national health care system, which relies heavily on health insurance provided by employers.

***GUNTHER* CASE** See ***County of Washington v. Gunther* (1981).**

HANDICAPPED EMPLOYEE A handicapped employee is a person who has mental or physical disabilities that limit his or her working potential. Extensive work in government rehabilitation programs and proper vocational guidance has permitted many of those persons previously considered handicapped to perform work in certain fields with equal or greater skill than those not considered handicapped.

A handicapped individual is defined by the Rehabilitation Act of 1973 as:

> any person who (1) has a physical or mental impairment which substantially limits one or more of such person's major life activities, (2) has a record of such an impairment, or (3) is regarded as having such an impairment. For purposes of sections 503 and 504 of this act as such sections relate to employment, such terms do not include any individual who is an alcoholic or drug abuser, whose current use of alcohol or drugs prevent such individual from performing the duties of the job in question or whose employment, by reason of such current alcohol or drug abuse, would constitute a direct threat to property or the safety of others.

The Fair Labor Standards Act defines a handicapped employee as "an individual whose earning capacity is impaired by age or physical or mental deficiency or injury for the work he is able to perform." Handicapped workers may be paid less than the prevailing rate with the approval of the Wage and Hour administrator.

Accommodations for persons with physical and mental disabilities are required under the government's contract compliance program, which is administered (as are all such efforts) by the Department of Labor's Office of Federal Compliance Program pursuant to the Rehabilitation Act of 1973. In 1990, Congress enacted the Americans with Disabilities Act (ADA), which prohibits discrimination because of disabilities in connection with public facilities as well as in the employment relationship. The ADA prohibits employers from discriminating against a "qualified individual with a disability." An individual with a disability is defined as one who has a physical or mental impairment that substantially limits one or more major life activities, who has a record of such an impairment or who is regarded as having such an impairment. Specifically excluded from this definition are homosexuals, bisexuals, transvestites, transsexuals, pedophiles, exhibitionists, voyeurs, and persons with gender identity disorders not resulting from physical impairments. Also excluded are compulsive gamblers, kleptomaniacs, pyromaniacs, and those who are currently engaged in the use of illegal drugs. Employers may hold alcoholics to the same qualifications and job performance standards as other employers, even if their unsatisfactory performance is related to alcoholism.

The remedies for employment discrimination under both the Civil Rights Act of 1964 and the Civil Rights Act of 1991 also apply to the ADA. In other words, punitive and compensatory damages are available as well as more traditional relief, although damages are limited by the statute. The Equal Employment Opportunity Commission has jurisdiction over claims of disability discrimination. Affirmative action and fair employment standards for the handicapped are provided by the Rehabilitation Act of 1973 and Executive Order 11758.

See also **Americans with Disabilities Act of 1990; Civil Rights Act of 1964; Civil Rights Act of 1991; Equal Employment Opportunity Commission; Fair Labor Standards Act; Rehabilitation Act of 1973.**

HIRING HALL A type of employment office established to meet the needs of workers in the casual trades, such as the construction trades, maritime trades, or food services. It is permitted by Section 8(f) of the National Labor Relations Act. When the closed shop existed, hiring halls were operated exclusively by the unions for the benefit of their members. Since 1947, when the Labor-Management Relations Act of 1947 (the Taft-Hartley Act) outlawed the closed shop, hiring halls commonly have been operated jointly by labor and management, often with state assistance or supervision. A common practice of many hiring halls is the assignment of workers in strict order of their registration for jobs, thus preventing discrimination in job assignments.

The distinctive feature of a hiring hall is that a union can select from among its members and nonmembers the workers to be hired by an employer. Under other types of union security arrangements, the initial employee selection is the responsibility of the employer. [*NLRB v. Radio Officers' Union* (1952)]

In an exclusive hiring hall arrangement the union acts as the sole supplier of labor to the employer, through a collective bargaining agreement, an oral understanding, or a tacit understanding. [*International Brotherhood of Teamsters v. NLRB* (1961)] A hiring hall arrangement may exist without a written contract; however, where no hiring hall contract exists, a union may not insist that an employer hire solely through the union's hiring hall. [*Laborer's International Union v. NLRB* (1974)] Under an exclusive arrangement, any person hired by an employer must be referred by a union. Exclusive hiring hall arrangements are not a form of union security and thus are legal in right-to-work states under the National Labor Relations Act. [*NLRB v. Tom Joyce Floors* (1965)]

In a nonexclusive hiring hall arrangement, the union is only one of several sources of employees available to an employer or a group of employers. A union has no duty of fair representation on job referrals from a nonexclusive hiring hall. Thus, a union's refusal to refer a former member who had previously accepted employment with a nonunion employer is not unlawful. Unions may legitimately refuse to aid nonmembers who seek to use their nonexclusive referral services.

A union hiring hall arrangement is a mandatory subject of bargaining and is considered a matter of negotiation between the parties. The National Labor Relations Board (NLRB) has no authority to compel, directly or indirectly, the inclusion of a hiring hall provision in a collective bargaining agreement. Nor can the NLRB compel the exclusion of such a provision.

A union acts lawfully in refusing to refer an applicant to the employers using the union's hiring halls when it wishes to afford preferential treatment to those workers who have been union members longer than the applicant. [*Plumbers, Local 741 (Stearns-Roger Corp.)* (1972)] However, preferential treatment of certain workers on grounds other than union affiliation may be an unfair labor practice.

See also **Closed Shop; Collective Bargaining Agreement; Discrimination in Employment; National Labor Relations Act; Right-To-Work Laws; Unfair Labor Practice.**

HISPANICS: EMPLOYMENT ISSUES

Persons of Mexican, Puerto Rican, Cuban, Central or South American, or other Spanish culture or origin, regardless of sex. Persons who may have adopted the Spanish culture are to be treated according to their racial identity. Under

Title VII of the Civil Rights Act of 1964, Hispanics are considered a part of a protected class and one of the racial/ethnic categories for which data is reported to the federal government.

The nation's Hispanic population totaled 27 million in 1994, an increase of 28 percent since 1990. Over one-third of American Hispanics were born outside the United States, compared with 3 percent of non-Hispanic whites. Poverty rates for Hispanic families are more than twice as high as for non-Hispanic families. Hispanics, however, have made significant gains in recent decades in their high school completion rates. Slightly over 5 in 10 Hispanics aged 25 and over were high school graduates in 1994, compared to 4 in 10 in 1980. Hispanics, however, have by far the highest high school dropout rates of any group in the nation.

Mexican-Americans are the single largest group of Hispanics in the United States and the second largest ethnic minority group. Mexican-Americans and European Americans tend to interpret the work environment differently due to cultural differences and therefore experience different levels of job satisfaction. Mexican-American employees are also a more cohesive cultural group than European Americans. Hispanics earn considerably higher pay in public sector jobs relative to their pay in the private sector, and the wage gap between Hispanics and European Americans is very low in the public sector. Some surveys have suggested that over time, rates of pay for Europeans and Hispanics are gradually moving together.

The Mexican workforce in the United States is becoming increasingly diverse in terms of geographic origin in Mexico and in educational levels. Women and children are present in increasing numbers, and settlement is increasing as well. States such as California are rapidly acquiring an age-race-stratified population. By the year 2030, the working-age segment of the population will be increasingly composed of Hispanics and other minorities while the older, nonworking segment will be increasingly European American.

See also **Civil Rights Act of 1964; Protected Class.**

HOLIDAY

HOLIDAY Time off from work made available to employees in observance of religious, patriotic, and other events or to honor a person.

Legal holidays are established by state and federal law. Despite the fact that certain days are traditionally referred to as "legal holidays," there is no legal requirement that the employer give his employees any days off.

However, most employees do provide paid holidays. The seven most common holidays are Thanksgiving, Christmas Day, Labor Day, Independence Day, New Year's Day, Martin Luther King, Jr. Day, and Memorial Day. Half-holidays may also be designated, such as the day before New Year's Day or Christmas. Holidays may also be granted on a worker's birthday.

When work is required on a holiday, collective bargaining agreements provide for compensation at a premium rate, based on the theory that work on a holiday is a sacrifice on the part of the worker, deserving of a special reward. Many part-time employees also receive holiday pay according to the number of hours they work in a day.

Though nearly every employment contract contains a paid holiday clause, the number and identification of the holidays are matters of individual preference and bargaining strength. Employers often insist on the traditional "day before and day after" language that requires an employee to work his last scheduled day before and first scheduled day after the holiday in order to receive holiday pay. Also, employment contracts often specify what happens to an employee's holidays when he or she is laid off or takes a leave of absence. Many state that if an employee is laid off more than a fixed number days before the holiday, the employee is not entitled to holiday pay.

See also **Collective Bargaining Agreement.**

HOSPITAL BENEFITS Service and/or cash benefits provided under basic health insurance plans to cover inpatient hospital charges, such as room and board, intensive care, necessary medical services, and inpatient drugs. Some outpatient services, such as pre-admission testing or emergency treatment as a result of an accident, may also be covered.

The plan may have separate limits for certain types of care. For example, room and board benefits may be limited to a maximum number of days, and total hospital benefits may be limited on a per admission basis. Maternity benefits are usually included in the hospitalization plan. Coverage is generally available to dependents under most plans.

HOT CARGO AGREEMENT Provisions in collective bargaining agreements (most commonly found in the construction and trucking industries) stating that employees need not handle nonunion, unfair, or struck goods of their employers. "Hot goods" are those products produced by an employer with whom the union has a dispute. These agreements also frequently include subcontracting clauses, which preclude contracting work to a nonunion employer.

Until the Landrum-Griffin Act in 1959, the legality of these hot cargo agreements under the Taft-Hartley Act was judged under the National Labor Relations Act's (NLRA) prohibiting secondary boycotts. The Landrum-Griffin Act amended the NLRA with the so-called "hot-cargo" section, making it an unfair labor practice for a union and an employer to enter into an agreement, express or implied, under which the employer must stop handling, using, selling, transporting, or otherwise dealing in the products of any other employer or to stop doing business with any other person. Agreements of this type previously entered into were declared unenforceable and void. It also was made an unfair labor practice under Section 8(b)(4)(A) of the NLRA for a union to use secondary boycott pressures to force an employer to enter into such an agreement.

The reason for this prohibition is that such contracting provisions have a "secondary objective": to influence the labor relations policies of the primary employer by organizing workers through an innocent third party—the employer who has signed the contract. On the other hand, subcontracting clauses to preserve the bargaining unit's work (e.g., agreements that prohibit subcontracting work to employers who provide substandard working conditions) are lawful.

The Landrum-Griffin Act created exceptions, under Section 8(f) of the NLRA, for agreements on job-site subcontracting in the construction industry and for agreements in the garment industry covering employers involved with jobbing and subcontracting.

See also **Collective Bargaining Agreement; National Labor Relations Act; Secondary Boycott; Subcontracting; Unfair Labor Practice.**

HOURLY RATE

The rate of pay, expressed in dollars and cents per hour, paid on a time basis. It is not the same as the amount actually earned in an hour since it does not include overtime or other premiums and bonuses. In the context of incentive wage payments, the term is sometimes used synonymously with "an earned rate per hour."

"Average hourly earnings" refers to the actual earnings of workers, including premium pay. The Bureau of Labor Statistics derives average hourly earnings by dividing gross payrolls by total hours. The rate does not represent total labor costs per hour to the employer because it excludes retroactive payments and irregular bonuses, fringe benefits, and the employer's share of payroll taxes.

"Straight-time average hourly earnings" refers to earnings that are approximated by advising average hourly earnings by eliminating premium pay for overtime at a rate of time and one-half. No adjustments are made for other premiums such as holiday work, late-shift work, and overtime rates other than at time and one-half.

See also **Bonus; Overtime.**

HOURS OF LABOR The time that a person spends at work. Typical collective bargaining provisions cover such issues as daily and weekly work schedules, requirements for overtime premiums, regulations for the distribution of overtime work, length of lunch and rest periods, and rules governing pay for time lost on a day of injury or time spent traveling to and from work.

The Fair Labor Standards Act (FLSA) does not restrict the number of hours employees may be compelled to work. It simply requires that employees not specifically exempt from the minimum wage and overtime provisions be paid at least the minimum wage from the first 40 hours they work in a work week and one and one half times their regular rate of pay for all additional hours worked. The FLSA does state that compensable hours worked include the principal activities of regular work, regardless of when they are done, and incidental activities like setting up equipment, picking up mail, completing paperwork, waiting time during regular work hours, and traveling during work hours.

Activities excluded from hours of labor are travel to and from work and activities integrated with principal activities, when performed before and after regular hours.

See also **Collective Bargaining; Fair Labor Standards Act; Minimum Wage; Portal-to-Portal Act of 1947.**

***HOWARD JOHNSON CO. V. DETROIT LOCAL JOINT EXECUTIVE BOARD* (1974)** In this case, the Grissom family operated a motel and restaurant as a Howard Johnson franchise.

The Grissoms' collective bargaining agreement with the union provided for the arbitration of disputes and intended to bind any successors to the employer. During the agreement, the Grissoms sold all the personal property involved in the enterprise and leased the real property to the Howard Johnson Corporation. Howard Johnson fired all of the Grissoms' employees and supervisors and hired new employees, only a few of whom had been with the Grissoms. The union filed a lawsuit to compel Howard Johnson to arbitrate its dismissal of the Grissoms' employees, relying on *John Wiley & Sons, Inc. v. Livingston.* The Supreme Court held that Howard Johnson had no duty to arbitrate and distinguished this case from *Wiley* on three grounds. First, the parties in *Wiley* knew of the existence of state law making the successor liable for the debts of the predecessor. Second, in *Howard Johnson* the predecessor still existed as an entity available for relief, although the particular relief requested by the union, continued employment for the employees, was admittedly unavailable. Third, and most important, in *Wiley* all of the predecessor's employees had been hired by the successor whereas in *Howard Johnson* only a few had been rehired. Thus, there is no duty of a successor to arbitrate unless there is continuity in the work force.

The Court suggested some circumstances where this result might not be reached. One is where the successor is the "alter ego" (the same entity) of the predecessor. Another is where the change in ownership is "a paper transaction having no meaningful impact on the ownership or operation of the enterprise." The Court also cryptically suggested that the union might have attempted to secure presale injunctive relief, ignoring the difficulty that unions ordinarily have in discovering pending sales prior to their implementation.

Howard Johnson offers an important incentive for employers, upon taking over another's business, to discharge present employees and make sure that the new group of employees is not substantially comprised of employees of the predecessor. The new employer cannot avoid hiring the old workforce if that workforce has expertise required by the new employer and lacked by available replacements. But if new employees are readily available, the employer can probably insure the lack of workforce continuity by interviewing actively on the open market. Furthermore, although the Court in *Howard Johnson* noted that the employer cannot avoid successorship by discriminating against the predecessor's employees, it did not seem to appreciate how difficult it would be for the union to prove such discrimination and how easy is it for the predecessor to accomplish it. Standards for new hires are usually vague, and unlike many cases where a hiring employer does not know the union affiliation of an applicant, a successor will know from an application form whether an applicant was an employee of the predecessor. Some commentators have argued that continuity of the workforce should control the outcome of the case only where the successor makes a basic alteration in the operation requiring a change in the composition of the work force or a reduction in the workforce. The kind of wholesale discharge that the Howard Johnson Company accomplished with Supreme Court approval is, in these commentators' view, no different than the mass discharge of employees by an employer attempting to destroy a union's majority status.

See also **Collective Bargaining Agreement;** ***John Wiley & Sons, Inc. v. Livingston; NLRB v. Burns International Security Services, Inc.;*** **Successor Employer.**

HUMAN RESOURCES MANAGEMENT A term that carried no special significance for several years and until the 1980s was used interchangeably with personnel management. Many companies in the nonunionized private sector recently adopted human resource management approaches, which are policies and procedures to treat employees fairly. Common contemporary management practices such as progressive discipline and grievance policies were advocated by unions, then carried over into human resource management programs.

The field of human resources has dramatically changed over the last 50 years. In the 1940s, the profession centered on labor relations, time and motion studies, work simplification, and supervision. Concepts from mass production dictated the way employees worked, the way they thought about work, and the way they learned about work. During the 1950s, psychology was increasingly incorporated into training and the need to involve upper management in the training was recognized. Scientific management was applied with increasing rigor, work was simplified and subdivided. During the 1960s, group and individual behavior became the focus of training as well as organization development and programmed instruction. (Organization development integrates selection, development, organization structure, management methods, interpersonal relations, and group dynamics.) Specifically, human resource theorists focused on the psychology of influence, motivation, and attitude change.

Management by objectives and social issues, such as pollution, racism, and feminism, were the training subjects during the 1970s. In the 1980s, quality became a popular training topic as well as behavior modeling, teamwork, empowerment, and diversity. Quality Circles and Quality of Work Life theories, for example, became popular in the United States 30 years after quality-management theory was introduced in Japan. Other popular training topics have included adventure learning, feedback, corporate culture, trainers' competencies, and cost-benefit analysis. Learning organizations, performance support systems, and re-engineering emerged as the popular topics in the 1990s. Training also has won new emphasis in the public sector. In 1992, Bill Clinton was elected president on a platform that endorsed training, and Robert Reich, a pro-training economist, became secretary of labor and established the Office of Work-Based Learning. Some of the leading training topics include learning organizations, performance-support systems, re-engineering, reorganization and transformation of work, customer focus, global organizations, "visioning," and balancing work and family.

Beginning in the 1980s, in particular, human resources emerged as a dramatically different approach to the management of people at work from "personnel management." Human resource management involves all management decisions and actions that affect the nature of the relationship between the organization and employees—its human resources. Thus, human resource management is more involved with central strategic management objectives than personnel management, since it involves human resources as the most valued company resource to be managed, it is involved in the achievement of business goals, and it is concerned with expressing senior management's preferred organizational values.

See also **Grievance Procedure; Management by Objectives; Progressive Discipline; Quality Circles; Quality of Work Life; Diversity; Scientific Management.**

Immigration Reform and Control Act (IRCA) of 1986 The federal statute that prohibits private employers with more than three employees from discriminating on the basis of national origin and citizenship. IRCA prohibits national origin discrimination by employers and other persons against any individual, other than an unauthorized alien, with respect to hiring, recruitment, or referral for employment, or discharge from employment. However, IRCA does not prohibit citizenship discrimination if citizenship is required by law, regulation, or executive order, or by federal, state, or local government.

In determining whether an employer is subject to IRCA's antidiscrimination prohibitions, only the part-time and full-time employees who were employed on the date the alleged discrimination occurred are counted.

Although aliens are generally protected from job discrimination by Title VII of the Civil Rights Act of 1964, the Age Discrimination in Employment Act (ADEA) of 1967, and the Equal Pay Act when they are authorized to work inside the United States, the protections available to unauthorized aliens under Title VII remain in doubt, particularly after the passage of IRCA, which permits citizenship discrimination against them in certain cases. The Equal Employment Opportunity Commission (EEOC) has ruled that Title VII protects unauthorized aliens, and at least one court agrees with the EEOC's position that Title VII protects aliens, whether or not they are authorized to work here.

The law authorized employer audits, whereby the Immigration and Naturalization Service randomly inspects employers who were required to complete the I-9 form, which discloses the legal status of their employees. The IRCA also establishes four different amnesty programs under which illegal aliens who have lived in the United States for several years may legalize their status. By providing for the admission of additional aliens in certain circumstances, the IRCA also addresses the concerns of some employers—especially those who depend on seasonal agricultural workers—that IRCA's penalty provisions will prevent them from hiring enough workers.

Whether the statute has been effective in controlling illegal immigration remains controversial. Because the statute penalizes employers who hire illegal aliens, employers may react by refusing to hire all noncitizens, or generally discriminating against "foreign-looking" individuals. Consequently, the IRCA makes it an unfair immigration-related practice for an employer to discriminate against any individual (other than an unauthorized alien) because of national origin, or in the case of a citizen or an intending citizen, because of citizenship status. However, the absence of an effective identification system, along with inadequate funding for enforcement and the statute's lack of attention to the powerful forces of population growth, poverty, unemployment, and corruption in the immigrants' countries of origin all suggest that illegal immigration will continue at high and possibly increasing levels.

The IRCA was amended in 1990 to address the concerns of civil rights groups that employers were discriminating against immigrant workers based on their national origin. The amendments strengthen the IRCA by increasing the monetary penalties for violations of the act by extending coverage to agricultural workers and by specifying two new discriminatory offenses: (1) retaliation against those who bring charges; and (2) abuse by employers who request applicants to provide additional documentation or refuse to honor documents that reasonably appear to be genuine.

Both the IRCA and Title VII prohibit national origin discrimination. Title VII does protect undocumented aliens, and the IRCA does not remove this protection. [*EEOC v. Tortilleria "La Mejor"* (1991)]

See also **Age Discrimination in Employment Act; Civil Rights Act of 1964; Equal Pay Act of 1963.**

IMPASSE In negotiations, a situation in which no agreement can be made. Either party may determine the point at which impasse has been reached. In the public sector, technical impasse occurs when agreement had not been reached by a specified time before the deadline for budget submission, even though the parties are continuing to bargain in good faith. In both private and public employment, impasses are often resolved by the intervention of a neutral third party, such as a mediator or factfinder.

INDEPENDENT CONTRACTOR Generally, a person who, in exercising an independent employment, contracts to do cer tain work according to his or her own methods, without being subject to the control of the employer, except regarding the product or result of the work.

The term "independent contractor" has been defined in several ways: (1) as one who carries on an independent employment pursuant to a contract by which he or she has the entire control of the work and the manner of its performance; (2) as one who contracts to perform a specific job, furnishing his or her own assistants and executing the work in accordance with either entirely his or her own ideas or a plan previously given to him or her by the person for whom the work is done, without being subject to the orders of the latter on the details of the work; (3) as any person following a regular independent employment in the course of which he or she offers services to the public to accept orders and execute commissions for all who may employ him or her in a certain line of work, using his or her own means for the purpose of being accountable only for the final result; (4) as one who contracts to perform a job at his or her own risk and cost, the workmen being his servants and he or she being liable for their misconduct. One of the basic factors of the independent contractor relationship, according to most courts, is whether the contractor has an independent business or occupation. In situations where an employer may prescribe what shall be done but not how it shall be done or who shall do it, an independent contractor relationship exists.

In general, whether an individual is considered an employee or an independent contractor under federal statutory law is covered by two different tests: 1) a relatively expansive "economic realities" test and (2) a more narrow "right-to-control" test.

The economic realities test extends broad coverage to employment relationships under the Fair Labor Standards Act (FLSA). The standard is whether, as a matter of economic fact, the individual is in business for him or herself. Use of the "independent contractor" label by either the employer or employee is not relevant. Several factors are considered in determining "economic independence," including the degree of control exercised over the individual, the skill required to perform the job, the location of the work, and the control over the basis of compensation. Also, an employee may work for more than one employer without losing coverage under the FLSA.

In contrast to the FLSA, Section 530 of the Revenue Act of 1978 provides broader latitude to consider an individual an independent contractor for tax purposes. The Internal Revenue Service uses a 20-factor common law test to determine whether an employer exercises sufficient control over when, how, and where an individual works for the employer to be classified as an employee. If according to this test, an individual is an independent contractor rather than an employee, the employer is not liable for withholding income taxes or making Social Security contributions on behalf of the individual. Independent contractors must make their own income tax payments as well as the Social Security self-employment contribution, which roughly equals the combined employer-employee Social Security taxes.

The National Labor Relations Act (NLRA) applies a more narrow "right to-control" test to determine whether an individual is an employee. Under the NLRA, an employment relationship exists if the employer controls both the work result and the "manner and means" by which the parties achieve those results. These facts are determined by examining the intent of the parties, industry norms, the relationship of the work to the employer's regular business, the level of supervision, and the duration of employment.

Section 2(3) of the NLRA specifically excludes from its definition of employee any individual who is classified as an independent contractor. The NLRA, however, does not provide a definition of independent contractor. Therefore, the National Labor Relations Board (NLRB) must determine on a case-by-case basis which employees are and which employees are not independent contractors.

Generally, an employer or master is not liable for the torts committed by an independent contractor. The commonly accepted theory behind this principle is the fact that the employer has no right of control over the manner in which the contractor's work is done. Thus the work is regarded as the contractor's own enterprise. Independent contractors are not ordinarily covered by statutes dealing with "employees," including workers compensation statutes. Nor are they protected by Title VII of the Civil Rights Act of 1964, which prohibits discrimination in hiring, firing, compensation, terms, conditions, or privileges of employment on the basis of race, color, religion, sex, or national origin.

A company that misclassifies an employee as an independent contractor can be held liable for back wages and overtime. It can also be charged for back taxes with penalties and can risk losing some of the tax benefits of certain qualified profit-sharing pension plans, group term life insurance plans, and other employment benefit plans.

According to the U.S. Department of Labor, independent contractors are the largest group of workers in indirect work arrangements. Currently, approximately 8.3 million workers are identified as independent contractors. They are much more likely to be men, more educated, and older than workers in traditional arrangements. Approximately 83 percent of independent contractors prefer that type of work arrangement.

See also **National Labor Relations Act.**

INDUSTRIAL RELATIONS Traditionally understood, the term refers to the relations between employers and employees in work arrangements.

The American industrial relations system is diverse and complicated. Its bargaining structure is decentralized, especially compared to European standards. A policy of laissez-faire in industrial relations was adopted at the time of the Norris-LaGuardia Act in 1932. This policy, however, was abandoned when the National Labor Relations Act (NLRA) became law in 1935. The NLRA established the right to engage in collective bargaining and has, to some extent, shaped industrial relations in the United States.

Since the mid-twentieth century, the labor market has been undergoing a significant structural change. Traditional occupations are being replaced by new ones, especially in the information sector. The necessity for constant retraining in these new occupations has established a permanent role for vocational training, which has become an essential element of the common employment service. Collective bargaining has declined due to the transformation in the U.S. economy from a unionized, blue-collar production economy to an unorganized, white-collar service economy. In addition, many jobs have moved from the traditionally unionized frost-belt states to the less unionized Sunbelt, and employers have shown increasing antipathy toward unions. The sanctions imposed by law against unfair labor practices are now criticized as ineffective in view of employer resistance to unions. Also, existing labor law does not allow for workers who want independent representation outside of unions. Some commentators believe that the New Deal system of industrial relations is in need of substantial reform in order to adequately serve the country's needs.

See also **Blue-Collar Worker; Collective Bargaining; National Labor Relations Act; Norris-LaGuardia Act; Unfair Labor Practice; White-Collar Worker.**

INDUSTRIAL UNION A labor union representing all employees, both skilled and unskilled, in a plant or industry.

See also **Labor Union.**

INITIATION FEE Payment to a union required of an employee when he or she joins the union, usually pursuant to the union's constitution. The Labor-Management Relations Act of 1947 (the Taft-Hartley Act) prohibits excessive or discriminatory fees in union shops, where workers are required to join the union to remain employed.

See also **Labor-Management Relations Act of 1947; Union Shop.**

INJUNCTIONS AGAINST UNIONS An injunction is a court order restraining individuals or groups from committing acts the court has determined will cause irreparable harm. The order can either prohibit a person, group, or company from performing a given action or order that certain action be taken. Employers believed that labor injunctions were an important means to control the actual or threatened violence, property destruction, and personal injury associated with labor picketing. Thus it is possible for an employer to go to court and obtain an injunction forbidding a union to picket its plant, conduct a boycott, or undertake any activities that it considers detrimental to its business prior to the passage of the Norris-LaGuardia Act in 1932.

At common law, injunctions were the most effective weapon against concerted labor activities. Throughout the nineteenth and early twentieth century, the judiciary defined the relatively narrow and unchanging limits of allowed collective actions. Beginning in the 1880s, however, courts greatly enlarged their role in regulating and policing industrial conflict through labor injunctions. When union activities were found to violate state tort law or federal tort law, prior to the Supreme Court's decision in *Erie Railroad v. Tompkins* (1938) or federal antitrust law, an injunction could promptly end a strike, picketing, or a boycott.

During the Progressive era, labor injunctions were increasingly attacked as a "judicial usurpation" of the legislature's prerogative to establish social policy. Congress had attempted to restrict the court's use of the injunction through Section 20 of the Clayton Act, which stated that no restraining order or injunction could be granted by any U.S. court in "any cases between an employer and employees, or between employed and persons seeking employment, involving, or growing out of, a dispute concerning terms of conditions of employment rules unless a showing of irreparable injury was made, and there was therefore no adequate remedy at law."

In 1932, Congress passed the Norris-LaGuardia Act, which rejected the injunction as a remedy in labor disputes unless there was violence or other legislation authorizing an injunction. The act also provided in Section 7 that an injunction could only be issued after notice to all parties and a hearing in which the court found that (a) an unlawful act had been threatened or committed and will be committed in the future unless restrained, (b) substantial and irreparable property damage will follow, (c) greater injury will result to the complainant from denying the injunction than to the defendant from granting it, (d) the complainant has no adequate remedy at law, (e) public officers are unable or unwilling to furnish adequate protection, and (f) the complainant has complied with every legal obligation involved in the dispute and has made every reasonable effort to settle the dispute by negotiation. The Norris-LaGuardia Act accomplished more than the withdrawal of the remedy of injunction; it declared that federal courts did not have a mandate to formulate rules to govern labor policy. The government was expected to be neutral, and this was expected to permit union growth.

The National Labor Relations Act (NLRA) as amended by the Taft-Hartley Act (1947) provided that injunctions may be issued in labor disputes that imperil the nation's health and welfare and in national emergencies, and to prevent certain unfair labor practices. (See sections 10(i) and 10(1) of the NLRA.) There are two types of injunctions: temporary restraining orders, which are issued for a limited time before a complete hearing, and permanent injunctions, which are issued after a full hearing and remain in force until such time as the conditions that gave rise to their issuance have been changed.

State courts still have the power to issue injunctions to maintain public order in a labor dispute. To obtain an injunction, the employer must show possession of a right requiring protection, immediate and irreparable injury without the injunction, probable success on the merits of the case, and no adequate remedy at law. Compared to the tightly restricted federal injunctions, state court injunctions are easier to obtain, as they are typically not subject to as stringent restrictions as are injunctions in federal court. Typically, state courts enjoin three types of conduct in a strike or misconduct action: mass picketing; the "time, place, or manner" of picketing; and harassing or intimidating statements made while picketing.

See also **Boycott; Clayton Antitrust Act; Collective Action; Common Law: Employment Doctrines; Labor Dispute; Norris-LaGuardia Act; Picketing; Strike; Tort; Unfair Labor Practice.**

INSUBORDINATION An employee's refusal or failure to obey a management directive, to comply with an established work procedure, or to obey some order that a superior officer is entitled to give and have obeyed. The term suggests a willful or intentional disregard of the lawful and reasonable instructions of the employer. [*Porter v. Pepsi Cola Bottling Co. of Columbia*]

Under certain circumstances, use of objectionable language or abusive behavior toward supervisors may be considered to be insubordination because it reveals disrespect of management's authority. Insubordination is considered a cardinal workplace offense since it violates management's traditional right and authority to direct the workforce.

The proven facts of a "classical case of insubordination" include: (1) the employee was given orders, (2) the employee refused to obey the orders, (3) the orders came from the employee's supervisors, who were known to him, (4) the orders were reasonably related to the job and within the language or the contract, (5) the orders were clear, direct, and understood by the employee, (6) the employee was forewarned of the possible and probable consequences of his continued actions by specific reference to the contractual guidelines . . . and (7) the employee was neither insulated nor protected from possible disciplinary action by his role as a representative of the employees. . . ."

The "obey now, grieve later" rule generally governs arbitral decisions in cases involving insubordination. The leading exception to the rule is refusing to follow an order that would endanger the employee's health or safety or that of other workers. Some arbitrators have found that employees are not insubordinate if they disobey an order they consider to be illegal or which would jeopardize their position, e.g., a union representative.

INSULATED PERIOD The 60 days immediately preceding the expiration of a collective bargaining agreement when no representation petition may be filed. This period gives the employer and the incumbent union the opportunity to negotiate a new contract without rival claims for recognition.

See also **Collective Bargaining Agreement; Contract Bar Rules.**

INSURANCE PROGRAMS

The organized means to insure, or assure, a group of employees against loss by accident or death.

In unionized settings, the employer either contributes to a union fund or provides its own group insurance benefits. Unless the employer has a philosophical objection to contributing to the union fund, or unless it needs the claims experience of the bargaining unit group (often younger than the management group) to lower the premiums for its nonunion employees, most employers find it advantageous to contribute to the union fund, provided there is a limit on the amount of contributions. Employers very seldom agree to an uncapped contribution to a union fund where the trustees have the right to determine the amount needed to maintain existing benefits. Union health and welfare funds (as well as pension funds) often require the employer to agree to be bound by the "agreement and declaration of trust" that sets up the fund, as well as by the rules and regulations of the fund. Before signing such a clause, the negotiator reviews the trust agreement and rules.

When an employer provides benefits directly to the bargaining unit, it generally reserves the right to select the insurance carrier, and the agreement is usually limited to the level of benefits. Employers also attempt to negotiate a limit on their contributions in order to protect themselves from experience-based premium increases.

A common technique used in some contracts is to substitute a co-pay hospitalization plan similar to that used for major medical benefits for the "first-dollar" coverage. Under this arrangement, the employee is responsible for a deductible as well as a copayment. In addition to being much less expensive to purchase, this plan discourages employee abuse, since they must pay from their own funds before taking advantage of the plan. To overcome obvious union resistance to this plan, employers occasionally agree to fund some or all of the deductible, arguing that even with this additional cost, the premium savings will result in a lower-cost health package.

INTERNATIONAL BROTHERHOOD OF TEAMSTERS, CHAUFFEURS, WAREHOUSEMEN, AND HELPERS OF AMERICA

Organized in 1899 as the Team Drivers' International Union. A group seceded in 1901 and established the Teamsters National Union. The two organizations reunited in 1903 and formed the International Brotherhood of Teamsters. With the advent of automobiles, the union extended its jurisdictions to chauffeurs and truck drivers and in 1909 changed its name to the International Brotherhood of Teamsters, Chauffeurs, Stablemen and Helpers. It adopted its present name in 1940. The union was expelled from the American Federation of Labor-Congress of Industrial Organizations (AFL-CIO) for corruption in December 1957. The union was easily the nation's most powerful and allegedly one of its most corrupt, when James R. Hoffa was its president between 1957 and 1971. On November 1, 1987, the Teamsters reaffiliated with the AFL-CIO. Currently, there are 1.4 million members of the Teamsters Union.

Ron Carey, a former United Parcel Service (UPS) driver and the Teamsters' President since 1991, has made considerable progress in reforming what some observers had called America's most mob-infested union and is credited for innovative strategies to organize workers and pressure employers. Carey was reelected as Teamsters' President in 1996 in a close race with James P. Hoffa, the son of James R. Hoffa. Hoffa and his supporters argued that membership and power had dwindled under Carey and that the contracts he had negotiated were deeply flawed. For example, they criticized the union's main trucking contract because it allowed freight companies to ship more goods by rail.

Unions that have merged with the Teamsters include the Allied Independent Union, in January 1957; the Laundry, Dry Cleaning, and Dye House Workers International, in March 1962; the American Communications Association, in December 1966; and the Brewery Workers, on November 6, 1973.

See also **American Federation of Labor-Congress of Industrial Organizations.**

INTERNATIONAL UNION The national organization of a labor union, so called because many unions have affiliates in Canada. In practice, international unions are understood to be synonymous with national unions. Financially supported by a per capita tax on all its members, its chief functions are extending union organization, chartering local unions, setting jurisdictional boundaries, conducting educational programs, doing research in areas related to trade union objectives, lobbying, aiding local unions in bargaining, and where multiemployer bargaining is used, negotiating directly with industry representatives if certified by the National Labor Relations Board.

See also **Multiemployer Bargaining.**

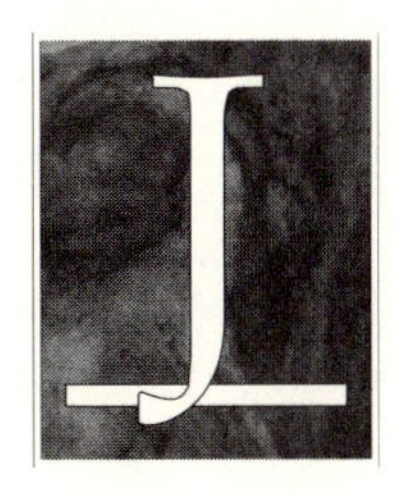

Job Action

A legal, concerted action by employees on the job which disrupts normal business activity and puts pressure on management without resorting to a strike. The term frequently covers sick-calls, work slowdowns, or work speed-ups.

See also **Concerted Action; Strike.**

Job Description

Written summary of the main features or characteristics of the job. It may include a description of the duties, responsibilities, promotional opportunities, general working conditions, employee qualifications, and the extent of the individual's responsibility. The description may be based on an analysis of the actual job performance of an incumbent or may be set up as a listing of the component parts of a job.

It is considered unfair to expect employees to perform effectively when they are not informed of the exact duties of their job. Oral job descriptions are subject to misinterpretation. Written descriptions are, thus, useful in clarifying and reinforcing oral descriptions. Written job descriptions can also help convince employees of the fairness of an employer's expectations because they show that the same requirements are imposed on all employees in a particular job classification.

Job Enlargement

A management action expanding a job to include more tasks. If a job is enlarged "vertically," duties of increasing complexity are assigned, thus placing added responsibility on the employee. This is also known as job enrichment. If a large number of similar tasks are added to a job, the job enlargement is called "horizontal."

JOB ENRICHMENT A management action that gives an employee added responsibility and more autonomy in the workplace by broadening his or her tasks and duties. It is argued that job enrichment makes many employees' jobs more meaningful. Job enrichment is also called "vertical" job enlargement.

JOB MOBILITY A worker's movement between one job and another. In the mid-to-late 1980s, both employment and income rose. By the early 1990s, more people were leaving jobs than entering them. Between 1900 and 1992, almost 43 million people left wage and salary jobs, while almost 40 million entered them.

Adults, aged 25 to 54 who changed jobs between 1990 and 1992 (and were jobless for at least one month in the interim) were more likely to have moved from a full-time to a part-time job than from a part-time to a full-time job (13 percent compared with 7 percent compared for men, 18 versus 12 percent for women). The longer someone remained jobless after having left a full-time job, the greater his or her chances of returning to a part-time job.

Men, aged 25 to 54, who left a full-time job and then, after a period of joblessness, sought full-time employment, saw their average weekly earning drop 20 percent—from $529 in their old job to $423 in their new in their new one. For women, the comparable decline was from $397 to $305.

More than 4 million workers who left their jobs between 1990 and 1992 lost their employer-provided health insurance as a result. This meant they had to either obtain coverage through some other means or try to manage without insurance.

See also **Unemployment Compensation.**

JOB SECURITY Protection of workers against job loss due to lay off or discharge. The protection consists of actions by the employer to avert the threat of layoff or severance or, if the threat becomes a reality, active help for the employees in finding suitable jobs with other employers. Job security typically means that during times of economic hardship, the employer retrains the employees rather than laying them off. Many union contracts contain provisions that protect jobs for bargaining unit members and provide for fair dismissal or just cause procedures for handling employee termination cases. Collective bargaining agreements may include job security measures such as work preservation or guarantees, work sharing, and seniority clauses.

When an employee alleges that his or her employer promised some form of job security, a court may look closely at the context of the alleged promise to determine whether the employer was seeking something in return from the employee. Evidence of such a "bargained for exchange" undermines an employer's argument that the promise was a gratuity or a mere statement of intent or policy. In fact, in the context of job negotiations between an employer and applicant, the employer's assurances of job security are difficult to describe as anything but an inducement for the employee's acceptance of employment. A court is quite likely to view such an assurance as a binding promise made in exchange for the employee's acceptance of the job.

After 30 years of improved treatment and increased job security for American workers, the risk of job loss has grown during the 1980s and 1990s. Increasingly, American workers fear job losses in an environment of corporate downsizing and shrinking payrolls that reduced the costs to corporations but that also made job security elusive. Moreover, American workers have far fewer protections against large layoffs than their European counterparts. Laws requiring notice of impending layoffs exist in almost every country in Europe, with Germany requiring the longest notice—12 months. Until recently, the major protection for displaced American workers was unemployment benefits, which tend to be insufficient.

Aside from unemployment insurance, nonunion workers have virtually no protection from large layoffs. Union workers have only slightly more. The language of union contracts may include procedures on reductions in force and plant closings, but it is generally ineffective in prohibiting an employer from closing all or part of its operations. For example, the National Labor Relations Board has ruled in two cases that employers do not have to bargain over transfer of work unless the collective bargaining agreement requires them to do so. Moreover, an employer is not required to bargain at all if a plant move is due to factors other than reducing labor costs.

Congress enacted the Worker Adjustment and Retraining Notification Act in 1989, which requires employers of 100 or more employees to provide advance notice of anticipated plant closings or other mass layoffs. It does not address the business necessity of reductions in the workforce. Nevertheless, by requiring proper notice, Congress may have established a rudimentary concept of just cause for mass layoffs. Recent proposed legislation could offer even more protection to groups of employees. New statutes and case law may require employers to meet stringent criteria related to the selection of displaced workers, provide longer notification periods, retrain and outplace employees to other companies, increase extended insurance benefits, or maintain displaced workers on preferred re-employment lists. Even more constraining for employers, new laws may require severance pay, relocation expenses, maintenance of minimum employment levels, or payment of a "super" unemployment tax for layoffs.

See also **Collective Bargaining Agreement; Downsizing; Layoff; National Labor Relations Board; Unemployment Compensation; Worker Adjustment and Retraining Notification Act.**

Job Sharing An arrangement where two employees hold a position together. They can either serve as a team, jointly responsible for the whole or responsible separately for each half of a position. The two workers combined have the workload and hours of one person.

This arrangement is often helpful to employers because it means extended hours of coverage; it is also helpful for the worker who wishes to work fewer hours. Because the job is shared, someone with the necessary expertise is always available. Job sharing, variously labeled as sharing, splitting, pairing, twinning, and tandem employment, was initiated during the 1960s in order to provide more part-time opportunities. It has been seen as a means of enhancing the work participation of women, the young, and older workers and is thought to promote greater leisure time and more work flexibility.

Job Training Partnership Act (1982) See **Job Training Programs, Federal.**

Job Training Programs, Federal Systematic instruction and training programs for the purpose of teaching job skills to individuals. National efforts to provide training for the hardcore disadvantaged, displaced workers, youth, unemployed, minority groups, and women, among others, have been implemented by statutes such as the Manpower Development and Training Act of 1962, the Comprehensive Employment Training Act of 1976, and the Job Training Partnership Act of 1982.

Beginning in the early 1960s, government-sponsored training programs became part of the nation's overall strategy for reducing unemployment and poverty. However, these measures were often criticized by civil rights activists and liberals, who believed that they did not adequately meet the needs of the disadvantaged, and by private employment agency representatives, who feared competition and bureaucratic centralization. During the 1970s and the early 1980s, additional emphasis was placed on efforts to create jobs in the public sector and to provide economic incentives for hiring in industry and business. The central purpose of the Comprehensive Employment and Training Act (CETA) of 1973 was "to provide training and employment opportunities for economically disadvantaged, unemployed or underemployed persons . . . and to assure that training and other services lead to maximum employment opportunities and enhance self-sufficiency by establishing a flexible, coordinated, and decentralized system of Federal, state, and local programs."

The responsibility for managing CETA programs rested with state and local governments, which were called "prime sponsors." The federal government provided prime sponsors with block grants, permitting local officials to tailor employment and training programs to meet the needs of their areas. A major CETA program dealt with public service employment, which by 1978 accounted for 60 percent of all CETA expenditures. The act was amended eight times, with the 1978 amendments reauthorizing it through September 1982. CETA was replaced by the Job Training Partnership Act of 1982 (JTPA).

The JTPA was the cornerstone of the Reagan administration's human resources development program, and it remained the single largest training program in the Bush administration. Both administrations wanted the JTPA to stand apart from the job training programs of the 1970s, especially CETA. Hence, JTPA provides a much greater role for state and business leaders in the daily operations of the program. The governors of each state, who are largely responsible for oversight of the program, establish service delivery areas. Each area has a Private Industry Council (PIC) that develops all training contract services jointly with local elected officials. No public service jobs were provided by the JTPA, so the PICs rely solely on the market to absorb the trained workers.

After a decade of operation, the JTPA continues to be controversial. In 1989, Secretary of Labor Elizabeth Dole described the JTPA as the "most successful training undertaken, with 68 percent of those who finish the training program being placed in jobs." Critics of JTPA charge, however, that its high placement rates during the 1980s resulted from "creaming"—that is, serving individuals who are the most employable at performance standards. Creaming created incentives that encourage the local PICs to choose those most likely to become employed after they complete their training.

JTPA's funds, like CETA's, are vulnerable to fraud, waste, and abuse when the program is controlled locally. Critics argue the lack of accountability is based on the wide discretion given to local businesses to determine who is trained and how. This problem is inherent in any system based on annual contracts rather than established institutions, where program directors do not see themselves as professionals with public responsibility for improving their programs over an extended period of time. It is this controversial power that is most criticized by those in Congress who want to exercise greater control.

Congress in the late 1980s and early 1990s attempted to make fundamental reforms in the JTPA. In 1988, an effort to make the program more accountable failed when the states were confronted with a proposed revamping of funding formulas and a resultant threat of revenue loss. Legislation was also under consideration to tighten the loopholes that allowed fraud and abuse to enter the old system. The Clinton Administration has been considering changes in JTPA in areas such as local control, the types of needs the training programs serves, and how the program evaluates its own performance.

Despite the repeated calls for reform, there seems to be an enduring faith in JTPA's underlying structure. The JTPA is centered on the idea that society greatly benefits when government and industry collaborate to train disadvantaged workers rather than relying on public service employment as CETA did. Current training efforts are generally directed at combating skill obsolescence by upgrading and developing worker skills in meeting global competition, high technology requirements, and the movement from a manufacturing to a service economy.

John Wiley & Sons, Inc. v. Livingston (1964)

In this case, the original employer, Interscience, a publisher, was purchased by and merged with John Wiley & Sons, another publishing firm, and ceased to do business as a separate entity. Interscience employees were represented by a union that had a collective bargaining agreement that contained no provision to bind successor employers to the agreement. Wiley, which had hired all of Interscience employees, was larger than Interscience and its employees were not represented by a union. Wiley refused to recognize the union or to honor the collective bargaining agreement, and the union filed a lawsuit under Section 301 of the National Labor Relations Act to force Wiley to arbitrate its grievances under the Interscience agreement. In this case, the U.S. Supreme Court ruled that the successor company was required to settle certain disputes that had arisen under the terms of the collective bargaining agreement between Livingston and the union representing its employees through arbitration. The Court held that the issue of whether the arbitration provisions of the predecessor's bargaining agreement survived the merger is for the courts to decide. The union relied on state corporation law making the successor liable for the debts of the predecessor and on national labor policy favoring arbitration. The Court held that the change in ownership would not automatically eliminate the duty to arbitrate since such a result would frustrate national labor policy. Rather, a court in a lawsuit to compel arbitration needs to balance the management prerogative to rearrange the nature of the business against the need of employees for continued protection. Noting that collective bargaining agreements are not completely the product of consensual undertakings, the Court held that Wiley could be bound to arbitrate even though it had not in fact consented to the agreement. But the duty to arbitrate does not exist in every case of changes in ownership. The test is whether there is a "substantial continuity of identity in the business enterprise before and after a change." Furthermore, the union can lose its right to arbitrate by not making its demand known in a timely fashion.

The Court also pointed out the limited nature of the claims made by the union in this case. No question was raised as to the union's right to continue to represent employees following the change in ownership, nor was the union asserting that it had any rights independent of the predecessor's bargaining agreement. The union did not seek to negotiate a new agreement. The Court avoided the potentially difficult question of how the union could secure any rights in the Wiley plant for a minority of employees without raising the issues that a "members-only" bargaining agreement ordinarily entails. The bargaining agreement with Interscience had expired, but the union only contended that certain rights under the expired agreement had accrued, or vested. The Court indicated that the union was not seeking to acquire new rights against Wiley by arbitration.

Identification of which substantive provisions of the Interscience bargaining agreement survived the change in ownership was left to an arbitrator.

Wiley failed to resolve several difficult issues but the most difficult was the question of standards for an arbitrator who must decide which provisions of the bargaining agreement carry over. This arbitration process resembles interest arbitration, where the arbitrator actually selects the terms and conditions of a bargaining agreement for consenting employers and unions, rather than the grievance arbitration given deference by the Court in the Steelworkers Trilogy. *Wiley* has subsequently been superseded by cases such as *NLRB v. Burns International Securities Services, Inc.*

Many legal scholars after *Burns* believed that the *Wiley* decision was no longer good law, mainly for the reason that none of the grounds upon which it was distinguished by the Court seemed persuasive. Other scholars saw *Burns* as not a successorship case at all and deplored the effect that *Burns* was likely to have on sale-and-purchase of assets cases. In *Golden State Bottling Co. v. NLRB* (1973), however, the Supreme Court continued to apply the *Wiley* case when it held that a National Labor Relations Board (NLRB) order remedying an unfair labor practice could apply against a purchaser of the enterprise who bought the business with notice of the outstanding NLRB order. The Court relied on *Wiley* and rejected an argument that *Wiley* is applicable only in merger situations.

See also **Collective Bargaining Agreement; *Howard Johnson Co. v. Detroit Local Joint Executive Board; NLRB v. Burns International Security Services, Inc.*; Successor Employer.**

JURISDICTION

In the labor context, jurisdiction often refers to those areas within which any agency or court is authorized to act. It also refers to the rights claimed by a union to organize a class of employees without competition from any other union.

See also **Federal-State Jurisdiction; Jurisdictional Dispute.**

JURISDICTIONAL DISPUTE

A disagreement, controversy, or conflict between two or more unions on the assignment of, or the right to perform, certain types of work. It is also a dispute over the right to represent employees in a particular company or industry. Organizational disputes involving two or more unions may be resolved by the American Federation of Labor-Congress of Industrial Organizations (AFL-CIO), by agreement of the two unions. Since the National Labor Relations Act (NLRA) as amended by the Labor-Management Relations Act (LMRA) of 1947 (the Taft-Hartley Act) prohibits jurisdictional strikes, unions face substantial pressure to resolve their own jurisdictional problems.

The questions of which group of employees should perform the work in a particular plant creates several disputes, particularly when changes in operation or materials involve the use of new equipment, machinery, or work products. A work stoppage resulting from a dispute between two or more competing unions is known as a "jurisdictional strike." The respective federations and the combined AFL-CIO have tried to reduce, if not completely eliminate, jurisdictional disputes because they harm not only the unions involved but also the public and the entire labor movement.

Though it is as disruptive as any other strike, a jurisdictional strike is particularly objectionable to employers. An employer subject to a jurisdictional strike may have no way of extricating itself. Providing the work to either of the two contending groups of employees will simply precipitate a strike by the other group. Congress, believing that these disputes should be controlled, enacted Section 8(b)(4) of the NLRA.

Section 8(b)(4) makes it an unfair labor practice for a union to induce a strike or a concerted refusal to handle goods in order to compel an employer to assign particular work to employees represented by one union rather than to employees represented by the other union. If a charge is filed alleging a jurisdictional dispute, the parties are given ten days to settle their dispute voluntarily. Section 10(k) provides that if the parties have not agreed upon a settlement within ten days, the National Labor Relations Board (NLRB) can hear the dispute and make an affirmative assignment of the disputed work.

The NLRB requires that there be reasonable cause to believe that Section 8(b)(4)(ii)(D) has been violated before a hearing is conducted to resolve the dispute. A field examiner will then preside over a hearing, as authorized under Section 10(k) of the NLRA. This official is empowered only to collect evidence with respect to the jurisdictional dispute. He or she does not render a recommended decision and makes no factual or credibility determinations. The purpose of the hearing is to determine which of the two contending unions has the better claim to the disputed work.

Once the record of the hearing reaches the NLRB, the board will render a Section 10(k) opinion. It will determine if there is a reasonable cause to believe that the dispute in this case is a jurisdictional dispute. If not, it will dismiss the charge. If it finds reasonable cause to believe that the dispute is jurisdictional, the NLRB will then draft an opinion considering the various factors supporting an assignment of the work to one union or to the other and issue an award declaring which union has the greater entitlement to the work. These factors include practice in the industry, skills of the workers involved, contracts between the parties, and efficient operation of the employer's business.

After the NLRB issues a Section 10(k) award, the regional office contacts the losing union and asks for a commitment that it will not continue to seek the work by prohibited means. If the union agrees, the case is ended. If, however, the union refuses to accept the NLRB's award, the Section 8(b)(4)(D) complaint goes forward. Since the evidence on whether the dispute is jurisdictional has already been collected in the Section 10(k) hearing, any Section 8(b)(4)(D) hearing before an administrative law judge is likely to be procedural, and the NLRB may issue a summary judgment at that point. When the case returns to the board after the 8(b)(4)(D) hearing, the NLRB will not relitigate the merits of the Section 10(k) award and is likely to defer to its original finding that the dispute was jurisdictional. A cease and desist order will then be issued against the losing union, forbidding it from engaging in prohibited conduct to gain the disputed work.

The employer is not bound to follow a Section 10(k) award. The award does not mean that the union the NLRB has found to have the greater entitlement to the work will actually be assigned the work. Its only effect is that the losing union will not be able to strike for the work without violating Section 8(b)(4)(D). If the unions do not comply with the NLRB determination or voluntary adjustment, an unfair labor practice complaint will be issued against the offending union. The NLRB will enter a cease and desist order and seek court enforcement. If the employer refuses to assign the work to the union the NLRB has favored by the Section 10(k) award, that union will then be able to strike or take other coercive action without violating Section 8(b)(4)(D).

See also **American Federation of Labor-Congress of Industrial Organizations; Charge; Labor Movement; National Labor Relations Act; National Labor Relations Board; Unfair Labor Practice.**

JURY DUTY LEAVE

Under the Jury System Improvements Act, an employee is protected from discharge, intimidation, and coercion by an employer because of the employee's service on a jury in federal court.

Every state except Montana has a statutory provision protecting an employee from discharge because of serving on a jury in a state or federal court. Like the protection afforded under the Jury System Improvement Act, several states prohibit an employer from threatening or coercing an employee because of jury service. However, many states focus merely on protections against wrongful discharge.

Employers find that jury duty clauses, like funeral leave clauses, often cause debate out of proportion to their cost. They usually limit the clause to the number of weeks during which jury duty pay will be available and often indicate that jury duty pay is the difference between the employee's regular rate of pay and the jury pay itself. The regular rate is often limited to straight time only. Unions will sometimes bargain to expand the scope of jury duty clauses to include pay for time lost when the employee is responding to a subpoena.

See also **Coercion; Wrongful Discharge.**

JUST CAUSE Standards or restrictions on management's right to discharge or discipline employees covered under a collective bargaining agreement. Also known as "justifiable cause," "proper cause," "obvious cause," or "cause." The term is commonly found, but seldom defined, in collective bargaining agreements, and the labor arbitrator is often called upon to determine whether there was just cause for the discipline or discharge action. Although there is no uniform definition of what constitutes just cause, a commonly accepted set of guidelines has been developed by arbitrators in determining whether the conduct of the discharged or disciplined employee was defensible and the penalty just. One of the most popular versions of the guidelines was articulated by Professor Carroll Daughtery, who in *Enterprise Wire Co.* (1966) suggested seven test questions involving just cause. A "no" answer to any of them would normally mean that just cause did not exist.

1. Was the employee given advance warning of the possible or probable disciplinary consequences of the employee's conduct?
2. Was the rule or order reasonably related to the efficient and safe operation of the business?
3. Before administering discipline, did the employer make an effort to discover whether the employee did, in fact, violate a rule or order of management?

4. Was the employer's investigation conducted fairly and objectively?
5. Did the investigation produce substantial evidence or proof that the employee was guilty as charged?
6. Had the company applied its rules, orders, and penalties without discrimination?
7. Was the degree of discipline administered in the particular case reasonably to (a) the seriousness of their employee's proven offense, and (b) the employee's record of company service?

See also **Collective Bargaining Agreement.**

Labor Department, U.S.

See **U.S. Department of Labor.**

Labor Dispute

A controversy between employers and employees, between employers and unions, between two unions, or between a union and its members. Although the term is sometimes used as a synonym for strike, a labor dispute need not lead to a work stoppage. In the current labor environment, disgruntled workers are more likely to participate in work slowdowns known as "holdouts" than to strike. This trend coincides with a rise in the willingness of employers to replace striking workers with permanent employees.

Section 13(c) of the Norris-LaGuardia Act (1932) defines labor disputes to include "any controversy, concerning terms or conditions of employment, or concerning the association or representation of persons in negotiating, fixing, maintaining, changing, or seeking to arrange terms or conditions of employment, regardless of whether or not the disputants stand in the proximate relation of employer and employee." Those who may be involved in a labor dispute it defines as persons in the same occupations or having interest therein or who work for the same employer or who are members of the same or affiliated union. The courts have frequently and scrupulously examined the extent to which a controversy constitutes a labor dispute within the meaning of the Norris-LaGuardia Act. Section 2(9) of Title I of the National Labor Relations Act, as amended, defined the term "labor dispute" in the same manner as it is defined under the Norris-LaGuardia Act.

Labor disputes may be distinguished according to the nature of the matter at issue. Rights disputes, sometimes called legal labor disputes, are controversies surrounding the application, interpretation, or existence of rights arising out of the collective bargaining agreement. Labor disputes are often categorized as (1) those related to the interpretation or violation of the terms of the collective bargaining agreements; (2) jurisdictional disputes; (3) interest disputes; and (4) disputes concerning the bargaining agent, recognition, or related issues.

Negotiating a lasting settlement in an employment dispute may require attention to several issues, including financial matters such as wages; fringe benefits such as health insurance, stock options, and retirement benefits; payment of fees and costs related to the mediation procedure; the emotional needs of both employees and management; the type of termination, which may be voluntary resignation, involuntary termination, layoff, or retirement; references; confidentiality; releases and waivers; and breach of the agreement.

Business leaders sometimes welcome certain disputes, because they allow executives a chance to show leadership by showing concern for the employees and to align their personal agendas with the corporation. When disputes are encountered, they are isolated from their emotional aspects by ventilating emotions and letting the parties discuss important issues. The intentions of the parties concerned then are fused and an action plan to correct the problems involved in the disputes.

See also **Benefits; Collective Bargaining; Mediation; Norris-LaGuardia Act; Termination.**

LABOR FORCE Includes all persons in the population 16 years of age and older who (1) worked as paid employees, in their own business, profession, or on their own farm, or who worked 15 hours or more per week as unpaid workers in an enterprise operated by a member of the family; (2) have a job but are not at work because of illness, bad weather, vacation, labor-management dispute, or personal reasons; (3) are not at work but made specific efforts to find a job within the past four weeks, were available for work from which they had been laid off, or were waiting to report to a new job within 30 days. Employed citizens of foreign countries who are temporarily in the United States but not living on the premises of an embassy are also included. The U.S. Department of Labor draws a distinction between the civilian labor force and the total labor force, with the total labor force including military personnel.

Those not included in the labor force are all other persons 16 years and older who are also engaged in their own home housework, in school, unable to work because of long-term physical or mental illness, retired, or "other." The "other" group is composed of those too old or temporarily unable to work, voluntarily idle, seasonal workers who were not working, those who did not look for work, and discouraged workers—persons who did not look for work because they believed that no jobs were available or that they could not qualify for the available jobs.

The full-time labor force includes persons working on full-time schedules (35 hours or more), those who worked less than 35 hours for economic or noneconomic reasons but usually work full time, and persons with a job who were not at work but who usually work full time. The part-time labor force consists of persons voluntarily working part time (less than 35 hours); those who want to work full time but worked part time for economic reasons, i.e., persons who could find only part-time work; and those with a job but not at work and who usually work part time.

See also **Part-time Employment.**

LABOR INJUNCTIONS

See **Injunctions against Unions.**

LABOR LAWS

Usually refers to all federal or state legislation designed to protect or improve the conditions of workers as well as the rights of labor unions, employers, and the public. Protection may deal with such diverse areas as collective bargaining, wage and hour regulation, the employment of children, safety, and other areas directly or indirectly related to employment conditions.

In understanding the term "law" or "labor law," one must first realize that there are four important bodies of law: (1) statutory law, which consists of legislation passed by individual state legislatures or by the Congress; (2) case law, which is composed of court interpretations of statutes; (3) administrative law, the regulations and decisions promulgated by duly authorized agencies; and (4) industrial jurisprudence, which consists of the decisions arising out of the daily collective bargaining relationship of the parties and the administration of the contract. Industrial jurisprudence may also be thought of as the common law of industrial relations. It may be given substance in arbitration awards or accepted by the parties themselves as a basis for working out their relationships.

In labor relations, it is also important to understand how the respective authority of state and federal governments is divided. Over the years, Supreme Court case law has changed the boundaries between state and federal jurisdiction until, in practice, the division of authority between the state and federal law is somewhat flexible.

On the federal level, the National Labor Relations Act of 1935, also known as the Wagner Act, guaranteed workers the right to choose their collective bargaining representatives by majority vote and required employer recognition and good faith bargaining. Recognizing the imbalance of power between the employer and the employee in the workplace, a central purpose of the Wagner Act was to regulate employer tactics and reduce the level of fear and intimidation felt by employees.

The passage of the Labor-Management Relations Act of 1947 (also known as the Taft-Hartley Act) heralded a period of the law's hostility to unions. Courts have generally constrained labor's ability to act while giving management greater freedoms. Because management's right to manage had been challenged during World War II, management became increasingly concerned about organized labor's refusal to accept any list of the specific functions reserved only to management and not subject to union influence or bargaining. Stability and undisputed control over strategic business decisions were management's major postwar aims. The Taft-Hartley Act gave priority to management's right to control work and to the individual worker's right not to join the union over the rights of workers to bargain collectively and to engage in other concerted activity.

National Labor Relations Board (NLRB) regulation was largely consistent with the economic model of bargaining that emerged out of unionized labor's position of power after World War II. Labor, not the NLRB, developed a model of centralized bargaining in which most issues are reduced to an extension of the economic wage agreement.

Industrial restructuring after World War II disrupted collective bargaining relationships in most American industries. Increased competition significantly reduced the foundation of union bargaining power, producing the most sustained period of union concessions during the 1980s. The increasing willingness of employers to actively resist unionization and the ineffectiveness of labor unions in redressing violations of labor laws has been accompanied by a decline in the number of representation elections, in the number of representation elections won by employees, and where elections have been won, in the securing of first contracts. Even with a substantial majority favoring organization, employees seeking independent representation have less than a one in four chance of obtaining an initial contract.

Many labor law experts advocate comprehensive labor law reform similar to the reform of commercial codes earlier in the century. Because American society is litigious and dynamic, and because labor law will evolve over the coming years, the legal struggle against discrimination may eventually convince the courts and legislatures that protection against arbitrary employer treatment for all workers is good policy and good law. The difficulty thus far has been that neither labor nor business had actively promoted legal safeguards for unorganized workers not protected by union-negotiated bargaining agreements.

Pro-union commentators argue that employers should not be allowed to inhibit the exercise of organizational rights through campaign delays and coercive behavior or to benefit from unlawful behavior. Unionists, to remedy these problems, advocate the use of interim injunctions to guarantee the speedy reinstatement of employees illegally discharged during organizing campaigns, the use of first contract arbitration when newly certified unions are unable to obtain initial agreements through collective bargaining, and limitations of the right of business entities to employ permanent replacements during economic strikes.

See also **Collective Bargaining; Grievance Arbitration; Hours of Labor; Labor Union; Management Rights; National Labor Relations Act; National Labor Relations Board; Permanently Replaced Employees; Wages.**

LABOR LEADER

Usually designates an individual devoting full time to the labor movement, or who has achieved prominence in leading a labor union. Leadership ranges from those active in local and regional areas to those who have important roles in major policy objectives of the labor movement on a national level.

Proponents of the Labor-Management Relations Act of 1947 (the Taft-Hartley Act) believed that workers would accept offers their supposedly "militant and unreasonable leaders" were unable or unwilling to accept. That theory has proved remarkably incorrect. When a last offer has been rejected, it is much more likely to be the rank and file workers who are pushing the union leaders and the leaders who are urging restraint. Also, any vote conducted by an outside agency (usually the

National Labor Relations Board) is likely to become a confrontation between the union and the employer and a vote over whether the workers support their union.

See also **Labor-Management Relations Act of 1947; Labor Movement; National Labor Relations Act; National Labor Relations Board.**

LABOR LOBBY Those groups of trade unionists or individuals assigned to the state or federal legislatures to influence action and win support of special labor legislation or legislation designed to protect or assist members of their organization.

LABOR MOVEMENT This generally inclusive term covers several organized group actions on behalf of working people in particular industries or workplaces. Essentially economic in its nature, the labor movement also engages in political activity. Thus the term encompasses all union activity in the fields of collective bargaining and social welfare. Although generally applied to organized workers and wage earners and concerned with their growth, structure, and activities, it sometimes also refers to the total mass movement of a working population not merely limited to union members.

The American labor movement is not monolithic but includes a diverse set of actors and situations. There are substantial differences, for example, between craft and industrial unions in ideology, structure, tactics, and social composition.

The labor movement is motivated by more than just economic goals. Like the politically disenfranchised who seek a greater voice in how government is run, the labor movement works to give the industrially disenfranchised some voice in the workplace. It provides not only an essential service by identifying workplace problems but also a vehicle by which working people can articulate their needs for improved workplace conditions.

There are several other ways of analyzing the labor movement. One is through a "functional analysis," which views the American labor movement as one of those elite power holders that can be relied upon to preserve harmony, stability, and support the status quo. A second is through a "conflict theory," which sees organized labor in a continuous struggle over power and resources. And third, a "humanistic theory" that emphasizes the ideal workplace environment and urges a new examination of accepted truths and unexamined assumptions. In the labor-management relations, the humanistic approach has led to surprising results. For example, a union-management coalition that sought to gain control of United Airlines was warned that unions and employee ownership are not compatible. Their successful effort was an example of an environment where unionized and profitable employee ownership work well together.

See also **Collective Bargaining.**

LABOR ORGANIZATION

A group of workers combined in a voluntary association for the common purpose of protecting or advancing the wages, hours, and working conditions of their members.

Section 2(3) of the National Labor Relations Act (NLRA) defines the term labor organization as "any kind, or any agency or employee representation committee or plan, in which employees participate and which exists for the purpose, in whole or in part, of dealing with employers concerning grievances, labor disputes, wage rates of pay, hours of employment or conditions of work." The NLRA does not require that the labor organization have a constitution, by-laws, or any form of structure.

Under Title VII of the Civil Rights Act of 1964 or the Age Discrimination in Employment Act, a labor organization is "engaged in an industry affecting commerce" if it either maintains or operates a hiring hall that provides employment opportunities for employees, or if it has a specified number of members and meets one of the following tests:

1. It is the certified representative of employees under the NLRA or the Railway Labor Act.
2. It is a national or international labor organization or a local labor organization recognized or acting as the representative of employees of an employer or employers engaged in an industry affecting commerce.
3. It has chartered a local labor organization or subsidiary body that is representing or actively seeking to represent employees of employers within the meaning of paragraphs (1) and (2).
4. It has been chartered by a labor organization representing or actively seeking to represent employees within the meaning of paragraphs (1) or (2) above as the local or subordinate body through which those

employees may enjoy membership or become affiliated with the labor organization.

5. It is a conference, general committee, joint or system board, or joint council subordinate to a national or international labor organization engaged in an industry affecting commerce within the meaning of (1), (2), (3), or (4). [*Ballinger v. Arlington Park Thoroughbred Race Track* (1989)]

The National Labor Relations Board's (NLRB) assertion of jurisdiction over an industry supports the belief that the industry affects commerce, and that labor organizations engaged in the industry are, therefore, subject to Title VII. Also, a labor organization can be subject to Title VII even when the NLRB has declined to assert jurisdiction over an industry.

The U.S. Supreme Court has rejected the argument that employee "committees," as opposed to unions, are excluded from the term "labor organization" as it is used in Section 8(a)(2) of the NLRA. Thus, an employer who dealt with such employee committees in matters involving the whole scope of the employment relationship, including matters commonly considered and deal with in collective bargaining can be guilty of an unfair labor practice under Section 8(a)(2). [*NLRB v. Cabot Carbon* (1959)]

Employee committees that addressed issues involving safety, fitness, recreation, health, programs, and publicity are also labor organizations. On the other hand, cooperative programs that would not be labor organizations include a group of employees that makes an ad hoc proposal in an isolated instance; a brainstorming group whose only purpose is to develop ideas rather than to make proposals; a committee with the exclusive purpose of sharing information with the employer; and a suggestion box procedure where employees make specific proposals to management on an individual basis. [*E.I. DuPont & Co.* (1993)]

Four out of the five largest increases in union membership corresponded with periods of war. The only growth period that does not fit this pattern is the New Deal period (1933–1939), which was characterized by a serious domestic crisis. Labor, some commentators believe, does not control its destiny. This view holds that throughout American history, workers and labor organizations are more often the acted upon rather than the actors.

See also **Age Discrimination in Employment Act; Civil Rights Act of 1964; National Labor Relations Act; National Labor Relations Board; Railway Labor Act; Unfair Labor Practice.**

LABOR ORGANIZER A person commonly referred to as a "representative," generally employed by a union, usually the international union, who is assigned to particular districts or regions or may work out of central headquarters and travels to where the union has members or potential members. Initially, the labor organizer's job is to recruit new members and establish new local organizations. After the new local is established, the organizer acts as an adviser to all of the locals within the assigned region on both internal union affairs and the union's relations with employers. The labor organizer plays an important role in interpreting the aims and policies of the international to the local officers and members and in keeping the international officers informed of the conditions and problems of the local unions.

Organizers are still considered the vanguard of the labor movement, the front-line troops in the effort to expand unionization. But union organizing has suffered serious setbacks, especially in the 1980s. Recognizing this problem, the AFL-CIO and its affiliates have vigorously initiated new ways to attract and organize new members. They have used associate membership to introduce workers to unions and to what unions can do for them. They have also developed new and quite promising approaches in recruiting and training new organizers. They have instituted new ways to target and organize potential bargaining units, using innovative tactics to reach the fastest growing sector—the service sector. The labor movement is seeking more organizers and a new breed of organizer. The AFL-CIO is doing this through its Organizing Institute, expanding resources for union organizers and matching organizers more closely with targets.

See also **American Federation of Labor-Congress of Industrial Organizations; International Union; Labor Movement; Union.**

LABOR RACKETEERING The use of union office or power for personal gain. Examples include embezzling funds; arranging "sweetheart agreements"; accepting a bribe by a union officer to overlook the violation of a rule in the labor agreement; accepting payments for calling off a strike or a campaign to organize a firm when the tactics are required by the tenets of union; accepting payment for so-called strike insurance; colluding with employers and union officers to create monopolies that are in the interest of employers, vendors, and union officers rather than the union members; and accepting kickbacks and rebates for the placement of union health and welfare contracts. Organized crime families and syndicates have played a large role in union corruption throughout the history of the modern American labor movement.

Four federal statutes prohibit racketeering that affects interstate or foreign commerce: the Racketeer-Influenced and Corrupt Organizations Act (RICO); the Anti-Racketeering (or Hobbs Act), which prohibits labor unions from blackmailing employers or accepting bribes for not calling strikes; Section 602 of the Labor-Management Reporting and Disclosure Act, which makes extortionate picketing a crime; and the Labor-Management Relations Act of 1947 (the Taft-Hartley Act), which makes interstate truckers' demands for unloading fees subject to criminal prosecution and an injunction.

Through its enactment of the Hobbs Act in 1934, Congress indicated its intention that racketeering activities in the labor context be punished. The Hobbs Act does not prohibit all demands pertaining to a labor dispute, however—it prohibits only those demands that are motivated by an intent to commit extortion. The Hobbs Act provides criminal penalties for a person who obstructs commerce "by robbery or extortion" or "commits or threatens physical violence to any person or property" in furtherance of a plan to do some action in violation of the statute.

"Legitimate labor activities" refers to actions taken in disputes over recognition and over terms and conditions of employment performed in accordance with the law, as opposed to extortion for personal gain. Such illegal activities include the use of coercive measures to obtain wage increases or carry out bargaining agreement, and the right to picket. [*United States v. Gibson* (1984)] Legitimate labor activities do not include the acceptance of payments by union representatives for their own gain, from which the union members can derive no benefit. Nor do they include an attempt by a union and its agent to obtain money, through the use of actual and threatened force, violence, and fear, to be paid employees for unwanted, superfluous, and fictitious services. Those who commit such acts can be held liable under the Hobbs Act.

Legitimate labor activities are not made illegal by the Hobbs Act. The U.S. Supreme Court specifically held that the statute does not apply to the use of force to achieve legitimate labor ends. Even violence is not prohibited by the Hobbs Act when it is used to achieve a legitimate union objectives, such as higher wages in return for services which the employer seeks, or when it is committed during a lawful strike for the purpose of inducing an employer to agree to legitimate collective bargaining demands. [*United*

States v. Billingsley (1973); *United States v. Enmons* (1973)] Picket-line violence is always illegal; the only question is whether it will be treated as a state crime on its own merits or will be made a federal felony because the motive for the violence is extortion. The problem with the concept of extortion in labor relations is that labor unions do indeed seek to use force to obtain something of value (increased wages) from the employer—a process that could fit the common-law definition of extortion.

Congress enacted RICO in 1970 as part of the Organized Crime Control Act to combat the influence of organized crime in interstate and foreign commerce. The statute provides another federal tool to combat racketeering activities in relevant labor settings. A primary purpose of the statute is to prevent organized crime from infiltrating legitimate economic enterprises, illegally acquiring such enterprises, and to prohibit organized crime from using both. RICO created four new crimes that are particularly applicable to the area of labor-management racketeering. In essence, RICO makes it unlawful for any person to use a pattern of racketeering activity to participate in the business of a formal or informal enterprise. Section 1963(a) prohibits the acquisition of an enterprise using any income derived from illegal activity; Section 1962(b) prohibits the illegal acquisition or maintenance of any interest or control of an enterprise; Section 1962(c) is designed to reach persons who are employed by or associated with an enterprise, and who use that enterprise to engage in unlawful activities; and Section 1962(d) prohibits any conspiracy to violate any of the subsections (a), (b), or (c) of 1962. However, there is no conspiracy where the only actors are the union, the members, and officers.

The U.S. Department of Justice sued the International Brotherhood of Teamsters under RICO in 1980. The consent decree provided for court-appointed officers who would oversee certain union operations after the Teamsters' 1991 election.

Some commentators believe that all matters involving labor relations should be governed by federal labor laws with RICO playing no role. These proposals envision a remedy under labor law as opposed to RICO. Any acts of violence still would be treated as crimes under state law or, for certain conduct (kidnapping or using explosives), as violations of federal criminal law. An employer seeking compensatory damages for injury suffered still would have access, where appropriate, to state tort remedies and to federal remedies for secondary actions. Civil RICO actions, however, would be excluded because Congress did not intend those activities to be criminalized.

See also **Consent Decree; Injunctions Against Unions; Labor Movement; Labor-Management Reporting and Disclosure Act; National Labor Relations Act.**

LABOR RELATIONS BOARDS

LABOR RELATIONS BOARDS Administrative agencies authorized by national or state labor statutes to issue and adjudicate complaints alleging unfair labor practices; to require such practices to be stopped; and to certify bargaining agents for employees.

On the national level, the current national labor relations boards include the National Labor Relations Board (NLRB), which administers the National Labor Relations Act, as amended; the National Mediation Board; and the National Railroad Adjustment Board under the Railway Labor Act. They may deal with unfair union and employer practices, representation elections, and a variety of policy matters that are incorporated into the statutes.

State labor relations boards, in both the private and public sectors, concern themselves with problems similar of those handled by the NLRB and may have, in addition, mediation and arbitration functions.

See also **Grievance Arbitration; Mediation; National Labor Relations Act; National Labor Relations Board; Railway Labor Act; Unfair Labor Practice.**

LABOR UNION

LABOR UNION In the broad sense, a continuous association of wage-earners for the purpose of maintaining or improving the conditions of their working lives. Contemporary labor unions are responsibile for maintaining and improving its members' terms and conditions of employment through collective bargaining with the employer and through other means.

The two generally recognized types of labor unions are the industrial union and the craft union. The craft union consists of an association of workers in a particular trade or skill, whereas the industrial union cuts across craft lines to unite all the workers in a particular industry into a coherent central organization. Labor unions, such as the Knights of Labor, included all workers regardless of craft, industry, profession, and without regard to differences suggesting the concept of the "solidarity of the working class" and the "brotherhood of man." Because the Knights of Labor appealed to all workers, it was quite different from earlier craft unions, which limited entry into their unions, or the American Federation of Labor (AFL), which originally consisted of independent national unions organized on the basis of crafts or trades. Some historians believe the development of American craft and industrial unions was influenced by the fact that the United States is not characterized by a rigid economic class and because it is, theoretically, the land of social mobility. Therefore, there was no perceived need for an ideology of the American working class because there was no class struggle. Instead, the AFL advocated "business unionism," that is, it would work to improve its members' wages, hours, and working conditions.

Another division of labor unions may be made in terms of local union, international union, and federation. A local union consists of employees in one or more bargaining unit(s) at a single plant or in a limited geographical area. It is chartered by the national or international union with which it is affiliated. A local union is the basic unit of labor organization. An international union is a parent union composed of affiliated locals in the United States and other countries. The United Steelworkers of American and the United Automobile Workers of America are two international unions. A federation is a league or alliance of national and international unions designed to provide mutual assistance on a federal level regarding legislation and policy formation and at the same time to provide autonomy to the unions affiliated or federated with it. The AFL-CIO is a labor federation.

The relations between the international unions and labor federations can be examined by focusing on two key principles of the American Federation of Labor—the "autonomy of the international unions" and the "principle of exclusive jurisdiction." With the 1955 merger of the American Federation of Labor and the Congress of Industrial Organizations, the concept of "established bargaining relationship" replaced "exclusive jurisdiction" as the basic principle governing relationships among affiliates. An international union, however, has the power to suspend the autonomy of a local union through a trusteeship.

From a high point of 35.7 percent of the private nonagricultural workforce in 1953, the United States currently has the lowest rate of union membership (15 percent of the private sector labor force) of all industrialized countries except France. This is approximately the same portion of the workforce that unions represented in the 1920s. If current trends continue, unions may represent only 5 percent of the U.S. labor force by the year 2000. Absent reform of the labor relations system, unions are likely to remain a significant force only in government employment, big city commercial construction, rail and air transportation, and certain shrinking mining and manufacturing industries.

The decline of union membership is due to (1) the changing demographic structure of the workforce; (2) a relative decline in the industries that have been most heavily unionized; (3) the impact of international competition; (4) the geographical migration of industry from prounion to right-to-work states; (5) the provision by government of many of the previous objectives of labor unions; (6) the intensification of employer opposition; and (7) the declining effectiveness of labor law, and its weak enforcement.

The structure of the American labor relations system required to meet the challenges of today's competitive global markets causes the following problems for labor unions: First, the system is decentralized, largely because unions seek elections on the basis of the smallest organizing unit. National Labor Relations Board (NLRB) elections are held at the plant level, usually among a subset of the workers, with the craft workers and professionals having the right to choose separate representation. Multiemployer bargaining units are formed only by consent—that is, it requires a clear and unequivocal intent by the unit members of each employer to be bound in collective bargaining by group rather than individual action. Second, the system is based on an adversarial model of labor-management relations. Though the system does not require adversarial unions or management, an essential concept behind the National Labor Relations Act is that there is a fundamental conflict of interest between labor and management, and that a structural guarantee is required to keep separate their respective spheres of influence. Thus, employers may play no role in forming or assisting labor organizations. Similarly, management representatives, including supervisors and nonsupervisory personnel with a role in making or implementing policy, may not form unions.

Unions have also been criticized for being less than democratic. Some unions have long been regarded as both undemocratic and corrupt, including the Teamsters, Longshoremen, Laborers, and Hotel and Restaurant Employees. The 1976–1977 Steelworkers' election campaigns of antiadministration challenger Edward Sadlowski and incumbent administration choice Lloyd McBride raised questions about the relations between the unions and the workers they represented. Other similar issues involve nonmembers' refusal to pay agency fees, the union duty of fair representation for nonmembers, and union discipline for a member's failure to observe a strike action.

After several years of declining membership, labor unions have recently begun to grow again. During the early to mid 1990s, approximately 200,000 new workers have joined unions. Strong recruitment drives, effective strikes, and innovative labor actions have increased union popularity. In order to continue reversing their long history of membership decline, labor unions must organize traditionally nonunionized workers by developing a more appealing public image, using more innovative organizing techniques, and focusing more energy on the needs of an increasingly female, nonwhite, service-sector labor force.

White-collar workers in the large corporations that now propel the U.S. economy are especially reluctant to join unions, which they often consider corrupt, unnecessary, and at best suitable only for blue-collar workers. The future vitality of the U.S. labor movement depends upon labor's ability to serve the needs of the late-twentieth-century workforce, increasingly composed of corporate workers employed in large, participatory, professionalized, postindustrial workplaces. Unions must address white-collar workers' desire for upward mobility by addressing their professionalism and careerism, their desire to engage in self-supervised, self-directed work, and their goal of high performance. White-collar antiunionism originates in the technological and educational similarity of white-collar work to the work of the supervisor or employer, the physical nearness to him or her; the prestige borrowed from him or her; the rejection of wage-worker types of organizations for prestige reasons; the greater privileges and security; and the hope of upward mobility—all of which lead the white-collar employee to identify with the boss.

Organized labor will strengthen itself by expanding its role to facilitate worker self-management. It must adjust to the transformation of the work world and the concomitant changes in workers' lives in order to reclaim its dignifying and democratizing influence in the workplace and society.

See also **American Federation of Labor-Congress of Industrial Organizations; Blue-Collar Worker; Craft Union; Duty of Fair Representation; Industrial Union; Labor Movement; Labor Organization; National Labor Relations Act; National Labor Relations Board; Right-To-Work Laws; White-Collar Worker; Union Trusteeship.**

LABOR-MANAGEMENT COOPERATION Joint efforts by labor and management to increase areas of agreement and to work toward common objectives as allies instead of adversaries. The concept of alliance sets cooperative programs apart from the traditional collective bargaining process, although both are problem-solving techniques.

There are a variety of labor-management cooperation plans. Terms such as codetermination, participative management, employee/worker involvement, organizational change and development, integrative bargaining, labor-management committee, quality of work life (QWL), productivity bargaining, quality circles (QCs), and gainsharing (Scanlan Plan, Rucker Plan) describe cooperative ventures. Each program seeks to obtain specific goals. The primary goal of gainsharing plans, for example, is productivity improvement; QCs seek to reduce costs and improve quality; labor-management committees look to improve labor-management relations and communication; and QWL programs attempt to improve the psychological well-being of the worker and increase job satisfaction.

The theories of labor-management cooperation, some of which are simply extensions of existing perspectives on labor relations, extend across the ideological spectrum. The centrist and leftist views of cooperation are linked to traditional industrial pluralism, while the rightist view is profoundly antiunion and seeks to reorient workers toward management objectives.

Many commentators argue that the traditional adversarial relationship between labor and management has not provided optimal results. Therefore, more cooperative employee involvement programs and less confrontational labor-management relationships have been proposed. These proposals include amending Section 8(a)(2) of the National Labor Relations Act, which prohibits the employer domination of labor organizations and might preclude work participation plans that include managerial personnel, in order to permit bona fide employee-involvement programs that would supplement rather than supplant union representation.

Labor management cooperative programs, which under certain circumstances may include employee committees or as they are commonly called, quality circles, can be legally established. However, employee committees set up by an employer to confer with management over such issues as absenteeism and attendance bonuses are considered labor organizations and act in a representative capacity, as union committees do. [*Electromation* (1991)]

Employee committees that address issues involving safety, fitness, recreation, health, programs, and publicity are also considered labor organizations. Cooperative programs that would not be considered labor organizations include a group of employees that makes an ad hoc proposal in an isolated instance, a brainstorming group whose only purpose is to develop ideas rather than to make proposals, a committee with the exclusive purpose of sharing information with the employer, and a suggestion box procedure where employees make specific proposals to management on an individual basis. [*E.I. DuPont & Co.* (1993)]

Union leaders generally distrust collaborative or cooperative management proposals, believing that collective bargaining is the best way to achieve healthy relationships between workers and management. They view employer offers of workplace cooperation as another means of trying to obtain more production with less labor, simply replacing the old time-and-motion with new offers of job enrichment.

Despite the history of adversarial labor-management relations, innovations such as employee involvement, team production, gainsharing—all aimed at tapping employee knowledge and skills—can make major improvements in productivity, product quality, and economic competitiveness. But many current efforts do not live up to their potential. Indeed, employee involvement is still in an embryonic state, partly because it is seldom pursued vigorously, thoroughly, openly, and with full commitment and mutual trust. In part, "lean and mean" corporate strategists who aggressively pursue downsizing, thereby destroying employee job security and trust, are to blame for the meager results of employee involvement programs. Another culprit is the largely nonunion environment of the American business environment.

Employee participation tends to work most effectively in a union environment—at least when the union is involved in and supports the participation process. Employee involvement and labor-management cooperation are most effective when labor is given considerable input, not only into the design and operation of the participation process but also into crucial strategic corporate decisions. Employee training, product quality and design, introduction of new technology, work design, investment, and location of production are all examples of strategic decisions. Employee participation in designing and operating involvement programs occurs almost exclusively in unionized corporations because the union entails representation as well as directs employee participation.

One effective form of labor-management cooperation in the organized sector is the "enterprise compact," which is guided by seven objectives: (1) mutually established productivity growth targets, (2) compensation goals consistent with productivity growth, (3) price-setting targets, (4) quality targeted to international standards, with quality assurance becoming a "strikable" issue, (5) employment security, (6) profit sharing or gainsharing, and (7) joint decision making throughout the firm, including labor representation on the board of directors and the abolition of traditional management rights clauses.

See also **Collective Bargaining; Job Enrichment; Job Security; Labor Organization; Management Rights; Quality Circles; Quality of Work Life.**

LABOR-MANAGEMENT COOPERATION ACT OF 1978

By the 1970s, the increased caseload of the National Labor Relations Board (NLRB) had placed considerable strain on the NLRB's ability to operate and caused serious delays. To remedy these problems, Congress enacted this statute as part of the Comprehensive Employment and Training Act Amendments of 1978, which authorizes and directs the Federal Mediation and Conciliation Service to provide grants and assist in the establishment and operation of labor-management committees. These committees are intended to improve organizational effectiveness, working conditions, and working relationships; to provide mechanisms to resolve problems; to enhance employee decision making and participation in workplace matters; and to encourage free collective bargaining.

See also **Collective Bargaining; Federal Mediation and Conciliation Service; National Labor Relations Board.**

LABOR-MANAGEMENT RELATIONS

A subset of industrial relations, labor-management relations refers to unionized employment situations. Usually it also refers to the procedures that union representatives and managements have created to settle disputes. Most disagreements are resolved by negotiation. When the negotiation process results in a written contract, it is called collective bargaining. On the other hand, labor-management relations have often been characterized by extreme actions such as lockouts, strikes, or even violence.

See also **Collective Bargaining; Employment Contract; Lockout; Strike.**

LABOR-MANAGEMENT RELATIONS ACT (LMRA) OF 1947 Popularly known as the Taft-Hartley Act, this statute represents the first major successful effort to amend the National Labor Relations Act of 1935 (NLRA). The legislation was called the "Taft-Hartley Act" after the respective chairmen of the Senate Labor and Public Welfare Committee, Robert A. Taft (R-OH), and the House Labor Committee, Rep. Fred A. Hartley, Jr. (R-NJ). Its avowed purpose was "to define and proscribe practices on the part of labor and management which affect commerce and are inimical to the general welfare." The act was passed by both houses of Congress. On June 20, 1947, President Truman vetoed the bill, but it became law after Congress overrode Truman's veto.

Following World War II, several widespread and often crippling strikes, drives for higher wages, and the perceived threat of labor unions prompted Congress to enact the Taft-Hartley Act. During this time, several states passed statutes that ordered new restrictions on unions, 16 of them prohibiting the closed shop, 21 requiring strike notices and cooling-off periods, and 12 forbidding secondary boycotts. Ten forced unions to file financial reports, and six removed prohibitions against the use of injunctions in labor disputes.

The Taft-Hartley Act provides a series of union unfair labor practices to parallel the employer unfair labor practices in the original NLRA. Provisions of the law dealt with matters such as the filing of certain financial statements with the U.S. Department of Labor and limitations on certain types of strike activity. The Taft-Hartley Act also limited union security provisions of the NLRA by outlawing the closed shop and the automatic checkoff and, under certain circumstances, substituting a form of a union shop. The statute also provides special procedures for handling national emergency disputes, including an injunction that delays a strike for approximately 80 days, during which time a board of inquiry gathers facts on the basic issues, elections are held on the company's last offer, and mediation efforts assist the parties in reaching agreement. It also provides methods of enforcing the collective bargaining agreement through lawsuits in the federal courts, and transfers the mediation and conciliation functions of the U.S. Conciliation Service in the U.S. Department of Labor to a separate and independent agency known as the Federal Mediation and Conciliation Service.

The Taft-Hartley Act marked a shift away from a federal policy encouraging unionization toward a more neutral position. While some commentators interpret the statute as encouraging collective bargaining, others believe that the Taft-Hartley Act was intended to protect free choice and individual rights of employees. Legislative confusion and contradictions in the act's purpose, due to inconsistencies among several of its important provisions, have given those charged with implementing it considerable freedom to apply their own values and beliefs.

The Taft-Hartley Act was amended in 1959 by the Labor-Management Reporting and Disclosure Act (the Landrum-Griffin Act). In spite of the Taft-Hartley restrictions, labor unions managed to increase their membership from 15 million in 1950 to more than 20 million in 1971.

See also **Closed Shop; Federal Mediation and Conciliation Service; Injunctions Against Unions; Labor-Management Reporting and Disclosure Act; Mediation; National Labor Relations Act; Secondary Boycott; Strike; Unfair Labor Practice; Union Security Clause; Union Shop; Wage.**

LABOR-MANAGEMENT REPORTING AND DISCLOSURE ACT (LMRDA) OF 1959 Following the McClellan Hearings with their disclosures of violence, corruption, and abuse in certain labor unions and the undemocratic governance of other unions, Congress passed the Labor-Management Reporting and Disclosure Act of 1959 (also known as the Landrum-Griffin Act). A largely procedural statute, it was intended to provide greater internal union democracy by establishing a bill of rights for union members, regulating trusteeships, and formulating standards for holding elections of union officers and for the financial obligations of union officers. The statute also provides criminal sanctions for violations of some of its provisions.

Title I of the LMRDA, which provides a bill of rights for union members, declares that every union member has the right to equal protection. It specifically requires freedom of speech and assembly in the conduct of union meetings; equality of rights regarding voting in elections, nomination of candidates, and attendance at meetings; secret balloting on increases in dues or assessments, after reasonable notice of a meeting and of intention to vote upon the proposal; safeguards in disciplinary actions against employees, such as written charges, time to prepare a defense, and a fair hearing; and it granted members freedom to sue unions and their officers. In connection with disciplinary actions against employees, the Landrum-Griffin Act guarantees rights only to union members, not to all employees represented by the union. The union member may not necessarily have the right to be represented by an attorney. Many union constitutions forbid union members from being represented by lawyers at these hearings but do permit representation by fellow union members.

The Landrum-Griffin Act, under Title IV, provides that members have the right to elect their officials and guarantees the right to an election every three years.

In order to prevent corruption, Titles II and III set requirements for union activities and require labor organizations to file annual financial reports, constitutions, and bylaws with the U.S. Department of Labor. Unions must also report such information as dues, fees, and assessments, qualifications for membership, financial auditing, and authorization for disbursement of funds. Union financial reports must show assets and liabilities at the beginning and end of the fiscal year; receipts of any kind and their source; salaries; expense reimbursements; and loans to any officer, employee, member, or business enterprise. Officers and employees (as opposed to the union itself) may be required to file reports that would disclose personal financial interests that may conflict with duties owed to union members and any transactions or business interests that might influence them in their union duties. These titles also impose reporting duties on employers if they make any payments or loans to a union or any of its officers or employees.

The LMRDA focused particularly at limiting when unions may impose a trusteeship, an administrative device whereby the national or international labor organization suspends the autonomy of a subordinate local union. The law provides conditions under which a trusteeship may be imposed and administered; it also requires that reports on trusteeships be filed with the secretary of labor.

The Landrum-Griffin Act also amended the Taft-Hartley Act to strengthen the hot cargo clauses [Section 8(e)], limited various types of picketing and secondary boycotts, and granted jurisdiction to the states where the National Labor Relations Board fails to handle a dispute.

Major unfair labor practice protection under the Landrum-Griffin amendments outlaws organizational or recognitional picketing to secure recognition for the union without the preferred method of selection through a secret ballot vote—or, more specifically, without the support of a majority of employees in the appropriate unit. This procedure was enacted in reaction to the use of "blackmail" picketing to pressure an employer to recognize a union without any consultation with the workers. Congress found that some unions (particularly the International Brotherhood of Teamsters) often picketed a firm (particularly one whose workforce was composed of racial minorities), forced the employer's recognition, and negotiated an agreement without the workers' interests at heart. The union's objective was simply to persuade workers to authorize payroll deductions for union dues. The employees often received poor representation from the union and little assistance in improving substandard working conditions.

See also **Hot Cargo Agreement; National Labor Relations Board; Picketing; Secondary Boycott; Unfair Labor Practice; Union Trusteeship.**

LANDRUM-GRIFFIN ACT

See **Labor-Management Reporting and Disclosure Act.**

LAW OF LABOR COMBINATIONS

See ***Commonwealth v. Hunt* (1842).**

LAYOFF

A permanent layoff (or "cutback") occurs when an employer discharges employees because of "business necessity," that is, because of an unexpected reduction in business.

Every year millions of employees are adversely affected by economic exigencies experienced by their employers. If the job loss results from a plant closing or a mass layoff, the employees are protected by the Worker Adjustment and Retraining Notification Act, which became effective in 1989. The statute requires employers of 100 or more workers to give employees 60 days' advance notice of a plant closing or mass layoff.

A temporary layoff or indefinite suspension occurs when the employer temporarily removes an employee from the payroll, usually during a period of slack work, materials shortage, or a temporary decline in the market. This action was not caused by any misconduct on the employee's part. Employees in layoff status usually retain certain seniority rights and other protection under contract or company practice. It is assumed that the employee will be returned to the payroll when additional work becomes available. The term is occasionally confused with discharge. The term "disciplinary discharge" is sometimes used to refer to the temporary suspension of employees that results in loss of pay (and sometimes seniority) and mars the employee's record.

Bumping is the practice used during layoffs where the employee with greater seniority has the right to displace an employee of lesser seniority. Generally, unless stated otherwise, a worker may displace any worker who has less seniority, not merely the least senior worker. This process is more widely used in companies with plantwide seniority where jobs are somewhat interchangeable or the work not too highly skilled. It is also designed to protect the job rights of the employees with greater length of service. In some plants the right to bump a lower-seniority employee is limited to employees in the same department. The bumping process is utilized during periods of layoff, reorganization, or automation that causes job elimination.

An employer commits an unfair labor practice when it lays off an employee for filing charges or testifying in National Labor Relations Board proceedings. In fact, an employee's participation in an unfair labor practice hearing is protected against a layoff, whether or not he has been subpoenaed to attend. The employer also commits an unfair labor practice by saying or implying that some employees may have to be laid off if unionization occurs. But statements implying that layoffs may result from economic duress are lawful when made in the course of efforts to obtain contract concessions, if the statements are supported by facts.

Troublesome conflicts regarding layoffs emerged in the 1970s between negotiated seniority clauses and the national labor policy mandated by Title VII of the 1964 Civil Rights Act. During times of recession, layoffs according to the principle of "last hired, first laid off" tended to erode the equal employment opportunities won by minorities and women in the late 1960s, when employment was expanding. The AFL-CIO and its affiliated unions have been working to change seniority systems to avoid discriminatory results.

See also **American Federation of Labor-Congress of Industrial Organizations; Civil Rights Act of 1964; Employment Contract; National Labor Relations Board; Worker Adjustment and Retraining Notification Act.**

LEAVE OF ABSENCE

In general, a grant to an employee of time off from the job without pay. A leave of absence allows workers to leave their jobs temporarily because of illness, pressing family difficulties, union business, school work, and other personal or civic reasons. Employee leaves are governed by both federal and state laws, which determine the types of leaves that a company must grant, the required duration of leaves, and the employee's reinstatement rights when the leave expires.

Under collective bargaining agreements, individuals may be permitted to remain away from their jobs for a limited period of time without loss of seniority and benefit coverage and with reinstatement rights. The leave may be for a short period of time in case of illness requiring hospitalization of a family member, death of a family member, or jury duty. Or it may be for a longer period, but generally not longer than one year. The types of leave normally covered under collective bargaining agreements include personal leave, union business leave, maternity leave, funeral leave, jury duty leave, sick leave, and military leave.

In defining leave-of-absence policies, employers recognize absences for medical, maternity, personal, and civic reasons. They define whether the absence will be paid or unpaid and explain any eligibility requirements for leave, such as a copy of military orders for military leave or a doctor's statement for medical leave.

Leaves of absence have become an important workplace issue in the 1980s and 1990s. As women continue to enter the workforce—and remain there after having children—maternity leave has become more important. Moreover, as the population ages, more employees are finding themselves needing time off from work to care for their elderly patents. Medical disabilities and personal crises can also compel employees to take leaves of absence. Parental leave, too, became an active area of legislative interest at the federal and state levels in the early 1990s. Several states enacted statutes permitting private and public sector employees an unpaid leave of absence for either parent for the birth or adoption of a child; for the employee's own serious illness; or to care for a seriously ill child, parent, or spouse. These state laws were the precursors of the Family and Medical Leave Act.

Employers find it important to formulate a clear leave-of-absence policy and to publish it in the employee handbook. Such a policy makes employees who wish to take leaves aware of both their entitlement and their obligations. Further, a clearly stated, standardized policy is easier to apply consistently to all employees—a crucial matter, since inconsistent leave-of-absence administration can lead to charges of employment discrimination.

The language on employees' rights when the leave of absence expires is often important. The customary options are (1) the right to return to the same job, (2) the right to comparable employment, and (3) the mere promise to be placed on a preferential hiring list if there are vacancies. Often the leaves-of-absence clause lists approved purposes for a leave. Employers customarily require that the length of the leave be specified and adequate advance notice given. They also retain the right to give consent.

Leaves-ofabsence clauses address the accumulation of seniority while the employee is on leave. Employers generally do not want a clause that permits employees on leaves to accumulate vacation time during the leave. Employers often agree, however, that seniority continues while an employee is on leave, so that when the employee returns from leave he or she may be entitled to additional vacation as a result of accumulated seniority.

Funeral leaves can be hotly debated issues. Generally, the employer wishes to appear sympathetic to employees who are in the midst of grief but also suspects that a funeral leave clause can be abused. With that suspicion comes the tendency to impose restrictions, but suggesting these restrictions in contract negotiations will often produce protests from the unions and accusations that the employer is heartless or cruel. Conceptually, the employer must decide whether it is going to agree to funeral leave or to bereavement leave. Funeral leave requires attendance at the funeral. It limits the days off to certain days surrounding the funeral or certain prearranged days after the death plus the day of the funeral. It may even require proof that the employee attended the funeral. Unions prefer bereavement leave. Such a provision simply guarantee employees a certain number of days off in the event of death and does not require them to attend the funeral. Employers often want funeral leave clauses to contain the provision that if a death occurs when the employee is otherwise off work, such as on a weekend, holiday, or vacation, a funeral leave will not be used to grant the employees additional days off with pay. Some unions, however, argue that at least one of the paid funeral leave days should be a business day, so that the employee can take care of death-related business.

See also **Employee Handbook; Family and Medical Leave Act of 1993; Jury Duty Leave; Military Leave; Preferential Hiring.**

LIMITATION OF ACTIONS These statutes generally prescribe limitations on the right to sue; that is, they declare that in certain instances, lawsuits must be filed only within a specified period of time after the cause of the action occurred.

All lawsuits for unpaid minimum wages, unpaid overtime compensation, or liquidated damages under the Fair Labor Standards Act (FLSA), including lawsuits for injunctive relief by the U.S. Department of Labor, must be brought within two years after the cause of action occurred, except in the case of a willful violation, where a lawsuit must be brought within three years. Time limitations apply both to actions brought by employees and to actions brought by the government for the benefit of employees.

The FLSA's statute of limitations applies only to actions brought under it and not to similar cases brought under state law in a state court. Accordingly, where a state statute is more favorable to an employee than the FLSA, resulting in a higher rate of remuneration than that specified by federal law, the employee's claim may be based on the stricter state statute, and the appropriate state statute of limitations applies. However, FLSA's time limits supersede any limits specified in a state statute if an employee sues under FLSA, whether in a state court or federal court.

Section 10(b) of the National Labor Relations Act (NLRA) contains a six-month limitations period for filing unfair labor practice charges, against either the union or the employer, with the National Labor Relations Board. As an example, employer domination of a union is prohibited as an unfair labor practice under 8(a)(2) of the NLRA. However, if the employer domination occurred more than six months after the filing and service of the charge, no finding of employer domination can be made. Section 10(b) specifically prohibits a charge where a party has "notice of a clear and unequivocal contract repudiation." At that point, the moment of repudiation, the unfair refusal to bargain occurs, and the legality of the refusal depends on the evidence the parties present regarding the repudiator's right to take actions at that time.

Prior to the six-month limitations period, the U.S. Supreme Court distinguishes between two different circumstances: (1) where unfair labor practices occur within the six-month limitations period, earlier events may be used as evidence to show what occurred during the limitations period; and (2) where the alleged unfair labor practice, which occurs within the limitations period, can be charged only through reliance on an earlier unfair labor practice. [*Local Lodge 1424 Machinists v. NLRB* (1960)]

See also **Fair Labor Standards Act; National Labor Relations Act; National Labor Relations Board; Unfair Labor Practice.**

LINDEN LUMBER V. NLRB (1974) In this case, the union recognition was based on authorization cards signed by a majority of employees in the appropriate bargaining unit. When the employer refused to recognize the union, the union petitioned for an election. The employer stated that it would not abide by the results of a National Labor Relations Board (NLRB) election if one were conducted, on the grounds that the union had been improperly assisted by company supervisors in violation of Section 8(a)(2) of the National Labor Relations Act (NLRA), making it a company-assisted union. The union withdrew its election petition and renewed its claim for recognition, but the company again declined to recognize the union. Thereupon, the union struck for recognition and filed an unfair labor charge based on the company's refusal to bargain. The NLRB held that the employer was not guilty of an unfair labor practice solely because it refused to accept evidence of the union's majority status other than the result of a NLRB election. The question of whether the employer acted in bad faith was not deemed relevant by the NLRB. The Court of Appeals reversed the NLRB. It held that if the employer had doubts as to the union's majority status it could and should test its doubts by petitioning for an election. The decision was appealed to the U.S. Supreme Court.

The Supreme Court in *Linden Lumber v. NLRB* introduced a crucial factor into initial employee attempts to organize for the purpose of collective bargaining. In 1972, the NLRB ruled in effect that employers could, whenever confronted with a card majority and a demand for recognition, lawfully refuse that demand and force the union, as a condition for recognizing its bargaining rights, to demonstrate majority support in a secret-ballot election. In 1974, the Supreme Court approved the NLRB's new decision that an employer could refuse a union's request for recognition even in the face of substantive evidence of majority employee support, such as signed authorizations for a strike by a majority of the employees. The Court also specifically approved the board's abandonment of a "good faith" test for employer refusals to bargain in this context.

The Court held that since employers may properly be suspicious of union-gathered authorization cards, and even more so of apparent majority support for a strike (which may be generated principally by fear or sympathy for the strikers and not by support for the union), the Board was entitled to establish a legal rule that would make it unnecessary to examine the employer's state of mind. The Court agreed with the NLRB that industrial peace would be fostered through the expeditious settling of representation claims through elections rather than through unfair labor practice proceedings under Section 8(a)(5). The Court also rejected the argument that the failure of the employer to file a representation petition demonstrated the lack of a good faith doubt of the union's majority status. In cases such as these, the union must file for the election.

The NLRB has accepted at least one exception to its rule that the employer may reject an authorization card majority, and that is when the employer actually agreed to abide by a union demonstration of majority status—typically by authorization cards—rather than by an election. If the employer repudiates the agreement after a union victory, the NLRB will find an unfair labor practice violation under Section 8(a)(5) of the NLRA. [*Snow & Sons* (1961); *Harding Glass Indus. Inc.* (1975)]

See also **Authorization Card; National Labor Relations Board.**

***Lochner v. New York* (1905)** In *Lochner,* the U.S. Supreme Court struck down a New York law that prohibited bakers from working more than 60 hours a week. The Court reversed its earlier position of deference to labor-protective legislation and began an era of striking down first state legislation and then federal legislation in the name of the constitutional doctrine of freedom of contract. *Lochner* came to represent an era of Supreme Court jurisprudence that lasted until the New Deal era. Throughout this period, the court granted the employer an advantage. Although the *Lochner* era came to be designated as the period of "economic due process," only the employer's economic interests were protected, while the workers' interests were ignored.

The statute was defended on two grounds: that it was a valid labor statute and that it protected the health and safety of the workers. The Court quickly rejected the labor law justification for the statute and ruled that the legislature's police power extended only to protection of the "public welfare." The readjustment of bargaining power between bakery employees and their employers, the Court implied, was not of sufficiently public (as opposed to private) concern, especially in view of the law's infringement of the freedom of contract. The Court suggested that if bakers were not as intelligent as other workers, or for some reason needed unusual protection, the statute might be valid as a labor law. But the Court found no reason to believe that bakers as a class needed such special protection.

The *Lochner* majority clearly disbelieved that the legislature had in fact acted in part for safety and health reasons. The law's natural effect, the Court believed instead, was to regulate labor conditions, not to protect anyone's health and safety. The Court also said that only certain legislative objectives were acceptable. Regulation of health and safety was permissible, but readjustment of economic power or economic resources was not. Thus, to the extent that the New York statute in *Lochner* was merely a "labor law" that readjusted bargaining power, rather than a true health regulation, it served an impermissible objective.

Another crucial element of the *Lochner* holding was its refusal to defer to legislative findings of fact. The Court insisted on reaching its own conclusions on the factual issue of whether the health and safety of bakers, or of the bread-eating public, needed special protection. For instance, the Court stated that "[in] our judgment it is not possible in fact to discover the connection between the number of hours a baker may work in the bakery and the healthful quality of the bread made by the workman."

Four justices dissented in *Lochner.* Justice John M. Harlan, in his dissent, argued that there was enough evidence that the statute would promote the health and safety of bakers that the legislature's judgment on this issue should have been accepted. Justice Oliver Wendell Holmes, in his dissent, contended that the Court had no right to impose its own views of correct economic theory on legislatures. He made one of the most famous statements in constitutional law: "The Fourteenth Amendment does not enact Mr. Herbert Spencer's social statics," a reference to a then popular social Darwinism–laissez-faire theory. Holmes went on to assert that "[a] constitution is not intended to embody a particular economic theory, whether of paternalism and the organic relation of the citizens of the state or of laissez-faire." Liberty, as the term is used in the Fourteenth Amendment, should be found to be violated only when a "rational and fair man necessarily would admit that the statute . . . would infringe fundamental principles as they had been understood by the traditions of our people and our law." By that test, Holmes contended, the statute was valid.

The majority opinion in *Lochner* can be criticized on several grounds, including how it interpreted the freedom of contract. The freedom of contract the *Lochner* majority purported to protect was an illusion. The bakery employees in *Lochner* were not truly "free," in any meaningful sense, to contract for a 40-hour work week rather than a 60-hour one, as long as there were no scarcity of bakers and no effective labor unions.

Lochner also seems to have taken an unduly narrow view of what legislative objectives are permissible. While the Court recognized the health and safety of bakery employees, and of the public as a whole, as a legitimate objective, it refused to regard "labor" objectives, such as redressing the inequality of bargaining power, as legitimate legislative ends.

Subsequent legal scholars believe that the *Lochner* court erred in treating freedom of contract as a "fundamental interest" so that the counterbalancing state interest had to be subjected to strict-scrutiny rather than minimal-rationality review. The specific holding of *Lochner* was effectively overruled by *Bunting v. Oregon* (1917), which sustained a law setting a ten-hour maximum day for factory workers with an additional three hours of overtime allowed at time-and-a-half. But the *Lochner* philosophy calling for protection of freedom of contract and close scrutiny of economic regulation endured until the late 1930s.

LOCKOUT The closing by an employer of a workplace, or a suspension of work initiated by the employer, to pressure workers into agreeing to the employer's terms. A lockout is the employer's counterpart of a strike. Lockouts are also used by employers to prevent a union from "whipsawing," which means striking one employer while allowing another to operate, in order to bring pressure on the struck employer to settle.

The National Labor Relations Act (NLRA) does not explicitly state whether lockouts are lawful or unlawful. The U.S. Supreme Court, however, has established the legal limits of employer lockouts in several crucial cases. If the purpose of the lockout is to punish employees for joining or designating a labor organization or otherwise to obstruct their free choice of a representative, than it is clearly a "discouragement of union membership" through the intentional deprivation of job opportunities. As such, it violates Section 8(a) of the NLRA. It also violates Section 8(a) if its purpose is to force a favored union on the employees. Lockouts violate Section 8(a)(5) if their purpose is to evade the duty to bargain or to force the union to agree to an illegal bargaining position.

Lockouts are lawful for legitimate business reasons. There are three important Supreme Court cases in which lockouts were found lawful. The first, *Truck Drivers Local 449 v. NLRB (Buffalo Linen)* (1957), concerned a multiemployer bargaining group. The union, in order to divide and conquer the employers, resorted to a "whipsaw" strategy: it struck one member of the group at a time. The intent of this strategy was to pressure a weak link, get a favorable settlement, and then pressure others to follow suit. The U.S. Supreme Court held that the other members of the multiemployer group could lawfully lock out their employees in order to preserve a united front. In a later case, *NLRB v. Brown Food* (1965), the Court also held that employers locking out under these circumstances may continue to operate with temporary replacements. Since this decision, appellate courts have disagreed on whether or not a single employer may continue operating with temporary replacements after locking out.

The third important case, *American Ship Building Co. v. NLRB* (1965), dealt with a single employer. After bargaining had reached an impasse, a strike appeared imminent. The employer wished to control when the stoppage occurred, both to minimize the disruption and to exert pressure on the negotiations. In this case, the Court found the lockout lawful because (1) the harm to employee rights was "comparatively slight," (2) the business end served was substantial, and (3) an unlawful purpose could not be inferred without proof of antiunion motive. In this case, the U.S. Supreme Court ruled that the lockout may be used by management to protect its collective bargaining position. There was no evidence that the employer was hostile to the employees' interest in organizing or the purpose of collective bargaining or that the lockout was used to "discipline" employees for engaging in the bargaining process. Thus, the Court held that it was not the employer's intention to "destroy or frustrate the process of collective bargaining" and that there was no indication that the union would be diminished in its capacity to represent the employees in the unit.

Lockouts have recently become an important bargaining tactic for employers. The question is to what extent the employer may exercise its right to lock out the employees. Currently, the test appears to be whether the union continues to function in the collective bargaining process despite the employer's tactics. However, it is difficult to precisely define the parameters of union and employer economic pressure under such a test. Some of the factors considered in determining whether a union continues to function are: Does it collect dues? Is it able to negotiate a union security agreement requiring collection of dues and conditions of employment, thereby to establish a relatively secure position of itself? Does it continue to process grievances? Is it able to exert economic pressure after the lockout or the replacement of strikers? The case law continues to be unsettled on many of these issues.

See also **Collective Bargaining; Grievance; National Labor Relations Act; Strike; Union Security Clause; Whipsawing.**

Loewe v. Lawlor (1908) In this case, also known as the "Danbury Hatters' case," the U.S. Supreme Court ruled that the Sherman Antitrust Act applied to combinations of workers, specifically meaning labor unions.

The case involved a secondary boycott engaged in by the United Hatters of North America, which had called a strike against the D.E. Loewe Company for the purpose of unionizing the company. The union called a strike for recognition against the employer and instituted a nationwide boycott of the employer's products handled by wholesalers and retailers. The union and its allies, the American Federation of Labor (AFL) and other affiliates, attempted to boycott not only the company but any person who patronized the company. Because the union's efforts were aimed at parties other than the employer, the tactics were referred to as "secondary" activities. The employer sued the union for treble damages under the Sherman Act.

The Supreme Court held that the Sherman Act applied to the union and that the union had violated that statute. The Court ruled, in part, "the combination [the union] described in this declaration is a combination 'in restraint of trade or commerce among the several states,' in the sense in which those words are wed in the act. . . . [T]he Act prohibits any combination whatever to secure action which essentially obstructs the free flow of commerce between the States, or restricts, in that regard, the liberty of a trader to engage in business." Chief Justice Melville Fuller, in the majority opinion, wrote that "the records of Congress show that several efforts were made to exempt, by legislation, organizations of farmers and laborers from the operation of the act and from all of these efforts failed, so that the act remained as we have it before us."

The impact of Danbury Hatters was devastating for organized labor. The unions and many others felt that the antitrust statute had been interpreted improperly, because organized labor was not the focus of congressional debate over that legislation. Moreover, because the Sherman Antitrust Act provides for treble damages rather than the actual amount of the losses incurred (as well as criminal sanctions), the final judgment after fourteen years of litigation in the Danbury Hatters was $250,000. The unionists were individually and personally liable. The case was settled in

1917 for slightly more than $234,000 and the AFL was able to obtain $216,000 in voluntary contributions from union members, but the fact that labor had to raise these funds to avoid foreclosures on members' homes made the case unforgettable.

Immediately after the decision, the labor movement began an effort to reverse the decision and the applicability of the Sherman Antitrust Act to trade unions. In 1908 the Democratic Party promised to amend antitrust legislation to reverse the Court's decision, and in 1912, it promised again in the following language: "Labor organizations and members should not be regarded as illegal organizations in the restraint of trade." After Woodrow Wilson was elected president in 1912, these efforts resulted in the Clayton Antitrust Act of 1914, which was intended to diminish union exposure to antitrust liability. Samuel Gompers hailed the enactment of this statute as labor's Magna Carta and Bill of Rights and the most important legislation since the abolition of slavery.

See also **Boycott; Clayton Antitrust Act; Secondary Boycott; Sherman Antitrust Act of 1980.**

LONGSHOREMEN'S AND HARBOR WORKERS' COMPENSATION ACT (LHWCA) OF 1927 In response to the problems created by the U.S. Supreme Court's decision in *Southern Pacific Co. v. Jensen* (1917), which resulted in the doctrine that state law could not constitutionally grant compensation to maritime employees, Congress passed the Longshoremen's and Harbor Workers' Compensation Act of 1927 in order to provide workers' compensation for persons in marine employment except masters and crews of vessels in U.S. navigible waters. Longshore and ship repair workers were the principal employees who Congress originally provided coverage for under the LHWCA. Seamen were included in the original bill of the LHWCA, but were dropped under pressure from the seamen's unions, which argued that seamen preferred their rights under the general maritime law and the Jones Act to workers compensation.

In 1972, the Longshoremen's and Harbor Workers' Compensation Amendments made substantial changes in this statute by redefining the basis of coverage, raising benefit levels, and limiting access by longshore workers to remedies under general maritime law. The LHWCA is administered by the office of Workmen's Compensation Programs.

See also **Workers' Compensation.**

McGann v. H&H Music Co. (1991) The fifth circuit in *McGann* allowed a self-insuring employer to lower the limit on medical benefits for AIDS after an employee submitted his first claim. The court ruled that Section 510 of the Employee Retirement Income Security Act does not prevent employers from making changes to group health plans to lower the maximum benefits for workers with AIDS.

The case involved an employee who submitted insurance claims for AIDS treatments. The employer subsequently changed the group health plan from one that provided a lifetime maximum of $1 million in benefits for AIDS treatments to a self-insured plan that provided a maximum of $5,000. The Court held that the employer's action did not constitute discrimination because the policy applied to all employees, even though the plaintiff was the most affected. The decision was limited to self-insurers, as self-insuring employers are exempted from state regulation, whereas commercial health insurance is subject to regulation by each state. In many states, changes without notice to policyholders and the exclusion, differentiation, or elimination of coverage for particular medical conditions are unlawful. Indeed, following *McGann,* Texas amended its insurance laws to prohibit the cancellation of an accident or sickness policy during its term because the insured has been diagnosed with the HIV infection or AIDS.

See also **Acquired Immune Deficiency Syndrome; Employee Retirement Income Security Act of 1974; Group Insurance.**

McJobs Originally, the term referred to the McDonald's program to hire and train the disabled. Under the program, the company has hired and trained more than 9,000 mentally and physically disabled workers since 1982.

Douglas Coupland's novel *Generation X* expanded the term's meaning to refer to minimum wage jobs in retailing, restaurants, and service industries that offer little chance for promotion. However, McJobs offer more opportunities than they seem to, especially since the rate of unemployment and underemployment for 15- to 29-year-olds is much higher than that of other age groups. Though many of these jobs pay the minimum wage to start, an employee can become an assistant manager within 12 months.

See also **Minimum Wage; Underemployed; Unemployment.**

MAINTENANCE OF MEMBERSHIP A form of union security, which appears as a contract clause, providing that individual union members or those employees who join a labor union must maintain their membership for the duration of the contract. It imposes no obligation to join a union. The concept was developed by the public members of the National War Labor Board during World War II to resolve the conflict between the opposing positions of the labor and industry members of the board. The labor members urged the extension of the union and closed shop during the war period, while the employers sought to limit union security in existing forms, including the open shop. The compromise was designed to protect both union security and the employer's position. Qualifying language incorporated into individual contracts provided a fifteen-day escape period during which employees were free to decide whether to remain in the union or to withdraw. This language protected, in part, the freedom of choice of the individual employees. There were many variations in this provision in the National War Labor Board decisions and also many variations following the termination of the board after the war.

Following the passage of the Labor-Management Relations Act of 1947 (the Taft-Hartley Act) and the outlawing of the closed shop, both the union shop and maintenance-of-membership clauses became much more common for companies engaged in interstate commerce. Whether states may lawfully prohibit maintenance-of-membership agreements has apparently never been judicially determined.

See also **Closed Shop; Labor-Management Relations Act of 1947; National Labor Relations Act; Open Shop; Union Security Clause.**

MAJOR MEDICAL BENEFITS These are composed of two types of benefits, supplemental and comprehensive. Supplemental major medical plans cover some services that are excluded under basic plans and may also cover the same services (inpatient and outpatient hospital care, special nursing care, prescription drugs, medical appliances, durable medical equipment, and outpatient psychiatric care) but with higher coverage limits. Comprehensive major medical plans provide the combined coverage of a basic plan and a supplemental plan. Unlike a basic medical benefit plan, major medical plans cover a broad range of health care services and are designed to protect against large medical expenses.

See also **Benefits.**

MAJOR UNION CONTRACT See **Collective Bargaining Agreement.**

MANAGEMENT Employees or executives of a business who are responsible for the administration and direction of an enterprise and the functions of leadership. The term also refers to general management or administrative functions, which include planning and organizing the activities of a corporation or other business enterprise so that it achieves its objectives most efficiently and economically. Managerial employees are excluded from coverage of the National Labor Relations Act (NLRA) regardless of whether their policy making activities affect labor relations. [*NLRB v. Bell Aerospace Co.* (1974)]

Traditionally, the employee-management relationship is commonly viewed as a constant conflict between management's need to control the business' and employees' economic needs. This conflict tends to diminish in an atmosphere of continued learning, open communication, and trust. If employees are well trained and confident that management trusts their ability to effectively operate the systems, they can offer their opinions on the causes of system failures, make recommendations to avoid future failures, and take direct action.

In most large manufacturing organizations, front-line leaders are responsible for obtaining the best work out of both the people and the system (materials, equipment, and procedures) provided by management. Often these leaders operate in the midst of conflict between the interests of the employees and the interests of management. Management, for its part, wants these front-line leaders to ensure employee compliance to the system, maximize output, maintain product conformity, and protect trade secrets. Employees want their leaders to be fair, compassionate and trusting, to share information, allow a degree of autonomy and risk taking in their work, and involve them in decision making.

Management's rights under the NLRA include the right to express its views to employees regarding their decision to join or vote for or against union representation, as long as management's response is free from unlawful promises of benefits, interrogations, threats, and surveillance. [*NLRB v. Gissel Packing Co.* (1969)]

See also **Managerial Employees; National Labor Relations Act.**

MANAGEMENT BY OBJECTIVES (MBO)

Peter Drucker, credited with the first use of the term, described Management By Objectives as a management philosophy that provides full scope to individual strength and responsibility and at the same time provides common direction of vision and effort, establishes teamwork, and harmonizes the goals of the individual with the common weal. MBO involves the setting of specific targets for subordinate managers relating to each of their tasks so that the individual efficiency of each unit of an organization can be monitored regularly.

MANAGEMENT RIGHTS

The need of management to run a profitable and efficient enterprise as accommodated in the labor agreement. With the possible exception of the no-strike clause, the management rights clause is often regarded as the single most important clause for management in a collective bargaining agreement. Prudent employers do not rely too heavily on such agreements because of the possibility that arbitrators' will either ignore these clauses or read loopholes into them.

Management has the need to increase productivity—to obtain more output from a given set of inputs of labor and capital. In the absence of a union, this right is unrestricted, except for relevant labor and employment statutes. Its power to do so is always restricted by what the labor market will tolerate; after all, a demoralized workforce is unlikely to be very productive. The emergence of labor unions placed formal restrictions on management power and management rights.

The management rights theory that developed after labor unions arose in the 1930s and 1940s was that management retained all rights not specifically granted in the collective bargaining agreement. The notion of the modified "residual rights theory" emerged, consisting of the following principles: (1) that management prerogatives are exercised in a reasonable and rational form, (2) that the intent of an action may not subvert the letter or spirit of the agreement, and (3) that long-established practices are not easily discounted. Explicit management rights clauses, however, became common and accepted by both management and labor unions.

In contract negotiations with a union, businesses normally attempt to win a strong management rights clause, which conveys to unionized employees that the employer still manages the business, controlling how its product is manufactured and how everyday business is conducted. It also reinforces the notion that rights not delegated to the union are reserved to management. The more detailed the management rights clause the better for the employer. If the management rights clause specifically states, for example, that the employer retains the sole right to set hours of work, it may discuss grievances, based on shortened work weeks or changed starting time. Similarly, the management rights clause may be an effective way to insure the right to subcontract. By including such clauses "as management reserves the right to determine how and by whom these products shall be manufactured," the employer can argue to the arbitrator that management has retained the right to contract out bargaining-unit work.

See also **Collective Bargaining Agreement; Employer; Grievance; Labor Union.**

MANAGERIAL EMPLOYEES Employees who "formulate and effectuate management policies by expressing and making operative the decisions of their employer." This definition, developed by the National Labor Relations Board (NLRB) in *Palace Laundry Dry Cleaning Corp.* (1947), has been accepted by the courts in the absence of specific mention of the term in both the National Labor Relations Act (NLRA) and the Labor-Management Relations Act of 1947 (Taft-Hartley Act). The U.S. Supreme Court in *NLRB v. Yeshiva University* (1980) restates previous court decisions which hold that "managerial employees must execute discretion within or even independently or established employer policy and must be aligned with management. . . . [Normally] an employee may be excluded [from the coverage of the NLRA] as managerial only if he represents management interests by taking or recommending discretionary actions that effectively control or implement employer policy." The majority of the U.S. Supreme Court in *NLRB v. Bell Aerospace Co.* (1974) ruled that it was the intention of Congress to exclude all persons properly defined as "managerial employees" from the coverage of the NLRA. The Court, in *Bell Aerospace*, defined "managerial employees" as "those who formulate and effectuate management policies by expressing and making operative the decisions of their employer, and those who have discretion in the performance of their jobs independent of their employer's established policy. " The *Bell* court also provided the following distinction between managerial and rank-and-file workers: "[M]anagerial status is not conferred upon rank-and-file workers, or upon those who perform routinely, but rather it is reserved for those in executive-type positions, those who are closely aligned with management as true representatives of management."

See also **National Labor Relations Act; National Labor Relations Board.**

MARITAL STATUS Traditionally considered the legal union of one man and one woman as husband and wife, relating to or connected with the status of marriage. To refuse to hire married women is considered sex discrimination under the Civil Rights Act of 1964, along with any discrimination based on pregnancy, childbearing capacity, sterilization, fertility, or related medical conditions. Several states have expanded their civil rights statutes to cover areas not included by federal statute, such as prohibiting discrimination based on marital status. Title VII of the Civil Rights Act of 1964 makes it unlawful for an employer to discriminate against an applicant or employee because the individual is married to or associates with members of another racial, religious, or ethnic group.

Unless marital status is a bona fide occupational qualification, it cannot be an issue in hiring interviews. The applicant may not be asked questions about marital status or family orientation, such as: Are you married? Do you have a family? What is your (or your spouse's) maiden name? Are you pregnant? Do you plan to have a family? What daycare arrangements have you made? However, some of these questions that were illegal before hiring may be asked afterwards. They include questions about dependents who will be covered by an employment-sponsored insurance plan.

The issue of whether same-sex marriages should be legally recognized is one of the most controversial issues in contemporary American society. Hawaii in 1993 became the first state in the nation to legalize marriage between same-sex couples when the state supreme court found a ban on same-sex marriage unconstitutional. Concerns that Hawaii would legalize such marriages spurred legislation nationwide. The federal Defense of Marriage Act, signed by President Bill Clinton in 1996, defines marriage as the union of one man and one woman, denies federal benefits to same-sex couples, and allows states to refuse to recognize same-sex marriages sanctioned by other states.

See also **Bona Fide Occupational Qualification; Civil Rights Act of 1964; Sex Discrimination in Employment.**

***Massachusetts Board of Retirement v. Murgia* (1976)** An equal protection case involving a Massachusetts statute that required all uniformed state police to retire at the age of 50. The statute's purpose was to help keep the police force free of officers whose physical health was not sound enough for them to perform their duties. The plaintiff argued that the statute unfairly discriminated against him on the basis of age.

The U.S. Supreme Court upheld the statute, even though some (perhaps many) officers over 50 were not in poor physical health, making the statute overinclusive. The Court, however, found the connection between being older than 50 and being physically unfit was not so thin as to be irrational. And the fact that better means of measuring physical health were available and were being used (such as an annual physical examination) did not mean that the less-than-best means selected by the statute was impermissible.

The Court found that the state had a legitimate interest in protecting the public by assuring that state police officers could respond to the demands of their jobs. The Court reasoned that, although particular individuals over 50 can perform the functions of a police officer, the evidence presented clearly established that the risk of cardiovascular failure and the effects of stress increased with age. The Court, applying the mere-rationality standard, found that this statute was rationally related to a legitimate state interest.

In *Murgia* the Court declined to treat the classification based on age as a "suspect" class, on the theory that old age "marks a stage that each of us will reach if we live out our normal span." The Court also held that "while the treatment of the aged in this Nation has not been wholly free of discrimination, such persons, unlike say, those who have been discriminated against on the basis of race or national origin, have not experienced a 'history of purposeful unequal treatment' or been subjected to unique disabilities on the basis of stereotyped characteristics not truly indicative of their abilities." Therefore, the court ruled that the elderly are not a "discrete and insular group . . . in need of 'extraordinary protection'." The difference between this type of discrimination and others is that it is based on ignorance rather than on hate. People do not despise or have intolerance for older people; instead they merely have false assumptions about their ability to work.

Justice Thurgood Marshall dissented in *Murgia,* arguing that the elderly have been subjected to "repeated and arbitrary discrimination in employment." Marshall believed that the statute certainly could not survive the intermediate scrutiny of the equal protection analysis because of its over-inclusiveness.

Because of the *Murgia* decision, it is unlikely that any state statute or policy on mandatory retirement will be stricken for violating the equal protection clause of the Constitution. Mandatory retirement requirements may fail on age discrimination in employment grounds as well. However, since *Murgia,* virtually all cases involving mandatory retirement ages for police officers have been brought under the Age Discrimination in Employment Act.

See also **Age Discrimination in Employment Act.**

MASTER AGREEMENT A collective bargaining agreement covering several plants of a single employer. The master agreement is often supplemented by local agreements covering conditions that vary among the individual plants or companies within the overall bargaining unit.

The master agreement helps to establish uniform conditions of employment throughout an industry or company. Some international unions suggest the master agreement as a guide but will permit variations to meet special circumstances of a union or company.

See also **Collective Bargaining Agreement.**

MEDIATION One of the modes of labor dispute resolution most commonly used in the United States. Mediation involves the attempt by a third party, appointed by labor and management or by government, to bring the parties together to resolve a labor dispute. The mediator has no power, even to make recommendations to the parties as to how the matter should be resolved. Even so, mediators often play innovative and important roles in dispute resolution. The mediator's function is to clarify the issues, appeal to the parties' reasoning processes through persuasion, and (when specifically authorized by the parties), to make recommendations. The mediator must have the parties' confidence. They must be able to entrust their secrets and confidences to the mediator without fearing that this information will be divulged to the other side. A skillful mediator is able to utilize such information in making suggestions, structuring the dialogue, or formulating proposals.

Though they are not synonymous, the terms "conciliation" and "mediation" are often used interchangeably. The difference is primarily the nature of the activity of the person acting as conciliator or mediator. In conciliation generally, the conciliator merely attempts to bring the parties together and permits them to act by themselves in resolving their problems. In mediation, the mediator is more active and attempts to suggest various proposals and methods for the resolution of the problem. Neither the conciliator nor the mediator renders a final decision. Possible areas for compromise and additional points of view may be suggested, but fundamentally, the parties are required to resolve the dispute themselves. If the parties are unwilling to help find a solution, the role of the conciliator or mediator is of little value.

As a practical matter, however, there is little need to make any sharp distinction between conciliation and mediation. The roles of intermediaries can shift between conciliation to mediation, depending on which technique is most effective and best designed to bring the parties to the point where they themselves can find solutions.

One of the key factors in the mediation process is the attempt to determine the actual needs of the parties. Through exchanging of ideas and concepts and clarifying which issues are of prime concern and which are peripheral, the mediator is able to bring the parties to the point where a solution is advanced, either by the mediator or by the parties themselves. The mediator rarely acts to pressure either party to accept a solution that the mediator has placed on the table for discussion and rarely participates in the debate on the merits of a particular issue except when it comes to matters of fact that can be determined by reference to statistical or other data, to court decisions, or to the actual language of a statute.

See also **Labor Dispute.**

MERIT SYSTEM See **Civil Service.**

MIGRANT LABOR

Migrant workers are individuals who have migrated from underdeveloped (usually rural) areas and are commonly engaged in temporary employment that native workers reject. The American supply of migrant labor is composed of (1) the "old" immigration from Northwestern Europe, which dominated early economic development; (2) the "new" immigration from Southern and Eastern Europe, which predominated in the late nineteenth and early twentieth centuries and ended with World War I and the 1923 legislation restricting immigration; (3) the internal migration of African Americans, Hispanics, and rural whites, who moved from the agricultural South and Southwest, Puerto Rico, and secondarily out of Mexico to the urban, industrial Northern American cities; (4) the "new" new immigration of the late 1960s and 1970s, which is dominated by immigrants from Mexico and the Caribbean basin.

Migrant farm workers are classified as independent contractors if they engaged in harvesting of crops, if they could refuse to work for any particular landowner in preference for another, and if the details of the methods by which they conducted the harvest were not controlled by the landowner. [*Donovan v. Horn (Walston Farms)* (1984); *Donovan v. Brandel* (1984)] In contrast, courts have found migrant workers to be employees rather than independent contractors when they were dependent on the grower for their continued employment and livelihood. [*Secretary of Labor, United States Department of Labor v. Lauritzen* (1987); *In re Kokesch* (1987)]

A firm that hires an independent farm labor contractor to supply its workers can be the employer of those workers, if as a matter of economic reality, the workers are dependent on that firm. Congress has specifically endorsed the use of the following factors, identified by the Fifth Circuit, in determining joint employment of farm workers: (1) whether the employment occurred on the alleged employer's premises; (2) how much control the alleged employer had over the workers; (3) whether the alleged employer could hire and fire workers or modify their employment conditions; (4) whether the workers performed "specialty jobs" within the line of production; and (5) whether the workers could refuse to work for the alleged employer and choose to work for others.

The most important federal law protecting migrant workers (or "farm labor contractors") is the Migrant and Seasonal Agricultural Worker Protection Act. This statute regulates the housing, transportation, pay, and recruitment of migran workers. It protects "any person, other than an agricultural employer, an agricultural association, or an employee of an agricultural employer or agricultural association, who, for any money or other valuable consideration paid or promised [performs farm work]."

Farm labor contractors or crew leaders who are involved in the employment process are required to register with the U.S. Department of Labor and obtain a certificate that authorizes them to recruit, drive, transport, and house the workers.

See also **African Americans: Employment Issues; Employee; Hispanics: Employment Issues; Independent Contractor.**

MILITARY LEAVE A provision incorporated into a collective bargaining agreement or a statement of company personnel policy granting a long-term leave of absence for active service in the U.S. Armed Forces and incorporating provisions of federal military training statutes and state laws. The employee's seniority and right to reinstatement upon return from service may be protected under some arrangements.

Time off for military reserve, National Guard training, and emergency military duty is provided in many agreements. The federal Veterans' Reemployment Act requires that employees leaving a job for short-term training duty must be reinstated in their former position without change in seniority, status, or pay unless the change affects all employees similarly situated. [*Monroe v. Standard Oil* (1981)] Most contracts provide pay for a stated period, usually in an amount equal to the difference between full pay and the money received for the training.

A leave of absence for military service is one area where an employer's personnel practices are subject to specific government regulations. In order to comply with government requirements, the employer's policy should permit full-time and part-time employees to schedule a leave of absence for military reserve training or active duty and grant reinstatement to the same or a similar job upon timely application following military discharge. There is no permissible limit on the length of leave for military service. [*King v. St. Vincent's Hospital* (1971)]

See also **Leave of Absence; Part-Time Employment; Reinstatement; Seniority.**

MINIMUM WAGE Lowest wage rate allowed by either federal or state law. Most employees covered by the Fair Labor Standards Act (FLSA) are subject to a minimum wage specified in the act as amended. The provisions of the FLSA that establish a minimum wage for employees engaged in commerce or in the production of goods for commerce represent a valid exercise by Congress of its power to regulate interstate commerce. Similarly, the provisions of the FLSA assigning to the administrator of the Wage and Hour Division of the U.S. Department of Labor authority to determine the "reasonable cost" of board, lodging, or other facilities provided to an employee in lieu of or in addition to cash wages is a legitimate exercise by Congress of its power to delegate to administrative agencies authority to issue regulations having the force and effect of law.

The FLSA does not excuse noncompliance with any federal, state, or municipal law establishing a minimum wage higher than that established by the FSLA. For example, a regulation adopted by the Minimum Wage Board of Puerto Rico, which required that certain hospital employees be paid a minimum wage higher than that established by the FLSA, was enforceable. Thus, the act does not invalidate other statutes requiring the payment of wages in cash, prohibiting or regulating the issuance of company scrip, preventing or restricting wages in services or facilities, controlling company stores, outlawing kickbacks, or restricting the assignment and garnishment of wages.

State minimum wage statutes enjoy wide applicability only in states that have set a higher rate for most employees than that set in federal law. In other states, local minimum wage laws operate only in those areas not covered by the federal minimum wage law. A few states have no minimum wage statutes and therefore rely on the federal government to set minimum rates for the payment of wages within their jurisdiction. Most states establish a specific minimum rate for wage payments by statute, although a significant number authorize state agencies to set minimum wage rates, often for specific industries or categories of employees by administrative order.

Generally, besides white-collar workers, employees who do not have to be paid minimum wages include cleaning people in private homes, people who work on commission, baby-sitters, newspaper delivery people, and members of the employer's immediate family. In most states a specified rate that is less than the minimum wage may be paid to apprentices in skilled occupations, learners in semiskilled occupations, and disabled workers, including those employed in a sheltered workshop, with the permission of the state commissioner of labor.

Federal statute allows employers to credit up to 50 percent of the tips employees received toward payment of the minimum wage. In order for the employer to legally do this, however the job must be one where employees would customarily expect to receive tips (examples: waitpersons, bartenders, dock attendants, cab drivers) and the employee must be allowed to keep all of the tips. Some states allow less in tip credits than the federal law does.

See also **Fair Labor Standards Act; White-Collar Workers.**

MODEL EMPLOYMENT TERMINATION ACT

See **Employment Termination Model Act.**

MOMMY TRACK

A concept that provides a separate employment track for women who want to pursue serious careers while participating actively in child rearing.

Some commentators note that factors such as maternity, tradition, and socialization prevent women from gaining leadership positions. To provide upward mobility opportunities for high performance "career and family" women, theorists have advocated that employers plan for and manage maternity and provide the flexibility that will allow these women to be as productive as possible. Employers can take an active role in helping to support families and in making high-quality, affordable child care available to all women. Job arrangements, such as flexible work hours, part-time work, and job sharing, will enable employers to retain their best employees and allow women to maintain high performance and job satisfaction levels.

The "mommy track" has been criticized by some observers as a way for employers to treat women unequally and as illegal sex discrimination.

See also **Child and Other Dependent Care; Part-Time Employment; Sex Discrimination in Employment; Women: Employment Issues.**

MONOPOLY The ability of a single producer to control the output of a particular product or service and thereby exercise substantial control over price. It is sometimes argued that labor unions exercise monopoly power through their ability to regulate the supply of labor and therefore significantly affect the price of labor. The term *labor monopoly* is applied to the control that labor unions are supposed to have over the supply of labor and the labor market in order to obtain working conditions favorable to a particular group of employees. The term was also used to describe a union with a closed shop as well as a closed union that denied employee entry into a particular trade and thus controlled the supply of potential labor in the labor market.

MONOTONY A state during work in which the employee's interest is low, and listlessness and boredom are manifested. Boredom and listlessness can result from the nature of the work—a job that is so routine that it requires little attention or concern—or from the lack of opportunity for creativity. Monotonous work is a critical problem because it affects production as well as safety and morale.

MOONLIGHTING Also known as "dual employment" or "multiple job-holding," moonlighting is holding more than one job at a given time. The term suggests that the extra job is performed by moonlight and referred to workers who have one full-time job and take another job in the evenings or over the weekend. A moonlighter is an employed person who (1) has a job as a wage and salary worker with two employers or more, or (2) was self-employed and also held a wage or salary job, or (3) worked as an unpaid family member on the primary job but also had a secondary wage or salary job. Among the reasons given for moonlighting are the need to meet regular household expenses, to pay off debts, to save for the future, and to obtain work experience in a different occupation. Among occupational groups with the highest rates of moonlighters are professional specialty workers, and protective service workers.

MOTION STUDY

See **Scientific Management.**

MOTOR CARRIER ACT (MCA)

A federal statute enacted in 1935, the MCA brought commercial motor vehicles operating in interstate and foreign commerce within the jurisdiction of the Interstate Commerce Commission, now the U.S. Department of Transportation. The statute subjects the rate structure and the services of these companies to the regulations of the transportation secretary. It states that the secretary of transportation may prescribe qualifications and maximum hours of service of employees and standards of safe operation and equipment of motor carriers.

The statute contains special provisions for certain motor carriers under its jurisdiction. Employees subject to the act, for example, are exempt from the overtime requirements of the Fair Labor Standards Act (FLSA). The third circuit ruled that field engineers who frequently traveled interstate as part of their job duties, carrying tools, component parts, and equipment to install and maintain customers' computers, are exempt from the overtime compensation requirements of the FLSA, pursuant to the MCA exemption. The fact that they operated passenger vehicles in interstate activities which required them to transport property essential to their job duties placed them within reach of the MCA. [*Friedrich v. US Computer Services* (1992)]

The administration of the MCA was transferred to the U.S. Department of Transportation in 1966. Following amendments to the transportation statutes in 1983 and 1987, the MCA was repealed. Sections of the statute, however, are revised without substantive changes and recodified in various sections of Title 49 of the United States Code, which compiles the federal transportation statutes.

See also **Fair Labor Standards Act; Jurisdiction.**

MULTIEMPLOYER BARGAINING Collective bargaining involving more than one company and resulting in a master agreement. Multiemployer bargaining takes various forms, such as areawide bargaining, industrywide bargaining, and regional bargaining. This type of negotiation is responsible for agreements covering 40 percent of American workers. The circumstances under which an employer may withdraw from a multiemployer bargaining unit without committing an unfair labor practice have been extensively litigated.

Several employers within a single area or industry may join to bargain as a group with a single labor union which represents employees at all of the companies—a common if not dominant bargaining pattern in such industries as clothing, construction, longshore and maritime, trucking and warehousing, coal mining, wholesale and retail trades, and newspaper printing. The multiemployer pattern may reflect the desire of several small employers for greater leverage in dealing with a common union (such as in the clothing, trucking, and retail industries), or the desires of unions representing employees whose work for any given employer is likely to be short-lived (such as in the construction and maritime industries).

See also **Collective Bargaining; Master Agreement; Unfair Labor Practice.**

NATIONAL EMERGENCY STRIKE A strike not specifically forbidden by the Railway Labor Act and Sections 206–210 of the Labor-Management Relations Act (Taft-Hartley Act) but which may be enjoined (restrained by an injunction) for up to 80 days if, in the opinion of the president of the United States and the appropriate court of competent jurisdiction, it threatens the nation's health or safety. An injunction in these cases requires action by the attorney general in any federal district court that has jurisdiction of the parties. The procedure is essentially a cooling-off process, with a requirement that the attorney general petition the court for the dissolution of the injunction at the end of the 80 days.

See also **Jurisdiction; Labor-Management Relations Act; Strike.**

NATIONAL LABOR RELATIONS ACT (NLRA) Also known as the Wagner Act of 1935, it was one of the first federal statutes enacted to regulate labor-management relations. It was envisioned by its creators as significantly more effective in guaranteeing industrial peace than breaking strikes by injunction. Today it forms the basis for legal regulation of collective bargaining in the private sector. The authority for the statute is the commerce clause of the U.S. Constitution (Article I, Section 8), which allows Congress to regulate commerce among the American states. The statute is based on the constitutional theory that statutory regulation of labor and management is necessary to diminish the possibility of industrial strikes that could disrupt interstate commerce.

The NLRA guarantees workers the "right to self-organization, to form, join, or assist labor organizations, to bargain through representation of their own choosing, and to engage in concerted activities for the purpose of collective bargaining or other mutual aid or protection." With the passage of the statute, Congress ended its laissez-faire attitude toward labor relations and began regulating collective bargaining in order to encourage equality in bargaining. The concept of the free play of economic forces, the statute's foundation, is based on the belief that Congress intended to modify the balance of power between labor and management by enacting the NLRA and also intended to leave the parties free to use economic pressure to support their positions.

The NLRA created a national administrative agency, the National Labor Relations Board (NLRB) to oversee the NLRA. Its main functions are conducting representation elections to determine whether a union is entitled to represent employees as their exclusive bargaining representative, and determining whether certain unfair labor practice violations have occurred. Its establishment was a highly significant advance for industrial relations in the United States, because in applying the NLRA, it must give specific meaning to broad statutory language. By interpreting unclear congressional or statutory language and filling in gaps in the law, the NLRB has had and continues to play a crucial role in shaping American labor policy.

Generally, the NLRA governs employment relations in the private sector that affect interstate commerce. Therefore, employees of the federal government are not covered by the NLRA; their labor relations are controlled by separate federal statutes. Nor are most state employees covered; most states have passed their own statutes providing employees of state and local government with some organization rights.

Other entities that are exempt from the NLRA include international organizations located within this country, such as the World Bank, the Inter-American Development Bank, and the International Monetary Fund. The NLRA has been applied, however, to foreign employers doing business within the territorial United States. In a series of cases, the NLRB announced clear guidelines for several industries in order to prevent application of the statute to the smallest of employers and to bring about some predictability.

Several categories of workers are excluded from the coverage of the NLRA, including (1) supervisors (those who may hire, transfer, suspend, lay off, promote, and discipline); (2) managerial employees (those who represent management interests by taking or recommending discretionary actions that effectively control or implement employer policy); (3) agricultural laborers; (4) independent contractors; (5) domestic servants; (6) children or spouses of a sole proprietor or substantial stock owner in a closely held corporation; (7) confidential employees (those who assist managerial employees with responsibility for labor relations); and (8) employees of a "carrier" such as a railway or airline.

The NLRA preempts state efforts at regulation in two principal ways. First, it preempts any state regulation of conduct that is either "arguably protected" or "arguably prohibited" by the act. Second, it may preempt even matters not addressed in the NLRA on the ground that the federal scheme is intended to preserve economic power for both labor and management and for the parties to be free from restriction in this respect.

The U.S. Supreme Court recently issued its most significant interpretation of the NLRA in the past decade with its decision in *NLRB v. Town & Country Electric and Ameristaff Personnel Contractors, Inc.* (1995). The case establishes clear protections for permissible organizing activities by clarifying the intersection of the scope of duty owed to one's employer and the breadth of protections to be afforded the employer's rights to engage in Section 7 activities, such as the right to organize and assist unions.

See also **Collective Bargaining; Concerted Activity; Employee; Employer; Injunction; Labor-Management Relations; National Labor Relations Board; Unfair Labor Practice.**

NATIONAL LABOR RELATIONS BOARD (NLRB)

The federal administrative agency created by National Labor Relations Act (NLRA) to enforce the provisions of that statute. The board itself is composed of five members appointed by the president and confirmed by the Senate. Its primary duties are to conduct elections to determine representation and to interpret and apply the statute on unfair labor practices. The NLRB (frequently referred to as simply "the board") regulates dealings between organized labor groups and employers to ensure that neither takes advantage of the other or of employees. The NLRB is intended to protect the right of employees to organize and bargain collectively. It resolves cases where an employer or labor organization is accused of an unfair labor practice that would interfere with that right.

The NLRB was established in 1935 with the basic goal of fostering meaningful collective bargaining through its powers to investigate claims of employer unfair labor practices (ULP), to provide remedies for violations of the law, and to determine an appropriate bargaining unit for which the majority union would be the exclusive representative. The board's decisions can be enforced by court action unless the parties themselves voluntarily implement its mandates. The NLRB usually announces new legal principles and repudiates old ones through adjudicating cases. The board does, however, have rule-making authority to make substantive law. [*NLRB v. Gordon Manufacturing Co.* (1969)] It has used that power in instances such as the announcement of minimum jurisdictional requirements in cases involving private colleges and universities.

Most of the more than 40,000 unfair labor practice charges processed each year by the NLRB involve allegations of discriminatory discipline and discharge of workers, frequently during organizational campaigns. Since the NLRB is engaged in more litigation than any other federal agency, a complaint must pass through several stages that filter out the great majority of charges. Most are dismissed and most cases not initially dismissed are settled. The board itself decided only 2.5 percent of all unfair labor practice cases closed in 1990, for example. The higher the level in the filtering process, the greater the proportion of complaints that are directed against employers.

ULP charges are first investigated by the regional director. This office makes the initial decision in representation decisions and determines whether to issue complaints in ULP cases. If a charge is found to have insufficient merit, the regional office director dismisses the charge or allows it to be withdrawn. If it has merit, the regional office seeks informal compliance with the law. If those attempts fail, the regional director prepares a formal complaint against the accused, who is called the "respondent." The general counsel of the NLRB supervises the regional offices and has ultimate responsibility for whether complaints would be issued in ULP cases. The general counsel also issues advice memoranda, which either generally or specifically advise the regional directors of the types of cases in which ULP complaints should be issued. Once a formal complaint is issued, a hearing before an administrative law judge (ALJ) is scheduled. ALJs hear testimony in ULP cases and issue recommended decisions for review by the NLRB.

Appealed cases are first assigned on a rotating basis to three-member panels of the board in which one panel member is designated as the "originating board member." Each member relies heavily on his or her staff to evaluate ALJ recommendations and exceptions filed and to draft recommendations. All five board members receive a copy of the panel's proposed decision and proposed dissents, if any, for every case. There is no formalized step in which members discuss cases with one another; however, some boards have engaged in informal discussions prior to making decisions. When disputes appear to be especially important or complex, all five members may vote. Any member may request that all members vote if a case involves new areas of law, or if the members seek to redefine policy or set new policy.

The NLRB's decisions on representation elections are final. Its orders on unfair labor practices, however, are not self-enforcing. They are enforced through the federal circuit courts of appeals. If labor or management does not comply with an order enforced in the court, contempt proceedings can be invoked by the court, resulting in criminal and civil penalties.

See also **Administrative Law Judge; Appropriate Bargaining Unit; Charge; Collective Bargaining; Employee; Employer; Jurisdiction; Labor Organization; National Labor Relations Act; Unfair Labor Practice.**

NATIVE AMERICANS: EMPLOYMENT ISSUES Native Americans is the designation now given to the aboriginal inhabitants of the United States. Individuals of mixed blood have been held to be Indians by the courts within the meaning of treaties and statutes. Indians born in the United States are citizens with the full range of rights and privileges accorded any other citizen. Native Americans have the shortest life expectancy of any group in the United States: as a whole, Native Americans live only two-thirds as long as the non-Native American population. Native Americans also suffer from a high rate of unemployment (more than 70 percent on many reservations), and they fall well below the national average in income, quality of housing, and education (half of the Native American population does not have a high school diploma).

A central problem facing Native Americans is the complex and confusing pattern of laws, especially federal laws, that dominate their lives. No other ethnic or cultural group is so heavily regulated. Although some federal laws were intended to benefit Indians, as a whole they have greatly restricted Native Americans politically and economically.

Federal labor and employment statutes are of "general applicability," that is they cover all persons and entities that fall under their definitions of "employers" and "employees." For example, Title VII of the Civil Rights Act of 1964 protects all Americans, including Native Americans, against job discrimination on the basis of race, ethnicity, or national origin. Native Americans are also protected under the Reconstruction Era Civil Rights Acts such as 42 U.S.C. Section 1981 and Section 1983, which prohibit race and ethnicity discrimination in employment as well. Title VII and the Americans with Disabilities Act, however, *expressly exclude* Indian tribes from their definitions of covered employers.

Many Native Americans believe that regulation by federal labor or health and safety law of tribally sponsored employment that subjects Indian tribes to litigation, damages, administrative proceedings, or fines necessarily thwarts the goals of tribal self-determination and economic development. The issue of whether the Occupational Safety and Health Act (OSHA) applies to tribes has been analyzed with respect to whether OSHA would interfere with treaty rights and sovereign rights. In *Donovan v. Navajo Forest Products Industries* (1982), the court held that applying OSHA would violate a specific treaty right retained by the Navajo Nation, as well as the Nation's sovereign right to exclude outsiders from its territory, and that Congress did not intend to infringe upon those rights in enacting OSHA.

National Labor Relations Act (NRLA) cases have largely been decided on grounds of tribal sovereignty; they focus on the tribe as an employer, not the job or the employee group in question, and accord tribal employers the status of governing entities. The National Labor Relations Board has determined Native American tribes generally to be exempt from coverage under the NLRA's exclusion of governmental entities as employers. [*Fort Apache Timber Co.* (1976)]

Native Americans have received employment preferences under affirmative action. These preferences have been upheld as constitutional in federal government hiring and training in the Bureau of Indian Affairs (BIA). [*United Steelworkers of America v. Weber* (1979)] These preferences have been extended to include preferences in job retention during reductions in force for Native Americans who are employed by the federal government in both the BIA or the Indian Health Services. [*Mescalero Apache Tribe v. Rhoades* (1992); *Morton v. Mancari* (1974)]

Affirmative action has also been sanctioned on the state level. Minnesota's Court of Appeals, using a rational basis standard of review, held that a state statute allowing public employer school districts to give preference to Native Americans during reductions in force did not violate equal protection under the Fourteenth Amendment. [*Krueth v Independent School District* (1993)]

See also **Civil Rights Act of 1964; National Labor Relations Act; Occupational Safety and Health Act.**

NEGOTIATION The process by which representatives of labor and management bargain to set terms and conditions of work, such as wages, hours, benefits, working conditions, and grievance procedures. The results of these negotiations are usually agreed to in writing and comprise the collective bargaining agreement.

See also **Collective Bargaining Agreement.**

NLRB See **National Labor Relations Board.**

***NLRB v. Burns International Security Services, Inc.* (1972)** In this case, the Wackenhut Company provided plant guard services under a contract with Lockheed Aircraft at a California location. Wackenhut lost its contract with Lockheed when it was underbid by Burns International Securities Services. When Burns began providing guard services, it employed 42 employees of which 27 had previously been employed by Wackenhut. Burns refused both to bargain with the union that had represented Wackenhut workers and to honor the union's collective bargaining agreement with Wackenhut.

Unlike *John Wiley & Sons, Inc. v. Livingston,* where the union had sought to compel arbitration in a lawsuit under Section of 301 of the National Labor Relations Act (NLRA), the union in *Burns* filed a National Labor Relations Board (NLRB) charge that Burns had refused to bargain in violation of Section 8(a)(5) of the NLRA.

The NLRB held that the security guards at the Lockheed location constituted an appropriate bargaining unit, thus rejecting Burns' argument that the only appropriate unit was a California-wide unit of Burns employees. The Board then found that Burns had violated Section 8(a)(5) and (1) by refusing to recognize the union, and by refusing to honor the collective bargaining agreement that the union had negotiated with Wackenhut. The U.S. Supreme Court granted certiorari on the bargaining agreement and recognition issues, but declined to review the question of unit appropriateness.

The Court upheld the NLRB's decision. Crucial to the 5 to 4 majority on the question of the union's right to continued recognition was the fact that the NLRB had found the bargaining unit to be still appropriate, and that a majority of the workers hired by Burns had been employed by Wackenhut. It was undisputed that Burns knew all the relevant facts concerning Wackenhut's labor status before Burns took over the security operations at Lockheed.

On the issue of representation, four dissenting Justices argued first that the appropriateness of the bargaining unit was fairly in doubt and that the Court's result prevented Burns' employees from having the free choice guaranteed them by the NLRA. Although 27 of Burns' 42 employees were formerly Wackenhut employees, there was nothing in the record to indicate how many of these employees had approved of being represented by the union when they were employed by Wackenhut, or whether considerations that might have influenced some of them to vote for the union at Wackenhut would still pertain after Burns had taken over.

The Court was unanimous in rejecting a duty of Burns to honor the collective bargaining agreement. The Court relied on the congressional policy of noninterference with collective bargaining agreements as evidenced by Section 8(d) of the NLRA, and found this case to be a departure from prior Board precedent. The Court also distinguished the *Burns* case from *Wiley* on several grounds. First, *Wiley* was brought as a Section 301 suit in which there is no Section 8(d) limitation. Second, it rested on a preference for arbitration and left the ultimate decision of which contract provisions survived to a labor arbitrator. Third, *Wiley* involved a merger which was governed by a state law that the surviving corporation is liable for the debt of its predecessor; whereas in *Burns* there was no buy-sale arrangement, nor any contact between the two employers. The policy of avoiding disruptions and securing industrial stability is not the only labor policy worth protecting, especially where, as in Burns, there was no voluntary assumption of the bargaining agreement. Forcing the agreement on the new employer might impede the sale of businesses and might also disadvantage the union, which would be unable to take advantage of changes in circumstances. Furthermore, it would mean that the new employer could not replace his predecessor's employees with new employees of his own choosing.

The Court suggested that the successor employer might voluntarily assume the provisions of a bargaining agreement or that with respect to other forms of sales and exchanges of capital, the Board might find such an assumption as a matter of law.

The Court turned finally to the NLRB ruling that Burns could not deviate from Wackenhut's collective bargaining agreement without first bargaining to impasse with the union-unilateral action would violate Section

8(a)(5). The Court agreed that Burns had a duty to bargain but held that Burns was not necessarily required to continue the terms and conditions of the Wackenhut bargaining agreement pending current bargaining. Such an obligation turns on whether the new employer plans to retain a majority of the employees in the unit. If it is clear that the firm will retain a majority, then it is appropriate for the firm to consult the union before it fixes employment terms. But where continuity of the predecessor's workforce will not be apparent until the successor's full complement of employees is hired, it has freedom to set unilaterally the initial terms and conditions of employment.

See also ***Howard Johnson Co. v. Detroit Local Joint Executive Board; John Wiley & Sons, Inc. v. Livingston;*** **National Labor Relations Act; National Labor Relations Board; Successor Employer.**

***NLRB v. Exchange Parts Co.* (1964)** The U.S. Supreme Court in *Exchange Parts* held that an employer violates Sections 8(a)(3) and (1) of the National Labor Relations Act (NLRA) by granting or withholding economic benefits in order to interfere with an incumbent bargaining representative or an employee organizing effort. Section 8(a)(1) of the NLRA gives employees the right to organize without employer interference. Benefits conferred on employees prior to a representation election interfere with this right, as do threats or promises of benefit. It must be presumed that the benefits were given to influence the outcome of the election. Therefore, the granting of benefits in this case interfered with the employees' exercise of their right to organize under Section 7 of the NLRA and Section 8(a)(1) of the NLRA.

Similarly, a National Labor Relations Board (NLRB) election may be set aside and a new election ordered where a labor union waives its initiation fees for those who join the union before the election. [*NLRB v. Savair Manufacturing Co.* (1973)] Under the authority of *Exchange Parts,* employers are prohibited from changing terms and conditions of employment for the purpose of affecting the outcome of a pending NLRB election.

In 1959, the International Brotherhood of Boilermakers, Iron Shipbuilders, Blacksmiths, Forgers, and Helpers began an organizational campaign at the Exchange Parts Company plant, seeking to be certified as the collective bargaining agent for the respondent's employees. The NLRB set March 18, 1960, as the date for the election. Prior to the vote, the employer mailed its employees a letter outlining several employee benefits. It contained the sentence: "The Union can't put any of those things in your envelope—only the company can do that." Among the benefits detailed in the letter were a new system for computing overtime during holiday weeks, which had the effect of increasing wages for those weeks, and a new vacation schedule allowing employees to extend their vacations by sandwiching them between two weekends. The letter was the first general announcement of these new benefits. The union lost the election.

The NLRB found that this conduct was an unfair labor practice. The court of appeals, however, refused to enforce the board's order because the new benefits became effective unconditionally on a permanent basis and there was no indication that the benefits would be withdrawn if the employees voted for the union. The unanimous Supreme Court reversed this decision, holding that the broad purpose of Section 8(a)(1) of the NLRA was to establish "the right of employees to organize for mutual aid without employer interference. . . . The action of employees with respect to the choice of their bargaining agents may be induced by favors bestowed by the employer as well as by his threats or domination." The Court, in referring to "the danger inherent in well-timed increases in benefits is the suggestion of a fist inside the velvet glove," explained that "Employees are not likely to miss the inference that the source of benefits now conferred is also the source from which future benefits must flow and which may dry up if it is not obliged."

See also **Collective Bargaining; National Labor Relations Act; National Labor Relations Board; Unfair Labor Practice.**

***NLRB v. Gissel Packing Co.* (1969)** The U.S. Supreme Court ruled in *Gissel* that (1) the National Labor Relations Board (NLRB) may require bargaining on the basis of authorization cards, (2) an employer is not obligated to rely on authorization cards as a proof of majority status and may request a representation election, and (3) the NLRB may order bargaining where an employer rejects a union card majority while at the same time committing unfair labor practices that tend to undermine the union's majority and make a fair election unlikely.

Four cases were consolidated under the *Gissel* caption for a hearing before the Supreme Court; three of them pertaining to the issue of the union obtaining bargaining rights without an election after substantial employer violations of the National Labor Relations Act (NLRA). In each of the three cases, the union conducted an organizational campaign, obtained authorization cards from a majority of the employees in an appropriate unit, and then demanded recognition. Each employer refused to recognize the union on the grounds that authorization cards are inherently unreliable indicators of employee desires and conducted its own antiunion campaign in which each of the employers committed various unfair labor practices. In the first company, the union did not petition for an election but filed unfair labor practice charges. At the second company, the union petitioned for an election, but it was not conducted because the union filed unfair labor practice charges. An election was conducted at the third company, and the employees rejected the union, but the NLRB set the election aside because of the employer's unfair labor practices. To remedy the unfair labor practices, each employer was ordered by the NLRB to bargain with the union. The employers appealed the board's action.

In *Gissel* the employers challenged the used of authorization cards as a basis for a bargaining order on three main grounds: (1) the employer may have no chance to campaign and present its views to the employees prior to the union's solicitation of card support; (2) absent a secret ballot election, employees will succumb to group pressure to sign cards or will be coerced into doing so; and (3) too often union authorization cards are obtained by misrepresentation and coercion. The Supreme Court would reject all three of these arguments in *Gissel*.

The Supreme Court was asked to decide (1) the worth of the authorization cards in this case a means of determining union representation status and (2) the issue of whether the NLRB acted properly in relying on employer reelection misconduct to justify recognizing the union without an election.

The Court found that the legislative history of neither the original NLRA nor the Labor-Management Relations Act of 1947 (the Taft-Hartley Act) would preclude union recognition on the basis of authorization cards without NLRB certification. Although the Court noted the "acknowledged superiority" of the election process, it held that authorization cards were not "inherently unreliable." Indeed, the Court stated that cards "may be the most effective—perhaps the only way of assuring employee choice" where unfair labor practices have made it impossible to test employees' free choice through the ballot box. Thus, the Court ruled that a union may establish its majority status and require an employer to bargain with it by means other than an NLRB election.

The Court, in deciding whether cards signed by employees authorizing the union to present them are sufficiently reliable to establish the majority status of the union, ruled that an employee who signs a card that already authorizes a union to represent him should be bound by it unless he is deliberately misled by union supporters as to the language on the card. The subjective motivation of the employee in signing the card is not relevant.

Gissel makes it clear that the union could obtain recognition on the basis of authorization cards where it has a majority, particularly if an unfair labor practice makes it impossible for the union to collect a majority and if, more specifically, the union alleges that but for the employer's unfair labor practices it would have obtained a majority or had a reasonable chance of obtaining majority status. The employer in this situation would profit from its wrongdoing by curtailing the union organizational drive before it could have established itself. When the employer has committed unfair labor practices designed to thwart the union activity of the employees, authorization cards may be the only reliable method of ascertaining the true wishes of employees. Thus, under appropriate circumstances, a union may establish its majority status by authorization cards signed by employees.

The Court ruled that the remedy of ordering an employer to bargain with the union is appropriate where the employer's unfair labor practices interfere with the holding of a fair election. The lesser penalty of posting a notice signed by the employer informing employees of their rights and assuring them that the employer will not violate the act in the future may not be adequate after the employer has succeeded in destroying the union's majority status or the conditions necessary for a fair election. The most suitable remedy for extensive unfair labor practices in those circumstances would be a bargaining order. On the other hand, minor or less extensive unfair labor practices, because of their minimal impact on the election machinery, would not warrant the issuance of a bargaining order. In such cases, the authorization cards are important only for obtaining the showing of interest necessary to initiate the NLRB's election procedure. The Supreme Court then remanded (sent back) the cases to the NLRB for a determination of the effect of the unfair labor practices and whether a fair election could be conducted.

See also **Authorization Card; *Linden Lumber v. NLRB;* National Labor Relations Act; National Labor Relations Board.**

NLRB v. Hendricks Co. (1981) The U.S. Supreme Court in *Hendricks Co.* ruled on the issue of whether it was an unfair labor practice to terminate a secretary who had access to confidential management information for activities which, if engaged in by a statutory employee, would have been protected by Section 2(3) of the National Labor Relations Act (NLRA). Her duties did not involve access to any labor matters. The Court, in distinguishing this case from *NLRB v. Bell Aerospace* (1974), ruled that she was not a managerial employee and was therefore protected by the statute.

The National Labor Relations Board (NLRB) has developed two tests to determine if an individual is a confidential employee (an employee assisting, in a confidential capacity, those who formulate, determine, and effectuate management relations policies). One of these is the "labor-nexus" test, which asks whether the employee acts in a confidential capacity to an individual who formulates, determines, and effectuates management policies in the field of labor relations. The board bases its labor-nexus test on the theory that "management should not be required to handle a labor relations matter through employees who are represented by the union with which the [c]ompany's position with regard to contract negotiations, the disposition of grievances, and other labor relations matters." This policy excludes from the coverage of the act only those employees who exercise managerial functions in labor relations matters.

The decision in *Hendricks Co.* actually involved two cases. In the first, the personal secretary of the chief executive officer of a corporation was discharged after she signed a petition urging reinstatement of an employee who had been dismissed. In the second, a corporation challenged the inclusion in the collective bargaining unit of 18 employees who had access to confidential business information. In each case, the seventh circuit rejected the board's labor-nexus policy.

The Supreme Court reversed and remanded (sent back to the lower court for further action) the lower court's ruling in an opinion by Justice William Brennan. The Court held that under the NLRA, the term "employee" includes any employee with the exception of agricultural laborers, supervisors, and independent contractors. The NLRB had rejected the argument that all individuals with access to confidential information should be excluded; the Court held that the NLRB's determination was entitled to great deference because the statute granted it broad discretion to determine appropriate bargaining units.

See also **Appropriate Bargaining Unit; Collective Bargaining; Employee; National Labor Relations Act; National Labor Relations Board; Termination; Unfair Labor Practice.**

NLRB v. Jones & Laughlin Steel Corp. (1937)

The U.S. Supreme Court in *Jones & Laughlin* upheld the constitutionality of the National Labor Relations Act (NLRA) by a five to four vote. In earlier Supreme Court decisions, the Court had held it beyond the power of Congress to regulate a "local" business, such as production, that had only an "indirect" effect on interstate commerce. In the early and mid 1930s, the U.S. Supreme Court had declared many of the Roosevelt administration's social and economic reform laws unconstitutional. The Roosevelt administration reacted by attempting to expand the Court in order to change the outcome of those decisions. Chief Justice Hughes joined the majority of the Court in *Jones & Laughlin* in declaring that statute constitutional. Specifically, the court held first that the employer unfair labor practice provisions of the NLRA did not constitute denial without due process of law of the employer's liberty to contract. Second, it held that the power of Congress under Article I to regulate commerce among the states extended to the business of the respondent, a manufacturer of steel.

The decision was highly significant in that it broadened the reach of the commerce clause of the Constitution and construed the NLRA as providing the National Labor Relations Board jurisdiction to the fullest extent permitted by the commerce clause. With this decision, the Court accepted the constitutional theory that Congress could regulate labor relations in order to avoid interference with the shipment of goods across state lines. The Supreme Court also noted the importance of collective bargaining, since an individual employee who resists unfair or arbitrary treatment by an employer both lacks equal bargaining power and depends on the employer for "his daily wage for the maintenance of himself and family."

See also **National Labor Relations Act; National Labor Relations Board; Unfair Labor Practice.**

NLRB v. MacKay Radio and Telegraph Co. (1938)

The U.S. Supreme Court held in *MacKay* that although striking is protected conduct, employers may permanently replace striking employees with strikebreakers. In other words, even though an employer may not discharge or discipline workers for engaging in a strike, the employer, in order to maintain production, has a "business justification" for permanently replacing strikers through the recruitment of strikebreakers. Thus an employer may just as effectively deprive employees of their job security as would be the case if they were dismissed or disciplined from striking. The U.S. House of Representatives voted to reverse *MacKay* in 1991, but the Senate filibustered the bill to death in 1992. During the 1992 campaign, President Clinton supported the legislation, and it was reintroduced in 1993.

The *MacKay* doctrine provides employers with a means to eliminate employees, pension obligations, and the labor union. The employer, under the Labor-Management Relations Act of 1947 (the Taft-Hartley Act), may petition for a National Labor Relations Board election if there is a question over union representation after the workers involved in the decision to select the union are no longer in the workforce. Only with the 1959 amendments to the National Labor Relations Act (NLRA) were strikers allowed to vote until twelve months after the commencement of the strike. To a limited degree, this provision of the NLRA amendments has mitigated some of the harsh effects of the *MacKay* doctrine.

The *MacKay* doctrine is also limited in cases where the strike is partially caused by an employer's unfair labor practices. In those instances, the employees are entitled to reinstatement. If after the unfair labor practice and the strike the employees offer unconditionally to return to work, they may be entitled to back pay as well. And even in an economic strike, such as that which occurred in *MacKay,* the Supreme Court has held (in a decision that is difficult to reconcile with *MacKay)* that an employer may not offer extra seniority to strikebreakers—even if the employer can show that such an offer was necessary to maintain production.

See also **Back Pay; National Labor Relations Act; National Labor Relations Board; Protected Activity; Reinstatement; Seniority; Strikebreaker; Unfair Labor Practice.**

NO MAN'S LAND

In labor disputes, the lack of clear jurisdiction between federal and state governments. The expression was popular in the 1950s, but since then the law has been clarified so that the states have jurisdiction over labor disputes when the National Labor Relations Board (NLRB) lacks or declines jurisdiction. The case law also affirmed the NLRB's primacy in labor disputes in which interstate commerce is involved. [*Guss v. Utah Board* (1957); *Automobile Workers v. O'Brien* (1950)]

See also **Labor Dispute; Jurisdiction; National Labor Relations Board.**

No Raiding Agreement An agreement among individual international unions in which they promise not to persuade employees to leave one labor union to join another when the first union has established a bargaining relationship. AFL-CIO–affiliated unions in good standing are participants in a general no raiding agreement. In addition, several unions have signed bilateral agreements on the organization of unorganized employees.

See also **American Federation of Labor-Congress of Industrial Organizations; Labor Union; International Union.**

Norris-LaGuardia Act (1932) Congress, through this statute, successfully acted to curb federal court abuses of the injunctive process and protect the right of workers to bargain collectively. The Norris-LaGuardia Act limited and restricted the jurisdiction of federal courts to issue injunctions and restraining orders in labor disputes, both of which were aimed at restricting the activities of labor unions. Section 1 stated that no federal court would have "jurisdiction to issue any restraining order or permanent injunction in a case involving or growing out of a labor dispute, except in a strict conformity with the provisions of this Act." This statute withdrew from federal courts all jurisdiction to issue injunctions against peacefully striking, assembling, patrolling, or publicizing facts in the context of a labor dispute. [Section 4] The act defines "labor dispute" to encompass disputes over organizing into unions and establishing "terms or conditions of employment," and to encompass all persons in the same industry or occupation or the same labor organization, or having a direct or indirect interest therein [Section 13] Section 13 also attempted to reverse the impact of the narrow definition of "labor dispute" arrived at in *Duplex Printing Press Co. v. Deering* (1921) by referring to nearly all labor disputes, including secondary stoppages. The act also provides that in the rare case when the concerted activities threaten to cause serious harm to person or property, the federal court must comply with stringent procedural safeguards and an injunction may be issued. [Section 7]

Congress, in drafting this statute, attempted to avoid having the Norris-LaGuardia Act interpreted like the Clayton Act was by the U.S. Supreme Court in *Duplex, Bedford Cut Stone Company v. Journeymen Stone Cutters' Association* (1927), and *American Steel Foundries v. Tri-City Central Council* (1921). A report of the House Judiciary Committee stated that the Norris-

LaGuardia Act is "intended to overcome the qualifying effect of the decisions of the court in protecting labor unions from injunctions."

The Norris-LaGuardia Act does not apply to state courts, but many states have followed the lead of Congress and enacted what are known as "little Norris-LaGuardia Acts." A federal labor statute might preempt the power of a state court to issue an injunction that would be more intrusive than a federal court injunction permitted by the *Boys Market* exception to the Norris LaGuardia Act. In fact, one of the principal exceptions to the statute's restrictions is that a federal court issue an injunction to stop a strike activity in order to enforce a no-strike clause in a collective bargaining agreement. [*Boys Market, Inc. v. Retail Clerks' Local 770* (1970)]

The Supreme Court ruled in *United States v. Hutcheson* (1941) that the Norris-LaGuardia prohibitions have a broader scope than the denial of jurisdiction to federal courts in connection with injunctions. The statute also prohibits the yellow-dog contract, in which employers require workers to stay out of unions as a condition of employment. These agreements were declared to be contrary to federal public policy and thus unenforceable in any federal court—an important first step in support of unions because, since it articulated a public policy in favor of free collective bargaining.

The Norris-LaGuardia approach to the yellow dog contract reflects the statute's general philosophy. Although the statute promoted the doctrine of freedom of association for all workers as a matter of public policy, it mandated no procedures for implementing this freedom. Instead, Norris-LaGuardia followed a laissez-faire approach to industrial relations by merely forbidding federal court intrusion into labor disputes. However, in 1947 the Taft-Hartley Act restored some injunctive power to the courts.

While the Norris-LaGuardia Act forbade the formulation of rules governing labor policy by the federal courts and declared that the government was to be neutral, the Wagner Act (The National Labor Relations Act) of 1935 was intended to represent affirmative federal government support of unionization and collective bargaining. The Wagner Act enumerated this principle chiefly through Section 7, which protects the rights of employees to engage in concerted activity for mutual aid and protection from employer restraint and coercion.

See also **Concerted Activity; *Duplex Printing Press Co. v. Deering*; Industrial Relations; Injunctions against Unions; Labor Dispute; Labor-Management Relations Act of 1947; National Labor Relations Act; National Labor Relations Board; Yellow Dog Contract.**

NORTH AMERICAN FREE TRADE AGREEMENT (NAFTA) After a hard fought struggle, the North American Free Trade Agreement won congressional approval in November 1993 and went into effect as planned on January 1, 1994. The agreement creates a free trade area in North America by gradually removing all tariffs and other trade barriers among the United States, Canada, and Mexico over a fifteen year period. In the process, it builds on the United States–Canada Free Trade Agreement of 1988 (implemented by the United States–Canada Free Trade Agreement Implementation Act, which took effect on January 1, 1989, and began the process of removing many trade barriers between the United States and Canada. All of the trade barriers between those two countries are scheduled to be eliminated on January 1, 1998.

Congressional approval for NAFTA was not a foregone conclusion and came only after an intense debate about the future of U.S. jobs and labor unions, the environment, immigration from Mexico, and the nature of the world economy in the twenty-first century. Indeed, even immediately prior to the vote, approval seemed in doubt, especially in the House of Representatives. Only an intense effort by President Bill Clinton, who made the vote one of the tests of his presidency, won a victory in the House, which passed implementing legislation in 1993.

The theory behind NAFTA was that American consumers would benefit from having relatively cheaper commodities to purchase and that it would aid development in Mexico. Furthermore, as the Mexican economy develops, there would be a greater demand for products produced in the United States and Canada.

Labor unions in both the United States and Canada have opposed free trade because of the immediate loss of employment resulting from competition with the lower labor costs in Mexico. It was estimated that the loss of American jobs will be primarily among assembly-line and relatively low-skilled workers. Opponents estimated that as many as 900,000 American jobs may be lost to Mexico as a direct result of NAFTA. The protests of the unions were rejected by some as protectionist.

One of the labor unions' concerns is how American labor law will function under NAFTA. Unions argue that the same labor laws that make the U.S. and Canadian economies viable consumer economies have failed to defend American and Canadian workers from labor competition from less-developed countries where American wage and work standards have no public policy protections. The arguments of NAFTA's supporters, who relied on abstract and long-term projections, have provided little comfort to workers already fearing for their jobs in a sluggish U.S. manufacturing economy during an era of corporate downsizing.

NO-STRIKE CLAUSES

Although the National Labor Relations Act (NLRA) protects the rights of employees to strike, that right may also be waived for the term of a collective bargaining agreement through clear contract language. In most collective bargaining agreements, a no-strike clause is included in return for the employer's agreement to resolve contract grievances through arbitration. If employees ignore the clause and strike, they waive federal protection and may be disciplined. Under these circumstances, the employer's paramount concern generally is the availability of injunctive relief.

The Norris-LaGuardia Act was passed in response to labor dissatisfaction with federal judges who had restricted strike activity. It specifies that federal courts shall not have jurisdiction to issue injunctions against strikes unless findings of "unlawful acts" and "irreparable harm" can be made. Since a breach of contract does not normally threaten to cause serious harm to persons or property, the Norris-LaGuardia Act was understood to forbid injunctions to enforce contractual no-strike clauses. No-strike clauses, however, can be enforced under Section 301(b) of the NLRA, which permits unions to be sued for breach of contract. Congress also intended through the Labor-Management Relations Act of 1947 (the Taft-Hartley Act) to induce both parties to the labor contract to incorporate grievance and arbitration provisions on one hand and on the other a no-strike, no-lockout clause. This inducement came from permitting the union to sue and be sued and to make arbitration and no-strike promises enforceable.

Employers were not satisfied with damage actions for breach of no-strike clauses; they wanted the strike enjoined. In *Sinclair Refining Co. v. Atkinson* (1962), the Supreme Court held that the anti-injunction provision of the Norris-LaGuardia Act precludes a federal district court from enjoining a strike in breach of a no-strike clause. The Court held that Section 301 of the NLRA did not expressly nor impliedly repeal the Norris-LaGuardia Act in this context. The Court left open the questions of whether state courts are bound by the anti-injunction provisions of Norris-LaGuardia and whether federal courts are required to overturn any injunctions that might have been given by the state courts.

The application of Norris-LaGuardia to injunctions against strikes in breach of a no-strike clause was taken up again in *Boys Market, Inc. v. Retail Clerks' Local 770* (U.S. 1970), where the Supreme Court reversed *Sinclair.* The Court held that federal courts are not precluded by the Norris-LaGuardia Act from enjoining a strike in breach of a no-strike clause where the strike is over a grievance that both parties are contractually bound to arbitrate. A court asked to issue such an injunction is to order the employer to arbitrate as a condition of obtaining the injunction. The enjoining court must also consider ordinary principles of equity in determining whether the injunction is warranted. Equity is justice administered according to fairness, as opposed to the strictly formulated rules of common law. These include whether the breaches are occurring and will continue or are threatened, whether the strike will cause irreparable injury to the employer, and whether the employer will suffer more from denial of an injunction than will the union from its issuance.

The Supreme Court in later cases refused to expand the *Boys Market* exception to the Norris-LaGuardia Act to cover every strike in breach of a collective bargaining agreement. [*Buffalo Forge v. United Steelworkers* (1976)]

A no-strike clause, however, does not apply to employees who strike to protest a serious unfair labor practice of their employer, partially because an unfair labor practice is defined as "destructive of the foundation on which collective bargaining must rest." [*Arlan's Department Store* (1961)]

Employers regard no-strike clauses as the most important management clause in labor agreements. Without it, there is no reason for management to agree to any request by the union, since agreement will not prevent mid-contract strikes, should the union decide that it wishes to improve the agreement or dispute its interpretation. Employers often bargain for a no-strike clause that covers all work stoppages, including sympathy strikes, even though there is considerable case authority for the argument that a sympathy strike cannot be enjoined, even if it is specifically mentioned in the no-strike clause. The no-strike clause usually applies to all strikes or work stoppages for any reason whatsoever, in case the union argues that its strike is over an issue not contemplated at the bargaining table and therefore not covered by the no-strike clause.

See also **Collective Bargaining Agreement; Grievance; Grievance Arbitration; Jurisdiction; Labor-Management Relations Act of 1947; National Labor Relations Act; Norris-LaGuardia Act; Unfair Labor Practice.**

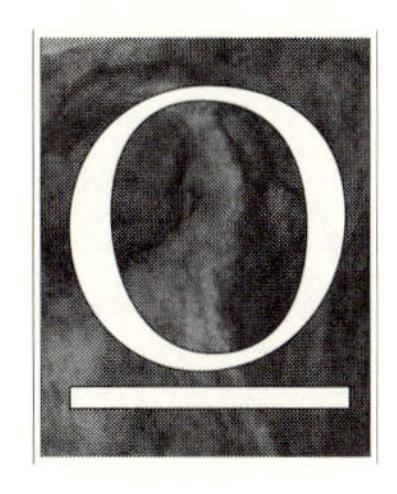

OBESITY DISCRIMINATION A still-developing legal concept, which basically states that a qualified individual who is considered obese may not be discriminated against because of that obesity in regard to job application, procedures in hiring, advancement, discharge, compensation, job training, and other terms or conditions of employment.

The federal Rehabilitation Act of 1973, which applies to holders of government contracts, recipients of federal grants, and government agencies and departments, does not specifically mention obesity as a potential disability, nor do the regulations enforcing the statute. The federal Americans with Disabilities Act (ADA) of 1990 augmented the Rehabilitation Act by prohibiting private employers as well as state and local entities from discriminating against the handicapped. Like the Rehabilitation Act, the ADA does not specifically mention obesity as a disability. The regulations enforcing the ADA, however, do discuss potential weight-based claims. These Equal Employment Opportunity Commission regulations exclude weight within a "normal range" as a recognized impairment.

In *Cook v. State of Rhode Island* (1993), a federal appellate court ruled for the first time that employment discrimination against obese individuals is illegal. The plaintiff in *Cook,* a morbidly obese woman, was denied a position as an attendant for the mentally retarded at a government-funded institution. The court, in a unanimous decision, endorsed the position that severely overweight people are protected from discrimination under federal disability law. As Judge Selya, author of the opinion, stated, "in a society that all too often confuses 'slim' with 'beautiful' or 'good,' morbid obesity can present formidable barriers to employment." *Cook* offered an approach of protecting obese individuals from employment discrimination under federal law that is consistent with relevant statutory, administrative, and case law, as well as modern medicine. Because obesity is not a disability per se under federal law, *Cook* requires potential claimants to prove discrimination on a case-by-case basis through either an actual or perceived disability theory under the test provided in Section 504 of the Rehabilitation Act of 1973.

The relevant case law indicates that the courts have not been willing to apply the Rehabilitation Act of 1973, the ADA, and state fair employment statutes to find overweight job seekers disabled in any and all circumstances. A federal district court in California, which heard a case of an applicant who was rejected for a job as an airline attendant because he exceeded the maximum weight limit, held that the plaintiff was not handicapped under the Rehabilitation Act. The applicant, whose weight appeared to be the voluntary result of avid body building, was not substantially limited in any major life activity. [*Tudyman v. United Airlines* (1984)]

A California Supreme Court held that an overweight condition must have a "physiological" or "systemic" basis in order to be considered a disability under the California Fair Employment and Housing Act. Ruling against a 305-pound woman who was denied employment in a health food store, the court said the woman failed to show that the employer perceived her as having a physiological disorder.

Michigan is the only state which has a specific statutory prohibition against employment discrimination based on weight. Other states have more general statutes prohibiting discrimination against the disabled. State courts have treated weight-based employment discrimination claims differently. A majority of weight-based discrimination claims filed pursuant to state law have been denied for various reasons. Several state cases have dealt with obesity as a disability. Some courts uphold the employer's decisions not to hire or promote because the courts find weight restrictions to be a bona fide occupational qualification or because obesity is not a disability or an immutable condition. Other courts have not required immutability and are more amenable to evidence that obesity is a disability. With the passage of the ADA and the trend toward defining obesity as a disability, more state and federal courts are likely to find obesity a disability justifying protection against discrimination.

See also **Americans with Disabilities Act of 1990; Bona Fide Occupational Qualification; Rehabilitation Act of 1973.**

OCCUPATIONAL SAFETY AND HEALTH ACT (OSHA) OF 1970

A federal statute that grants the federal government authority to develop and enforce nationwide safety and health standards for private sector employers. It was preceded by a series of piecemeal federal statutes that had extended federal work safety regulation from one industry to another. The U.S. Supreme Court stated that the purpose of OSHA was to ensure "safe and healthful working conditions" for every working American. In enacting OSHA, Congress was not concerned with promulgating absolute safety, but with the elimination of significant harm. The statute was not designed to eliminate all occupational accidents; rather, it is designed to require a good-faith effort to balance the needs of workers to have a safe and healthy work environment against the need of industry to function without undue interference.

OSHA, which has withstood several constitutional challenges, establishes the "general duty" of each employer to provide a safe workplace, one which is free from recognized hazards causing or likely to cause serious harm to his or her employees. The statute requires employers to comply with the prescribed health and safety standards, submit to inspections, maintain records, and report accidents and illnesses. An employer violates the "general duty" clause when it is proven that: (1) the employer failed to make its workplace "free of a hazard which was (2) "recognized" and (3) "causing or likely to cause death or serious physical harm." [*National Realty and Construction Co., Inc. v. OSHRC* (1973)] A hazard may be "recognized" in either of two ways: (1) the employer may know of the hazard or (2) the hazard may be one that is known as a hazard in the industry which the employer is operating.

OSHA grants employees the right to: (1) question unsafe conditions and request a federal inspection of the workplace; (2) assist OSHA inspectors on a limited basis; (3) aid a court in determining whether certain imminently dangerous conditions exist; and (4) bring a lawsuit to compel the U.S. Department of Labor to seek injunctive relief.

Employees have the right to refuse to perform hazardous job activities where they reasonably believe there is a real danger of death or injury and there is no time to rely on administrative action to remedy the problem. The U.S. Supreme Court, however, ruled that employees risk termination if they acted "unreasonably or in bad faith." [*Whirlpool v. Marshall* (1980)] OSHA prohibits discrimination against any employee who has filed a complaint, testified in a proceeding, or otherwise exercised a right under OSHA.

Employees have a duty to comply with all OSHA standards, rules, regulations, and orders. There are, however, no legal sanctions for employees who violate OSHA standards or obstruct its purposes. [*Atlantic & Gulf Stevedores, Inc. v. Occupational Safety & Health Review Commission* (1976)]

OSHA provides for a wide range of penalties. The violations are categorized in order of increasing severity are: a notice of a violation, nonserious, serious, repeated, willful, and failure to abate notice. The good faith of the employer, the seriousness of the violation, the employer's past history of compliance, and the size of the employer are all considered in assessing the penalty. Criminal penalties, including fine and imprisonment, may be imposed for persons who knowingly make false statements, representations, or certifications on documents filed with the agency.

OSHA authorizes the Occupational Safety and Health Administration, an agency of the U.S. Department of Labor, to issue and enforce detailed health and safety regulations. Compliance officers have the primary responsibility for direct enforcement of OSHA and may make unannounced workplace inspections and issue citations for violations of OSHA standards. The Labor Department, in designing regulations on particular toxic materials or harmful physical agents, must prove that an exposure limit is "reasonably necessary or appropriate to provide safe and healthful employment." The Occupational Safety and Health Review Commission, an independent body created by the OSHA, conducts enforcement proceedings against alleged OSHA violators. It also hears and rules on appeals by employers cited for violations. It is composed of three members appointed for six-year terms by the President, with the advice and consent of the U.S. Senate.

See also **Safety.**

Occupational Safety and Health Administration

See **Occupational Safety and Health Act of 1970.**

Open Shop

A business establishment in which employees are declared by the employer to be free to join or not to join any labor union. Union membership is neither a condition of employment nor a condition of continuing employment. Theoretically, the workers are employed regardless of union affiliation, though open shops have generally employed nonunion workers throughout American labor history. Unionists believe that the open shop effectively bars union members from employment.

Employer-sponsored open shop drives from 1903 to 1916 and during the 1920s were basically antiunion efforts, along with such devices as the yellow dog contract, designed to eliminate existing unions or to prevent their entrance.

In the construction industry, the open shop sector has increased noticeably in recent times. Its success depends upon the ability of contractors to recruit and flexibly deploy skilled craftsmen in combination with relatively large numbers of semiskilled workers who are paid at subunion rates. The decline in union representation began especially around 1970, spurred by the recession and rising unemployment, and continues to the present. Since that time, the disparity between union and nonunion wages has increased, due largely to the rising cost of union fringe benefits. Unions have been forced to engage in concession bargaining in order to make union contractors more competitive. In 1984 the open shop lobby persuaded the U.S. Department of Labor to amend the rules for determining the prevailing wages. These regulations made it more difficult for the union rate to prevail, thus enabling open shop contractors to exploit their lower labor costs in competitive bidding. Although state prevailing wage laws continue to support the collective bargaining system in the construction industry, the new regulations have made it easier for open shop contractors to win government construction contracts, further eroding union power and control.

See also **Collective Bargaining; Davis-Bacon Act of 1931; Labor Union.**

OUTSOURCING Contracting out work to another plant or procuring parts from other manufacturers. Partly in reaction to competitive pressures from the "global" economy and perhaps in response to congressional actions regulating employment rights and benefits, companies began using outsourcing in the 1980s to reduce labor costs and obtain greater workplace flexibility. Poor sales and increased foreign competition have forced the automobile industry, for example, to use outsourcing to lower production costs. Industry executives held that outsourcing in the automobile industry was prompted by the relative rise in workers' wages, the availability of suppliers of auto products, and the desire of industry to maintain access to some foreign markets.

OVERTIME The hours worked by an employee in excess of the standard workday or workweek established by statute, by the collective bargaining agreement, or by company policy. Hours in excess of the standard are generally paid for in "penalty" or overtime rates. Frequently, the overtime rate is one and one-half times the regular rate. Overtime regulations, like minimum wage statutes, supersede any contractual provisions.

The Fair Labor Standards Act (FLSA) established basic weekly hours and set premium or overtime rates beyond those hours, except in exempted industries or where other conditions are met under the statute. The FLSA does not prohibit overtime work; it simply requires that one and one-half times the employee's regular rate be paid for each hour worked in excess of 40 hours per week. Overtime is payable on a workweek basis. The "workweek" is defined as any regularly recurring period of seven consecutive 24-hour days.

Wage and hour provisions requiring overtime pay under the FLSA and similar state laws apply only to "nonexempt" employees, who must be paid the minimum wage (either federal or state, whichever is higher) and at a rate not less than one and one-half times the employee's regular rate for all hours worked in excess of 40 in a weekly pay period, or if state law mandates, for all hours worked in excess of eight hours a day.

The employees who are exempt from overtime payments under federal law include those who hold an "executive, administrative, or professional position," or whose primary duty (50 percent or more of their time) is devoted to such work and who earn a salary of $250 per week (regardless of the number of hours worked that week, inclusive of board, lodging, or other allowances and facilities) or are salesmen. Highly but hourly-paid computer personnel are also exempt. To be classified as an executive, one must regularly direct the work of two or more other employees and primarily manage, at the least, a recognized subdivision of a department. The executive must have the authority to hire and fire, or to effectively recommend the same, and must regularly exercise discretionary powers.

See also **Collective Bargaining Agreement; Fair Labor Standards Act; Hours of Labor.**

Parental Leave

See **Family and Medical Leave Act of 1993.**

Parol Evidence Rule

Generally, this evidence rule is intended to preserve the integrity of written agreements by refusing to allow contracting parties to attempt to change the meaning of their contract through the use of oral statements made at the time of the contract. As applied to employment contracts, the rule states that once two parties have made a written employment contract and agreed that it is the complete and accurate representation of their agreement, evidence, whether oral or otherwise, of prior understandings and negotiations will not be admitted for the purpose of varying or contradicting the contract. The only exceptions to the parol evidence rule are in cases of fraud, duress, or mutual mistake.

See also **Employment; Grievance Arbitration; Negotiation.**

Participatory Management

A means of more actively involving the individual employees in determining management goals related to their work. It is intended to reduce costs, increase productivity, improve communications within the company, and enhance greater worker understanding of company goals and company welfare. It generally refers to employee involvement in the decision-making processes traditionally reserved for management, involving employees with decisions that affect them both directly and indirectly.

In the 1970s, decades after Japan implemented participatory management, this concept began to interest American employers. Workers' participation is sometimes viewed as a solution to labor-management relations problems and sometimes as a synonym for industrial democracy. Workers' participation can be as indirect as the use of suggestion boxes or as direct as conferences between employees and management or committees of employee representatives that meet periodically with company executives.

Worker participation differs from collective bargaining in two ways. Worker participation includes decisions that relate to the daily performance of the job, while collective bargaining is typically limited to general matters, such as wages and working hours, that affect the employees of an entire industry or region. Worker participation emphasizes and facilitates cooperation rather than the union-management conflict that characterizes collective bargaining.

See also **Collective Bargaining; Employee; Labor-Management Relations; Management.**

PART-TIME EMPLOYMENT Employment with a workweek of less than 35 hours.

The voluntary part-time employed includes workers who do not want or are not available for full-time work, including workers who accept part-time employment while their young children are in school but are not generally able or willing to accept full-time employment.

Part-time employees are those who do not work a full schedule or are not considered full-time employees. They may work only part of a schedule or perform only certain limited work. While many employers create part-time positions in order to reduce costs, unions advocate part-time work for those that want it as well as benefits for those part-timers. Part-time work is considered by these unionists as an important means of flexibility for many working families.

Involuntary part-time workers are persons who work less than 35 hours a week, not by choice but for economic reasons—slack work, the inability to find full-time jobs, or for other reasons—and who usually work full time. They are included in the full-time labor force by the Bureau of Labor Statistics.

See also **Employee.**

PATERNITY LEAVE See **Family and Medical Leave Act of 1993; Leave of Absence.**

PATTERN BARGAINING A negotiation technique in which crucial terms reached in a settlement with one company are closely followed by other companies. U.S. Steel, for example, has traditionally set the pattern in the steel industry, while in the auto industry the first employment contract reached with one of the Big Three auto manufacturers (General Motors, Ford, and American Motors) sets the pattern for the rest of the companies.

See also **Employment Contract.**

PENDLETON ACT (1883) Also known as the Civil Service Act, this statute created the federal merit system and provided the first civil service protections for federal employees.

The statute emerged from the civil service reform movement of the 1870s and 1880s, led by George W. Curtis, who headed the Civil Service Commission created by President Ulysses S. Grant in 1871 and was one of the founders of the National Civil Service Reform League, currently the National Civil Service League. (The assassination of President James Garfield by a disappointed office seeker also persuaded Congress to enact the statute.) In 1881, Senator George Pendleton of Ohio introduced a bill drafted by the New York Civil Service Reform Association. The measure became law on January 16, 1883.

The Pendleton Act contained the following provisions: (1) it created the U.S. Civil Service Commission, an independent bipartisan commission appointed by and responsible to the president, charged with enforcing the statute; (2) it introduced the merit principle and selection by open competitive examinations; and (3) it freed employees from any obligations to make political contributions and strictly prohibited officers from receiving or soliciting such funds. It did not, however, address the issue of terminations. Indeed, Congress rejected a proposal that terminations be permitted only for cause. Only when the Lloyd-LaFollette Act was enacted in 1912 did federal employees receive protection against termination except for cause.

Gradually, civil service protection has been extended to almost all federal and state and most local government employees. Beginning in the late 1960s, constitutional protections against wrongful dismissals were added to civil service protection, at least for employees below the federal level.

See also **Civil Service; Wrongful Discharge.**

PENSION Payments, usually monthly, to individuals who retire from employment with a company after reaching a specified age or period of service, or because of accident, illness, or some other reason. Previously, pensions were variously known as superannuations, service retirement allowances, or service apportionments.

A pension plan is an organized program, usually developed by administrators and supervised by trustees of the funds set aside for the payment of benefits. It is maintained by an employer in order to provide specific benefits following the employees' retirement. It is, in effect, a contract between an employer and employee. Usually pension plans consist of deferred payments to a former employee (or surviving spouse) for past services rendered. They usually specify a normal retirement age at which time benefits begin to accrue to the employee as well as the formula employed to calculate benefits and how they are integrated with social security benefits.

The Employee Retirement Income Security Act (ERISA) of 1974 defines a pension plan as "any plan, fund, or program . . . established or maintained by an employer or by an employee organization, or by both . . . [which] (i) provides retirement income to employees, or (ii) results in a deferral of income by employees for periods extending to the termination of covered employment or beyond ." In 1988, approximately 834,000 pension plans with 54 million participants were governed under ERISA.

The different forms of pension plans include (1) the "floor plan," a defined benefit pension plan, the benefits of which are reduced by the actuarial equivalent of an amount held under a profit sharing plan (a system in which an employer pays compensation or benefits to employees in addition to their regular wages, based on the profits of the company); (2) the "multiemployer plan," a plan maintained under a collective bargaining agreement between an employee organization and more than one employer to which more than one employer must contribute; and (3) the "governmental plan," any plan established or maintained by the federal government, any state or political subdivision, or any agency or instrumentality of the United States, or to which the Railroad Retirement Act of 1935 or 1937 applies.

Since the early 1970s, private pension plan coverage has stabilized at between 51 and 53 percent of full-time workers. At the same time, coverage under defined contribution plans has decreased. These trends are due to several factors, including shifts in employment from large, heavily unionized, high-wage companies to smaller, nonunion, low-wage firms and the increasing costs and administrative burdens imposed by ERISA and its subsequent amendments.

Bargaining on pensions gained momentum after World War II, facilitated by the National Labor Relations Board's Inland Steel ruling in 1948 that pension plans were a negotiable issue and the 1949 steel industry fact-finding board recommendation to subject pension and welfare plans to negotiation.

See also **Benefits; Collective Bargaining; Employee Retirement Income Security Act of 1974; National Labor Relations Board; Railroad Retirement Acts.**

PERFORMANCE APPRAISAL One of the most frequently used methods to measure employee performance. Organizations use performance appraisal systems for several purposes, including: determining wage and salary adjustments, making promotion decisions, identifying retraining needs, human resources planning, developing skill inventories, layoff decisions, and measuring communications between supervisors and subordinates. The range of criteria that might be measured when assessing performance includes quality and quantity of work, initiative, cooperation, dependability, job knowledge, attendance, and need for supervision. Performance assessment techniques including rating scales, essays and diaries, checklists, the so-called critical incidents technique (which uses observers to record examples of effective and ineffective behavior), management by objectives, behaviorally anchored rating scales, ranking, and forced distribution (use of set minimums or maximums for the percentage of rating in each category of performance).

The traditional "top-down" performance appraisal system, in which managers rate their subordinates on a variety of job duties, is currently being supplanted with "upward appraisal systems" in which peers, subordinates, and managers complete questionnaires about the employee. These systems are used as direct reports on a supervisor's communication, teamwork, and leadership skills.

See also **Management by Objectives.**

PERFORMANCE REVIEW The means for the employer to discuss his or her expectations of the employees and to inform them how their work is progressing and what changes (if any) are necessary.

The review is a tool used to evaluate the value, special abilities and contributions, weaknesses, and development of the employee.

Most employers conduct regular (annual or semiannual) performance reviews and record them in a standard written form. Supervisors normally complete a section rating employee performance in areas such as accuracy and productivity, attendance, cooperation, public relations, initiative, job knowledge, and responsibility, commenting on good job performance and offering recommendations for improvements. Salaries, bonuses, transfers from probationary to permanent status, and job terminations are based, in part, on the outcomes of the performance reviews. They are also an important part of the personnel audit, which involves a survey of the operation of personnel policies, including their impact on individual employees.

See also **Personnel Policy.**

PERMANENT INJUNCTION See **Injunctions against Unions.**

PERMANENT UMPIRE An arbitrator selected by both a labor union and management to serve for a specified period of time, usually for the duration of the employment contract. The contract outlines the duties of the arbitrator.

See also **Employment Contract; Grievance Arbitration.**

PERMANENTLY REPLACED EMPLOYEES Under current labor law, termination of striking employees is unlawful; however, they may be "permanently replaced." The distinction is irrelevant to most employees, who are not allowed to return to work after a strike ends. The employer's characterization of the replacement as permanent rather than temporary will usually not be contradicted by the courts. [*Texas Company* (1951)] There are, however, profound differences in the legal rights of a permanently replaced worker as opposed to one who is dismissed. A permanently replaced employee does not lose all job rights, as does a terminated employee. Though the employer is not obligated to remove permanent replacements in order to create work opportunities, former strikers must be kept on a preferential rehire list and be given the chance to return to work as soon as vacancies occur.

More than any other aspect of current labor law, unions perceive this doctrine as shifting power unduly in the direction of employers. In 1995, President Clinton issued an executive order which provides that federal agencies may not contract with employers who permanently replace employees engaged in a lawful strike. The order was, however, enjoined in the federal court pending appeal. While the federal district court upheld the order, it said that it represented a radical departure from long-established policy; therefore an injunction was needed to preserve the status quo. [*Chamber of Commerce v. Reich* (1995)]

See also **Preferential Hiring; Strike; Termination.**

PERSONAL LEAVE

See **Leave of Absence.**

PERSONNEL FILES

Contain information on employees, including the employee's job description, resume, salary history, vacation schedule, performance reviews, and employment authorization forms.

Apart from providing ready access to necessary employee information, these files also serve a "defensive" purpose for management: they facilitate the compilation of performance reviews and the compilation of disciplinary and other similar reports, and they document inferior performance if a disgruntled employee claims entitlement to a promotion or raise, or a terminated employee files a wrongful discharge lawsuit. Similarly, sick leave and vacation information may be used to refute claims of terminated employees. Several federal and state statutes and regulations (the Fair Labor Standards Act and the Immigration Regulation and Control Act, for example) require that employers maintain records for specified periods on employee wages, hours, employment authorization, and other designated items. Every personnel file should include the same categories of information. Inconsistent documentation (e.g., performance reviews only of "problem" employees) may result in claims of disparate treatment (that is, unlawful discriminatory treatment) by terminated or disciplined employees.

Several state and federal statutes govern employees' access to their personnel file. For example, employers must permit employees to inspect their own medical records (under regulations issued pursuant to the Occupational Safety and Health Act). Federal agency records are governed under federal privacy law, and nearly all states have statutes, regulations, or case law regarding access to personnel files.

In general, personnel file access laws cover topics such as the time and place of access, the right to make copies, right to correct, right to protest and seek removal, and the right to insert explanations. To ensure confidentiality, prudent employers control access to personnel files so they do not become available to unauthorized personnel, and expose the employer to a possible invasion of privacy or defamation lawsuit. Most employers restrict employee access to their personnel files to those with a "need to know."

Many states award damages and/or attorneys' fees for failure to provide access. However, nearly all personnel file access laws have exceptions and limitations. Some states limit their applicability to state employees, and others extend coverage to private and public employees. Some states apply the right of access only to private sector employees.

See also **Fair Labor Standards Act; Immigration Reform and Control Act; Job Description; Occupational Safety and Health Act; Performance Review; Wrongful Discharge.**

PERSONNEL POLICY An organization's guiding principles on its treatment of employees, very often embodied in a statement by management. It specifies the actions that are to be taken in various cases and the principles upon which they are based. The personnel policy is intended to state the company's philosophy toward its employees and the means by which it will attain its goals.

The practice of giving employees policy manuals or handbooks allows large employers to provide standardized instruction on company policy that is more cost-effective than individual training. Employment manuals range from general statements of the firm's policies to detailed descriptions of discharge, discipline, grievance, promotion, vacation, compensation, and benefit policies.

Prior to the 1980s, courts usually held that promises and statements by employers in employee manuals did not constitute contractual obligations. Some courts reasoned that the promises in the manuals were unenforceable because they lacked legal "consideration"—in other words, the personnel policy manual was not considered an inducement or a cause for the contract of employment negotiated by the employer and the employee. The employee's labor was seen as the consideration supporting the employer's promise to pay wages, and additional consideration, beyond the employee's continued labor, was required to support any other promises the employer made. Although few employees could satisfy this requirement, some cases have arisen in which the necessary additional consideration support promises of job security existed. For instance, quitting an existing job, especially one with protection from arbitrary discharge, or moving to another city to take an offered job, was sometimes found sufficient to support employer promises of job security. A related aspect of the doctrine of additional consideration prevented the enforcement of any employer or promises made after the employee began work because the employee would have nothing left to give as consideration.

If an employee handbook contains detailed procedures for discipline and discharge and expressly contains an obligation to discharge only for good cause, then the courts will recognize that the at-will rule has been modified. An employer may, however, include a disclaimer preventing the handbook from becoming a part of a binding contract. To minimize the risk of fraud claims by employees, employers have deleted from employee manuals any assurances that might form the basis of a misrepresentation theory. In addition to removing statements implying that the employer requires "cause" to terminate an employee, companies have deleted or amended representations on promotions, pay increases, reductions in force, and transfers. Firms that cover these topics in their manuals qualify any discussion by stating that the ultimate decision is made at management's complete discretion.

The federal equal employment opportunity statutes enacted in the 1960s and 1970s significantly influenced the private sector's design of equal employment opportunity–affirmative action personnel policies. Studies indicate that most firms either changed or instituted most of their equal employment opportunity policies after one or more of these statutes had been passed. The policies in question typically govern recruitment and selection, training and development, and labor-management relations.

See also **Affirmative Action; Employee Handbook; Labor-Management Relations.**

PICKETING Publicizing the existence of a strike or other labor dispute by patrolling at or near the employer's place of business, with placards or banners announcing the nature of the dispute and the parties to it.

Picketing takes many forms. Mass picketing occurs when large numbers of striking workers assemble at a plant gate to discourage nonstrikers from entering or to prevent delivery of materials. Organizational or recognition picketing is an attempt by the labor union to force the employer to recognize the union or to persuade the unorganized employees to join the union. Informational picketing occurs when off-duty employees picket to inform the public of the union's position in a dispute. During informational picketing, strikers do not attempt to keep people from passing through the picket line as they do in other forms of picketing. Consumer picketing involves direct appeals to a secondary (or neutral) employer to cease patronizing that employer.

The activities of picketers have been limited by legislation. The Labor-Management Relations Act of 1947 (the Taft-Hartley Act) and the Labor-Management Reporting and Disclosure Act of 1959 (the Landrum-Griffin Act), in particular, limit certain types of organization or recognition picketing. However, the terms "picket" and "picketing" are not defined in the Taft-Hartley Act; in fact, they did not appear in the law until the 1959 amendments in Section 8(b)(4) and 8(b)(7) of the National Labor Relations Act (NLRA). The NLRA protects picketing by employees that is peaceful and for a proper purpose under Sections 7 and 8(a)(1). The definitions of proper purposes have been developed from case law, so what constitutes recognition or organizational picketing, and thus is subject to Section 8(b)(7) limitations, depends almost entirely on the particular circumstances of the case.

The U.S. Supreme Court has ruled that picketing on private property is not constitutionally protected. In *Hudgens v. NLRB* (1976), a case involving a shopping center, the Court concluded that constitutional protection was available against private landowners only when their property assumed all of the attributes of a municipality (post office, streets, sewers, and other semiofficial municipal functions) and not merely the location of its business. Justice William O. Douglas wrote that, "picketing by an organized group is more than free speech since the very presence of a picket line may induce action irrespective of the nature of the ideas which are being disseminated."

In reality, the belligerence of the picket line varies greatly. Passersby do not feel threatened if a solitary worker stands silently with a sign. But often picketing is associated with the use of force, and the psychological impact of a picketer carrying a large placard in a crowded shopping mall might be significant. Handbilling offers a less threatening and a constitutionally protected alternative. The employer has a right to a state court injunction against trespass on private property unless the union can show that the picketing is "protected" by Section 7 of the NLRA. [*Sears Roebuck & Co. v. San Diego District Council of Carpenters* (1978)]

The right to picket also depends on who is picketing. Employees have a greater right of access to the employer's' private property for picketing than do nonemployee union representatives.

See also **Labor Dispute; National Labor Relations Act; Strike.**

"PINK SLIP"

See **Termination.**

PINK-COLLAR WORK

Tasks performed predominantly by women. Traditionally, there have been dramatic distinctions in terms of compensation and prestige between pink-collar work and the work predominantly performed by men. Among the occupations referred to as the "pinkest" of pink-collar occupations are registered nurse, typist, secretary, hairdresser, sewer and stitcher, private household worker, and homemaker. The socialization process that determines the occupational choices of women is still largely a matter of class as well as gender.

See also **Women: Employment Issues.**

PLANT CLOSING Termination of operations that occurs when an employer relocates or goes out of business. Economic considerations, which may include the availability of cheaper labor in another region or country, are primary causes of plant closings. It does not matter that the employer expects to reopen at a time six months after the shutdown, only that it is totally shut down.

Section 462(e) of the Job Training Partnership Act of 1982 requires the U.S. Department of Labor to maintain statistical data on mass layoffs and plant closings, including the numbers of plant closings and workers displaced and the localities and types of industries affected. During the 1970s, business closings, relocations, and permanent physical cutbacks resulted in the loss of as many as 38 million American jobs. In the 1980s, congressional concern over plant closings led to the enactment of the Worker Adjustment Retraining Notification Act of 1988 (WARN), the leading statute on large-scale employment reductions. It requires employers with 100 or more workers to provide a 60-day advance notice of plant closing affecting at least 50 employees. In addition, 11 states have laws regulating plant closings and work relocations. Some impose obligations upon employers, while others merely suggest voluntary conduct.

A "plant closing," according to WARN involves "the permanent or temporary shutdowns of a single site of employment, or one or more facilities or operating units within a single site of employment, if the shutdown results in an employment loss at a single site of employment during any 30-day period for 50 or more employees excluding any part-time employees." A "plant closing" includes the closing of a distinct "operating unit" within the plant. But to determine whether the 50-employee threshold has been reached, does one count only the jobs within the closed unit or all the plant jobs lost as a result of the unit's closing? One federal district court held that the so-called employee count may include employees of the same plant who were not employed within the closed unit but who lost their jobs as a result of that unit's work. [*Pavao v. Brown & Sharpe Manufacturing Co.* (1994)] Also, determining whether a plant closing or mass layoff has occurred may require identification of a "single site" affected by the closing or layoff. But WARN does not define what constitutes a single site. That issue arose in *Williams v. Phillips Petroleum* (1994), and the fifth circuit held that plants hundreds of miles apart did not constitutes a single site.

WARN requires that the employer notify (1) the affected nonunion employees, (2) the representatives of affected unionized employees, (3) the state's dislocated workers' unit, and (4) the local government where the closing or layoff is to occur. The "affected employee" is one who may be reasonably expected to experience an employment loss as a result of a plant closing or mass layoff. Part-time employees—those employed for an average of fewer than 20 hours per week or who have been employed for fewer than 6 of the 12 months preceding the date of a required notice—are not included in determining whether there is a plant closing or mass layoff. However a part-time worker who does qualify as an "affected employee" is therefore entitled to notification.

WARN specifies three very limited conditions under which the 60-day notice requirements may be reduced. The statute still requires that the employer provide as much notice as practicable along with a brief statement explaining the reasons for reducing the notification period. The conditions under which the 60-day period may be reduced are (1) the faltering company exception, which is a private company attempting to remain in business if that employer reasonably and in good faith believed that giving notice for the full 60 days would have lessened the chance of getting the required capital or business; (2) if the closing or layoff is caused by business circumstances that were not reasonably foreseeable 60 days prior to the mass layoff or plant closing; or (3) when a natural disaster occurs.

In addition to the provisions that allow for reduction of the 60-day notice period, WARN provides two complete exemptions. No notice is required (1) for employees terminated or laid off at the end of a project, if they were hired with the understanding that their employment was limited to the duration of the project, or (2) in the case of a plant closing or mass layoff that constitutes an economic strike or lockout not intended to evade the WARN requirements.

Many states and municipalities have enacted plant closing legislation. These statutes often place greater restrictions on the employer by mandating a longer notice period than does the federal law. WARN's notification period runs together with any other period of notification required by employment contract or state or municipal law.

See also **Employment Contract; Layoff; Worker Adjustment and Retraining Notification Act.**

PORTAL-TO-PORTAL ACT OF 1947 An amendment to the Fair Labor Standards Act (FLSA) enacted to limit the liabilities under the FLSA based on pay for "walking" or "clean up" time.

Originally, portal-to-portal payment referred to payment for time employees spent on coal company premises traveling from the entrance of a mine to the actual place of work, at both the start and completion of a day's work. Later, this standard was adopted in other industries where travel time is a factor. For example, the time employees at a meat packing plant spent waiting at the knife room for sharpened knives was held to be compensable, since the use of sharpened knives was clearly crucial to their work. In addition, the time spent walking back and forth between the work station and the knife room was compensable because it occurred during the workday. [*Reich v. IBP, Inc.* (1994)]

Courts, in interpreting the FLSA, have held that portal-to-portal pay constitutes an appropriate standard and that the employer must pay wages for all time employees spend on the work premises, including time spent in preparation for work and activities following the completion of work, until leaving the workplace. The Supreme Court held in the *Mount Clemens Pottery Company* (1946) case that employers were liable for portal-to-portal pay under the provisions of the FLSA. Following the decision, many claims were filed under the statute, and in 1947 Congress passed the Portal-to-Portal Act, which limited such claims.

The act exempts from compensable time such matters such as travel to and from work, when performed before and after regular hours.

See also **Fair Labor Standards Act.**

POSTAL REORGANIZATION ACT OF 1970

The federal statute, whose primary purpose was to modernize and create an independent U.S. Postal Service to replace the Post Office Department. The statute also gave the Postal Service the right to sue and be sued, which the Courts have interpreted as a waiver of sovereign immunity—the legal doctrine holding that a governmental body can not be sued for torts occurring as a result of activities which were governmental in nature.

Like other federal employees, the rights of postal workers to unionize and engage in collective bargaining prior to 1970 were established by executive orders issued by Presidents John F. Kennedy and Richard Nixon. During the 1960s, labor unrest in the postal service became so widespread that it became apparent that reform was needed, a need which Congress sought to address in this statute.

Chapter 12 of the Postal Reorganization Act, which covers employee-management regulations, made the Postal Service the only federal entity subject to the jurisdiction of the National Labor Relations Board (NLRB). Chapter 12 also granted postal employees certain collective bargaining and organizing rights guaranteed by the National Labor Relations Act (NLRA). In addition, the Chapter made the NLRA's prohibitions against unfair labor practices [Sections 8(a) and 8(b)] applicable to the postal service and its employees. Because the NLRB rules and regulations now govern representation issues involving the postal service, the NLRB was authorized to determine bargaining units and conduct elections. Postal employees, however, do not have the right to strike and are excluded from coverage of the union shop provisions of the Labor-Management Relations Act (the Taft-Hartley Act). The reporting and disclosure provisions of the Labor-Management Reporting and Disclosure Act of 1959 (the Landrum-Griffin Act) also now applied to postal unions.

Despite a decline in union membership nationwide, organized labor at the U.S. Postal Service has fared relatively well. The American Postal Workers Union and the National Association of Letter Carriers have maintained union representation while providing comparatively good contracts for postal workers. This result is largely due to two factors: the preservation of the quasi-monopoly status of the Postal Service (which the unions have contributed a great deal toward politically); and the recognition of collective bargaining rights for postal workers in the Postal Reorganization Act.

See also **Collective Bargaining: National Labor Relations Act; National Labor Relations Board; Unfair Labor Practice.**

POVERTY An insufficiency of material goods and services; a situation in which the basic needs of individuals or families exceed their means to satisfy them.

Poverty in the United States is measured by the threshold index established by the Bureau of Census. Figures are based on the location of the family (urban or rural), family size, age of family members, and income levels. An individual or family with income below the determined level is living below the poverty level.

Various criteria have been established over the years by the U.S. Department of Labor, Social Security Administration, Department of Agriculture, and others to distinguish the poor from the nonpoor. These criteria include the presence of hunger; a nutritionally inadequate diet; expenditures for food, clothing, shelter, and other services below those currently required for a minimum-decency standard of living; and an income or level of consumption expenditure that places the family in the lowest percentiles of the population. The poor, then, include individuals or families whose income falls below a minimum or subsistence level of living, or "one who fails to have resources to purchase a particular bundle of goods and services perceived necessary for the minimally acceptable standard of living." The term "poor" is frequently applicable to the sick, the disabled, the disadvantaged, the aged, and the unemployed.

Throughout much of the twentieth century, poverty among working families has declined noticeably. In 1900, more than half of all American families were poor by contemporary standards, compared with 7.2 percent of families with at least one worker in 1988. In recent years, however, the numbers of the poor have increased. In 1990, 33.6 million persons were below the poverty level in the United States, an increase of 2.1 million from 1989.

The concept of combating poverty originated as a political objective in planning the reelection campaign of President John F. Kennedy. His successor, President Lyndon B. Johnson attempted to help the poor with his ambitious "War on Poverty" program during the 1960s.

PRE-EMPLOYMENT CONTRACTS Methods such as printed or published advertisements, word-of-mouth advertisements, and referrals used by employers to recruit job applicants. Equal employment opportunity statutes require that such procedures be free of preferences or limitations based on race, color, religion, sex, national origin, age, disability, or veteran status. In addition, the job description must reflect the requirements of the position being advertised. Section 8(f) of the National Labor Relations Act permits a construction industry union and an employer in the industry to sign a collective bargaining agreement before the employer has hired its employees and thus before the union has attained majority status. This provision enables the employer to use the union hiring hall; otherwise, the short duration of many construction jobs would preclude unionization.

See also **Hiring Hall; National Labor Relations Act.**

PREEMPTION Doctrine adopted by the U.S. Supreme Court holding that certain matters are of such national, as opposed to state or local, significance that federal law preempts or takes precedence over state law. Thus a state may not pass a law inconsistent with federal law. The doctrine is intended to prevent potential conflicts between state and federal rules of law, remedies, or administration.

In the National Labor Relations Act (NLRA), and the Labor-Management Relations Act of 1947 (the Taft-Hartley Act), Congress intended to define carefully the role of the courts and the National Labor Relations Board (NLRB) in labor relations. Because the NLRA has no express preemption provision, the U.S. Supreme Court should not find a state labor law provision preempted unless: (1) the provision conflicts with federal law or would frustrate the federal scheme, or (2) the court discerns from the totality of the circumstances that Congress sought to occupy the field. [*Building & Construction Trades Council v. Assoc. Builders & Contractors, Inc.* (1993)] The NLRA is the most comprehensive federal labor relations statute, extensively regulating the conduct of employers, unions, and employees. A particularly detailed set of principles and precedents for determining how preemption affects this interplay has been developed. [*San Diego Building Trades Council v. Garmon* (1959)] The amendments clearly state that collective bargaining agreements are enforceable in court and that most allegations of unfair labor practices may be heard only by the NLRB and ultimately by the federal courts.

Where Congress has the constitutional authority to legislate, the federal law may be supreme—and state jurisdiction precluded completely. The supremacy of federal law is based on Article VI of the U.S. Constitution. The courts fashioned a doctrine of preemption that is based on the supremacy clause and the commerce clause. Whenever Congress has extensively legislated in an area, the courts consider whether Congress intended to deprive the states of jurisdiction in the particular field (in other words, whether Congress intended to "occupy the field"). It was not until 1957, however, that the U.S. Supreme Court formally recognized that the courts must fashion a policy of national labor laws rather than state law. [*Guss v. Utah Board* (1957)]

The basis for the doctrines of preemption and occupation of the field is that conflicting interpretations of a law by 50 state court systems may frustrate the objective of the national legislation. Therefore, the Supreme Court has held that whenever the subject matter involved in a labor controversy is "arguably" protected by Section 7 of the NLRA, which protects labor's right to organize, or prohibited by the unfair labor practice provision applicable to both unions and employers in Section i, federal and state courts are deprived of jurisdiction. In applying the doctrine of preemption to the NLRA, the Supreme Court has stated that usually the NLRB has primary jurisdiction to determine the question of whether the subject matter involved in a labor dispute is protected or prohibited by the NLRA before the courts intervene. The NLRB is the "expert agency," meaning that it has been entrusted with the special responsibility to interpret the statute. If the courts were to hear a case without the benefit of the board's interpretation, their exercise of jurisdiction and interpretation of the statute and national labor policy could disrupt the uniform federal arrangement Congress intended to apply in labor-management relations.

There are exceptions to the preemption doctrine. The NLRA and its amendments do not completely preempt all authority in the labor relations field. The remaining state jurisdiction is determined on a case-by-case basis. A departure from general preemption guidelines may be allowable when (1) a significant state interest exists in protecting the state's citizens from the challenged conduct, and (2) the exercise of state jurisdiction over the action entails little risk of interference with the NLRB's jurisdiction. In one case, because a retail store challenged only the location of the pickets, trespass and not union recognition was at issue, and the state's interest in maintaining public order and protecting private property was based on local control. [*Sears Roebuck & Co. v. San Diego District Council of Carpenters* (1978)] The method of regulation adopted by the state and the formal descriptions of the governing legal standards are irrelevant to finding whether a state is properly exercising jurisdiction in a labor relations case. [*Amalgamated Association of Streetworkers [etc.] v. Lockridge* (1971)]

Another example is where a lawsuit is brought for breach of collective bargaining agreement, the state retains jurisdiction even where the subject matter also involves an unfair labor practice. Cases involving the duty of fair representation are another exception to the rule. The U.S. Supreme Court has permitted the states to assume jurisdiction where lawsuits have been brought alleging libel or harm suffered under statutes designed to protect an individual against emotional injury, or to enjoin trespass by union organizers seeking to bring their message to employees or the public on private premises, or to prevent violence or a threat to public order. The Supreme

Court has also inferred congressional intent to confer regulatory authority on the states when federal statutes provide some room for state action on the subject matter in question.

See also **Collective Bargaining Agreement; Duty of Fair Representation; National Labor Relations Act; National Labor Relations Board; Unfair Labor Practice.**

PREFERENTIAL HIRING

A form of union security under which the employer agrees to give first preference to union members or to workers made available by the labor union, so long as the union is able to supply the necessary number and quality of employees. The preferential hiring list establishes a waiting list of individuals who are eligible for employment, arranged in order of priority. Nonunionists are hired after all of the qualified union members have been placed.

In some industries, unions have been able to secure an agreement that provides preference in hiring decisions to union members. Though they do not require the employers hire only union members, these agreements effectively give union members an advantage in securing employment.

Although racial affirmative action programs are the most controversial, they are not the only form of preferential treatment. The most common use of affirmative action has been preferential opportunity for veterans.

See also **Affirmative Action; Union Security Clause.**

PREGNANCY DISCRIMINATION ACT OF 1978

An amendment to Title VII of the Civil Rights Act of 1964, the Pregnancy Discrimination Act expanded the prohibition against employment discrimination "because of sex" or "on the basis of sex" to cover "pregnancy, childbirth, or related medical conditions." The statute states that "women affected by pregnancy, childbirth, or related medical conditions shall be treated the same for all employment-related purposes . . . as other persons not so affected but similar in their ability to work."

The act was prompted by *General Electric v. Gilbert* (1976), in which the U.S. Supreme Court allowed the exclusion of pregnancy from an employer's disability plan. The Court ruled that a private employer did not violate Title VII by excluding pregnancy coverage in its disability benefit plan. The Court ruled that the disability plan did not exclude anyone because of gender but merely removed one physical condition, pregnancy, from its list of compensable disabilities.

The statute provides that an employer cannot treat a pregnant employee any differently from employees with other temporary medical disabilities for the purposes of hiring, transfer, or accumulation of benefits while on leave. Nor can pregnant employees be forced to begin or return from a maternity leave at preset times. The only exception to the mandate of equal treatment is the provision that employers are not required to pay for health insurance benefits for abortion, except where the life of the mother would be endangered if the fetus were carried to term or where "medical complications from an abortion, medical payments and disability, and sick leave benefits for the treatment of these complications" would be covered by an employer's comprehensive health and disability insurance.

The statute has been interpreted to mean that employers may not require maternity leave of a certain length that bears no relation to the woman's ability or inability to work; employers must offer those returning from maternity leave reinstatement to the same or an equivalent job, benefits, and seniority; employers must offer leaves of absence for pregnancy and childbirth-related "disabilities" under the same terms as they offer it for other disabilities.

In order to comply with the statute, employers adopted several pregnancy disability and maternity leave policies. Often they provided a pregnant employee not only leave time for disabilities due to pregnancy and childbirth but also leave time to care for the infant. Such leave programs, though satisfying the employer's duty to avoid discrimination against pregnant employees, may violate other provisions of Title VII. The Equal Employment Opportunity Commission (EEOC) warned that child-care leave offered only to female employees may violate Title VII by discriminating against male employees. The EEOC said that the employer must provide, or refuse to provide, child-care leave to male and female employees on an equal basis. To ensure that its leave policy is lawfully administered, employers were advised to distinguish carefully between child-care leave (which must be provided to both males and females if it is provided at all) and pregnancy disability leave (which is available only to females).

The Pregnancy Discrimination Act is the precursor to the federal Family and Medical Leave Act of 1993. Many states have passed statutes prohibiting discrimination because of pregnancy. The first state laws on family and medical leave were simply extensions of the Pregnancy Discrimination Act.

See also **Civil Rights Act of 1964; Equal Employment Opportunity Commission; Family and Medical Leave Act of 1993; Sex Discrimination in Employment.**

PREMIUM PAY An extra rate of pay for especially hazardous, dangerous, inconvenient, or unpleasant work. Employees also often receive premium pay for working overtime, on late shifts, on holidays, or in hazardous working conditions.

See also **Holiday; Overtime.**

PRIVACY See **Employee Privacy.**

PROBATIONARY EMPLOYEE Generally a new employee who is on trial status and attempting to establish a right to permanent status. During the probationary period, the individual usually does not have seniority rights and may be discharged without cause, except when the discharge is discriminatory. The probationary period is intended to allow an employer the opportunity to determine whether the employee is qualified to perform the work for which the individual was hired. During the probationary period, employees are often paid a probationary rate that is below the job minimum during probationary period.

Many private and public sector employees must successfully complete a probationary period before becoming permanent employees. Whether a special probationary period exists depends on employee manuals, written employment contracts, or statutory law.

The effect of having a probationary period varies. Frequently, the agreement will specify that probationary employees may be discharged at will, whereas permanent employees may be discharged only for cause. Public employees may have no property interest in their jobs until after the successful conclusion of the probationary period.

See also **Employment Contract; Employee Handbook; Property Rights; Seniority.**

PROBLEM EMPLOYEES See **Troubled Employees.**

PRODUCTION WORKER An employee connected directly with manufacturing or operational processes in industry, as contrasted with a supervisory or clerical employee. For example, an assembly line worker in the automobile industry. A production worker is also frequently called a blue-collar worker.

See also **Blue-Collar Worker.**

PRODUCTIVITY A measurement of the efficiency of production: a ratio of output to input. Labor productivity is measured by output per hour.

PRODUCTIVITY BARGAINING A collective bargaining arrangement that provides for wage increases based on the increased productivity of the operation. In many cases wage increases are the tradeoff for the labor union's agreement to abandon certain work practices that have tended to inhibit productivity.

See also **Collective Bargaining; Productivity.**

PROFESSIONAL EMPLOYEE Individuals whose work is predominantly nonroutine and intellectual in character. (See Section 2(12) of the National Labor Relations Act.) They generally exercise a substantial degree of discretion and judgment in the performance of their work.

Professional employees work in occupations that require specialized and theoretical knowledge usually acquired through college training or work training including specific experience in the application of professional skills. Professional positions commonly require high educational levels and offer relative freedom from direct supervision and the status associated with professional positions. They provide higher levels of satisfaction and motivation than nonprofessional jobs. These positions include the engineering, law, education, and medical professions. Under Section 2(12) of the National Labor Relations Act and most state labor relations statutes, professional employees may determine for themselves whether they wish to bargain in a separate professional bargaining unit or be in the same unit with nonprofessional employees.

See also **National Labor Relations Act.**

PROFIT SHARING

A system or procedure whereby an employer pays compensation or benefits to employees in addition to their regular wages, based on the profits of the company. Profit-sharing provisions are intended to link the employees' economic fortunes with those of the employer. Often they serve as incentives for employees to expend greater efforts on behalf of the company.

Usually a profit-sharing plan takes one of two forms: (1) a cash plan that provides employees a share of the profits on a regular basis (quarterly, semiannually, or annually); or (2) a deferred plan , in which a trust fund is established and payments are made to employees at the time of their retirement, death, illness, disability, or severance of employment. The profit-sharing plan generally is based on a definite, determined formula specifying the percentage of profit to be distributed and how the profit is to be computed. The payments an employer makes to a bona fide profit-sharing plan are not included in the employee's regular rate of pay.

PROGRESSIVE DISCIPLINE

Also known as corrective discipline, progressive discipline is the principle underlying systems designed to achieve employee compliance with company rules by progressively increasing the penalties. Typically, the progressive penalties are warnings (or counselings), reprimands, and suspensions short of discharge.

Although not required by any law, progressive penalties are the basis for all nonsummary disciplinary action. A progressive discipline system is one that provides to employees, prior to termination, one or two warnings of unacceptable conduct. The progressive nature is usually twofold: the system "progresses" through a series of warning steps, and each step in the process contains some added element to impress on the employee the growing urgency of compliance.

Arbitrators generally find progressive discipline appropriate in cases involving attendance problems and low productivity levels. But when such conduct is repeated following corrective measures, arbitrators have recognized management's right to impose harsher penalties, including termination. Conduct that is inherently wrong or destructive to a continuing employment relationship—theft, willful destruction of property, and unauthorized work stoppages—is considered so serious that no specific warning or prior discipline need precede discharge. Incompetence, like carelessness, is considered a special case where progressive discipline is inappropriate and unproductive.

See also **Suspension; Termination.**

PROMOTION The advancement of employees among the departments of a company or within a department, generally to positions that entail greater responsibility, more prestige, greater skill, or higher pay. Most collective bargaining agreements establish procedures for handling transfers and promotions on the basis of ability, length of service, or a combination of these. Where the advancement occurs within the same general classification, it is referred to as horizontal promotion; in a vertical promotion, the employee moves to a different or higher classification.

Employees who are members of a protected class and believe that a test to determine promotion is discriminatory (on the basis of race, sex, or national origin) may file a complaint with the Equal Employment Opportunity Commission. The test can be challenged successfully by proving a pattern of discrimination against a protected class. Once that has been done, the employer will be required to implement steps to change the composition of its workforce to remedy past imbalances created by the testing procedure.

See also **Collective Bargaining Agreement; Equal Employment Opportunity Commission; Protected Class.**

PROPERTY RIGHTS The Fifth and Fourteenth Amendments of the U.S. Constitution guarantee against the deprivation of property without due process of law. In the employment context, both employers and employees have property rights under certain circumstances.

Section 7 of the National Labor Relations Act (NLRA) guarantees employees the right to engage in concerted activities for mutual aid and protection. In most cases involving Section 7 rights, there is no dispute that the activity is concerted or that acting in concert for mutual aid and protection is protected by Section 7. However, the section is silent on both employer property rights and the employer's interest in managing its business. It has never been seriously contended, though, that these employer interests can be ignored in interpreting Section 8(a)(1) of the NLRA.

Nonemployee union organizers do not have a statutorily protected right to distribute union literature on the employer's property, except in the limited instance that the union lacks reasonable access to employees outside the employers' property (e.g., where they are isolated from ordinary flow of information by virtue of working or living in logging or mining camps, or mountain resort hotels), and then after an unspecified balancing test between employees' Section 7 and employer's private property rights. [*Lechmere, Inc. v. NLRB* (1992)]

Public employment can be a property interest entitled to constitutional protection when the employee has a reasonable expectation, created by the employer, of continued employment—that is, the expectation that he or she is subject to termination only for cause or through statutorily defined procedures. There is some uncertainty whether procedural protections alone constitute a valid property interest.

In public employee dismissal cases, proving infringement of a property interest is conceptually similar to proving a breach of an implied-in-fact contract at common law. To establish a contractual entitlement, public sector plaintiffs must establish that the promise was not forbidden by statute. The plaintiff claiming a constitutional violation must prove (1) that a property interest in the job existed, usually resulting from a state promise of employment security, and (2) deprivation of the property interest by breach of the promise. The property interest created by an expectation of continued employment is illustrated by two Supreme Court cases: *Board of Regents v. Roth* (1972) and *Perry v. Sindermann* (1972).

See also **Concerted Activity; National Labor Relations Act; Termination.**

PROTECTED ACTIVITY Section 7 of the National Labor Relations Act protects the right of employees to "self-organization," which includes not only the right to "form" or "join" labor organizations and to "bargain collectively." It also protects their right to engage in "other concerted activities" for "mutual aid or protection."

For activities to be protected, they must be "concerted"—that is, activities where individual employees seek to initiate, induce, or prepare for group action, or bring group complaints to the attention of management. Though it seems clear that employees' protests must be aimed at group concerns, concerted activities can include the activities of one employee if that employee is acting for the "mutual aid or protection" of the employees.

Typical protected concerted activity involves union organizing, the discussion of unionization among employees, or the attempt by one employee to solicit union support from another employee. However, concerted activity need not involve a union. Activities by groups of non-union employees to improve their work situation are deemed protected concerted activities.

If an activity is protected, employees are immunized from discipline or discharge for engaging in the activity. If it is prohibited, the National Labor Relations Board may obtain a cease and desist order against the conduct through its own administrative process and may eventually enforce it through a petition to the circuit court of appeals. Activity that is neither protected nor prohibited is a gray area of the law; employees may be dismissed or disciplined for engaging in it. Unprotected activities, or any conduct for which employees may be discharged or disciplined by an employer, include violence or sit-down strikes in defiance of the owner's possessory rights; partial strikes, in which employees refuse to perform some tasks within the scope their duties while remaining on the premises and accepting pay; attacking the quality of the employer's product or service; mutinies; strikes for a purpose in violation of law or public policy; strikes in violation of the statutory notice requirements; and national emergency strikes enjoinable for a cooling-off period at the request of the U.S. president.

A strike or other concerted activity is protected by statute, and at the same time, it is an economic weapon employees can use to bring bargaining pressure to bear on their employer. An employer cannot take reprisals against employees for exercising Section 7 rights, but the employer retains the right to continue production despite the strike and to bring bargaining pressure of its own to bear on the union and the employees.

See also **Cease and Desist Order; Concerted Activity; National Labor Relations Act; National Labor Relations Board; Strike.**

PROTECTED CLASS

A generic term with no precise legal meaning, "protected class" describes individuals whom the courts and Congress intend to protect from employment discrimination. Except for certain exclusions from statutory protection, federal job discrimination laws protect most persons having or seeking an employment relationship with an employer. Generally, antidiscrimination statutes prohibit unfavorable treatment of two broad groups of persons: those who share a particular status or condition characteristic (those who are over 40, or female, or union members) and those who have engaged in certain conduct specified in the statute (such as going on strike or performing military service).

Title VII of the Civil Rights Act of 1964 protects persons against employment discrimination because of their sex, race, religion, or national origin. Many attorneys, in wrongful dismissal cases, consider whether the facts warrant a Title VII claim. According to one broad interpretation, everyone is a member of a protected class under Title VII. Whites are protected as well as African Americans; men as well as women; Protestants as well as Catholics; Moslems as well as Jews. [*St. Francis College v. Al-Khazraji* (1987)] The Supreme Court held in *McDonald v. Santa Fe Transportation* (1976) that Title VII's prohibition of race discrimination applies not only to historically excluded "minorities" but to all racial groups. The Court in that case held that when an unequal treatment of similarly situated employees is premised on race, it violates Title VII.

All persons are protected by Title VII against a certain type of discrimination: discrimination because of their race, sex, religion, or national origin. There is some authority for the proposition that discrimination by a dark-skinned African American against a lighter-skinned African American because of color is prohibited by Title VII. Adverse action indirectly based on sex is also prohibited, such as pregnancy discrimination and sexual harassment. The majority view, however, is that discrimination based on sexual orientation does not violate Title VII.

Persons between 40 and 69 years of age, Vietnam veterans, and disabled persons are also protected classes under other federal law. The Age Discrimination in Employment Act of 1967 (ADEA), for example, prohibits employers from discriminating because of age against nonexecutive employees over age 40. Members of this age group are protected against any discrimination based on age; thus, it violates the act to favor a 60-year-old over a 45-year-old or to favor a 45-year-old over a 60-year-old, based on age. Although precedent is mixed, a plaintiff in an ADEA case should not be required to show that someone outside the protected class was preferred to the plaintiff.

See also **African Americans: Employment Issues; Age Discrimination in Employment Act of 1967; Asian Americans: Employment Issues; Civil Rights Act of 1964; Discrimination in Employment; Hispanics: Employment Issues; Native Americans: Employment Issues; Sex Discrimination in Employment; Sexual Harassment; Sexual Orientation; Women: Employment Issues.**

PUBLICITY PICKETING

See **Picketing.**

Quality Circles (QCs) A problem-solving technique involving a group of employees who meet regularly to solve workplace problems. Quality circles are not ad hoc bodies created to solve specific problems; they are established on a permanent basis. Circle members decide the problem areas to be studied, which may include productivity, cost, safety, and product quality. Recommendations are presented to management, and circle members assist in implementing recommendations accepted by management. These employee decision-making teams were first used in Japan, with apparent success.

In the late 1970s, surveys indicated that many employees were interested in improving productivity and becoming more involved in decision making, which they believed would serve as an incentive to increase productivity. While not every effort has been successful, several case studies indicate quality circles have generally improved productivity, increased employee satisfaction, and reduced absenteeism and turnover problems at many corporations. [*Electromation, Inc. v. NLRB & Teamsters* (1994)]

See also **Employee; Management.**

Quality of Work Life (QWL) A concept usually associated with labor and management efforts devoted to improving both productivity and the intangible or QWL factors that determine the workplace experience of employees: physical and psychological safety at work as well as opportunities to learn new skills, accept greater responsibility, and obtain greater satisfaction from work. Efforts focus on improvement through "multidimensional change" designed to provide "greater democratization of the workplace," greater control for the employee over his or her environment, and more joint problem solving between labor and management. It is a process by which an organization attempts to involve employees in decisions affecting their work lives. The process of improving the QWL is distinguished by the fact that its goals are not simply extrinsic, focusing on the improvement of productivity and efficiency powers; they are also intrinsic, regarding what the worker sees as self-fulfilling and self-enhancing as ends in themselves.

QWL programs typically include one or more of the following elements: job redesign, quality circles, flextime, autonomous work groups, job enlargement, and participative management. QWL encompasses such activities as employee involvement, harmonization of work, work reform, work redesign, work improvement, and job enrichment.

Essential to efforts to improve the QWL is the direct involvement of the workers in the decision-making process. Unions often play a major role in establishing programs for employee participation in efforts to improve productivity along with job satisfaction—if management regards unions as equal partners in the efforts. The success of worker participation in decision making in a unionized setting requires a cooperative collective bargaining relationship. For QC's to be effective, there must be a climate of mutual respect in which solving problems is emphasized over competing with each other.

See also **Flextime; Job Enrichment; Participatory Management; Quality Circles.**

QUESTION CONCERNING REPRESENTATION (QCR)

A question exists whether one or more unions represent a majority of employees in a bargaining unit.

QUICKIE STRIKE

See **Wildcat Strike.**

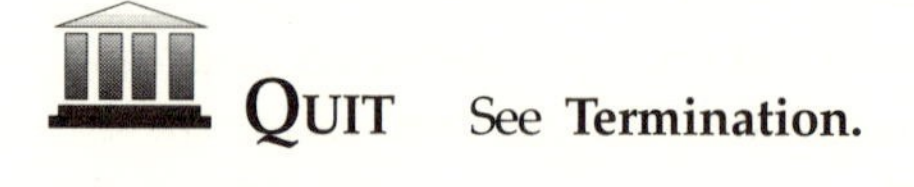

QUIT

See **Termination.**

RACE DISCRIMINATION See **Discrimination in Employment.**

RACKETEER INFLUENCED AND CORRUPT ORGANIZATIONS ACT (RICO) See **Labor Racketeering.**

RAIDING The efforts of a labor union to enroll members of another union, thereby encroaching on the other union's jurisdiction. A union's efforts to enroll unorganized employees who may be in another union's jurisdiction is not, however, considered raiding.

Raiding occurs for several reasons. Among the most frequent are the union's desire to bring within its jurisdiction employees organized by a union that does not technically have jurisdiction over them; to strengthen its own membership for bargaining purposes by increasing the number of employees within its control; and to retaliate against or harass another labor organization that has refused to work with it or has tried to organize its employees.

The two American Federation of Labor-Congress of Industrial Organizations (AFL-CIO) no-raiding programs currently handle different kinds of disputes: one program handles representation disputes between affiliates of the AFL-CIO; a separate program handles representation disputes between unions that are members of the Industrial Union Department of the AFL-CIO (IUD). The first program arose when the AFL and the CIO were still separate entities, out of an agreement originally designed to discourage an attack by a constituent of one federation upon the established bargaining relationship enjoyed by a constituent of the other federation. The program was continued following the 1955 merger of the AFL and the CIO. Since 1962 it has applied to all affiliates as part of the AFL-CIO constitution (now as article XX). The second program is designed to eliminate organizing disputes between unions that are members of the IUD, whether or not an "established bargaining relationship" is involved. Thus, whenever two IUD unions find themselves competing for the same employees, the director of the IUD seeks to resolve the dispute by persuading one of the unions to withdraw from the case.

See also **American Federation of Labor-Congress of Industrial Organizations; Jurisdiction.**

RAILROAD RETIREMENT ACTS Federal statutes that provide benefits to railroad employees who retire because of age or disability. The first of these statutes was enacted in 1934 and was later declared unconstitutional by the U.S. Supreme Court in *Railroad Retirement Board v. Alton Railroad Company* (1935). In a 5-4 decision, the Court argued that the statute deprived the railroads of due process because it provided pensions for persons who were at one time but are not currently in railroad service, and because the pension provisions had nothing to do with railroad safety and efficiency. Congress responded by enacting a second statute in 1935; it in turn was succeeded by a 1974 statute.

The Railroad Retirement Act of 1974 establishes a broad program of benefits to employees and their survivors based on earnings and length of service. Both employees and employers share the costs of treatment, survivor benefits, and Medicare through a special payroll tax. Workers or their survivors may file claims for benefits with the Railroad Retirement Board or at any of its regional offices.

RAILWAY LABOR ACT (RLA) (1926) The federal statute that today is the basis for collective bargaining in the railroad and airline industries. The RLA was drafted with the express purpose of protecting the rights of railroad employees to bargain collectively. It was originally based on a proposal by representatives of both labor unions and management to resolve labor disputes in the railroad industry by mediation and voluntary arbitration, with special provisions for emergency disputes. The RLA was upheld as constitutional in *Texas & New Orleans R.R. v. Brotherhood of Railway Clerks* (1930)] This case was decided prior to both the enactment of New Deal legislation and a dramatic change in the Court's jurisprudence towards congressional power in the field of interstate commerce. The coverage of the RLA was extended to the airlines by amendment in 1934, and a further amendment in 1951 made union shop and check-off agreements lawful. Congress, through this statute, intended to establish a system that fosters the resolution of labor disputes and avoids interruptions to commerce in the airline and railroad industries.

While many of the RLA's policies are similar to those of the National Labor Relations Act (NLRA), its internal operations and procedures differ significantly. The RLA is administered by two agencies: the National Mediation Board (NMB) and the National Railroad Adjustment Board. The RLA protects the rights of employees in collective bargaining and provides for the establishment of the NMB. The NMB holds representation elections, determines appropriate bargaining units, mediates collective bargaining disputes, persuades parties to arbitrate, and when necessary, requests that the president appoint emergency boards to decide disputes. Written collective bargaining agreements must be filed with the board. The act also established a National Railroad Adjustment Board, which makes final decisions on grievances arising under the terms of contracts between employers and employees.

Collective bargaining in the railroad industry predated the RLA by 50 years and was becoming an established practice in the railroad industry. When the RLA was applied to air carriers, where there was no broad tradition of collective bargaining, labor and management based their application of the act on different labor-relations models, including that established by the NLRA. Thus the statute has been applied differently in the railroad and airline industries.

All provisions of the RLA except those on the Adjustment Board were made applicable to air carriers and their employees. Instead of a national adjustment board, each air carrier and the representatives of its employees must establish a separate board of adjustment to resolve disputes regarding the management and application of their contracts.

Because the RLA is a relatively simple statute, enacted within a well-established system of labor relations and collective bargaining, its provisions raise several questions that must be resolved by the parties, the NMB, and the courts. Since the NMB lacks an unfair labor practice jurisdiction similar to that of the National Labor Relations Board, there is less case law under the RLA. The only unifying court decisions are the relatively small number of opinions by the U.S. Supreme Court.

See also **Collective Bargaining; Grievance Arbitration; Labor Dispute; Labor-Management Relations; National Labor Relations Act; National Labor Relations Board; Unfair Labor Practice.**

RANK AND FILE Ordinary members of an organization. Usually, the term refers to the individual members of a labor union, who have no special status as either union officers or shop stewards. They are the workers the union represents and to whom the union leadership is ultimately responsible.

REASONABLE ACCOMMODATION See **Americans with Disabilities Act of 1990.**

RECOGNITION A formal acknowledgment by an employer that the majority of its employees in a certain bargaining unit want a specific labor union to represent them in collective bargaining.

Recognition is a basic and essential element of collective bargaining. One of the major objectives of labor's early organizing efforts was persuading the employer to recognize the union as the bargaining agent and representative of the employees. Frequently employers insisted that they would deal with their own employees but would not deal with a union. Failure to accord recognition to the union has historically been a leading cause of industrial conflict.

With the passage of the National Labor Relations Act in 1935, Congress held that strikes could be eliminated through the use of the election procedures through which the National Labor Relations Board (NLRB) would determine the majority status of employees and the appropriate bargaining unit, then certify the union that had received a majority. The certified organization would become the exclusive bargaining agent of the employees in the appropriate unit, and the employer was required under the law to recognize that union for bargaining proposes.

The employer's duty to bargain with the union can arise when the employer voluntarily recognizes the union. An employer can insist on an NLRB election before recognizing the union if he does not engage in substantial unfair labor practices that would make a fair election impossible.

Under the current practice of the NLRB, and approved by the U.S. Supreme Court in *Linden Lumber v. NLRB* (1974), an employer may refuse a union's request for recognition even in the face of substantial evidence of majority employee support for the union, such as authorization card signatures or a strike by a majority of the employees. Authorization cards are somewhat suspect and "[f]ear may . . . prevent some [employees] from crossing a picket line; or sympathy for stikers, not a desire to have a particular union in the saddle, may influence others." The Court approved the NLRB's abandonment of a good faith test for employer refusals to bargain in this context. The Court also rejected the contention that the failure of the employer to file a petition demonstrates the lack of a good faith doubt of the union's majority status.

See also **Appropriate Bargaining Unit; Collective Bargaining; National Labor Relations Act; National Labor Relations Board.**

RECONSTRUCTION CIVIL RIGHTS ACTS

See **Civil Rights Act of 1866; Civil Rights Act of 1871.**

REDUCTION IN FORCE

See **Layoff.**

REFUSAL TO BARGAIN

Findings made by the National Labor Relations Board (NLRB) under Sections 8(a)(5), 8(b)(3), or 8(d) of the National Labor Relations Act (NLRA) that either the employer or the labor union has not fulfilled the collective bargaining requirements of the statute.

What constitutes a refusal to bargain will depend upon specific circumstances or the total behavior of the union or the company. The conduct of the parties is often probed for evidence of good faith—or evidence of its absence. But certain types of conduct have been viewed as independent or per se refusals to bargain, without regard to any consideration of good or bad faith. These include (1) unilateral changes of mandatory subjects of bargaining; (2) bargaining directly with the employees; (3) failure to sign a written memorandum of agreement; (4) refusing to meet at reasonable times, to attend a minimal number of meetings, or to meet in person; (5) failure to confer in good faith; and (6) insisting to an impasse on incorporating in a contract a permissive subject of bargaining (a subject that may be included in the collective bargaining agreement, but as to which the parties are not forced to bargain).

The proposed Labor Reform Act that failed to pass Congress in 1978 attempted to broaden the NLRB's remedial powers in refusal-to-bargain cases. The bill proposed that the board be allowed to award employees compensation for bargaining delays. The amount of the monetary award would equal the average wage settlements negotiated at plants where bargaining was not thwarted by illegal employer practices. The award would be retroactive from the beginning of the illegal bargaining. Since the Labor Reform Act was not passed, the board's remedial powers in good faith bargaining cases are still limited to cease and desist orders. Union supporters argued that this limitation seriously impairs the effectiveness of American labor laws. Though the NLRB has been empowered to protect employer interests in secondary boycotts and jurisdictional disputes by use of the injunction, similar remedies are unavailable to protect worker interests.

See also **Cease and Desist Order; Collective Bargaining; Compensation; Impasse; Injunctions Against Unions; Jurisdictional Dispute; National Labor Relations Board; Secondary Boycott.**

***REGENTS OF THE UNIVERSITY OF CALIFORNIA V. BAKKE* (1978)** The first U.S. Supreme Court decision on the legality of an affirmative action program voluntarily undertaken by a school to remedy enrollment imbalances by providing preferential treatment to minority groups. This so-called reverse discrimination case was initiated by a white male who was denied admission to a medical school that had reserved openings for minority students as part of a special admissions program to increase minority enrollment. A divided Court struck down a university admissions plan that set aside a specific number of places for minority applicants. A key holding of the case was that while affirmative action was constitutional and that it might sometimes be appropriate to undo past wrongs, an affirmative action plan had to be based on proved constitutional or statutory violations. *Bakke,* therefore, was the first legal setback to voluntary affirmative action.

The Court held that the admissions plan violated Title VII of the 1964 Civil Rights Act since it used race as the sole basis for excluding a nonminority applicant from a federally funded program. Race or ethnic origin, however, can be considered as "one element—to be weighed fairly against other elements" in the selection process. The Court noted that a substantial interest may be served by a properly devised admissions program involving the competitive consideration of race and ethnic origin.

The opinion sanctioned all but the cruder forms of affirmative action. Numerical quotas became constitutionally suspect, unless used to remedy specified instances of prior discrimination. Minority preferences in education admissions, however, were deemed constitutionally legitimate. While neither side in the affirmative action controversy "won" in *Bakke,* the decision did clearly establish two points: (1) the view of the Constitution as strictly color blind had not prevailed and (2) the door remained open to racial preferences in integrating higher education and by extension all aspects of American life.

See also **Affirmative Action; Civil Rights Act of 1964.**

REHABILITATION ACT OF 1973 Prohibits discrimination based on a person's disabilities by federal agencies and departments, and by private employers, individuals, and organizations working under federal contracts or receiving federal grants and assistance. This act was the first major federal statute prohibiting employment discrimination on the basis of handicap. It also promotes vocational rehabilitation services, expands federal responsibility and research and training programs for disabled individuals, and promotes affirmative action and nondiscrimination.

Section 503 of the statute requires federal contractors to "take affirmative action to employ and advance in employment qualified individuals with disabilities"; it is administered by the Office of Federal Contract Compliance Programs (OFFCCP). The rules and regulations of the OFFCCP specify that every government contractor or subcontractor holding a contract of $50,000 or more and having 50 or more employees is required to prepare and maintain an affirmative action program at each establishment. Moreover, all covered contractors must include an affirmative action clause in each covered contract and reasonably accommodate the physical and mental limitations of employees or applicants unless it can be proved that the accommodations would impose an undue hardship on the conduct of business. Though the Americans with Disabilities Act (ADA) is a more significant and encompassing statute, the Rehabilitation Act remains important for special categories of employers (federal agencies, recipients of federal funds, and federal contractors). The Rehabilitation Act also served as the model for key provisions of the ADA. Therefore, many of the decisions under the Rehabilitation Act are also useful for interpreting the ADA.

See also **Affirmative Action; Americans with Disabilities Act of 1990; Discrimination in Employment; Handicapped Employee.**

REINSTATEMENT Generally, the restoration of an employee to his or her former position without the loss of seniority or other benefits. Reinstatement also may mean return of an individual to union membership following disqualification resulting from various offenses, including failure to pay dues.

The nature and circumstances of reinstatement may vary. One form of reinstatement occurs under an arbitration award, if an employee has been improperly discharged; in this case the arbitrator may order reinstatement without loss of seniority and other rights, but without back pay. Another form involves an employee discharged because of an employer unfair labor practice. The National Labor Relations Board (NLRB), in enforcing the provisions of the National Labor Relations Act (NLRA), may order reinstatement of the employee without loss of benefits and require back pay. (Back pay is customarily awarded beginning five days after their unconditional offer to return to work.) Reinstatement also arises under the provisions of the NLRA for the return of veterans to their previous positions following the end of hostilities or the completion of the term of enlistment with the armed forces.

If the NLRB has found that an employee was discharged illegally, it will ordinarily order that he or she be reinstated upon unconditional application for reinstatement, even if this means discharging an employee hired as a replacement. In many cases the NLRB also will order the employer to reimburse the employee for any loss of wages he or she has suffered as a result of the discharge. If a union caused the employer to discharge the employee unlawfully, the back pay order may be directed against either the union or the employer, or it may be directed against both.

See also **Award; Back Pay; Benefits; Grievance Arbitration; National Labor Relations Act; National Labor Relations Board; Seniority; Unfair Labor Practice.**

REINSTATEMENT RIGHTS OF ECONOMIC STRIKERS

Governed by the *MacKay* rule, under which employers may permanently replace economic strikers without proving business necessity for their offer of permanency. [*NLRB v. McKay Radio & Telegraph Co.* (1983)] There seems to be a paradoxical inconsistency between the legislative protection of the right to strike and an unqualified right of employers to permanently replace striking employees.

The National Labor Relations Act (NLRA) distinguishes between terminating and permanently replacing strikers. The NLRA makes it illegal for employers to terminate striking workers. But in economic strikes (those involving disputes over the terms and conditions of employment), it is legal for employers to *permanently replace* strikers.

There seems to be strong evidence that prohibiting the hiring of "permanent replacement" strikers would increase the frequency and duration of strikes. More important, because an economic strike does not involve illegal acts on the part of the struck employer, the employer has a strong case for asserting its right to carry on business activities with replacement workers.

Economic strikers have only limited rights: they may claim their former jobs if permanent replacements have not been hired. Prior to the strikers' application for reinstatement, however, the employer may protect his business by hiring replacements or by discontinuing jobs for business reasons. If permanent replacements are hired before the strikers apply for reinstatement, the employer may legally reject the strikers' application pursuant to the *McKay* rule. However, replaced economic strikers have been ordered reinstated where reinstatement was "crucial to the effectiveness of a bargaining order that had been issued against the employer."

See also **National Labor Relations Act; Strike; Termination.**

RELIGIOUS DISCRIMINATION

Practices, policies, or procedures that deny equal employment opportunity on the basis of religion. When religious discrimination cases arise, they usually center on two related questions: (1) Did the employer make a reasonable accommodation to the religious needs of the employees? and (2) Was the employer excused from accommodating its employees on the grounds of undue hardship?

Under Title VII of the Civil Rights Act of 1964, employers must make reasonable efforts to accommodate religious observance or practices of employees or job applicants unless it is demonstrated that the accommodation would impose "undue hardship" on the conduct of business. Examples of reasonable accommodation include reassignment or transfer; restructuring of job duties; allowing time off for religious practices; flexibility in dress and appearance standards; and allowing voluntary exchanges of work schedules.

An employer is not required to incur more than minimal costs in order to accommodate employee religious practices and need not take steps inconsistent with a valid seniority system. [*Trans World Airlines v. Hardison* (1977)] Courts have considered these factors in determining whether a requested accommodation would constitute an undue hardship: the size of the employer, the nature of the employer's business, the type of accommodation required, the cost of the accommodation, whether the employee provided reasonable notice to the employer of the desired accommodation, and the composition and structure of the workforce.

On the issue of union membership, the Taft-Hartley amendments of 1980 (now known as Section 19 of the National Labor Relations Act) provide that employees whose religious convictions prevent them from joining or supporting a union are not required to join a union as a condition of employment. Such employees, however, may be required by the collective bargaining agreement to contribute a sum equal to the union dues and fees "to a nonreligious, nonlabor organization charitable fund" and to pay costs of using the grievance procedures.

In a recent case involving a similar issue, *EEOC v. American Federation of State, County & Municipal Employees (AFSCME)* (1996), a federal district court held that allowing a Roman Catholic employee who objected to a union's positions on abortion and the death penalty, to donate his shop fees to a charitable organization was a reasonable accommodation of the employee's religious beliefs.

A recent Ninth Circuit case, *Tucker v. State of California Department of Education* (1996), involved state employees who challenged their employer agency's prohibition against employees' engaging in religious advocacy in the workplace or displaying religious materials outside their offices and cubicles, despite the fact that employees could post materials on many other subjects. The state argued that the ban was justified in the interest of maintaining church and state separation. The court rejected the state's argument and struck down the prohibition as overbroad and as a violation of the employees' First Amendment rights.

Title VII clearly does not apply to those who are employed to conduct the religious activities of a religious corporation, such as a Baptist church hiring only ministers of the Baptist church. In addition, if an employer can show that its employment practices are closely connected with its religious practices, the relatively broad exceptions for religious entities will also apply. For example, Title VII does not cover the employment relationship between a church and its ministers, even when a minister complains of sex discrimination. [*McClure v. Salvation Army* (1972)]

See also **Civil Rights Act of 1964; Collective Bargaining Agreement; Discrimination in Employment.**

REOPENING CLAUSE

A provision in a collective bargaining agreement stating the circumstances under which either party may reopen the contract to renegotiate terms of the agreement, usually while other terms of the agreement remain in force and prior to the expiration of the agreement. It is often called a "reopener."

The reopening clause is used when unions and employers negotiate contracts which cover an extended period of time. Unless the contract provides for automatic adjustments, it is common to make some provision to reopen to avoid freezing wages for a long period and to take care of unusual circumstances that might result from rapid price increases or a period of wage instability.

See also **Collective Bargaining Agreement.**

REPRESENTATION ELECTION

Procedure in which employees in a bargaining unit determine which bargaining agent, if any, will represent them for collective bargaining purposes. These elections are regulated by federal and state law to allow employees to designate their bargaining agent without restraint, interference, or domination.

The Labor-Management Relations Act of 1947 (the Taft-Hartley Act), as amended in 1959, provides for three general types of elections: (1)

representation (as described above); (2) decertification, to determine whether employees wish to withdraw bargaining rights from a previously certified union; and (3) deauthorization, to determine whether employees wish to rescind a union shop agreement. Ordinarily, only one election may be held in a bargaining unit within any 12-month period. State election procedures tend to follow those developed by the National Labor Relations Board (NLRB), although this is not required.

In order for the NLRB to conduct a representation election, a party must request or petition the NLRB to do so. (It is important to note that the NLRB is not empowered to determine the bargaining representative or to investigate union claims of majority status on its own initiative. An election petition must be filed.) A petition is a formal request to the NLRB that it determine whether a majority of employees in a bargaining unit wish to be represented by a particular labor organization for the purposes of collective bargaining. A petition for an NLRB-conducted certification election can be filed by an employee or a group of employees, a labor organization acting on behalf of the employees, or an employer. If the petition is filed by employees or on their behalf by a labor organization, the petition must be accompanied by a showing of support by employees wishing union representation by at least 30 percent of the employees. The petition must also state that the employer declined to recognize the labor organization. If the employer files, the petition must state that one or more labor organizations have requested to be the employees' exclusive bargaining representative.

See also **Collective Bargaining; Employee; National Labor Relations Board.**

RETIREMENT A severance of employment, either voluntary or forced, because of age, disability, or illness. Generally, the retired individual withdraws permanently from gainful work and lives on a retirement allowance or a pension.

The retirement age—the age at which a person becomes eligible for retirement or a pension—is usually set between 60 and 65 years. A more flexible approach is to assess the individual's productive capacity. In this approach the issue of retirement age is based primarily upon the employee's ability to continue to make a productive contribution to the work of the employer.

Mandatory retirement is distinct from voluntary retirement. Mandatory retirement is a provision in collective bargaining agreements, personnel policy, or statutes that compels retirement of employees at a fixed age. The Age Discrimination in Employment Act (ADEA) amendments of 1986 prohibited mandatory retirement for virtually all private sector and state and local government employees. The ban has also applied to public safety officers (police, firefighters, and prison guards) and tenured college and university faculties since 1994.

The ADEA continues to allow the termination or forced retirement of any employee who does not meet the physical, mental, or other demands of the job. For example, the Federal Aviation Agency's regulatory ban on the employment of airline pilots after they reach the age of 60 years has been found to come within the exception for bona fide occupational qualifications under the ADEA. If provisions in an employment contract provide for retirement of employees, benefits usually depend on length of service and earnings with the company. Compulsory and automatic retirement are treated differently under the terms of the pension plan. An employee may work beyond the compulsory retirement age if the employer consents, but automatic retirement prevents the use of this option.

Voluntary retirement is the company's policy of setting no formal age of retirement but permitting employees to work as long as they are physically and mentally capable of performing their work.

Early retirement allows the worker to cease employment at age 55 rather than the normal retirement age of 65. Early retirement can be an attractive way for employers to structure a workforce while providing benefits to the employee. Through early retirement, an employer can reduce the workforce without inflicting the pain of mass layoffs and implement affirmative action programs or provide promotion opportunities the younger employees.

See also **Age Discrimination in Employment Act; Benefits; Collective Bargaining Agreement; Pension; Personnel Policy.**

RETROACTIVE PAY

A delayed wage payment for work previously performed at a lower rate. This income is due to workers when a new employment contract provides for a wage increase for work completed prior to the date the contract becomes effective, often beginning at the expiration of the previous contract.

In cases involving the National Labor Relations Board or a state board reinstating an employee to remedy an unfair labor practice discharge, the employee may be made whole and receive retroactive pay from the time of the discharge, less other earnings during that period. For most purposes, the terms "retroactive pay" and "back pay" are used interchangeably.

See also **Back Pay; Employment Contract; National Labor Relations Board; Unfair Labor Practice; Wage.**

REVERSE DISCRIMINATION Discrimination against those who historically have been favored in employment. Since exercising a discriminatory preference in employment for any racial group, minority or majority, is unlawful under both Title VII of the Civil Rights Act of 1964 and the early civil rights acts, unless accomplished pursuant to a valid affirmative action plan, preferences for African Americans are unlawful not only where Caucasians are better qualified, but where they are equally qualified. [*Butta v. Anne Arundel County* (1979)]

The same standards that prohibit race discrimination against nonwhites apply to whites. Thus two white employees who were discharged for wrongfully taking cargo that was in their employer's keeping stated a Title VII claim where an African American employee who also did the same thing was not discharged. [*McDonald v. Santa Fe Trail Transportation Co.* (1976)] A white plaintiff's ultimate burden in a disparate treatment case under Title VII is the same as an African American plaintiff's—that is, to prove intentional discrimination based on race. [*Fischbach v. Government of District of Columbia Dist. of Corrections* (1991)]

To establish a prima facie case of reverse discrimination, some courts require a claimant to prove background circumstances that are sufficient to raise the inference that the employer has discriminated against the majority. This requirement acts as a modification of the first element of a typical *McDonnell-Douglas* case—belonging to a racial minority—since, in a reverse discrimination situation, this element does not apply. The standard analysis of individual claims of disparate treatment of discrimination was established by the U.S. Supreme Court in *McDonnell Douglas Corp. v. Green* (1973). The Court held that the plaintiff, who had alleged racial discrimination in hiring, had the burden of producing evidence that:

1. He belongs to a racial minority;
2. He applied and was qualified for a job for which the employer was seeking applicants;
3. Despite his qualifications, he was rejected; and

4. After his rejection, the position remained open and the employer continued to seek applications from persons of the complainant's qualifications.

As a result, the *McDonnell-Douglas* analysis may still be used, and once an inference of discrimination is raised, the plaintiff need not show direct evidence of discrimination. [*Parker v. Baltimore & Ohio R.R. Co.* (1981)]

See also **Civil Rights Act of 1964.**

RIGHT TO JOIN A UNION

See **Right To Organize.**

RIGHT TO ORGANIZE

The federally protected right of workers to organize for the purposes of collective bargaining.

Section 7 of the National Labor Relations Act (NLRA) protects the right of employees to organize, to bargain collectively, and to engage in other concerted activities. Section 8(a)(3) of the NLRA treats any employer action as an unfair labor practice if it results in "discrimination in regard to hire or tenure of employment or any term or condition of employment to encourage or discourage membership in any labor organization." This section prohibits employer discrimination against an employee to encourage or discourage membership in a labor organization. A violation occurs when an employer purposefully discourages union membership, but also when discouragement is the "natural consequence of [the] employer's action." Most Section 8(a)(3) cases involve little or no dispute over the employer's action in changing employment tenure; rather the dispute is over the employer's purpose or motive or over the effect of the employer's action.

In a typical discharge case involving the "right to organize" under the NLRA, the employee alleges that the discharge was motivated by his or her union activity. For example, in *NLRB v. Associated Milk Producers, Inc.* (1983), the employee claimed his dismissal was caused by his support of a union organizing campaign. The employer claimed the dismissal was caused by the employee's failure to report an accident. The National Labor Relations Board (NLRB) found that the employer failed to prove that it would have discharged the employee regardless of his union advocacy and therefore had committed an unfair labor practice under Sections 8(a)(1) and 8(a)(3) of the act.

The NLRB has applied the *Mt. Healthy* (1977) standard in "pretext" and "dual motive" cases, where the employer presents a legitimate justification for dismissal. The justification is then treated as an affirmative defense (in pleading, matter constituting a defense or new matter which, assuming the complaint to be true, constitutes a defense to it). The effect is placing a heavier burden of proof on the plaintiff at the beginning of the case and shifts the burden of proof to the defendant to prove the absence of a pretext. [*Wright Line Board* (1980)]

See also **Concerted Activity; Labor Organization; National Labor Relations Act; National Labor Relations Board; Union Membership, Rights of; Unfair Labor Practice.**

RIGHT TO STRIKE

RIGHT TO STRIKE The U.S. Supreme Court has held that a right to strike cannot be inferred from the U.S. Constitution. Generally, however, the right to strike is available to employees in the private sector under federal and state statutes, especially the National Labor Relations Act, except that in some situations certain procedural steps must be taken before a strike may occur.

Although a few statutes provide the limited right to strike in the public sector, public employment strikes are almost uniformly prohibited. Laws usually provide for alternative methods of settling disputes. Neither the right of public employees to bargain collectively nor the right to strike are protected by the U.S. Constitution. The two main arguments against allowing public employees to strike are that (1) the strikes by at least some public employees would create a substantial and imminent threat to the health and safety of the public and (2) that unions in the public sector may apply pressure on their employers through the political process. The argument favoring granting the public sector the right to strike is that it is impossible for the collective bargaining process to operate the way it was intended without the possibility of strikes. Unless the employer faces the prospect of inconvenience or injury, there is no inducement to compromise or negotiate seriously on wages, hours, and working conditions.

The U.S. Supreme Court has ruled that while striking is "protected concerted activity," employers may permanently replace strikers with strikebreakers.

See also **Collective Bargaining; Concerted Activity; National Labor Relations Act; Strike; Strikebreaker.**

RIGHTS OF UNION MEMBERS

See **Union Membership, Rights of.**

RIGHT-TO-WORK LAWS

State laws, permitted by Section 14(b) of the National Labor Relations Act (NLRA), that prohibit employers from entering into agreements with labor unions to require employees to join or support unions as a condition of employment. In other words, right-to-work laws expressly forbid employment discrimination based on membership or nonmembership in a labor union. Specifically, these state laws may prohibit the union shop, maintenance of membership clauses, preferential hiring, and any other contract provision calling for compulsory union membership. Right-to-work laws are controversial because they impact labor's right to organize, to solidify its strength, and to preserve the group interest as well as the individual's right to obtain and keep his job without organizational affiliations he or she may not want.

The right-to-work conflict focuses on union security clauses, all of which establish the status of a union at a given workplace. The NLRA as enacted in 1935 (the Wagner Act) provides that a union may agree to include one of these clauses in a collective bargaining contract. The four types of union security clauses are (1) the closed shop, which requires that all employees belong to the union in order to retain their jobs and that the employer hire *only* union members; (2) the union shop, which requires that all employees, *after* they are hired, become and remain members of the union as a condition of employment; (3) the agency shop, which requires nonmembers to pay the equivalent of full union dues and initiation fees as a condition of employment but limits the union's use of these funds to covering the expenses incurred in representing all of the employees; and (4) maintenance of membership, which requires that all present and future union members remain members for the duration of the contract as a condition of continued employment, while employees who are not union members and who do not join the union in the future may continue employment without union membership.

The present NLRA allows both the union shop and agency shop. The Labor-Management Relations Act of 1947 (the Taft-Hartley Act) amended the NLRA by adding Section 14(b) to expressly outlaw the closed shop and to allow states to enact right-to-work laws that would outlaw union shop and agency shop agreements. Under the authority of Section 14(b), twenty states have adopted such laws. Right-to-work laws, which vary from state to state, are enacted as either a state constitutional amendment or as a state statute. Some states vaguely prohibit an employment monopoly by a labor union, while others expressly prohibit requiring union dues as a condition of employment. State right-to-work laws affect only those workers covered by the NLRA or those remaining under state authority. Railroad and airline employees, for example, are covered by a different federal statute (the Railway Labor Act) and therefore are not subject to right-to-work laws.

The right-to-work movement began at the state level in response to organized labor's ability to win maintenance-of-membership guarantees during World War II. The movement successfully won antiunion legislation in several states, particularly in the South, and in 1947 was successful in persuading Congress to enact the Taft-Hartley Act (which is sometimes referred to as Section 14[b]). Both the American Federation of Labor (AFL) and the Congress of Industrial Organizations (CIO) were unable to prevent this legislation.

After the Taft-Hartley Act was passed, however, labor became increasingly active in the Democratic party and more involved in electoral politics. The labor movement won significant victories in 1948 in stopping the passage of right-to-work statutes in some states and actually repealing them in two. Cooperation between the AFL and CIO in stopping right-to-work legislation in the early 1950s played a significant role in facilitating the merger of the two organizations in the mid 1950s. A well-financed AFL-CIO Committee on Political Education skillfully defeated right-to-work initiatives in several critical states—including Ohio and California in 1958—and laid the groundwork for electoral activism that contributed to the election of John F. Kennedy in 1960. The AFL-CIO, however, failed to repeal Section 14(b) in the 1960s, despite a liberal Congress and support from President Lyndon B. Johnson. Since the mid-1960s, organized labor's struggle against right-to-work laws has been fought primarily at the state level.

In prohibiting union shop and agency shop arrangements, right-to-work laws may permit employees who do not voluntarily pay these funds to become free riders. A free rider is a nonunion employee who receives benefits, such as union representation in pursuing grievances, but is not required to pay to the union either the actual costs of these benefits or the dues and assessments that union members pay to offset the union's expenses. However, unions in right-to-work states are still required by the NLRA to fully represent all employees, including the free riders. Unions consider it unfair to allow free riders, since nonunion employees share in the benefits of the union's efforts in bargaining without paying a fair share of the costs.

Right-to-work laws have been bitterly controversial ever since permitted by the Taft-Hartley Act, but their practical importance is somewhat exaggerated. These laws do not significantly reduce union strength or union membership. Where unions are well established, employees have tended to ignore right-to-work statutes. Also, state governments have generally declined to rigorously enforce these laws. Right-to-work laws may, thus, be more a symptom than a cause of union weakness in certain industries and regions of the country.

But even in states without a right-to-work law, the courts have ruled that employees have minimal obligations to the union, even under a union shop arrangement. An employee, for example, need not participate in a strike or fulfill other formal membership obligations. An employee in a union shop arrangement must pay the regular union dues and fees but may recover any portion of those funds that would otherwise be spent for union activities unrelated to collective bargaining, such as political or social causes.

The strongest support of right-to-work laws generally has come from small business. The states with right-to-work laws are concentrated in the South and West and do not include any major industrial state. Supporters of right-to-work laws maintain that they guarantee a person's right to work without being forced to join a union. They also argue that such laws do not weaken the bargaining power of unions but merely permit a worker to bargain on an individual basis if he or she so chooses. Opponents argue that the name right-to-work law is misleading, because such laws do not guarantee employment to anyone. On the contrary, they tend to reduce workers' job security by weakening the bargaining power of unions. Besides weakening unions and dividing the workforce, these laws virtually ensure the failure of any strike.

Right-to-work laws have been found valid under the U.S. Constitution and the constitutions of several states. Generally, the courts have held that these laws do not violate constitutional due process or equal protection.

Further, most courts have found that these laws do not infringe on workers' freedom of speech and assembly, nor do they violate freedom of contract, referring to an individual employee's right to freely bargain the terms of employment with an employer. The issue of which persons or associations were intended to be covered by the law is frequently litigated. Right-to-work laws do not cover members of professional organizations, such as bar associations, or of political parties, because these organizations do not represent their members in matters of wages or working conditions and bargain with no one.

Right-to-work laws have periodically become important political issues, even though the right-to-work controversy peaked as a national issue in the 1950s. In 1966, President Johnson attempted to eliminate these laws by repealing Section 14(b). The effort was defeated in a filibuster led by Senator Everett Dirksen of Illinois. Since that time, there has been no serious effort to repeal Section 14(b).

See also **American Federation of Labor-Congress of Industrial Organizations; Closed Shop; Collective Bargaining Agreement; Due Process Rights; Free Riders; Freedom of Contract; Grievance; Maintenance of Membership; National Labor Relations Act; Maintenance of Membership; Preferential Hiring; Union Security Clause.**

RUNAWAY SHOP Involves a permanent shutdown of a plant with a reopening of a plant at a new site, usually in a distant city, to replace the closed plant. Sometimes considered a variant of a lockout, this sort of relocation is usually undertaken by an employer in order to avoid dealing with a union. Though it appears in different forms, the runaway shop always involves a transfer of work—to another plant, to other employees within the same plant, or to an alter-ego corporation. If an employer moves its business in order to discourage union membership or to avoid collective bargaining, it violates Section 8(a)(3) of the National Labor Relations Act (NLRA), but if it moves for legitimate economic reasons, such as lower wage rates in the new area, it does not violate the NLRA. An employer also violates 8(a)(3) of the NLRA if it closes part of its business, transfers work to another plant, or opens a new plant to replace a closed plant if the purpose of the partial closing is to discourage unionism in the remaining parts of the business and the employer reasonably can foresee that the closing will have that effect. [*Textile Workers v. Darlington Mfg.* (1965)]

The U.S. Supreme Court distinguished the shutdown in *Textile Workers v. Darlington Mfg.* from runaway shops and partial shutdowns; it held that the employer has the absolute right to close his entire business for any reason he chooses, including antiunion bias. In that case, the Court found that Darlington had sufficient business reasons to shut down its plant and therefore did not violate the NLRA.

See also ***Darlington*** **Case; National Labor Relations Act.**

SAFETY Efforts by management, labor unions, and government to reduce accidents by identifying causes of accidents; taking corrective action, including proper training; and instituting safety rules and control procedures. Safety programs are any organized set of plans designed to meet safety problems at a workplace. The programs may be educational in nature; they may involve job training or an examination of the particular equipment and machinery to establish better safety conditions in the plant.

The National Labor Relations Board considers safety rules a mandatory subject of bargaining. Safety clauses in collective bargaining agreements vary widely, ranging from a general statement of responsibility for the safety and health of employees to detailed provisions on such issues as safety equipment, first aid, physical examinations, investigation of accidents, employee obligations, hazardous work, safety committees, and substance abuse.

Safety regulations are federal and state statutes and regulations and employer policies and rules that promote workplace safety and health. The Occupational Safety and Health Act is one of the most comprehensive statutes affecting labor-management relations. Its coverage extends to all employees whose activities affect interstate commerce. Basically, it requires employers and employees to comply with the safety and health regulations of the U.S. Department of Labor. There are stringent penalties for violations.

See also **National Labor Relations Board; Labor-Management Relations; Occupational Safety and Health Act.**

***SAINT FRANCIS COLLEGE V. MAJID GHAIDAN AL-KHAZRAJI* (1987)** The U.S. Supreme Court held that Civil Rights Act of 1866 (also known as Section 1981) prohibited discrimination against an Iraqi-born U.S. citizen who claimed that his employer had discriminated against him because he was an Arab. The plaintiff had been an associate professor at St. Francis College for five years before he was ultimately denied tenure. After the Equal Employment Opportunity Commission issued a right to sue letter, he filed a lawsuit against the college for employment discrimination under Section 1981.

At issue was whether Arabs, who are taxonomically considered Caucasians, are permitted to bring race discrimination claims under Section 1981. The section was originally interpreted by the courts as applying only to discrimination on the basis of race (against African Americans) and color. The Court noted that the general understanding of the term *race* was very broad, and that when Section 1981 was enacted in 1866, *race* included groups that are now considered "ethnic groups": Arabs, Jews, Scandinavians, Germans, Greeks, Finns, Irish, Spanish, Hungarians, Russians, and Italians. Because the Court found that Congress intended to protect several groups from discrimination when it enacted this statute, the Court expanded the scope of Section 1981 protection to include those identifiable classes of persons who are subject to discrimination "solely because of their ancestry or ethnic characteristics." In so doing, the Court rejected the use of current anthropological-racial classifications.

The Court also interpreted Section 1981 as protecting individuals against discrimination on the basis of race, ethnicity, and ancestry. Therefore, *St. Francis College* requires the proponent of a racial class to prove that (1) the group is definable by and limited by some clearly identifiable factor, (2) a common thread of attitudes, ideas, or experiences runs through the group, and (3) a community of interests exists among the members. Since *St. Francis College,* Section 1981 has been interpreted to encompass most claims of ethnic discrimination because the crucial issue is the meaning of *race* when the act was passed in 1866. As the term was used at the time, *race* often referred to different ethnic groups.

The Supreme Court later applied the *St. Francis College* holding to protect the property rights of Jewish persons, as Jews were considered a separate class distinct from whites. The lower federal courts have also applied the *St. Francis College* analysis to different ethnic groups. Italian Americans were judicially defined as a cognizable racial group because they "share a common experience and culture, often share the same religious and culinary practices, often have commonly identifiable surnames, and have been subject to stereotyping, invidious ethnic humor, and discrimination." [*United States v. Biaggi* (1988)]

Section 1981 has long been understood to have been enacted to protect freed African American slaves. Some recent commentators, however, believe that the section was instead enacted to protect Chinese immigrants. The constitutional rights of Asian Americans, therefore, are protected to the extent that they are similar to African Americans, as both groups were subject to racial discrimination.

See also **African Americans: Employment Issues; Discrimination in Employment; Equal Employment Opportunity Commission; Property Rights.**

Salary Compensation paid by the week, month, or year, rather than by the hour. Salaried positions are generally nonproduction, nonroutine supervisory or managerial jobs that are exempt from the provisions of the Fair Labor Standards Act (FLSA), though some nonexempt jobs are salaried as well.

A salaried employee is generally an individual who does not receive compensation on the basis of the number of hours worked, although white-collar employees are expected to work a definite number of hours. The salary rate is the rate of pay expressed in terms of dollars per week, per month, or per year for employees hired on a weekly, monthly, or yearly basis. Salaried white-collar employees, such as executive and professional employees, are exempt from the overtime pay provisions of the FLSA. The time, place, and method of paying salaries is regulated by state law and varies from state to state.

See also **Compensation; Fair Labor Standards Act; White-Collar Employee.**

Scab A colloquialism for any employee who refuses to go on strike with his co-workers. Also refers to a worker who is hired to replace a striking employee, or to any person who crosses a picket line to work.

See also **Strike.**

***Schecter Poultry Co. v. United States* (1935)** The National Industrial Recovery Act (NIRA) was enacted in 1933 to help the United States recover from the Great Depression.

Section 7(a) of the statute covered labor matters. This section declared that employees had the right to organize and engage in collective bargaining through representatives of their own choosing. Basically, it outlawed employer conduct that interfered with the collective bargaining process.

Pursuant to this statute, a code was established for the live poultry industry in and around New York City. It required a 40-hour work week and a minimum wage of 50 cents per hour, prohibited child labor, set a minimum number of employees based on sales volume, and prohibited various unfair methods of competition. In New York City, where 96 percent of the live poultry marketed came from other states, Schechter Poultry Corporation owned a wholesale poultry slaughterhouse that sold only to local New York retailers. Charged with violating various parts of the code, Schechter contended that the code was an unconstitutional delegation of legislative power and that it attempted to regulate intrastate transactions beyond the authority of Congress.

In *Schecter,* the U.S. Supreme Court declared the NIRA unconstitutional. The Court concluded the legislation constituted an illegal delegation of power by Congress to the administrator of the National Industrial Recovery Administration, without standards sufficiently definite to limit his discretion in any way. The Court also ruled that the statute's particular application in the Poultry Code exceeded congressional authority to regulate interstate commerce. The Court said that only intrastate practices "directly" affecting interstate commerce were subject to the federal power.

The NIRA was in existence for only two years. Though Section 7(a) was not the subject of the *Schechter* decision, this important provision was invalidated when the legislation was struck down by the Supreme Court. Despite the short life of the NIRA, it substantially impacted federal labor law. The legislation represented an important change in the attitude of government toward unions. Instead of being laissez-faire, as was the Norris-LaGuardia Act, Section 7(a) of the NIRA extended legal protections to workers' rights to organize and engage in collective bargaining. Shortly after the NIRA was declared unconstitutional, Congress passed new legislation (the Wagner Act, which became known as the National Labor Relations Act) that marked a complete departure from the preexisting attitude of government toward unions. With the passage of the Wagner Act, Congress declared as national policy the encouragement of the practice and procedures of collective bargaining. The Wagner Act was held constitutional by the U.S. Supreme Court in *NLRB v. Jones & Laughlin Steel Corporation* (1937).

See also **Collective Bargaining; *NLRB v. Jones & Laughlin Steel Corp.***

SCIENTIFIC MANAGEMENT A concept created and largely popularized by Frederick W. Taylor, who was considered the father of scientific management. The three essential tenets of this theory, according to Taylor, were (1) the substitution of science for the individual judgment of the worker, (2) the scientific selection and development of the worker (after each man had been studied, taught, trained, and experimented with) instead of allowing the men to select themselves and develop in a haphazard way; and (3) cooperation between management and the workers, so that they perform their work in accordance with the scientific laws instead of leaving the solution of each problem in the hands of the individual worker.

The term now includes the general philosophy, methods, and principles concerned with the improvement of efficiency, reduction of operating costs, and the maximum utilization of human and material resources in the operation of a company, in the production of a product, or the development of a particular service. One of the main tools of scientific management is the motion study.

Motion study, sometimes called "methods study," is the observation of the movements of machinery and materials to determine the "preferred methods of doing work." The purpose is to make performance easier, economize motion, and increase productive time. Classic Taylorist time and motion studies are intended to standardize job tasks and result in the requirement that employees adhere strictly to formally specified motions. This rigid standardization goes along with the no-slack principle of lean production—that is, assignments must be rigorously specified to achieve the sixty-seconds-per-minute load for all workers.

The Taylor system of scientific management consisted primarily of three elements. First, Taylor advocated paying workers according to a system of "differential piece rates," in order to give faster workers an incentive to outperform the others. Second, he advocated systematic time study so that the work of each laborer could be measured individually. Third, he insisted that all thinking and planning work be removed from the laborers and concentrated in the planning department. The last aspect of scientific management underlies the rigid boundaries so prevalent in traditional industrial relations thought.

Taylor insisted on removing all thinking work from the shop floor, because he claimed that when workers held a monopoly of knowledge about production, they could control the pace of work and thus limit production. The planning department, like time and motion study, was designed to reduce the skill level of the worker and place knowledge about production exclusively with management. And just as Taylor advocated removing the workers' hold on knowledge, he also believed that the management function and the laborer's function could not be shared.

Time and motion studies had long played a role in management and they continue to do so. They are also used in the government enforcement of regulations. California, as early as 1914, has been using time-studies to determine if the contract price would ensure that minimum wages were paid. In 1993, the state of California issued an executive order creating a joint enforcement strike force to target the "underground economy," including garment sweatshops. Despite widespread and highly publicized abuses, manufacturers feigned ignorance of conditions in the garment sweatshops. But after the strike force had performed a time and motion study, it became obvious that, with the extremely low contract prices manufacturers forced subcontractors to accept, the subcontractors obviously could not afford to pay minimum wages.

See also **Industrial Relations; Minimum Wage.**

Scope of Bargaining

The subject matter of bargaining, or the issues deemed appropriate to be negotiated in a collective bargaining agreement. Sections 8(a)(5) and 8(d) of the National Labor Relations Act (NLRA) require the employer to bargain with his employees' union over "wages, hours, and other terms and conditions of employment." The scope of bargaining depends to a large extent on diverse factors such as the size and nature of the bargaining unit, attitudes of unions and employees, length of the contract term, the industry involved, legislation, and the positions of the courts and the National Labor Relations Board (NLRB).

The provisions generally found in collective bargaining agreements include recognition, bargaining unit, union security, wages, hours, working conditions, layoffs, transfers, promotions, vacations, overtime, the grievance procedure, and provisions for the duration of the agreement.

In *NLRB v. Wooster Division of Borg-Warner Corporation* (1958) (known as the "Borg-Warner case"), the U.S. Supreme Court recognized three categories of bargaining proposals under the NLRA and established rules for them:

1. Illegal Subjects of Bargaining. These are proposals that would be illegal and forbidden under the act, such as a proposal for a closed shop. Bargaining on such proposals is not required, and they may not be included in the contract even if both parties agree.

2. Mandatory Subjects of Bargaining. Under Section 8(d) of the NLRA, both employers and unions are required to bargain in good faith with respect to "wages, hours, and other terms and conditions of employment." Either party must bargain about proposals falling in this category, and the party advancing the proposals may insist on their inclusion in any contract executed.
3. Voluntary (or Permissive) Subjects of Bargaining. These are proposals that fall outside the mandatory category of "wages, hours, and other terms and conditions of employment." They may be placed on the table for voluntary bargaining and agreement. But the other party is not be required either to bargain or to agree to their inclusion in the contract. Insistence on including these proposals as a condition to the execution of a contract is a violation of the bargaining duty under the NLRA.

If an impasse is reached over one of the mandatory subjects of bargaining, a lawful economic strike may ensue. Failure to bargain over a mandatory subject of bargaining is an unfair labor practice under the NLRA. Permissive subjects of bargaining (e.g., pension improvements for retirees) may not be taken to impasse and a strike may not occur over permissive items. If there is a dispute over whether a given demand falls within the appropriate subject matter, that dispute is resolved by the administrative agency or, after it, by the courts.

See also **Appropriate Bargaining Unit; Collective Bargaining Agreement; Grievance Procedure; Impasse; National Labor Relations Act; National Labor Relations Board; Unfair Labor Practice; Union Security Clause.**

SEASONAL EMPLOYMENT AND SEASONAL EMPLOYEES

Work opportunities available only during certain times of the year, such as jobs in the fruit canning, logging, or the retail industry. Seasonal employment may, for example, involve employees hired for peak activity periods such as during the Christmas season.

A seasonal industry is an industry that has high peaks of employment at certain times of the year and troughs during other seasons. The term is specifically defined in the Fair Labor Standards Act (FLSA) as an industry that is forced to curtail or cease production periodically during the year. The FLSA grants relief from statutory overtime pay standards to seasonal industries qualifying for these exemptions, limited to a fixed number of weeks per year.

Seasonal employees are workers who work from 25 to 149 days per year. They make up 33 percent of the agricultural labor force and account for 25 percent of farm work. Many seasonal and casual workers are students, housewives, and others wanting temporary work. Because of their limited workforce commitment, they are often poor prospects for unionization. Casual workers—those who work less than 25 days—account for 45 percent of the agricultural labor force, although they do only 5 percent of the work.

Workers employed by amusement or recreational establishments whose business is "seasonal" within the meaning of the FLSA are exempted from the minimum wage, equal pay, and overtime pay requirements under Section 13(a)(3) of the statute. The business of an establishment is "seasonal" if the establishment does not operate for more than seven months in any calendar year, or if the establishment's average receipts for any six months of the year were not more than one third its average receipts for the other six months of the year.

See also **Fair Labor Standards Act; Equal Pay for Equal Work; Minimum Wage; Overtime.**

SEASONAL UNEMPLOYMENT

See **Unemployment.**

SECONDARY BOYCOTT

The pressure exerted by a union (in the form of a refusal to work for, purchase from, or handle products of) against a neutral party (an employer with whom the union has no dispute) with the object of forcing that employer to place pressure on the actual object of the strike (the employer with whom the union has a dispute). A secondary boycott is indirect pressure exerted by a union on a neutral party, who then exerts pressure against the business that is the actual object of the strike action. The immediate object of the action is to induce the neutral party to bring pressure against the business from whom the economic concessions are sought.

Secondary boycotts are prohibited by Section 8(b)(4) of the National Labor Relations Act (NLRA) in order to "prevent the spread of economic disputes." However, the NLRA tends to be economically deceptive and ideologically confusing. The provision is economically deceptive because, as applied, it inhibits construction unions' efforts to close minor job sites while large industrial unions may strike with enormous impact on neutral employers. However, strikes by large industrial unions and resulting losses for neutrals are inevitable in a system based on free collective bargaining and the use of economic weapons to settle disputes. The absence of any limitation on concerted strikes by employees of competing employers magnifies such losses.

Most forms of secondary boycotts are considered unfair labor practices in all industries except interstate airlines and railroads. Since airlines and railroads are governed by the Railway Labor Act and the Norris-LaGuardia Act, secondary boycotts against these transportation entities may not be enjoined by the federal courts. Thus, airlines and railroads as well as the general public, are subject to secondary boycotts by labor unions.

Before it was made illegal, the secondary boycott was effective in obtaining recognition from nonunion employers. The carpenters' union, for example, had jurisdiction over factories making millwork and other lumber products. These plants were numerous, small, and often difficult to organize. They were organized, in part, when the union carpenters on construction sites began to refuse to install millwork from nonunion factories. This refusal forced the building contractors to buy from union plants only. The nonunion plants found their market reduced or even destroyed, and so were forced to recognize the union.

See also **Ally Doctrine; Boycott; Collective Bargaining; Common Situs Picketing; National Labor Relations Act; Norris-LaGuardia Act; Railway Labor Act; Strike; Unfair Labor Practice.**

SENIORITY

SENIORITY An individual employee's length of service with an employer or in one unit of the employer's business. There are two kinds of seniority: competitive seniority, which is used to determine which employees should secure advantages at the workplace (such as promotion, shift assignment, or layoff survival), and benefit seniority, which is used to measure employee entitlement to benefits.

Seniority rights are the privileges, rights, and other benefits that accrue to an individual because of length of service or in the performance of certain work. These rights may be construed and protected by arbitrators or the courts in interpreting the collective bargaining contract. Seniority may be established for various units, such as an individual craft or operation, department, entire plant, or in some cases, all of the plants of a company in a particular geographic area. Seniority systems are the procedures established in the workplace to protect the rights of individuals who have been with the company for long periods of time. They exist not only in organized plants but also in nonunion and unorganized plants.

Often a company has a policy that describes its seniority system. Where the workplace is unionized, collective bargaining agreements often have clauses that apply the seniority principle to the employment relationship, delineating the nature of seniority and its application to various situations, such as layoffs, promotions, and rehires. Typically such clauses relate an individual's length of service to job retention and recall in case of a layoff. They may also make seniority a factor in promotion or transfer, in choice of vacation, and in other aspects of employment.

In situations involving employers who have recently adopted an affirmative action policy and hired more minority workers than in the past, layoffs in accordance with a "last hired, first fired" seniority system would frustrate the purpose of the affirmative action policy. The U.S. Supreme Court has recognized that parties may adopt affirmative action programs that extend beyond what a court can order as a remedy under Title VII of the Civil Rights Act of 1964. [*United Steelworkers v. Weber* (1979)]

In *Lorance v. AT&T Technologies, Inc.* (1989), the U.S. Supreme Court held that the statute of limitations for a claim alleging that a seniority system was adopted for a discriminatory purpose begins to run at the time the system was adopted, not the time it was applied. Lorrance alleged that AT&T's 1979 collectively bargained seniority system from plant seniority to job seniority was motivated by intentional sex discrimination—to protect senior male jobholders against new female entrants. The statute of limitations, if calculated from the time the company adopted the policy, had run. Lorance argued that the limitations should not have begun until the company applied the policy to her. The Court, however, ruled that actionable discrimination occurs at the time the system is adopted for a discriminatory purpose; subsequent applications do not constitute either new instances of actionable intentional discrimination or continuing violations relating back to the initial discriminatory intent. The decision has been criticized for wrongly shielding existing seniority systems from employment discrimination claims.

Retroactive seniority is an appropriate remedy for unlawful employment practices under Title VII. As with back pay, victims of discrimination ought ordinarily to receive retroactive seniority with a hiring or reinstatement order. Remedial seniority allows the victim of discrimination to receive seniority credit from the date of the discriminatory act. Although this approach affects the rights of innocent incumbent employees, the Supreme Court found more significant the interests of victims of discrimination to receive complete relief. [*Franks v. Bouman Transportation*, Inc. (1976)]

The remedy of retroactive seniority is distinguishable from challenges to seniority systems as themselves discriminatory. A seniority system that perpetuates the effects of past discrimination is not subject to challenge as disparate impact discrimination because Section 703 of Title VII insulates bona fide seniority systems from attack on the grounds that pre–Title VII discrimination is perpetuated by the system after the act. The Supreme Court held that the proviso protects bona fide seniority systems from challenge on the same basis as other employment rules. The Court found the "unmistakable purpose" of the provision was to make clear that the routine application of a bona fide seniority system would not be unlawful under Title VII. [*International Brotherhood of Teamsters v. United States* (1977)]

See also **Affirmative Action; Civil Rights Act of 1964; Collective Bargaining Agreement; Disparate Impact Discrimination; Sex Discrimination in Employment; *United Steelworkers v. Weber.***

SEPARATION

See **Termination.**

SERVICE CONTRACT ACT (1965)

Also known as the O'Hara-McNamara Services Act, this is one of the three federal statutes that require employers to pay "prevailing wages," as determined by the U.S. Department of Justice, to employees involved in the performance of federal contracts. The Service Contract Act supplements the Fair Labor Standards Act (FLSA), and its provisions apply only when they do not conflict with those of the FLSA. The statute does not apply to contracts governed by the Walsh-Healey Act or to construction contracts, which are governed by the Davis-Bacon Act.

The statute was enacted to ensure that government contractors compensated their blue-collar service workers and some white-collar workers fairly, but it does not cover executive, administrative, or professional employees. It requires employers engaged in performance of service contracts for government agencies where contracts are valued at more than $2,500 to pay their employees not less than the minimum wages and benefits determined by the U.S. Department of Labor to be prevailing locally. Since the statute does not define "locality," a problem arises when the place of contract performance cannot be established at the time of bid solicitation. In no event may employers pay their employees less than the minimum wage under the FLSA.

A 1972 amendment to the statute requires a successor contractor providing substantially the same services to pay its employees at least as much as the predecessor paid unless the U.S. Department of Labor determines, after a hearing in the locality, that such an amount varies from rates "which prevail for services of a character similar in the locality." This successorship requirement applies to all contracts for substantially the same services also furnished in the same locality.

See also **Davis-Bacon Act; Fair Labor Standards Act.**

SERVICE WORKER An employee whose job is to provide personal assistance, protective service, or current maintenance for buildings or residences. Some examples of service workers are parking lot attendants, beauticians, hospital orderlies, bartenders, and custodians.

SETTLEMENT See **Labor Dispute.**

SEVERANCE INTERVIEW See **Exit Interview.**

SEVERANCE PAY Compensation to an employee permanently separated from a company for any reason. Often, severance pay is given as a result of a permanent reduction of the workforce, introduction of labor-saving machinery, plant shutdown, or any other cause for which the worker is not responsible.

SEX DISCRIMINATION IN EMPLOYMENT Practices, policies, or procedures that deny equal employment opportunity on the basis of sex. Title VII of the Civil Rights Act of 1964 states that it is an unfair employment practice for an employer to limit, segregate, or classify employees in any way that tends to deprive any individual of employment opportunities or adversely affects that person's status as an employee because of sex. Under Title VII, discrimination on the basis of pregnancy, childbirth, or related medical conditions is included in the meaning of sex discrimination. Sex discrimination includes actions such as labeling jobs as either "men's" or "women's" for hiring or promotion purposes, maintaining separate seniority lists based on sex, or discriminating between men and women in regard to benefits. Employment practices constituting sexual harassment are also considered sex discrimination. Discrimination against homosexuals, however, is not prohibited by Title VII.

In addition to the Title VII's prohibition against sex discrimination, Executive Order 11246 (1965) requires federal contractors to take affirmative action to ensure that their employment practices do not discriminate based on sex, and Executive Order 11478 (1978) prohibits discrimination on the basis of sex in federal employment.

However, the employer may legally specify a preference for a member of one sex over another for a particular job or class of jobs if the employer can show that being a female (or male) is a bona fide occupational qualification (BFOQ). The Equal Employment Opportunity Commission said that the BFOQ exception to the general ban on sex discrimination should be construed narrowly. A BFOQ will not generally be recognized if the refusal to hire an individual was based because of the preferences of co-workers, the employers, clients, or customers, except where it is necessary for authenticity or genuineness, such as the preference for actresses to play female parts.

The Equal Pay Act of 1963 makes it unlawful to pay a lower wage to members of the opposite sex for equal work in jobs that require equal skill, effort, and responsibility under similar working conditions in the same establishment.

See also **Affirmative Action; Bona Fide Occupational Qualification; Equal Pay Act of 1963; Sexual Harassment.**

SEXUAL HARASSMENT Sexual harassment is defined by the Equal Employment Opportunity Commission (EEOC) as:

> Unwelcome sexual advances, requests for sexual favors, and other verbal or physical conduct of a sexual nature . . . when (1) submission to such conduct is made either explicitly or implicitly a term or condition of an individual's employment, (2) submission to or rejection of such conduct by an individual is used as the basis for employment decisions affecting such individual, or (3) such conduct has the purpose or effect of unreasonably interfering with an individual's work performance or creating an intimidating, hostile, or offensive working environment.

Sexual harassment in the workplace is considered a violation of Title VII of the Civil Rights Act of 1964. The principle behind this prohibition is that an individual on the job should be free from sexual threats, persuasion, or humiliation; and that acceding to sexual demands should not be a condition for promotion, favorable treatment, or pay increases. There are two types of sexual harassment: quid pro quo harassment and hostile environment harassment.

Quid pro quo harassment (literally, "something for something") was the first type of sexual harassment recognized as actionable under Title VII of the Civil Rights Act of 1964. The Civil Rights Act of 1991 states that sexual harassment "is established when the complaining party demonstrates that . . . sex . . . was a motivating factor for any employment practice, even though other factors also motivated the practice." Quid pro quo harassment occurs when an employee is threatened with firing, nonpromotion, or other consequences if he or she does not submit to "unwelcome sexual advances, requests for sexual favors, and other verbal or physical conduct of a sexual nature" initiated by another employee. Plaintiffs must show that the unwelcome advances were a condition of receiving job benefits or that the plaintiff suffered an adverse employment action as a result of refusing such advances.

Hostile environment discrimination was first recognized as actionable under Title VII in *Bundy v. Jackson* (1981) and the principle was affirmed by the U.S. Supreme Court in *Meritor Savings Bank v. Vinson* (1986). In that case, the employee had voluntary—but not consensual—relations with her manager—she did so because the manager's propositions included threats of losing her job.

The Court, however, defined this type of harassment as one which does not affect the economic aspect of the plaintiff's employment, such as promotion, discharge, or salary but rather deprives an employee of the "right to work in an environment free from discriminatory intimidation, ridicule, and insult." Thus, hostile environment harassment occurs when the behavior in question "has the purpose or effect of unreasonably interfering with an individual's work performance or creating an intimidating, hostile, or offensive working environment."

In *Harris v. Forklift Systems, Inc.* (1993), the U.S. Supreme Court came closer to establishing a working definition for hostile work environment sexual harassment claims. It reaffirmed the applicability of Title VII to sex harassment cases and endorsed a standard using the perspective of a person in the same or similar circumstances of the victim.

The EEOC's *Guidelines on Discrimination Because of Sex* holds the employer, its agents, or supervisors responsible for the sexual harassment of employees, "regardless of whether the specific acts complained of were authorized or even forbidden by the employer and regardless of whether the employer knew of or should have known of their occurrence." An employer, along with its agents and supervisory employees, who knows or should have known of harassing conduct is also responsible for conduct between fellow employees and possibly for the acts of nonemployees unless it can show that "immediate and appropriate corrective action" was taken. Some courts have ruled that the employer's failure to respond to an employee's repeated complaints of sexual harassment gives rise to a finding of intentional infliction of emotional distress. [*Ford v. Revlon* (1987)]

Since the courts have generally upheld sexual harassment claims and have found employers liable for the actions of supervisory employees, employers should take these claims seriously and investigate them immediately. For an investigation procedure to be effective, the individual responsible for handling the complaints should have the full support of top management as well as the personnel skills to investigate situations that often become complicated. Investigations must be conducted with sensitivity and must uncover the details of who, what, when, where, why, and how often. Because both these types of harassment are deeply rooted in the popular culture, charges of sexual harassment often accompany other complaints of discrimination.

Sexual harassment takes many forms, ranging from mild verbal banter to violence or the threat of violence. It is a particularly insidious form of workplace discrimination with severe economic and psychological repercussions for its victims. Women who are victims of sexual harassment at work suffer from stress symptoms, including feelings of powerlessness, fear, anger, nervousness, decreased job satisfaction, and diminished ambition. Both an occupational health hazard and an economic barrier, sexual harassment also operates to confine women to traditionally "female" jobs.

Some courts have ruled that same-sex harassment is not actionable under Title VII of the Civil Rights Act. [*Hopkins v. Baltimore Gas & Electric Co.* (1996); *Garcia v. Elf Auto Chem* (1994)]

See also **Equal Employment Opportunity Commission.**

SEXUAL ORIENTATION A review of 20 surveys conducted across the country between 1980 and 1995 indicates that 16 to 44 percent of gay and lesbian respondents believed they encountered some form of employment discrimination, primarily in hiring, firing, promotion, and performance evaluation. A 1987 *Wall Street Journal* poll of Fortune 500 chief executive officers indicated that 66 percent of them would hesitate to offer a management job to a homosexual. Given evidence of potential and actual sexual orientation discrimination, U.S. Representatives Barney Frank and Gerry Studds of Massachusetts first authored, sponsored, and introduced the Employment Nondiscrimination Act (ENDA) in the 103rd Congress in 1994.

The central mandate of ENDA is contained in Section 4 of the act, which prohibits employers and other covered entities from "subject[ing] an individual to a different standard of treatment on the basis of sexual orientation." It then calls for extending this protection from employees' sexual orientation to their right of actual or perceived association with others of the same orientation. In the language of the act, employers shall not "discriminate against an individual based on the sexual orientation of a person with whom such individual is believed to associate or to be associated." Sexual orientation is defined in Section 3(9) as "homosexuality, bisexuality, or heterosexuality, whether such orientation is real or perceived." With the inclusion of heterosexuality, the theoretical integrity of sexual orientation as a fair and all-inclusive legislative category is insured. The strongest support for this legislation comes from gay and lesbian groups such as the Human Rights Campaign Fund, Lambda Legal Defense Fund, and the National Gay and Lesbian Task Force. Several civil rights groups, such as the Leadership Conference on Civil Rights and the U.S. Civil Rights Commission, also support ENDA.

See also **Sexual Orientation Discrimination.**

SEXUAL ORIENTATION DISCRIMINATION Federal law does not prohibit discrimination based on sexual orientation. Title VII of the Civil Rights Act of 1964 prohibits discrimination on the basis of sex but not on the basis of sexual orientation. The legislative history of Title VII has not been interpreted by the courts to support the extension of sex discrimination to include homosexuality. There have been several unsuccessful attempts since 1975 to amend Title VII of the Civil Rights Act of 1964 to prohibit discrimination based on sexual orientation. More recently, Congress has expressly declined to include sexual orientation among the protected classes in the Americans with Disabilities Act (ADA). However, the AIDS epidemic has created new discrimination problems for homosexuals and has led to special regulations on food handling in connection with the ADA.

Most states and many municipalities have statutes to promote fair employment practices. Some of these statutes specifically protect homosexuals. California, Connecticut, Hawaii, Massachusetts, Wisconsin, New Jersey, Vermont, and the District of Columbia, all have statutes prohibiting discrimination on the basis of sexual orientation. In *Gay Law Students Association v. Pacific Telephone and Telegraph Co.* (1979), the Supreme Court of California held that homosexuality is the equivalent of political activity or affiliation within the meaning of that state's labor code, which prohibits discrimination in this area. A California lower court held that this decision applies to sex discrimination in the workplace, and the dismissal of a homosexual employee in California resulted in a $5.3 million damage award.

The workplace rights of homosexuals is one of the most difficult and controversial issues of the 1990s, complicated by the absence of clearly articulated legislative federal policy on homosexual rights. Gays and lesbians are excluded from the scope of Title VII, and homosexual relationships are not recognized for purposes of federal entitlement or employee benefits programs. In the absence of federal legislative standards, the courts, as well as state and local governments, have attempted to fill the gaps. The result has been a patchwork of case law and state and local statutes that provide employers with few clear guidelines on issues involving gay and lesbian employees.

In the 1990s, there have been several legislative, administrative, and judicial developments on the state level regarding the rights and status of homosexuals. Several employees have brought charges of sexual preference discrimination against their employees on constitutional and other grounds. At the same time, some federal courts have suggested that homosexuality may be a "status" that merits heightened scrutiny. [*Steffan v. Aspin* (1993)] The courts have generally held that employees may not be discharged solely because they are homosexuals, though discharges of homosexuals for other reasons have been upheld. One court of appeals held that a federal employee's discharge for an off-duty homosexual advance was improper. [*Norton v. Macy* (1969)]

At the federal level, issues of discrimination can be expected to interact increasingly with the Employment Retirement Insurance Security Act of 1974, AIDS, and the ADA in intricate and unanticipated ways. Complicating the problems are difficult questions of ethics and social policy on the shared responsibility of employers and government to provide health care for those who are ill.

See also **Americans with Disabilities Act of 1990; Employment Retirement Insurance Security Act of 1974; Fair Employment Practice Laws;** ***Gay Law Students Association v. Pacific Telephone and Telegraph Co.*** **(1979); Sex Discrimination in Employment.**

SHELTERED WORKSHOP A work-oriented rehabilitation facility for handicapped persons with a controlled working environment. Sheltered workshops emphasize individual vocational goals and assist handicapped persons in progressing toward productive lives.

SHERMAN ANTITRUST ACT OF 1890 Enacted by Congress in 1890, this statute prohibits trusts and conspiracies that restrain interstate commerce and forbids parties to monopolize trade or commerce among the states. This statute was passed to control the trusts that had achieved prominence in the late nineteenth century. Labor unions were not specifically mentioned in the act, and it appeared that the statute was intended to curtail industry monopolistic and antitrust practices. For several years, only business activities restraining interstate commerce were prosecuted under the Sherman Act. Employers soon began to argue that unions and the economic pressure they applied achieved the same objectives as trusts and therefore violated the statute. The courts then began to apply the statute to labor unions. Under its terms, the federal courts decided several historic labor disputes and restrained, by injunction, strikes, boycotts, and the use of blacklists.

The first test of the applicability of antitrust legislation to labor came before the U.S. Supreme Court in the case of *Loewe v. Lawlor* (Danbury Hatters' case) in 1908. The court in that decision concluded that antitrust laws applied to labor. The labor unions subsequently lobbied to have legislation passed (the Clayton Act) in order to invalidate court decisions under the Sherman Act. But even the Clayton Act did not resolve the problems created for unions by the antitrust laws. Many of these problems were eventually resolved by the Norris-LaGuardia Act and by the National Labor Relations Act.

See also **Clayton Antitrust Act;** ***Loewe v. Lawlor;*** **Norris-LaGuardia Act.**

SHOP COMMITTEE A group of employees elected by fellow workers or appointed by union officials to represent the bargaining unit in considering grievances and related matters, with workplace management above the level of supervisor.

SHOP STEWARD The union representative of a group of employees who conducts union duties at the workplace, such as handling grievances, collecting dues, and recruiting new members. Elected by union members at the plant or appointed by higher union officials, the shop steward (also called "union steward") usually continues to work at his or her regular job while handling union duties only on a part-time basis.

The steward is protected while holding that position under the super seniority provisions with regard to layoff and frequently is paid for the time spent handling grievances.

SICK BENEFITS See **Benefits.**

SICK LEAVE See **Leave of Absence.**

SLOWDOWN While not a work stoppage, a slowdown is a concerted and intentional reduction of production by employees in an attempt to win concessions from an employer. The slowdown is a modified form of a strike, since it is designed to achieve the same general purpose through different means. [*NLRB v. Insurance Agents International Union* (1960)]

SMOKING REGULATIONS Whether or not and when employees choose to smoke in the workplace has become an issue for many employers. Traditionally, smoking was a matter left to the discretion of individuals and employers became involved only when necessary, resolving employee complaints on a case-by-case basis.

Recently, however, many nonsmokers, claiming a right to smoke-free environment, have requested court or legislative intervention, often seeking to prohibit or severely restrict smoking. Public commentary on environmental tobacco smoke, including the surgeon general's 1986 report on smoking's health effects, has enhanced awareness of this issue. Some employers now believe that they risk the prospect of lawsuits if they do not institute restrictive policies. Increasingly, employers are restricting cigarette smoking in the workplace. Though many of the restrictions are mandated by state and local laws, the increased activism of nonsmokers and the employer's desire to reduce health insurance and workers' compensation costs also have contributed to the growth of restrictions on workplace smoking.

Statutes restricting workplace smoking may be viewed as a subset of laws restricting smoking in public places. Virtually every state restricts smoking in public places. Statutes typically prohibit smoking in conference and meeting rooms, classrooms, auditoriums, restrooms, medical facilities, hallways, elevators, company cafeterias, office lounges, and other areas of common use. Many of these statutes require employers to adopt a smoking policy or to take some other action (such as establishing separate smoking or nonsmoking areas) to protect nonsmoking employees from the hazards of environmental smoke. Twenty states restrict smoking in both public and private sector workplaces. There are, as of yet, no federal statutes regulating smoking in the workplace.

Generally, lawsuits that seek to require a smoke-free work environment, whether based on the Constitution, statute, or case-law, have been unsuccessful. Since 1976, only one lower-level court has actually enjoined an employer to restrict smoking in its workplace. What might constitute an appropriate workplace smoking policy—one that would balance the rights of nonsmokers to be protected from tobacco smoke and the rights of smokers to be free from unnecessary or unreasonable smoking restrictions—is still under debate.

Many employers have been refusing to hire smokers in order to contain health care costs and to improve safety conditions. These hiring bans have prompted many state legislatures to pass statutes specifically to protect smokers. No such laws existed in 1989, but by 1994, 28 states had enacted legislation to protect smokers. These statutes, which generally require employers to abolish the hiring restrictions, were promoted by the tobacco industry and organizations such as the American Civil Liberties Union, which views the hiring ban on smokers as discriminatory and a violation of privacy.

The New York Court of Appeals recently held that where a bronchial asthma condition was aggravated by exposure to excessive amounts of second-hand smoke, the condition qualifies as a compensible "accidental injury" under New York's workers' compensation statute. [*Johannsen v. New York City Department of Housing Preservation & Development* (1994)] The court's position on the nature of smoke-related injuries makes clear that employers have an affirmative obligation to ensure that the workplace complies with all state and local smoke-free requirements.

SOCIAL SECURITY ACT (1935)

A federal statute enacted in 1935 establishing a national social insurance program and an agency to administer it. The two cash assistance programs for the elderly created by the Social Security Act were Old Age Insurance and Old Age Assistance (later substantially federalized under the Supplemental Security Income program in 1972). Social Security was devised to "provide some safeguard against insecurity of modern life through cooperative action by federal and state governments, thus making possible the fullest consideration of the local economic and social problems . . . while maintaining a national unity of programs and purposes."

The Social Security Act was held constitutional by the U.S. Supreme Court in *Steward Machine Company v. Davis* (1937). The Court upheld the state unemployment insurance laws and provisions for the payment of federal old age benefits and taxes, which were set up under the statute. The Court's rationale for the decision was that the levying of federal taxes for old age pensions was a valid exercise of the power to tax for the general welfare, and that the offer of federal rebates to states for unemployment insurance did not violate due process or amount to coercion of the states.

Congress broadened Old Age Insurance and transformed it into a family program in 1939 by adding benefits for spouses and dependents as well as for survivors of deceased workers. A series of subsequent liberalizing amendments broadened the statute's coverage and expanded its benefits. The following major programs are currently provided under the act.

1. Retirement insurance
2. Survivors' insurance
3. Disability insurance
4. Hospital and medical insurance for the aged and disabled
5. Black lung benefits
6. Supplemental security income
7. Unemployment insurance
8. Public assistance
9. Food stamps
10. Child support enforcement
11. Maternal/child health and welfare
12. Workers' compensation
13. Railroad retirement, sickness, and unemployment insurance
14. Veterans' benefits
15. Federal, state, and local government employees' retirement

Social Security eventually became instrumental in encouraging widespread retirement. Before the New Deal, more than half of the men age 65 and older remained in the labor force. As Old Age Insurance benefits increased and private sector pensions became more common, the proportion dropped to 33 percent by 1960 and to 17 percent by 1989.

The act was amended in 1983 to alleviate the social security program's $168 billion deficit. The National Commission on Social Security Reform, established by the president, presented its recommendations to the president and the Congress in 1983. Based on these recommendations, Congress enacted amendments that, among other changes, provided for a higher tax rate and taxable wage base, decreased benefits, taxed some benefits, extended coverage to federal employees hired after 1983 and employees of nonprofit organizations, raised the retirement age, revised the cost-of-living adjustment of benefits, and prevented the withdrawal of state and local governments from the social security system.

See also **Black Lung Benefits; Railroad Retirement Acts; Unemployment Insurance; Workers' Compensation.**

State of New Jersey v. Shack and Tejeras (1977)

Tedesco, a farmer, employed migrant workers for his seasonal needs. As part of their compensation, these workers were housed at a camp on his property. Defendant Tejeras was a field worker for the Farm Worker Division of the Southwest Citizens Organization for Poverty Elimination (SCOPE), a nonprofit corporation founded by the Office of Economic Opportunity (OEO). The role of SCOPE included providing for the health services of the migrant farm workers. Defendant Shack was a staff attorney with the Farm Workers Division of Camden Regional Legal Services, Inc. (CRLS), also a nonprofit corporation funded by the OEO. Their mission of CRLS included legal advice and representation for these workers.

Differences had developed between Tedesco and these defendants before the events that led to the trespass charges in this case. Hence, when defendant Tejeras wanted to go on Tedesco's farm to find a migrant worker who needed medical aid, he called upon the defendant Shack for legal help. Shack also needed to go to Tedesco's farm to discuss a legal problem with another migrant worker. The defendants then agreed to go to the farm together.

Defendants entered Tedesco's property and as they neared the campsite where the farm workers were housed, they were confronted by Tedesco, who inquired as to their purpose. Tejeras and Shack stated their missions. In response, Tedesco offered to find the injured worker and to locate the worker who needed legal advice. However, Tedesco insisted that the consultation would have to take place at Tedesco's office and in his presence.

Defendants declined, saying they had the right to see the man in the privacy of his living quarters and without Tedesco's supervision. Tedesco, thereupon summoned a state trooper, who, however, refused to remove defendants except upon Tedesco's written complaint. Tedesco then executed the formal complaints charging violations of the trespass statute.

The Supreme Court of New Jersey ruled that the defendants invaded no property rights of the farmer-employer. Therefore, their conduct was outside the reach of the state's trespass statute. Finding that the farmer had no legitimate need for a right to deny the worker the aid available from government or charitable organizations seeking to assist him, the court ruled that the employer may not deny the worker his privacy or interfere with his opportunity to live with dignity and to enjoy associations customary among American citizens.

STATUTE OF LABORERS See **Common Law: Employment Doctrines.**

STATUTE OF LIMITATIONS See **Limitation of Actions.**

STEELE V. LOUISVILLE & NASHVILLE R.R. CO. (1944)

In this case the U.S. Supreme Court first announced the principle that a bargaining representative must represent fairly all employees within the bargaining unit, regardless of race and regardless of union membership. The duty of fair representation was first enunciated in two cases involving racial discrimination by labor unions certified as exclusive bargaining representatives under the Railway Labor Act (RLA).

In *Steele*, a railroad company and the union representing its firemen negotiated several contract provisions that imposed a ceiling on the number of African American employees to be assigned to work within the bargaining unit and restricted altogether the access of African American workers to certain positions. Many unit employees were African American and were, because of their color, barred from membership in the union that was their bargaining representative. A lawsuit was brought against both the railroad and the union on behalf of a number of African American firemen who had been removed from their jobs because of the defendant's discriminatory agreement. The state courts ruled that the authority of the statutory bargaining representative to negotiate and modify the job rights of employees within the unit was "plenary" and dismissed the complaint as stating no cause of action.

The Supreme Court reversed the lower court's decision, striking down a bargaining agreement that discriminated against African American members of the bargaining unit. The Court found embedded in the principle of exclusive representation an implied obligation to represent employees in bargaining fairly and without hostile discrimination. It observed that the RLA had granted the union power to bargain for all firemen employed by the railroad, including the African American plaintiffs, and that the statute forbade the workers within the unit to bargain individually or to select a minority union to represent them. Since Congress could not have intended that a minority union be formed within the unit, the Court found an implied duty in the RLA to refrain from "hostile discrimination" against any minority groups within the bargaining unit and that race discrimination was "irrelevant and invidious" and therefore in violation of the RLA.

See also **Duty of Fair Representation; Railway Labor Acts.**

STEELWORKERS TRILOGY In these three decisions, the Supreme Court established principles that served to protect and strengthen grievance arbitration by limiting judicial participation in the process. These cases involved the United Steelworkers of America and its separate litigation with the American Manufacturing Company, Warrior Gulf and Navigation Company, and Enterprise Wheel and Car Corporation.

These cases clearly demonstrated that the arbitration was accepted by the courts as a desirable method for handling grievances during the life of the collectove bargaining agreement. The decisions also insulated the arbitration process from the review of the courts. Both the *United Steelworkers of America v. American Manufacturing* and the *United Steelworkers of America v. Warrior Gulf & Navigation* cases involved actions to enforce agreements to arbitrate; the *United Steelworkers of American v. Enterprise Wheel and Car* case involved an action to enforce an arbitration award. In *American Manufacturing,* the Supreme Court stated that courts must arbitrate even frivolous claims of arbitrability and should rule only on arbitrability questions and should not be involved in judging the merits of the grievance. The Court, in *Warrior Gulf & Navigation,* ruled that if doubts exist on arbitrability, they should be resolved in favor of arbitration, and that grievances are arbitrable unless specifically excluded by the contract. *Enterprise Wheel and Car* provided that courts should not review the merits of an arbitration award "so long as it draws its essence from the collective bargaining agreement. When the arbitrator's words manifest an infidelity to this obligation, courts have no choice but to refuse enforcement of the award."

Generally, the Steelworkers Trilogy helped clarify the important role of grievance arbitration in the American industrial relations system. Arbitration was identified as the preferable means for resolving disputes over the interpretation or administration of the contract. If the parties included an arbitration clause in their agreement, the Steelworkers Trilogy ensured that an arbitrator would be able to determine the arbitrability of the grievance, examine the merits of the case, and render a decision relatively free from interference by the judicial system. When a court is asked to determine the arbitrability of a dispute covered by federal law, the court is limited to deciding only whether the reluctant party agreed to arbitrate the grievance or agreed to grant the arbitrator the power to make the award rendered. Any doubts over whether the arbitration clause covers the asserted dispute should be resolved in favor of coverage. The issue of arbitrability involves the question of whether a particular dispute is properly subject to arbitration. It involves two aspects: (1) substantive arbitrability and (2) procedural arbitrability. Substantive arbitrability is a claim that the subject matter of a grievance is not arbitrable because there is no valid contract in force, because the contract does not deal with certain issues or the arbitration clause does not seem to include them, or because specific exclusions from the contract or the arbitration clause prohibit arbitration. Procedural arbitrability deals with claims that procedural requisites to arbitration have not been met. It includes arguments that there is not a proper grievant or that time limitations or other specified formalities have not been complied with. Under federal law, the Court has the jurisdiction to decide the question of substantive arbitrability unless the decision is expressly reserved by the collective agreement for the arbitrator.

There have been several challenges to arbitration awards since the *Enterprise Wheel and Car* decision. These cases have been successful on at least one of the following grounds: (1) lack of jurisdiction or authority for the award (i.e., the arbitrator was not authorized to make the award); (2) procedural unfairness or irregularity (i.e., where the award was obtained through corruption or fraud, or where the arbitrator was biased; (3) gross error or irrationality (i.e., cases where an arbitrator made an admittedly erroneous assumption of fact; made a capricious or unreasonable interpretation of the facts; or made an award which was totally baseless or without reason); (4) violation of public policy involves only a determination of the lawfulness of enforcing an award, not a review of the correctness of the arbitrator's interpretation of the contract public policy (i.e., courts would not enforce an arbitration award requiring discriminatory treatment; and (5) incompleteness, ambiguity, or inconsistency (i.e., where the award is defective in itself). Most courts, when confronted with a contract that is too incomplete, ambiguous, or inconsistent to enforce, would resubmit to the arbitrator for clarification or as opposed to amending the award.

The Supreme Court held that arbitration of grievances is the tradeoff for a no-strike agreement and is the preferred means of handling industrial disputes. It also directed that a lower court should set aside an arbitration award only if the arbitrator exceeds his or her jurisdiction. The courts are not permitted to vacate an award on the merits of the decision.

The legacy of the Steelworkers Trilogy, then, is the strong federal labor law policy favoring the submission of labor disputes to arbitration and enforcing the results of arbitration.

See also *Alexander v. Gardner-Denver;* **Grievance Arbitration; No-Strike Agreement; United Steelworkers of America.**

STOCK PURCHASE PLAN

See **Employee Stock Ownership Plan.**

STRIKE

A temporary, concerted withdrawal from work by a group of employees of an establishment or several establishments to express a grievance or to enforce demands affecting wages, hours, and working conditions. It is a "concerted" withdrawal from work, since it is the action of a group, and it "temporary" since the employees expect to return to work after the dispute is settled. Strikers consider themselves employees of the company with a right to return to the job once the dispute has been resolved.

Although strikes date back at least to the fourteenth century, the word "strike" was not commonly used in its modern sense in Great Britain until the late eighteenth century. Historians disagree about the dates of the early strikes in American labor history and which unions were involved. In the late eighteenth century, the strikes commonly mentioned are the New York Journeymen Tailors' Strike of 1786, the New York Printers' Strike of 1778, the Philadelphia Seamen's Strike of 1779, the New York Shoemakers' Strike of 1785, and the Philadelphia Printers' Strike of 1786.

The strike is the principal weapon available to labor unions in the event of deadlocked talks. Most of the state and local laws regarding strikes address public employee strikes; many attempt to define a strike, and some indicate the penalties which result from an illegal strike. On the federal level, the National Labor Relations Act (NLRA) protects the right of employees to engage in strikes and does so without any requirement that an impasse be reached before employees resort to a strike. Indeed, employees will be protected from retaliation if they strike even prior to negotiations—for example, to compel their employers to recognize the union as their bargaining representative. However, if a collective bargaining agreement has been in effect and negotiations for a successor agreement are expected, one rather technical limitation of strike rights exists. The union must provide the employer 60 days notice of its wish to amend the agreement, and 30 days later it must notify federal and state mediation services of the dispute. It must then refrain from striking for a 60-day period.

An employee's right to strike and picket is also protected under Section 7 of the Labor-Management Relations Act (LMRA) of 1947 (the Taft-Hartley Act) governing "concerted activities for the purpose of collective bargaining or other mutual aid or protection." This provision limits the use of injunctions, damage actions, and discipline in response to a strike. There are two types of "protected activities": "economic" strikes over disputed negotiation matters, and "unfair labor practice" strikes in response to an employer's unfair labor practices. An *unfair labor practice strike,* as opposed to an economic strike, refers to any strike resulting from an employer's bad faith bargaining. An employer has the right to have permanent replacements for economic strikers, but unfair labor practice strikers can only be temporarily replaced.

However, the right to strike is not absolute. Employers have the right to use such devices as injunctions and damage actions when the activity is unprotected. Activity becomes "unprotected" when the right to strike is partly or entirely limited by the labor contract, by public policy as established by the courts and the National Labor Relations Board (NLRB), and by statutory limitations. In addition, certain kinds of strike activity have been held to exceed the protections of the statute. Sit-down strikes (in which employee seek to control the employer's property from inside the workplace), partial strikes (in which employees decline only certain work), sabotage, and picket-line violence have all been found to exceed the protections of the NLRA.

Boycotts that affect employers other than the struck employer (i.e., "secondary employers") are covered by the NLRA's complex regulations governing "secondary boycotts." Pickets at a struck employer's premises may appeal to employees of other businesses who arrive to perform work "related to" struck work, encouraging them not to cross the picket line. It is illegal, however, for a union to go to a secondary employer's premises and encourage its employees to strike or refuse handling of struck merchandise (or otherwise coerce that secondary employer) in order to persuade it to apply pressure to the struck employer. In Congress' view, this tactic unduly embroils an outsider in the dispute. If the struck employer, however, arranges to have struck work performed by the second business, the secondary employer is no longer treated as an innocent outsider to the dispute. It has become an "ally," subject to direct picketing. [*NLRB v. Business Machine and Office Appliance Mechanics Conference Board, Local 459 (Royal Typewriter Co.)* (1955)]

Sympathy strikes are strike actions by a union in support of the objectives of another organization for the purpose of influencing the outcome of a dispute in another enterprise or a dispute in which the union has no direct or immediate interest and the possible benefits to itself from such a strike are indirect and remote. Absent a specific contractual limitation, sympathy strikes are protected activity. The sympathy striker is entitled to the legal status of the primary striker. Thus, when an employee honors the lawful picket line of economic strikers at their common place of business, only permanent replacement, as opposed to outright discharge, is permitted. Honoring an unlawful picket line, however, is not protected activity. Employees who do so may be terminated.

Discharging strikers is a major strike-related issue. "Discharge" means the employee has been terminated without a permanent replacement having been hired. Striking employees may not ordinarily be discharged for engaging in "protected activities," though strikers who engage in "unprotected activities" may be discharged. Discharge also may be lawful if strikers engage in serious misconduct during the strike (including verbal threats) that reasonably tend to intimidate others.

Strikes often end with a *back to work agreement*, which is the accord reached between an employer and a union representing the employees that establishes the terms and conditions governing the return of striking employees to work. Disputes involving back to work agreements are covered by federal and state laws on labor-management relations.

A *back to work movement* is an organized effort to compel striking employees to return to work. Employees opposed to the strike and the business community, sometimes with police assistance, participate in these efforts. Frequently the action is instituted by employers to persuade the workers to abandon the strike. Unions generally regard such efforts as union-busting.

Strikes have become less effective in recent years. The number of strikes involving at least 1,000 workers fell from about 425 in 1974 to only 31 in 1995, the fewest since the federal government started tracking such data in 1947. A changing economic situation and changing attitudes have created a difficult environment for unions, and most unions now view a general strike as a last-resort bargaining tactic. In most cases, the union faces a dilemma: it loses member confidence if it makes too many concessions during contract talks; on the other hand, if the union calls a strike, it threatens members' jobs by weakening the company and risks losing members' jobs to replacement workers.

Economic changes are also impacting the traditional industry-pattern contract negotiating process. When unions negotiate a base contract and benefits package with one company, they have traditionally insisted that other major corporations in that industry accept—or better—the terms agreed to by their competitors. The negotiation trend today has moved toward writing labor contracts that not only meet the needs and competitive requirements of individual companies but also the needs of their different operating units—and even separate plants—as well.

See also **Ally Doctrine; Boycotting; Collective Bargaining Agreement; Economic Strike; Pickets.**

STRIKE BENEFITS

STRIKE BENEFITS Payments from a labor union, usually a small portion of regular income, to employers during a strike. Many unions do not supply payments but distribute groceries and other types of aid to needy striking families.

See also **Labor Union.**

STRIKE FUND Money held by an international union or a local union for allocation during a strike to cover costs of matters such as strike benefits, legal fees, and publicity. Some international unions assess each member a small amount each month to support the fund. The amount of the fund often determines the staying power of the workers and, consequently, the success or failure of the strike. Strike funds are often designated in union financial statements as "emergency," "reserve," or "special funds."

See also **Strike Benefits.**

STRIKE NOTICE A notice advising the employer and filed with the Federal Mediation and Conciliation Service (FMCS) or appropriate state agency that the labor union has rejected the company's latest offer and a strike is pending. The National Labor Relations Act (NLRA) requires that, if a collective bargaining agreement exists between a labor union and the employer, the union may not call a strike until 60 days after it has notified the employer of its desire to modify or terminate the existing agreement. The union must also notify the FMCS within 30 days of notifying the employer. If the union strikes without obeying these rules, the strikers lose the rights granted to them by the NLRA.

The NLRA also requires a labor union representing health care institution employees to provide ten-day written notice to the employer and to the FMCS of its intention to go out on strike.

See also **Collective Bargaining Agreement; Federal Mediation and Conciliation Service; National Labor Relations Act.**

STRIKE REPLACEMENTS Individuals who are hired by the employer to replace striking employees. An employer has the right to continue to operate his business by replacing economic strikers. An employer is not required to re-employ a replaced economic striker when the strike is terminated. The National Labor Relations Board (NLRB) has recognized significant differences in the rights of economic strikers (those who seek some economic benefit or recognition of his union) as opposed to unfair labor practice strikers (those who seek, as one of their purposes, to protest an unfair labor practice of the employer).

The status of replacement workers and striking workers after a strike has been an issue before the NLRB and the courts beginning with *NLRB v. McKay Radio & Telegraph Co.* (1938). If an employer has bargained in good faith, the employer's only obligation is to place the returning economic strikers on a preferential hiring list. Today, the NLRB principle on strike replacements and reinstatement rights of striking employees generally provides that

1. In an unfair labor practice strike—one conducted in response to an employer unfair practice or a strike that becomes an unfair labor practice strike because of employer unfair actions during the strike— strikers are entitled to reinstatement when the striking employees offer to return to their jobs. The replacements must be laid off to make room for the returning strikers. Failure to return unfair labor strikers to work will result in a backpay order from the date of their offer to return. [*Pecheur Lozenge Co.* (1953)]
2. In an economic strike—a strike carried out to enforce economic demands—strikers' rights follow *Laidlow* (1968), which states that "economic strikers who unconditionally apply for reinstatement at a time when their positions are filled by permanent replacements (a) remain employees; (b) are entitled to full reinstatement upon the departure of replacements unless they have in the meantime acquired regular and substantially equivalent employment, or the employer can sustain his burden of proof that the failure to offer full reinstatement was for legitimate and substantial business reasons.
3. Following the beginning of a strike, an employer generally does not need to bargain over the wages, hours, and working conditions it establishes for striker replacements, regardless of the presence of a bargaining impasse.

The NLRB's *Laidlow* ruling followed the Supreme Court decisions in *NLRB v. Great Dane Trailers, Inc.* (1967) and *NLRB v. Fleetwood Trailers Co.* (1967). The Court in *Fleetwood* held that "if and when a job for which the striker is qualified becomes available, he is entitled to an offer of reinstatement." This right can be defeated only if the employer can show "legitimate and substantial business justifications." Thus, the employer is generally obligated to reinstate economic strikers who have not been permanently replaced, barring a "legitimate and substantial business justification" for not doing so. The NLRB principle has been variously applied in numerous cases coming before the board.

Legislation to protect the rights of striking employees and to restrict the employer's ability to hire permanent replacement workers has been introduced in several sessions of Congress, but thus far Congress has failed to act on these bills.

See also **Impasse; National Labor Relations Board;** ***NLRB v. MacKay Radio and Telegraph Co.*** **(1938)**.

STRIKEBREAKER

A person, not a regular employee, who accepts employment in a struck plant. He or she is an outsider brought in by employer to fill a job temporarily vacated by a striker. A strikebreaker is distinguished from a scab, an employee who continues to work during a strike. A strikebreaker may pretend to work, or may be a guard or an informer.

Often an employer attempts to break a strike by hiring outsiders, thus maintaining production and lowering the strikers' morale. The purpose of strikebreaking is to destroy an existing union. Strikebreaking is particularly effective when the issue in the strike is employer recognition of the union. Since labor unions must be recognized by employers as collective bargaining agencies before they can bargain in the employees' behalf over economic issues, employers have frequently used one of the following methods to break strikes: (1) they have fortified the plant with munitions and private plant police, the latter hired not to protect property against theft, fire, and the like, but for the purpose of intimidating workers who would strike; (2) they have hired professional strikebreakers; and (3) they broken down of the morale of strikers by instituting back to work movements.

See also **Collective Bargaining; Scab.**

STRUCTURAL UNEMPLOYMENT

See **Unemployment.**

SUBCONTRACTING

Taking a portion of a contract from a principal contractor or subcontractor and giving it to a subcontractor to do the work. Often companies "sublet" certain parts of the operation to contractors rather than having their own employees perform the work, frequently because the work can be performed more efficiently and with less expense by the subcontractor. Subcontracting occurs when one enters into a contract for the work with a person who has already contracted for its performance. The term "privatization" is used to refer to the subcontracting of public services to private industry. Services commonly privatized include, among others, building construction, janitorial services, and refuse collection.

Subcontracting worries labor union members when they could have performed the work themselves. When work is subcontracted, less work is available for members of the bargaining unit. As a result, unions have sought to limit the employer's flexibility to subcontract work.

In 1964, the U.S. Supreme Court ruled that management has a legal obligation to bargain on subcontracting. In this dispute, which involved the Fibreboard Papers Corporation and the United Steelworkers of America, the existing collective bargaining agreement was to expire in July 1959. When the union sought to establish a time and place for negotiating the renewal of the agreement, the employer responded that subcontracting the work would be more efficient and that it was therefore not necessary to negotiate a new contract. In July 1959, the company terminated the employees of its maintenance staff. The court held that the company was obligated to bargain with the union before making the decision to subcontract work that otherwise would have been performed by members of the bargaining unit.

A key point of the *Fibreboard Paper Products Corp. v. NLRB* (1964) decision is that the law does not forbid an employer from changing working conditions. Rather, the employer must first bargain with the union on the subcontracting decision. If an impasse is reached, the employer can make the change. The application of this doctrine has presented some serious problems for employers. Before making a change involving subcontracting, employers are obligated to bargain to an impasse. As a result, employers may have not been able to take immediate advantage of economic benefits that would have resulted from a change.

Bargaining was also required over economically motivated decisions to subcontract bargaining unit to an outside firm, the Court held, emphasizing that the subcontract did not alter the employer's basic operation but merely replaced existing employees with those of a contractor to do the same work under similar conditions. However, the Court limited its holdings "to the facts of the case" and said its ruling did not encompass other forms of subcontracting. [*Fibreboard Paper Products Corp. v. NLRB* (1964)]

Agreements negotiated between the unions and companies specify the conditions under which work may be contracted out. One such agreement reads, "Work usually performed by employees in this bargaining unit will not be contracted out if it will result in a layoff of the employees covered by this agreement." Subcontracting for the purpose of avoiding or evading the duty to bargain with a union is an unfair labor practice under the Labor-Management Relations Act of 1947 (the Taft-Hartley Act).

See also **Collective Bargaining Agreement; Labor-Management Relations Act of 1947.**

SUBSTANTIVE DUE PROCESS RIGHTS An absolute check on certain governmental action notwithstanding the fairness of procedures used to implement them. [*Love v. Pepersack* (1995)]

Broadly defined as the constitutional guarantee that no person shall be deprived of his life, liberty, or property, substantive due process is primarily concerned with protection from arbitrary and unreasonable governmental action. Equal protection is similar to substantive due process, however, equal protection is also available even when no liberty of property interest is at issue. If a state action discriminates against suspect classes or discriminates based on fundamental rights (essentially the same as liberty interests under substantive due process analysis), the government must have a compelling state interest to justify the discrimination.

In *Mugler v. Kansas* (1887), the U.S. Supreme Court had recognized that there were substantive limits to the powers of legislatures. Relying largely on the notion that persons and business should be "free" to negotiate on any basis they saw fit, the Court had by 1900 accepted the notion of "substantive due process" in the context of economic relations. The Court used this doctrine to invalidate much of the social legislation enacted by Progressives throughout the United States, including that which governed the workplace, as interference with the rights of parties to contract freely with each other, and thus violation of due process clauses of the Fifth and Fourteenth Amendments to the U.S. Constitution.

The Court's most stringent applications of substantive due process came in cases involving workplace reform laws. The judicial enforcement of the laissez-faire economic theory reached its high point in the case of *Lochner v. New York* (1905). There, the Court found a New York statute limiting a baker's work to 60 hours a week, or ten hours a day, to be an unconstitutional interference with the liberty of the employer and employee to enter into a contractual relationship, a liberty that was protected by the due process clause of the Fourteenth Amendment. Similarly, the Court struck down minimum wage laws for women in *Adkins v. Children's Hospital* (1923).

The Court applied *Lochner* to federal legislation as well. Congress had enacted the Erdman Act in 1907 to prohibit the so-called yellow dog contract in the railroad industry, both out of a realization that these contracts were inherently coercive and out of a concern over industrial unrest. The Court struck down the Erdman Act as unconstitutional in 1907 on the grounds that it interfered with the substantive due process of freedom to contract. Following this approach, the Court in *Hammer v. Dagenhart* (1918) and *Bailey v. Drexel Furniture Co.* (1923) struck down two Congressional efforts to enact a federal child labor statute.

In the years that followed, the Court retreated and finally rejected the *Lochner* approach. The Court sustained legislation regulating the number of hours that women could work, or that men could work in certain dangerous industries. Likewise, substantive due process was found not to preclude state legislation regulating business when the public interest was at stake. In *Nebbia v. New York* (1934), the Court declined to follow the *Lochner* approach by ruling that "a state is free to adopt whatever economic policy may reasonably be deemed to promote public welfare, and to enforce that policy by legislation adopted to this purpose." The Court, instead of expressly overruling *Lochner,* instead relaxed the standard of review it applied to socioeconomic legislation. In *United States v. Carolene Products Co.* (1938), the Court adopted a standard of "mere rationality" to challenges to the power of state government in the area of economic regulation. In other words, the Court said it would uphold such legislation if any known or reasonably inferable state of facts supported the legislature's judgment. The Court has followed this approach since that time.

The Court has continued to hold that the concept of due process of law can, in some circumstances, offer the individual protection from governmental action in areas not concerned with economic or property rights. Judicial use of substantive due process, however, began to focus on a different set of rights not expressly protected by the Constitution—a diverse group of claims that have been referred to as the "right of privacy."

The Fourteenth Amendment, as interpreted by contemporary courts, protects both the substantive and procedural rights of employees. There are several cases interpreting the principle that the Fourteenth Amendment imposes on governments the requirements to use fair procedures in deciding to deprive a person of a benefit such as employment. Substantive due process has occasionally been invoked as a source of a right of privacy. In *Eckman v. Board of Education of Hawthorn* (1986), a federal district court held that a school teacher had a substantive right to conceive and raise a child out of wedlock and may not be disciplined for doing so. And in *Stoddard v. School District No. 1, Lincoln County* (1977), a federal court held that the nonrenewal of a teacher's employment because of a lack of church attendance and the conduct of her personal life violated her constitutional privacy rights.

Some cases have interpreted the Fourteenth Amendment broadly regarding public employment. In *Hyde v. Jefferson Hospital Dist. No. 2* (1981), for example, a Louisiana federal district court held that a public hospital is required to afford substantive due process to an applicant for admission to a medical staff, that is, it is required to consider the applicants only on grounds that are reasonably related to the purpose of providing adequate medical care.

Substantive due process and equal protection issues frequently arise in state wrongful dismissal cases. The law of equal protection extends the influence of traditional substantive due process requirements in order to protect against classifications that impermissibly discriminate against individuals similarly situated. Any wrongful dismissal statute that limits claims or plaintiffs, classifies individuals as either protected under the statute or outside the statute's protections. These classifications must be analyzed to determine whether they discriminate against a protected class of persons or infringe upon a fundamental right.

The history of American employment law has been the history of adding legally recognized employee interests. Once a new category of interests is recognized, these interests are weighed against legitimate employer interests—either in a statutory formula or in individual cases. Formulating a standard for substantive fairness in wrongful dismissal legislation, for instance, requires a consideration of all the recognized interests. Employee interests are reinforced by societal interests in favor of certain types of conduct by employees. Opposing these interests are employer and societal interests favoring effective management of organizations. Free enterprise, the preference for regulating economic relations by market forces instead of by law, is a social value on the employer's side. The free enterprise value operates against intrusive legal regulation of discharge decisions. Balancing these opposing interests in a substantive fairness analysis requires at a minimum that employers use their power over the employment relation in a way that does not jeopardize important social policies, and at most that the employer's decisions meet objective criteria of rationality.

See also **Discrimination in Employment; Equal Protection; *Lochner v. New York* (1905); Protected Class; Wrongful Discharge; Yellow Dog Contract.**

SUCCESSOR EMPLOYER An individual or corporation purchasing a company or its stock, leasing a business, or forming a new company, or companies that merge or take over the operations of other companies inherit the predecessor's obligations under the National Labor Relations Act (NLRA). When a new owner purchases an entire going business and continues its operations, or when two firms merge to form a new enterprise, civil liability for violations of the rights of the employees of the "old business" will usually attach to the new entity. Despite changes in ownership or management, the successor is subject to the predecessor's obligations under the law regarding continuity in the workforce (the majority issue), continuity in the employing industry, continuity in the appropriateness of the bargaining unit, and the impact of a hiatus in operations. Although the courts have held that the substantive terms of a collective bargaining agreement may not be imposed on the new owner, the successor employer may be liable for a predecessor's unfair labor practices or may be compelled to arbitrate employee rights under the old contract.

Successorship clauses in union contracts provide that any change in the management of the organization may not invalidate the contract and that the new management must assume the contractual obligations of the predecessors. The legal obligations of the acquiring organizations with respect to such clauses have been addressed in three U.S. Supreme Court decisions: *John Wiley & Sons v. Livingston* (1964); *NLRB v. Burns International Security Services Inc.* (1972); and *Howard Johnson Co. v. Detroit Local Joint Executive Board* (1974). These decisions indicate that under certain conditions the successor employer has little legal responsibility.

When a union has secured bargaining rights for the employees of an employer, and perhaps has negotiated a bargaining agreement, the union naturally hopes to maintain the bargaining rights and the agreement if that employer should be replaced by a second employer. U.S. Supreme Court cases on the rights of a union in successorship situations have traveled a convoluted path reaching results that lend themselves to manipulation by a successor employer who wants to eliminate a union.

In its last landmark successorship case, *Fall River Dyeing & Finishing Corp. v. NLRB* (1987), the Supreme Court first held that where a majority of a firm's employees have worked for the firm's predecessor, there is a conclusive presumption of majority status even if the union was not recently certified, as the union had been in *Burns.*

The test for successorship, as enunciated in *Fall River,* is twofold: there must be substantial continuity between the two enterprises, and a majority of the successor's employees must have been employed by the predecessor. "Substantial continuity" was described as "whether the business of both employers is essentially the same; whether the employees of the new company are doing the same jobs in the same working conditions under the same supervisors; and whether the new entity has the same production process, produces the same products, and basically has the same body of customers."

The Court then held that the National Labor Relations Board (NLRB) was justified in finding substantial continuity in this case notwithstanding a business hiatus. The Court also approved the Board's "substantial complement" and "continuing demand" rules.

An employer's bankruptcy is another form of successorship situation, although the incumbent managers may remain, as the firm is controlled by the debtor-in-possession under supervision of the bankruptcy court. In *NLRB v. Bildisco & Bildisco* (1984), the Court addressed whether a debtor-in-possession may reject a collective bargaining agreement as it can other executory agreements, and whether unilateral rejection or modification violates the NLRA's duty to bargain requirement.

The Court held that a bankruptcy court should permit rejection of a collective bargaining agreement "if the debtor can show that the collective agreement burdens the estate, and that after careful scrutiny, the equities balance in favor of rejecting the labor contract." The Court then held that a collective bargaining agreement is not an "enforceable contract" under Section 8(d) of the NLRA from the time that the firm files a bankruptcy petition, and so a unilateral termination or modification cannot be prevented by the NLRB.

Bildisco was soon modified by Congress. The bankruptcy statute was amended to require court approval before a debtor can reject a collective bargaining agreement. Rejection should be allowed only if the union has refused the debtor's proposed contract modifications "without good cause" and if the balance of equities clearly favors rejection of the union contract.

See also **Collective Bargaining Agreement;** ***Fall River Dyeing & Finishing Corp. v. NLRB; Howard Johnson Co. v. Detroit Local Joint Executive Board; John Wiley & Sons v. Livingston*** **(1964); National Labor Relations Act;** ***NLRB v. Burns International Security Services, Inc.***

SUPERVISOR A person with management responsibilities, usually including the right to hire and fire or to recommend such action. Section 2(11) of the National Labor Relations Act (NLRA) defines the term supervisor as

> any individual having authority, in the interest of the employer, to hire, transfer, suspend, layoff, recall, promote, discharge, assign, reward, or discipline other employees, or responsibly to direct them, or to adjust their grievances, or effectively to recommend such action, if in connection with the foregoing the exercise of such authority is not of a merely routine or clerical nature, but requires the use of independent judgment.

Supervisory employees are excluded from coverage under the NLRA and the Civil Service Reform Act (CSRA). Section 14(a) of the NLRA allows supervisory employees to form units composed exclusively of supervisors, and the "employer may bargain voluntarily with such groups." The Labor-Management Relations Act of 1947 (the Taft-Hartley Act), however, expressly excludes "any individual employed as a supervisor" from its definition of "employee." The bargaining rights of supervisors, therefore, are not protected by the NLRA. Supervisors may join unions, but, per Section 14(a) of the NLRA , employers are not required to recognize unions of supervisors or bargain with a union that purports to represent them.

Congress, in considering Taft-Hartley, wanted to ensure that rank-and-file employees could unionize and choose their leaders free from undue influence by supervisors, but more important to ensure that supervisors—whether organized within a rank-and-file union or organized independently—would not ally or become accountable to employees whom they were charged to supervise and thereby compromise the undivided loyalty to the employer.

Since supervisors are excluded from the jurisdiction of the National Labor Relations Board, some state courts have ruled that the regulation of their economic weapons and bargaining rights are subject to state law. [*Safeway Stores, Inc. v. Retail Clerk Association* (1953)] More recently, however, the U.S. Supreme Court has held that state court injunctions against labor activities by supervisors are proper, unless preempted by federal labor law, only because they are consistent with Congress' primary motivation in the Taft-Hartley Act to relieve employers from any compulsion under the act and under state law to bargain with any union of supervisory employees. [*Hanna Mining Co. v. District 2, Marine Engineers* (1965)]

Section 7135(a)(2) of the CSRA allows the "renewal, continuation, or initial according of recognition of units of management officials or supervisors represented by labor organizations which historically or traditionally represent management officials or supervisors in private industry and which hold exclusive recognition for units of such officials or supervisors in any agency on the effective date of this chapter."

See also **Civil Service Reform Act; Labor-Management Relations Act; National Labor Relations Act.**

SUPPLEMENTAL UNEMPLOYMENT BENEFIT (SUB) PLANS Private plans providing compensation for wage loss to laid-off workers, usually in addition to public unemployment insurance payments. The automobile, glass, and steel industries have the highest percentage of these plans. SUB plans originated in 1955 as a compromise when the United Auto Workers demanded a guaranteed annual wage plan from Ford Motor Company. These plans are financed by employers.

See also **Unemployment Insurance.**

SUSPECT CLASSES See **Discrimination in Employment.**

SUSPENSION A disciplinary action less drastic than termination, usually resulting from an infraction or violation of company rules or policies. Part of the progressive discipline system, a suspension or "disciplinary layoff" frequently serves to warn the individual that a continuation of certain conduct will result in termination. A suspension results in loss of pay, and occasionally seniority, for a set period ot time. When discharged employees are reinstated by arbitrators without backpay, the result is similar to a suspension.

In several cases, a suspension has constituted unlawful discrimination against an employee when it resulted from filing charges or giving testimony:

- where an employee who had testified against the employer at an unfair labor practice proceeding was suspended, allegedly for violating established rules, but the rules were not enforced against other employees;
- where an employee was suspended for attempting to leave work to file a charge with the National Labor Relations Board (NLRB), despite an employer's normal practice of allowing employees to leave work for union business; and
- where an employer suspended a worker before he would provide testimony on the General Counsel's behalf at an NLRB hearing.

See also **Progressive Discipline; Seniority.**

SWEATSHOP A workplace where work conditions are substantially below accepted standards. Sweatshops are usually characterized by low wages, long hours, and an unsanitary work environment. Historically, sweatshops were often found in the garment industry. Recently, public awareness of third world sweatshop conditions has been aroused by broad media coverage of cases involving celebrity-endorsed products sold in the United States but apparently produced abroad under sweatshop conditions.

SWEETHEART CONTRACT A collective bargaining agreement usually between a racketeer head of a local union (which may or may not be a legitimate body) and a corrupt employer. Such an arrangement is advantageous to the employer because legitimate unions have difficulty organizing the shop and the employer pays less in wages and other benefits and contends with fewer restrictions. The union racketeer benefits through payoffs from the grateful employer or the dues collected from the employees or both. Sweetheart contracts are denounced by the AFL-CIO in its code of ethical practices.

See also **American Federation of Labor-Congress of Industrial Organizations; Labor Racketeering.**

SYMPATHY STRIKE A concerted work stoppage by employees not directly involved in a labor dispute to support the objectives of striking workers of another employer when the resolution of the dispute will not directly benefit the sympathy strikers.

See also **Strike.**

SYSTEMATIC DISCRIMINATION See **Discrimination in Employment.**

TAFT-HARTLEY ACT See **Labor-Management Relations Act of 1947.**

***TAMENY V. ATLANTIC RICHFIELD CO.* (1980)** *Tameny* is the first significant case in the development of California wrongful discharge law. This case articulated the principle that a tort action exists when an employer discharges an employee for reasons that violate public policy.

Gordon Tameny, a retail sales representative, sued his former employer, Atlantic Richfield Company (ARCO), alleging that ARCO had discharged him because he refused to participate in an illegal scheme to fix retail gasoline prices. Tameny sought recovery from ARCO, contending that the company's conduct in discharging him for refusing to commit a criminal act was tortious and subjected the employer to liability for compensatory and punitive damages under ordinary tort law principles. ARCO conceded that, under California law, an employee who has been discharged for refusing to perform an illegal act may recover from his former employer for "wrongful discharge." ARCO contended, however, that employees may seek only contractual remedies rather than those in tort. Contractual remedies are the rights a party may exercise on the breach of a contract. A remedy in tort (wrong) is a recovery for a private or civil wrong by a party, other than a breach of contract. The trial court accepted ARCO's argument and Tameny then appealed to the California Supreme Court.

The California Supreme Court first acknowledged case law recognizing that in the absence of contractual limitations, an employer enjoys broad discretion to discharge an employee. Nonetheless, the court held that an employee who refuses to obey an employer's demand to engage in criminal conduct and suffers damages as a result may maintain a tort action for wrongful discharge against that employer on the basis of public policy.

Therefore, the court found that Tameny was wrongfully discharged in violation of public policy.

To prove successfully a tort claim for wrongful discharge based on public policy, the employee is required to show that (1) the employer instructed the employee to engage in conduct constituting an illegal act; (2) the employee refused to follow these instructions; and (3) as a result of this refusal, the employee was discharged.

The *Tameny* case led the way for the development of two additional theories that limit the employment-at-will doctrine: the implied-in-fact covenant and the implied covenant of good faith and fair dealing. While California courts, like those in many states, continue to struggle with applying these theories, most courts have found the public policy concept to be relatively clear. Indeed, the public policy exception presents fewer problems of proof than the other exceptions to the employment-at-will rule.

See also **Employment-at-Will; Tort; Wrongful Discharge.**

TARDINESS Considered a form of absenteeism, tardiness is a lack of punctuality in arriving at the workplace. Sometimes it is defined as any absence of less than one-half day. Tardiness may, under proper circumstances, be a valid ground for discharge. However, a discharge allegedly for tardiness is discriminatory if an employee is discharged after his or her first offense of tardiness; where an employee is dismissed suddenly when he or she is two minutes late; or where no policy on tardiness was undertaken until after union activity began.

TEAMSTERS UNION See **International Brotherhood of Teamsters, Chauffeurs, Warehousemen, and Helpers of America.**

***TEAMSTERS V. U.S.* (1977)** The U.S. Supreme Court decision, which along with *United Airlines, Inc. v. Evans* (1977), was the first review of lower court decisions brought under Title VII of the Civil Rights Act of 1964 challenging seniority systems as discriminatory. In *Teamsters v. U.S.*, the U.S. Justice Department sued the Teamsters Union and

T.I.M.E.-D.C. Inc., alleging that the defendants had engaged in a pattern or practice of discrimination against African Americans and Hispanic Americans in hiring line drivers (over-the-road, long-distance drivers). The government claimed that minority employees of the company were given lower paying, less desirable jobs as servicemen or city drivers. Servicemen service trucks, unhook tractors and trailers, and perform other similar tasks. City drivers pick up and deliver freight within the immediate area of a particular terminal. The government further alleged that the seniority system established by the collective bargaining agreement between T.I.M.E.-D.C. and the International Brotherhood of Teamsters was racially discriminatory with respect to transfers and promotions.

Under the union contract, bargaining unit seniority determined the order in which employees were permitted to bid for jobs, were laid off, or were recalled from a layoff. A line driver's seniority took into account only the length of time he had been a line driver at a particular terminal. When transferring to a line driver's job, all employees forfeited all seniority accumulated in a previous position. Before the passage of the 1964 Civil Rights Act, African Americans and Hispanic Americans had been denied an equal opportunity to become line drivers. The government argued that employees should receive retroactive seniority dating to the time the employee was hired, as the seniority system locked in past discrimination. The labor union and company opposed retroactive seniority based on pre-act discrimination, because the company had granted seniority based on a bona fide seniority plan.

The federal district and appeals courts ruled for the government, but the U.S. Supreme Court reversed. The Court held the employer's seniority system to be bona fide because: (1) It applied "equally to all races and ethnic groups," i.e., the system equally discouraged all employees from transferring; (2) the placement of line drivers in a separate bargaining unit was found to be not only reasonable, but also in accord with the industry practice; and, (3) the "seniority system did not have its genesis in racial discrimination." The standard for determining when a seniority system has its "genesis in discrimination," however, remained unclear after the decision. In finding that the seniority system was "bona fide," the court found that it had complied with Title VII.

The Court, in *Teamsters,* also articulated the distinction between disparate impact discrimination and disparate treatment discrimination, a distinction that is still recognized. *Teamsters* involved a case of disparate impact discrimination, which is based on the unjustified exclusion caused by some hiring device that disproportionately disadvantages a group defined by race, color, religion, sex, or national origin, rather than disparate treatment, which requires that the plaintiff establish that the defendant acted intentionally to treat the plaintiff class or individual differently. Disparate impact claims involve job requirements which are "facially neutral" (they do not overtly discriminate). In these cases, however, it is not necessary for the plaintiff to prove discriminatory intent. Rather, if the plaintiff shows that an employment practice produces an adverse impact upon the protected class, a legal presumption of discrimination is raised, which the defendant must refute. The plaintiff, however, must prove that the acts of discrimination were more than isolated, accidental, or sporadic. The employer must then demonstrate the practice is a business necessity.

The Court also ruled that retroactive seniority may be an appropriate remedy for individuals who had been discouraged from applying for more desirable jobs because of the employer's well-known discriminatory policies. It declared that "an incumbent employee's failure to apply for a job does not totally prevent an award of retroactive seniority. Individual nonapplicants must be given an opportunity to undertake their difficult tasks of proving that they should be treated as applicants and therefore are presumptively entitled to relief accordingly."

See also **African Americans: Employment Issues; Civil Rights Act of 1964; Discrimination in Employment; Disparate Impact Discrimination; Disparate Treatment Discrimination; Hispanics: Employment Issues; Protected Class.**

TEMPORARY DISABILITY

An injury resulting in the temporary incapacity to perform work. The disability may be partial or total. Temporary partial disability means that the disabled worker has returned to work but is earning less than before and still has not reached maximum recovery. Temporary total disability means that the employee is totally disabled but is expected to recover fully and return to work.

Temporary disability insurance, sometimes referred to as cash sickness benefits, is a compulsory program providing weekly cash benefits measured by prior earnings, payable to workers during periods of sickness or injury incurred while engaged in nonwork connected activities. Benefits can also be paid to eligible unemployed workers who become sick or disabled while employed and for a disability due to pregnancy. It is different from health insurance, which aims to minimize the cost of medical and hospital care and provides benefits measured primarily by the cost of the services needed. It is also distinct from social security disability benefits (cash payments for long-term cases to a worker and his or her beneficiaries) and workers' compensation (both cash and service benefits for work-connected cases).

Under statutes enacted by California, Hawaii, New Jersey, New York, Puerto Rico, and Rhode Island, and by the federal government for railroad employees under the 1946 amendments to the Railroad Unemployment Insurance Act of 1938, benefits are provided over a limited period of time. New York, for example, provides benefits amounting to one-half the workers' average weekly wages, with a minimum of $20 and a maximum of $95 a week, for a maximum of 26 weeks; employees contribute one-half of 1 percent of the first $60 of weekly wages and the employer pays the balance of the cost.

See also **Social Security Act; Workers' Compensation.**

TEMPORARY EMPLOYEE A worker hired for a limited time only, frequently to meet a peak demand or to complete a special rush job. Such an employee is hired with the understanding that employment will end with the completion of the particular task. A temporary employee does not accumulate seniority.

A temporary employee may also be a worker supplied to a business by a temporary employment agency on a contractual basis and whose salary is paid by the agency. The temporary employment industry is described as the fastest growing industry in the economy. Under these arrangements, the payroll functions and the recruiting and selection functions—including reference checks, testing, and training in some cases—are handled by the temporary employment agency. The agency has full responsibility for the employee, although the employee works under the supervision of the employing company. Temporary workers have tended to be disproportionately female, young, and African American, and heavily concentrated in clerical and industrial help occupations.

See also **Employee; Independent Contractor; Seniority; Training.**

Temporary Layoff See **Layoff.**

Temporary Replacement Workers

Employers may not retaliate against employees for striking, but they may attempt to continue operations. To do so, employers may hire temporary replacement workers to perform the work of striking employees.

If strike replacements are hired only temporarily, commonly for the duration of the strike, the striking workers—even the economic strikers—are entitled to reinstatement upon making unconditional application. [*Pioneer Flour Mills v. NLRB* (1970)] The employer violates the National Labor Relations Act (NLRA) if it discriminates against these employees by requiring them to appear for an interview or to submit applications as new employees. [*Spencer Auto Electric Inc.* (1947); *Philanz Oldsmobile, Inc.* (1962)]

In terms of voting in a collective bargaining election conducted during the strike, the eligibility of economic strikers and unfair labor practice strikers differs—as does the eligibility of their replacements. While both economic and unfair labor practice strikers are entitled to vote (whether or not the employer has purported to replace them), this privilege expires for the economic striker if the election is conducted more than 12 months after the beginning of the strike as provided in Section 9(c)(3) of the NLRA.

In the Supreme Court case *NLRB v. Brown Food* (1965), a strike was called against one employer in a multiemployer bargaining unit, and the other employers in the unit locked out their employees in order to lessen the effectiveness of the whipsaw strike and preserve a united bargaining front. When the struck employer chose to continue operating with temporary replacements, the other employers also reopened with temporary replacements rather than their locked out employees. The U.S. Supreme Court overruled the National Labor Relations Board's finding of illegality and held that the use of temporary replacements by the nonstruck employers violated neither Section 8(a)(1) nor 8(a)(3) of the NLRA. The Court appeared to hold that both sections require proof of antiunion animus (that is, the desire to evade bargaining, destroy the union, or penalize the employees for bargaining) or of employer conduct that is "demonstrably so destructive of employee rights and so devoid of significant service to any legitimate business end that it cannot be tolerated consistently with the Act." Here, the impact of the temporary replacement was "comparatively slight" (over and above the already lawful lockout), and it was "reasonably adapted to achieve legitimate business ends or to deal with business exigencies."

See also **Employee; Lockout; Multiemployer Bargaining; National Labor Relations Act; Reinstatement; Strike; Unfair Labor Practice; Whipsawing.**

TENURE A form of job security under which employment is continued until retirement, barring special circumstances such as dismissal for cause or financial exigency. Tenure is generally acquired through seniority and satisfactory job performance over a period of time.

Tenure is achieved after a specified probationary period has been served. An individual with tenure is assured continuous employment and can be terminated only because he or she has reached the mandatory retirement age, because of unusual financial exigencies, or for just cause. In the case of termination for just cause, the employee is protected by due process.

Customarily, tenure is confined to employees in the education system, although civil service employees also have a form of tenure. In the public service, security of tenure is required to deal with factors such as the danger of making employment contingent upon factors other than the employee's performance. Meeting this threat was precisely the aim of the "security of tenure" advocated by the early civil service reformers and implied in the tradition of "merit system" laws.

Upon the termination of an employment, the law implies, in the absence of an agreement to the contrary, that the employee will discontinue the use of all property of his former employer, returning it wherever possible.

Where a discharge violates only the public policy of a state other than the forum state, and such other state does not recognize a public policy exception to the general rule that an employee is dischargeable at will, an employee may not bring an action for wrongful discharge.

See also **Civil Service; Job Performance; Job Security; Retirement; Seniority.**

TERMINATION The severing of an employee's relationship with an employer. At common law the right of the employer to terminate the employment is unconditional and absolute.

The traditional American common law rule of employment-at-will states: unless a definite period of services is specified, hiring is presumed to be at will, meaning that an employer has the right to discharge at any time, without notice, for good or bad reasons, or for no reason at all. An employer's otherwise unfettered right to discharge at will can be limited, however, by statute, contract, and case law.

Labor separations, those terminations that occur at the will of the employer, without prejudice to the worker, include discharges and layoffs. Discharges and layoffs may be due to a lack of business, technical changes, or an interruption of the flow of parts or materials to the job. A quit is a voluntary termination or resignation from employment initiated by the employee. Although the right to discharge an employee depends on the nature of the employment and the terms of the contract, as a general rule, an employer has the power to discharge an employee, even though the discharge constitutes a breach of the contract of employment.

Employers and employees can also agree to alter an at-will relationship by fixing a definite term of employment or by establishing some grounds upon which either or both parties may sever the employment relationship. A claim that the employment termination breached an express or an implied-in-fact contract may be based on a number of sources including employee handbooks, policy statements, oral representations, and a course or pattern of dealing with the employee—the "totality of the parties' relationship."

Commonly, individual employees acting alone lack the leverage with their employer to bargain for job security. Some employees, therefore, find it advantageous to form labor unions in order to strengthen their bargaining positions. Unions, in turn, typically bargain for contracts that contain "just cause" provisions, which limit the employer's right to terminate employees. Where an employment contract exists, whether it is an individual employment contract or a collective bargaining agreement, an employer is bound to adhere to the terms of that contract.

In various circumstances, a claim for a breach of an employment contract resulting in termination of the employment is governed by the law of a particular state, such as the state with the most significant contacts with the case, the state in which the employee was hired, or the state in which the employee was employed. A tort claim on the termination of an employment relationship is not necessarily limited by state laws on contract claim. State statutory law has been held to govern a tort claim, such as the state with the most significant contacts with the case. One such tort claim is the "intentional infliction of emotional distress." Under this theory, the plaintiff claims that, the employer's actions are so extreme and outrageous as to go beyond all possible bounds and to be regarded as atrocious, and utterly intolerable in a civilized society. Some examples of this would be where an employer allegedly launched a campaign of outrageous and harassing conduct, including purported false and defamatory claims of theft and various alleged threats that are "outside the scope and normal risks of employment."

A second tort claim, defamation and invasion of privacy, may arise where the plaintiff claims injury by false adverse post-employment references, or by loose investigative procedures, with accompanying gossip, during a pre-termination investigation. In either event, the plaintiff claims on this theory that statements made or distributed in connection with an employment termination are false and injure the discharged employee by making re-employment difficult.

The courts and legislatures have expanded recognized employee interests in the following ways. First, when the reason for termination is based on a racial, religious, gender, or age characteristic or a mental or physical disability, or when it is based on certain conduct, legislatures have said that the termination is at least prima facie illegal. Remedies are available to employees terminated for these reasons, unless the employer can offer overriding justification. Second, termination by a public employer is prima facie illegal when the reason for the termination is conduct within constitutional guarantees against government interference with free speech, association, privacy, and religion. To escape liability, a government employer must offer legally adequate justification to escape liability. Third, when the reason for the discharge is a tort, unless the employer can offer justification. Fourth, when the employer has promised that it will terminate only for certain reasons, or only after following certain procedures, the employee's expectations created thereby are protected by enforcing the employer's promise in a common law breach of contract lawsuit. If the employer is the government, its promises may be enforced under the constitutional guarantee against governmental deprivation of property without due process. Fifth, when a private sector employer acts in bad faith, for reasons extraneous to workplace management, or to deprive an employee of compensation, a common law action for breach of an implied covenant of good faith and fair dealing may exist.

There are several major federal laws which limit an employer's right to discharge: the National Labor Relations Act (prohibits discharge for union activity, protected concerted activity, or filing charges or giving testimony under the Act); the Fair Labor Standards Act (FLSA) (prohibits discharge for exercising rights guaranteed by minimum wage and overtime provisions of the FLSA); the Occupational Safety and Health Act (OSHA) of 1970 (prohibits the discharge of employees in reprisal for exercising rights under OSHA); Title VII of the Civil Rights Act of 1964 (prohibits discharge based on race, color, religion, sex, or nation origin and reprisals for exercising Title VII rights); Age Discrimination in Employment Act of 1967 (prohibits age-based discharge by private employers and the federal government of persons between the ages of 40 and 70 and reprisals for exercising statutory rights); the Employee Retirement Income Security Act of 1974 (ERISA) (prohibits discharge of employees in order to prevent them from attaining vested pension rights); the Vietnam Era Veterans' Readjustment Assistance Act (provides protection, for a limited period, against discharge, without just cause of returning service people); Consumer Credit Protection Act (prohibits discharge of employees because of the garnishment of wages for any one indebtedness); and the Civil Service Reform Act of 1978 (prohibits removal of federal service employees except "for such cause as will promote the efficiency of the service").

The National Conference of Commissioners of Uniform Laws has drafted a proposed Model Employee Termination Law, and hearings have been conducted on this proposal. Under the law, employees would be protected from "unjust dismissal" from employment and employers would benefit by avoiding trials on a variety of tort and contract theories. The Conference, which drafts laws for consideration by the 50 states and the District of Columbia, has been working on the proposed law for several years. Although the Conference's work is advisory only, it does enjoy some influence among state legislators.

See also **Age Discrimination in Employment Act; Civil Service Reform Act; Collective Bargaining Agreement; Common Law: Emploument Doctrines; Consumer Credit Protection Act; Employee Handbook; Employee Retirement Income Security Act of 1974; Employer-Employee Relationship; Employment Contract; Employment-at-Will; Fair Labor Standards Act; Job Security; National Labor Relations Act; Vietnam Era Veterans Readjustment Act.**

TERMINATION PAY

See **Severance Pay.**

TEST Any device or questionnaire, written or oral, for the purpose of measuring a person's abilities, interest, aptitude, and other qualities for the purpose of hiring, promotion, or for special training. The use of objective tests in employment decisions remains one of the most controversial areas of employment discrimination law, because these tests generally show average numerical score differentials among African American, Hispanic, and European American test takers.

The Supreme Court in *Griggs v. Duke Power Co.* (1971) established the principle that employers must prove the job relatedness of any testing device that operates to exclude a group covered by Title VII of Civil Rights Act of 1964. Once the plaintiff establishes a prima facie case showing the disparate impact of the test, the burden shifts to the defendant to demonstrate the validity of the device. The tests involved in *Griggs* were the Bennett and Wonderlic aptitude tests, which had a disproportionate impact on the basis of race.

One of the goals of Title VII is to ensure that if testing is used, it is not used as a guise for discrimination. An employer who wishes to discriminate, for example, could construct a testing device that would discriminate against minorities in favor of whites. For this reason, the Equal Opportunity Commission insists that the tests be valid and that there be a correlation between high scores on the test and good job performance. However, any adverse effect on the basis of race, gender, or national origin is irrelevant so long as the employer can establish the validity of the examination. The problem for employers is that the validity of the test cannot be established prior to litigation.

Section 106 of the Civil Rights Act of 1991 prohibits so-called race-norming, whereby test scores are adjusted or used differently according to the test taker's race or ethnicity. Race-norming had its most widespread application in the use of the General Aptitude Test Battery (GATB) by state-administered offices of the U.S. Employment Service. This test is a general aptitude test developed by the federal government and used for vocational counseling and job referral for several public and private sector jobs. African American job applicants score significantly lower on the test, on average, than European Americans. Therefore, the use of unadjusted GATB scores for job placement and referral may lead to disproportionately greater job opportunities for white applicants.

See also **African Americans: Employment Issues; Civil Rights Act of 1964; Civil Rights Act of 1991; Discrimination in Employment; *Griggs v. Duke Power Co.*; Equal Employment Opportunity Commission; Hispanics: Employment Issues.**

Time and Motion Study

See **Scientific Management.**

Title VII

See **Civil Rights Act of 1964.**

Title IX of the Education Amendments of 1972

Prohibits sex discrimination in any education program or activity that receives federal financial assistance. Educational institutions covered by the act include "any public or private preschool, elementary or secondary school, or any institutional, professional, or higher education." Title IX does not cover religious and military schools, social fraternities or sororities, voluntary youth service organizations, and father-son or mother-daughter activities.

In 1984, the U.S. Supreme Court ruled in *Grove City College v. Bell* (1984) that federal tuition grants to college students did not mean that Title IX covered all the institution's programs except the school's financial aid office. This narrow interpretation limited the enforcement of Title IX only to those educational programs and activities directly receiving federal funds. The Civil Rights Restoration Act of 1988 was enacted to "restore the . . . broad . . . institution wide application" of Title IX.

See also **Civil Rights Restoration Act of 1988; Sex Discrimination in Employment.**

Tort

A civil wrong. The elements for recovery under any tort theory in an employment case are duty (the employer's duty to act in a nonnegligent manner toward the employee), breach of the duty, proximate cause, and damages. Although many aspects of modern employment law differ greatly from earlier common law rules, the tort consequences of the employment relationship still closely follow traditional common law doctrines. In particular, liability principles of employment law today are substantially based on the common law of master and servant. The relation of master and servant was said to exist where one person, for pay or other valuable consideration, enters into the service of another and devotes to him his personal labor for an agreed period. These rules remain extremely important and govern several tort actions, including the liability of an employer for the torts committed by an employee within the scope of employment. Generally, a master is liable for the torts of a servant when the servant commits a tort against a third party while acting within the scope of employment (the doctrine of respondent superior). The term "employer" has largely displaced the term "master" in statutes and case law, and the terms are now used interchangeably.

Traditionally, employers have had wide discretion over all conditions of employment, because the employer owns the property and the business and is therefore entitled to decide the means of operation and employee conduct in the workplace. Employer negligence is generally alleged under two theories: negligent hiring and negligent retention. Negligent hiring occurs when the employer knew or should have known of the employee's unfitness before the employee was hired. In this instance, the issue of liability focuses on the adequacy of the employer's preemployment investigation into the employee's background. Negligent retention occurs when employer becomes aware or should have become aware of problems with an employee during his or her employment that indicated unfitness. In this case, the employer may be negligent if it fails to take further action, such as investigating, discharging, or reassigning the employee.

Several other negligence claims arise within the employer-employee relationship. *Negligent entrustment* claims arise when an employer assigns an employee to operate equipment (such as an automobile) without investigating whether the employee is fit or capable doing so. *Negligent supervision* claims contend that an individual was harmed due to the employer's failure to supervise the employee adequately. Unlike theories of negligent hiring and negligent retention, the theory of negligent supervision is similar to the respondeat superior doctrine, because it relied upon a connection to the employer's premises or property. An employer is under a duty to exercise reasonable care to control its employees acting outside the scope of their employment if the employees are on the employer's premises or using the employer's property. Several jurisdictions have recognized a separate tort category known as the *negligent infliction of emotional distress.* An employer could be liable for an employee's foreseeable illness or bodily harm if the employer should have realized that its conduct involved an unreasonable risk of causing emotional distress. Emotional disturbance alone, without bodily harm or other compensable damage, is not ground for a successful suit. A person is liable for *negligent misrepresentation* if, in the course of his business, profession, or employment, he supplies false information for the guidance of others in their business transactions and is liable for financial loss caused to them by their justifiable reliance upon the information, if he or she fails to exercise reasonable care or competence in obtaining or communicating the information.

Employers can also be liable in a tort to their employees. The number of conditions subject to state regulation has increased as the identity and relationship of the workers changes and new issues arise. Sexual harassment as a social matter has arisen because of new working relationships and a new societal ethos. Also, the range of employee interests deemed worth protecting through legislative action or litigation will likely continue to expand. The privacy of employment records and the right to be free of employer interference with off-work activities are examples of employee interests that have been asserted only recently.

Some of the specific grounds employees have asserted against employers include

- Breach of an express or implied agreement.
- Breach of a covenant of good faith and fair dealing, meaning that neither party to a contract may do anything that injures or interferes with the rights of the other to enjoy benefits of their employment bargain.
- Defamation, a false statement about the plaintiff published to a third person that damages the plaintiff's reputation, a situation that frequently occurs if a discharged employee claims that his former employer gave unfavorable references to prospective employers.
- Intentional infliction of emotional distress. The plaintiff is required to prove that: (a) the defendant acted intentionally or recklessly, (b) the conduct was extreme and outrageous, (c) the actions caused the plaintiff emotional distress, and (d) the emotional distress suffered by plaintiff was severe, which covers egregious conduct such as a calculated campaign of harassment by supervisors.
- Invasion of privacy, which encompasses four theories: unreasonable intrusion upon an individual's solitude, public disclosure of private facts, false light, and misappropriation of an individual's likeness. Many state courts have held that discharging or disciplining employ-

ees in violation of privacy rights can give rise to claims for wrongful termination or for the tort of invasion of privacy.

- Fraud and misrepresentation. The elements of fraud are misrepresentation, knowledge of falsity; intent to defraud, justifiable reliance upon the defendant's representation, and resulting damage.

See also **Common Law; Jurisdiction; Sexual Harassment.**

TOTAL QUALITY MANAGEMENT (TQM)

Understood as a program, process, methodology, or management strategy. As a management strategy, TQM redefines the purpose of work in terms of customer satisfaction and provides feedback to continuously improve the process by which work is performed in order to achieve this purpose. It also sees every employee in every function at every level as a learner with the responsibility of continually discovering new and better ways to perform his or her job.

TQM is designed to improve the quality of work life, the product, and customer support while reducing the cost of doing business. The key to TQM is the redistribution of power, responsibility, and accountability from the few at the top of the organizational hierarchy to the entire workforce. In the United States, the TQM movement was prompted, beginning in the late 1970s, by foreign trade competition, successive recessions, deregulations, the trade deficit, low productivity, downsizing, and increased consumer awareness.

TQM involves continuous improvement in products and processes to meet the needs of customers. The common themes of all TQM programs are a focus on the customer, continuous improvement based on measurements, preventing rather than detecting errors, top management commitment and involvement, a strategic business focus on quality, and employee involvement.

See also **Quality of Work Life; Management.**

TRADE UNIONS

See **Labor Unions.**

TRAINING Systematic instruction and programs of activities and learning for the purpose of acquiring skills for particular jobs.

National efforts to provide training for the disadvantaged, displaced workers, youth, hardcore unemployed, minority groups, and women, among others, have been authorized by legislation such as the Manpower Development and Training Act of 1962, Comprehensive Employment and Training Act of 1973, and the Job Training Partnership Act of 1982. Current training efforts are directed at combating skill obsolescence by upgrading and developing worker skills to meet global competition and high-technology requirements and to adjust to the movement from a manufacturing to a service economy.

See also **Job Training Programs, Federal.**

TRILOGY See **Steelworkers Trilogy.**

TROUBLED EMPLOYEE An individual with personal or work-related problems. The troubled employee's problems are generally more frequent and serious than those of the "normal" employee—higher rates of absenteeism and tardiness, more accidents, inferior work, low productivity, and interpersonal conflict. Alcoholism, drug abuse, emotional or mental illness, and marital and financial problems are some of the factors contributing to poor job performance of troubled employees. The term is often used synonymously with "problem employee."

See also **Employee Assistance Programs**.

TRUSTEESHIP See **Union Trusteeship.**

TURNOVER The rate at which employees move into and out of employment, usually expressed as the number of accessions and separations during a given period. Monthly turnover rates, by industry and by selected states and regions, are compiled by the Bureau of Labor Statistics.

UNAUTHORIZED STRIKE A strike that does not have the approval of the labor union. An unauthorized strike is also called a wildcat, illegal, quickie, or an outlaw strike. These strikes are unprotected activities where the strikers are essentially usurping the collective bargaining function from the union.

When employees have selected an exclusive representative to bargain with their employer, concerted activity on the part of a minority of employees, not authorized by the union, is commonly held unprotected. Although the activities themselves—concerted activity for mutual aid—fall within the literal coverage of Section 7 of the National Labor Relations Act (NLRA), they have been viewed as inconsistent with the philosophy of exclusive representation embodied in the NLRA. Control over bargaining and the use of economic force in this regard should be centralized in the union.

Professor Harry Shulman of Yale University, an umpire in a case involving Ford Motor Company, summarized the effects of a wildcat strike: "An illegitimate strike is a serious blow against the union itself. It manifests a lack of confidence in the union. It mars the union's efforts to achieve compliance by the company. It weakens the union's bargaining power in future negotiations. The illegitimate strikers must be told without equivocation that they are fighting the union as well as the company."

Despite statutory prohibition of unauthorized strikes, the courts have restricted whom the employers may hold liable for monetary damages. Section 301 of the Labor Management Relations Act of 1947 does not authorize lawsuits for damages against individual employees who engage in a wildcat strike without union sanction. [*Complete Auto Transit, Inc. v. Reis* (1981)]

Unauthorized strikes are not always unlawful. For instance, an unauthorized strike by employees at a nursing home was protected because the strikers were not attempting to bargain with the employer and the resulting inconvenience was minor. [*East Chicago Rehabilitation Center, Inc.* (1982)]

See also **Collective Bargaining; Concerted Activity; Labor-Management Relations Act; National Labor Relations Act.**

UNDEREMPLOYED Working in a job that does not fully use or develop one's abilities or that is beneath one's skill level.

UNDUE HARDSHIP See **Civil Rights Act of 1964.**

UNEMPLOYMENT The state of being not employed or lacking employment. Under the Current Population Survey (CPS) of the Bureau of Labor Statistics, persons are considered unemployed who are (a) engaged in some specific job-seeking activity (going to the Employment Service, applying with an employer, answering a want-ad, being listed on a labor union or a professional register) within the past four weeks, (b) they were waiting to start a new job within 30 days, or (c) they were waiting to be recalled from a layoff. In all cases, for an individual to be considered unemployed, he or she must be currently available for work.

The CPS definition of unemployed does not include passive or inactive work seekers who would be looking for work but believe that no work is available. If these inactive work seekers have made no effort to find work in the past four weeks, they are not considered part of the current labor force. Persons holding a job but not at work during the survey due to illness, vacation, leave of absence, bad weather, or strike are now classified as employed.

The CPS identified three categories of unemployment: cyclical, hard-core, and structural. Cyclical unemployment means the loss of work resulting from periodic fluctuations of the economy. In the past, the impact on employment of cyclical economic fluctuations was far greater than that due to seasonal, technological, or other factors in the economy. (Seasonal unemployment is due to the seasonal variations in the need for labor. Agricultural workers, lumber workers, and some construction workers are unemployed only for a certain period each year because of weather conditions.)

The hard-core unemployed are those who can work and are willing to work but are unable to obtain employment, even during periods when labor is in short supply. These people are usually unemployable because of mental or physical disabilities, lack of education or suitable skills, inability to relocate, or lack of information about the job market.

Structural unemployment is that caused by changes in the structure of the economy, such as the emergence of new industries and the decline of older industries, the growth of automation, relocation of industry, and foreign competition. These changes cause mismatches between the changing character of the demand for labor and the skills and education of the available supply of labor. Thus, imbalances arise between geography and skill: the jobs are in a different location than the qualified workers needed to fill them. If wages were completely flexible and if costs of occupational or geographic mobility were low, market adjustments would quickly eliminate this type of unemployment. Among the solutions advanced to eliminate structural unemployment are the creation of new job opportunities, retraining, and relocation allowances for dislocated workers. Structural unemployment also refers to sociological factors such as discrimination against workers on the basis of age, sex, or race.

Generally, the pace of economic recovery following the recession of the early 1990s has been insufficient to dramatically reduce the number of persons who have been unemployed for more than a half year. In fact, it took 15 months after the recession officially ended for long-term unemployment to decrease slightly—twice as long as it took after the prior two major recessions. In addition, the long-term jobless of the nineties were more likely to be of prime working age and less likely to be young than they were in past. They were also far less likely to return to the same jobs when the economy improved.

See **Seasonal Employment.**

UNEMPLOYMENT COMPENSATION The terms "unemployment insurance" and "unemployment compensation" are used interchangeably. They are programs that provide cash benefits or income to individuals who lose their jobs through no fault of their own. A 26-week benefit period is set under most state laws. Some states, such as Massachusetts and California, have extended unemployment compensation to domestic partners.

The federal-state social insurance program was established by Titles III, IX, and XII of the Social Security Act of 1935 to provide cash benefits to individuals who incur financial loss caused by involuntary unemployment. Unemployment insurance (UI) funds are derived from employer payroll taxes levied by both the federal government (to defray administrative costs) and states (for regular UI benefits). The taxing provisions under Title IX were transferred to the Internal Revenue Code by the Federal Unemployment Tax Act (1939).

Adjusted for inflation, the average weekly benefit has declined by 12 percent from 1971 to 1990. The maximum duration of benefits has been significantly reduced since the 1970s, and benefit payments—tax-free until 1979—are now fully subject to federal income taxes.

Unemployment insurance may increase joblessness because workers are more likely to become unemployed and remain so if they have a cushion to fall back upon. Also, firms may be able to save money by temporarily laying off workers, who will not switch employers because unemployment insurance tides them over until they are recalled to work.

See also **Social Security Act.**

UNFAIR LABOR PRACTICE

Section 7 of the National Labor Relations Act (NLRA) establishes the basic rights of employees to organize and participate in "concerted activities." Section 7 rights are protected through the prohibition of activities by employers and unions that are deemed unfair labor practices. Section 8 of the NLRA lists the employer-union unfair labor practices under federal law.

Employer unfair labor practices include:

1. Interference with employee rights protected under the NLRA.
2. Domination of unions
3. Discrimination against employees for union or concerted activities
4. Retaliation against employees for invoking their rights under the NLRA
5. Refusal to bargain with a majority representative of the employees

The union unfair labor practices include:

1. Restraining or coercing employees or employers in the exercise of their statutory rights
2. Causing an employer to unlawfully discriminate against an employee
3. Refusing to bargain with an employer
4. Striking, inducing others to strike, and threatening, coercing, or restraining any person for the objects of forcing an employer or self-employed person to join a union or enter into a hot-cargo contract,

forcing any person to stop doing business with another person (a secondary boycott), forcing another employer to bargain with a union not certified as bargaining agent, or forcing an employer to assign work to a particular union, trade, or craft (a jurisdictional strike)
5. Requiring employees covered by union security agreements to pay excessive or discriminatory union fees
6. Causing an employer to pay for services not to be performed (featherbedding)
7. Engaging in recognitional or organizational picketing where (a) another union is lawfully recognized as bargaining agent, (b) a valid election has been conducted within the preceding one year, or (c) the picketing is conducted without an election petition being filed within a reasonable period of time

The National Labor Relations Board (NLRB) has the duty of preventing unfair labor practices by both employers and employees. It has the exclusive jurisdiction to determine whether or not an unfair labor practice has been committed, subject to judicial review. If the NLRB finds violations, it may issue cease and desist orders. It is also empowered by the amended NLRA to petition the appropriate federal court of appeals for enforcement of its orders after it has found an unfair labor practice to exist.

See also **Cease and Desist Order; Featherbedding; Jurisdiction; Hot Cargo Agreement; National Labor Relations Act; National Labor Relations Board; Secondary Boycott; Union Security Clause.**

UNION MEMBERSHIP, RIGHTS OF Protection that may be available to union members in relation to both their employers and their labor union. Nearly all rank-and-file employees in private U.S. businesses of any substantial size are protected by federal law against antiunion discrimination. The Railway Labor Act applies to the railroad and airline industries. The National Labor Relations Act (NLRA) applies to all other businesses whose operations affect interstate commerce in any way. Separate federal statutes protect federal employees. About 30 of the 50 states have enacted statutes ensuring the right to organize on the part of some or most of the state and municipal employees. However, the NLRA is by far the most significant legislation protecting private sector employees. For example, it comprehensively prohibits antiunion discrimination.

Administrative and judicial decisions interpreting the statute have been generous in expanding the substantive rights of unions.

The bill of rights for union members, as contained in the Labor-Management Reporting and Disclosure Act of 1959 defines certain rights held by union members and grants the district courts jurisdiction to redress any violation of those rights. It imposes reporting requirements and allows the U.S. Department of Labor to sue in federal district court to enforce those requirements. It permits either the U.S. Department of Labor or a union member to sue to enforce its provisions on trusteeships and allows the department to sue in federal district court to challenge improperly held union elections. Finally, it allows lawsuits by union members in any federal district court for relief against union representatives who have violated the fiduciary responsibilities imposed on them by the statute.

Rules may restrict membership to persons engaged in, or qualified to perform, the tasks of a specific occupation. Most of the older restrictions, such as the closed shop, eligibility only of offspring or other relatives of members, and race, have been made illegal by statute. However, several union constitutions still prohibit membership to employers, Fascists, Communists, and other specified groups.

See also **National Labor Relations Act; Railway Labor Act; Labor-Management Relations Act; Union Trusteeship.**

Union Organizing

The selection of representatives for collective bargaining through elections conducted by the National Labor Relations Board (NLRB) and preelection activities of employers and unions.

The National Labor Relations Act (NLRA) guarantees employees' right to engage in union organizing activities. This right encompasses the right of union officials to discuss organization with employees and the right of employees to discuss organization among themselves or to act in support of a union including distributing union literature. This right is a fundamental right guaranteed by Section 7 and cannot be waived by the employees.

The primary task for the labor union is to convince a majority of the voting members in the bargaining unit to vote for union representation in the upcoming election. In an organizational campaign, unions and employers are concerned with union attempts to surmount obstacles to communications with employees, union efforts to protect adherents in the workplace, the tactics that can be employed, and the circumstances under which recognition can be compelled.

Employees have the right to self-organize and to form and join unions, and an employer may not restrict that right unless it can demonstrate that a particular restriction is necessary to maintain discipline or production. Employees are generally entitled to speak to one another on subjects pertaining to union organizing, if it does not interfere with their work, and an employer's lawful no solicitation rule cannot bar such discussion.

Nonemployees have no inherent right of access to employers' premises for the purposes of union activities. An employer is entitled to bar nonemployee organizers from his property, provided they have reasonable access to employees outside of the workplace. Moreover, an employer need not accommodate nonemployee organizers unless they are trying to reach employees. An employer may not deny nonemployee union supporters use of its premises for handbilling and picketing when it has allowed individuals from other organizations unlimited access for sales and solicitation.

In circumstances where nonemployee organizers' access to employees is infeasible, the employers' property rights are balanced against the accommodation that must be made for nonemployees to have access to employees. In such cases, the employer is obligated to give nonemployees reasonable access to the employees at the work site, because employees are beyond the feasible reach of union organizers.

Union organizers are prohibited from engaging in practices that interfere with employee free choice. Examples include threatening employees with physical harm if they do not vote for the union; threatening employees with expulsion from the union and the loss of their jobs if they support another union in the upcoming election; and serious acts found to violate Section 8(b)(1) of the NLRA. If the NLRB finds that the union has engaged in any of these activities, it can set the election aside.

Union organizers may not engage in organizational picketing if it falls within one of the three broad categories under Section 8(b)(7) of the NLRA: (a) where the employer has lawfully recognized another union and a question of representation may not be raised under Section 9(c) of the NLRA; (b) where within the preceding 12 months a valid election has been conducted; and (c) where organizational picketing has been conducted without an election being filed within a reasonable time that may not exceed 30 days from the commencement of such picketing.

See also **Collective Bargaining; Labor Union; National Labor Relations Act; National Labor Relations Board.**

UNION SECURITY CLAUSE Provisions in a collective bargaining agreement that aim to protect the labor union against employers, nonunion employees, and raids by competing unions. The typical union security clause is the union shop. In this case, the union negotiates with an employer a collective bargaining agreement that requires workers to pay periodic dues and initiation fees as a condition of employment. In the absence of such provisions, employees in the bargaining unit are free to join or support the union at will, and in union reasoning, receive union negotiated benefits at no personal expense, thus getting a "free ride." States, under Section 14(b) of the Labor-Management Relations Act of 1947 (the Taft-Hartley Act), may forbid union security agreements, even if both the union and employer desire to enter into such agreements.

See also **Collective Bargaining Agreement; Free Rider; Labor-Management Relations Act; Union Shop.**

UNION SHOP A bargaining unit covered by a union security clause that permits employers to hire workers of their choice but requires all new employees to become union members within a specified period of time, usually within the first 30 days of employment. The employee may also be required to remain a member or pay union dues for the duration of the collective bargaining agreement. If a worker refuses the union's request to pay membership dues, he or she may be dismissed from employment unless the worker's objection is religious.

A variation of the union shop is the modified union shop, which requires new employees to join the union and requires present employees and all who join in the future to maintain their union membership. However, it allows pre-existing employees who are not union members to continue to stay out of the union.

The union shop provision is now the dominant form of union security provision. It has replaced the closed shop provision that had been the most common form of security. From management's viewpoint, the principal difference between a union shop and a closed shop is that management is free to make hiring decisions without reference to the union membership of applicants for employment.

See also **Closed Shop; Collective Bargaining Agreement; Union Security Clause.**

Union Shop Deauthorization Election

See **Deauthorization.**

Union Summer

During the summer of 1996, the American Federation of Labor-Congress of Industrial Organizations sent 1,000 college students and workers to 18 communities to organize and rally support for labor-backed legislation. Called "Union Summer," the campaign was inspired by the 1964 "Freedom Summer" movement that mobilized young people to promote civil rights. Organizing efforts focused on women, people of color, and recent immigrants. Its organizers hoped that the campaign would produce both a generation of Americans interested in the union movement and a "living wage" for American workers.

See also **American Federation of Labor-Congress of Industrial Organizations.**

Union Trusteeship

The assumption of control over a local labor union by an international union. Under a trusteeship, the normal governmental process of the local union is suspended and the international takes over management of the local's assets and the administration of its internal affairs. The constitution of many international unions authorizes their officers to establish trusteeships over local unions in order to prevent corruption, mismanagement, and other abuses.

A union trusteeship is defined by the Labor-Management Reporting and Disclosure Act (LMRDA) of 1959 (the Landrum-Griffin Act) as any receivership, trusteeship, or other method of supervision or control whereby a labor organization suspends the autonomy otherwise available to a subordinate body under its constitution and bylaws. As a result of union abuses and corruption publicized during the McClellan Committee hearings, Congress enacted Title III of the LMRDA, which sets forth the conditions under which the trusteeships may be established and continued. Most labor union constitutions contain procedures for placing local unions under a trusteeship supervised by the parent body.

The LMDRA also imposes some strict controls on such trusteeships. The statute requires reporting and public disclosure by labor organization acting as steward in the trusteeship to the US Department of Labor. The parent organization must file a report on the trusteeship with the U.S. Department of Labor within 30 days. Thereafter, a report must be filed every six months while the trusteeship remains in effect. Among other requirements, these reports must provide a detailed statement of the reasons for the trusteeship and a complete record of the trusteed organization's financial condition when the trusteeship was imposed.

The LMRDA also places specific limitations on the purposes for which a trusteeship may be established. The trusteeship may be imposed only in accordance with the parent organization's constitution and bylaws and only for these purposes: correcting corruption or financial malpractice; assuring the performance of collective bargaining agreements or other duties of a collective bargaining representative; restoring democratic procedure; and otherwise carrying out the legitimate objective of the local.

It is unlawful to count the votes of the delegates of a trusteed union participating in the convention of a parent body unless they are democratically elected. It is also unlawful to transfer funds from the local to the supervisory organization, unless permission is granted through the courts or through the U.S. Department of Labor.

See also **Collective Bargaining Agreement; International Union; Labor Union; Labor-Management Reporting and Disclosure Act.**

UNION-BUSTING

Firms using this approach attempt to make the costs of forming a labor union so great that a union will not be certified. To be effective, this approach necessitates that the employee be willing to ignore his or her rights to engage in concerted activities for mutual aid or protection as articulated in Section 7 of the National Labor Relations Act (NLRA). For example, once a union-organizing campaign is underway, one tactic is to discharge employees known to be sympathetic to the union. This action would constitute an employer unfair labor practice under Section 8(a)(1) of the NLRA, which prohibits employers from actions that would "interfere with, restrain, or coerce employees in the exercise of the rights guaranteed in Section 7."

Union leaders believe that union busting is popular among employers because it is cost-effective, in that employers can violate the law, pay the back wages ordered by the National Labor Relations Board (NLRB) or the courts plus the lawyers' fee, and still be better off financially than when a union represents their employees. This situation arises because the penalty that the NLRB can impose on unfair labor practice cases is limited to awarding back wages.

See also **National Labor Relations Act; National Labor Relations Board; Unfair Labor Practice.**

UNIONS: POLITICAL ACTIVISM Although American labor unions are not affiliated with a political party, they are very much involved in the political process. Unions have established special political organizations to support those who support organized labor.

While some observers have suggested that the two world wars and the Great Depression brought about the spectacular growth of unions during the first half of the twentieth century, others credit the policies and programs of the Democratic party and its receptive attitude toward unionism as the primary forces behind the union growth. Many workers saw in the mid 1930s, probably for the first time, a compelling need for an organization that would represent their interests in the battle for economic power. Workers realized they were too weak individually to obtain for themselves the security they desired, and they found in the trade union a means to satisfy their needs.

Union involvement in the political process is limited by law. Section 304 of the Labor-Management Relations Act of 1947 (the Taft-Hartley Act) criminalizes labor union contributions in federal elections. Under the Federal Election Campaign Act of 1971, as amended, unions and corporations may use their funds for the purpose of sending political messages to their own members or shareholders, for conducting partisan registration and get-out-the-vote campaigns directed at such groups, and as seed money to solicit contributions to a union or corporate political action committee. But any direct contribution by labor unions to the treasuries of federal political candidates is prohibited. The U.S. Supreme Court, however, has held that a union may use funds contributed voluntarily outside the normal dues structure by union members as contributions to federal candidates. Congress has explicitly rejected the idea that tax exemption of unions should be terminated where union dues are used in political campaigns.

See also **Committee on Political Education; Labor Union; Labor-Management Relations Act.**

UNITED AUTO WORKERS (UAW) One of the major industrial unions to emerge in the 1930s. The UAW was formed in 1935 by the American Federation of Labor following the passage of the National Industrial Recovery Act, and it became an integral part of the Congress of Industrial Organizations (CIO). With the other CIO unions, the UAW became part of the AFL-CIO in 1955, but it withdrew in 1968 because of dissatisfaction with the AFL-CIO policy and leaders. In 1978 it returned to the federation.

In the 1970s and 1980s, cooperation increased between the UAW and the American auto industry. The UAW agreed to major concessions to help keep Chrysler Corporation out of bankruptcy, and in May 1980, Douglas A. Fraser, president of the United Auto Workers, became a member of Chrysler Corporation's board of directors. The UAW also supported federal legislation to regulate plant closings. It required that employers provide workers and communities advance notice of plant closings, provide workers with some form of job and income security (transfer rights and severance pay, for example) and compensate local communities for tax losses.

The UAW has established a reputation for being a democratic union. It has set up a public review board to review charges by union members against union officials and elects its national officers at a convention. The UAW currently has about 771,000 members.

See also **American Federation of Labor-Congress of Industrial Organizations.**

UNITED MINE WORKERS OF AMERICA (UMWA) The UMWA was organized in Indiana in 1890 and became the first successful industrial union. The first interstate coal agreement, which followed a strike called by bituminous coal workers in 1897, resulted in recognition of the UMWA and the establishment of grievance and negotiating machinery. Efforts to organize anthracite workers followed around 1899. By 1902 the UMWA was strong enough to engage in a major strike that received nationwide attention. President Theodore Roosevelt intervened in the strike and established the Anthracite Coal Commission, which investigated the conditions in the industry and settled the dispute.

Originally an American Federation of Labor (AFL) affiliate, the union became part of the Congress of Industrial Organizations (CIO) in 1935. Many

CIO unions, including the UMWA, had used communists as organizers prior to World War II. John L. Lewis, for one, considered the strongly motivated communists essential to his early organizing efforts. These ideological differences between Lewis and CIO leaders led to the withdrawal of the UMWA from the CIO in 1940. The union affiliated with the American Federation of Labor-Congress of Industrial Unions (AFL-CIO) in 1989, after more than 40 years of being an independent union.

See also **American Federation of Labor-Congress of Industrial Organizations; Grievance Procedure.**

UNITED STATES ARBITRATION ACT (1947) The federal statute that made valid and enforceable the written agreements that called for arbitration of disputes arising out of contracts, maritime transactions, or commerce among the states or territories or with foreign nations. Several courts have held that the act manifests a 'clear federal policy' favoring the enforcement of arbitration agreements.

The U.S. Supreme Court has created some doubt on the applicability of the United States Arbitration Act to disputes arising from collective bargaining agreements. The Court has made no reference to the relationship between that statute and arbitration clauses in collective bargaining agreements when it ruled that such provisions were enforceable under the contract enforcement provisions of the National Labor Relations Act. [*Textile Workers Union v. Lincoln Mills of Alabama* (1957); *General Electric Co. v. United Electrical, Radio & Machine Workers* (1957); *Goodall-Sanford, Inc. v. United Textile Workers* (1957)] There are major groups of employees excluded from the statute. The United States Arbitration Act does not apply to contracts of employment executed by seamen, railroad employees, or other workers engaged in foreign or interstate commerce.

Outside the collective bargaining context, an individual employee can waive the right to judicial review of statutory claims. The Supreme Court held that an agreement to arbitrate employment disputes was enforceable under the United States Arbitration Act. [*Gilmer v. Interstate/Johnson Lane Corp.* (1991)] The United States Arbitration Act expressly provides that in wrongful discharge or defamation cases, a prospective arbitration agreement will support a stay of the employee's lawsuit and an order compelling arbitration.

Arbitration is contractual, so parties can design their own procedures. They can specify what discovery will occur, the identity and qualifications of their decision maker, the standards of proof for evidence, and the rules of evidence. The statute empowers arbitrators in proceedings mandated by the act to issue subpoenas to force persons to attend arbitrations. The awards resulting from an arbitration proceeding are binding, essentially unappealable, and subject to court enforcement. Under the act, however, a court has the power to overturn an arbitrator's award if the "rights of any party have been prejudiced."

Since arbitration is largely a matter of private contract between labor and management, few statutes, either federal or state, impact the process. Furthermore, the controlling decisions of the U. S. Supreme Court in the area basically hold that the courts should not interfere with the arbitration process. Nevertheless, certain statutes and cases significantly affect the rights of the parties in arbitration, as in cases applying Title VII of the Civil Rights Act of 1964. [*Alexander v. Gardner-Denver Co.* (1974)]

See also **Civil Rights Act of 1964; Collective Bargaining Agreement; Employment Contract; Grievance Arbitration; Wrongful Discharge.**

U.S. DEPARTMENT OF LABOR One of the executive departments of the federal government headed by a secretary who is a member of the president's cabinet. Established by federal statute in 1913, its primary functions are to promote employment and to improve the working conditions and general welfare of wage earners.

It is responsible for the collection of major labor statistics including data on wages, hours, other working conditions, and collective bargaining agreements. The Labor Department consists of the following agencies: Bureau of Labor Statistics, Women's Bureau, Bureau of International Labor Affairs, Employment and Training Administration, Office of Labor-Management Standards, Pension and Welfare Benefits Administration, Labor-Management Relations and Cooperative Programs, Employment Standards Administration, Occupational Safety and Health Administration, the Mine Safety and Health Administration, and the Veterans Employment and Training Service.

From its origin in 1913, the Labor Department was responsible for mediation and conciliation functions until they were separated from the department by Labor-Management Relations Act (the Taft-Hartley Act) in 1947 and vested in the Federal Mediation and Conciliation Services, a separate and independent agency. As a matter of policy and operation, however, the department is still responsible for the problems involved in labor relations because of the president's labor responsibilities, particularly in issues involving the public interest or a national emergency. The department is also concerned with the general problems of employment and, through the Employment and Training Administration, operates and cooperates in the program with the respective states.

See also **Federal Mediation and Conciliation Services; Mediation; National Labor Relations Act.**

***UNITED STATES V. DARBY LUMBER CO.* (1941)** The U.S. Supreme Court decision that upheld the constitutionality of the minimum wage provision (Section 6) and the maximum hours provision (Section 7) of the Fair Labor Standards Act (FLSA). Specifically, the Court found that neither provision violated the due process clause of the Fifth Amendment of the U.S. Constitution.

Based on its constitutional power to regulate commerce, Congress enacted the FLSA in 1938. It prohibited the shipment in interstate commerce of goods manufactured by employees earning less than the prescribed minimum wage. A Georgia Lumber manufacturer challenged the statute on Tenth Amendment grounds, arguing that the FLSA encroached on the powers reserved to the states. The Court unanimously upheld the direct regulation of wages and hours. In *Darby,* the Court reversed much of its prior commerce clause jurisprudence, including its ruling in *Hammer v. Dagenhart* (1918), and held that the congressional power to regulate interstate commerce was not limited to formal distinctions between manufacturing and commerce. The opinion by Justice Stone was first to recognize the plenary power of Congress to set the terms for interstate transportation; that was clearly "commerce among the states." The Court also recognized that the Tenth Amendment did not serve as a basis for restricting the commerce power. Although the FLSA has been amended several times since 1939, its basic structure has remained essentially unchanged.

See also **Fair Labor Standards Act; Minimum Wage; Hours of Labor.**

UNITED STEELWORKERS OF AMERICA (USWA)

After the failure of the major efforts to organized the steel industry at the end of World War I, the Steel Workers Organizing Committee (SWOC) of the Congress of Industrial Organization (CIO) finally organized the industry. In 1942, the United Steelworkers of America succeeded SWOC. In 1967, the unaffiliated International Union of Mine, Mill, and Smelter Workers merged with the Steelworkers, adding some 30,000 members to the USWA.

Over the years, the steel industry has been characterized by labor unrest. (For example, the industry incurred a 116-day strike in 1959.) During contract negotiation years, a disruptive pattern of behavior developed. In anticipation of a strike, the steel companies and their customers stockpiled large amounts of steel. As a result, union members were able to work large amounts of overtime. But then, if an agreement was reached without a strike, partial plant shutdowns and worker layoffs occurred as the companies worked off the stockpiles. If negotiations led to a strike, especially a lengthy one, foreign steel manufacturers were able to gain a greater American market share.

To avoid this boom-bust cycle and permanent loss of customers to foreign competition, the USWA and the steel companies developed the experimental negotiating agreement (ENA). It was adopted by the parties in 1973 to govern the administration of the agreement in 1974. Its most significant provision was an agreement not to strike or lockout at the expiration of the contract and to submit all national issues not resolved through collective bargaining to a panel of impartial arbitrators for final and binding arbitration. The parties thus guaranteed that there would be no interruption of steel production in the following year. The ENA was credited for bringing greater stability to the steel industry.

In 1962, the United Steelworkers negotiated extended vacations of 13 weeks called "sabbatical vacations." Employees with 13 or more years of service were eligible for a sabbatical every five years. The objective of these extended vacations was to provide greater leisure time for long-service employees and to create additional jobs in the steel industry. This sabbatical vacation has not been widely adopted outside the steel industry.

The USWA has benefited from mergers with many smaller unions. In January 1971, the United Stone and Allied Products Workers of America merged with the union. District 50, an independent union formerly affiliated with the United Mineworkers of America, merged with the Steelworkers in August 1972, and the Upholsterers' International Union of North America in 1985. The USWA currently has 615,000 members.

See also **Collective Bargaining; Lockout.**

***UNITED STEELWORKERS V. WEBER* (1979)** In *Weber,* the U.S. Supreme Court, by a 5-2, vote endorsed a contractual affirmative action plan negotiated between Kaiser Aluminum and Chemical Corporation and the United Steelworkers Union that reserved 50 percent of the openings in a job training program for African American employees. The Court held that the affirmative action plan and Title VII of the Civil Rights Act of 1964 worked to eliminate "old patterns of racial segregation and hierarchy." Both companies' affirmative action plans were developed to "open employment opportunities for Negroes in occupations which have been traditionally closed to them." The Court found the plan to be "permissible" because it

> does not unnecessarily trammel the interest of the white employees. The plan does not require the discharge of white workers and their replacement with new African American hires. Nor does the plan create an absolute bar to the advancement of white employees; half of those trained in the program will be white. Moreover, the plan is a temporary measure; it is not intended to maintain racial balance, but simply to eliminate a manifest racial imbalance. Preferential selection of craft employees . . . will end as soon as the percentage of black skilled craft workers . . . approximates the percentage of blacks in the labor force.

The decision was criticized by some because it permitted an employer to institute a racial quota in order to determine who should be promoted.

The Civil Rights Act of 1991 did not express either approval or disapproval of *Weber* or other judicial decisions on court-ordered remedies, affirmative action, or conciliation agreements. These cases seem to establish that an employer may institute an affirmative action program consistent with Title VII based on "manifest imbalance" in traditionally segregated job categories. Nor did that statute purport to resolve the question of the legality under Title VII of affirmative action programs that grant preferential treatment to some on the basis of race, color, religion, sex, or national origin.

See also **Affirmative Action; Civil Rights Act of 1964; Civil Rights Act of 1991.**

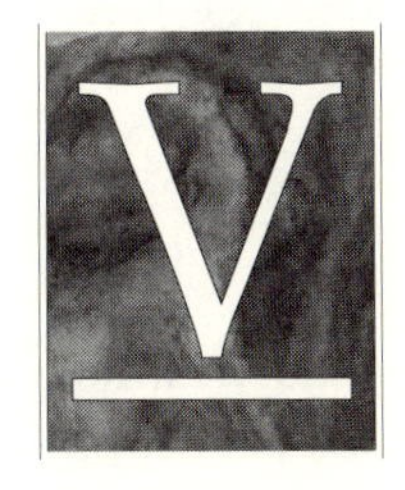

VACATIONS Specific periods during which employees are relieved of job obligations without loss of pay or any benefit or privilege of employment.

Almost exclusively a privilege of white-collar workers for many years, paid vacations were extended to manual workers relatively late. The growth of paid vacations is credited, in part, to the influence of labor unions, who viewed vacations as necessary to combat fatigue and maintain good health; to provide relaxation and recreation; to promote morale, efficiency, and a reasonable standard of living; and to deter labor turnover. Employers, too, contributed to the growth of paid vacations when they recognized the benefits workers derive from them. The National War Labor Board's policy of ordering vacations in collective bargaining contracts to ensure maximum individual and plant production also contributed to the popularity of vacations. The board extended paid vacation to production workers, reasoning that paid vacations were not inflationary. The usual award was one week with pay for one year's service and two weeks after five years. One of the first fringe adjustments to gain widespread popularity, paid vacation, along with paid holidays, is the most common and extensive of all fringe benefits.

Since World War II, the amount of vacation time and number of paid holidays provided in collective bargaining agreements has increased dramatically. An advantage of holidays and vacations for unions is that they reduce the amount of work done by an individual union member, thereby increasing the number of people employed and the number of union members. For the union member, longer vacations and more holidays provide time for leisure time activities. For an employer, providing employees with time off may increase their productivity on the job, and vacation time that increases with length of service provides a reward for longevity and reduces labor turnover.

See also **Benefits.**

VETERANS PREFERENCE Advantages in employment and promotion, both in the civil service and private employment, to veterans of the armed forces who have been honorably discharged. Preferential treatment has also been given to veterans by some labor unions, who accept them into membership without initiation fees, and in some cases have waived formal apprenticeship where the veteran had acquired reasonable skill in the trade while serving in the armed forces.

Independent of the civil service statutes' preferential treatment for veterans, statutes in many jurisdictions give veterans a preferential right to appointment to minor civil service offices. Where a veteran possesses equal capabilities with others, the rule is that the veteran's preference is based upon a reasonable relationship between the qualifications demonstrated by his or her service to the country and the nature of the duties of the public office involved. It is legally sufficient that the statutes require that the veterans possess the minimum qualifications necessary to the discharge of the public duties involved.

The general validity of such statutes has been upheld by the courts against a variety of constitutional objections. However, statutes that make the preference compulsory for the appointing body, regardless of the veteran's fitness or capacity, have been held unconstitutional. Also found unconstitutional was a veterans' preference law providing that upon application of a veteran deeming himself aggrieved, any district court judge shall have original jurisdiction to determine whether the applicant shall be preferred for employment and to order the appointing authority to employ the applicant. The statute was deemed unconstitutional because it confers an executive function upon the judiciary. Moreover, such a statute lacked due process by failing to provide notice to and an opportunity for a hearing of the appointing power.

The power to determine whether a veteran possesses such fitness and competency as well as the general qualifications for the office or employment rests largely in the discretion of the appointing body. As a general rule, the decision of the appointing body is conclusive unless it acts arbitrarily, unwarrantably, and in abuse of discretion.

See also **Apprenticeship; Civil Service.**

VETERANS' REEMPLOYMENT RIGHTS ACT See **Vietnam Era Veterans' Readjustment Assistance Act of 1974.**

Vicarious Liability

Vicarious Liability A common law doctrine of indirect legal responsibility. The foundation of vicarious liability is negligence, but under certain circumstances the law broadens liability for the fault by imposing it upon an additional, though innocent, defendant. The fault remains negligence, however, and the ordinary rules of negligence liability apply to it. The most familiar context is the liability of a master for the torts of his servant in the course of his employment or, in the employment context, the liability of an employer for the acts of an employee.

The modern justification for vicarious liability is a rule of policy, a deliberate allocation of risk. The losses caused by the torts of employees, which as a practical matter are sure to occur in the conduct of the employer's enterprise, are placed upon that enterprise itself as a required cost of doing business. The employer, having engaged in an enterprise that will, on the basis of all past experiences, involve harm to others through the torts of employees, and having sought to profit by it, should bear the losses rather than the innocent injured plaintiff. The employer is better able to absorb them and to distribute them, through prices, rates, or liability insurance, to the public and to society. Vicarious liability is also justified by the argument that an employer who is held strictly liable is under the greatest incentive to be careful in the selection, instruction, and supervision of his employees, and to take every precaution to see that the enterprise is conducted safely.

See also **Common Law: Employment Doctrines; Employee; Employer; Tort.**

Vietnam Era Veterans' Readjustment Assistance Act of 1974

Originally enacted in 1972, this statute prohibits employment discrimination against qualified disabled veterans and Vietnam era veterans by certain government contractors and federal agencies. Employers with federal contracts in the amount of $10,000 or more are required to "take affirmative action to employ and advance in employment qualified special disabled veterans and veterans of the Vietnam era." Federal agencies must draft and implement an affirmative action program for the hiring, placement, and advancement of veterans covered by the statute.

This statute is intended to cover any "an eligible veteran in any part of whose active military, naval, or air services was during the Vietnam era."

The Office of Federal Contract Compliance Programs specifically defines an eligible veteran as

> a person who served in active duty for a period of more than 180 days, any part of which occurred between August 5, 1964 and May 7, 1975, and was discharged or released therefrom with other than a dishonorable discharge; or who was discharged or released from active duty for a service-connected disability if any part of such active duty was performed between August 5, 1964 and May 7, 1975; and who was so discharged or released within 48 months preceding an alleged violation of the Vietnam Era Veterans Readjustment Assistance Act of 1974, the affirmative action clause, or the regulations issued pursuant to the act.

The long-standing reemployment and related rights of returning veterans are codified in this statute. Under the act, an employer is required to grant an employee's request for a leave of absence for the period required to perform military duty and military training in the reserves. The employee is entitled to retain his or her job and to be restored to his position without loss of promotion or other employment advantage due to his reserve obligations, and the employer is prohibited from discriminating against the employee because of his reserve obligations. In the absence of evidence from the civilian employer that the reservist's request for leave pursuant to military orders was unreasonable, the request must be honored by the employer. One very important provision of the statute restricts the termination of returning servicemen except for cause. All veterans are protected from dismissal without cause for one year after discharge from the military. The plain language of the statute imposes no limitation of reasonableness on the job guarantee, despite the fact that such a long leave places a burden on the employer and coworkers.

See also **Affirmative Action; Discrimination in Employment; Leave of Absence; Military Leave.**

VOCATIONAL REHABILITATION Programs designed for and directed to physically and mentally disabled individuals who need to be retrained and prepared for new jobs. Prior to the passage of the Federal Vocational Rehabilitation Act of 1920, some programs had been instituted by the states in this area. With the passage of the Social Security

Act of 1935 and subsequent amendments, funding was authorized to meet the costs of approved state vocational rehabilitation programs.

The Vocational Rehabilitation (Smith-Fess) Act of 1920 was enacted to aid workers who suffered a disabling injury at work, which arose out of the scope and course of their employment, and provide funds to augment rehabilitation programs being started by several states. In 1943, with the passage of the LaFollete-Barden Act, the present vocational rehabilitation program was established. Services were extended to include the blind and the mentally disabled, and the definition of rehabilitation service was expanded to include medical restoration and all services necessary to return disabled persons to satisfying, gainful employment.

See also **Social Security Act.**

WAGE The price paid for a particular type of work or service performed by an employee. Technically, the compensation paid to executive and professional employees are included in wages, although some suggest that this type of pay should be considered salary. In common usage, the term wage applies to compensation to unskilled, semiskilled, and skilled workers who are paid on an hourly or incentive basis. Payments to white-collar employees and professionals are generally referred to as salary.

See also **Compensation; Salary.**

WAGE COLLECTION Regulations established either by state departments of labor or by state statute to assure that individuals working for wages receive the full amount due them. The regulations may cover the frequency of the wage payment intervals and require explicit indication to the employee of the amount earned and of any deductions from the wages due. Wage collection problems often arise in the case of unscrupulous enterprises that seek to defraud individual wage earners. In some cases, legal aid societies have assisted low income employees in collecting the wage due them.

See also **Complaint; Fair Labor Standards Act; Wage**

WAGE STRUCTURE The existence of a wage structure implies a series of relationships based on compensation. The wage structure of a plant, an office, or more broadly, of a national economy may be viewed as a series of wage rates designed to compensate workers for the varying skills and abilities required in the production process. The concept of structure also has dimensional aspects. In the case of wages, the significant factor is the number of workers at each rate in the scale. A wage structure is determined, therefore, not only by a particular series or hierarchy of rates, but also by the relative importance of the jobs reflected in each rate.

A firm's wage structure is determined through job analysis, wage surveys, job evaluation, pricing jobs, wage progression, and negotiation with the union. Job analysis is the process of studying jobs in an organization with the purpose of identifying the tasks and duties involved in the performance of a job as well as the employee characteristics necessary to perform these tasks. Job surveys, such as those conducted by the Bureau of Labor Statistics, focus on clerical and blue-collar occupations and cover manufacturing and nonmanufacturing industries. They provide pay data for selected jobs and include data such as average wage rates and the dispersion in wages. Job evaluation is a process used to determine or estimate the relative worth of jobs in an organization.

The two dimensions of labor rates—local labor market rates and industry wage patterns—are the most important factors in setting wages. In nonunion organizations, the local labor rate appears to be more important than industry patterns; in unionized organizations, the reverse is true, probably due to the union's emphasis on achieving uniform wage rates within an industry.

See also **Blue-Collar Worker; Wage.**

WAGNER-CONNERY ACT (1935) See **National Labor Relations Act.**

WAGNER-PEYSER ACT (1933) The federal statute establishing the U.S. Employment Service to assist in developing a nationwide system of public employment offices that will bring workers and employers together and to promote interstate clearance of labor. These offices match employers and potential employees through "job orders," employment offers filed by the employer and displayed to potential employees. Employers wishing to recruit outside their state can file an interstate job order.

The state public employment services established under the act are responsible for providing job seekers—both unemployed and employed—with job placement and other employment services and for providing employers with recruitment services and referrals of job-seeking applicants. Because they are subject to the Wagner-Peyser Act, state employment services are bound to observe rules and regulations promulgated by the U.S. Department of Labor. One such regulation prohibits state employment agencies from making a job referral that will aid directly or indirectly in filling a job that is vacant because the former jobholder is on strike or being locked out in the course of a labor dispute, or is otherwise an issue in a labor dispute involving a work stoppage.

Waiting Period Variously defined as, among others, (1) a cooling-off period prior to calling a strike, which may be required by law or a collective bargaining agreement; (2) the period employees must wait, under sickness and accident insurance plans, to establish eligibility to receive benefits; (3) the period before an employee receives unemployment insurance payment; or (4) idle time because of a breakdown in machinery or because of a delay in receiving materials.

See also **Collective Bargaining Agreement; Cooling-off Period; Strike; Unemployment Compensation.**

Walkout Synonymous with a strike, but more like a "quickie" or a wildcat strike. There is usually no formal procedure for calling a walkout. It is a spontaneous reaction to a specific problem in the plant rather than the calculated preplanned action or strike.

See also **Strike; Unauthorized Strike.**

Walsh-Healey Public Contract Act (1936) Federal statute to establish labor standards for work performed on government manufacturing and supply contracts. The Walsh-Healey Public Contract Act applies to employees working on government contracts in excess of $10,000 for materials, articles, supplies, equipment, or naval vessels. Office and custodial employees are not covered, and the exemptions under the Fair Labor Standards Act (FLSA) for executive, administrative, and professional employees also apply under this act. Several contracts, including those for certain agricultural products, those with common carriers and communication companies, and those for purchase of commodities in the "open market," are specifically exempt from the statute's requirements.

Under the minimum wage standards, covered employees must be paid at least the prevailing minimum wage rates as determined by the U.S. Department of Labor. They also must be paid time and one-half their "basic" rate for work in excess of 40 hours per week. Learners, disabled workers, and apprentices may be employed at rates below the applicable minimum rate in accordance with special regulations issued under the statute. The child labor provisions forbid the employment of both female and male minors under the age of 16 for government work. Convict labor is also prohibited. The act also forbids employment on government contracts where the working conditions are unsanitary, hazardous, or dangerous to the health and safety of the employees.

The U.S. Department of Labor is authorized to investigate and decide cases involving alleged violations of the statute. The government may sue in the federal courts to recover liquidated damages (where the amount of damages has been ascertained by the judgment in the case), or it may deduct the damages from the amount due the contractor under the contract. For minimum wage and overtime pay violations, the liquidated damages equal the underpayments to employees. A penalty of $10 a day is assessed for each day a minor or convict is knowingly employed on government work. Serious and willful violators are subject to the blacklist penalty barring them from participation in government contracts for a period of three years. The act is administered by the Wage and Hour Division in the U.S. Department of Labor.

The FLSA, Davis-Bacon Act, and the Walsh-Healey Act were amended by the Portal-to-Portal Act to specify standards for determining compensable working time and to provide additional defenses to liability under the act, including a two-year statute of limitations on liquidated damage claims.

The Walsh-Healey Act parallels the Davis-Bacon Act in that the U.S. Department of Labor identifies the prevailing wages and fringe benefits for the relevant occupations and industry in the geographic area of the employer who has the contract. These prevailing rates constitute the minimum standard for the wages and fringe benefits of the contractor. These rates prevent the downward spiral of wages and hinder reliance on wage cutting as the prime competitive strategy. Businesses have not criticized the Walsh-Healey Act as much as they have the Davis-Bacon Act. However, when the prevailing wages and benefits for a locality are defined to be those negotiated in relevant collective agreements, the same criticisms would appear to apply, specifically that the law increases labor costs and decreases competition.

See also **Child Labor Laws; Davis-Bacon Act of 1931; Fair Labor Standards Act; Minimum Wage; Portal-to-Portal Act of 1947; U.S. Department of Labor.**

WARDS COVE PACKING CO. V. ATONIO (1989)

The U.S. Supreme Court, on a 5–4 vote, in *Wards Cove,* held that a statistical showing of a racial imbalance between classes of workers in the workplace does not establish a prima facie case of disparate impact or racial discrimination under Title VII of the Civil Rights Act of 1964.

There were two general types of jobs at the Wards Cove Packing Company: low-paid unskilled line jobs in its salmon canning facility in Alaska and the higher-paid "noncannery" jobs (such as machinists, engineers, accountants) which were filled at the company offices in Washington and Oregon. Nonwhite workers, mainly Filipinos and Alaska Natives, filled a high percentage of the cannery worker positions; white workers primarily held the noncannery worker positions. The employer argued that the disparity resulted from a lack of minority employees who had the requisite skills necessary to be considered for the noncannery jobs.

A panel of the Ninth Circuit found the statistical disparity in this case sufficient to establish a prima facie case of disparate impact. The U.S. Supreme Court reversed and remanded (sent back the case) on the grounds that the statistical proof the plaintiffs offered did not reflect an appropriate comparison of the relevant qualified labor pool and the jobs at issue.

To compare the number of nonwhites with whites in skilled jobs "is nonsensical," according to the Court, which ruled that when considering the issue of racial composition of at-issue jobs, the analyses must reflect the pool of qualified job applicants or the qualified population in the labor force. The minority workers in this case claimed that the company's employment practices violated Title VII because minorities held unskilled low-paying cannery jobs and not the skilled noncannery positions. The court found that the absence of nonwhites from the noncannery positions was because of a lack of qualified nonwhite applicants. This absence was not the employer's fault and thus, the employment practices of Wards Cove did not have a disparate impact on nonwhites.

In order to prove disparate impact discrimination, the court ruled that the workers must present evidence that the cannery workforce did not represent the pool of qualified applicants or the qualified population in the labor force and show that a particular employment practice caused the statistical disparity. They also were required to specifically demonstrate that each of the alleged discriminatory practices, such as nepotism, separate hiring channels, rehire preferences, "has a significant disparate impact on employment opportunities for white and nonwhites." Thus, while employers have the lesser burden of producing evidence of business justification for their employment practices, the burden of proving discrimination rests with the workers or the plaintiffs, to disprove the employer's assertion that "the adverse employment action was based on a legitimate neutral consideration."

The Court's decision in *Wards Cove* was severely criticized by the civil rights community and plaintiff's attorneys who asserted that the Court had eviscerated disparate impact analysis as formulated in *Griggs v. Duke Power* (1971) and later cases. The proponents of new civil rights legislation in 1990 and 1991 proposed three measures designed to overturn perceived changes in the disparate impact analysis announced in *Wards Cove.* Among these included a proposal that an employer should not be permitted to engage in an employment practice that results in a disparate workforce without showing that the practice is "essential." *Wards Cove* had ruled that it was not essential for the challenged practice to be "indispensable" to the employer's business because such a level of scrutiny would be almost impossible for most employers to meet and would effectively require an employer to implement a quota system of employee selection or face litigation to defend the business necessity of their business practices. The final version of the 1991 Act, however, represented less than full victory for civil rights advocates in undoing the effect of *Wards Cove* on disparate impact analysis.

See also **Civil Rights Act of 1964; Disparate Impact Discrimination; *Griggs v. Duke Power Co.***

WELFARE AND PENSION PLANS DISCLOSURE ACT (WPPDA) OF 1958 Also known as the Teller Act, this federal statute covered all nongovernmental welfare and pension plans affecting employers with more than 25 employees. It provided for the registration, reporting, and disclosure of employee welfare and pension benefit plans and pertinent data. The statute lacked substantive requirements and did not grant the government enforcement authority. In 1962, it was amended to grant the U.S. Department of Labor interpretive, investigative, and enforcement powers. Kickbacks, embezzlement, conflicts of interest, and false entries by fund officials or employees were made federal crimes and subject to stiff penalties. Interest in pension reform continued, stimulated by the termination of underfunded plans, media attention, and by a public perception that pension plans were not delivering on their promises. Conflicting interest groups and political infighting prevented the passage of any pension reform legislation until 1974. The WPPDA was then repealed with the enactment of the Employee Retirement Income Security Act (ERISA) of 1974, which established additional fiduciary standards for plan administrators. It also provided for mandatory vesting of benefits and funding of plans. A division within the Labor-Management Services Administration of the U.S. Department of Labor was established to insure benefits in the event of the termination of a plan.

See also **Employee Retirement Income Security Act; Pension.**

WHIPSAWING A labor union strategy to obtain benefits from a number or group of employers by imposing demands on one of them. The objective is to win favorable terms from the one employer and then use the settlement as a pattern or base to obtain the same or greater benefits from the other employers, under the same threat of pressure (including a strike) used against the first employer.

Whipsawing can also be a management strategy—assigning work to the plants on the principle that the low-cost operation receives the business. Though the unions in the past were successful in combating management's divide-and-conquer strategy, they are no longer successful in many industries. They currently find themselves able to develop safeguards to contend with competitive threats coming from a higher management level, namely cross-plant comparisons.

WHISTLEBLOWER An employee who discloses improper employer practices or policies. Manufacture of defective products, corruption, and cost overruns are among the practices that have been exposed by whistleblowers. Case law and statutory law have now evolved to protect employee whistleblowers from the retaliatory actions of their employers. Retaliation can take the form of discharge, suspension, threats of discrimination, or actual discrimination against an employee regarding his or her compensation, terms, conditions, or privileges of employment.

The Civil Service Reform Act of 1978 protects federal employees against reprisal for such disclosure. Employees of federal agencies are protected by the Whistleblower Protection Act, which protects employees from retaliation resulting from their attempts to prevent illegal activity or to assist or cooperate in the investigation of illegal activity. Employees discharged for blowing the whistle against their employers have sometimes used the provisions of whistleblower protection acts as the basis of lawsuits against their employers. In addition, employers of federal defense contractors are protected by another special whistleblower statute.

Several states also prohibit employers from discriminating against employees who have reported violations or cooperated in investigation of violations. Currently at least 34 states have statutes that provide protections for public employees similar to the protections provided on the federal level. However, the scope of protected activities varies from state to state. In 18 states, this protection extends to employees who report violations of the law, gross waste of public funds, abuse of authority, or any act that poses a substantial and specific risk to public health or safety.

See also **Civil Service Reform Act of 1978.**

WHITE-COLLAR WORKER A broad category of employees other than production and blue-collar service employees and farm workers. The term normally refers to office, clerical, sales, technical and professional employees, executives, managers, and administrative employees. Whether a certain position is a white-collar job depends on a salary level that is above a specified minimum, the primary duty of exempt work (which refers to the provisions in the Fair Labor Standards Act exempting professional, administrative, and executive employees from the act's overtime pay requirement), and regularly exercised discretion.

The Department of Commerce, in its *Standard Occupational Classification Manual,* eliminated the broad categorization of jobs as white-collar or blue-collar for the 1980 census and the Current Population Survey beginning in January 1983. These titles were discontinued because of the favorable impression given by "white-collar" and the more pejorative notion of "blue-collar jobs." Also, the terms are unevenly applied and commonly misunderstood. For example, it is often assumed that the two together include all occupations, though neither category covers service and farm groupings.

As white-collar workers increasingly comprise a greater proportion of the labor force, some labor unions have developed strategies to increase the attractiveness of unions to white-collar workers. The two issues that can persuade white-collar workers to support a union are job satisfaction and the ability to influence work conditions. If unions bargain for and help establish quality of work life programs and quality circles, they will be perceived by white-collar workers as instrumental in attaining highly desirable results.

See also **Blue-Collar Worker; Quality Circles; Quality of Work Life; Salary.**

WILDCAT STRIKE

See **Unauthorized Strike.**

WILLIAMS ENTERPRISES V. NLRB (1992)

The U.S. Court of Appeals for the District of Columbia held that, if compliance with the terms of a health or safety standard would place employees in a greater peril than they face under existing conditions, then the employer may appropriately raise the "greater hazard defense." In order to establish this affirmative defense, however, the employer must prove that (1) the hazards of compliance are greater than the hazards of a noncompliance; (2) alternative means of protecting employees are unavailable; and (3) a permanent variance application would be inappropriate. The evidence of a greater hazard, however, must be clear. The "mere verbalized fears" of employees and an employer's unsupported opinion have been held to be inadequate. Similarly, it is not enough that compliance with the standard will cause momentary lapses of protection or inconvenience to employees.

Williams also defined a violation as willful

> if committed with intentional, knowing, or voluntary disregard for the requirements of the Act, or with plain indifference to employee safety. It is not enough for the Secretary to show that an employer was aware

of conduct or conditions constituting a violation; such evidence is necessary to establish any violation, serious or nonserious. A willful violation is differentiated by a heightened awareness—of the illegality of the conduct or conditions—and by a state of mind—conscious disregard or plain indifference.

WOMEN: EMPLOYMENT ISSUES Federal and state governments have, in the past, actively discouraged women, especially wives and mothers, from working. With strong public approval, governments sought to deny jobs to wives during the 1930s because of concern that women would displace male breadwinners. Many school districts refused to hire wives and fired women who were married. The "marriage penalty" in the federal income tax during the 1970s also placed working couples at a disadvantage compared with more traditional family arrangements.

Women were not originally included in the Civil Rights Act of 1964. But through amendment, prohibitions against sex discrimination in employment were included in the final legislation. The moral force of the law, combined with the creation of a legal enforcement mechanism, provided the emerging feminist movement with leverage to attack barriers that had previously prevented women from fully participating in the labor market.

The pace of change was also stimulated by the prolonged period of inflation that occurred during the 1970s and early 1980s. The decrease in real family incomes forced many women to find jobs. In the wake of these events, the number of female heads of households has surged: 16.2 percent of all families in 1985 were headed by women, up from 10.8 percent in 1979. For African-American families, the percentage headed by women increased from 28.3 percent in 1970 to 43.7 percent in 1985. Widowhood, divorce, and pregnancies outside of marriage have caused an increasing number of women to be the sole breadwinners for their families; many of these women have been forced to seek employment whether they wished to or not. Many want to pursue careers, but many others work outside the home simply because their contribution is essential to their own or their family's well-being.

Between 1950 and 1980, the proportion of working-age women in the labor force nearly doubled, rising from 30 to 57 percent of all women. Since the 1960s, women have had the largest share of labor force growth, and women accounted for 7 of 10 additions to the labor force during the

1980s. Current trends indicate that women will comprise some 47 percent of the labor force by the year 2000, and 61 percent of women will be employed. Between 1985 and 2000, some three-fifths of the new entrants into the labor force will be women, but the trend is expected to peak by the year 2000. The slowdown is based on the declining labor force participation rate of women aged 55–64 and the desire of working mothers to avoid full-time jobs.

In 1991, some 56.8 million women workers, 16 years of age and older, comprised more than 45 percent of the civilian labor force and 57.3 percent of the total female population in the United States, compared to 68.4 million men workers representing 55 percent of the total labor force and 75.5 percent of the male population. The unemployment rate for women was 6.3 percent, and for men, 7.0 percent. Labor force participation was highest among women in the 25–34 (14.7 million) and 35–44 year (14.4 million) age brackets. Approximately 48.1 million (or 57.4 percent) of European American women were in the labor force in 1991, with a 5.5 percent unemployment rate; there were 6.7 million (or 57 percent) African American women in the labor force with a 11.9 percent unemployment rate; and 3.8 million (or 52.3 percent) Hispanic women in the labor force with a 9.5 percent unemployment.

Some commentators still justify discrimination against women on the basis that gender determines worker preferences for jobs and that female workers mean higher costs for employers, since women's work patterns are more likely to be intermittent and their health care costs high, primarily because of their care-giving and child-bearing responsibilities. Thus, by extension, occupational segregation and lower pay for women are inevitable. However, such arguments ignore the discrimination women have historically faced in attempting to be treated fairly in employment and society.

Women constitute a substantial majority of the working poor in the United States, largely because of the traditional assumption that women will be provided for through private arrangements with male breadwinners. The U.S. wage labor system is structured around the vision of an ideal worker: a male primary breadwinner with a dependent spouse and children. In this model, a woman, if she enters the wage labor force at all, will be the secondary wage earner.

State legislation was once intended to protect the woman worker and restrict the number of hours a woman could work. Current federal legislation prohibits such discrimination based on sex. The Equal Pay Act of 1963 calls for equal pay for equal work regardless of sex, and Title VII of the Civil Rights Act of 1964 prohibits discrimination in employment on the basis of race, color, religion, national origin, or sex. Executive Order 11246 also forbids employment discrimination by federal contractors on the basis of sex.

Major concerns for single, head-of-household women with children or working wives include child care, flextime, maternity leave, and sexual harassment.

See also **Civil Rights Act of 1964; Discrimination in Employment; Equal Pay Act of 1963; Flextime; Glass Ceiling; Mommy Track; Sex Discrimination in Employment.**

WORKER ADJUSTMENT AND RETRAINING NOTIFICATION (WARN) ACT OF 1988 Federal statue requiring, with certain exceptions, employers with 100 or more employees to provide a 60-day advance notice of (1) a plant closing affecting at least 50 employees and (2) a mass layoff affecting at least one-third of the workforce or 50 or more employees.

Increased foreign competition, technological change, and structural changes in industry have left many states with plant closings that have resulted in large numbers of displaced workers. Advance notification provisions were originally enacted as part of the Omnibus Trade and Competitiveness Act, which was vetoed by President Reagan on May 24, 1988, because of his opposition to the mandatory notification requirement. Enacted on August 4, 1988, the WARN became effective February 4, 1989. The purpose of WARN is to provide:

> protection to workers, their families, and communities by requiring employers to provide notification 60 calendar days in advance of plant closings and mass layoffs. Advance notice provides workers and their families some transition time to adjust to the prospective loss of employment, to seek and obtain alternative jobs, and if necessary, to enter skill training or retraining that will allow these workers to successfully compete in the job market.

The 60-days advance notice is served to affected employees or their representatives, the state dislocated worker unit, and the chief elected local government official of the affected jurisdiction. The notice period is necessary to significantly reduce dislocated workers' earnings losses and the probability of their experiencing one or more weeks of unemployment. Any employer who orders a plant closing or a layoff in violation of the law is liable for back pay and fringe benefit payments to each employee suffering employment loss for each day that notice was not given. An employer may also be subject to a penalty up to $500 a day (maximum $30,000) for each day notice was not given to the local government. Employees, their representatives, or the local government may seek redress to enforce an employer's liability in federal district court, and the court may order reasonable attorneys fees to the prevailing party.

Whether workers actually receive advance notice of layoff and how much notice they receive vary according to the characteristics of the lost job. Compliance with WARN has been low, for reasons of either ignorance or evasion on the part of employers. Many employers were uncertain, at least initially, of their obligations under the law. Also, only fairly large firms are subject to the legislation. Firms with fewer than 100 employees employ 35 percent of the workforce, yet are automatically exempt from WARN. The one-third rule also played a significant role in the statute's apparent lack of effectiveness. In 1993, for example, roughly 50 percent of the layoffs involving 50 or more workers were exempt from WARN due to the one-third rule.

See also **Back Pay; Benefits; Layoff; Unemployment.**

WORKERS' COMPENSATION The intent of these statutes is to provide some protection in the event of work-connected injury, illness, or death. Workers' compensation statutes are based on the principle of liability without fault. Under this principle, employers contribute to a fund providing compensation for employees involved in work-connected accidents and injuries. The benefits are not provided because of liability or negligence on the part of the employer but as a matter of public duty. Prior to workers compensation laws, employees injured on the job had to bring a lawsuit against the employer to receive any compensation for their injuries, and employers were responsible only when their negligence resulted in the injury.

The basic principles of workers compensation laws were developed in Germany around 1884 and spread to various parts of Europe. Workers' compensation laws were advocated in the United States when the common law provisions of employer liability became inadequate and when it was found that an injured worker could recover damages only if it could be proven that the injury was caused by the negligence of the employer. The first workers' compensation statute enacted in the United States applied only to a limited group of federal employees. Major developments in workers compensation legislation then occurred in the states. Maryland was the first state to establish a workers' compensation statute in 1902 to protect disabled miners.

The primary purpose of workers compensation was to provide financial aid through a system of insurance to compensate employees for injuries related to their employment. Injured workers no longer had to establish negligence attributable to their employer in order to obtain legal redress. They merely had to demonstrate that their conditions arose out of and during the course of their employment. Furthermore, the traditional common law defenses—contributory negligence, the fellow servant rule, and assumption of risks—were abolished. Even workers who sustained injuries as a result of their own carelessness were entitled to workers' compensation.

The legislative acceptance of the liability without fault concept significantly benefited covered workers and also provided employers with several benefits. While injured employees were guaranteed medical coverage and specified amounts for lost earnings, the liability imposed upon employers was limited. Workers' compensation statutes generally precluded the awarding of compensatory or punitive damages. In addition, by creating the exclusive remedy for employee injuries, these laws gave employers immunity against most tort actions arising from the employment relationship.

Present statutes mandate employer liability for medical care and partial replacement of wages for injury, death, occupational disease, or safety code violations without regard to negligence or carelessness on the part of employees. The focus of safety regulation has been twofold, with the Occupational Safety and Health Act providing resources to encourage injury prevention and workers' compensation laws aimed at providing medical and income security to injured employees.

Employers insure workers' compensation risks through state-funded plans, private insurance companies, or self-insurance.

See also **Common Law: Employment Doctrines; Compensation; Fellow Servant Rule; Occupational Safety and Health Act; Tort.**

WORKPLACE VIOLENCE Physical force applied to persons and property in an employment setting. Extreme instances of workplace violence include assaults and murder.

In 1994, 2.2 million Americans were physically attacked at work and another 6.3 million were threatened. Furthermore, approximately 15 percent have been physically assaulted on the job at least once. During the 1980s, homicide accounted for 7,600 deaths in the workplace, making it the third leading cause of death from injury in the workplace.

The factors causing frustration resulting in workplace violence include a constantly evolving society; stress among employees; the ready availability of guns; and the increasing presence of women and minorities in the workforce, who provide convenient scapegoats for anger.

In addition, aggressive corporate downsizing is creating a large number of psychologically troubled "walking wounded" who have seen their job prospects and self-respect evaporate. In the 1970s, 80 percent of all displaced employees could find a comparable replacement job. In the 1990s, that total has fallen to less than 25 percent.

Workplace violence is contributing to making workplace liability one of the fastest growing and most rapidly evolving areas of civil litigation. Generally speaking, the principle of "second occurrence" carries weight among the states nationwide. If a rape takes place at a work site and little or nothing is done in response, company officials will be hard-pressed to present a credible liability defense if a second incident occurs.

Where the law is less clear, and is changing, concerns the initial occurrence of violence. Courts are asking both: Were there signs of danger? Was the company negligent in failing to see them? There is a subtle shift of momentum toward finding liability if the answer to these questions is in the affirmative. In a landmark California case, a Sonoma County jury awarded $5.5 million to the family of a winery employee who was murdered by a co-worker. The assailant had a criminal record, and the employment agency that helped him get the winery job was found liable for failing to perform a proper background check.

There are several legal theories under which an employer may potentially be liable to victims of workplace violence, including

1. Negligent hiring, which may arise if the employer knew or should have known that the employee was either unfair for the job or potentially dangerous;

2. Negligent supervision and retention, involving personal injuries or property damage inflicted by employees on third persons, which may create liability for an employer where the employer knew the employee had a record of, or the potential for, violence;
3. Liability under the Occupational Safety and Health Act, which requires employers to provide a workplace free from hazards that are likely to cause death or serious harm;
4. Liability under Worker's Compensation, which is generally an employee's exclusive remedy for a job-related injury, including injuries caused by a co-worker; and
5. Sexual harassment and other prohibited harassment, which may make the employer liable for either engaging in or allowing sexual harassment that creates a hostile work environment.

WRONGFUL DISCHARGE An unjust termination of an employee. The theory of wrongful discharge is based on judicially created exceptions to the at-will termination doctrine: (1) terminations in which the employer's motivation is contrary to public policy, (2) the employer's promises of continued employment (also known as an expressed or implied agreement to terminate only for cause), and (3) violation of an implied covenant of good faith and fair dealing inherent in the employment contract.

In some wrongful discharge cases, the courts have tempered the rigidity of the employment-at-will doctrine by finding an employer breach of the covenant of good faith and fair dealing said to be present in every contract. The covenant has been described as creating a duty that is unconditional and independent in nature. It essentially states that neither of the parties to a contract will do anything that would injure the right of the other to receive the benefits of the agreement. Judicial enforcement of this covenant provides a measure of minimal fairness into the employment-at-will doctrine without abolishing the doctrine itself.

The public policy wrongful discharge cases have generally involved employer conduct that violates a policy embodied in a state statute or regulation. They can be divided into three broad categories: (1) those where the employee is fired for refusal to commit an unlawful act; (2) those where the employee is fired for performing an important public obligation, such as jury duty or "whistleblowing" on illegal employer conduct; and (3) those where the employee is fired for exercising a statutory right or privilege, such as filing a workers' compensation claim. All three of these involve public policy grounded in state substantive law.

American common law has traditionally recognized that employment relationships are terminable at the will of either party, absent a contractual commitment to the contrary. Several federal and state statutes have limited the applicability of this doctrine, protecting employees from discharge because of race, religion, sex, national origin, age, or union activities. Despite these protections, employers until very recently had considerable freedom in deciding whether or not to discharge a nonunion employee. Since the late 1970s, however, an increasing number of jurisdictions have recognized a cause of action for wrongful discharge or termination. (The state courts, rather than the legislatures, are responsible for this development.) The reasoning behind the wrongful discharge doctrine has usually imposed implied contractual obligations upon employers in their dealings with individual employees. State and federal courts developed the wrongful discharge theory in the 1980s as a "justification" for penalties imposed on employer conduct perceived to be arbitrary and capricious. Through mid 1992, some 43 states have adopted the public policy-exception to the doctrine of employment at will.

In many states the common law employment-at-will doctrine has been eroded during the 1970s and 1980s by state court rulings. In addition to the three legal exceptions to the employment-at-will doctrine, courts have also accepted some common law causes of action such as fraud and intentional or negligent infliction of emotional distress. The new employment-sometimes-at-will common law doctrine has produced uncertain and incomplete property rights to jobs, often leaving employers and employees unsure of the legality of personnel actions. Moreover, when disputes arise over improper dismissals, the current judicial system imposes large transaction costs and only variable awards on the parties.

Wrongful discharge legislation is more likely to be proposed in states where the departure from the traditional employment-at-will doctrine by the courts has been the most pronounced. When proposed, this legislation is typically designed to limit employer liability, expedite dispute settlements, reduce legal costs, and clarify property rights. There is a possibility, of course, that wrongful discharge legislation could at least, at first, increase uncertainty and disputes over property rights.

The prospects for the passage of wrongful discharge legislation are linked to the erosion of the common law employment-at-will doctrine.

The doctrinal erosion of common law in particular is not easily stopped because precedents make it difficult for courts to reverse themselves and because state judges typically serve for long terms.

See also **Common Law: Employment Doctrines; Employment Contract; Employment-at-Will; Property Rights; Whistleblower; Workers' Compensation.**

Wygant v. Jackson Board of Education (1986)

The U.S. Supreme Court held 5-4 that the Jackson Board of Education violated the equal protection clause of the Fourteenth Amendment in adhering to a collective bargaining agreement that required the board to maintain a percentage of minority teachers on the faculty during layoffs. The layoff provision sought to maintain racial balance in the workforce in order to remedy past discrimination. The Court, however, ruled that the education board could not lay off the European-American teachers in order to retain minority teachers with lesser seniority. The Court found the layoffs "too intrusive" to achieve racial equality and recommended other means, such as adopting hiring goals, to "satisfy the demands of the Equal Protection Clause." Justice Lewis Powell's opinion seemed to focus on the idea that the loss of an existing job on the basis of racial considerations was particularly intrusive compared to the denial of future employment opportunities.

The plurality and concurring opinions noted several problems with the plan, including its generalized desire to make the composition of the teachers represent the community rather than to address the underutilization of qualified teachers, its permanent nature, and its layoff policy that unduly trammeled the interests of the senior European-American teachers.

Wygant also stands for the principle that the voluntary affirmative action plan of public employers that involve government classifications on the basis of race and ethnicity are "inherently suspect and thus call for the most exacting judicial examination."

See also **Affirmative Action; Collective Bargaining Agreement; Layoff; Seniority.**

YELLOW DOG CONTRACT An agreement (either written or oral) between an employer and an employee that provides that as a condition of employment the worker will refrain from joining a labor union or, if the worker is a member, will leave the organization. These agreements, when reinforced by court injunction, were an effective means for limiting union organizing activities in the early twentieth century.

In 1917, the U.S. Supreme Court in *Hitchman Coal & Coke Co. v. Mitchell* (1917) upheld yellow dog contracts on the grounds that the employer and the nonunion employee "are entitled to be protected by the law in the enjoyment of benefits of any lawful agreements they may make." Prior to the *Hitchman* decision, workers who signed such an agreement probably felt no moral compulsion when they violated it. The effect of the contract was primarily psychological. After the *Hitchman* case, however, breaching the "yellow dog" contact violated the law.

The Norris-LaGuardia Act (1932) both denied the courts their primary device for discouraging unions—the injunction—and made the yellow dog contact unenforceable in court. Section 3 of that statute states:

> Any undertaking or promise, such as is described in this section, or any other undertaking or promise in conflict with the public policy declared in section 2 of this Act, is hereby declared to be contrary to the public policy of the United States, shall not be enforceable in any court of the United States and shall not afford any basis for the granting of legal or equitable relief by any such court, including specifically the following:
>
> > Every undertaking or promise hereafter made, whether written or oral, express or implied, constituting or contained in any contract or agreement of hiring or employment between any individual, firm, company, association, or corporation, and any employee or prospective employee of the same, whereby (a) Either party to such contract or agreement undertakes or promises not to join, become, or remain a

> member of any labor organization or of any employer organization; or (b) Either party to such contract or agreement undertakes or promises that he will withdraw from an employment relation in the event that he joins, becomes, or remains a member of any labor organization or of any employer organization.

This statute made yellow dog contracts practically useless as a means by employers to deter unionization.

One of the legacies of the "yellow dog contract" is the great emphasis on security agreements by unions. The unions have sought to ensure that employees will support the union that represents their interests in terms of union membership dues and other financial support.

See also **Injunctions Against Unions; National Labor Relations Act; Norris-LaGuardia Act; Union Security Clause.**

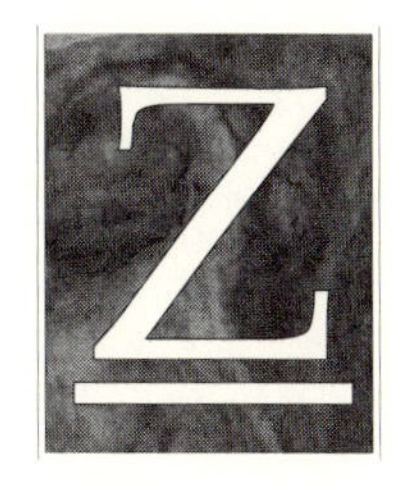

ZIPPER CLAUSE Clause that seeks to close all employment terms for the duration of the labor contract by stating that the agreement is "complete in itself" and sets forth all the terms of the agreement. It is an abbreviated form of the waiver provision in a collective bargaining agreement sometimes referred to as a "wrap up" clause, considered to mean a waiver of the right of either party to require the other to bargain on any matter not covered in an agreement during the life of the contract, thus limiting the terms and conditions of employment to those set forth in the contract. A clause of this type would read: "This contract is complete in itself and sets forth all the terms and conditions of the agreements between the parties hereto." These terms have been considered mandatory bargaining subjects in cases such as *NLRB v. Tomco Communications* (1978).

Frequently litigation occurs over the duty to bargain during the term of the contract and the employer's right to refuse to do so when it has negotiated a "zipper clause" which, in the employer's view, zips up all future obligations to negotiate. A party to a collective bargaining agreement may lawfully require midterm negotiation over mandatory subjects not "contained in" the agreement. When a party, however, has acquiesced during negotiations to the exclusion of a mandatory subject by effectively "agreeing to disagree" on the issue, and the matter is not incorporated in the contract, midterm bargaining on the subject cannot be required. For the zipper clause to waive a duty to bargain, it must do so clearly and unequivocally.

A zipper clause does not serve as a waiver of the parties' right to bargain over a new policy not discussed during negotiations because the clause waived only demands and proposals made during negotiations.

See also **Collective Bargaining Agreement.**

Aboud, Antone, ed. *Plant Closing Legislation.* Ithaca, NY: ILR Press, 1984.

Alder, Jonathan L. *Sexual Harassment: Discrimination and Other Claims.* Charlottesville, VA: Michie Butterworth, 1994.

American Arbitration Association. *The Future of Labor Arbitration in America.* New York: American Arbitration Association, 1976.

American Bar Association. *Developing Labor Law.* 3d ed. Washington, DC: BNA, 1994.

Anderson, Bernard E., and Isabel V. Sawhill. *Youth Employment and Public Policy.* St. Louis: American Assembly, 1980.

Aswad, Nadya. *AIDS-HIV in the Workplace: A Fact Sheet for Employees.* Washington, DC: BNA, 1994.

Atkinson, Lynn, ed. *State and Federal EEO Compliance Encyclopedia.* Madison, WI: Business Legal Reports, 1989.

Atleson, James B. *Values and Assumptions in American Labor Law.* Amherst, MA: University of Massachusetts Press, 1983.

Baird, Charles W. *Opportunity or Privilege: Labor Legislation in America.* New Brunswick, NJ: Transaction Pubs., 1984.

Baker, Elizabeth. *Protective Labor Legislation.* Temecula, CA: Report Service, 1993.

Bakke, E. Wight, Clark Kerr, and Charles Anrod. *Unions, Management, and the Public.* 3d ed. New York: Harcourt, Brace, 1967.

Begin, James P., and Edwin Beal. *The Practice of Collective Bargaining.* 8th ed. Homewood, IL: Richard D. Irwin, Inc.,1989.

Benson, Herman, Wilham Scherdel, John Donaldson, John Reimann, and Frank Schonfeld, eds. *Union Democracy in the Construction Trades.* Brooklyn, NY: Association for Union Democracy, 1985.

Berman, Harold J., and William R. Greiner. *The Nature and Functions of Law.* 3d ed. New York: Foundation Press, 1972.

Bloom, Gordon F., and Herbert R. Northrup. *Economics of Labor Relations.* 9th ed. Homewood, IL: Richard D. Irwin, Inc., 1981.

Blum, Leo. *A History of the American Labor Movement.* Washington, DC: American Historical Association, 1972.

BNA's Business and Human Resources Services Staff. *State Labor Laws.* Washington, DC: BNA, 1954.

Bompey, Stuart H., Max G. Brittain, and Paul I. Weiner. *Wrongful Termination Claims: A Preventive Approach.* New York: Practising Law Institute, 1991.

Bok, Derek C., and John C. Dunlop. *Labor and the American Community.* New York: Simon and Schuster, 1970.

Brooks, Thomas. *Toil and Trouble: A History of American Labor,* 2d ed. New York: Dell Publishing Co., Inc., 1971.

Calavita, Kitty. *U.S. Immigration Law and the Control of Labor, 1820–1924.* San Diego: Acad Press, 1984.

Canan, Michael J. *Qualified Retirement and Other Employee Benefit Plans, 1990.* St. Paul, MN: West Publishing, 1989.

Cavanagh, John, Lance Compa, Allan Ebert, Bill Goold, Kathy Selvaggio, and Tim Shorrock. *Trade's Hidden Costs: Worker Rights in a Changing World Economy.* Washington, DC: International Labor Rights, 1988.

Chamberlain, Neil W., and Jane M. Schilling. *The Impact of Strikes.* New York: Harper and Brothers, 1954.

Clark, Gordon L. *Unions and Communities under Siege: American Communities and the Crisis of Organized Labor.* New York: Cambridge University Press, 1989.

Collier, Rohan. *Combatting Sexual Harassment in the Workplace.* Bristol, PA: Taylor & Francis, 1995.

Commons, John R., and Associates. *History of Labour in the United States.* New York: Macmillan, 1991.

Commons, John R., and John B. Andrews. *Principles of Labor Legislation.* 4th Reprint ed. W. Caldwell, NJ: Kelley, 1967.

Connolly, Walter B., Jr. *Strikes, Stoppages, and Boycotts, 1976.* New York: Practising Law Institute, 1976.

Cox, Archibald. *Law and the National Labor Policy.* Los Angeles: University of California, Institute of Industrial Relations, 1960.

Cullen, Donald E. *National Emergency Disputes.* Ithaca, NY: New York State School of Industrial and Labor Relations, 1968.

Decker, Kurt H. *Privacy in the Workplace: Rights, Procedures and Policies.* Horsham, PA: LRP Pubns, 1994.

Dereshinsky, Ralph M. *The NLRB and Secondary Boycotts.* Philadelphia: University of Pennsylvania Press, 1972.

Dewar, K. *A Guide to Employment Law.* Salem, NH: Butterworth Legal Publications, 1991.

Dickson, Mary, and Philip Gerould, eds. *Supervising Employees with Disabilities.* Menlo Park, CA: Crisp Publications, 1993.

Dolson, William F., ed. *Second Annual Labor and Employment Law Institute: New Directions in the Labor and Employment Field*. Littleton, CO: Rothman, 1986.

Donahue, John D. *Shortchanging the Workforce: The Job Training Partnership Act and the Overselling of Privatized Training*. Washington, DC: Economic Policy Inst, 1990.

Drucker, Peter F. *The Practice of Management*. New York: Harper, 1954.

Dulles, Foster R. *Labor in America*. 3d ed. New York: Crowell, 1966.

Dunlop, John T. *Dispute Resolution, Negotiation, and Consensus Building*. Dover, MA: Auburn House, 1984.

———. *Industrial Relations Systems*. New York: Holt, 1958.

Duston, Robert L., and Scott Robbins. *A Practical Guide to Implementing the Family and Medical Leave Act*. Washington, DC: College & University Personnel, 1993.

Eggert, Gerald G. *Steelmasters and Labor Reform, 1886–1923*. Pittsburgh: University of Pittsburgh Press, 1981.

Ernst, Daniel R. *Lawyers against Labor: From Individual Rights to Corporate Liberalism*. Champaign, IL: University of Illinois Press, 1995.

Feliu, Alfred G. *Primer on Individual Employee Rights*. Washington, DC: BNA, 1992.

Fix, Michael, ed. *The Paper Curtain: Employer Sanctions' Implementation, Impact, and Reform*. Washington, DC: Urban Institute, 1991.

Flood, Lawrence, ed. *Unions and Public Policy*. Urbana, IL: Political Studies, 1989.

Foner, Philip S., ed. *We, the Other People: Alternative Declarations of Independence by Labor Groups, Farmers, Woman's Rights Advocates, Socialists, and Blacks, 1829–1975*. Ann Arbor, MI: Books on Demand, 1988.

French, Wendell. *Human Resources Management*. Boston: Houghton Mifflin, 1986.

Friedman, Sheldon, ed. *Restoring the Promise of American Labor Law*. Ithaca, NY: ILR Press, 1994.

Frierson, James G. *Employer's Guide to Americans with Disabilities Act*. 2d ed., Washington, DC: BNA, 1995.

Fritz, Richard J., and Arthur M. Stringari. *Employer's Handbook for Labor Negotiations*. 3d ed. Detroit: Management Labor Relations Service, Inc., 1968.

Gelman, Jon L. *Workers' Compensation Law*. St. Paul, MN: West Publishing, 1988.

Getman, Julius G., Steven B. Goldberg, and Jeanne B. Herman. *Union Representation Elections: Law and Reality*. New York: Russell Sage Foundation, 1976.

Goad, Lynn. *Uniform Contract Compliance: A Working Labor Compliance Program.* Whittier, CA: Paige Publications, 1988.

Goldberg, Arthur J. *AFL-CIO: Labor United.* New York: McGraw-Hill, 1956.

Goldman, Alvin L. *The Supreme Court and Labor-Management Law.* Lexington, MA: D.C. Heath, 1976.

Gould, William B., *A Primer on American Labor Law.* 3d ed. Cambridge: MIT Press, 1993.

Gould, William B. *Strikes, Dispute Procedures, and Arbitration: Essays on Labor Law.* Westport, CT: Greenwood, 1985.

Green, Ronald M., William A. Carmell, Peter S. Gray, and Laura B. Kaiser, eds. *State by State Guide to Human Resources Law.* New York: Panel Publications, 1991.

Gregory, Charles O. *Labor and the Law.* New York: W.W. Norton, 1946.

Groat, George G. *Trade Unions and the Law in New York: A Study of Some Legal Phases of Labor Organizations.* New York: Columbia University Studies in the Social Sciences, 1988.

Grodin, Joseph R. *Union Government and the Law: British and American Experiences.* Los Angeles: UCLA Industrial Relations, 1961.

Gross, James A. *Broken Promise: The Subversion of U.S. Labor Relations, 1947–1994.* Philadelphia: Temple University Press, 1995.

Gunningham, Neil. *Safeguarding the Worker: Job Hazards and the Role of the Law.* Holmes Beach, FL: W.W. Gaunt, 1984.

Haber, William, and Merrill G. Murray. *Unemployment Insurance in the American Economy.* Homewood, IL: Richard D. Irwin, Inc., 1966.

Higgins, George C. *Voluntarism in Organized Labor in the United States, 1930–40.* Reprint ed. N. Stratford, NH: Ayer, 1971.

Hill, Herbert. *Black Labor and the American Legal System.* Washington, DC: BNA, 1977.

Holzschu, Michael. *The Complete Employee Handbook: A Guide for Small and Medium Businesses.* Wakefield, RI: Moyer Bell, 1995.

Horton, Janet L. *The Preemployment Process: Avoiding Impermissible Inquiries and the Effect of the Americans with Disabilities Act.* Topeka, KS: NOLPE, 1993.

Joseph, Joel D. *The Worker's Bible: The Last Word on Employees' Rights.* Chicago, IL: Krantz Co, 1991.

Justice, Betty W. *Unions, Workers, and the Law.* Washington, DC: BNA, 1983.

Kalet, Joseph E. *Primer on FLSA and Other Wage and Hour Laws.* 3d ed. Washington, DC: BNA, 1994.

Kochan, Thomas. *Collective Bargaining and Industrial Relations.* Homewood, IL: Richard D. Irwin, Inc., 1980.

Kohn, Stephen M. *The Whistleblower Litigation Handbook: Environmental, Health and Safety Claims.* New York: Wiley, 1991.

Koral, Alan M. *Conducting the Lawful Employment Interview: How To Avoid Charges of Discrimination When Interviewing Job Candidates.* 4th ed. New York: Wiley, 1994.

Leacock, Eleanor B., and Helen I. Safa. *Women's Work: Development and the Division of Labor by Gender.* Westport, CT: Greenwood, 1986.

Lee, R. Alton. *Truman and Taft-Hartley: A Question of Mandate.* Westport, CT: Greenwood, 1980.

Lehrer, Susan. *Origins of Protective Labor Legislation for Women, 1905–1925.* Albany: State University of New York Press, 1987.

Levitan, Sar A., Peter E. Carlson, and Isaac Shapiro. *Protecting American Workers: An Assessment of Government Programs.* Washington, DC: BNA, 1986.

Lewis, Paul. *Practical Employment Law: A Guide for Human Resource Managers.* Cambridge, MA: Blackwell Publications, 1992.

Leibig, Michael T., and Wendy L. Kahn. *Public Employee Organizing and the Law.* Washington, DC: BNA, 1987.

Lindemann, Barbara, and David D. Kadue. *Sexual Harassment in Employment Law.* Washington, DC: BNA, 1992.

Lipsett, Laurence. *How To Hire Winners Legally.* Amherst, MA: Human Res Dev Press, 1994.

Lockton, Deborah. *Employment Law.* Salem, NH: Butterworth Legal Publications, 1993.

Lopez, Antoinette S., ed. *Latino Employment, Labor Organizations, and Immigration.* New York: Garland, 1994.

McCallum, Ron, Greg McCarry, and Paul Rolfeldt, eds. *Employment Security.* Holmes Beach, FL: W.W. Gaunt, 1994.

McMahon, June, ed. *Organizing Asian Pacific Workers in Southern California.* Los Angeles: University of California LA Indus Rel, 1993.

McWhirter, Darien A. *Your Rights at Work.* 2d ed. New York: Wiley, 1992.

Mason, Alpheus T. *Organized Labor and the Law.* N. Stratford, NH: Ayer, 1972.

Millis and Brown, E. *From the Wagner Act to Taft-Hartley.* Chicago: University of Chicago Press, 1950.

Millis and Montgomery, Royal E. *Organized Labor* New York: McGraw-Hill, 1945.

Mills, Daniel Quinn. *Labor-Management Relations.* 2d ed. New York: McGraw-Hill, 1982.

Mintz, Benjamin W. *OSHA: History, Law, and Policy.* Ann Arbor, MI: Books on Demand, 1988.

Modjeska, Lee, and Abigail C. Modjeska. *Federal Labor Law: NLRB Practice.* Rev. ed. Deerfield, IL: Clark Boardman Callaghan, 1995.

Morris, Gillian S., Timothy J. Archer, and Gillian S. Morris. *Trade Unions, Employers and the Law.* 2d ed. Salem, NH: Butterworth Legal Publications, 1993.

Murphy, Betty S., and Elliot S. Azoff. *Practice and Procedure Before the National Labor Relations Board.* 2d ed. Washington, DC: BNA, 1989.

Myers, M. Scott. *Managing without Unions* Reading, MA: Addison-Wesley, 1976.

Myles, John, and Jill Quadgano, eds. *States, Labor Markets and the Future of Old Age Policy.* Philadelphia: Temple University Press, 1991.

Nester, Mary A. *Pre-Employment Testing and the ADA.* Horsham, NH: LRP Publications, 1994.

Northrup, Herbert R., and Amie D. Thornton. *The Federal Government as Employer: The Federal Labor Relations Authority and the PATCO Challenge.* Philadelphia: University of Pennsylvania Wharton Center for Human Resources, 1988.

O'Connell, Francis A. *Plant Closings: Worker Rights, Management Rights and the Law.* New Brunswick, NJ: Transaction Publications, 1987.

O'Meara, Daniel P. *Protecting the Growing Number of Older Workers: The Age Discrimination in Employment Act.* Philadelphia: University of Pennsylvania Wharton Center for Human Resources, 1989.

O'Reilly, James T., Gale P. Simon, and Jodi C. Aronson. *Unions' Rights to Company Information.* Ann Arbor, MI: Books on Demand, 1986.

Occupational Safety and Health Administration. *OSHA Technical Manual.* Washington, DC: OSHA, 1993.

Outten, Wayne N., Robert J. Rabin, and Lisa R. Lipman. *The Rights of Employees and Union Members: The Basic ACLU Guide to the Rights of Employees and Union Members.* 2d rev. ed. American Civil Liberties Union Handbook Series. Carbondale, IL: Southern Illinois University Press, 1994.

Pension and Benefits Law, 1993. Rev. ed. New York: Resources Institute of America, 1993.

Pension and Employee Benefits Code—ERISA—Regulations—Preambles: As of March 1, 1993. Chicago, IL: CCH, 1993.

Perlman, Selig. *History of Trade Unionism in the United States.* New York: Macmillan, 1937.

Peterson, Florence. *American Labor Unions, What They Are and How They Work.* 2d rev. ed. New York: Harper & Row, 1963.

Perritt, Henry H. *Workplace Torts: Rights and Liabilities.* New York: Wiley, 1991.

Peters, Edward. *Strategy and Tactics in Labor Negotiations.* New London, CT: National Foremen's Institute, 1955.

Piore, Michael J. *Birds of Passage: Migrant Labor and Industrial Societies.* New York: Cambridge University Press, 1979.

Plant Closings: A Selected Bibliography of Materials. Published, 1986–1990. Ithaca, NY: ILR Press, 1991.

Practical Lawyer's Manual on Labor Law. Philadelphia: American Law Institute, 1988.

Reed, Smith, Shaw & McClay Staff, *OSHA Compliance Handbook.* Rockville, MD: Government Institutes, 1992.

Reynolds, Lloyd G., Stanley H. Masters, and Colleta H. Moser. *Labor Economics and Labor Relations.* 10th ed. Englewood Cliffs, NJ: Prentice Hall, 1991.

Rothstein, Mark A., Charles Craver, Elinor Schroeder, Elaine Shoben, and Lea S. Vanderveld. *Human Resources and the Law.* Washington, DC: BNA, 1994.

Rothstein, Mark A., Charles B. Craver, Elinor P. Schroeder, Elaine W. Shoben, and Lea V. Velde, eds. *Employment Law.* St. Paul, MN: West Publishing, 1994.

Ruzicho, Andrew J., and Louis A. Jacobs. *Employment Practices Manual: A Guide to Minimizing Constitutional, Statutory and Common Law Liability.* Rev. ed. Deerfield, IL: Clark Boardman Callaghan, 1994.

Sale, Kirkpatrick. *Rebels against the Future: The Luddites and Their War on the Industrial Revolution—Lessons for the Computer Age.* Reading, MA: Addison-Wesley, 1995.

Salomone, William G. *Salomone on Mediation: A Practice and Procedure Handbook.* Sarasota, FL: W. G. Salomone, 1993.

Schachter, Victor, and Thomas E. Geidt. *Drugs and Alcohol in the Workplace: Legal Developments and Management Strategies.* 2d ed. New York: Wiley, 1994.

Scheuch, Joanne D., and Wendy E. Shannon. *Personnel and the Law.* Washington, DC: American Bankers, 1989.

Schlei, Barbara L., and Paul Grossman. *Employment Discrimination Law.* 2d ed. Washington, DC: BNA, 1983.

Schlossberg, Stephen I., and Judith A. Scott. *Organizing and the Law.* 4th ed. Washington, DC: BNA, 1991.

Schoonhaven, Ray, ed. *Fairweather's Practice and Procedure in Labor Arbitration.* 3d ed. Washington, DC: BNA, 1991.

Shepard, Ira M., Robert L. Duston, and Karen S. Russell. *Workplace Privacy: Employee Testing, Surveillance, Wrongful Discharge, and Other Areas of Vulnerability.* 2d ed. Washington, DC: BNA, 1989.

Simkin, William E. *Mediation.* Washington, DC: BNA, 1971.

Smith, Melissa K. *Southern Employer's Guide: A Handbook of Employment Laws and Regulations.* Austin, TX: Summers Press, 1993.

Somers, Gerald G., ed. *Collective Bargaining: Contemporary American Experience.* Madison: IRRA, 1980.

———. *Essays in Industrial Relations Theory.* Ames: Iowa State University Press, 1969.

Sovereign, Kenneth L. *Personnel Law.* 3d ed. Englewood Cliffs, NJ: Prentice-Hall, 1994.

Strohm, Richard L. *Your Rights in the Workplace.* 2d ed. Franklin Lakes, NJ: Career Press Inc., 1994.

Summer, Clyde W., Joseph L. Rauh, and Herman Benson. *Union Democracy and Landrum-Griffin.* Brooklyn, NY: Association for Union Democracy, 1986.

Taft, Philip. *Rights of Union Members and the Government.* Westport, CT: Greenwood Press, 1975.

Taylor, Benjamin J., and Fred Witney. *Labor Relations Law.* 7th ed. Englewood Cliffs, NJ: Prentice-Hall, 1995.

———. *U.S. Labor Relations Law: Historical Development.* Englewood Cliffs, NJ: Prentice-Hall, 1991.

Technical Assistance Manual on the Employment Provisions Title 1 of the Americans with Disabilities Act. Washington, DC: Government Printing Office, 1993.

Teplow, Leo. *Regulating Safety and Health: A Working Model.* Des Plaines, IL: ASSE, 1987.

Tomlins, Christopher L. *The State and the Unions: Labor Relations, Law and the Organized Labor Movement in America, 1880–1960.* New York: Cambridge University Press, 1985.

Treiman, Donald J. *Job Evaluation: An Analytic Review.* Washington, DC: National Academy of Sciences, 1979.

Treiman, Donald J., and Heidi Hartmann, eds. *Women, Work, and Wages: Equal Pay for Jobs of Equal Value.* Washington, DC: National Academy Press, 1981.

Trollip, A. T. *Power, Law and Procedure: A Contemporary Guide to Industrial Relations.* Salem, NH: Butterworth Legal Publications, 1992.

Turnbull, Bruce H., Ethan S. Naftalin, and Lawyers Committee for Human Rights Staff, eds. *Worker Rights under the U.S. Trade Laws.* New York: Lawyers Comm Human, 1989.

Turner, Margery A., Michael Fix, and Raymond J. Struyk. *Opportunities Denied, Opportunities Diminished: Racial Discrimination in Hiring.* Washington, DC: Urban Institute, 1991.

Volz, Marlin M., ed. *Sixth Annual Labor and Employment Law Institute, School of Law, University of Louisville: Evolving Applications and Consequences of Labor and Employment Law, June 29–30, 1989.* Littleton, CO: Rothman, 1994.

———. *Third Annual Labor and Employment Law Institute: Labor and Employment Relations in the Age of the Robot, Computer and Foreign Competition.* Littleton, CO: Rothman, 1987.

Walton, Richard, and Robert McKersie. *A Behavioral Theory of Labor Negotiations.* New York: McGraw-Hill, 1965.

Wellington, Harry H. *Labor and the Legal Process.* New Haven, CT: Yale University Press, 1968.

West, Ruth C., ed. *United States Labor and Employment Laws.* Ann Arbor, MI: Books on Demand, 1994.

Westman, Daniel P. *Whistleblowing: The Law of Retaliatory Discharge.* Washington, DC: BNA, 1991.

What Managers and Supervisors Need To Know about the ADA. Minneapolis, MN: Society for Human Resources Management, 1992.

What You Ought To Know about Family and Medical Leave: What Are the Rules—Who Is Eligible—What Is Required. Chicago: CCH, 1993.

Weisinger, Hendrie. *Anger at Work: Learning the Art of Anger Management on the Job.* New York: Morrow, 1995.

Wendling, Wayne R. *The Plant Closure Policy Dilemma: Labor, Law and Bargaining.* Kalamazoo, MI: W.E. Upjohn, 1984.

Wikander, Ulla, Alice Kessler-Harris, and Jane Lewis, eds. *Protecting Women: Labor Legislation in Europe, the United States, and Australia, 1880–1920.* Champaign,IL: University of Illinois Press, 1995.

Winter, Robert H., Mark H. Stumpf, and Gerald L. Hawkins, eds. *Shark Repellents and Golden Parachutes: A Handbook for the Practitioner.* Gaithersburg, MD: Aspen Law, 1983.

Wood, Horace G., R. H. Helmholz, and Bernard D. Reams, eds. *A Treatise on the Law of Master and Servant.* Buffalo, NY: W. S. Hein, 1981.

Woodiwiss, Anthony. *Rights v. Conspiracy: A Sociological Essay on the History of Labour Law in the United States.* Herndon, VA: Berg Publications, 1990.

A Working Woman's Guide to Her Job Rights. New York: Gordon Press, 1992.

Workplace Discrimination: How To Pursue Your Rights. New York: Service Fund of NOW NYC, 1993.

Yager, Daniel V. *Has Labor Law Failed? An Examination of Congressional Oversight and Legislative Proposals 1968–1990.* Washington, DC: EPF, 1995.

Yates, Michael. *Power on the Job: The Legal Rights of Working People.* Boston: South End Press, 1994.

Yoder, Dale. *Personnel Management and Industrial Relations.* 6th ed. Englewood Cliffs, NJ: Prentice-Hall, 1970.

Adair v. United States, 208 U.S. 161, 28 S. Ct. 277, 52 L. Ed. 436 (1908)

Adarand Constructors, Inc. v. Federico Pena, 515 U.S. ——, 115 S. Ct. 2097, 132 L. Ed. 2d 158 (1995)

Adkins v. Childrens Hospital, 43 S. Ct. 394, 67 L. Ed. 785 (1923)

A.F.S.C.M.E. v. State of Washington, 770 F.2d 1401 (9th Cir. 1985)

Alexander v. Gardner-Denver Co., 415 U.S. 35, 94 S. Ct. 1011, 39 L. Ed. 2d 147 (1974)

Allgeyer v. Louisiana, 165 U.S. 578, 17 S. Ct. 427, 41 L. Ed. 832 (1897)

Allen Bradley Co. v. I.B.E.W. Local 3, 325 U.S. 797, 65 S. Ct. 1553, 89 L. Ed. 1939 (1945)

Allis Chalmers v. Lueck, 471 U.S. 202, 105 S. Ct. 1904, 85 L. Ed. 2d 706 (1985)

Amalgamated Association of Streetworkers [etc.] v. Lockridge, 403 U.S. 274, 91 S. Ct. 1909, 29 L. Ed. 2d 473 (1971)

American Manufacturing Co. See *United Steelworkers of America v. American Manufacturing.*

American Newspaper Publishers Association v. NLRB, 345 U.S. 100, 73 S. Ct. 552, 97 L. Ed. 852 (1953)

American Nurses Association v. State of Illinois, 783 F.2d 716 (7th Cir. 1986)

American Ship Building Co. v. NLRB, 380 U.S. 300, 85 S. Ct. 955, 13 L. Ed. 2d 855 (1965)

American Steel Foundries v. Tri-City Central Council, 257 U.S. 184, 42 S. Ct. 72, 66 L. Ed. 189 (1921)

Anderson v. Mount Clemens Pottery Co., 328 U.S. 680, 66 S. Ct. 1187, 90 L. Ed. 1515 (1946)

Apex Hosiery Co. v. Leader, 310 U.S. 469, 60 S. Ct. 982, 84 L. Ed. 1311 (1940)

Arizona Governing Committee for Tax Deferrred Compensation Plans v. Norris, 671 F.2d 330 (9th Cir. 1982), 463 U.S. 1073, 103 S. Ct. 3492, 77 L. Ed. 2d 1236 (1983)

Arlan's Department Store, 133 N.L.R.B. —— (1961)

Atlantic & Gulf Stevedores, Inc. v. Occupational Safety and Health Review Commission, 542 F.2d 602 (3d Cir. 1976)

Automobile Workers v. O'Brien, 339 U.S. 454, 70 S. Ct. 781, 94 L. Ed. 978 (1950)
Autoworkers v. Johnson Controls, 499 U.S. 187, 111 S. Ct. 1196, 113 L. Ed. 2d 158 (1991)
B.F. Goodrich Company, 115 N.L.R.B. 722 (1956)
Bailey v. Drexel Furniture Co., 259 U.S. 20, 42 S. Ct. 449, 66 L. Ed. 817 (1923)
Bakke Case. See *Regents of the University of California v. Bakke*
Ballinger v. Arlington Park Thoroughbred Race Track, No. 87 C 1161 (N.D. Ill. 1989)
Bautista v. Pan American, 828 F.2d 546 (9th Cir. 1987)
Bedford Cut Stone Co. v. Journeymen Stone Cutters' Association, 274 U.S. 37, 47 S. Ct. 522, 71 L. Ed. 916 (1927)
Belknap v. Hale, 463 U.S. 491, 103 S. Ct. 3172, 77 L. Ed. 2d 798 (1983)
Biggers v. Wittek Industries, Inc., 4 F.3d 291 (4th Cir. 1993)
Black & Decker Manufacturing. Co., 147 N.L.R.B. 825 (1964)
Board of Regents v. Roth, 408 U.S. 564, 92 S. Ct. 2701, 33 L. Ed. 2d 548 (1972)
Bob's Casing Crews, Inc. v. NLRB, 458 F.2d 1301 (5th Cir. 1972)
Bonner v. City of Pritchard, 661 F.2d 1206 (11th Cir. 1981)
Bowen v. U.S. Postal Service, 459 U.S. 212, 103 S. Ct. 588, 74 L. Ed. 2d 402 (1983)
Boys Market, Inc. v. Retail Clerk's Local 770, 398 U.S. 235, 90 S. Ct. 1583, 26 L. Ed. 2d 22 (1970)
Bradley v. Pizzaco of Nebraska, 7 F.3d 795 (8th Cir. 1993)
Bradwell v. State of Illinois, 83 U.S. (16 Wall.) 130, 21 L. Ed. 442 (1872)
Brennan v. Kroger, 513 F.2d 961 (7th Cir. 1975)
Bricklayers Local 18, 191 N.L.R.B. 872 (1971)
Brooks v. NLRB, 348 U.S. 96, 75 S. Ct. 176, 99 L. Ed. 2d 125 (1954)
Brown v. Board of Education, 347 U.S. 483, 74 S. Ct. 686, 98 L. Ed. 873 (1954)
Buffalo Forge v. United Steelworkers, 428 U.S. 397, 96 S. Ct. 3141, 49 L. Ed. 2d 1022 (1976)
Bundy v. Jackson, 641 F.2d 934 (D.C. Cir. 1981)
Bunting v. Oregon, 243 U.S. 426, 37 S. Ct. 435, 61 L. Ed. 830 (1917)
Burrell v. LaFollette Coach Lines, 97 F. Supp. 279 (E.D. Tenn. 1981)
Butta v. Anne Arundel County, 473 F. Supp. 83 (D. Md. 1979)
California Trucking Association v. Brotherhood of Teamsters & Auto, Truck Drivers, 679 F.2d 1275 (9th Cir. 1981), *cert. denied,* 459 U.S. 970, 103 S. Ct. 299, 74 L. Ed. 2d 281 (1982)
Campbell Coal. See *Truck Drivers & Helpers Local 728 v. NLRB (Campbell Coal)*
Carpenters Local 1302 v. United Brotherhood of Carpenters, 477 F.2d 612 (2d Cir. 1973)

Chamber of Commerce v. Reich, 57 F.3d 1099 (D.C. Cir. 1995)
Chinese Exclusion Case, 130 U.S. 581, 9 S. Ct. 673, 32 L. Ed. 1068 (1889)
Christensen v. State of Ohio, 563 F.2d 353 (8th Cir. 1977)
City of Los Angeles Department of United Automobile Workers, 435 U.S. 702, 98 S. Ct. 1370, 55 L. Ed. 2d 657 (1978)
Clady v. County of Los Angeles, 770 F.2d 1421 (9th Cir. 1985), *cert. denied,* 475 U.S. 1109, 106 S. Ct. 1516, 89 L. Ed. 2d 915 (1986)
Clayton v. United Auto Workers, 451 U.S. 679, 101 S. Ct. 2088, 68 L. Ed. 2d 538 (1981)
Cleary v. American Airlines Inc., 111 Cal. App. 3d 443, 168 Cal. Rptr. 722 (Cal. 1980)
Cole v. Fair Oaks Fire Protection District, 43 Cal. 3d 148, 233 Cal. Rptr 308, 729 P.2d 743 (1987)
Commonwealth v. Hunt, 45 Mass. (4 Met.) 111 (1842)
Commonwealth v. Pullis (Philadelphia Mayor's Court, 1806)
Consolidated Rail Corporation v. Darrone, 465 U.S. 624, 104 S. Ct. 1248, 79 L. Ed. 2d 568 (1984)
Cook v. Peter Kiewit Sons' Co., 775 F.2d 1030 (9th Cir. 1985)
Cook v. State of Rhode Island, 10 F.3d 17 (1st Cir. 1993)
Cooper Tire & Rubber Co. v. NLRB, 443 F.2d 338 (6th Cir. 1971)
County of Washington v. Gunther, 452 U.S. 161, 101 S. Ct. 2242, 68 L. Ed. 2d 751 (1981)
Craig v. Boren, 429 U.S. 679, 101 S. Ct. 2088, 68 L. Ed. 2d 538 (1981)
D'Amico v. New York State Board of Law Examiners, 813 F. Supp. 220 (W.D.N.Y. 1993)
Denver Building Trades. See *NLRB v. Denver Building & Construction Trades Council*
Detroit Police Officers v. Young, 452 U.S. 938, 101 S. Ct. 3079, 69 L. Ed. 2d 951 (1981)
Donovan v. Brandel, 736 F.2d 1114 (6th Cir. 1984)
Donovan v. Horne & Walston Farms, 735 F.2d 1354 (4th Cir. 1984)
Donovan v. Navajo Forest Products Industries, 692 F.2d 709 (10th Cir. 1982)
Dothard v. Rawlinson, 433 U.S. 321, 97 S. Ct. 2720, 53 L. Ed. 2d 786 (1977)
Douds v. Metropolitan Federation of Architects, 75 F. Supp. 672 (S.D.N.Y. 1948)
Duplex Printing Press Co. v. Deering, 254 U.S. 443, 41 S. Ct. 172, 65 L. Ed. 349 (1921)
East Chicago Rehabilitation Center Inc., 710 F.2d 397 (7th Cir. 1987), 465 U.S. 1065, 104 S. Ct. 1414, 79 L. Ed. 2d 740 (1984)
Easter v. Jeep Corporation, 750 F.2d 520 (6th Cir. 1984)

Eastex Inc. v. NLRB, 437 U.S. 556, 98 S. Ct. 2505, 57 L. Ed. 2d 428 (1977)
Eckmann v. Board of Education of Hawthorn School District #17, 636 F. Supp. 1214 (N.D. Ill. 1986)
Edward G. Budd Manufacturing v. NLRB, 138 F.2d 86 (3d Cir. 1943), *cert. denied*, 321 U.S. 778 (1943)
E.E.O.C. v. American Federation of State, County & Municipal Employees (AFSCME), 937 F. Supp. 166 (N.D.N.Y. 1996)
E.E.O.C. v. Aramco Services, Inc., 499 U.S. 244, 111 S. Ct. 1227, 113 L. Ed. 2d 274 (1991)
E.E.O.C. v. Tortilleria "La Mejor", 758 F. Supp. 585 (E.D. Cal. 1991)
E.E.O.C. v. Wyoming, 460 U.S. 226, 103 S. Ct. 1054, 75 L. Ed. 2d 18 (1983)
E.I. DuPont deNemours & Co., 162 N.L.R.B. 413 (1966)
E.I. DuPont deNemours & Co., 311 N.L.R.B. 893 (1993)
E.I. DuPont deNemours & Co. v. Local 900 of the International Chemical Workers Assn., 968 F.2d 456 (5th Cir. 1993)
Electromation, Inc. and Teamsters Local 1049, 309 N.L.R.B. 990 (1992)
Electromation, Inc. v. NLRB & Teamsters, 35 F.3d 1148 (7th Cir. 1994)
Emporium Capwell Co. v. Western Addition Community Organization, 420 U.S. 50, 95 S. Ct. 977, 43 L. Ed. 2d 12 (1975)
Enterprise Wheel and Car. See *United Steelworkers of America v. Enterprise Wheel & Car Corporation*
Enterprise Wire Co., 46 Lab. Arb. (BNA) 356 (1966)
Erie Railroad v. Tompkins, 304 U.S. 64, 58 S. Ct. 817, 82 L. Ed. 2d 1188 (1938)
Espinoza v. Farah Manufacturing Co., 414 U.S. 86, 94 S. Ct. 334, 38 L. Ed. 287 (1973)
Fall River Dyeing & Finishing Corp. v. NLRB, 482 U.S. 27, 107 S. Ct. 2225, 96 L. Ed. 2d 22 (1987)
Farmer's Reservoir & Irrigation Co. v. McComb, 337 U.S. 755, 69 S. Ct. 1274, 93 L. Ed. 1672 (1949)
Farwell v. Boston & Worcester R.R., 4 Metcalf 49 (Mass. 1842)
Fibreboard Paper Products Corp. v. NLRB, 379 U.S. 203, 85 S. Ct. 398, 13 L. Ed. 2d 233 (1964)
Firefighters Local Union No. 1784 v. Stotts, 467 U.S. 561, 104 S. Ct. 2576, 81 L. Ed. 2d 483 (1984)
Fitzpatrick v. Blitzer, 519 F.2d 559 (2d Cir. 1975), *rev'd on other grounds*, 427 U.S. 445 (1976)
Fong Yue Ting v. U.S., 149 U.S. 698, 13 S. Ct. 1016, 37 L. Ed. 905 (1893)
Ford Motor Co. v. Huffman, 345 U.S. 330, 73 S. Ct. 681, 97 L. Ed. 1048 (1953)
Ford Motor Co. v. NLRB, 441 U.S. 488, 99 S. Ct. 1842, 60 L. Ed. 2d 420 (1979)

Hazen Paper Co. v. Biggins, 507 U.S. 604, 113 S. Ct. 1701, 123 L. Ed. 2d 338 (1993)

Held v. Gulf Oil Company, 684 F.2d 427 (6th Cir. 1982)

Hertzka v. Knowles, 503 F.2d 625 (9th Cir. 1974)

Hines v. Anchor Motor Freight, Inc., 424 U.S. 554, 96 S. Ct. 1048, 47 L. Ed. 2d 231 (1976)

Hitchman Coal & Coke Co. v. Mitchell, 245 U.S. 229, 38 S. Ct. 65, 62 L. Ed. 260 (1917)

Hod Carriers Local 840 (Blinne Construction Co.), 135 N.L.R.B. 1153 (1962)

Hopkins v. Baltimore Gas & Electric Co., 871 F. Supp. 822 (D Md. 1994), 77 F.3d 745 (4th Cir. 1996)

Houston Building and Construction Trades Council (Claude Everett, Construction Co.), 136 N.L.R.B. 321 (1962)

Howard Johnson Co. v. Detroit Local Joint Executive Board, 417 U.S. 249, 94 S. Ct. 2236, 41 L. Ed. 45 (1974)

Hudgens v. NLRB, 424 U.S. 507, 96 S. Ct. 1029, 47 L. Ed. 2d 196 (1976)

Humphrey v. Moore, 375 U.S. 335, 84 S. Ct. 363, 11 L. Ed. 2d 370 (1964)

Hunio v. Tishman Construction Corporation of California, 34 Cal. Rptr2d 557, 882 P.2d 248 (1994)

I.A.T.S.E. v. Compact Video Services, Inc., 50 F.3d 1464 (9th Cir. 1995), *cert. denied*, —— U.S. ——, 116 S. Ct. 335, 133 L. Ed. 2d 423 (1995)

In re American Provision, 44 Bank. 907 (D. Minn. 1984)

In the Matter of Kokesch, 411 N.W.2d 559 (Minn. App. 1987)

Inland Steel Company, 77 N.L.R.B. 1 (1948)

Inland Steel Company v. NLRB, 170 F.2d 247 (7th Cir. 1948), 336 U.S. 960 (1949)

International Brotherhood of Electrical Workers, Local 861 (Plauche Electric Co.), 135 N.L.R.B. 250 (1962)

International Brotherhood of Teamsters v. United States, 431 U.S. 324, 97 S. Ct. 1843, 52 L. Ed. 2d 396 (1977)

International Brotherhood of Teamsters Local 695 v. Vogt, Inc., 354 U.S. 284, 77 S. Ct. 1166, 1 L. Ed. 2d 1347 (1957)

International Brotherhood of Teamsters v. NLRB, 365 U.S. 667, 81 S. Ct. 835, 6 L. Ed. 2d 11 (1961)

International Ladies Garment Workers' Union v. NLRB [Bernhard-Altman Corp.], 366 U.S. 731, 81 S. Ct. 1603, 6 L. Ed. 2d 762 (1961)

International Rice Milling, 341 U.S. 665, 71 S. Ct. 961, 95 L. Ed. 1284 (1951)

Jane Doe v. United States Postal Service, 37 Fair Empl. Prac. Cas. (BNA) 1867 (D. D.C. June 12, 1985)

Loving v. Virginia, 388 U.S. 1, 87 S. Ct. 1817, 18 L. Ed. 2d 1010 (1967)
Mallinckrodt Chemical Works, 162 N.L.R.B. 387 (1966)
Marbro Co., 284 N.L.R.B. 1303 (1987)
Martin v. Wilks, 490 U.S. 755, 109 S. Ct. 2180, 104 L. Ed. 2d 835 (1989)
Maryland State Troopers Association, Inc. v. Evans, 993 F.2d 1072 (4th Cir. 1993)
Massachusetts Board of Retirement v. Murgia, 427 U.S. 307, 96 S. Ct. 2562, 49 L. Ed. 2d 520 (1976)
McClure v. Salvation Army, 460 F.2d 553 (5th Cir. 1972), *cert. denied*, 409 U.S. 896 (1972)
McDonald v. Santa Fe Trail Transportation Co., 427 U.S. 273, 96 S. Ct. 2574, 49 L. Ed. 2d 493 (1976)
McDonnell Douglas Corp. v. Green, 411 U.S. 792, 93 S. Ct. 1817, 36 L. Ed. 2d 668 (1973)
McGann v. H&H Co., 946 F.2d 401 (5th Cir. 1991), *cert. denied sub nom. Greenberg v. H&H Music*, 506 U.S. 981, 111 S. Ct. 1310, 121 L. Ed. 2d 387 (1991)
Meritor Savings Bank v. Vinson, 477 U.S. 57, 106 S. Ct. 2399, 91 L. Ed. 2d 49 (1986)
Mescalero Apache Tribe v. Rhoades, 755 F. Supp. 1484 (D. N.M. 1992)
Mike Yurosek & Son, Inc., 292 N.L.R.B. 1074 (1989)
Minnesota v. Century Camera, Inc., 309 N.W.2d 735 (Minn. 1981)
Monroe v. Standard Oil, 452 U.S. 549, 101 S. Ct. 2510, 69 L. Ed. 2d 226 (1981)
Moore Dry Dock. See *Sailors Union of the Pacific and Moore Dry Dock Company*
Morton v. Mancari, 417 U.S. 535. 94 S. Ct. 2474, 41 L. Ed. 2d 290 (1974)
Mount Healthy City School District Board of Education v. Doyle, 429 U.S. 274, 97 S. Ct. 568, 50 L. Ed. 2d 471 (1977)
Mourad v. Automobile Club Insurance Ass'n, 186 Mich. App. 715, 465 N.W.2d 395 (1991)
Muller v. Oregon, 208 U.S. 412, 28 S. Ct. 324, 52 L. Ed. 551 (1908)
Nashville Gas Co. v. Satty, 434 U.S. 136, 98 S. Ct. 347, 54 L. Ed. 2d 356 (1977)
National Post Office Mail Handlers v. U.S. Postal Service, 594 F.2d 988 (4th Cir. 1979)
National Realty and Construction Co., Inc. v. OSHRC, 489 F.2d 1257 (D.C. Cir. 1973)
National Treasury Union v. Von Raab, 489 U.S. 656, 109 S. Ct. 1384, 103 L. Ed. 2d 685 (1989)
Nebbia v. New York, 291 U.S. 502, 54 S. Ct. 505, 78 L. Ed. 2d 940 (1934)

NLRB v. Great Dane Trailers, Inc., 388 U.S. 26, 87 S. Ct. 1792, 18 L. Ed. 2d 1027 (1967)

NLRB v. Hendricks County, 454 U.S. 170, 102 S. Ct. 216, 70 L. Ed. 2d 323 (1981)

NLRB v. Insurance Agents International Union, 361 U.S. 477, 80 S. Ct. 1107, 8 L. Ed. 2d 230 (1960)

NLRB v. International Longshoremen's Association, 447 U.S. 490, 100 S. Ct. 2305, 65 L. Ed. 2d 289 (1980)

NLRB v. International Longshoremen's Association, 473 U.S. 61, 105 S. Ct. 3045, 87 L. Ed. 2d 47 (1985)

NLRB v. J. Weingarten, Inc., 420 U.S. 251, 95 S. Ct. 959, 43 L. Ed. 2d 171 (1975)

NLRB v. Jones & Laughlin Steel Corporation, 301 U.S. 1, 57 S. Ct. 615, 81 L. Ed. 893 (1937)

NLRB v. Katz, 369 U.S. 736, 82 S. Ct. 1107, 8 L. Ed. 2d 230 (1962)

NLRB v. Local 18, Bricklayers, Masons (et al.), 453 F.2d 863 (3d Cir. 1971)

NLRB v. Local 138, Operating Engineers, 377 F.2d 528 (2d Cir. 1967)

NLRB v. Local 1229, IBEW (Jefferson Standard Broadcasting Co.), 346 U.S. 132, 96 S. Ct. 2548, 49 L. Ed. 2d 396 (1976)

NLRB v. MacKay Radio & Telegraph Co., 304 U.S. 333, 58 S. Ct. 904, 82 L. Ed. 1381 (1938)

NLRB v. Magnavox of Tennessee, 415 U.S. 322, 94 S. Ct. 1099, 39 L. Ed. 2d 358 (1979)

NLRB v. Marine Workers, 391 U.S. 418, 88 S. Ct. 1717, 20 L. Ed. 706 (1968)

NLRB v. Radio Officers' Union, 196 F.2d 960 (2d Cir. 1952), 347 U.S. 17, 74 S. Ct. 323, 98 L. Ed. 455 (1954)

NLRB v. Retail Store Employees Union Local 1001, 447 U.S. 607, 100 S. Ct. 2372, 65 L. Ed. 2d 377 (1980)

NLRB v. Savair Manufacturing, 414 U.S. 270, 94 S. Ct. 495, 38 L. Ed. 2d 495 (1973)

NLRB v. Servette, 377 U.S. 46, 84 S. Ct. 1098, 12 L. Ed. 2d 121 (1964)

NLRB v. Tom Joyce Floors, 353 F.2d 768 (9th Cir. 1965)

NLRB v. Tomco Communications, 567 F.2d 871 (9th Cir. 1978)

NLRB v. Town & Country Electric, Inc., —— U.S. ——, 116 S. Ct. 450, 133 L. Ed. 2d 371 (1995)

NLRB v. Transportation Management Corporation, 462 U.S. 393 (1983)

NLRB v. Truitt Manufacturing Co., 351 U.S. 149, 76 S. Ct. 753, 100 L. Ed. 1027 (1956)

NLRB v. United Steelworkers [Nutrone and Avondale], 361 U.S. 39, 80 S. Ct. 1, 4 L. Ed. 2d 12 (1959)

NLRB v. Wooster Division of Borg Warner Corporation, 356 U.S. 342, 78 S. Ct. 718, 2 L. Ed. 2d 823 (1958)
NLRB v. Wyman-Gordan, 394 U.S. 759, 89 S. Ct. 1426, 22 L. Ed. 2d 709 (1969)
NLRB v. Yeshiva University, 444 U.S. 672, 100 S. Ct. 856, 63 L. Ed. 2d 115 (1980)
Norton v. Macy, 417 F.2d 1161 (D.C. Cir. 1969)
Otis Massey, 109 N.L.R.B. 275, *enf't denied*, 225 F.2d 205 (5th Cir. 1955), *cert. denied*, 350 U.S. 914 (1955)
Pacific Coast Association of Pulp and Paper Manufacturers, 121 N.L.R.B. 990 (1958)
Pacific Coast Association of Pulp and Paper Manufacturers v. NLRB, 304 F.2d 760 (9th Cir. 1962)
Palace Laundry Dry Cleaning Corp., 75 N.L.R.B. 320 (1947)
Parker v. Baltimore and Ohio R,R. Company, 652 F.2d 1012 (D.C. Cir. 1981)
Patterson v. McLean Credit Union, 491 U.S. 164, 109 S. Ct. 2363, 105 L. Ed. 2d 132 (1989)
Pavao v. Brown & Sharpe Manufacturing Co., 844 F. Supp. 890 (D. R.I. 1994)
Payne v. Western & A.R.R., 81 Tenn. 507 (Tenn. Sup Ct. 1884)
Pecheur Lozenge Co., 209 F.2d 393 (2d Cir. 1953)
Pena v. Brattleboro, 702 F.2d 322 (2d Cir. 1983)
Perry v. Sindermann, 408 U.S. 593, 92 S. Ct. 264, 33 L. Ed. 2d 570 (1972)
Peter Kiewit & Sons Co., 231 N.L.R.B. 76 (1977), *enf'd*, 595 F.2d 844 (1979)
Philanz Oldsmobile, Inc., 137 N.L.R.B. 867 (1962)
Pioneer Flour Mills v. NLRB, 427 F.2d 983 (5th Cir. 1970)
Plauche Electric. See *International Brotherhood of Electrical Workers, Local 861 (Plauche Electric Co.)*
Plessy v. Ferguson, 163 U.S. 537, 16 S. Ct. 1138, 41 L. Ed. 256 (1896)
Plumbers, Local 741 (Stearns-Roger Corp.), 198 N.L.R.B. 1056 (1972)
Porter v. Pepsi Cola Bottling Co. of Columbia, 247 S.C. 370 370, 147 S.E.2d 620
Price v. Teamsters, 457 F.2d 605 (3d Cir. 1972)
Price Waterhouse v. Hopkins, 490 U.S. 228, 109 S. Ct. 1775, 104 L. Ed. 2d 268 (1989)
Prickett v. Circuit Science, 518 N.W. 2d 602 (Minn. 1994)
Pruitt v. Cheney, 963 F.2d 1160 (9th Cir. 1992)
Public Service Co. of Colorado, 312 N.L.R.B. 459 (1993)
Railroad Retirement Board v. Alton Railroad Company, 295 U.S. 330, 55 S. Ct. 758, 79 L. Ed. 1468 (1935)
Railway Mail Ass'n v. Corsi, 326 U.S. 88, 65 S. Ct. 1483, 89 L. Ed. 2072 (1945)

Regents of the University of California v. Bakke, 438 U.S. 265, 98 S. Ct. 2733, 57 L. Ed. 2d 750 (1978)
Reich v. IBP, Inc., 38 F.3d 1123 (10th Cir. 1994)
Republic Aviation v. NLRB, 324 U.S. 793, 65 S. Ct. 982, 89 L. Ed. 1372 (1945), *reaffirmed in Eastex v. NLRB*, 437 U.S. 556, 98 S. Ct. 2505, 57 L. Ed. 2d 428 (1978)
Republic Steel Corp. v. Maddox, 379 U.S. 650, 85 S. Ct. 614, 13 L. Ed. 2d 580 (1965)
Retail Clerks Local 1625 v. Schermerhorn, 375 U.S. 96, 84 S. Ct. 219, 11 L. Ed. 2d 179 (1963)
Rex v. Journeymen Tailors of Cambridge, 8 Modern 10 (Great Britain)
Reynolds v. Brock, 815 F.2d 571 (9th Cir. 1987)
Rovira v. A T T, 817 F. Supp. 1062 (S.D.N.Y. 1993)
Safeway Stores, Inc. v. Retail Clerks Association, 41 Cal. 2d 567, 261 P.2d 721 (1953)
Sailors Union of the Pacific and Moore Dry Dock Co., 92 N.L.R.B. 547 (1950)
Saint Frances College v. Al-Khazari, 481 U.S. 604, 107 S. Ct. 2022, 95 L. Ed. 2d 582 (1987)
St. Mary's Honor Center v. Hicks, 509 U.S. 502, 113 S. Ct. 2742, 125 L.2d 407 (1993)
San Diego Building Trades Council v. Garmon, 359 U.S. 236, 79 S. Ct. 773, 3 L. Ed. 2d 775 (1959)
Schecter Poultry v. U.S., 295 U.S. 495, 55 S. Ct. 837, 79 P.Ed 1570 (1935)
Schultz v. Wheaton Glass Co., 421 F.2d 259 (3d Cir. 1981), *cert. denied*, 398 U.S. 905 (1981)
Sears Roebuck & Co. v. San Diego District Council of Carpenters, 436 U.S. 180, 98 S. Ct. 1745, 56 L. Ed. 2d 209 (1978)
Secretary of Labor, United States Department of Labor v. Lauritzen, 835 F.2d 1529 (7th Cir. 1987), *cert. denied*, 488 U.S. 898, 109 S. Ct. 243, 102 L. Ed. 2d 232 (1988)
Shelly & Anderson Furniture Manufacturing Co. v. NLRB, 497 F.2d 1200 (9th Cir. 1974)
Sinclair v. Auto Club of Oklahoma, 733 F.2d 726 (9th Cir. 1984)
Sinclair Refining Co. v. Atkinson, 370 U.S. 195, 82 S. Ct. 1328, 8 L. Ed. 2d 440 (1962)
Skinner v. Railway Labor Executive's Association, 489 U.S. 602, 109 S. Ct. 1402, 103 L. Ed. 639 (1989)
Smitley d/b/a Crown Cafetaria v. NLRB, 327 F.2d 351 (9th Cir. 1964)
Snow & Sons, 134 N.L.R.B. 709 (1961), *enf'd*, 308 F.2d 687 (9th Cir. 1962)

Soroka v. Dayton-Hudson, 1 Cal. Rptr. 2d 77, 235 Cal. App. 3d 654 (Cal. 1991)
South Prairie Construction Co. v. Operating Engineers, Local 627, 425 U.S. 800, 96 S. Ct. 1842, 48 L. Ed. 2d 382 (1976)
Southern Pacific Co. v. Jensen, 244 U.S. 205, 37 S. Ct. 524, 61 L. Ed. 1086 (1917)
Sparks Nugget, Inc., d/b/a John Ascaugas Nugget, 230 N.L.R.B. 275 (1977)
Sparks Nugget, Inc. v. NLRB, 968 F.2d 991 (9th Cir. 1992)
Spaulding v. University of Washington, 740 F.2d 686 (9th Cir. 1984)
Spencer Auto Electric, Inc., 73 N.L.R.B. 1416 (9th Cir.1947)
Stanley v. University of Southern California, 13 F.3d 1313 (9th Cir. 1993)
Steele v. Louisville & N.R. Railroad, 323 U.S. 192, 65 S. Ct. 226, 89 L. Ed. 173 (1944)
Steffan v. Aspin, 8 F.3d 57 (D.C. Cir. 1993)
Steward Machine Company v. Davis, 301 U.S. 546, 57 S. Ct. 883, 81 L. Ed. 1279 (1937)
Stoddard v. School Dist. No. # 1, Lincoln County, Wyoming, 429 F. Supp. 890 (D.C. Wyo. 1977), *aff'd in part, rev'd in part,* 590 F.2d 829 (10th Cir. 1979)
Swift v. United States, 649 F. Supp. 596 (D. D.C. 1986)
Syres v. Oil Workers, Local 23, 223 F.2d 739 (5th Cir.), *cert. granted,* 350 U.S. 892 (1955)
Syres v. Oil Workers, Local 23, 257 F.2d 479 (5th Cir. 1958), *cert. denied,* 358 U.S. 929 (1959)
Teamsters v. U.S., 431 U.S. 234, 97 S. Ct. 1843, 52 L. Ed. 2d 396 (1977)
Texas v. Hopwood, 78 F.3d 932 (5th Cir. 1996), *cert. denied,* 116 S. Ct. 2581 (1996)
Texas & New Orleans R.R. v. Brotherhood of Railway Clerks, 281 U.S. 548, 50 S. Ct. 427, 74 L. Ed. 1034 (1930)
Texas Company, 93 N.L.R.B. 1358 (1951), *enforcement denied,* 198 F.2d (9th Cir. 1952)
Texas Department of Community Affairs v. Burdine, 450 U.S. 248, 101 S. Ct. 1089, 67 L. Ed. 2d 207 (1983)
Textile Workers Union v. Darlington Manufacturing Co, 380 U.S. 263, 85 S. Ct. 994, 13 L. Ed. 2d 827 (1965)
Textile Workers Union v. Lincoln Mills of Alabama, 358 U.S. 448, 787 S. Ct. 912, 1 L. Ed. 2d 972 (1957)
Toussiant v. Blue Cross & Blue Shield of Michigan, 292 N.W.2d 880 (Mich. Sup. Ct. 1980)
Trans World Airlines v. Hardison, 432 U.S. 63, 97 S. Ct. 2264, 53 L. Ed. 2d 113 (1977)

Traux v. Raich, 239 U.S. 338, 36 S. Ct. 7, 60 L. Ed. 31 (1915)

Truck Drivers & Helpers Local 728 v. NLRB (Campbell Coal), 249 F.2d 512 (D.C. Cir. 1957), *cert. denied*, 355 U.S. 958, 78 S. Ct. 543, 2 L. Ed. 2d 533 (1959)

Truck Drivers Local 449 v. NLRB (Buffalo Linen), 353 U.S. 87, 77 S. Ct. 643, 1 L. Ed. 2d 676 (1957)

Tucker v. State of California Department of Education, 97 F.3d 1204 (9th Cir. 1996)

Underwood v. D.C. Armory Board, 816 F.2d 769 (D.C. Cir. 1987)

United Brotherhood of Carpenters v. Brown, 343 F.2d 872 (10th Cir. 1965)

United Independent Flight Officers v. United Airlines, Inc., 756 F.2d 1274 (7th Cir. 1985)

United States v. Biaggi, 853 F.2d 89 (2d Cir. 1988), *cert denied*, 489 U.S. 1052, 109 S. Ct. 1312. 103 L. Ed. 2d 581 (1989)

United States v. Billingsley, 474 F.2d 63 (6th Cir. 1973)

United States v. Darby Lumber Co., 312 U.S. 100, 61 S. Ct. 451, 85 L. Ed. 609 (1941)

United States v. Enmons, 410 U.S. 396, 93 S. Ct. 1007, 35 L. Ed. 2d 379 (1973)

United States v. Gibson, 726 F.2d 869 (1st Cir. 1984)

United States v. Hutcheson, 312 U.S. 219, 61 S. Ct. 463, 85 L. Ed. 788 (1941)

United States v. Carolene Products Co., 304 U.S. 144, 58 S. Ct. 778, 82 L. Ed. 1234 (1938)

United States Railroad Retirement Board v. Fritz, 449 U.S. 166, 101 S. Ct. 453, 66 L. Ed. 2d 368 (1980)

United Steelworkers of America v. American Manufacturing, 363 U.S. 564, 80 S. Ct. 1343, 4 L. Ed. 2d 1403 (1960)

United Steelworkers of America v. Enterprise Wheel & Car Corporation, 363 U.S. 593, 80 S. Ct. 1358, 4 L. Ed. 2d 1424 (1960)

United Steelworkers of America v. NLRB [Carrier Corp.], 376 U.S. 442, 84 S. Ct. 899, 112 L. Ed. 2d 863 (1964)

United Steelworkers of America v. United States, 361 U.S. 39, 80 S. Ct. 1, 4 L. Ed. 2d 12 (1959)

United Steelworkers of America v. Warrior Gulf & Navigation Co., 363 U.S. 574, 80 S. Ct. 1347, 4 L. Ed. 2d 1409 (1960)

United Steelworkers of America v. Weber, 443 U.S. 193, 99 S. Ct. 2721, 61 L. Ed. 2d 480 (1979)

Vaca v. Sipes, 386 U.S. 171, 87 S. Ct. 903, 17 L. Ed. 2d 842 (1967)

Wards Cove Packing Co. v. Atonio, 490 U.S. 642, 109 S. Ct. 245, 104 L. Ed. 2d 733 (1989)

Warrior Gulf and Navigation. See *United Steelworkers of America v. Warrior Gulf & Navigation*

Washington Coca Cola Bottling Works, 107 N.L.R.B. 299 (1953), *enf'd sub. nom. Brewery & Beverage Drivers Local 67 v. NLRB*, 220 F.2d 380 (D.C. Cir. 1971)

Watkins v. U.S. Army, 875 F.2d 699 (9th Cir. 1989)

Watson v. Fort Worth Bank & Trust, 487 U.S. 977, 108 S. Ct. 2777, 101 L. Ed. 2d 827 (1988)

Weber v. Kaiser Aluminum, 611 F.2d 132 (5th Cir. 1980)

Webster v. Motorola, 418 Mass. 425, 637 N.E.2d 203 (1994)

West Virginia University Hospitals v. Casey, 499 U.S. 83, 111 S. Ct. 1130, 113 L. Ed. 2d 68 (1991)

Wheeler v. Snyder Buick, Inc., 794 F.2d 1228 (7th Cir. 1986)

Whirlpool v. Marshall, 445 U.S. 1, 100 S. Ct. 883, 63 L. Ed. 2d 154 (1980)

Williams Enterprises v. NLRB, 456 F.2d 1226 (D.C. Cir. 1992)

Williams v. Phillips Petroleum, 23 F.3d 930 (5th Cir. 1994), *cert. denied*, 115 S. Ct. 582 (1994)

Woolley v. Hoffman-LaRoche, Inc., 99 N.J. 284, 491 A.2d 1257 (1985)

Wooster Division of Borg-Warner Corporation, 113 N.L.R.B. 1288 (1955), 358 U.S. 342 (1958)

Wright Line, Inc., 251 N.L.R.B. 1083 (1980), *enf'd*, 662 F.2d 899 (1st Cir. 1981), *cert. denied*, 455 U.S. 989 (1982)

Wygant v. Jackson Board of Education, 476 U.S. 267, 106 S. Ct. 1842, 90 L. Ed. 2d 260 (1986)

Yick Wo v. Hopkins, 118 U.S. 356, 6 S. Ct. 1064, 30 L. Ed. 220 (1886).

Note: a list of executive orders related to labor and employment issues appears at the end of this section.

Administrative Procedure Act
37 Stat. 736 (1913), 5 U.S.C. 551-921 (1988)

Age Discrimination Claims Assistance Act of 1988
102 Stat. 78 (1988); 29 U.S.C. 626 (1988)

Age Discrimination Claims Assistance Amendments of 1990
104 Stat. 1298 (1990); 29 U.S.C. 626 notes (1988)

Age Discrimination in Employment Act of 1967
81 Stat. 602 (1967), 29 U.S.C. 621, et seq (1988)

Age Discrimination in Employment Act of 1975
89 Stat. 728, 42 U.S.C. 6101 et seq (1988)

Americans with Disabilities Act of 1990
104 Stat. 327 (1990); 42 U.S.C. 1201 et seq., 47 U.S.C. 152, 221 (1988)

Anti-Kick Back Act
62 Stat. 740 (1948); 18 U.S.C. 874 (1988); 40 U.S.C. 1873 (1988)

Bankruptcy Reform Act of 1978
92 Stat. 2549 (1978); 11 U.S.C. 525 (1988)

Bankruptcy Amendments of 1984
98 Stat. 333 (1984); 11 U.S.C. 525 (1988)

Bankruptcy Amendments and Federal Judgeships Act of 1984
98 Stat. 333 (1984); 11 U.S.C. 1113, 1113 note (1988)

Black Lung Benefits Act of 1972
86 Stat. 150 (1972); 30 U.S.C. 901 et seq. (1988)

Black Lung Benefits Amendments of 1981
95 Stat. 1643-1645 (1981); 30 U.S.C. 901,902,921-923,932,940 (1988)

Black Lung Benefits Reform Act of 1977
92 Stat 95 (1978); 30 U.S.C. 901-904, 921-924a (1988)

Child Labor Act
52 Stat. 1067 (1938); 29 U.S.C. 212, 213 (1988)

Civil Rights Act of 1866
14 Stat. 27 (1866); 42 U.S.C. 1981 (1988)

Civil Rights Act of 1871
16 Stat. 433, 17 Stat 13 (1871); 42 U.S.C. 1983-1986 (1988)

Civil Rights Act of 1964
78 Stat. 241 (1964); 42 U.S.C. 2000d-2000e-17 (1988)

Civil Rights Act of 1991
105 Stat. 1071 (1991); 29 U.S.C. 626, 42 U.S.C. 1901, 1988, 2000e (1988)

Civil Rights Restoration Act of 1988
102 Stat. 28 28 (1988); 29 U.S.C. 706, 794 (1988)

Civil Service Reform Act of 1978
92 Stat. 111 (1978); 5 U.S.C. 7501-7504,7511-7514,7521,7541-7543 (1988)

Clayton Antitrust Act
38 Stat. 730 (1914), as amended, 15 U.S.C. 15, 17,26, 29 U.S.C. 52, 53 (1988)

Coal Mine Health and Safety Act
83 Stat. 742 (1969); 15 U.S.C. 633, 636; 30 U.S.C. 801-804 (1988)

Comprehensive Employment and Training Act (CETA) of 1973
87 Stat. 830 (1973); 29 U.S.C. 801 (1988)

Comprehensive Employment and Training Act Amendments of 1978
92 Stat. 1909 (1978); 29 U.S.C. 1273, 175a, 186 (1988)

Consolidated Omnibus Budget Reconciliation Act of 1985
101 Stat. 82 (1986); see tables to the U.S.C. (1988)

Consumer Credit Protection Act of 1968
82 Stat. 146 (1968); 15 U.S.C. 1601, et seq. (1988); 18 U.S.C. 891, et seq. (1988)

Contract Disputes Act of 1978
92 Stat. 2382 (41 U.S.C. 601-613 (1988)

Contract Work Hours and Safety Standards Act (1962)
76 Stat. 357 (1962); 40 U.S.C. 327-333 (1988)

Cooper Labor Jurisdiction Amendment
49 Stat. 457 (1935); 29 U.S.C. 164 (1988)

Copeland Anti-Racketeering Act
60 Stat. 420 (1946); 18 U.S.C. 874 (1988)

Crimes and Criminal Procedure Act of 1948
62 Stat. 683 (1948); 18 U.S.C. 1231 (1988)

Davis-Bacon Act of 1931
46 Stat. 1494, 40 U.S.C. 276a-276a5 (1931), amended by 49 Stat. 1001 (1935), (1940), (1964), 74 Stat. 418 (1960), and 78 Stat. 238 (1964)

Department of Labor Act
37 Stat. 736 (1913); 29 U.S.C. 1-49l-d, 551-567 (1988)

Department of Labor Executive Level Conforming Amendments of 1986
100 Stat. 3491 (1986); 29 U.S.C. 552, 553, 1721 (1988)

Displaced Homemakers Self-Sufficiency Assistance Act
104 Stat. 2751 (1990); 29 U.S.C. 2301-2314 (1988)

Drug-Free Workplace Act of 1988
102 Stat. 4181, 5151, et seq. (1988), 41 U.S.C. 701-707 (1988)

Economic Dislocation and Worker Adjustment Assistance Act
102 Stat. 1524 (1988); 29 U.S.C. 565,1502,1505,1532,1651-1662c,1732 (1988)

Employee Polygraph Protection Act of 1988
102 Stat. 646 (1988), 29 U.S.C. 2001 et seq. (1988)

Employee Retirement Income Security Act (ERISA) of 1974
88 Stat. 829 (1974); 29 U.S.C. 441, 1001-1461 (1988)

Equal Employment Opportunity Act
78 Stat 241 (1964); 42 U.S.C. 701, et seq. (1988), 42 U.S.C. 2000e (1988)

Equal Employment Opportunity Act of 1972
86 Stat. 103 (1972); 42 U.S.C. 200e-2000e-8, 200e-9,2000e-13,2000e-14, 2000e-16,2000e-17 (1988)

Equal Pay Act of 1963
77 Stat. 56 (1963); 29 U.S.C. 206 (1988)

Fair Labor Standards Act of 1938
52 Stat. 1060 (1938); 29 U.S.C. 201 et seq. (1988). Amended by 63 Stat. 910 (1949), 69 Stat. 711 (1955), 75 Stat. 65 (1961), 80 Stat. 830 (1966), 88 Stat. 55 (1974), and 91 Stat. 1245 (1977); 29 U.S.C. 201-219 (1988)

False Claims Act
12 Stat. 698 (1963); 31 U.S.C. 3729-3733 (1988)

Family Medical Leave Act of 1993
107 Stat. 6 (1993); 29 U.S.C. 2601-2654 (1988 supp.)

Federal Coal Mine and Health and Safety Act of 1969
83 Stat. 742 (1969); 30 U.S.C. 801 et seq. (1988)

Federal Employees Compensation Act
35 Stat. 556 (1908); 5 U.S.C. 8101, et seq. (1988)

Federal Employer's Liability Act (Sterling Act)
35 Stat. 65 (1908); 45 U.S.C. 51-60 (1988)

Federal Employment Service Act
48 Stat. 113 (1933); 90 Stat 2672 (1976); 29 U.S.C. 49-49l-1 (1988)

Federal Mine Safety and Health Amendment Act of 1977
91 Stat. 1290 (1977); 30 U.S.C. 801-804, 811-825, 842, 861, 878, 951-955, 958, 959, 961

Federal Rules of Civil Procedure, Rule 23
48 Stat. 1064 (1934); 28 U.S.C. 2072 (1988)

Federal Unemployment Compensation Act
42 USC 501-504, 1101-1105 (1988)

Fitzgerald Act (National Apprenticeship Act)
50 Stat. 664 (1937); 29 U.S.C. 50-50b (1988)

Fulbright Amendment
66 Stat. 308 (1952); 41 U.S.C. 43a (1988)

Glass Ceiling Act of 1991
105 Stat. 1081 (1991); 42 U.S.C. 2000e note (1988)

Government Contracts Act
105 Stat. 1081 (1936); 41 U.S.C. 35-45 (1988)

Government Employees Rights Act of 1991
105 Stat. 1088 (1991); 109 Stat. 40, 41 (1935); 2 U.S.C. 1201-1224; 42 U.S.C. 12209 (1988)

Handicapped Programs Technical Amendments Act of 1988
102 Stat. 3289 (1988); 29 U.S.C. 702-796i, 1904 (1988)

Hobbs Anti-Racketeering Act
49 Stat. 979 (1934); 60 Stat. 420 (1946); 18 U.S.C. 1951 (1988)

Immigration Act of 1990
104 Stat. 4878 (1990); 29 U.S.C. 1506 (1988)

Immigration Reform and Control Act of 1986
100 Stat. 3359 (1986). *See* tables to the U.S.C

Industrial Productivity and Labor Costs Act
54 Stat. 249 (1940); 29 U.S.C. 2b (1988)

Job Training Partnership Act
96 Stat. 1322 (1982); 29 U.S.C. 49-49l-1, 1505-1791 (1988)

Job Training Partnership Act Amendments of 1986
100 Stat. 1261 (1986); 29 U.S.C. 1503, 1511, 1516, 1518, 1531, 1534, 1582, 1602, 1603, 1630, 1632-1634, 1652, 1707, 1733, 1736 (1988)

Job Training Reform Amendments of 1992
106 Stat. 1021 (1992); 29 U.S.C. 1501-1792b (1988)

Jobs for Employable Dependent Individuals Act
102 Stat. 3248-3256 (1988); 29 U.S.C. 49-49l-1, 1502, 1504, 1505, 1514, 1516, 1531, 1583, 1602, 1791-1791j (1988)

Judicial Improvements Act of 1990
104 Stat. 5089 (1990); 9 U.S.C. 15, 16 (1988)

Ku Klux Klan Act (see Civil Rights Act of 1871)
16 Stat. 140 (1870); 18 U.S.C. 241, 242, 371, 372, 752, 1071 (1988)

Labor Disputes Act (Norris-LaGuardia Act)
47 Stat. 70 (1932); 29 U.S.C. 101-115 (1988)

Labor Injunction Act (Norris-LaGuardia Act)
47 Stat. 70 (1932); 29 U.S.C. 101-115 (1988)

Labor-Management Cooperation Act of 1978
92 Stat. 2020 (1978); 29 U.S.C. 173, 175a, 186 (1988)

Labor Management Relations Act of 1947 (Taft-Hartley Act)
61 Stat. 36 (1947), as amended by 73 Stat. 519 (1959); 83 Stat. 133 (1969), 87 Stat. 314 (1973); 88 Stat. 396 (1974); 29 U.S.C. 141-167, 171-187 (1988)

Labor-Management Reporting and Disclosure Act of 1959
73 Stat. 519 (1959); 29 U.S.C. 153, 158-160, 164, 186, 187, 401-531 (1988)

Landrum-Griffin Act (1959)
73 Stat. 519 (1959); 29 U.S.C. 153, 158-160, 164, 186, 187, 401-531 (1988)

Lloyd-LaFollette Act
37 Stat. 3555 (1912)

Longshore and Harbor Workers' Compensation Act of 1927
44 Stat. 1424 (1927); 33 U.S.C. 901-950 (1988)

Longshore and Harbor Workers' Compensation Act Amendments of 1972
86 Stat. 1251 (1972); 33 U.S.C. 902, 903, 905-910, 912-914, 917, 919, 921, 921(a), 923, 927, 928, 933, 935,939,940,944, 948a (1988)

Longshore and Harbor Workers' Compensation Act Amendments of 1984
98 Stat. 1639 (1984); 33 U.S.C. 901-910, 912-914, 917, 918, 921, 922, 928, 930-933, 938, 942, 944-947, 948a (1988)

Manpower Development and Training Act of 1962
76 Stat. 23 (1962)

Mechanics Lien Act
49 Stat. 793-794 (1935); 40 U.S.C. 270-270d (1988)

Migrant and Seasonal Agricultural Worker Protection Act
29 U.S.C. 1811-1815; 29 U.S.C. 1801-1872 (1988)

Miller Act (Public Works)
49 Stat. 793-794 (1935); 40 U.S.C. 270a-270d (1988)

Model Employment Termination Act
Uniform Law Commissioners' Model Employment Termination Act — 1991 Act. Uniform Laws Annotated. St. Paul, Minn: West Pub., 1996

Motor Carrier Act
49 Stat. 793 (1935)

Multi-Employer Pension Plan Amendments Act of 1980
88 Stat. 832 (1974); 29 U.S.C. 1001a, 1002, 1023, 1051, 1058, 1081, 1082, 1103, 1104, 1108, 1132, 1145, 1202, 1301, 1307, 1322-1366, 1381-1405, 1411-1461 (1988)

National Apprenticeship Act
50 Stat. 664 (1937); 29 U.S.C. 50-50b (1988)

National Employment Service Act
48 Stat. 113 (1982); 29 U.S.C. 49-49l-1 (1988)

National Labor Relations Act (1935)
65 Stat. 601 (1951); 72 Stat. 945 (1958); 73 Stat. 541 (1959); 88 Stat. 395 (1974); 29 U.S.C. 151-169 (1988)

Service Contract Act of 1965
79 Stat. 1034 (1965); 41 U.S.C. 351-358 (1988)

Servicemen's Readjustment Act of 1944 (G.I. Bill of Rights)
58 Stat. 284 (1944); 38 U.S.C.A. 1801 (1988)

Single Employer Pension Plan Amendments Act of 1986
100 Stat. 237 (1986); 29 U.S.C. 1001b, 1002, 1023, 1024, 1054, 1061, 1083-1086, 1135, 1143a, 1301, 1303-1306, 1322, 1322a, 1341, 1342, 1344, 1347-1349, 1362-1370 (1988)

Social Security Act
49 Stat. 620 (1935); 42 U.S.C. 301, et seq. (1988)

Taft-Hartley Act (1947)
61 Stat. 136, 29 U.S.C. 141-262 (1988)

Tax Reform Act of 1986
100 Stat. 2085 (1986); 29 U.S.C. 1002, 1052-1056, 1108, 1162, 1165-1167, 1349, 1461 (1988)

Technical and Miscellaneous Revenue Act of 1988
29 U.S.C. 1082, 1167 (1988)

Technology-Related Assistance for Individuals with Disabilities Act of 1988
102 Stat. 1044 (1988); 29 U.S.C. 2201, 2202, 2211-2217, 2231, 2241-2271 (1988)

Technology-Related Assistance for Individuals with Disabilities Act of 1994
108 Stat. 50 (1994); 29 U.S.C. 706, 761a, 771a, 2201, 2202, 2212-2216, 2231 etc. (1988)

Title VII. *See also* Civil Rights Act of 1964 (Bennett Amendment)
78 Stat. 257 (1964); 42 U.S.C. 2000e-2h (1988)

Title IX of the Education Amendments of 1972

Toxic Substances Control Act
100 Stat. 954 (1986); 15 U.S.C. 2622; 15 U.S.C. 2623 (1988)

Uniformed Services Employment and Reemployment Rights Act of 1994
108 Stat 3149; 38 U.S.C. 4301-4333 (1988)

United States Arbitration Act of 1947
61 Stat. 670; 9 U.S.C., et al. (1988)

Urban Mass Transportation Act
78 Stat. 302; 49 U.S.C. 5333 (1988)

Vietnam Era Veterans Readjustment Assistance Acts, 1972–1978
86 Stat. 1074 (1972); 88 Stat. 1578 (1974); 38 U.S.C. 101, et seq.; 38 U.S.C. 2011-2014; 38 U.S.C. 4211-4214, 4301-4306 (1988)

Wagner Act, see the National Labor Relations Act of 1935
49 Stat. 449 (1935); 29 U.S.C. 151-169 (1988)

Wagner-Connery Act of 1936
49 Stat. 449 (1935); 29 U.S.C. 151, et seq. (1988)

Wagner-Peyser Act
48 Stat. 113 (1933); 29 U.S.C. 49, 49c, 49d, 49g, 49h, 49j, 49k (1988)

Walsh-Healey Act Public Contracts Act of 1936
49 Stat. 2036 (1936); 41 U.S.C. 35-45 (1988)

Water Pollution Control Act
62 Stat. 1155 (1948); 33 U.S.C. 1367 (1988)

Whistleblower Protection Act of 1989
103 Stat. 16 (1989); 5 U.S.C. 1201-1222, 7502, 7512, 7521, 7542, 7701, 7703 (1988 supp.)

Women Apprenticeship and Nontraditional Occupations Act
76 Stat. 357 (1962); 29 U.S.C. 2501-2509 (1988)

Work Hours Act of 1962
40 U.S.C. 327-333 (1988)

Worker Adjustment and Retraining Notification (WARN) Act
102 Stat. 890 (1988); 29 U.S.C. 2101-2109 (1988)

Executive Orders on Labor and Employment

Executive Order 10988
Employee-Management Cooperation in the Federal Service, 27 Fed. Reg. 551 (January 17, 1962)

Executive Order 11246
Equal Employment Opportunity, 30 Fed. Reg. 12319 (September 24, 1965)

Executive Order 11375
Amending Executive Order No. 11246 Relating to Equal Employment Opportunity, 32 Fed. Reg. 14303 (October 13, 1967)

Executive Order 11478
Equal Employment Opportunity in the Federal
Government, 34 Fed. Reg. 12985 (August 8, 1969)

Executive Order 11491
Labor-Management Relations in the Federal Service, 34 Fed. Reg. 17605 (October 29, 1969)

Executive Order 11758
Delegating Authority of the President Under the Rehabilitation Act of 1973, 39 Fed. Reg. 2075 (January 15, 1974)

Index

Christopher Anglim, Government Documents and Special Collections Librarian at the South Texas College of Law, has an M.A. in history from Arizona State University, an M.L.S. from the University of Arizona, and a J.D. from the Arizona State University College of Law. The author of articles, books, and a special-collections catalogue, Mr. Anglim continues to research and write in the areas of librarianship, preservation, history, and law. He lives in Houston.